Y0-DFO-981

ADMINISTRATION OF DECEDENTS' ESTATES

Administration of Decedents' Estates

Eustace W. Tomlinson, J.D.
Of the New York Bar

Prentice-Hall, Inc. Englewood Cliffs, New Jersey

DR. NORMAN A. WIGGINS

PRENTICE-HALL INTERNATIONAL, INC., *London*
PRENTICE-HALL OF AUSTRALIA, PTY. LTD., *Sydney*
PRENTICE-HALL OF CANADA, LTD., *Toronto*
PRENTICE-HALL OF INDIA PRIVATE LTD., *New Delhi*
PRENTICE-HALL OF JAPAN, INC., *Tokyo*

© 1972, BY

PRENTICE-HALL, INC.
ENGLEWOOD CLIFFS, N.J.

ALL RIGHTS RESERVED. NO PART OF THIS BOOK MAY BE REPRODUCED IN ANY FORM, OR BY ANY MEANS, WITHOUT PERMISSION IN WRITING FROM THE PUBLISHER.

LIBRARY OF CONGRESS
CATALOG CARD NUMBER: 78–170030

"This publication is designed to provide accurate and authoritative information in regard to the subject matter covered. It is sold with the understanding that the publisher is not engaged in rendering legal, accounting or other professional service. If legal advice or other expert assistance is required, the services of a competent professional person should be sought.

. . . *From the Declaration of Principles jointly adopted by a Committee of the American Bar Association and a Committee of Publishers and Associations.*"

PRINTED IN THE UNITED STATES OF AMERICA
ISBN–0–13–005306–6

About the Author

Eustace W. Tomlinson, J.D., is considered one of the nation's leading authorities on estate administration. He has practised law for many years in New York, and at present is also an adjunct professor at Temple University (Philadelphia) School of Law, where he conducts graduate and undergraduate courses in estate planning and counselling. He is admitted to the Bars of New York and Iowa, and is a member of the American Bar Association (where he served on the Council of the Section of Real Property, Probate and Trust Law and as chairman of several committees), and of the New York State Bar Association and the Association of the Bar of the City of New York.

Mr. Tomlinson was formerly a senior trust officer and counsel to the Personal Trust Department of Chemical Bank (New York), and has appeared as chairman, lecturer, or panelist on programs of the Practising Law Institute, the New York University Institute on Federal Taxation, and a number of state and city bar associations, university seminars, and estate planning councils. His articles have been published in various law reviews in the field of wills, trusts, and taxation.

PREFACE

This book is distilled from many years' experience advising executors and administrators in the administration of decedents' estates. During that period it was increasingly felt that there was a need for a comprehensive guide to fiduciaries and their counsel through the many and often complex problems encountered in the management of estates, problems that seem to increase with the growing complexity of life and the law. What seemed needed, and not available, was a practical treatment of the whole field of estate administration, an alerting to the kind of problems that arise therein, and a consideration of means of minimizing or avoiding many of such problems or of resolving them as they confront one, without recourse, so far as it could be avoided, to construction proceedings, litigated surcharge claims, and other adversary measures, and with due protection both to beneficiaries and to fiduciaries. This book attempts to meet that need.

It emphasizes the fundamental principles of the executor's relationship to his estate, its creditors, and its beneficiaries, and the often overlooked area of duties and responsibilities before probate; and then proceeds with a treatment, chronological so far as feasible, of each of the main steps and areas of administration, from time of probate to final distribution and accounting. Stress is laid upon assembling information about the decedent's affairs; collecting, protecting, and managing assets; duties as to the decedent's lifetime income taxes as well as the income taxes of the estate; investigation of his gift tax liabilities, if any; and determination of estate and inheritance taxes. Rights of surviving spouses and children, and the sources of property to be used to satisfy such rights, are discussed. Claims of creditors, their relative rights inter se, the establishment of their claims and the time and manner of satisfaction of claims are treated, as are the necessity and manner of liquidation of assets to provide for payment of claims, taxes, and other cash requirements. The various elections available to the executor, especially those often grouped under the label "post mortem planning," and the duty of the executor to use them for the benefit of the estate or its beneficiaries, are emphasized.

There are treated the many problems that can arise, and may not be recognized, in the ascertainment and identification of beneficiaries, the determination of the property or share passing to each, conditions precedent and subsequent attached to bequests, the practical steps required in making satisfaction of legacies, and the very important area of apportionment of estate taxes, including the necessity, propriety, and basis of apportionment and the collection of apportioned shares of the tax.

The sometimes difficult, and again too often unrecognized, problems connected with the ascertainment and disposition of the residuary estate are considered in detail; the special problems and risks involved where the estate is insolvent, or insufficient for all dispositions, and the risks to the executor if his estate proves to be insolvent, are also fully discussed. Consideration is given to the matter of administration expenses, including the items properly comprised therein, and the payment thereof; the allowance, payment, or forfeiture of the executor's compensation is included in this category, as are problems of the amount and payment of counsel fees. The basic importance of record-keeping and accounting is stressed, as are the extent and limits of the protective effect of voluntary or judicial settlement of an account and discharge of the executor.

Questions as to what law governs, both as between laws in force at different times and laws of different jurisdictions, are an area which in estate matters has been surprisingly neglected. Herein these problems are given especial attention, and conclusions are reached on the basis of principle.

Throughout the book, there are stressed not only the rights of beneficiaries but also the potential liabilities of executors, and in all aspects of administration suggestions are made as to practical means of avoiding mis-constructions or surcharge proceedings by forethought and appropriate precautions before or as questions arise.

Because of the complexity of the subject matter and the interrelationships of many principles and problems, allusions in the text and cross-references in footnotes to other sections of the work have been somewhat freely provided, to guide the reader to or warn him of related matters.

In view of the substantial influence the Uniform Probate Code is expected to have on legislation and decisions in all jurisdictions, even those that have not enacted it at the time, the Code is cited where apposite. There are also frequent citations of bar journals and law reviews, where relevant discussion may be found. Citations of decisions are fewer than would be expected in many other fields, primarily because most administrative problems are raised and resolved in lower courts rather than in courts of appeal, and only in a minority of states are their decisions reported. However, at the headings of many sections will be found notes referring, with the permission of the respective publishers, to relevant topics in the Prentice-Hall Estate Planning Service ("P-H Est. Plng. Serv.") and the West Publishing Company digest system ("West Dig."), where the reader may find additional authorities collected.

As a further assistance to the practitioner, the book contains, as Appendix A, a specimen form of "tickler" or calendar of important dates and actions to be taken, and as Appendix B a detailed outline of an executor's duties. The latter is adapted from a chart that has appeared in Taxes and Estates (W. Gibbs McKenney, Baltimore), with the kind permission of its publisher.

Grateful acknowledgment is made to my secretary, Margaret Maloney, for invaluable help in the physical preparation of the manuscript, and to my wife for her forbearance during my many months of work thereon.

Eustace W. Tomlinson

Table of Contents

I. TERMINOLOGY

§ 1.1	Preliminary statement	(1)
§ 1.2	Legal representative	(1)
§ 1.3-1	Executor; in general	(2)
§ 1.3-2	———; "independent" executor	(2)
§ 1.3-3	———; "preliminary" executor	(2)
§ 1.3-4	———; substituted or successor executor	(3)
§ 1.3-5	———; literary executor	(3)
§ 1.4-1	Administrator; in general	(3)
§ 1.4-2	———; administrator d.b.n. or c.t.a.	(4)
§ 1.5	Temporary administrator	(4)
§ 1.6	Special administrator	(5)
§ 1.7	Ancillary executor or administrator	(5)
§ 1.8	Administrator de son tort	(6)
§ 1.9	Executorship and administratorship compared	(6)
§ 1.10	Administration	(7)
§ 1.11-1	Estate; in general	(7)
§ 1.11-2	———; as not an entity	(7)
§ 1.12	Letters testamentary or of administration	(8)
§ 1.13	Devise; bequest or legacy	(8)
§ 1.14	Children; issue	(8)

II. NATURE AND PHASES OF ADMINISTRATION

§ 2.1	In general	(10)
§ 2.2	Limitations	(10)
§ 2.3	Phases of administration; tickler and check-list; and copy of will	(11)
§ 2.4	Problems created or avoidable by draftsmanship	(12)

III. BASIC DUTIES AND RESPONSIBILITIES OF EXECUTOR

§ 3.1	Care, diligence, and prudence	(13)
§ 3.2-1	Discretionary powers; in general	(14)
§ 3.2-2	———; duty to exercise	(14)
§ 3.3	Advice and assistance	(14)
§ 3.4-1	Delegation; in general	(15)

§ 3.4-2	———; to co-executor (15)	
§ 3.5-1	Negligence; in general (16)	
§ 3.5-2	———; waste (16)	
§ 3.5-3	———; speculation (16)	
§ 3.5-4	———; errors of judgment distinguished (16)	
§ 3.6	Surcharge (17)	
§ 3.7-1	Liability as insurer; in general (17)	
§ 3.7-2	———; liability of third person participating (18)	
§ 3.8	Confidentiality (18)	
§ 3.9-1	Impartiality and conflicts of interest; in general (18)	
§ 3.9-2	———; interests of creditors (19)	
§ 3.9-3	———; conflicting interests of beneficiaries (19)	
§ 3.9-4	———; executor's own interests (20)	
§ 3.9-4a	———; ———; interest as creditor or beneficiary (20)	
§ 3.9-4b	———; ———; self-dealing (21)	
§ 3.9-4c	———; ———; executor as debtor (21)	
§ 3.9-5	———; interest of executor's attorney (21)	
§ 3.10	Exculpatory provisions (22)	
§ 3.11	Reliance on advice of counsel (22)	

IV. PRE-PROBATE RESPONSIBILITIES

§ 4.1	In general (24)
§ 4.2-1	Search for will; in general (24)
§ 4.2-2	———; peril of later discovery (24)
§ 4.3-1	Production or filing of will; in general (25)
§ 4.3-2	———; delivery to another (25)
§ 4.3-3	———; offer for probate (25)
§ 4.3-4	———; concealment of will (26)
§ 4.4	Examination of will (26)
§ 4.5-1	Decision whether to accept appointment; in general (26)
§ 4.5-2	———; renunciation (27)
§ 4.5-3	———; ineligibility (27)
§ 4.6	Power and duty to preserve assets (27)
§ 4.7	Funeral arrangements (28)

V. PROBATE OF WILL AND QUALIFICATION OF EXECUTOR

§ 5.1	Establishment of fact of death (30)
§ 5.2-1	Ascertainment of time of death; date and hour (31)
§ 5.2-2	———; standard or "daylight" time (32)
§ 5.2-3	———; time and date at domicile (32)
§ 5.3-1	Determination of "last" will; in general (32)

TABLE OF CONTENTS xi

§ 5.3-2	———; failure to discover other will, or codicil	(33)
§ 5.3-3	———; revocation of later will; revival	(33)
§ 5.3-4	———; dependent relative revocation	(34)
§ 5.3-5	———; revocation other than by later instrument or destruction	(34)
§ 5.3-6	———; joint will	(35)
§ 5.4-1	Determination of (a) domicile and (b) place of probate; in general	(35)
§ 5.4-2	———; domicile problems	(35)
§ 5.4-2a	———; ———; importance of determining domicile	(36)
§ 5.4-3	———; place of probate within state	(36)
§ 5.5-1	Probate of will of non-resident; in general	(36)
§ 5.5-2	———; jurisdiction to tax not affected	(37)
§ 5.5-3	———; statutes requiring original probate at domicile	(37)
§ 5.5-4	———; ancillary probate	(38)
§ 5.6-1	Probate; in general	(38)
§ 5.6-2	———; persons to receive notice	(39)
§ 5.6-3	———; "probate of heirship" distinguished	(39)
§ 5.7-1	Temporary administration; in general	(39)
§ 5.7-2	———; powers of temporary administrator	(40)
§ 5.8-1	Eligibility and qualification of executor; in general	(40)
§ 5.8-2	———; bond	(41)
§ 5.8-3	———; letters testamentary	(41)
§ 5.8-4	———; disqualification	(42)
§ 5.9	Review of will provisions	(42)
§ 5.10-1	Contests; in general	(43)
§ 5.10-2	———; in terrorem provisions	(43)
§ 5.11	"Small estates" statutes; dispensing with proceedings	(44)

VI. COLLECTION OF ASSETS AND PAPERS
Part A—In General

§ 6.1	Existence and nature of duty	(45)
§ 6.2	Preliminary steps; forwarding address; advices of death, etc.	(45)
§ 6.3	Identification of assets and familiarization with affairs	(46)
§ 6.4	Locating and opening safe deposit box	(46)
§ 6.5	Cash and valuables on decedent's person, etc.	(47)
§ 6.6	Cash in safe deposit box, home, or office	(47)
§ 6.7-1	Bank accounts; in general	(47)
§ 6.7-2	———; savings accounts	(48)
§ 6.8	Contents of home or office, and tangibles generally	(48)
§ 6.9	Assets of proprietorship or close corporation	(49)
§ 6.10	Rented home; apartment	(49)
§ 6.11-1	Receivables; in general	(50)
§ 6.11-2	———; accruals from fiduciaries; commissions as fiduciary	(50)

§ 6.11-3	———; compromise (51)	
§ 6.12	Brokerage accounts of decedent (51)	
§ 6.13	Collection of insurance payable to estate (51)	
§ 6.14	Facilitation of collection of benefits payable to others (52)	

VI. COLLECTION OF ASSETS AND PAPERS
Part B—Particular Assets and Problems

§ 6.15-1	Real property; in general (53)	
§ 6.15-2	———; leases and possessory claims (53)	
§ 6.15-3	———; encumbrances (54)	
§ 6.15-4	———; executory contracts of purchase or sale (54)	
§ 6.16-1	Joint ownership and other survivorship interests; real property (55)	
§ 6.16-2	———; personal property (55)	
§ 6.16-2a	———; ———; joint bank accounts (56)	
§ 6.16-2b	———; ———; bank account trusts; revocation (56)	
§ 6.16-2c	———; ———; United States Savings Bonds (57)	
§ 6.17	Decedent as legal life tenant (57)	
§ 6.18	Invalid or ineffective lifetime transfers; alleged gifts, etc. (57)	
§ 6.19	Appointive property (58)	
§ 6.20-1	Estates of professional men; in general (58)	
§ 6.20-2	———; lawyers (59)	
§ 6.20-3	———; physicians and surgeons (60)	
§ 6.20-4	———; accountants (61)	
§ 6.20-5	———; collection of fees (61)	
§ 6.21-1	Property in another jurisdiction; in general (61)	
§ 6.21-2	———; property disposed of by separate will (62)	
§ 6.22	Discovery proceedings (63)	
§ 6.23	Reverse discovery (63)	
§ 6.24	Death tax waivers or consents (64)	

VII. CUSTODY, PRESERVATION, AND MANAGEMENT OF ASSETS
Part A—Possession and Control

§ 7.1	Nature of duty (65)	
§ 7.2-1	Tangibles; in general (66)	
§ 7.2-2	———; "exempt" articles (66)	
§ 7.2-3	———; sale or other disposition of residuary tangibles (66)	
§ 7.2-4	———; insurance (67)	
§ 7.2-5	———; contraband (67)	
§ 7.3-1	Securities; in general (68)	
§ 7.3-2	———; margin accounts (68)	

TABLE OF CONTENTS xiii

§ 7.3-3	———; rental of safe deposit box (69)
§ 7.3-4	———; establishment of custodian or advisory account (69)
§ 7.3-4a	———; ———; corporate executor distinguished (70)
§ 7.3-5	———; registration in nominee's name (70)
§ 7.4-1	United States government bonds; in general (71)
§ 7.4-2	———; bonds applicable at par on Federal estate tax (71)
§ 7.4-3	———; Savings Bonds redeemable at par (72)
§ 7.5-1	Real property; in general (72)
§ 7.5-2	———; collection of rents (73)
§ 7.5-3	———; sale (73)
§ 7.5-4	———; liability and casualty insurance (74)
§ 7.5-5	———; realty in another jurisdiction (75)
§ 7.5-6	———; cemetery lots (75)

VII. CUSTODY, PRESERVATION, AND MANAGEMENT OF ASSETS
Part B—Liquidation, Investment, Other Management Problems

§ 7.6-1	Liquidation of assets; for cash requirements (76)
§ 7.6-1a	———; ———; redemption of corporate stock (77)
§ 7.6-1b	———; ———; borrowing (78)
§ 7.6-2	———; for distribution (78)
§ 7.6-3	———; sale to executor or beneficiary (79)
§ 7.6-4	———; corporate executor's own securities; "divided loyalty rule" (80)
§ 7.6-4a	———; ———; officer or director of corporation (80)
§ 7.6-5	———; retention for distribution in kind (81)
§ 7.6-6	———; liquidation of unauthorized or unsuitable investment (81)
§ 7.7-1	Money; opening bank account; commingling (82)
§ 7.7-2	———; duty to make productive; investments (82)
§ 7.7-2a	———; ———; sale of unproductive property (83)
§ 7.8-1	Closely-held corporations; in general (84)
§ 7.8-2	———; management, sale, merger, liquidation (84)
§ 7.8-3	———; buy-and-sell agreements (85)
§ 7.8-4	———; fee or salary to executor as director or officer (85)
§ 7.9	Proprietorships and partnership interests (86)
§ 7.10	Domestic and personal employees (87)
§ 7.11-1	Apartment or rented home; in general (87)
§ 7.11-2	———; cooperative apartment, or condominium (88)
§ 7.12	Suspension of utilities (88)
§ 7.13-1	Executory contracts of decedent; in general (89)
§ 7.13-2	———; purchase or sale of land; equitable conversion (89)
§ 7.14	Contracts and undertakings of executor (90)
§ 7.15	Torts of executor (90)
§ 7.16	Exculpation from liability (90)

VIII. VALUATION OF ASSETS

§ 8.1 Necessity and purposes of valuation (91)
§ 8.2 Accounting and tax values distinguished (92)
§ 8.3-1 Inventory value; basis and determination (92)
§ 8.3-2 ———; statutory inventory and appraisal (93)
§ 8.4-1 Tangible personal property; in general (93)
§ 8.4-2 ———; exempt property (94)
§ 8.5-1 Real property; as such (94)
§ 8.5-2 ———; mortgages (94)
§ 8.6-1 Securities; in general (94)
§ 8.6-2 ———; stock of closely-held corporation (95)
§ 8.6-3 ———; buy-and-sell agreements (96)
§ 8.7 Stock options, etc. (96)
§ 8.8 Proprietorships and partnership interests (96)
§ 8.9 Oil, gas, and mineral interests (97)
§ 8.10 Patents and copyrights (97)

IX. FUNERAL EXPENSES, DEBTS, AND CLAIMS

§ 9.1 Taxes and administration expenses (99)
§ 9.2-1 Funeral expenses; in general (99)
§ 9.2-2 ———; items included (100)
§ 9.2-3 ———; amount (100)
§ 9.2-4 ———; governmental funeral allowance (101)
§ 9.3-1 Debts and claims; in general (101)
§ 9.3-2 ———; unmatured or unliquidated liabilities (101)
§ 9.3-3 ———; secured debts; debts of business (102)
§ 9.3-3a ———; ———; effect of direction in will (103)
§ 9.3-3b ———; ———; life insurance policy loans (103)
§ 9.3-4 ———; personal liability of executor for payment (104)
§ 9.4-1 Presentation and consideration of claims; in general (104)
§ 9.4-2 ———; time of presentation; limitation (104)
§ 9.4-2a ———; ———; notice to creditors (105)
§ 9.4-3 Allowance or rejection (105)
§ 9.4-3a ———; ———; basis of decision; proof of claim (106)
§ 9.4-4 ———; claims barred by statute of limitation (107)
§ 9.4-5 ———; claims of foreign creditors (107)
§ 9.5 Time for payment of claims (108)
§ 9.6 Personal claim of executor (109)
§ 9.7 Interest on debts and claims (109)
§ 9.8-1 Source of payment of claims; in general (110)
§ 9.8-2 ———; provision in will (110)

TABLE OF CONTENTS   XV

§ 9.8-3 ———; property subject to power of appointment (110)
§ 9.8-4 ———; counterclaims (110)
§ 9.9-1 Compromise of claims; in general (111)
§ 9.9-2 ———; creditor's acceptance of bequest (111)
§ 9.10-1 Liability of decedent as a fiduciary; in general (111)
§ 9.10-2 ———; legal life tenant (111)
§ 9.11 Decedent's charitable pledges (112)

X. INCOME TAXES

§ 10.1 Priority of payment (113)
§ 10.2-1 Final return of decedent; in general (113)
§ 10.2-2 ———; joint return with spouse (113)
§ 10.2-2a ———; ———; division of tax on joint return (114)
§ 10.3 Examination of prior returns (114)
§ 10.4 Fraud of decedent (114)
§ 10.5 Failure of decedent to file returns (115)
§ 10.6 Income taxes of estate (115)
§ 10.7-1 Request for early audit; of decedent's returns (116)
§ 10.7-2 ———; of estate's returns (116)
§ 10.8 Closing agreements (117)

XI. GIFT TAXES

§ 11.1 In general (118)
§ 11.2 Gifts in quarter of death and preceding quarter (118)
§ 11.3 Past gifts (119)

XII. ESTATE AND INHERITANCE TAXES

Part A—In General; Payment

§ 12.1 Priority (120)
§ 12.2 Contest as to domicile and right to tax (120)
§ 12.3 Preliminary investigations; notices and returns (121)
§ 12.4-1 Payment of tax; in general (122)
§ 12.4-2 ———; source of initial payment (122)
§ 12.4-2a ———; ———; time; premature payment (123)
§ 12.4-3 ———; deficiency assessments (123)
§ 12.4-3a ———; ———; interest and penalties (124)
§ 12.4-4 ———; insufficiency of testamentary assets (124)
§ 12.4-5 ———; death taxes of foreign state or country (125)
§ 12.4-5a ———; ———; effect of direction in will (126)

§ 12.5	Discounts; additions to tax (126)
§ 12.6	Postponement of payment (127)
§ 12.7	Personal liability of executor for tax (128)
§ 12.8	Additional state tax to utilize Federal credit (129)
§ 12.9	Establishment of credit against Federal tax for state tax paid (129)

XII. ESTATE AND INHERITANCE TAXES
Part B—Apportionment; Waivers

§ 12.10-1	Apportionment of taxes; in general (130)
§ 12.10-2	———; inheritance taxes (131)
§ 12.10-3	———; direction in will as to apportionment (132)
§ 12.10-4	———; apportionment within residue (133)
§ 12.10-4a	———; ———; payment "as expense" distinguished (133)
§ 12.10-5	———; retention or recovery of apportioned shares; in general (134)
§ 12.10-5a	———; ———; collection by litigation (135)
§ 12.10-5b	———; ———; disposition of amounts recovered (136)
§ 12.10-5c	———; ———; inability to recover (136)
§ 12.10-5d	———; ———; interest on apportioned share (136)
§ 12.10-6	———; insufficiency of residue (137)
§ 12.11	Waivers and consents to transfer (137)

XIII. OPTIONS AND ELECTIONS

§ 13.1	In general (139)
§ 13.2	Estate tax optional valuation date (139)
§ 13.3	Claiming deductions for estate tax or income tax purposes (140)
§ 13.4	Increment on United States Savings Bonds (141)
§ 13.5	Administrative elections affecting income taxation (142)
§ 13.6	Other fiduciary elections (143)
§ 13.7	Non-fiduciary elections (143)

XIV. SATISFACTION OF LEGACIES
Part A—General Principles

§ 14.1-1	Classification of legacies; in general (145)
§ 14.1-2	———; legacies in trust; conditional and deferred legacies (145)
§ 14.2	Abatement, ademption, lapse (145)
§ 14.3	When title to legacy vests (147)
§ 14.4-1	Specific legacies; definition (147)
§ 14.4-2	———; identification of property bequeathed (148)
§ 14.4-2a	———; ———; description by provenance or location (148)

TABLE OF CONTENTS   xvii

§ 14.4-2aa   ———; ———; ———; contents of box, room, etc.   (149)
§ 14.4-2b   ———; ———; description by nature: "jewelry," "personal effects," "household effects"   (149)
§ 14.4-2bb   ———; ———; ———; coin or stamp collections, works of art, etc.   (150)
§ 14.4-2c   ———; ———; bequest of "all tangibles"   (150)
§ 14.4-2d   ———; ———; bequest of "all personal property"   (151)
§ 14.4-2e   ———; ———; corporate stock after capital changes   (151)
§ 14.4-3   ———; income from date of death   (152)
§ 14.4-4   ———; ademption   (153)
§ 14.4-4a   ———; ———; open-market securities   (153)
§ 14.4-4b   ———; ———; property sold by guardian of incompetent   (154)
§ 14.4-4c   ———; ———; insurance proceeds   (154)
§ 14.4-5   ———; property subject to encumbrance   (155)
§ 14.4-5a   ———; ———; obligations of business specifically bequeathed   (156)
§ 14.4-6   ———; availability for debts and expenses   (156)
§ 14.4-7   ———; letter or memorandum as to distribution   (156)
§ 14.4-7a   ———; ———; wishes orally expressed   (157)
§ 14.4-8   ———; division among legatees   (157)
§ 14.4-9   ———; delivery of tangibles   (158)
§ 14.4-10   ———; bequest or disposition of body or organs   (158)
§ 14.5-1   Demonstrative legacies; definition   (159)
§ 14.5-2   ———; bequest of bank account distinguished   (160)
§ 14.5-3   ———; general legacy to extent fund insufficient   (160)
§ 14.5-4   ———; ademption   (160)
§ 14.5-5   ———; availability of fund for charges and expenses   (160)
§ 14.6-1   General legacies; definition   (160)
§ 14.6-2   ———; legacy of securities   (161)
§ 14.6-3   ———; ademption by satisfaction   (161)
§ 14.7   Residuary legacies; definition   (162)

XIV. SATISFACTION OF LEGACIES
Part B—Special Problems

§ 14.8-1   "Marital deduction" legacies; in general   (163)
§ 14.8-2   ———; formula clauses: "pecuniary" and "share" formulae   (163)
§ 14.8-2a   ———; ———; importance of determining nature of formula   (164)
§ 14.8-2b   ———; ———; administrative problems under formulae   (164)
§ 14.8-2bb   ———; ———; ———; non-qualifying assets   (165)
§ 14.9-1   Legacies charged on land; in general   (166)
§ 14.9-2   ———; charge on specific devise   (166)
§ 14.10   Legacies subject to condition precedent   (167)
§ 14.11   Legacies upon condition subsequent; life estates; responsibility of executor   (168)
§ 14.12-1   Deferred legacies; in general   (168)

§ 14.12-2	———; administrative problems (169)
§ 14.13	Direction of authorization to purchase annuity (170)
§ 14.14-1	Charitable legacies; in general (171)
§ 14.14-2	———; cy pres (171)
§ 14.14-3	———; "honorary trusts" (172)
§ 14.15	Bequest to creditor (172)
§ 14.16-1	Bequest to debtor; forgiveness of debt (173)
§ 14.16-2	———; right of set-off or retainer (173)
§ 14.17	Bequest to executor eo nomine (174)
§ 14.18-1	Legatees not capable of taking; subscribing witness (175)
§ 14.18-2	———; unincorporated associations (175)
§ 14.18-3	———; person responsible for death of decedent (175)
§ 14.18-4	———; charitable or religious corporation (176)
§ 14.19-1	Legatees not permitted to receive; in general (176)
§ 14.19-2	———; infant legatees (176)
§ 14.19-2a	———; ———; will provision for payment to parent or another (177)
§ 14.19-2b	———; ———; powers of management during minority (177)
§ 14.19-3	———; persons in "iron curtain" countries (178)
§ 14.20	Incompetent and possibly incompetent legatees (179)
§ 14.21-1	Location and identification of legatees; in general (179)
§ 14.21-2	———; inability to locate legatee (181)
§ 14.21-3	———; illegitimate or adopted children as "issue," etc. (181)
§ 14.22-1	Doubt as to survivorship; in general (182)
§ 14.22-2	———; "common disaster" provisions of wills (182)
§ 14.23-1	Lapse; in general (183)
§ 14.23-2	———; non-lapse statutes (184)
§ 14.24-1	Class gifts; in general (185)
§ 14.24-2	———; what is a class gift (185)
§ 14.24-3	———; when class to be ascertained (186)
§ 14.24-4	———; applicability of non-lapse statute (187)
§ 14.25	Pour-over legacies (187)
§ 14.26-1	Renunciation or disclaimer; of legacy (187)
§ 14.26-2	———; of intestate share (188)
§ 14.27-1	Satisfaction of cash legacy in property; in general (188)
§ 14.27-2	———; marital deduction legacy (189)
§ 14.28	Legacy of share or fraction (190)
§ 14.29	Assignments by legatees (190)
§ 14.30	Satisfaction in lifetime; advancements (190)
§ 14.31-1	Time of payment or satisfaction; in general (191)
§ 14.31-2	———; partial satisfaction (192)
§ 14.31-3	———; interest on cash legacies (192)
§ 14.31-4	———; establishment of trusts (193)
§ 14.32	Duty of simultaneous payments or distributions (193)
§ 14.33	Payment to legal representative of afterdying legatee (194)

§ 14.34	Revocation of legacy by later instrument or by law (194)
§ 14.35-1	Construction questions; in general (195)
§ 14.35-2	———; perpetuities problems (195)
§ 14.36-1	Estate and inheritance taxes; waivers and consents (196)
§ 14.36-2	———; apportionment (196)

XV. DEVISES

§ 15.1	Importance of law of situs (197)
§ 15.2-1	Description and identification; in general (197)
§ 15.2-2	———; devise of "all" real property (198)
§ 15.2-2a	———; ———; oil, gas, and mineral interests (198)
§ 15.2-2b	———; ———; as specific devise (199)
§ 15.3	Encumbrances (199)
§ 15.4	Lapse; incapacity to take (200)
§ 15.5-1	Ademption; in general (200)
§ 15.5-2	———; sale by incompetent's guardian or committee (200)
§ 15.5-3	———; damage or destruction (201)
§ 15.6	Rents as belonging to devisee (201)
§ 15.7	———; availability for charges, expenses, and legacies (202)
§ 15.8	Cemetery lots (202)
§ 15.9	Renunciation (202)
§ 15.10	Estate tax apportionment (203)
§ 15.11	Establishing title to real property in another state (203)

XVI. PRINCIPAL AND INCOME

§ 16.1	Tax and accounting computations distinguished (204)
§ 16.2	Need for separate ascertainment (204)
§ 16.3-1	What is income; in general (205)
§ 16.3-2	———; capital gains and losses (205)
§ 16.4-1	Income received by executor; accruals before death (206)
§ 16.4-2	———; accruals after death; "income during period of administration" (206)
§ 16.5-1	Expenses payable out of income; in general (207)
§ 16.5-2	———; interest on debts and legacies (208)
§ 16.5-3	———; alteration of rules by will; attempts to define net income (208)
§ 16.6-1	Disposition of net income; in general (208)
§ 16.6-2	———; income from specific legacies and devices (208)
§ 16.6-3	———; general legacies; outright (209)
§ 16.6-3a	———; ———; in trust (209)
§ 16.6-3aa	———; ———; ———; payment to trustee or beneficiary (210)
§ 16.6-4	———; surplus income (210)
§ 16.7	Expenses payable out of principal (211)

XVII. RIGHTS OF SURVIVING SPOUSE OR CHILDREN

§ 17.1	"Exempt" property and allowances	(212)
§ 17.2	Widow's quarantine	(213)
§ 17.3	Dower and curtesy	(213)
§ 17.4-1	Spouse's election to take statutory share; in general	(213)
§ 17.4-2	———; measure of elective share; in general	(215)
§ 17.4-2a	———; ———; "limited" right of election	(215)
§ 17.4-3	———; waiver of right during testator's lifetime	(216)
§ 17.4-4	———; withdrawal of election	(216)
§ 17.4-5	———; source of satisfaction of elective share	(217)
§ 17.4-6	———; informing spouse of right to elect	(217)
§ 17.5	Dissolution of marriage	(218)
§ 17.6-1	Rights of children unprovided for; in general	(218)
§ 17.6-2	———; children living at execution of will	(218)
§ 17.6-3	———; after-born or after-adopted children	(219)
§ 17.6-4	———; sources of satisfaction of child's share	(219)
§ 17.7	"Excessive" or "late" gifts to charity	(220)
§ 17.8	Forced heirship	(220)
§ 17.9	Community property	(221)

XVIII. ASCERTAINMENT AND DISTRIBUTION OF RESIDUARY ESTATE

Part A—Residuary Clause; Property Passing

§ 18.1	Ascertainment of residuary estate	(222)
§ 18.2	Nature and effect of residuary clause	(223)
§ 18.3-1	Particular kinds of property; preliminary statement	(223)
§ 18.3-2	———; "exempt" property and allowances	(223)
§ 18.3-3	———; lapsed, renounced, and revoked legacies and other dispositions	(223)
§ 18.3-3a	———; revocation or ineffectiveness by operation of law	(224)
§ 18.3-3b	———; ———; revocation of "bank account trust"	(224)
§ 18.3-4	———; estate and inheritance taxes recouped	(224)
§ 18.3-5	———; real property; in general	(225)
§ 18.3-5a	———; ———; cemetery lots	(225)
§ 18.3-6	———; life insurance payable to estate	(225)
§ 18.3-7	———; life insurance payable to testamentary trustee	(226)
§ 18.3-8	———; appointive property	(226)
§ 18.4-1	Surplus income; in general	(227)
§ 18.4-2	———; where entire residue passes outright	(227)
§ 18.4-3	———; where residuary trust or life estate is created	(228)
§ 18.4-3a	———; ———; true residue rule	(228)
§ 18.4-3b	———; ———; majority rule	(229)

TABLE OF CONTENTS xxi

§ 18.4-4 ———; allocation among residuary beneficiaries (229)
§ 18.5 "Pour-over" (230)

XVIII. ASCERTAINMENT AND DISTRIBUTION OF RESIDUARY ESTATE

Part B—Distribution Problems

§ 18.6-1 Distribution of residuary estate; in general (232)
§ 18.6-2 ———; necessity of order of distribution (233)
§ 18.6-3 ———; partial distributions (233)
§ 18.6-4 ———; distribution in cash or in kind (234)
§ 18.6-4a ———; ———; shares or fractions of residue (234)
§ 18.6-4b ———; ———; cash distribution to one beneficiary (236)
§ 18.7-1 Lapse of residuary legacy; in general (236)
§ 18.7-2 ———; disposition of lapsed share; "residue of residue" (237)
§ 18.8 Partial intestacy (238)
§ 18.9-1 Assignment by legatee; in general (238)
§ 18.9-2 ———; revocability; direction for payment distinguished (239)
§ 18.9-3 ———; assignment before death of testator (239)
§ 18.10 Satisfaction in lifetime; advancements (239)
§ 18.11 After-acquired or after-discovered property (240)
§ 18.12 Worthless property; abandonment (240)
§ 18.13 Prolongation of administration (241)

XIX. INSOLVENT OR INSUFFICIENT ESTATES

§ 19.1 When estate "insolvent" (242)
§ 19.2 Priority and abatement (243)
§ 19.3 Liabilities of executor (243)
§ 19.4-1 Charges and expenses; in general (244)
§ 19.4-2 ———; administration expenses (244)
§ 19.4-3 ———; funeral expenses (245)
§ 19.4-4 ———; taxes (245)
§ 19.4-5 ———; debts of decedent (245)
§ 19.4-5a ———; ———; debts to Federal or state government (246)
§ 19.4-5b ———; ———; expenses of last illness (246)
§ 19.4-5c ———; ———; secured debts (246)
§ 19.4-5d ———; ———; other debts (246)
§ 19.5-1 Legacies and devises, in general (247)
§ 19.5-2 ———; devises; common law rules (248)
§ 19.5-2a ———; ———; statutory changes (248)
§ 19.5-3 ———; residuary legacies (249)

§ 19.5-3a	———; ———; legacy of amount out of residue	(249)
§ 19.5-4	———; general legacies	(250)
§ 19.5-4a	———; ———; legacy for specified purpose	(250)
§ 19.5-4b	———; ———; legacy to wife or child; marital deduction legacy	(250)
§ 19.5-5	———; demonstrative legacies	(250)
§ 19.5-6	———; specific legacies	(251)
§ 19.5-6a	———; ———; legacy charged on specific devise	(251)
§ 19.6	Appointive property	(252)
§ 19.7	Income	(252)
§ 19.8	"Exempt" property and allowances	(253)
§ 19.9	Totten trusts	(253)
§ 19.10	Intestate property	(253)

XX. ADMINISTRATION EXPENSES; FEES AND COMPENSATION

§ 20.1	Administration expenses defined	(255)
§ 20.2	Source of payment	(255)
§ 20.3-1	Counsel fees; in general	(256)
§ 20.3-2	———; amount and fixation	(257)
§ 20.3-2a	———; ———; agreement by executor	(257)
§ 20.3-3	———; co-executors' separate counsel	(258)
§ 20.3-4	———; time of payment	(258)
§ 20.3-4a	———; ———; partial payments	(258)
§ 20.3-5	———; pre-probate services	(259)
§ 20.3-6	———; contested probates	(259)
§ 20.3-7	———; executor as attorney	(260)
§ 20.4-1	Compensation of executor; in general	(260)
§ 20.4-2	———; basis, rate, and amount	(261)
§ 20.4-2a	———; ———; specification in will	(261)
§ 20.4-2b	———; ———; will providing for service without compensation	(262)
§ 20.4-2c	———; ———; legacy in lieu of compensation	(262)
§ 20.4-2d	———; ———; waiver of compensation	(262)
§ 20.4-2e	———; ———; executor dying, resigning, or removed during administration	(263)
§ 20.4-3	———; time of payment; allowance or approval	(263)
§ 20.4-3a	———; ———; premature payment	(264)
§ 20.4-4	———; commissions on principal and income	(264)
§ 20.4-5	———; assets includible in commissions base	(264)
§ 20.4-5a	———; ———; uncollected assets; assets subject to pledge	(265)
§ 20.4-6	———; compensation of co-executors	(265)
§ 20.4-6a	———; ———; agreement; waiver by one	(265)
§ 20.4-7	———; assignment of compensation	(266)
§ 20.4-8	———; denial of compensation	(266)

TABLE OF CONTENTS   xxiii

§ 20.5   Out-of-pocket disbursements   (266)
§ 20.6   Judicial review   (267)

XXI. AGREEMENTS WITH OR AMONG BENEFICIARIES

§ 21.1   Utility and advisability   (268)
§ 21.2-1 Scope and effectiveness; in general   (268)
§ 21.2-2 ———; public policy   (269)
§ 21.3-1 Who must join; in general   (270)
§ 21.3-2 ———; joinder of fewer than all beneficiaries   (271)
§ 21.4   Indemnification agreements   (272)

XXII. CONSTRUCTION AND INSTRUCTION PROCEEDINGS

§ 22.1   In general   (273)
§ 22.2   Proceeding for instructions   (274)
§ 22.3-1 Matters for construction; in general   (274)
§ 22.3-2 ———; precatory provisions   (274)
§ 22.4-1 Time; interim or special proceeding   (275)
§ 22.4-2 ———; on final accounting   (276)
§ 22.5-1 Necessary parties; in general   (276)
§ 22.5-2 ———; heirs or next of kin   (276)
§ 22.6   Prematurity; moot questions   (277)
§ 22.7   Expenses   (277)

XXIII. DEATH, RESIGNATION, OR REMOVAL OF EXECUTOR; SUCCESSORS

§ 23.1   Death   (278)
§ 23.2   Resignation   (278)
§ 23.3   Removal   (279)
§ 23.4-1 Successors; appointment   (279)
§ 23.4-2 ———; powers and responsibilities   (280)

XXIV. RECORDS AND ACCOUNTS; SETTLEMENT

§ 24.1   Accountability   (281)
§ 24.2   Records   (282)
§ 24.3-1 Accounts; in general   (282)
§ 24.3-2 ———; definitive and informational accountings distinguished   (282)
§ 24.3-3 ———; scope of account, and disclosure   (282)
§ 24.4-1 Time for accounting; intermediate and final accounts   (283)

§ 24.4-2	———; death, resignation, or removal of executor (284)	
§ 24.5-1	Settlement of account; in general (284)	
§ 24.5-2	———; judicial or voluntary settlement (284)	
§ 24.5-2a	———; ———; "general release" without account (285)	
§ 24.5-3	———; parties (285)	
§ 24.5-3a	———; ———; same person executor and trustee (285)	
§ 24.5-4	———; objections to account (286)	
§ 24.5-4a	———; ———; objection by fewer than all beneficiaries affected (287)	
§ 24.5-4b	———; ———; determination on rejected or unpaid claim (287)	
§ 24.5-5	———; effect of settlement (287)	
§ 24.5-5a	———; ———; as construction of will or determination of rights (288)	
§ 24.6	Failure to have account settled (289)	
§ 24.7	Compulsory accountings (289)	
§ 24.8-1	Expenses of settling account; in general (289)	
§ 24.8-2	———; cost of keeping records and preparing account (289)	
§ 24.9	Discharge of executor from liability or from office (290)	
§ 24.10	Accounting in respect of decedent as fiduciary or life tenant (291)	
§ 24.11	"Small" estates (291)	

XXV. WHAT LAW GOVERNS

§ 25.1	In general (292)
§ 25.2	Problems as to character of ownership distinguished (293)
§ 25.3-1	As between laws in force at different times; execution requirements (293)
§ 25.3-2	———; administrative powers (294)
§ 25.4-1	As between laws of different jurisdictions; in general (294)
§ 25.4-2	———; formalities of execution (294)
§ 25.4-3	———; real property (295)
§ 25.4-4	———; personal property; in general (296)
§ 25.4-4a	———; ———; direction that law of nondomiciliary state governs (296)
§ 25.4-4b	———; ———; administrative powers and duties (297)
§ 25.4-4bb	———; ———; ———; what is administrative or substantive (297)
§ 25.4-5	———; effectiveness of exercise of power of appointment (298)
§ 25.4-6	———; construction and interpretation (298)
§ 25.5	Intestate property (299)

XXVI. CONSTRUCTIVE TRUSTS

§ 26.1	Nature (300)
§ 26.2	Responsibility of executor (300)

TABLE OF CONTENTS   XXV

XXVII. TESTAMENTARY TRUSTS

§ 27.1   In general   (302)
§ 27.2   Validity of trust; importance to executor   (302)

§ 27.3   Qualification of trustee   (303)
§ 27.4   Functions of executor and trustee distinguished   (303)
§ 27.5   Pour-over to other trust distinguished   (304)

Appendix A
CALENDAR AND TICKLER   (309)

Appendix B
CHECK LIST OF EXECUTOR'S DUTIES   (310)

Appendix C
SUPPLEMENTARY CHECK LIST AS TO REAL PROPERTY HELD IN ESTATE   (315)

INDEX   (317)

ADMINISTRATION OF DECEDENTS' ESTATES

I

TERMINOLOGY

§ *1.1. Preliminary statement.* The term applied to the person or institution that is charged with administering the estate of a decedent is of significance in indicating whether the decedent died testate or intestate and whether such person's appointment comes from the testator or from a court.[1] The terms "estate"[2] and "administration"[3] are of less precise character, but have accepted meanings. Several other terms also distinguish one situation or relationship from another,[4] and in a will the differences may be vital. Accuracy in the use of terminology is, therefore, of importance, and the various terms should not be used without appreciation of their respective connotations, as discussed in following sections.

§ *1.2. Legal representative.* The term "legal representative" as used in respect of a decedent's estate is an inclusive one that refers to any person authorized or empowered to administer the decedent's property, whether the decedent died testate or intestate, and accordingly includes both executors and administrators,[5] and temporary[6] or special[7] administrators as well as others. It is sometimes treated as referring in a looser sense (in which, however, it is not used in this work) to the heirs or next of kin of a decedent, in their capacity as successors to the decedent's rights, properties, or obligations, at least where no executor or administrator has been appointed. The term is also applicable in respect of a living person, when it may include a guardian, tutor, or committee (by whatever name known) of an infant or incompetent. The term "personal representative" is sometimes used as synonymous with "legal representative"[8] but would seem to be less correct than the latter.

---

[1] Infra §§ 1.3-1 to 1.7 incl.
[2] Infra § 1.11.
[3] Infra § 1.10.
[4] E.g., §§ 1.4-2 to 1.8 incl., 1.12, 1.13, and passim.
[5] Capacities compared, infra § 1.9.
[6] Infra § 1.5.
[7] Infra § 1.6.
[8] So in Unif. Prob. Code sec. 1-201 (30).

§ 1.3-1. *Executor; in general.* The term "executor" is limited in its application to a person appointed by a testator in his will to carry out or "execute" its directions and dispositions.[9] Occasionally a will may authorize a third person to designate a person to be executor, but the appointment is nevertheless, in legal theory, made by the testator and not by the third person. An executor is properly referred to as "executor of the will" of the decedent, and not as "executor of the estate", although this solecism has crept into use in some jurisdictions.

§ 1.3-2. ———; *"independent" executor.* In a few states statutes permit a testator by appropriate provision in his will to relieve his executor from judicial supervision, or of the necessity of obtaining judicial authorization for or approval of his acts, other than the probate of the will and such matters as the making of an inventory or appraisal or a list of claims.[10] A will containing provisions designed to conform with such a statute is often called a "non-intervention" will, the executor thereof is called an "independent" executor, and administration of the estate is referred to an "independent" or "unsupervised" administration to distinguish it from the more customary administration subject to a greater or lesser degree to the court's control or supervision, which latter is then referred to as a "supervised" administration.[11] It is to be noted, however, that some other states,[12] which do not have express statutes of the kind referred to and do not use the quoted terms, nevertheless give the executor some degree, varying with the states, of power to act at his own initiative or discretion without first obtaining judicial authorization or approval, including, for example, power to sell real as well as personal property,[13] freedom from any duty to render an accounting except at the demand of a beneficiary,[14] and other matters that classically are required to be brought before the court; and so the concept of an independent executor is a relative one and not *sui generis*.

§ 1.3-3. ———; *"preliminary" executor.* While a temporary administrator[15] may be appointed where delay ensues or is to be anticipated in the probate of a will and the issuance of letters testamentary thereunder, the powers of a temporary administrator are so restricted and his functions so circumscribed[16] that the efficient protection and management of the decedent's assets may be hampered or prevented, and that state of affairs may continue for an extended period of time. In order to obviate these undesirable features, at least one jurisdiction has provided by statute[17] for the appointment, instead of a temporary administrator, of what

---

[9] "Domiciliary" executor, infra § 1.7.
[10] The Unif. Prob. Code contemplates such independence of administration in all cases unless otherwise ordered.
[11] Unif. Prob. Code sec. 3-501.
[12] E.g., New York, Pennsylvania.
[13] Infra § 7.5-3.
[14] Infra §§ 24.1, 24.7.
[15] Infra § 1.5.
[16] Ibid.
[17] N.Y. S.C.P.A. § 1412.

TERMINOLOGY

is termed a "preliminary executor", who has all the powers of an executor of the will in question except power to distribute assets, and thus falls somewhere between a temporary administrator and an ordinary executor. Where such an appointment is available, it may be preferable to temporary administration because of its greater freedom and, consequently, greater economy to the estate as well as greater expedition in its administration. Under such a statute, however, the pendency of a probate proceeding is a prerequisite to the appointment, whereas a temporary administrator may be appointed whether or not such a proceeding has been commenced. The preliminary executor, like a temporary administrator,[18] becomes *functus officio* when a will is admitted to probate or is denied probate, and is superseded by the executor or administrator then appointed.

§ 1.3-4. ———; *substituted or successor executor.* While ordinarily the distinctions have no significance other than a descriptive one, it is customary to refer to the person appointed by the will to act at the testator's death as the executor, or, when being distinguished from a substitute or successor, as the "primary" executor; one so appointed in lieu of the primary executor if the latter fails to qualify as a "substituted" executor; and one so appointed to succeed any preceding executor upon the latter's death, resignation, or removal[19] as a "successor" executor.[20] An executor appointed upon probate where there has previously been in office a "preliminary" executor[21] or a temporary administrator[22] is not referred to as a successor executor.

§ 1.3-5. ———; *literary executor.* The term "literary executor" seems not to have been defined by a court. It is occasionally used in the will of an author to designate a person authorized by the will to assemble unpublished works of the testator, to cull or edit them, to discard or withhold from publication those not deemed worthy, to arrange for publication of others, or the like. A person so designated would not seem to be an executor, even to the limited extent indicated in the foregoing, but more probably should be treated as the donee of a power, and as such subordinate to or acting only after the relevant acts of the executor in matters of the estate not directly related to or concerned with the matters committed to the donee.[22a]

§ 1.4-1. *Administrator; in general.* The term "administrator", used alone, refers to a legal representative who, instead of having been appointed by the decedent in his will and therefore being an executor,[23] is appointed by a court to administer the

---

[18] Infra § 1.5.
[19] Generally, infra Ch. XXIII.
[20] Appointment and powers of successor executor, infra §§ 23.4-1, -2.
[21] See last preceding section.
[22] Infra § 1.5.
[22a] Even less correctly, the quoted term seems sometimes to be used to refer to one to whom manuscripts, letters, etc., are bequeathed on a trust or quasi trust to cull, edit, publish, etc.
[23] Infra § 1.3-1.

decedent's estate. One so appointed is, therefore, properly referred to as "administrator of the estate" of the decedent. An administrator is appointed where the decedent died intestate, or left a will but failed to appoint an executor thereof, or where, by reason of renunciation,[24] ineligibility,[25] or disqualification,[26] or of death, resignation, or removal, no person designated in the will as executor thereof is in office as such.[27] More exotic terms are administrator *pendente lite,* a temporary administrator;[28] and administrator *ad colligendum,* one appointed as agent of the court to collect and preserve assets.[29] Statutes permitting settlement of "small estates" without judicial administration[30] may refer to a "voluntary administrator" to distinguish the person authorized under such statute to make such settlement from an administrator *de son tort*[31] as well as from an administrator appointed in a conventional proceeding.

§ *1.4-2.* ———; *administrator d.b.n. or c.t.a.*[32] Where an administrator is appointed to succeed another legal representative who has taken office but because of death, resignation, or removal[33] has failed to complete the administration of the estate, or after whose discharge from office additional property is discovered or received in the estate,[34] the administrator so appointed is often designated an administrator *de bonis non,* to indicate that he is successor to another representative and has been appointed to administer "assets not" administered by the predecessor. Where the decedent died testate but no executor is effectively appointed by the will or the executorship becomes vacant, the administrator is referred to as an administrator *cum testamento annexo,* which indicates that the estate is not one of an intestate and that the administrator's powers and duties are affected by a "will annexed" rather than merely by law. An administrator c.t.a. is, therefore, for most purposes to be treated as to his powers and duties as if he were the executor. Properly, an administrator with will annexed who succeeds another legal representative, whether an executor or an administrator c.t.a., by whom the administration of the estate was commenced but not completed, should be designated an administrator d.b.n. c.t.a., to indicate not only that a will is present but also that the administrator is a successor representative; but this is a somewhat seldom used and ordinarily unnecessary refinement of terminology.

§ *1.5. Temporary administrator.*[35] A temporary administrator is one appointed, where necessary, to administer an estate temporarily while search is made for a

---

[24] Infra § 4.5-2.
[25] Infra § 4.5-3.
[26] Infra § 5.8-4.
[27] Infra Ch. XXVIII.
[28] Infra § 1.5.
[29] As function of temporary administrator, infra § 1.5.
[30] Infra § 5.11.
[31] Infra § 1.8.
[32] West Dig., Exrs. & Admrs. Key Nos. 21, 37, 120-121.
[33] Generally, infra Ch. XXIII.
[34] Infra § 24.9. After-acquired or after-discovered property, infra § 18.11.
[35] West Dig., Exrs. & Admrs. Key Nos. 22, 122.

TERMINOLOGY

will,[36] a will contest pends,[37] or some other factor delays the admission of the will to probate or the granting of letters testamentary[38] to the executor or to an administrator c.t.a.,[39] and some action with respect to the estate or assets included therein is necessary in the meantime. The function of a temporary administrator is primarily a "holding" or protective one,[40] and he does not have the broad powers conferred by law or by a will upon an executor or administrator; ordinarily he cannot take any important action without prior authorization by the court in which he was appointed.[41] A temporary administrator ceases to be in office upon the appointment of the "permanent" legal representative, who is sometimes designated by the quoted adjective, or as a "general" representative, when it is necessary or desired to distinguish him from a temporary administrator.

§ 1.6. *Special administrator.*[42] Some statutes provide for a "special administrator", distinguishable from the general or "permanent" legal representative. Under such statutes the term may be synonymous with "temporary administrator",[43] or it may also, or instead, designate a legal representative appointed to perform particular acts, or acts with respect to particular property, usually where the executor or administrator is unable to do such acts or deal with such property as a result of a conflict of interest.[44]

§ 1.7. *Ancillary executor or administrator.*[45] As a general rule, an executor or administrator is not recognized as such, in the sense of having legal status or authority, in any jurisdiction other than that in which he was appointed, except as such other jurisdiction may by statute otherwise provide.[46] Accordingly, it is often necessary, where a decedent had property or property rights in a jurisdiction other than that of his domicile,[47] and his will has been admitted or letters of administration have been issued in the domiciliary jurisdiction, to obtain the appointment of a legal representative in such other jurisdiction for the purpose of collecting and dealing with the assets located therein,[48] or settling its death taxes.[49] A proceeding

---

[36] Infra § 4.2-1.
[37] Contests, infra § 5.10-1.
[38] Letters testamentary or of administration, infra § 1.12.
[39] See preceding sections. Under some statutes the term is also applied to a representative appointed for one who has an interest in property and who is absent from his abode, and cannot be located, or is a prisoner of war or detained by an enemy or in enemy-controlled territory.
[40] Temporary administrator, in general, infra § 5.7-1. Cf. "administrator ad colligendum", supra § 1.4-1.
[41] Powers generally, infra § 5.7-2.
[42] West Dig., Exrs. & Admrs. Key Nos. 22, 122.
[43] So in Unif. Prob. Code secs. 3-614 to 3-617 incl.
[44] Conflicts of interest, in general, infra § 3.9-1 ff.
[45] West Dig., Exrs. & Admrs. Key Nos. 518-526; P-H Est. Plng. serv. ¶¶ 2559-2562.
[46] Cf. Unif. Prob. Code sec. 4-201 ff. Capacity to sue and be sued in other jurisdiction, infra § 12.10-5a note 38.
[48] Voluntary payment of moneys or delivery of assets to foreign executor, and quittance therefor, Restatement, Conflict of laws 2d secs. 326-329.
[49] Death taxes of non-domiciliary jurisdiction, in general, infra § 12.4-5.

for the appointment of a representative in such circumstances is called an ancillary proceeding,[50] inasmuch as it is secondary to and in a sense in aid of the original proceeding, and the representative appointed in such proceeding is called an ancillary executor or ancillary administrator, as the case may be, to distinguish him from the representative appointed in the original proceeding, who is then referred to as the "domiciliary" executor or administrator. The term "ancillary administration" refers to the management and administration of the assets in the secondary jurisdiction, whether by an ancillary executor or by an ancillary administrator.[51] The powers and duties of the ancillary representative are controlled by the law of the jurisdiction in which he is appointed, and are usually confined to the collection, preservation, and perhaps liquidation of assets located in that jurisdiction, the satisfaction of such jurisdiction's taxes, and the payment of claims of creditors resident therein. He is usually required, upon completion of his function, to remit such assets as remain in his hands to the docimilary representative, to be disposed of by the latter as part of the general estate, but in some states statutes permit the court, in its discretion, to authorize an ancillary representative appointed by it to distribute directly to the beneficiaries in a proper case.[52]

§ *1.8. Administrator de son tort.*[53] One who, without proper appointment or qualification,[54] and so without authority, purports to administer a decedent's estate or to deal with a decedent's property is referred to as an administrator *de son tort*;[55] as will be obvious, he is not an administrator at all in the legal sense but acts "of his own wrong". By extension, the term is sometimes applied to an executor or administrator who, though duly appointed and qualified, so far exceeds his lawful powers in any particular respect that to that extent he partakes of the nature and incurs the liability of one who acts wholly without authority. An administrator *de son tort* is liable as an insurer to persons interested in the estate.[56]

§ *1.9. Executorship and administratorship compared.* As appears from the foregoing discussion, the distinction between an executor and an administrator is primarily as to the manner of appointment: the executor by a will, and the administrator by a court. Apart from that factor, the two capacities are substantially identical in essential nature and in the responsibilities they entail, except, of course, that an executor's powers and duties may be curtailed or enlarged by the will and those of an administrator, other than an administrator c.t.a.,[57] depend entirely upon the law.

---

[50] Ancillary probate, infra § 5.5-4.

[51] Ancillary administration in general, see McClain, Some Problems in Administration and Estate Planning When Assets are Located in Several States, 39 The Trust Bull. 30.

[52] Generally, see Restatement, Conflict of Laws 2d secs. 364–365; Unif. Prob. Code sec. 3-816.

[53] West Dig., Exrs. & Admrs. Key Nos. 6, 538–544.

[54] Qualification, infra § 5.8-1. Intermeddling in administration, in general, West Dig., Exrs. & Admrs. Key No. 6.

[55] By analogy to the term "trustee de son tort".

[56] Liability as insurer, in general, infra § 3.7-1.

[57] Supra § 1.4-2.

TERMINOLOGY

In this work the term "executor" is used at most places to refer to the legal representative, but it should be kept in mind that the principles stated apply equally to an administrator c.t.a. and, except where the matter under discussion depends upon terms of a will, are also applicable to an administrator as such and to an administrator d.b.n.[58]

§ **1.10.** *Administration.* While the term "administration"[59] is occasionally used in its restricted sense as referring to the procedures and actions of an administrator as distinguished from those of an executor, it properly applies to all matters having to do with estates of decedents, whether testate or intestate, since both an executor and an administrator are charged with the same essential functions of collecting assets,[60] settling liabilities,[61] and distributing net assets to beneficiaries.[62] It is in this wider sense that the term is used in this work.

§ **1.11-1.** *Estate; in general.* The term "estate" has several possible meanings, and whenever it is used it must be determined which of such meanings is intended. As used in this work, except where the context otherwise requires, the term refers to the assets (collectively) that are disposed of by will or descend as intestate property, as distinguished from the often wider category of property includible in the "taxable estate" for the purposes of computing death taxes.[63] In a few instances herein the term "testamentary estate" is used, for additional emphasis upon the distinction between property passing by will or intestacy and the taxable estate, and in particular as excluding property passing under a beneficiary designation, as in insurance policies, or by operation of law, as property in joint ownership with right of survivorship; as so used it corresponds to what is also called the "probate estate", and, like the latter term, does not intend to distinguish between a testate and an intestate estate. Assets other than those included in the "testamentary estate" or "probate estate" but passing at death or included in the taxable estate are usually referred to as "non-testamentary assets" or "non-probate property", and collectively as the "non-probate estate".

§ **1.11-2.** ———; *as not an entity.* It is to be borne in mind that the estate of a decedent is not an entity, and references apparently assuming or implying the contrary should correctly be read as referring either to the executor or administrator in his representative capacity, or to the assets collectively constituting the property passing by reason of death. Because, however, the usage is so prevalent and

---

[58] Defined, ibid.
[59] "Independent", "unsupervised", and "supervised" administration, supra § 1.3-2; ancillary administration, supra § 1.7.
[60] Infra Ch. VI.
[61] Infra Ch. IX.
[62] Infra Ch. XVIII.
[63] See also § 12.3, infra. It is to be observed that such terms as "gross estate" and "net estate" are chiefly death tax concepts, but not exclusively so, and the use of either term in a will may accordingly give rise to questions as to which of its meanings is intended.

convenient, decisions and writers customarily speak of the estate as if it were an entity.

§ 1.12. Letters testamentary or of administration. In legal theory an executor is appointed by the testator and not by the probate court,[64] but the appointment is confirmed by decree of the court and is then evidenced by the court's issuance of a document called letters testamentary.[65] Where an administrator,[66] instead of an executor, is appointed, the document evidencing such appointment is called letters of administration; if the administrator is appointed d.b.n. or c.t.a.[67] the letters of administration usually so indicate and are accordingly referred to with the addition of the relevant initials or words. Presumably letters testamentary or of administration and their names are historically descended from or analogous to the "letters patent" by which, in England, were evidenced titles of honors, or authority to represent the sovereign in some matter or capacity.

§1.13. Devise; bequest or legacy. Historically, the term "devise" relates to a disposition by will of real property or an interest therein,[68] and the terms "bequest" and "legacy" relate to such dispositions of personal property.[69] The term used accordingly indicates whether one is referring to real property or to personal property without the need of further specification;[70] and for that reason, among others, the historical distinction is maintained in the present work, as in the Restatement of Property.[71] In the Uniform Probate Code,[72] however, the term "devise" is used to refer to dispositions of real and personal property alike, under the Code's tendency to ignore or abolish the distinction between the two kinds of property. "Devise" may mean either the provision disposing of property or the property so disposed of.[73] Properly, a "bequest" is the provision disposing of personalty, and "legacy" is the property (which may be money, a tangible, or an intangible) so disposed of, but this distinction is not always observed in statutes or by writers.

§ 1.14. Children; issue. It is important to preserve the distinction between the term "children", which refers to descendants of the first generation, and the term "issue", which extends to descendants of any generation, including children.[74] While the former term has sometimes been given by courts the broader meaning of

---

[64] Supra § 1.3-1.

[65] Use and effect, infra § 5.8-3. Probate of will and issuance of letters as prerequisite in general to exercise of power or undertaking of duties, cf. Unif. Prob. Code secs. 3-102, -103, and 4-701.

[66] Defined, supra § 1.4-1.

[67] Supra § 1.4-2.

[68] Devises generally, infra Ch. XV.

[69] Legacies generally, infra Ch. XIV.

[70] "In propriety of language the word 'devise' means a testamentary disposition of land, while 'legacy' or 'bequest' are words appropriate to such dispositions of personalty." *Fetrow's Est.*, 58 Pa. 424, 427.

[71] Restatement of Property, sec. 12.

[72] Sec. 1-201 (h), and passim.

[73] Supra note 71.

[74] Adopted or illegitimate children as "issue" etc., infra § 14.21-3.

the latter in particular cases where an intention that it have such meaning has been discovered, the executor should not extend a gift or reference to children to any more remote descendants unless and until it shall have been judicially construed as having the more inclusive meaning.[75]

[75] Construction proceedings, infra Ch. XXII.

II

NATURE AND PHASES OF ADMINISTRATION

§ 2.1. In general.[1] In many respects the legal representatives[2] of a decedent "steps into the shoes of" the decedent and takes his place in all financial matters, or matters having to do with the decedent's property rights and financial obligations; and frequently this necessarily involves the executor in non-financial matters also, including personal relations of the decedent or among the beneficiaries. Any given estate accordingly may bring the legal representative face to face with any of the problems and situations that can confront an individual during his lifetime. The possible range of such problems is thus unlimited. Estate administration may ramify into any field of human activity; it may involve or be affected by problems of personalities and by all kinds and sorts of other human problems; it may open closet doors upon skeletons that during life the decedent had carefully concealed; it affords a cross-section of life, of business, of law, of economics, of human vanity and human nobility. And, it is not to be forgotten, it offers constructive opportunities, to minimize taxes and expenses, to preserve asset values, to bolster or enhance the security of beneficiaries.[3] The responsibility of a legal representative is great, which emphasizes the care that should be taken by a testator in selecting him; and his risks are correspondingly great, so that he should not accept his appointment without realization of his potential personal liabilities.[4]

§ 2.2. Limitations. While, as has been mentioned,[5] the executor is to be regarded for many purposes as standing in the place of his decedent as respects the latter's financial affairs, the executor obviously does not have the freedom of action in such matters that the decedent had during his lifetime or would have had if he had lived. The distinction, always to be kept in mind, is that the decedent was dealing with property or rights belonging to himself but the executor is dealing with property

---

[1] West Dig., Exrs. & Admrs. Key Nos. 1, 3.
[2] Term as including executors and administrators, supra § 1.2.
[3] Generally, infra Ch. XIII.
[4] Decision to accept or reject appointment, infra § 4.5-1.
[5] See last preceding section.

NATURE AND PHASES OF ADMINISTRATION 11

and rights of others. The decedent had all the powers not precluded by civil or criminal law or public policy; the executor has only the powers conferred by law and the will. The decedent was legally responsible, as to his own property and affairs, to no one, so long as he did not infringe the rights of others or of society; the executor is legally responsible to the beneficiaries, and for any dereliction of duty may be held pecuniarily liable by them.[6] An executor must, therefore, be fully familiar with his powers and duties, and with the restrictions upon them, and may not assume that some action which seems to him to be desirable, or which he thinks would have been in accordance with the decedent's wishes, is within his power merely for that reason.

§ 2.3. *Phases of administration; tickler and check-list; and copy of will.* As appears from following chapters of this work, the responsibilities of an executor may commence even before probate of the will by which he is appointed,[7] and continue through final accounting.[8] Many intermediate steps must be taken during this period, and many of those steps must be taken at specified times, or within specified periods, or in a particular order. It is therefore of great importance that the executor, promptly upon entering upon the discharge of his duties, prepare a tickler of important dates and other important stages of the administration of the estate, and a careful check-list of all important matters in connection with such administration;[9] and as each such matter is covered or each step in the administration accomplished the executor should so note on such check-list, with an entry of the date of so doing. Without an adequate tickler system and a detailed check-list it is highly likely that some important detail will be forgotten or some significant date will pass unregarded, with consequent damage to the interests of beneficiaries and liability on the part of the executor. The executor should also have always at hand, of course, an exact copy of the will under which he is operating; it is strongly recommended that he make or cause to be made for this purpose a photocopy or other facsimile, as only in that way can he be certain his copy agrees with the original in every detail;[10] also a facsimile made before the will is filed would be highly useful in case of any damage to or loss of the original in the office of the court clerk or enroute thereto.

---

[6] Surcharge, infra § 3.6.

[7] Infra Ch. IV.

[8] Infra Ch. XXIV.

[9] An illustrative form of such a tickler, and an outline of duties from which a check-list for a particular estate may be prepared, are set forth in Appendices A and B, respectively; but neither should be used without consideration of applicable law and practice and suitable modification accordingly. A corporate executor, in particular, for its own internal purposes, may find useful an additional and different type of memorandum or checklist, a specimen of which (geared to the operations of a particular trust company in a particular jurisdiction but adaptable to or suggestive in other situations) is set forth in Casner, Estate Planning (3d ed.) 41 ff. Attention may also be called to Schlesinger, Immediate Pre-Mortem Checklist, P-H Est. Plng. Serv. ¶ 3501, which, while relating primarily to actions before the testator's death, will suggest a number of things the executor should have in mind or may be concerned with after death.

[10] It is to be realized that in construing a will provision and determining its meaning or effect even punctuation and physical arrangement may be important.

§ 2.4. *Problems created or avoidable by draftsmanship.* As is implicit in the discussion at various places infra, many problems of administration of an estate are created by inadequate or unclear draftsmanship or by failure to recognize and provide for such problems, and many others can be avoided or minimized by draftsmanship which takes into account considerations of practical administration. These problems of draftsmanship include such things as directions for payment of debts,[11] bequests of tangible personal property,[12] *in terrorem* provisions relating to contests,[13] inadequate or inappropriate administrative powers,[14] precatory provisions,[15] etc. There is thus emphasized the importance of familiarity on the part of draftsmen of wills with the executor's problems in administering estates, to the end that it may be made entirely clear what in fact the executor is intended or expected to do with particular property or in particular kinds of situations, and that practical considerations as well as technical and theoretical ones are kept in mind and provided for.

---

[11] Infra § 9.3-3a.
[12] Infra § 14.4-2 ff.
[13] Infra § 5.10-2.
[14] See, e.g., §§ 14.13, 16.5-2 infra.
[15] Infra § 22.3-2.

III

BASIC DUTIES AND RESPONSIBILITIES OF EXECUTOR

§ *3.1. Care, diligence, and prudence.* This is inherent in any fiduciary capacity or relationship, including that of an executor,[1] the duty to use care, diligence, and prudence at all times in the exercise of his function and the performance of his duty. From this principle ultimately stem all the rules discussed in this work as to the executor's duties, responsibilities, and liabilities. So inextricably a part of the relationship is the principle stated that, as in the case of the executor's accountability to beneficiaries,[2] without it the fiduciary relationship would not exist or would be essentially meaningless. It follows that, at least in many jurisdictions, a provision in a will, however stated, cannot effectively relieve an executor from such inherent duty or protect him against liability to beneficiaries for any failure to perform it.[3] The executor, like any other fiduciary, is not required to have perfect judgment or to be right in all his decisions, so long as he has been careful, diligent, and prudent;[4] but any failure in the latter regard makes him answerable for any harm suffered by a beneficiary as a result of such failure.[5] Again like any other fiduciary, an executor is required to use all the skill he has in carrying out his responsibilities, even though his skill be greater than that of others;[6] on the other hand, notwithstanding that he does use all the skill of which he is capable, he is not relieved from liability if it is less than that of an ordinary prudent man.[7]

---

[1] Cf. Unif. Prob. Code sec. 3-703: executor "is a fiduciary, who shall observe the standards of care applicable to trustees . . .", which, under sec. 7-302 of the Code, include a duty to use any special skills or expertise he has or has represented himself to have.

[2] Infra § 24.1.

[3] Exculpatory provisions, in general, infra § 3.10.

[4] Generally, infra § 3.5-4.

[5] Generally, supra §§ 3.1-1 ff, 3.6.

[6] *Lohm's Est.*, 440 Pa. 268, 269 A.2d 451.

[7] Restatement, Trusts 2d, sec. 174, comment (a); Unif. Prob. Code sec. 7-302 (made applicable to executors by sec. 3-703).

§ **3.2-1.** *Discretionary powers; in general.* Even though a will contains a grant to the executor of a power or authority to be exercisable in his "absolute" or "uncontrolled" discretion, such power and its exercise are not beyond the control of the court, and no words can so far remove or render nugatory the essential nature of the fiduciary relationship as to enable the executor to act otherwise than upon a rational (as distinguished from a whimsical or capricious) basis or otherwise than in the interests of the estate and its beneficiaries. An executor accordingly should not be misled by words of the kind quoted above, and should at all times bear in mind that, notwithstanding their generality, his powers and authorities are at all times trammeled by his fiduciary responsibilities.[8]

§ **3.2-2.** ———; *duty to exercise.* It is a corollary to the basic duty of care, diligence, and prudence that an executor has a duty to exercise a power granted to him, whether by law or by the terms of the will, even though such power is discretionary, where its exercise is necessary or desirable in the interests of beneficiaries or of the estate. So an executor cannot refrain from taking an action on the ground that the power to take it is committed to his own discretion, where principles of care, diligence, and prudence dictate such action for the benefit of persons interested in the estate.[9]

§ **3.3.** *Advice and assistance.* An executor may seek advice or assistance in the performance of his duties from any source he chooses; but in doing so he is circumscribed by two principles, namely, the rules against delegation[10] and the rules relating to payment of the expenses of such advice or assistance. As to the latter, it is basic that, except as a statute may otherwise provide, an executor cannot pay from the estate, or reimburse himself for payments for, services which are a part of his executorial function and therefore covered by his compensation.[11] He may, however, obtain assistance at the expense of the estate in matters as to which by common consent services of a specialist or expert are required in the interest of the estate and which the executor as such would therefore not be expected to perform.[12] Familiar examples of the latter are the making of scales of securities or other property through a broker,[13] auctioneer, or the like, or the employment of an appraiser to advise as to the value of real of personal property proposed to be sold;[14] and, as pointed out infra, in some circumstances an executor may be justified in establishing a cus-

---

[8] For a useful discussion of the principles here applicable, see 1965 Proc. A.B.A. Sec. Real Prop. Prob. & Tr. Law, Part I, 185 ff.; while the treatment there is in terms of trustees, it is equally applicable to executors and administrators.

[9] Unif. Prob. Code sec. 3-703 would seem to make this explicit: "A personal representative . . . shall use the authority conferred upon him by this Code, the terms of the will, if any, and any order in proceedings to which he is a party for the best interests of successors to the estate". Options and elections available to executor, infra Ch. XIII.

[10] See next following section.

[11] Compensation as intended to cover all executorial services, infra § 20.4-1.

[12] Cf. Unif. Prob. Code sec. 3-715 (21). Counsel fees, infra §20.3-1 ff.

[13] Delegation of discretion improper, see next following section.

[14] Appraisal, in general, infra § 8.3-1.

todian or advisory account as to investments[15] or in employing assistance in the keeping of financial records and preparation of his account.[16] The elementary, and perhaps over-simplified, criterion to be applied in determining to whom the cost of advice or assistance is chargeable is whether the services in question are both necessary for the benefit of the estate, and not within the executor's own duties, in which case their reasonable cost is payable from the estate as a part of the administration expenses,[17] or instead the services are for the convenience or personal benefit of the executor, in which case they are payable by him personally.

§ 3.4-1. *Delegation; in general*.[18] Except, in some jurisdictions, where a statute or the will so provides, an executor may not lawfully delegate to any person other than a co-executor[19] the making of any decisions in connection with estate matters or the exercise of any power or authority involving discretion or judgment; and if he does so he is absolutely liable for the consequences.[20] He may, however, delegate to an agent or other third person purely ministerial acts, such as carrying out decisions duly made by the executor. Thus, for example, an executor may authorize a securities broker[21] to sell a security at a specified price or within a predetermined range, but is without power to confer discretion on the broker as to whether, when, or at what level to make a sale.

§ 3.4-2. ———; *to co-executor*. It appears that, in most if not all jurisdictions, where there are two or more co-executors in office one of them may effectively delegate some or all of his executorial functions to another or others.[22] This rule may be deemed to follow from the general principle that any one of two or more co-executors may act for all in at least some matters,[23] such as collecting or receiving assets; and even in jurisdictions in which or as to matters as to which the joinder of both or all executors is requisite, the delegation by one to another may be regarded as a concurrence in the action taken as a result of the delegation. The general rule permitting delegation does not, however, permit a delegation of such degree or for such period of time as to amount to an abrogation of the delegating executor's responsibilities to creditors and beneficiaries. Moreover, the rule ordinarily applies only as to transactions in which third persons are concerned, and is for the protection of third persons, and so a delegating executor is ordinarily liable to persons interested in the estate on a parity with and to the same degree as the delegee for the consequences of the latter's acts or omissions, except in the case of intentional wrongdoing or fraud in which the delegator had no part.

---

[15] Infra § 7.3-4.
[16] Infra § 24.8-2.
[17] Defined, infra § 20.1.
[18] West Dig., Exrs. & Admrs. Key Nos. 80, 139.
[19] See next following section.
[20] Liability as insurer, infra § 3.7-1.
[21] See last preceding section.
[22] Cf. Unif. Prob. Code sec. 3-717.
[23] Duties and powers of co-executors and co-administrators, in general, West Dig. Exrs. & Admrs. Key Nos. 123–127.

§ *3.5-1.* ***Negligence; in general.*** The concept of negligence in connection with an executorship or other fiduciary relationship is both broader and somewhat more specific than in the field of torts. In the fiduciary connotation, any unwarranted act or omission is negligence, inasmuch as the fiduciary is inherently under a duty to be careful, diligent, and prudent,[24] whether the act or omission is or is not such as would amount to negligence under the general principles of torts law. Any breach of such duty, or failure to sustain it, on the part of an executor is thus negligence, in the sense in which that term is used in connection with the administration of estates and other trusts, and the concept of negligence is accordingly the foundation for imposing liability upon an executor for any dereliction of duty.

§ *3.5-2.* ———; ***waste.***[25] One kind of negligence in the administration of an estate is the incurrence of unnecessary expense or the making of an unnecessary or excessive disbursement of estate funds. Negligent acts of that character are referred to as waste. An act or omission which results in avoidable depreciation of value or loss of potential value may also be regarded as waste.

§ *3.5-3.* ———; ***speculation.*** Since the duty of an executor is essentially to conserve the assets of an estate for the benefit of creditors and beneficiaries, rather than to increase their value, he is not justified in taking risks of loss or of depreciation of value in the hope of gain to the estate or an increase of value at some later time.[26] Such risk taking is called, in the terminology of estate administration, speculation, and may appear or exist in many indirect forms as well as direct ones. For example, an executor who fails promptly to effect necessary liquidation[27] to obtain funds with which to provide for cash requirements (for taxes, expenses, debts, and cash legacies) is guilty of speculation, for consciously or unconsciously he is taking the risk that the value of assets in his hands will decrease, rather than increase or remain level, before the funds are needed, and, of course, if a decrease occurs a greater amount of property will have to be liquidated to obtain the needed amount of cash.

§ *3.5-4.* ———; ***errors of judgment distinguished.*** Provided that an executor has acted with care, diligence, and prudence in connection with the exercise of a discretionary power or the omission of a discretionary action, he is not to be deemed guilty of negligence, or held liable for a resulting loss, merely because of an error of judgment on his part.[28] This rule is merely a statement in other words of the principle, mentioned in a preceding section,[29] that an executor is not required to be

---

[24] Supra § 3.1.

[25] West Dig., Exrs. & Admrs. Key Nos. 117, 118.

[26] Margin account as speculation, infra § 7.3-2. A possible exception to the rule of the text might exist where appreciation is quite clearly foreseeable; cf. *Christy v. Christy,* 225 Ill. 547, 80 N.E. 242.

[27] Infra § 7.6-1.

[28] Note, however, that the mere fact that an act is done in good faith does not of itself relieve the executor from liability for any want of care, diligence, or prudence. Cf. Unif. Piduciaries Act sec. 1(2), providing that, within the meaning of that Act, "A thing is done 'in good faith' . . . when it is in fact done honestly, whether it be done negligently or not". Cf. also § 3.11 infra as to reliance on advice of counsel.

[29] Supra § 3.1.

right but is required to apply and use his best efforts and abilities in carrying out his trust.

§ 3.6. Surcharge. An executor is subject to surcharge for any loss or damage to the estate that results from his negligence, wrongdoing, or other failure to carry out his duties.[30] The literal meaning of the term is its own explanation: The executor is charged with, and must turn over to beneficiaries, at the proper time for distribution,[31] all the assets then remaining in his hands, and is also charged, "over" or "above" such assets, with the amount of property that would have been in his hands if he had properly performed in his executorial duties. To say that an executor is, or may be held, personally liable to beneficiaries for a dereliction of duty is to say that he is subject to surcharge for the loss or damage resulting from such dereliction. The doctrine of negligence,[32] and surcharge as a remedy therefore, constitute the basic protections to beneficiaries of an estate, and references in this work to an executor's steps to protect himself against liability to surcharge are accordingly merely a way of referring to the rights and the protection of beneficiaries. Where surcharge is sought,[33] the burden of proof is generally upon the executor to demonstrate proper performance of his duty, rather than upon the objectant to prove the contrary; and the measure of liability is ordinarily the full amount of loss or damage to the objectant.[34]

§ 3.7-1. *Liability as insurer; in general.* While in general the liability of an executor for breach of duty is based upon the doctrine of negligence,[35] an executor who does a plainly unauthorized act[36] may be liable for any resulting loss or damage to the estate or its beneficiaries wholly without regard to whether he was guilty of any want of care, diligence, or prudence. Thus, where an executor invests funds of his estate without authority so to do, or in a security that is not of a character in which investments by the executor are authorized,[37] and later the market value of the purchased security declines, the executor may be liable to the beneficiaries for the loss even though the investment was prudent in the sense that, if made by one having authority so to do, it would not have been negligent nor subject to criticism. Liability under such circumstances is spoken of an liability as an insurer, inasmuch as, by exceeding or departing from his authority, the executor must be deemed to have guaranteed the estate against loss. A *fortiori*, the principles of liability as an insurer apply to an administrator *de son tort*.[38]

---

[30] Liability same as that of a trustee, Unif. Prob. Code sec. 3-712.
[31] Distribution of legacies, infra § 14.31-1 ff.; of residuary estate, infra § 18.5-1.
[32] Supra § 3.5-1 ff.
[33] Objection to account as method of raising issue, infra § 24.5-4.
[34] Unif. Prob. Code sec. 3-712. Who may participate in surcharge, and adjustments as to non-participants, infra § 24.5-4a.
[35] Supra § 3.5-1.
[36] Liability as insurer for unwarranted delay in distributing residuary, infra § 18.6-1.
[37] Investments by executor, infra § 7.7-2.
[38] Supra § 1.8.

§ 3.7-2. ——; *liability of third person participating.* It is to be noted that, where an act on the part of an executor is such as to make him liable as an insurer, any third person who participates in the act or takes steps without which it would not have been carried out may be jointly liable with the executor for any resulting loss or damage. Where, in the example given above[39] of an unauthorized purchase of a security, a bank with which the executor maintains a custody account transmits the order for purchase or pays for the security out of moneys in the account, or a broker executes the order, such bank or broker may be liable to beneficiaries for the subsequent loss in value of the security on the theory that one dealing for or with a fiduciary must be at his peril know the extent of or limitations on the power of the fiduciary to take the action involved.

§ 3.8. *Confidentiality.* Inherent in every fiduciary relationship is the duty of the fiduciary to keep confidential all information that he obtains in the course or as a result of his activities, and not to disclose any such information to any unauthorized person. This principle applies, of course, to an executor or administrator, who because of his intimate knowledge of his decedent's affairs may often become possessed of information that could be either highly damaging or embarrassing, or very valuable, to others.[40] While beneficiaries are entitled to be fully informed as to all matters of the decedent's estate that affect their rights therein, their right to information coming to the knowledge of the executor of administrator is not unlimited and cases may readily be envisaged where communication of certain kinds of information to beneficiaries or family members would serve no useful purpose and would merely produce unhappiness or anguish. Third persons have, of course, ordinarily no right to receive information concerning the decedent's affairs, at least beyond matters necessarily appearing in public records and such disclosures as necessarily must be made to the third persons in connection with dealings between them and the legal representative; and the latter must be very cautious to limit his disclosures to essentially necessary ones and to proper persons. Also, in seeking information from a third person about the decedent's affairs, the legal representative must take care not to disclose anything unnecessary to the inquiry, and in some instances it may be necessary to limit inquiries in order to prevent improper disclosure; the representative must in such a case take great care to perform his duty to obtain all needed information without violating his duty of confidentiality.

§ 3.9-1. *Impartiality and conflicts of interest; in general.* The executor, like every other fiduciary, owes a duty of faithfulness to his trust. The basic expression of that concept is the duty of care, diligence, and prudence.[41] A manifestation of the same principle underlying that duty is the duty to be impartial, as between the interests of creditors and those of the estate, as between or among the interests of

---

[39] See last preceding section.
[40] In estates of professional men, infra § 6.20-1 ff.
[41] Supra § 3.1.

beneficiaries *inter se*, and as between his interests and those of the estate or the beneficiaries.[42]

§ 3.9-2. ———; *interests of creditors.* As elsewhere stated, it is the duty of an executor to protect the estate against unjustified claims and to reject or refuse to allow those that are excessive or without lawful basis, and it is also his duty to satisfy lawful and proper claims.[43] Thus the executor must protect equally the interests of creditors and the interests of beneficiaries. He must maintain strict impartiality in that regard and neither impede the collection of a lawful claim nor facilitate in any way the collection of an unwarranted or excessive one. On the same principle as that relating to simultaneity of distribution among beneficiaries,[44] the executor must not favor one creditor by making prompt payment to him while delaying or postponing, without adequate reason, payment to another. If each of two persons claims to be the sole creditor in respect of a particular liability of the estate, or if two creditors interested in the same claim differ between themselves as to their respective rights or interests, the executor must be completely impartial between them. Of course, the executor should not satisfy any claim if that would result in a preference over any other creditor of equal or higher priority.[45]

§ 3.9-3. ———; *conflicting interests of beneficiaries.* The executor must at all times refrain from preferring in any way the interest of any beneficiary over that of another beneficiary; and where, as may sometimes be the case, a particular action or omission will be beneficial to one and detrimental to another, the executor must take great care to make his decision objectively and in the interests of the estate as a whole rather than in the interest of either beneficiary as such.[46] Further, the executor must preserve equality among the beneficiaries as far as concerns his treatment of them or their respective interests; thus, as pointed out elsewhere, tre executor must not make a distribution to one beneficiary without at the same time making corresponding distributions to all other beneficiaries of the same class,[47] or discriminate among beneficiaries in dividing a fund or group of assets into shares.[48] Where a question of construction or effect of a provision of the will, affecting the rights or interests of beneficiaries *inter se*, arises for determination, the executor must no take a position favorable to one beneficiary or interest as against another but must maintain impartiality;[49] if on submission of such a question to a court the executor deems a particular construction or result to be correct as a matter of law, he is not precluded from bringing to the court's attention authorities which support that point of view, and indeed may have a duty so to do if no person in

---

[42] See next following sections.
[43] Generally, infra § 9.4-1. Duty of executor for convenience of creditors to collect and administer appointive property that is subject to creditor's claims, infra § 19.6 note 89.
[44] Infra § 14.32.
[45] Relative priorities of claims, infra § 19.2.
[46] Post-mortem options and elections, infra Ch. XIII.
[47] Infra § 14.32.
[48] Infra § 18.6-4a.
[49] Infra § 22.1.

interest presents it, but his brief or argument should also give due consideration to any contrary authorities and should basically be not that of an advocate but rather than of an objective counsellor or friend of the court.

§ 3.9-4. ———; *executor's own interests*.[50] It will be obvious that, under his duty of faithfulness,[51] an executor must maintain impartiality as between himself and the persons interested in the estate, and he should avoid even any appearance of putting his own interests ahead of those of others concerned.[52] So fundamental is this duty that a court noticing an instance of action tending to benefit the executor personally will often raise the point *sua sponte* even though it is not raised by any beneficiary.[53] A conflict of interest may exist in either of two principal ways, as noted in the following sections.

§3.9-4a. ———; ———; *interest as creditor or beneficiary*. Where the executor is also, in his individual capacity, a creditor of the estate or one of two or more beneficiaries under the will, conflicts of interest are extremely likely to arise and should be carefully guarded against. As a creditor, the executor is in a peculiarly favorable position to obtain allowance and payment of his claim, and even if he acts in entire good faith some doubt or suspicion is likely to occur to other beneficiaries or, if the estate should be insolvent,[54] to other creditors; accordingly, as elsewhere discussed, special considerations apply as to payment of an executor's own claim.[55] Somewhat similarly, an executor who is also a beneficiary under the will is vulnerable to charges of administering the estate or making particular decisions in such manner as to favor his own interests, and it may be very difficult to avoid questions of that nature from arising. It has been observed elsewhere[56] that a nominated executor should consider possible conflicts of interest in determining whether to qualify; and indeed in cases of serious conflict of interest the executor may have a duty to take steps to resign. In those states where the concept of a special administrator exists,[57] cases of conflict of interest may afford occasion for the appointment of a special administrator to supersede the executor as to the matters in question.

---

[50] West Dig., Exrs. & Admrs. Key No. 115.

[51] Supra § 3.9-1.

[52] "Many forms of conduct permissible in a workaday world for those acting at arm's length, are forbidden to those bound by fiduciary ties. A trustee is held to something stricter than the morals of the market place. Not honesty alone, but the punctilio of an honor the most sensitive, is then the standard of behavior." *Meinhard v. Salmon*, 249 N.Y. 458, 464, 164 N.E. 545, 546, 62 A.L.R. 1, 5. "Divided loyalty" rule as to securities, infra § 7.6-4.

[53] *Est. of Binswanger*, N.Y.L.J. Apr. 21, 1967, p. 17: "No objection has been filed to this item. But the court has an affirmative duty with respect to the supervision of acts of fiduciaries when they deal with themselves. At least if the matter comes to the court's attention, the court has the power and the duty to inquire into the acts of self dealing whether or not objections are filed." Cf. *Whitney v. Whitney*, 317 Mass. 253, 57 N.E.2d 913 (so in the case of a trustee).

[54] Insolvent or insufficient estate, infra Ch. XIX.

[55] Infra § 9.6.

[56] Infra § 4.5-1.

[57] Special administrator, supra § 1.6.

BASIC DUTIES AND RESPONSIBILITIES OF EXECUTOR   21

§ 3.9-4b. ———; ———; *self-dealing.*[58] Apart from the matter of conflicting interests of an executor as a creditor or a beneficiary are the problems connected with transactions between the executor and the estate. One aspect of this is the clearly established rule that an executor cannot make a personal profit out of his trust, and therefore, in the absence of specific provision in the will, cannot be allowed to receive compensation (other than that allowed by law[59]) from estate funds for any services involving his executorial functions or any assets of the estate, as, for example, in the absence of an express provision in the will, a salary or fee as an officer or director of a corporation held in the estate,[60] or in any other way to realize personal gain from his official position.[61] More frequently, self-dealing involves the purchase of assets from the estate by the executor, or his sale of assets to it. Because of the confidential relationship of the executor to the estate and the opportunity afforded for over-reaching or personal profit, such transactions will usually be set aside and held void at the request of any beneficiary,[62] without a showing of actual unfairness or damage and regardless of the executor's good faith in effecting the transaction.[63]

§ 3.9-4c. ———; ———; *executor as debtor.* Where the executor in his individual capacity is a debtor of the estate, he is not permitted, in some jurisdictions, because of his duty not to put his personal interests ahead of those of the estate where a conflict exists, to interpose a statute of limitations to prevent having to pay the indebtedness.[64]

§ 3.9-5. ———; *interest of executor's attorney.* It has been laid down as a general rule of law,[65] and a requirement of professional ethics,[66] that if a transaction would be improper, under the principles relating to self-dealing,[67] if made by the executor, it is improper if made by the executor's attorney.[68]

---

[58] West Dig., Exrs. & Admrs. Key Nos. 144, 163.

[59] Lawful compensation as covering all executorial services, infra § 20.4-1.

[60] Infra § 7.8-4.

[61] Executor acting also as attorney, infra § 20.3-7; as accountant, infra § 24.8-2.

[62] The term "void" is sometimes used as to such transactions, but it would seem rather that they are voidable.

[63] See *In re Durston's Will*, 297 N.Y. 64, 74 N.E. 310, where not even ratification by disinterested co-fiduciary was held to validate the transaction. Cf. Unif. Prob. Code sec. 3-713, extending the rule to transactions with the executor's spouse, agent, or attorney, or any corporation in which the executor has a substantial beneficial interest. Transactions by executor's attorney, infra § 3.9-5.

[64] *Matter of Lipsit*, 21 A.D.2d 509, 251 N.Y.S.2d 979, aff'd. 15 N.Y.2d 588, 255 N.Y.S.2d 257, 203 N.E. 646 (rule applied to a co-executor). In a further proceeding in the same estate such co-executor was held precluded to act as a trustee under the will because of his concealment as an executor of his debt to the decedent and pleading the statute of limitations when it was discovered; *Matter of Lipsit*, N.Y.L.J. July 24, 1967, p. 11. Claims against estate and statute of limitations, infra § 9.4-4.

[65] *In re Robbins' Est.*, 94 Minn. 433, 103 N.W. 217, 110 Am.St.Rep.375

[66] A.B.A. Committee on Prof. Ethics (now Comm. on Ethics and Prof. Responsibility): It is as improper for the executor's attorney as for the executor to purchase assets from the estate (Inf. Op. 677), even at an auction (Inf. Op. 804); cf. 55 A.B.A.J. 448–449.

[67] Supra § 3.9-4b.

[68] Attorneys for executors, generally, infra § 20.3-1 ff.

§ 3.10. *Exculpatory provisions.* The grant by statute of the privilege[69] of disposing of property by will carries with it, as a general rule, the right to make such dispositions upon terms of the testator's own choice, and from this it would follow as a corollary that the testator may not only impose upon his executor such duties as he chooses but also may relieve him of obligations or responsibilities which he would otherwise have. Just as substantive dispositions, however, are subject to restraints and restrictions based upon public policy, as, for example, the rule against perpetuities, rules against restraints on alienation and restraints on marriage, and others, so the extent to which an executor may be relieved of responsibilities is also restricted by considerations of public policy. The chief one of these relates to an attempt to relieve an executor from the duty of care, diligence, or prudence,[70] or to exculpate him from liability for failure to exercise such a duty. That duty is, as has been seen, so inherent in the fiduciary relationship that, at least in many jurisdictions, a provision in a will, however stated, cannot effectively relieve an executor from sucr inherent duty or protect him as against beneficiaries from liability for failure to carry it out;[71] and the same is true as to other basic fiduciary duties.[72] Subject to this principle, an exculpatory provision in a will presumably may be effective; but because any such provision is almost certain to involve to some degree the matter of care or diligence or prudence, the executor may not be justified in relying upon it, and its presence in the will may result in entrapment of an executor who supposes that it affords a degree of protection considerably beyond that which a court will apply when a beneficiary seeks to impose a surcharge[73] upon the executor.

§ 3.11. *Reliance on advice of counsel.* The fact that in deciding to take or to omit to take a particular action, or in taking an action in a particular way, the executor obtained and relied upon the advice of legal counsel[74] does not of itself necessarily protect the executor against liability for resulting loss or damage if the executor (and his counsel) prove to have been wrong as a matter of law. A showing that the action or omission was considered with counsel and his advice was followed does, however, tend to demonstrate that the executor was careful and diligent in the matter and acted in good faith,[75] and, in many instances, will constitute protection to the executor on that basis, under the principle that the executor is not liable merely

---

[69] By the weight of authority, the disposition of property by will is a privilege, granted by the sovereign (the state), and not an inherent right, and so subject to such restrictions as the statute may provide.

[70] Supra § 3.1. Release by beneficiary, infra §§ 21.2-1, -2.

[71] *Matter of Curley*, 151 Misc. 664, 675, 272 N.Y.S. 489, 501 (mod. on other gds. 245 App.D. 255, 280 N.Y.S. 80, affd. 269 N.Y. 548, 199 N.E. 665), where it was said that attempted exoneration of executor from neglect or misconduct was "a waste of good white paper".

[72] Exculpation as to preservation and management of assets, infra § 7.6-1; from duty to account, infra § 24.1.

[73] Surcharges, supra § 3.6.

[74] *Mintz Trust*, (Pa.) 282 A.2d 295. Right to retain and pay counsel, infra § 20.3-1.

[75] "Good faith" distinguished from lack of negligence, supra § 3.5-4 note 28.

BASIC DUTIES AND RESPONSIBILITIES OF EXECUTOR

for errors of judgment.[76] The degree of the protection so afforded will, of course, be affected by the competence of the counsel[77] and by his care in advising the executor, and the executor should accordingly seek to obtain from his counsel a reasoned and judicious opinion, in writing, rather than oral advice or a mere categorical answer to his question. Also, it has been emphasized that whatever protection may be afforded by reliance upon counsel as to a matter of law or judgment does not apply as to a matter of fact.[78]

---

[76] Supra § 3.5-4.

[77] "The initial choice of counsel must have been prudent under all the circumstances, and the subsequent decision to rely upon this counsel must also have been a reasonably wise and prudent choice." *Lohm's Est.*, 440 Pa. 268, 269 A.2d 451, 455.

[78] Ibid.

IV

PRE-PROBATE RESPONSIBILITIES

§ *4.1. In general.*[1] It is a general proposition that an executor's duties and responsibilities commence when the will is admitted to probate and the executor duly qualifies as may be required by law;[2] and from this is follows, again speaking generally, that until that time he has no powers and hence no duties or responsibilities. This general rule is, however, subject to some qualifications or exceptions, as noted in following sections. Because the general rule is apparently logical and is often stated, the pre-probate responsibilities of the executor may be overlooked, and liability may be incurred accordingly.

§ *4.2-1. Search for will; in general.* Where a decedent is known to have executed a will and there is no reason to believe that it was thereafter revoked, or for any other reason he is believed to have died testate, but a will is not readily found, one knowing or believing himself to have been nominated in the will as executor thereof should assist in the search for the will.[3] If the will in question had been left or deposited with the nominated executor for safekeeping, he is particularly under a duty of producing it or accounting for its nonproduction, at the peril of liability to any person damaged by failure to produce it.[4]

§ *4.2-2. ———; peril of later discovery.* Particularly before accepting appointment as administrator of a decedent's estate on the theory or supposition that the decedent died intestate, one must use every reasonable effort, or make sure that every reasonable effort has been used, to discover any will that may exist; and one who administers an estate as that of an intestate may be liable to beneficiaries under a later-discovered will unless he can demonstrate that full diligence was used in searching for the will.[5]

---

[1] West Dig., Exrs. & Admrs. Key Nos. 77–79.
[2] Generally, infra § 5.8-1.
[3] Ascertainment of "last" will, infra § 5.3-1; failure to discover will, infra § 5.3-2.
[4] See also next following section.
[5] This danger apparently would be obviated by Unif. Prob. Code sec. 3-703 (b). Cf. Casner, Estate Planning, 3d ed., 37–38, as to protection of third persons dealing with administrator where will is later found. Failure to discover later will or codicil, in general, infra § 5.3-2.

PRE-PROBATE RESPONSIBILITIES

§ 4.3-1. *Production or filing of will; in general.* One who has possession of a decendent's will has the duty of producing it and filing it in the court which would have jurisdiction to admit it to probate; and in many jurisdictions a procedure to compel production is prescribed. It is not required that the possessor, even if he be nominated in the will as executor there of, offer it for probate or institute a proceeding for that purpose;[6] the purpose is merely to make sure that the existence of the will is disclosed and the will is brought forth so that any person in interest may offer it for probate and so that the decedent's estate will not mistakenly be administered under an earlier will or as that of an intestate.[7] The requirement ordinarily applies to every testamentary instrument, including codicils, and applies even if there is a will of later date that supersedes the one held, unless the holder of the latter is confident that such later will is valid and effective to supersede or cancel the instrument held. Even in the latter case, the instrument should, of course, be preserved, at least until the later instrument has been probated and any period of time allowed by law for contesting it has expired.[8]

§ 4.3-2. ———; *delivery to another.* In view of the rule requiring one having possession of a will of a decedent to file it in the appropriate court,[9] the holder of a will is subject to liability if he delivers it to another, even if such other be a lawyer or be the person nominated in the will as executor thereof, and the will is lost or destroyed, or for any other reason is not duly filed. A risk is especially present if the person to whom delivery is made is one who, as an heir or next of kin of the decedent, or as a beneficiary under a will of earlier date, would receive a larger share of the decedent's estate, or a greater of more immediate benefit, than under the will in question. The holder of a will should therefore himself file the will or cause it to be filed as required by law, and preserve an appropriate record of such filing.

§ 4.3-3. ———; *offer for probate.* As has been pointed out above,[10] the principle under which a will must be produced by the person having possession of it, or filed in the appropriate court, does not of itself require such person to offer the will for probate or commence a proceeding for that purpose. However, one nominated as executor in a will is a proper person to offer it for probate; and where a will is so produced or filed by the executor nominated therein, or he learns of the filing of the will by another without application for its probate, the nominated executor ordinarily has a duty to make such application, unless he is unwilling to act as executor and promptly renounces his appointment as such.[11]

---

[6] Nominated executor as a proper person to offer will for probate, infra § 4.3-3.
[7] Concealment of will, infra § 4.3-4.
[8] Contests, infra § 5.10-1; time as affected by form of probate, infra § 5.6-1.
[9] See last preceding section.
[10] Supra § 4.3-1.
[11] Renunciation, infra § 4.5-2.

§ 4.3-4. ———; *concealment of will.* In some jurisdictions statutes prescribe criminal penalties for concealment of a will or wilful failure to produce it. As in the case of the general rule requiring production or filing of a will by one having possession of it,[12] such a criminal statute does not require that the will be offered for probate by its holder, but only that its existence be not concealed.

§ 4.4. *Examination of will.* The executor nominated in a will should examine it, promptly upon learning of the testator's death and the existence of the will, to discover the nature of its provisions[13] and, in particular, whether it contains any directions with respect to such matters as the decedent's funeral, the burial or cremation of his body, and the like,[14] or the disposition of the body or of parts or organs thereof.[15]

§ 4.5-1. *Decision whether to accept appointment; in general.* Ordinarily before the offering of a will for probate, and in any case without delay after learning that it has been so offered, the person nominated therein as executor thereof should decide whether he is willing to accept his appointment as executor. The preliminary examination of the will referred to in the preceding section should accordingly extend to a consideration of the form and character of the will and its provisions, to such a degree as to enable the nominated executor to form a tentative opinion as to their adequacy and practicability; and he should also at least tentatively ascertain the nature and amount of the decedent's assets, and the existence and nature of any special problems in connection with the estate,[16] including any problems arising out of the personalities or interrelationships of the beneficiaries. Further, he should consider whether there are likely to exist or develop any conflicts of interest between him and creditors or beneficiaries.[17] In any case of doubtful acceptability, he will also wish to take into account his own prior relations, if any, with the testator or the beneficiaries, and whether he has led the testator to believe he would act as executor or for any other reason has a moral duty to accept the appointment.[18] He should then determine, in the light of all such matters, whether he is competent or equipped to handle the estate and perform the duties of executor, and whether, after considering the time and effort that will be involved, the probable duration of the administration, and the amount of compensation he can expect to receive,[19] he is willing to undertake the responsibilities of executorship.

---

[12] Supra § 4.3-1.
[13] As bearing on decision whether to accept appointment, infra § 4.5-1a; for construction problems, infra § 5.9; as to possibility of contest, infra § 5.10-2.
[14] Authority to arrange for funeral, infra § 4.7.
[15] Infra § 14.4-10.
[16] In terrorem provision as inviting contest, infra § 5.10-2.
[17] Generally, supra § 3.9-4 ff.
[18] Similarly, in the case of a proffered appointment by a court as administrator where a vacancy in the office of the legal representative of an estate exists or occurs, the appointee will wish to consider his relations with the court or judge and, particularly in the case of a "professional" fiduciary, his moral obligation to the court and the community to serve as and when needed.
[19] Compensation of executors, infra § 20.4-1 ff.

PRE-PROBATE RESPONSIBILITIES

§ 4.5-2. ———; *renunciation*.[20] It for any reason the executor nominated in a will feels unable or unwilling to act as such, he should affirmatively manifest his unwillingness,[21] by filing in the probate court a renunciation of his appointment or of all right to act as executor of the will, or by such other overt procedure as may be prescribed by local law or recognized under local practice. Any renunciation of appointment should be made promptly, as delay may subject the nominated executor to liability for failure to take steps that he should have taken, on the ground that persons in interest were entitled to assume that he would accept appointment and were misled by his failure to decline it.[22]

§ 4.5-3. ———; *ineligibility*. Statutes ordinarily prescribe the qualifications or eligibility of executors, in terms of who may or may not be appointed,[23] with reference to such matters as citizenship, moral character, criminal conviction, or the like, and, in some instances, residence within the jurisdiction or relationship to the decedent. Under many statutes a bank or trust company of another state is not permitted to act as executor, at least unless reciprocal statutes exist,[24] or unless it can and does "qualify" under general laws to do business in the jurisdiction as a foreign corporation.[25] Obviously, a nominated executor who by such a statutory provision is made ineligible to be appointed cannot accept the appointment, but for his own protection and the protection of persons interested in the estate he should consider, especially if the facts disqualifying him are not known to the proponent of the will or the right to qualify is in any way uncertain, whether he should file a renunciation[26] or at least make certain that the matter is brought to the court's attention. The matter of ineligibility arising after appointment, by reason of a change of circumstances, is hereinafter referred to.[27]

§ 4.6. *Power and duty to preserve assets*.[28] One who is aware that he is nominated in a will as executor thereof, and who has not renounced his appointment,[29]

---

[20] West Dig., Exrs. & Admrs. Key Nos. 16, 19; P-H Est. Plng. Serv. ¶ 2170.

[21] Renunciation of legacy, infra § 14.26-1. Just as a legacy is an offer to the legatee, the nomination of one to be executor is of the nature of an offer to him, which he is free to accept or reject, subject to the considerations mentioned in the last preceding section.

[22] Implied duty to preserve assets, infra § 4.6.

[23] "Qualification" in sense of steps necessary to receive letters testamentary, infra § 5.8-1 ff.

[24] Under most such statutes the ability of a bank or trust company of State A to act in State B exists only where State B's banks or trust companies are permitted to act in State A. Such "reciprocal" statutes differ in detail and should be carefully examined.

[25] Inasmuch as such "qualification", even where permitted to a bank or trust company (as is not always the case), may entail laborious assemblage and filing of certified copies of charter, submission of balance sheets or other financial statements, and periodic reporting, as well as subjecting the bank or trust company to all the consequences of taxation, service of process, etc., that attach to such qualification of any other foreign corporation, it may not be deemed advisable unless the bank or trust company has sufficient other reason to wish to do business in the foreign state, or in order to serve in a particular estate is willing to assume the burdens and risks referred to.

[26] See last preceding section.

[27] Infra § 5.8-4; removal upon becoming disqualified, infra § 23.3.

[28] West Dig., Exrs. & Admrs. Key Nos. 77–79.

[29] Renunciation, supra § 4.5-2.

may well have a duty, even before the probate of the will or the issuance to him of letters testamentary,[30] to take steps to preserve assets of the estate and prevent their dissipation, loss, or destruction.[31] Such a duty may be explicitly imposed by statute or decisional rule, or may be implied therefrom,[32] but probably exists as a necessary corollary to the principle that the executor's powers relate back in time so as to give beneficial acts done before the issuance of letters testamentary the same effectiveness as those done thereafter.[33] Such power, where it exists, is of a very limited character; it grows out of, and hence is restricted to exercise in, cases of necessity, where immediate steps are requisite to prevent loss and there is no one else having authority to act, and so in many instances any pre-probate responsibilities of the nominated executor may be obviated or ended by the appointment of a temporary administrator, which it may be the duty of the nominated executor to seek.[34] As in the case of every other power possessed by a fiduciary, the existence of the power connotes a duty to exercise it in a proper case, and, where a duty exists, a liability to anyone damaged by failure to exercise the power. A nominated executor should, of course, be very chary of taking any action before the will is probated or he receives his letters, and should limit his action to what is strictly necessary. In a case, however, where his action will preserve an asset or prevent a loss, the risk he incurs in taking the action is likely to be small or non-existent, and in any case usually less than his risk of being held liable for the loss or damage resulting from his inaction; and it would seem that this is so even if the will in which he is named should afterward be denied probate, or its probate should be set aside. It has been held that where the named executor, before probate, retained an attorney who performed necessary and valuable services, the attorney is entitled to be compensated out of the estate.[35]

§ *4.7.* *Funeral arrangements.*[36] The executor named in the will may, of course without waiting for probate, assist family members in arranging for, or himself arrange for, appropriate funeral services and the disposition of the decedent's body, or the shipment of the body elsewhere for the purposes of holding a funeral, in

---

[30] Letters testamentary as evidence of appointment and qualification, infra § 5.8-3.

[31] Protection and safekeeping of tangibles, infra § 6.8; of assets of business, infra § 6.9. Cf. *Cavanaugh v. Dore*, 358 Pa. 183, 56 A.2d 92 (one nominated as executor but who had not applied for or received letters directed, in action by a creditor, either to file answer or to renounce).

[32] Cf. N. Y. E.P.T.L. sec. 11-1.3, providing that a named executor has no power before receiving letters to interfere with the estate "other than to take such action as is necessary to preserve it".

[33] Unif. Prob. Code sec. 3-701 provides that, while the powers and duties of an executor "commence" upon his appointment, his powers "relate back in time to give acts by the person appointed which are beneficial to the estate occurring prior to appointment the same effect as those occurring thereafter"; and further provides that the executor may ratify and accept acts done by others where they would have been proper for a personal representative, thus extending the principle to others than the named executor and, presumably, to one named in a will he mistakenly believed to be the last will and not named in the latter.

[34] Infra § 5.7-1.

[35] *Est. of Baumgartner*, 274 Minn. 337, 144 N.W.2d 574. Attorneys' fees generally, infra § 20.3-1 ff.

[36] West Dig., Dead Bodies Key Nos. 1–6; P-H Est. Plng. Serv. ¶ 2147.

PRE-PROBATE RESPONSIBILITIES

accordance with the ascertained wishes of the family; and if no family member or other authorized person is available to instruct the named executor in such particulars, it is ordinarily appropriate for the latter, and the indeed probably his duty, at least to arrange for temporary care of the body until its disposition can be determined. The executor's responsibilities and discretions in these regards are, however, subject to any directions left by the decedent or contained in the will,[37] which ordinarily should be followed,[38] and particularly to any bequest or direction by the decedent pursuant to a statute permitting a bequest or disposition of bodies or organs thereof.[39] In general, however the nature and place of funeral services, if any, the disposition of the body, and like details are within the province of the family to decide,[40] subject as aforesaid and subject also, so far as concerns payment of expenses out of the estate,[41] to the reasonableness of the costs[42] in the light of such matters as the size of the estate, the decedent's style of life, and the like.

---

[37] Cf. Unif. Prob. Code sec. 3-701: before his appointment an executor may carry out written instructions of the decedent as to his body, funeral, and burial arrangements. Examination of will to ascertain directions if any, supra § 4.4.

[38] Effectiveness of directions, see 7 A.L.R.3d 747 note; in insolvent or insufficient estate, infra § 16.4-3 note 26.

[39] Bequest or direction for disposition of body or its parts or organs, infra § 14.4-10.

[40] Right of possession and disposition of body, in general, West Dig., Dead Bodies Key No. 1 ff.

[41] Funeral expenses as payable out of estate, infra § 9.2-1 ff.

[42] Excessive costs, infra § 9.2-3; in insolvent estate, infra § 19.4-3.

V

PROBATE OF WILL AND QUALIFICATION OF EXECUTOR

§ 5.1. *Establishment of fact of death*.[1] The executor or another offering a will for probate must, of course, establish that the testator has died.[2] In the ordinary case this will present no problem. In cases, however, where the fact of death is not subject to direct proof but is left to presumption or inference, the matter is more difficult. Such cases fall in general into one of two categories which must be distinguished from each other. Where death is to be presumed, or seems probable, merely because the testator has disappeared,[3] statutes usually require proof that his disappearance has continued for a specified period of years and, in addition, that diligent efforts have been made to locate him; for obvious reasons, such statutes are usually strictly applied and the proponent of the will must show full compliance with their requirements, particularly as to the search made. In such a case, even where death is deemed to have occurred, there may be little to indicate when it occurred, and a decision as to the latter may have to be somewhat arbitrary or empiric.[4] Where, however, death is to be inferred from the known or apparent involvement of the testator in an accident or catastrophe, the "waiting period" prescribed by statutes of the character above referred to does not apply and the fact of death, usually within a fairly narrow range of time, may be established by inference from the circumstances; but careful investigation is required, first, to establish the oc-

---

[1] West Dig., Exrs. & Admrs. Key No. 4; P-H Est. Plng. Serv. ¶ 371.

[2] For a discussion of the medico-legal problems as to what is death, and when or whether death has occurred, see Porzio, The Transplant Age, 23 ff. and 86–89. Death certificate as evidence, see next following section.

[3] To avoid jurisdictional problems, statutes often base the power of the court to appoint a representative in such cases upon absence rather than upon presumptive death.

[4] As to Federal tax returns and payments, see Rev. Rul. 66-286, 1966-2 Cum. Bul. 485: next responsible person, who may be the person who would be executor or administrator if the absentee were dead, has a duty to file all returns when and where appropriate; the time for the estate tax return is measured from the date of the transfer or vesting of the absentee's assets, unless an earlier date is indicated. Returns and payment of decedent's income taxes, in general, infra § 10.2-1 ff.; of estate taxes, infra § 12.3 ff.

PROBATE OF WILL AND QUALIFICATION OF EXECUTOR 31

currence of the accident or catastrophe and the testator's involvement therein or presence at the locality thereof, and, second, to rule out any reasonable possibility of intentional disappearance or of escape alive.[5] The case of one "missing" in military action is a special case of inferred death, and in such case the proponent of the will may ordinarily rely on the ultimate findings of the military authorities.

§ 5.2-1. *Ascertainment of time of death; date and hour.* The date of the testator's death ordinarily is the date as of which his estate must be valued, for both administrative and tax purposes,[6] and in that sense fixes the values to be used. Moreover, since such values are to be determined as of that date whether the death occurred in the first few minutes of the day, or the last few, or any time in between, the ascertainment of the hour may also be necessary for the same purposes; it is apparent that if death occurred shortly before midnight of one day the values as of the day then ending govern whereas if it occurred shortly after midnight the values as of the day then beginning govern. Apart from and in addition to questions of valuation, the date of death may fix the due date of estate or inheritance tax returns and the period within which various administrative steps must or may be taken; and, as an entirely different matter, with the increased number of instances of organ transplantation and the like the executor of the "donor" may have a possible cause of action, and responsibility to investigate, where there is room for doubt as to whether death occurred before the transplant or was hastened by it.[7] Perhaps of even more substantive importance in some cases is the fact that ascertainment of the date and even of the hour of the testator's death may be essential to a determination of the rights of a legatee, when his death and that of the testator were within a short space of time of one another, whether the deaths occurred in a common disaster or quite independently and perhaps at widely separated places.[8] The executor accordingly has the duty of ascertaining when death occurred, and in any case of doubt, particularly where a short period of continued life or survivorship would have substantive results, the executor should make careful and adequate investigation to ascertain the facts. Ordinarily, a death certificate, or authenticated copy of a record or report of a governmental agency,[9] is accepted, and is adequate, to establish both the fact and the time (date and hour[10]) of deaths; but it should not be relied upon alone where doubt exists or exactness is of importance, and especially

---

[5] For an example of thorough investigation in a case of disappearance in trans-marine flight, see *Est. of Currier*, N.Y.L.J. Mar. 20, 1967, p. 17, illustrating the kinds of questions that may arise and the kinds of proof concerning them that may be necessary.

[6] Infra § 8.2.

[7] See Porzio, op. cit. supra note 2, at 78 ff.; Corday, Life-Death in Human Transplantation, 55 A.B.A.J. 629. Bequests of body, or parts of organs thereof, for transplantation or other purposes, infra § 14.4-10.

[8] Doubt as to survivorship, infra §§ 14.22-1, -2, Such problems may be eased where a statute requires survivorship for a specified length of time in order to inherit, take as legatee or devisee, etc; cf. Unif. Prob. Code secs. 2-104, 2-601 (120 hours, unless will makes other provision).

[9] Person missing in military action, see last preceding section.

[10] Unif. Prob. Code sec. 1-107.

in such cases, as in those where the person certifying death is unable to certify the exact date or time, it may be necessary for the executor to obtain additional medical evidence and, in some cases, police evidence. Certainly, if the facts are not ascertainable, or cannot be established with certainty, the executor should not proceed, as to any matter significantly affected by the doubt, on the basis of any assumption, but should obtain judicial instructions or a judicial determination.[11]

§ 5.2-2. ———; *standard or "daylight" time.* Where it is important to determine the hour of death, as where the date is thereby fixed or for any other reason, the time to be applied is standard time. Where "daylight saving" time, by whatever name known, is in use, it therefore does not govern the hour if it is actually a departure from standard time; but there is to be distinguished the case of a statutory change, even though a temporary one or for only a limited period, of standard time, so that the advanced or "daylight" time is itself standard time, as is the case under the Uniform Time Act of 1966.[12]

§ 5.2-3. ———; *time and date at domicile.* Where the decedent died at a place other than that of his domicile, and in a different time zone, the time of his death as indicated by clocks at the domicile, rather than that so indicated at the place of his death,[13] governs for most purposes in the administration of his estate. It will be apparent that this principle may affect the date, as well as the hour, at which death is to be regarded as having occurred, as where at the place of death the hour was before midnight and at the domicile was after midnight, or vice versa. So questions of survivorship, or length of survivorship,[14] as between the decedent and a beneficiary, the date as of which assets are to be valued for purposes of Federal or domiciliary death taxes, and periods of time measured from the date of death, must be determined in the light of such principle. The case is similar where the International Date Line intervenes between the place of death and the domicile. There is to be distinguished, however, the case of ancillary administration[15] in a time zone other than that of the domicile; in such case it seems clear that local clock and calendar time will be applied in the ancillary proceeding for such purposes as the computation of the period after death within which, under local law or practice, particular actions must or may be taken, and presumably also for ascertaining the date of valuation for purposes of a local death tax.

§ 5.3-1. *Determination of "last" will; in general.*[16] It is of course important that the will offered for and admitted to probate be the decedent's last will, and the

---

[11] Instruction and construction proceedings generally, infra Ch. XXII.
[12] U. S. C. A. Sec. 260a.
[13] This rule is prescribed for Federal tax purposes by Rev. Rul. 66-85, 1966-15 Cum.Bul. 8.
[14] Cf. Unif. Prob. Code secs. 2-104, 2-601, providing that heir or beneficiary failing to survive decedent by 120 hours is to be treated as not surviving him.
[15] Supra § 1.7.
[16] Determination of intestacy, West Dig., Exrs. & Admrs. Key No. 5.

principles hereinbefore stated with respect to the search for and discovery of a will extend to the ascertainment of what is the last will, and of any codicils. Moreover, it is always to be kept in mind that a will of later date does not wholly revoke one of earlier date unless it specifically so provides or is fully inconsistent therewith; and the executor must endeavor to assure himself that no instrument, other than or in addition to the one offered for probate, is in force as a part of the decedent's "will", or, if there be any such other instrument, that it is offered for probate along with the later instrument. It may also be in mind that in a number of states a lost or destroyed will may be admitted to probate on production of a copy or other proof of its execution and contents, if the circumstances are not such as to raise a presumption of intention to revoke.

§ 5.3-2. ———; *failure to discover other will, or codicil.* There has been discussed above the liability of one who administers an estate as that of an intestate decedent where, at some later time, a will of the decedent is discovered.[17] The principles there stated extend to the case of administration of an estate under a particular will where another instrument constitutes a part of the decedent's will,[18] as where there is a will of later date, or a codicil, that affects but does not completely revoke or supersede the instrument probated, or, conversely, where the will admitted to probate does not, either expressly or by necessary implication, revoke a will of earlier date, which accordingly remains in force in whole or in part.[19] In any such case the executor may be liable to beneficiaries affected by the other instrument, unless he can show that all proper diligence was used in searching for any other testamentary instrument in force at the time of the decedent's death, or in endeavoring to ascertain with assurance that the instrument probated was in fact the decedent's last will and the whole of his will.[20]

§ 5.3-3. ———; *revocation of later will; revival.*[21] In some jurisdictions there is applied the doctrine that, upon the revocation by a testator of a particular will, his last preceding will, if it is still existent, is revived or restored to effectiveness. In other jurisdictions, however, the doctrine does not obtain, and, upon the revocation of a will which revoked earlier wills, no earlier instrument is restored to effectiveness[22] and the decedent is held to have died intestate unless he executed a new will after such revocation. The law to be applied in determining whether the doctrine

---

[17] Duty to search for will, and peril of late discovery, supra § 4.2-2.

[18] Cf. *Appln. of Spitzmuller*, 279 App.D. 233, 109 N.Y.S.2d 1, affd. w/o op. 304 N.Y. 608, 151 N.E. 91, applying the rule in the case of a trustee making distribution after inquiry and in absence of knowledge of will, exercising power of appointment, that was discovered later.

[19] See last preceding section.

[20] Separate will disposing of property in particular jurisdiction, or except in particular jurisdiction, infra § 6.21-2.

[21] P-H Est. Plng. Serv. ¶ 475.

[22] So in Unif. Prob. Code sec. 2-509, "unless it is evident" that the testator intended the first will to be effective.

applies is apparently that of the domicile of the decedent, rather than that of the place of probate, if the two are different.[23]

§ 5.3-4. ———; *dependent relative revocation*.[24] A number of states apply the doctrine that a revoked will is nevertheless to be given effect, if the testator revoked it only in contemplation of executing a new will but he failed to do the latter or the will he executed was for some reason ineffective. In other jurisdictions, however, the doctrine is not recognized. Where it is applied, the doctrine is one of presumed intention, on the assumption that the testator would rather have his property pass under the "revoked" will than to die intestate, and is in that respect related to the rule of revival of an earlier will on revocation of a later one.[25]

§ 5.3-5. ———; *revocation other than by later instrument or destruction*.[26] It is to be borne in mind that a will may be revoked otherwise than by a later instrument or by destruction *animo revocandi*. In some jurisdictions, a will is revoked by the marriage of the testator, or his marriage and the birth of issue to him, after its execution;[27] and statutory provisions in other jurisdictions giving a spouse a right to elect to take a statutory share of the estate,[28] or to the effect that a spouse married to the testator after the execution of the will, or a child born to the testator after such execution, at least if not mentioned or provided for the will,[29] takes an intestate share, so that the will is operative only as to the remaining balance of the estate, may be regarded as equivalent to a statutory revocation of the will *pro tanto*. In some states, but not in the majority of them, divorce of the testator or annulment of the marriage revokes a previously executed will, either entirely or, as in most instances, only as to its provision for the benefit of the spouse.[30] A will may in effect be revoked or annulled by the acquisition by the testator of a new domicile in a jurisdiction under whose laws the will is invalidly executed, unless a statute in such jurisdiction makes effective any will that was validly executed under the law of the place of its making.[31]

---

[23] This would be consistent with the general rule that the validity and effect of a will (except as to real property situate in another jurisdiction) are governed by the law of the testator's domicile; see § 25.4-4 infra.

[24] P-H Est. Plng. Serv. ¶ 468.

[25] See last preceding section.

[26] P-H Est. Plng. Serv. ¶¶ 469–474.

[27] At common law, the marriage of a female testator, or the marriage of a male testator and birth of issue to him, revoked a previously executed will. It will be in mind, however, that this rule did not necessarily result in passing any part of the estate to the spouse, inasmuch as a spouse was not an heir, but merely prevented the testator from disposing of his property to others of his choice without executing a new will after the event that caused revocation. Cf. Bliss, Implied By Law Revocation of Wills, 42 Notre Dame L. 71.

[28] Infra § 17.4-1 ff.

[29] Infra § 17.6-1 ff.

[30] Infra § 17.5.

[31] What law governs as to formalities of execution, infra § 25.4-2.

§ 5.3-6. ———; *joint will*.[32] It will of course be kept in mind that a joint, or joint and mutual, will may be probated as the last will of each testator, if it remains in force at such testator's death; but that such a will may be revoked, as to his own estate, by either testator, even if the other has died,[33] and so that it ceases to be effective as to the revoking testator and the rights, if any, of the beneficiaries named in it depend upon contract, as a claim against the estate,[34] if a contract between the testators can be established,[35] or, in some circumstances, on the doctrine of constructive trust.[36]

§ 5.4-1. *Determination of (a) domicile and (b) place of probate; in general.* The decedent's domicile and the place of probate of his will are not necessarily the same. In every case, for reasons noted in a following section,[37] the executor must determine the domicile of the testator, regardless of the place of probate. Ordinarily, of course, a will is offered for probate in the jurisdiction in which the decedent's domicile was at the time of his death.[38] There is, however, no inflexible requirement that that be done,[39] and it may well be advisable in some cases to offer the will for probate in another jurisdiction, so that the estate may be administered in the latter. Accordingly, before offering a will for probate at the decedent's domicile, or arranging to have it so offered, the executor should consider the pertinent factors and, where a choice of forum may exist, should endeavor to obtain probate where the interests of the estate will be best and most economically served.[40]

§ 5.4-2. ———; *domicile problems*.[41] Difficult problems can arise in determining the domicile of a decedent,[42] and such problems arise with increased frequency under present conditions because of the mobility of the population and also because of the increased number of persons who have more than one residence. Employees of businesses operating in several sections of the country may be shifted from place

---

[32] P-H Est. Plng. Serv. ¶¶ 490–495.

[33] Cf. *Rubenstein v. Mueller*, 19 N.Y.2d 228, 225 N.E.2d 540, referring to a joint will by husband and wife as irrevocable by the husband after the wife's death, but where the point decided as that a second wife could not elect against such will after the husband's death. Election by surviving spouse, in general, infra § 17.4-1 ff.

[34] Claims generally, infra § 9.3-1 ff.

[35] Unif. Prob. Code sec. 2-701 provides that a joint will gives rise to no presumption of a contract, and specifies how (only) a contract may be established.

[36] Infra Ch. XXVI.

[37] Infra § 5.4-2a.

[38] Jurisdiction at domicile, West Dig., Exrs. & Admrs. Key No. 10.

[39] Where will may be probated, in general, Restatement, Conflict of Laws 2d, sec. 314.

[40] Stallings, Choosing Foreign Forum for Probate and Administration, 1959 Proc. A.B.A. Sec. Real Prop. Prob. & Tr. L, Part I, 25; cf. Hendrickson, Planning Wills for Nonresidents, 105 Trusts & Estates 315. Probate of wills of non-residents, infra § 5.5-1 ff.

[41] West Dig., Domicile Key No. 1 ff.

[42] For an excellent discussion of domicile problems in this context, see Chrystie, What Is or Was or Will Be Your Client's Domicile, 1 The Practical Lawyer 13. Conclusiveness of probate decree as to domicile, see Bozeman, The Conflict of Laws Relating to Wills, Probate Decrees and Estates, 49 A.B.A.J. 670, 671–673; cf. Unif. Prob. Code sec. 3-203.

to place as changing needs of the business dictate or for the purpose of broadening their experience; and persons in military or other public service are also frequently transferred from place to place. The question in each such case is whether there is a change of domicile, so that a new domicile is acquired with a particular change of residence or location, or instead the original domicile is retained. Since domicile is dependent in part upon intention and in part upon overt action, many factors may have to be considered; it may be conjectured that a business employee is more likely to effect a change of domicile with a change in location than is a person in the military or another public service. Questions may also arise as to the domicile of one who has a place of residence in each of two or more jurisdictions; and there is even the occasional case of an individual so peripatetic that it is difficult to determine whether he has any fixed place or places of residence and whether he has ever acquired a domicile other than that of origin.

§ 5.4-2a. ———; ———; *importance of determining domicile.* It is important, and necessary in practically every estate, to determine the domicile of the decedent, not only for the purpose of determining what jurisdiction has power to impose an estate or inheritance tax on the estate but also because of the general rules, elsewhere discussed, as to governance of many matters connected with the disposition of the decedents property by the law of his domicile.[43] In the usual case no doubt as to the matter may exist, but, as pointed out above, where any doubt does exist the problem may be very difficult of solution, and the executor should not proceed as to any matters significantly affected by domicile without making a full investigation and, very often, instituting such judicial proceeding as may be available under the circumstances to determine or adjudicate the question.

§ 5.4-3. ———; *place of probate within state.* Statutes ordinarily provide for the probate of a will in the county (or other political subdivision) in which the testator was domiciled at his death, or, if he was not domiciled in the state, in any county (or subdivision) in which any of his property was located.[44] Where, under such a statute, probate is permissible at either of two or more places in the state, it is usually further provided that the court in which a proceeding is first commenced has exclusive jurisdiction or right to proceed as to that and all subsequent proceedings in the administration of the estate.[45]

§ 5.5-1. *Probate of will of non-resident; in general.*[46] It has been pointed out above that a will need not in every case be probated at the testator's domicile, and that instead it may be possible and advisable to probate it elsewhere.[47] The executor does not, however, have a free choice to select a particular jurisdiction as the

---

[43] Infra § 25.4-1 ff.
[44] So in Unif. Prob. Code secs. 3-201, -202.
[45] Op. cit., sec. 1-303.
[46] West Dig., Exrs. & Admrs. Key Nos. 8–12 and Wills Key Nos. 238–246; "foreign" administration generally, op. cit. Exrs. & Admrs. Key No. 517 ff.
[47] Supra § 5.4-1.

place of probate merely on the basis of whim or personal preference. Ordinarily, a court of probate is not required, by the law governing it, to take jurisdiction of a proceeding for the original probate of the will of a person not domiciled within the state, but in a majority of states it may in its discretion accept jurisdiction if it deems sufficient reason therefor to exist. The factors that may lead a court to accept jurisdiction under such a discretionary authority are very similar to those that may cause a proponent to seek non-resident probate.[48] Among them are the physical location within the state of the bulk of the decedent's assets,[49] the residence within the state of the principal beneficiaries under the will, the fact that the executor named in the will is a resident of the state or a trust company therein, particularly if he or it would be unable under the law of the testator's domicile to qualify as executor there,[50] and the presence in the will of a direction or request that the will be offered for probate in the court's state or, under a statute or rule of law permitting it, of an election that the validity and effect of the dispositions made in the will be governed by the law of such state.[51] Conversely, a court will ordinarily refuse to take jurisdiction of the probate proceeding if none of such factors is present, as there would not seem to be any reason why its state should lend its judicial processes to the case of a will having no connection with the state.

§ 5.5-2. ———; *jurisdiction to tax not affected.* It is probably unnecessary to point out that the place of probate of a will does not affect the power of a state to impose an estate or inheritance tax on or in respect of the estate or assets included therein. The taxing power remains with the state of domicile, except as to assets having a situs for tax purposes in another jurisdiction,[52] and the probate of the will in a particular state neither confers upon such state any right to impose a tax nor deprives any other state of such right.[53]

§ 5.5-3. ———; *statutes requiring original probate at domicile.* Where a statute of the state of the decedent's domicile requires that the will be offered for original probate in that state, or imposes a penalty for its probate elsewhere,[54] an executor residing in another state in which, under its own laws, the will may be admitted to probate as that of a non-resident[55] must consider the effect, if any, of such a statute upon him. It would seem unlikely, under general principles, that such a statute would be given effect by the courts of any other state, and that any penalty could

---

[48] Ibid.
[49] *Matter of Heller-Baghero,* 26 N.Y.2d 706, 257 N.E.2d 49 (where 90% of assets were in the state, and the executor and certain, legatees resided therein, jurisdiction to grant original probate was justified (although not compelled), even though an earlier will had been probated as the "last" will in Austria where decedent was domiciled at death).
[50] Disqualification of non-resident or a foreign trust company, supra § 4.5-3.
[51] Will provision as to place of probate, cf. Hendrickson, Planning Wills for Non residents, 105 Trusts & Estates 315, 318. Direction as to what law governs, infra § 25.4-4a.
[52] Infra § 12.1.
[53] Contest as to domicile and right to tax, infra § 12.12.
[54] E.g., Fla. Stat. Ann. sec. 732.36.
[55] Supra § 5.5-1.

be imposed upon the executor for its violation, at least unless he were found within the borders of the domiciliary state. Where the statute further purports to provide that title to property of the decedent does not devolve unless and until it has been administered in the domiciliary jurisdiction, a somewhat more serious question may be presented, for if it be recalled that the disposition of property by will is generally regarded as a privilege rather than a right,[56] upon which privilege the sovereign may presumably impose such conditions as it may determine, an argument can be made that such a statutory provision is effective as to all property of the decedent not having a situs in another jurisdiction.

§ 5.5-4. ——; *ancillary probate.*[57] Original probate of a will in a jurisdiction other than that of the domicile of the testator[58] is, of course, to be distinguished from ancillary probate. The latter term connotes a "secondary" establishment in one jurisdiction of a will that had previously been established in another jurisdiction as the testator's last will, and, as has been indicated in a preceding section,[59] is ordinarily required, if at all, only where the testator left property in a state other than that of the original probate which cannot be collected or managed,[60] or as to which state death taxes cannot be fixed, without the appointment in such state of a legal representative.[61] The term "ancillary administration" refers to administration[62] under ancillary probate.

§ 5.6-1. *Probate; in general.* Probate of a will in some jurisdictions requires the institution of a formal proceeding, upon notice to next of kin and others in interest, while in other jurisdictions probate is *pro forma* and notice, if any, is given after the will has been admitted to probate. The chief difference between the two kinds of probate is that in the former case (called "probate in solemn form" or "formal probate"[63]) persons who receive the required notice or appear in the proceeding must therein assert any objections they may have to the admission of the will to probate[64] and, if they fail to do so, are, in general, precluded by the entry of a decree of probate from thereafter contesting the will or objecting to its validity;[65] while in the latter case (called "probate in common form" or "informal

---

[56] Supra § 3.10 note 69.
[57] West Dig., Exrs. & Admrs. Key No. 578 ff.; P-H Est. Plng. Serv. ¶ 2560.
[58] Supra § 5.5-1.
[59] Supra § 1.7.
[60] Necessity of ancillary probate, in general, Goodrich & Scoles, Conflict of Laws, secs. 171–174; power of executor outside state of appointment, op. cit. secs. 185–186. Suits by or against executor appointed in another jurisdiction, Restatement, Conflict of Laws 2d, secs. 354–358; Ehrenzweig, Conflict of Laws, pp. 48–49, 60 ff.; Leflar, American Conflicts Law (1968 rev.) sec. 204.
[61] Defined, supra § 1.2.
[62] Term as applicable in testate as well as intestate estate, supra § 1.10.
[63] Cf. Unif. Prob. Code sec. 3-401 ff.
[64] Contests, infra § 5.10-1.
[65] Conclusiveness of probate in another jurisdiction, Bozeman, The Conflict of Laws Relating to Wills, Probate Decrees and Estates, 49 A.B.A.J. 670, 672–674.

PROBATE OF WILL AND QUALIFICATION OF EXECUTOR 39

probate"[66]) the will is first admitted to probate and any objections and contests may be asserted after probate, either within a specified period or, under some statutes, at any time before distribution of the estate has been made.[67] The duties of an executor as to production of a will[68] and as to offering it for probate[69] have been elsewhere discussion. Ordinarily, the probate of a will involves or comprehends the appointment[70] of an executor[71] or an administrator c.t.a.[72]; but in at least one jurisdiction[73] there exists a practice of probating a will to prove title to property without the appointment of a legal representative.

§ 5.6-2. ———; *persons to receive notice*.[74] Where in the jurisdiction involved probate of a will is in solemn form,[75] by a formal proceeding, upon notice to heirs or other specified classes of persons in interest, it is important that due notice be given to all such persons, as any person not duly served is not precluded from raising an objection as to the validity of the will or contesting its provisions; and the executor, even if he is not the proponent, will therefore want to be sure that all necessary persons have been so given notice. At least where the executor is the proponent, it is his duty to search for and identify the heirs or other persons entitled to notice. On similar principles, where probate is in common form,[76] the executor must consider whether formal notice to any persons that the will has been probated is required by the applicable statutes, for, if a required notice is not given, a person entitled thereto may presumably object to or contest the will at any time thereafter regardless of the running of an otherwise applicable statute of limitation.

§ 5.6-3. ———; *"probate of heirship" distinguished*. In a number of states statutes provide a proceeding to establish that a decedent died intestate, or to determine who are his heirs. Such a proceeding is often called "probate of heirship", but resembles a proceeding for probate of a will only in that both are directed toward the eventual ascertainment of the persons entitled to receive the property of the decedent.[77]

§ 5.7-1. *Temporary administration; in general*. Where factors exist, of the character referred to in a preceding section, that make necessary or advisable the ap-

---

[66] Unif. Prob. Code sec. 3-301 ff.
[67] See Bozeman, op. cit. supra note 65.
[68] Supra § 4.3-1.
[69] Supra § 4.3-3.
[70] Proceedings for appointment, in general, West Dig., Exrs. & Admrs. Key No. 20.
[71] Supra § 1.3-1.
[72] Supra § 1.4-2.
[73] Texas.
[74] West Dig., Exrs. & Admrs. Key No. 20 (4), (4½). P-H Est. Plng. Serv. ¶ 2128.
[75] See last preceding section.
[76] Ibid.
[77] In states not having a statute of the character referred to, presumably the result is usually reached by a conventional intestacy proceeding for the administration of the decedent's estate.

pointment of a temporary administrator,[78] or, where a statute provides therefor, a "preliminary executor",[79] the named executor of a will has a duty, of the same nature as other pre-probate responsibilities,[80] to seek the appointment of himself or another in such temporary or preliminary capacity, unless another party in interest makes such an application; and for failure so to apply in a proper case the named executor may incur liabilities for resulting loss or damages to the estate.

§ 5.7-2. ———; *powers of temporary administrator.*[81] A temporary administrator has only such powers as are granted to him by statute or granted by the court pursuant to a statute,[82] and specifically he does not have the powers conferred by the will or the inherent powers of an executor. His statutory powers are ordinarily closely circumscribed, and even the additional powers or authority that may be granted to him by the court are usually of limited character. The theory of statutes providing for temporary administration appears clearly to be merely that of meeting an emergency or urgent situation, and the temporary administrator is little more than an arm of the court. Thus the temporary administrator usually must apply for and obtain express judicial authorization for any action other than the barest minimum necessary for preservation of the estate, and for any action taken without proper authorization by statute or by the court the temporary administrator acts at his peril of begin held liable to any person damaged by it.[83] Moreover, even if the court purports to confer additional power or authority upon the temporary administrator, it would seem that the latter does not possess and should not exercise any such authority unless it is within the scope of the powers that the statute authorizes the court to confer upon him.[84]

§ 5.8-1. *Eligibility and qualification of executor; in general.*[85] The term "qualification" with respect to an executor is sometimes used in two different senses. The first of these relates to his right or capacity to be an executor, as, for example, under a statute precluding or restricting service as an executor by a non-resident of the state, or a trust company not qualified to do business in the state; the term "eligibility" would seem more correctly to describe a question of this nature. The second, and more accurate, sense refers to the steps to be taken by the appointed executor to entitle him to receive letters testamentary[86] and to act as executor[87] as, usually, by taking an oath of office, perhaps manifesting in some prescribed man-

---

[78] Supra § 1.5.
[79] Supra § 1.3-3.
[80] Supra § 4.6.
[81] West Dig., Exrs. & Admrs. Key No. 122.
[82] Appointment, functions, and termination, in general, cf. Unif. Prob. Code secs. 3-614 to 3-618 incl.
[83] Liability as insurer, in general, supra § 3.7-1.
[84] Broader powers of a "preliminary executor", supra § 1.3-3.
[85] West Dig., Exrs. & Admrs. Key Nos. 15, 18, 25.
[86] Infra § 5.8-3.
[87] Unif. Prob. Code sec. 3-103.

PROBATE OF WILL AND QUALIFICATION OF EXECUTOR 41

ner his acceptance of appointment and willingness to serve,[88] in some states designating the clerk of the court as his agent to receive service of process in any action or proceeding affecting the estate, and, as discussed in the next following section, furnishing a fidelity bond. It is in this second sense that the term "qualification" is used in this work.[89] A third person dealing with an executor should require evidence, usually in the form of a certified copy of the letters testamentary or, in some states, a certificate that such letters have been issued and remain in force,[90] that the executor has qualified as required by law, and so is entitled as the legal representative of the estate to receive assets of the estate and to deal with its property and affairs, as in the absence of such qualification the executor may be without authority[91] and the third person may incur liabilities to beneficiaries of the estate.[92]

§ 5.8-2. ———; *bond*.[93] The qualification required of an executor ordinarily includes the furnishing of a bond for the protection of creditors and beneficiaries,[94] unless the will effectively exonerates the executor from furnishing bond. Even where the will directs that a bond be not required, the court of probate may have power in its discretion to require a bond, as, for example, where the executor is a non-resident of the state. In some jurisdictions banks and trust companies are excepted from the requirement of a bond, or are not required to furnish any surety on the bond. One delivering property of the decedent to an executor must ascertain whether the latter was required to furnish bond and, if so, whether the bond given is sufficient in amount to cover the property being delivered, and may refuse to make delivery until an adequate bond has been furnished; if without sufficient investigation, or with notice of the absence or inadequacy of bond, the third person delivers property to the executor, he may be held liable to persons harmed by any loss or misappropriation of the property by the executor. In this connection it is to be kept in mind that evidence that a bond of a specified amount has been given is not necessarily protective to one delivering property to the executor, without in addition evidence as to how much, if any, property has already come into the executor's hands and hence whether the bond is sufficient to cover the additional property being delivered.

§ 5.8-3. ———; *letters testamentary*.[95] Statutes ordinarily provide that upon the due qualification[96] of the executor, the court of probate shall issue to him letters

---

[88] Op. cit. sec. 3-601.
[89] "Disqualification", infra § 5.8-4.
[90] Letters as evidence of appointment and qualification, infra § 5.8-3.
[91] As executor de son tort, supra § 1.8. But failure of a co-executor to qualify does not affect the powers of an executor who does, unless the will otherwise provides; Unif. Prob. Code sec. 3-718.
[92] Supra § 3.7-2.
[93] West Dig., Exrs. & Admrs. Key No. 26.
[94] Unif. Prob. Code sec. 3-601. Liabilities on bond and enforcement thereof, West Dig., Exrs. & Admrs. Key No. 527 ff. Release of bond on discharge of executor, infra § 24.9.
[95] West Dig., Exrs. & Admrs. Key Nos. 27, 28.
[96] Supra § 5.8-1.

testamentary,[97] evidencing the fact that he is the executor of the will; and in general the executor cannot act as such until letters have been so issued.[98] The executor retains the letters, as his own evidence of his authority, and may exhibit them to anyone to demonstrate his official capacity. Where, however, proof of such capacity is to be filed with another the executor should instead furnish a certified copy of his letters, or, under the practice in some jurisdictions, a certificate of the clerk of the probate court (often called a "short-form certificate") to the effect that the letters have been issued and remain in force. The letters, or such certificate, are adequate evidence that formal qualification requirements have been complied with, but are not evidence that the bond, if any, given by the executor is sufficient to cover any particular amount or value of property, except as, under the practice in some jurisdictions, they specify the amount of the bond given.[99] Letters testamentary are revoked, either automatically or by express order, when an executor is permitted to resign or is removed.[100] Accordingly, one shown or furnished with the letters or a copy of them should satisfy himself that they have not been revoked, and by the same token any short-form certificate relied upon should be of recent date.

§ 5.8-4. ———; *disqualification.*[1] An executor who, after having been appointed and qualified as such, becomes ineligible to serve, by reason of a change in circumstances such that if the change had occurred before his appointment he would not have been eligible to be appointed,[2] is spoken of as having become "disqualified" to serve,[3] and is subject to removal.[4]

§ 5.9. *Review of will provisions.* Reference has been made earlier[5] to the advisability or review of the will promptly upon the death of the testator to determine whether the executor wishes to accept his appointment as such and what, if any, special problems can be noted at the outset. Unless such review also included a detailed analysis of the terms and provisions of the will,[6] such an analysis should be made, promptly after the admission of the will to probate, in the light of what is then known as to the nature and character of the assets of the estate and the identities and problems of beneficiaries, in order to determine at least tentatively what problems of management or administration[7] or of construction[8] may arise and at

---

[97] Defined, supra § 1.12.
[98] So in Unif. Prob. Code sec. 3-103. Pre-probate powers and responsibilities, supra §§ 4.6, 4.7.
[99] See last preceding section
[100] Resignation and removal, infra §§ 23.2, 23.3. Revocation of letters, in general, West Dig., Exrs. & Admrs. Key No. 32.
[1] West Dig. Exrs. & Admrs. Key No. 34.
[2] Supra § 4.5-3.
[3] The term unfortunately suggests that its antithesis is "qualified", which, however, has a different connotation (cf. § 5.8-1 supra), and it should not be confused with the matter of eligibility or ineligibility.
[4] Infra § 23.3.
[5] Supra §§ 4.4, 4.5-1.
[6] Cf. P-H Est. Plng. Serv. ¶ 2145. Tickler and check list of dates and duties, supra § 2.3.
[7] Generally, infra Ch. VII.
[8] Infra § 14.35-1. Construction proceedings, infra Ch. XXII.

PROBATE OF WILL AND QUALIFICATION OF EXECUTOR 43

what time, or at what stage of the administration of the estate, they will have to be resolved. It will often be found helpful to prepare at this stage a brief outline of the important dispositive and administrative provisions of the will, together with notations of the construction or other problems that are apparent or probable, and to keep such outline at the top of a file dealing with estate matters, so that it will be noticed each time the file is referred to and will serve as a ready index to or reminder of the nature and problems of the estate.

§ 5.10-1.   *Contests; in general*.[9] It is, on general principles, ordinarily a part of the duty of the executor named in a will that is the subject of objections or contest to defend the validity of the will, and hence the interests of those named in it as beneficiaries, at least unless the latter participate actively in the proceeding and thereby themselves protect their interests.[10] The executor is therefore not necessarily justified in standing mute when objection is made or a contest is initiated; on the other hand, where a contest involves the rights of heirs against beneficiaries, or of beneficiaries among themselves or those under one will against those under another, it would not seem that the executor is bound to take or indeed warranted in taking an adversary position for or against objectants or contestants,[11] except to the limited extent indicated above.

§ 5.10-2.   ———;   *in terrorem provisions*.[12] Where a will contains a provision for the deprivation of benefits from a beneficiary who institutes or participates in a contest of the will, the primary question to be decided is as to the validity or efficacy of such provision.[13] The modern tendency appears to be against such validity; and even if it is not invalid on general principles, it seems to be usually (although not universally) the rule that, at least so far as concerns personal property,[14] a provision to the effect that a contestant shall lose his benefit is merely *in terrorem*, and without legal effect, unless it is coupled with a gift over of the "lost" benefit to another. It may be commented that an executor considering whether to qualify[15] under a will should give special attention to an anti-contest provision, inasmuch as the presence of such a provision may suggest vulnerability and thus tend to invite a contest, for it is ordinarily possible for potential objectants to find a beneficiary whose interests are

---

[9] P-H Est. Plng. Serv. ¶¶ 2129, 2130. For a detailed study of contests, including the grounds therefor and the effects thereof, see 1965 Proc. A.B.A. Sec. Real Prop. Prob. & Tr. L., Part I, 149 ff.

[10] Existence *vel non* of duty to defend will, see op. cit. prec. note, 166. Attorney's fees in contest proceedings, infra § 20.3-6.

[11] Duty of impartiality among beneficiaries, supra § 3.9-3; in construction proceedings, infra § 22.1.

[12] P-H Est. Plng. Serv. ¶¶ 375.16–18.

[13] Cf. Unif. Prob. Code sec. 3-905: Such a provision is unenforceable if "probable cause" exists for instituting proceedings; it is not clear how or at what stage the existence or non-existence of probable cause would be determined.

[14] *Matter of Arrowsmith*, 162 App.D. 623, 147 N.Y.S. 1016, affd. 213 N.Y. 104, 108 N.E. 1089. As to real property, cf. *Hogan v. Curtin*, 88 N.Y. 162.

[15] Generally, supra § 4.5-1.

so small or slight that he can be persuaded, for an appropriate consideration, to act as cat's-paw for the others in contesting the will.[16]

§ 5.11. *"Small estates" statutes; dispensing with proceedings.* In a number of jurisdictions statutes provide a simplified procedure, as a substitute for conventional probate or administration, for the settlement of estates not exceeding in size some specified amount or value.[17] Especially as the statutes are mostly recent, and differ considerably among themselves, cases construing them are rare, and procedure under them is ordinarily prescribed in detail, they are not discussed in this work.[18] Closely allied with such statutes are those laws or procedures in various jurisdictions permitting a person in possession of property of the decedent, or a debtor of the decedent, including a depositary bank, to deliver specified kinds of property, or pay money up to a specified amount, to the decedent's spouse or children without the appointment of a legal representative or other judicial proceeding.[19] In both cases the purpose is, of course, to facilitate the devolution of small estates and avoid the formalities, delays, and expense of conventional administration.[20]

---

[16] As to *in terrorem* clauses and their effects, in general, see 1965 Proc. A.B.A. Sec. Real Prop. Prob. & Tr. L., Part I, 162–164.

[17] Cf. Unif. Prob. Code sec. 3-1201 ff; see also Model Small Estates Act, 9C U.L.A. (Pkt. Part) 95. "Voluntary administration" under such a statute, supra § 1.4-1.

[18] For a study of problems of small estates and special statutory treatment thereof, see 1965 Proc. A.B.A. Sec. Real Prop. Prob. & Tr. L., Part I, 142 ff.

[19] E.g., U.S. Savings Bonds (31 Code Fed. Reg. 315.73(b)), Federal income tax refunds (I.R.S. Form 1310), Social Security benefits (42 U.S.C.A. Sec. 404(d)), and, under various state statutes or practices, wages, small life insurance payments, bank balances not exceeding specified amounts, small amounts of stock, etc.

[20] Accounting and settlement under such statutes, infra § 24.11.

VI

COLLECTION OF ASSETS AND PAPERS

Part A—In General

§ 6.1. *Existence and nature of duty*.[1] An essential duty of the executor after his appointment is to collect all assets of the decedent, in order that they may be identified and administered.[2] Not only is he responsible in this respect as to all the decedent's property of the existence of which he knows, but it is also his responsibility to inform himself of the full extent of the decedent's assets, and, if he has reason to believe that any asset exists or may exist, even though his knowledge is incomplete, he must make all necessary investigations to discover the facts.[3] One of his first duties, therefore, is to familiarize himself as fully as possible with the decedent's affairs. Some of the methods of doing this, some of the kinds of assets to be searched for, and some of the methods of making as sure as possible that all assets are discovered, are discussed in following sections. While not every step to which the discussion relates must necessarily be taken in every estate, the executor may be held liable by beneficiaries for failure to discover any asset, or any significant fact relating to the decedent's interests and rights, that proper investigation would have disclosed, with resulting failure to collect and preserve any asset or value that with due attention could have been preserved.

§ 6.2. *Preliminary steps; forwarding address; advices of death, etc.* In order to be sure that any mail directed to the decedent will receive proper attention, and as a part of his actions looking toward full familiarization with the decedent's affairs, the executor should file with the relevant post office a direction for forwarding all such mail to him; and as a further precaution the executor should advise each person known or believed to have had a business relationship, or any kind of business or financial dealings, with the decedent of the latter's death and the identity and

---

[1] West Dig., Exrs. & Admrs. Key Nos. 38 ff, 83–89; P-H Est. Plng. Serv. ¶ 2189 ff.
[2] Preservation and management of assets, infra Ch. VII. Inventory and valuation, infra § 8.1 ff.
[3] Discovery proceedings, infra § 6.22.

address of the executor.[4] In this connection, it is also ordinarily advisable for the executor to file a notice of his fiduciary relationship with the Federal tax authorities, so that he may receive any notices, assessments, and the like relating to the decedent's tax matters.[5]

§ 6.3.   *Identification of assets and familiarization with affairs.* In carrying out the executor's duty to verify the existence and nature of the decedent's assets, and otherwise to familiarize himself with the decedent's affairs,[6] a number of steps, taken promptly after the executor's entry upon his duties, will be found helpful and in many cases essential. A review of the decedent's personal and business records and correspondence, covering at least the last year or two before his death, will assist the executor in becoming conversant with the decedent's activities and his affairs generally, and may supply clues to rights or interests belonging to him and enterprises or transactions in which he was or had been engaged. Examination of his checkbook and of bank and brokerage statements, credit and debit advices, duplicate deposit tickets, and the like will help to disclose the sources of the decedent's income and thus the nature and existence of assets and property rights. Checks for dividends and interest, and other items of income, as they are received by the executor, should be checked against securities on hand and other known assets to determine whether all income-producing assets have been located. A review of the decedent's income tax returns for the five years next preceding his death will provide additional or confirmatory information as to the nature and sources of his income and hence of the identity and existence of capital assets.[7] Any information or indications disclosed by such examinations and reviews should be promptly investigated by the executor, to the end of making sure that he discovers all assets of the estate and has full information concerning the decedent's affairs. As is elsewhere pointed out,[8] the executor's investigations should extend not only to assets that will or should come into his hands or control but also to other assets, if any, that will be includible in the taxable estate for the purposes of an estate or inheritance tax. While the emphasis here is on business and financial matters, it is not to be overlooked that there may also be disclosed information as to personal affairs that will be of importance to the executor in the administration of the estate.

§ 6.4.   *Locating and opening safe deposit box.* Unless the executor knows, or discovers in the course of the preliminary investigations referred to in the last preceding section, the location of the decedent's safe deposit box or other safekeeping facilities, or is fully satisfied that no such box or other facility (or no other than the one discovered) exists, it is his duty to make whatever search for such a facility is appropriate under the circumstances to establish its existence or nonexistence. It

---

[4] Suspension of utilities, infra § 7.13.
[5] I.R.S. Form 56; see Reg. 301.6903-1.
[6] Supra § 6.1.
[7] Examination of returns as to possible deficiency assessment, infra § 10.3.
[8] Infra § 12.3.

COLLECTION OF ASSETS AND PAPERS 47

may be necessary for the executor to address inquiries to all banks and safe deposit companies in the city or other area in which the decedent lives or conducted his affairs. If a safe deposit box key is found among the decedent's possessions, the executor must, of course, discover the box to which the key relates; and, inasmuch as such keys ordinarily are not marked with the name of a bank or safe deposit company or with a box number, the executor may have to make fairly widespread inquiries to locate the box, usually on the basis of the type of key and its serial number, which will enable a bank or safe deposit company to determine readily whether the box is one in its vaults. When a box or other safekeeping facility is located, it must be promptly opened[9] and its contents examined; apart from securities or other valuables contained in the box, any papers and records found therein may, of course, afford clues to assets, or to property or business interests, not previously located or identified, and should be carefully examined from that point of view.

§ 6.5. *Cash and valuables on decedent's person, etc.* Especially where the decedent died suddenly or away from his own home, the executor must make due investigation as to what money and other property was on his person or in his possession at the time of his death, and take appropriate steps to gain possession of such assets or to recover them from a person who has them. Where the decedent was in a hospital or sanitarium, the executor should make sure that he learns of and collects all property that was kept by the decedent in his room as well as whatever property was held by the institution for him in its safe or safekeeping facility. Particularly if the decedent was a wealthy person or in the habit of carrying considerable sums of money, and dies away from home, the executor should carefully and fully investigate the facts as to what money was found and what became of it, having in mind not only his fiduciary duty to the estate and its beneficiaries but also the questions on the point that are likely to be asked by death tax authorities on audit of tax returns.

§ 6.6. *Cash in safe deposit box, home, or office.* Where a sum or sums of cash are found in a decedent's safe deposit box, in his home or office, or otherwise among his papers or possessions, the executor should carefully preserve any envelopes or folders in which cash was contained, and examine any notations thereon and any accompanying or relevant memoranda, to aid in ascertaining or determining when or how the cash was received, whether it is the property of the decedent or of another, and its nature as income or otherwise.[10] This is particularly important in order that the executor may be in a position to meet the presumption applied for federal and at least some state income tax purposes that cash held by a decedent at the time of his death is to be regarded as income received in the year of death, and accordingly is taxable for such year, unless the contrary can be established.

§ 6.7-1. *Bank accounts; in general.* The investigation of the decedent's records and papers referred to in a preceding section[11] will ordinarily disclose the existence

---
[9] Necessity of state death tax waiver, infra § 12.11.
[10] Cash presumed to be income in year of death, *Evelyn Hickok*, P-H Memo. T.C. ¶ 52005.
[11] Supra § 6.1.

and location of any bank accounts and other deposit accounts maintained by the decedent at the time of his death.[12] Unless, however, the executor is fully satisfied that he knows of all such accounts, it may be necessary for him, as in the case of safe deposit boxes,[13] to make inquiries of all banks and other depositaries, including savings and loan organizations, in the area in which the decedent lived, conducted his affairs, or for any other reason might have maintained any such account. If the decedent was employed, investigation should be made as to his participation in an employees' credit union or savings plan. All deposit accounts of the decedent should be closed[14] and the funds therefrom transferred to an account in the name of the executor or the estate.[15]

§ 6.7-2. ———; *savings accounts.* Where funds of the decedent are at the time of his death on deposit in a savings or other interest-bearing account, on which interest is paid only at periodic dates on the then balance, the executor ordinarily should postpone closing such account, or transferring the funds thereof to an estate account, until the next interest-payment date, in order not to deprive the estate of interest for the current period.[16] An exception to this rule would, of course, exist if the executor has any reason to doubt the solvency or reliability of the depositary institution, in which case the safety of the fund outweighs the accrual of interest and the account should be closed immediately.

§ 6.8. *Contents of home or office, and tangibles generally.* It is the duty of the executor to ascertain and preserve assets located in the decedent's home or office just as any other assets, and to that end whatever steps are reasonable and appropriate should be taken. If the decedent resided alone, his home or apartment should be locked or sealed by the executor at the earliest possible moment, even before the latter's qualification,[17] in order to prevent or minimize the possibility of removal of or interference with assets and records by any unauthorized person; often installation of new locks in addition to or in place of those existing at the time is advisable. If the decedent lived with another, or if another or others have access to his home, the executor must, again very promptly, take whatever steps are necessary and reasonable in the circumstances to prevent interference with or loss or removal of assets and records, including removal from the premises of valuables and disappearance, damage, or destruction of papers or records belonging to the decedent or relating to his affairs, or property or papers belonging to others. In any case, the executor should promptly make a search of the premises for money, valuables, bankbooks, records, papers, and the like,[18] and should take into his own possession all such prop-

---

[12] Joint accounts, infra § 6.16-2a; bank account trusts, infra § 6.16-2b.
[13] Supra § 6.4.
[14] Savings accounts, see next following section.
[15] Bank account of executor, infra § 7.7-1.
[16] Avoidable loss of income as waste, supra § 5.2.
[17] Pre-probate responsibility to preserve assets, supra § 4.6.
[18] Search for will, supra § 4.2-1.

COLLECTION OF ASSETS AND PAPERS 49

erty that is found, at the risk of being surcharged, if he does not do so, for any assets that are lost or disappear or any loss resulting from failure to preserve relevant records. A prompt inventory of the contents of the home should be made, for the protection of the executor as well as for estate or inheritance tax purposes; in a proper case the contents of the home or some of them should be put into storage or appropriate safekeeping for safety and preservation. These same principles apply also to an office or place of business of the decedent,[19] which, like his home, should be promptly searched for valuables, papers, and records belonging to him or in his custody[20] and, in a proper case, should be protected by sealing or otherwise to prevent unauthorized entry, damage, or loss.

§ *6.9. Assets of proprietorship or close corporation.* In addition to examining business premises for assets and papers of the decedent,[21] the executor must promptly take such steps as are necessary to preserve the assets of a business conducted or controlled by the decedent, particularly in the case of a sole proprietorship or a corporation owned and operated wholly or largely by the decedent.[22] A going business presents special problems in this regard, as, on the one hand, it is ordinarily undesirable from the standpoint of preserving its value that the business be closed at once but, on the other hand, continuance of its operation is likely to afford many opportunities to employees or others to appropriate, lose, or damage its inventories, funds, and equipment. Inasmuch as the executor is liable for all assets belonging to the decedent at death and all amounts receivable after his death, his position with respect to such a business may be particularly precarious. In order to sustain his responsibility in this regard, it may be necessary for the executor, if the business is not suspended and the business premises secured, to station a reliable person on the premises and put him, temporarily at least, in control and supervision of employees and business activities. In any case, the executor should take all steps that are reasonable and necessary under the circumstances to preserve the assets and records of the business and, at least temporarily,[23] to preserve the business as a going concern,[24] and may be held liable by beneficiaries for any loss or damage that results from failure to carry out his duties in that regard.

§ *6.10. Rented home; apartment.* If the decedent occupied a rented home or an apartment, the executor should inform himself as to the terms of the tenancy, in order that he may know the rights and liabilities of the estate in respect thereof and may determine whether he may terminate the tenancy in order to eliminate the rental or maintenance burden upon the estate.[25] In the case of an apartment, the executor

---

[19] Assets of proprietorships and close corporations, see next following section.
[20] In case of professional man, infra § 6.20-1 ff.
[21] See last preceding section.
[22] Partnerships, infra § 7.9.
[23] Continuance of business and management problems, in general, infra §§ 7.8-8, 7.9.
[24] Duties and responsibilities as to management of closely-held corporation, infra § 7.8-1.
[25] Generally, infra § 7.11-1 ff.

must ascertain whether it was rented in the conventional fashion, or was a "cooperative" apartment held under a proprietary lease, or was owned in condominium, and, of course, govern his subsequent acts accordingly.[26]

§ 6.11-1. Receivables; in general.[27] As a part of his duty to collect all assets of the decedent, the executor must, of course, ascertain whether any causes of action were possessed by the decedent at his death, and what if any moneys were owing to or receivable by the decedent from others[28] at the time of his death, and take all lawful steps to collect such moneys.[29] Obviously, if it is clear that a debtor is insolvent and will doubtless remain so, or that the expense of endeavoring to collect a sum would exceed the sum or the collectible portion of it, the expenditure of estate funds in an effort at collection would be waste and the executor would not be justified in incurring the expense.[30] In such a case, the facts would be a sufficient defense to the executor against any charge of dereliction of duty, but he should bear in mind that the burden of establishing the facts is upon him if his action or non-action is questioned.

§ 6.11-2. ———; accruals from fiduciaries; commissions as fiduciary.[31] If the decedent at the time of his death was a beneficiary of a trust, or interested in an estate not yet wholly distributed, the executor must ascertain the nature and extent of his rights or interest and take appropriate steps to collect accrued income,[32] or capital assets, as the case may be. Inasmuch as an executor is liable for all assets that belonged to the decedent or to which his estate becomes entitled, the executor has the affirmative duty to make sure he receives all such income or principal that is properly payable to him, and in order to assure himself of the amount payable it may be necessary for him to compel the fiduciary of the trust or estate in question to render an accounting.[33] If the decedent was himself a fiduciary, the executor must ascertain what, if any, compensation is payable to him in respect of his services as such, and take appropriate steps to collect it, as well as to obtain reimbursement out of the fund of proper expenses that had been incurred by the decedent in his fiduciary activities; if the amount of such compensation depends on the amount or value of assets received or paid out by the decedent as a fiduciary,[34] an accounting may first be necessary to enable computation of the compensation, as well as to discharge the decedent's estate from liability.[35]

---

[26] Cooperative or condominium, infra § 7.11-2.
[27] West Dig., Exrs. & Admrs. Key Nos. 48–52.
[28] Fees owing to deceased professional man, infra § 6.20-5. Executor's own debt to estate, supra § 3.9-4c; generally, West Dig., Exrs. & Admrs. Key No. 50, and P-H Est. Plng. Serv. ¶ 2190.2.
[29] Set-off or retainer as against legatee-debtor, infra § 14.16-2.
[30] Waste in general, supra § 3.5-2.
[31] West Dig., Exrs. & Admrs. Key No. 45.
[32] Accruals as part of corpus of estate, infra § 16.4-1.
[33] Compulsory accounting, infra § 24.7. If under applicable law a legal life tenant (or the like) is treated as a fiduciary, the same principles apply as to compelling an accounting by him where the decedent was a remainderman; cf. § 9.10-2 infra.
[34] Compensation and computation thereof, infra § 20.4-2.
[35] Accounting for protection of estate, infra § 24.10.

COLLECTION OF ASSETS AND PAPERS 51

§ *6.11-3.* ———; *compromise.* By express statute in some jurisdictions, but, even in the absence of such a statute, as a part of his duty to collect amounts owing to the decedent or the estate,[36] the executor has power to compromise claims held by the estate,[37] provided, of course, the compromise is reasonable and is justified by the circumstances. Advance judicial approval of a proposed compromise may be required under local law, or if it is not required or obtained the executor is accountable to the court or the beneficiaries for the propriety of the compromise as for all his other acts and omissions.[38]

§ *6.12.* *Brokerage accounts of decedent.* It is particularly important that an executor take prompt steps to notify each securities broker with whom the decedent maintained an account of the death of the decedent and to cancel any orders for purchase of securities that had been given by the decedent during his lifetime and remain unexecuted at his death.[39] This is partly because the executor may not have authority to make an investment of estate funds,[40] or at least an investment of the kind or quality that would be involved in the purchase, and partly because, even if neither of these considerations applies, the particular security may not be of a character permitted for the investment of estate funds, or may be deemed by the executor not to be of satisfactory quality or not to be suited to the investment needs of the estate. The basic reason underlying all these factors is that if the executor allows a purchase order that had been given by the decedent to be carried out, he makes it his own order and so assumes the same responsibilities and liabilities in respect of the investment involved as if he had given the order on his own initiative. For a like reason, any orders so given and remaining unexecuted for the sale of securities should be promptly canceled if in the judgment of the executor such sale should not be made at the time, although in the usual case the executor is likely to be content to allow the sale to be made.[41] If the brokerage account involved purchases on margin, additional considerations apply, as discussed in a later section.[42]

§ *6.13.* *Collection of insurance payable to estate.* The executor must of course collect all insurance on the decedent's life, including in an appropriate case travel insurance and other accident insurance providing a death benefit, that is payable to the estate.[44] Accordingly, he must examine all policies to ascertain what, if any, amounts are payable thereunder to the estate. In that connection he must keep in mind the usual policy provision that makes its proceeds payable to the insured's estate if no designated beneficiary survives; thus, the executor may have the task of ascertaining whether a designated beneficiary did or did not survive the decedent.

---

[36] Supra § 6.11-1.
[37] So in Unif. Prob. Code sec. 3-715 (17). Compromise of claims against the estate, infra § 9.9-1.
[38] Accountability in general, infra § 24.1.
[39] For protection and management, infra § 7.3-1.
[40] Investment by executor, infra § 7.7-2.
[41] Liquidation of assets, in general, infra § 7.6-1 ff.
[42] Infra § 7.3-2.
[43] West Dig., Exrs. & Admrs. Key No. 46.
[44] Benefits payable to others, infra § 6.14.

Similarly, under life insurance policies providing double (or other special) idemnity in case of accidental death, and under accident insurance policies providing death benefits, where the proceeds of the policy are payable to the estate the executor must make sure whether the decedent did or did not die by accident within the meaning of the policy provision, and will be liable to persons interested in the estate if he fails to assert his claim to such benefits in a proper case.

§ 6.14. *Facilitation of collection of benefits payable to others.* While it probably is not, in a strict legal sense, a part of the executorial function or duty so to do, it is often advisable that an executor assist in or take appropriate action to facilitate the collection of various benefits payable to others than the estate,[45] such as life insurance, death benefits and survivors' benefits under the Social Security system, and a funeral expense allowance under that system or in the case of a decedent who was in or a veteran of military service,[46] not only because the executor is ordinarily in the best position to facilitate the establishment of a right to and the collection of such benefits, and can thus be of substantial assistance to family members or others, but more directly because at least such benefits as life insurance and a funeral expense allowance must usually be taken into account for purposes of estate and inheritance taxes on the decedent's estate,[47] and, in a case of apportionment of death taxes, for the purposes of such apportionment.[48] The executor is also concerned with such insurance if, under applicable law, the estate as a whole (as distinguished from the insurance beneficiary) is liable for repayment of indebtedness secured by the insurance.[49]

---

[45] Benefits payable to estate, see last preceding section.

[46] Funeral allowance as applicable against funeral expenses, infra § 9.2-4.

[47] Estate and inheritance taxes in general, infra Ch. XII. At least in a case where the insurance is includible in the taxable estate for the purposes of such a tax, the executor should procure from the insuring company a statement (I.R.S. Form 712) showing the amount of the insurance, return of premium, dividends, interest, indebtedness, etc.

[48] Apportionment of death taxes, infra § 12.10-1 ff.

[49] Life insurance policy loans, in general, infra § 9.3-3b.

VI

COLLECTION OF ASSETS AND PAPERS

Part B—Particular Assets and Problems

§ *6.15-1. Real property; in general.* The executor must ascertain whether the decedent was the owner of any real property or interest therein, and, if so, whether he was sole owner or one of two or more co-owners; further, if the latter was the case, the executor must ascertain whether the decedent was a tenant in common, or instead was a joint owner with right of survivorship. For these purposes the executor must examine all relevant deeds and other title documents, and in some cases may be required to cause a search to be made of public records either to determine whether property was owned at death or to determine the character or quantum of ownership. Even though, as in practically all jurisdictions, real property owned by the testator vests by operation of law in the devisee,[1] and the executor may have little or no control of the property or responsibility for its management,[2] he usually must know the existence and nature of the ownership in order that he may correctly report the property for estate or inheritance tax purposes, and apart from such considerations he may have a duty to collect the rents of the property,[3] or a duty to resort to it for payment of charges or expenses if the estate should be insolvent or otherwise insufficient,[4] or if the distinctions between real and personal property as to availability for those purposes has been abolished by applicable statute.[5]

§ *6.15-2.* ———; *leases and possessory claims.* Where under applicable law the executor has no power, or at least no duty, to collect rents of real property owned by the decedent at his death,[6] or where the real property was held in joint tenancy or tenancy by the entireties with a surviving owner, the executor may not have need

---

[1] Infra § 7.5-1.
[2] Ibid.
[3] Infra § 7.5-2.
[4] Infra § 19.5-1.
[5] Infra § 15.7.
[6] Collection of rents, infra § 7.5-2.

to inquire into or concern himself with the matter of existing leases or possessory tenancies thereof,[7] except as to rents accrued and unpaid at death,[8] inasmuch as the devisee, heir, or surviving owner, as the case may be, in most or all jurisdictions takes title directly at the death of the decedent and is entitled to rents from that date. If, however, the law requires the executor to collect the rents or otherwise to manage or control the property, or if the executor appropriately exercises a power so to do,[9] he must ascertain whether any person is in possession or claims possessory rights, and, if so, the basis of the occupancy or claim, and accordingly he must examine all leases and other pertinent documents or records and satisfy himself as to any contractual arrangement, including those for month to month tenancies and tenancies at will.

§ *6.15-3.* ———; *encumbrances.*[10] Where under applicable law[11] the title of a devisee of encumbered real property passes to him subject to the encumbrance,[12] the executor must nevertheless ascertain the nature and amount of the encumbrance, not only for the purposes of valuation of the property for estate or inheritance tax purposes[13] but also because of the liability of the general estate to discharge the encumbrance if and to the extent hat it is not satisfied by the devisee or after the creditor's resort to the property. *A fortiori,* if the property passes to the devisee free of the encumbrance, and the general estate must discharge the latter, the executor must know its nature and amount so that he may provide funds for the purpose.[14] If there is doubt on the point, as where a will provision may or may not be such as to change the rule that would otherwise be applicable,[15] the executor must assume until a determination is made to the contrary that the estate may have to discharge the encumbrance, and the considerations mentioned in the last preceding sentence accordingly apply.

§ *6.15-4.* ———; *executory contracts of purchase or sale.*[16] As a part of familiarizing himself with the decedent's assets and affairs, the executor must ascertain whether the decedent during his lifetime had entered into any contracts of purchase or sale of real property that remain unperformed at his death,[17] and must examine all such contracts to determine the rights and liabilities of the estate thereunder. As is pointed out at another place, questions of equitable conversion may be involved

---

[7] Decedent as tenant or lessee of another's property, infra § 7.11-1.
[8] As corpus of estate, infra § 14.4-1.
[9] Infra § 7.5-2.
[10] West Dig., Exrs. & Admrs. Key No. 133.
[11] Law of situs as governing, infra § 25.4-3.
[12] Burden of encumbrance, infra § 15.3.
[13] Infra § 8.1.
[14] Provision for cash requirements, infra § 7.6-1.
[15] Infra § 9.3-3a.
[16] West Dig., Exrs. & Admrs. Key Nos. 95–100, 135, 156.
[17] Executory contracts of decedent in general, infra § 7.13-1.

in such contracts and affect the duties and powers of the executor as well as the rights of beneficiaries.[18]

§ 6.16-1. *Joint ownership and other survivorship interests; real property.* Where real property is held in the names of the decedent and another the executor must first determine whether a right of survivorship exists and generally the nature of the tenancy. Language which would create joint ownership with right of survivorship under the law of one state may not do so under the law of another, and vice versa.[19] In some states tenancy by the entireties in real property[20] is recognized, and indeed in certain states a conveyance to husband and wife may create such a tenancy by the mere fact or mention of the relationship of the grantees, if no contrary provision appears; in other states such tenancy has been abolished. The determination of the nature of the decedent's ownership as to whether he was a tenant in common, a joint tenant, or a tenant by entireties involves, in addition to a consideration of the governing law, examination of the deed or will by which title was acquired; and, in the case of a deed not recorded in the decedent's lifetime, the executor should satisfy himself that wording appearing to create a co-tenancy with or a right of survivorship of another was contained in the deed when it was delivered, and was not added later, perhaps even after the testator's death.[21] Where a valid joint tenancy or tenancy by entireties was created by the instrument which is the source of the testator's title, the executor must of course determine whether any co-owner survived the testator;[22] if one did, the propery is not an asset of the estate, but if no co-owner survived the testator obviously is sole owner.

§ 6.16-2. ———; *personal property.* While joint tenancy, if not tenancy by the entireties, in real property[23] appears to be universally recognized, in the case of personal property probably tenancy by the entireties does not exist in any state, and in a number of states it is not clear that there may be joint tenancy of personalty with right of survivorship, at least in the absence of a statute, such, for example, as one permitting joint bank accounts.[24] The first matter for determination by the executor when joint ownership of personal property is asserted or has been attempted to be created is whether such ownership is recognized or the attempt effective. If the law recognizes joint ownership of personal property, much the same kind of considerations arise as in the case of real property, although very often there is no recorded title or "label" of ownership in the case of personalty other than, for

---

[18] Infra § 7.13-2.
[19] Law of situs as governing, infra §§ 15.1, 25.4-3.
[20] Personal property, see next following section.
[21] Any difference between the writing or typing at this point in the deed and that at other places therein, or any erasure, crowding, or other indication of change or afterthought, should put the executor upon inquiry.
[22] Questions of time of death, and survivorship, in general, supra § 5.2-1 and infra § 14.22-1.
[23] See last preceding section.
[24] Infra § 6.16.2a.

example, a registered security or a bank account and so there may be no available evidence of the creation of the joint ownership, especially in view of the statutes in many jurisdictions precluding one asserting rights against an estate from testifying to transactions with the decedent; accordingly, in the absence of proof to the contrary the executor should take the view that the personalty in question was the individual property of the decedent, or at the least that he was an owner in common, until the contrary is established. Subject to the considerations discussed in this section, however, the executor has no power and no responsibilities with respect to jointly owned personal property, except with respect to death taxes.[25]

§ 6.16-2a. ———; ———; *joint bank accounts.* Even in states in which joint bank accounts are recognized, the executor should not assume that such an account in the name of the decedent and another necessarily passes to the surviving depositor. He should have in mind that in some jurisdictions the entitlement of an account in joint names merely creates a rebuttable presumption that it was intended to pass to the survivor; and under some statutes the rule is different as to accounts with savings banks and those with commercial banks. In case of an account affected by such a presumption the executor should not permit the account to pass into the control of the surviving depositor or its funds to be withdrawn by the latter until pertinent facts and circumstances have been investigated to ascertain whether the presumption is or can be rebutted.

§ 6.16-2b. ———; ———; *bank account trusts;*[26] *revocation.* In some jurisdictions the law recognizes the creation of a bank account, or at least a saving account, in the name of the depositor "in trust for" another, and provides, in general, that on the death of the depositor such account become the property of the beneficiary so designated. Such trusts are variously known as Totten trusts,[27] savings bank trusts, or bank account trusts. The "trust" created by the establishment of such an account is not only fully revocable by the depositor during his lifetime, by withdrawal of its funds, but also may be cancelled or terminated by the depositor by his will, either explicitly or by a bequest of the account to a third person or by other disposition inconsistent with the implication of the style of the account,[28] as, for example, in some instances, bequests of more property than the testator possessed exclusive of the account.[29] Where a decedent has created such an account in his lifetime and it remains at the time of his death, the executor must not permit the funds to be withdrawn by the designated beneficiary without first determining that the

---

[25] Apportionment and collection of share of tax, infra § 12.10-1 ff.

[26] P-H Est. Plng. Serv. ¶¶ 3603.1–3604.14.

[27] So called in view of *Matter of Totten*, 179 N.Y. 112, 71 N.E. 748, 1 Ann. Cas. 900, 70 L.R.A. 711.

[28] Cf. *Matter of Krycun*, 24 N.Y.2d 710, 301 N.Y.S.2d 970, 249 N.E.2d 753, recognizing the rule but holding that a bequest of "all funds on deposit to my credit in any bank" did not evidence the necessary clear intention to revoke Totten trust where the testatrix also had bank accounts in her individual name. See also *Matter of Deneff*, 44 Misc.2d 947, 255 N.Y.S.2d 347.

[29] *In re Koster's Will*, 119 N.Y.S.2d 2; *Rodgers Est.*, 374 Pa. 246, 97 A.2d 789, 38 ALR 2d 1238. Charge on trust account for benefit of creditors where estate insufficient, infra § 19.9.

COLLECTION OF ASSETS AND PAPERS 57

account is not so cancelled or terminated by any provision of the will, or, if it is, must take control of it as against the designated beneficiary.

§ 6.16-2c. ———; ———; *United States Savings Bonds.* Although the registration of United States Savings Bonds in the name of one "or" another, or in the name of one "payable on death" to another, as permitted by the Treasury regulations governing the issuance and registration of such bonds,[30] does not accord with the laws of most states governing the passage of property at death, it appears to be established that such regulations override state laws and are effective to pass ownership of such bonds so registered, or at least to entitle no one other than the designated alternate or successor owner to re-register or redeem such bonds, so that the decedent's estate has no right to the bonds or their proceeds. Accordingly, as in the case of conventional joint ownership,[31] the executor has no duties with respect to bonds registered in either style mentioned, except as to estate and inheritance taxes.

§ 6.17. *Decedent as legal life tenant.* Where the decedent held real or personal property as a legal life tenant, or the like, as distinguished from having been beneficiary of a trust,[32] the executor must examine the instrument by which the tenancy was created and satisfy himself as to the decedent's rights and obligations thereunder and under law[33] and in that regard, in addition to collecting any accrued rents and other income,[34] the executor must consider particularly what if any duties he may have to release or deliver the subject property to a successor tenant or remainderman, or to render an accounting of the decedent's holding or management of the property under any statute requiring such an accounting.[35]

§ 6.18. *Invalid or ineffective lifetime transfers; alleged gifts, etc.* Not infrequently, after the death of a decedent, a third person asserts that particular personal property was given to him by the testator before death, or was transferred to him in consideration of a promise of care or the like.[36] Under his duty to collect all property receivable by the decedent from others,[37] it is the duty of the executor to ascertain whether any purported or alleged transfer by the decedent during his lifetime was in fact made and was valid and effective. If doubt exists on either score, the executor should require the claimant, if he does not have possession of the property in question, to file an appropriate claim or bring an appropriate proceeding to establish his ownership; or, if the claimant does have possession of the property, the executor should institute a discovery proceeding or take other appropriate action to recover the property or determine its ownership.[38] The first question to be determined

---

[30] 31 Code Fed. Regs. sec. 315.7.
[31] Supra § 6.16-2.
[32] Accruals from fiduciaries, supra § 6.11.
[33] Life tenant as fiduciary, infra § 9.10-2.
[34] As corpus of estate, infra § 16.4-1.
[35] Infra § 24.10.
[36] Ascertainment of taxable gifts, infra § 11.1 ff.
[37] Supra § 6.11-1.
[38] Discovery proceedings, infra § 6.22.

may be whether in fact any transfer of ownership appears to have been made or attempted to have been made by the decedent, and if so whether it was completed by due delivery; and, even if the facts in those regards be established, it may then be necessary to consider whether the transfer was induced by fraud, duress, or undue influence and whether the decedent was competent to make the transfer at the time it was made. In at least some circumstances a person claiming to have received property as a gift from a decedent has the burden of proving the fact, and the executor must have in mind statutes, such as exist in a number of jurisdictions, barring or restricting testimony by a claimant as to transactions with the decedent. A special case of an ineffective lifetime gift is one made to a charity or for charitable purposes within a period before death specified in a statute making such gifts within such period void or voidable;[39] the executor must, of course, enforce the return of the amount or subject matter of a gift invalidated by or under such a statute.

§ 6.19. *Appointive property.* Where the decedent was possessed at the time of his death of a power of appointment which he exercised by an appointment to his legal representatives or his estate, the executor must collect the property so appointed, just as any other property comprising a part of the estate.[40] Similarly, where the power was a general one and was exercised by the decedent in favor of one other than the estate, and under applicable law the appointed property is subject to debts of the testator if his own property is insufficient,[41] the executor must collect the appointed property to the extent required for payment of such debts. Except in the cases hereinabove referred to, however, the executor has no concern with property subject to a power of appointment held by the testator, and therefore no right or duty to collect it or take possession of it.

§ 6.20-1. *Estates of professional men; in general.* In addition to the general considerations, hereinabove discussed, affecting the collection of assets and papers of the decedent,[42] and the basic duty, also discussed above, to keep confidential all information that comes to the attention of the legal representative,[43] special problems in both these areas arise in connection with the estates of lawyers, medical men, accountants, and other professionals.[44] At the outset, the executor or administrator must segregate and protect all files and records that belong or pertain to clients or patients of the decedent, and to that end must take all proper steps not only to ascertain ownership but to prevent improper disclosure of information. The confidentiality that attaches to the office of executor has special significance in the case of the estate of a professional person, and the sensitive nature of many of his records and of many documents in his possession makes the problem of the executor

---

[39] Infra § 17.7.
[40] Infra § 18.3-8.
[41] Infra § 19.6.
[42] Supra § 6.1.
[43] Supra § 3.8.
[44] See following sections.

particularly acute; great harm to others, legal, economic, or penal, or at least embarrassment or violation of privacy, could come from revealing to an unauthorized person any information that the executor obtains therefrom. Moreover, many books, documents, and records, including correspondence and copies thereof, even if they be in their physical sense the property of the decedent, may as to their contents belong in a real sense to the client or patient because they were obtained or created in his behalf or for his benefit; and they are often of continuing value and importance to the client or patient, as, for example, when they relate to business transactions or negotiations, in the case of a lawyer or accountant, or to medical histories, tests, or procedures and treatments, in the case of a physician or surgeon. Where the decedent was a member of a professional firm,[45] and the client or patient was that of the firm rather than of the decedent individually, the records and files belong to, or the custody of, the firm, and there is no problem for the executor as to their disposition. Where, instead, the decedent was a sole practitioner, or was acting as an individual for the client or patient, the executor should on request turn over pertinent records and files to the successors chosen by the respective clients or patients,[46] but as to any records or files that remain after a suitable length of time the executor may have no choice but to destroy them. The executor's purpose, however, should be the preservation of records and files for the benefit of clients or patients and of the decedent's professional successors, and the preservation also of the confidentiality of them against unauthorized access or inspection; and for the accomplishment of both purposes the executor should make sure that he does not deliver or make available any such material except to a person duly authorized by the client or patient to receive it.

§ 6.20-2. ———; *lawyers.* Where the decedent was a lawyer, the executor must distinguish carefully between documents, records, and files that belonged to the decedent and are includible in his estate,[47] on the one hand, and, on the other hand, items of similar character that belong to clients or others and are not part of the estate. Such non-owned items may have been held by the decedent in escrow, or safekeeping, for others, or may have come into his possession on a temporary basis for such a purpose, for example, as study or reference in connection with a client's affairs or use as evidence in pending or potential litigation, or may have been ac-

---

[45] Business partnerships and proprietorships, infra § 7.9.

[46] The executor, of course, cannot employ or retain a new lawyer, physician, etc. to represent or serve the client or patient; that is the prerogative of the latter.

[47] Such items relating to the decedent's practice are includible in the estate in the sense that the executor has the responsibility for and disposition of them, but not in a sense of monetary value; for under established principles all contracts and arrangements with a lawyer cease at his death, his practice is thus without good will in the economic sense, and his files cannot be sold any more than his practice as such. See Fulrath, The Lawyer's Estate: Composition of Sole Practitioner's Assets, 1964 Proc. A.B.A. Sec. Real Prop. Prob. & Tr. L., Part I, 27; Limbaugh, The Lawyer's Estate: Responsibilities and Rights of Clients, op. cit., 29; and cf. Stevens, The Lawyer's Estate: Key Tax Problems in Disposition of Practice, op. cit., 34, where there are discussed some substantive problems as well as tax matters.

quired by him as the client's agent. A familiar example of a document not the property of the lawyer is the will of a client; the will is at all times the property of the client, even though it was prepared by the lawyer and retained by him for safekeeping. It will be apparent that the considerations of special confidentiality hereinabove discussed[48] apply in full force, in the case of the lawyer's estate, to the contents of records and documents,[49] but it should not be overlooked that, in addition, the very existence of some items, or the fact that they had come into the possession of the lawyer or his client, may also be a matter of great confidence, as, for example, in some business negotiations or where litigation or criminal prosecution is pending or threatened. The executor accordingly should not even let it be known, to others than the respective clients concerned, what he has found in a lawyer's office or possession, and may cause harm or incur liability if he does so even though he does not disclose information derived from what he has found. Inasmuch as a lawyer's practice cannot be sold,[50] the executor has no duties of management with respect to it,[51] other than to preserve confidentiality as hereinabove discussed in disposing of the lawyer's own property and to deliver to clients, or upon their order, documents and other items that, as above mentioned, are the property of the clients and not of the estate.

§ *6.20-3.* ———; *physicians and surgeons.* The special degree of confidentiality, and the problems of disposal of files and records, that apply in estates of professional men generally are fully applicable in the case of medical men. A further problem of a different character arises with respect to drugs and medicines in the decedent's office or possession at his death; the executor must take all adequate precautions to safeguard such materials, not only to preserve whatever values they may have but, perhaps more importantly, to minimize the risk of their coming into the hands of others and being misused or causing harm. Within the generality of that responsibility, the laws and regulations relating to narcotic drugs must in particular be regarded by the executor, and before, or immediately upon, taking possession or control of any narcotic drugs the executor must comply with the rules of the Bureau of Narcotics of the United States Treasury Department as to surrender of such drugs to the Bureau.[52] There is no provision in the statute or regulations for payment for drugs so surrendered, and hence they are to be treated by the executor in his inventory[53] and for other accounting purposes[54] as without monetary value.

---

[48] See last preceding section.

[49] Obligation to preserve confidences and secrets of client as continuing after lawyer's death, A.B.A. Code of Prof. Responsibility EC 4–6 and DR 4–101(A).

[50] Ibid.; and Op. 266, A.B.A. Standing Committee on Professional Ethics (now Standing Comm. on Ethics and Prof. Resp.).

[51] Duties of management of estate assets, in general, infra Ch. VII.

[52] Narcotics Regs. No. 5, sec. 151.474 (a), (b), and (c) (the drugs are to be forwarded, not by mail, with Bureau Form 142). Contraband articles or items of property in general, infra § 7.2-5.

[53] Infra § 8.3-1.

[54] Account as listing all assets, infra § 24.3-3.

COLLECTION OF ASSETS AND PAPERS 61

§ 6.20-4. ———; *accountants.* The estate of an accountant presents problems to the executor much like those he faces in the estate of a lawyer,[55] and similar considerations apply.

§ 6.20-5. ———; *collection of fees.* As a part of his duty to collect all assets of his decedent's estate[56] the executor must, of course, endeavor to collect fees owing to the deceased professional man, not only for services completed during his lifetime but also for uncompleted services.[57] In the absence of any fixed scale or criterion for fixing fees, particularly in the case of a lawyer,[58] the basis must be *quantum meruit*. Of course, if the client's arrangement or agreement was with a firm of which the decedent was a member, the fee is payable to the firm and not to the decedent individually. Further, however, in the case of a deceased partner, the executor must collect from the firm the decedent's share of its profits, and so must inform himself as to the terms of the partnership agreement. Because such an agreement, particularly in the case of a law firm, is usually desired to be kept confidential among the surviving partners, the will of a lawyer often provides in substance that his executor shall accept and rely without investigation upon statements rendered to him by the firm, and such a provision is effective at least for administration purposes; the executor may need to consider separately whether it is fully effective for estate and inheritance tax purposes.[59]

§ 6.21-1. *Property in another jurisdiction;*[60] *in general.* Where property of a decedent was at the time of his death located or kept in a jurisdiction other than that in which the executor is appointed, the executor must consider whether he has power to collect such property or take it into his own custody; this may depend upon such factors as whether such other jurisdiction recognizes the legal existence and powers of an executor appointed elsewhere,[61] or by statute protects its residents in paying or delivering property to such an executor,[62] whether there are or may be creditors of the decedent in the jurisdiction where the property is located or kept,[63] and whether the determination and settlement of such jurisdiction's death tax (if any)[64] may be obtained without the appointment of a representative in such

---

[55] Supra § 6.20-2.

[56] Supra § 6.1; receivables, supra § 6.11-1.

[57] Cf. Flomenhoft, Is an Unrealized Contingent Fee an Asset of a Deceased Illinois Attorney's Estate, 58 Ill. Bar J. 216.

[58] Estates of lawyers, supra § 6.20-2. See also Fulrath, op. cit. supra note 47, and Limbaugh, op. cit. ibid.

[59] Valuation of partnership interests, infra § 8.8. Estate and inheritance taxes in general, infra Ch. XII.

[60] West Dig., Exrs. & Admrs. Key Nos. 518–526; P-H Est. Plng. Serv. ¶ 2201.

[61] Generally, supra § 1.7. When foreign executor may receive payment of amounts owing to estate and give quittance therefor, Restatement, Conflict of Laws 2d secs. 326, 328, 329; delivery of assets to foreign executor, op. cit. sec. 331.

[62] Such statutes are sometimes limited to deposits in financial institutions; but not so in Unif. Prob. Code sec. 4–201 ff.

[63] Claims of foreign creditors as payable by domiciliary representative, infra § 9.4-5.

[64] Right of non-domiciliary jurisdiction to impose death tax, infra § 12.2.

jurisdiction.[65] If for these or any other reasons the executor is unable to have the property paid or delivered to him, an ancillary proceeding may be necessary,[66] and if so the domiciliary executor should institute such a proceeding or arrange for it to be instituted. The executor should ascertain, however, whether in the jurisdiction in which the property is located or kept any statute provides for filling exemplified copies of the will, and perhaps of the papers in the proceeding for its probate, in lieu of the institution of an ancillary proceeding; and in particular should ascertain whether such filing is necessary, and sufficient, in the case or real property.[67]

§ *6.21-2.* ———; *property disposed of by separate will.* Occasionally a testator executes two wills, one for the disposition of property located in a jurisdiction other than that of his domicile, as in another state of a foreign country, and the other disposing of property at the domicile or, more generally, the balance of his property.[68] The domiciliary executor in such a case must ascertain what property is disposed of by the will of which he is executor and what property instead passes under the "foreign" will. If the domiciliary will is later in date than the foreign will, it may well have the effect (under the principle that a will is revoked by a later will to the extent the latter is inconsistent with the former, even though no express words of revocation appear[69]) of superseding the latter, unless the domiciliary will expressly excludes from its operation the property referred to in the foreign will, or otherwise clearly leaves the foreign will in force; and, of course, the foreign will may on similar principles supersede an earlier domiciliary will entirely instead of merely as to the foreign property. Even if neither of the two wills has the effect of entirely revoking or superseding the other, substantial questions may arise as to which of them governs the disposition of particular property. For example, a reference to property "located" or "situate" within, or elsewhere than within, the foreign state or country leaves doubt as to many kinds of intangibles; it may have to be determined under such a provision which will governs as to a bank account in a bank in the foreign jurisdiction (having in mind the rule of the common law *mobiliae personam sequuntur* and possibly a different rule in the foreign jurisdiction), or whether the disposition of corporate stock is affected by the physical location of the stock certificates at the time of death or by a rule of law of the incorporating jurisdiction that stock is to be deemed to be located at the place of incorporation, or whether bonds issued in one of the two jurisdictions but physically present in the other at the time of death are to be regarded as located in

---

[65] Cf. Shriver, The Multi-State Estate, 3 Real Prop. Prob. & Tr. J. 189, 192–194.
[66] Ancillary probate, supra § 5.5-4.
[67] Real property in jurisdiction other than that of executor's appointment, infra § 7.5-5.
[68] This device is used most often where some property is in a foreign country the law of which (as in the case of civil law countries) differs so widely from that of the domicile, as to form or execution of the will or as to estates that may be created, as to make impracticable or ineffective any attempt to dispose of such property and property at the domicile by a single instrument.
[69] Supra § 5.3-1.

the latter in view of the usual rule in common law jurisdictions that bonds are themselves property and not merely evidence of property. Questions of this character are very likely to arise unless each of the wills has been very carefully drawn with recognition of the existence of the other and in contemplation of the nature and kinds of the assets involved, and the executor should be alert to the troublesome possibilities that inhere in any case of plural wills.

§ 6.22. Discovery proceedings.[70] Statutes ordinarily provide a procedure whereby an executor may, in a proceeding in the probate court, and without the technicalities of a common law action, recover tangible personal property belonging to the decedent that is in the possession of another, or may obtain information from another as to the whereabouts or existence of a tangible. Such a remedy is known as discovery; but perhaps the term should be understood more nearly in the sense of "uncovering" property wrongfully withheld, or information about it, than in the sense of seeking and finding, and it is not available merely as an instrument for a speculative search. With that limitation, and subject to the terms of the statute by which it is created, the remedy is available not only to recover possession but also to determine ownership as between the decedent and the holder, as in (but not limited to) the case of a third person claiming by way of *inter vivos* gift from the decedent;[71] and also, as indicated above, it affords a means in a proper case for the executor to examine a person having information concerning a tangible, in order to discover its whereabouts or its holder so that he can proceed against the latter. From the general duty of an executor to collect all assets of the estate,[72] it follows that the executor must bring a discovery proceeding where that is necessary or advisable to effect or facilitate his recovery of a tangible that is believed to have belonged to the decedent, and it is an obvious corollary that the executor must investigate all reasonable possibilities that an asset of the estate may be in the possession or under the control of another.[73] The remedy of discovery is ordinarily not available for the recovery of money or a monetary claim, and so to enforce a money payment the executor must bring a conventional action.

§ 6.23. Reverse discovery.[74] Just as discovery is often provided by statute as a convenient remedy for the recovery of tangibles belonging to the decedent and held by or in the possession of another,[75] a procedure often exists by which a third person claiming ownership of tangibles that were in the hands of the decedent at death or come into the possession of the executor may establish his title thereto and recover possession thereof, by a proceeding in the probate court, instead of being compelled to resort to conventional legal remedies. Where such a procedure is pro-

---

[70] West Dig., Exrs. & Admrs. Key No. 85.
[71] Supra § 6.18.
[72] Supra § 6.1.
[73] See 3 Warren's Heaton, Surrogate's Court, sec. 232 par. 1(b).
[74] P-H Est. Plng. Serv. ¶ 2227.
[75] See last preceding section.

vided, it is ordinarily of the same character as discovery and applicable in corresponding situations, except that it is the converse of discovery and operates in the opposite direction, and so for convenience it is often spoken of a "reverse discovery."

§ *6.24.* *Death tax waivers or consents.* Where, in states having inheritance or estate tax laws, it is required that waivers of notice of or consents to the transfer of personal property that belonged to a decedent by any person in possession of it be obtained before any such transfer may be made,[76] it is ordinarily the function of the executor, when collecting any money, securities, tangibles, or other personal property, to obtain and furnish to the payor or holder all necessary waivers and consents.

---

[76] Infra § 12.11.

VII

CUSTODY, PRESERVATION, AND MANAGEMENT OF ASSETS

Part A—Possession and Control

§ 7.1. Nature of duty.[1] It is the duty of an executor, promptly upon coming into office (and probably even before probate of the will, if necessary to preserve them[2]), to reduce the assets of the estate to his own possession or bring them under his own control, except in some cases of real property,[3] and in general to safeguard and preserve them.[4] This duty grows out of the fact that it is a basic responsibility or function of an executor to collect and manage the assets of his estate,[5] and he is accordingly not justified in allowing another person to hold, possess, or control such assets.[6] If he does leave assets in the hands of another, and loss, damage, or diminution in value occurs, the executor can be held liable for his negligence, and may perhaps be liable as an insurer,[7] that is, without regard to negligence or fault other than that he did not bring the assets into his own possession or under his own control. Apart from the considerations mentioned, not only prompt collection of debts owing to the decedent and other cash receivables,[8] but also prompt reduction to possession of other property of value,[9] will make moneys available to the executor when they are needed and meanwhile capable of being made productive of income,[10] and other property available for liquidation if and when necessary or appropriate.[11]

---

[1] West Dig., Exrs. & Admrs. Key Nos. 90 ff., 153–172, 413.
[2] Supra § 4.6.
[3] Supra § 7.5-1.
[4] Unif. Prob. Code sec. 3-709.
[5] Supra § 6.1.
[6] Delegation, supra § 3.4.
[7] Supra § 3.7-1.
[8] See *Matter of Foster*, N.Y.L.J. Aug. 1, 1966, p. 8, holding executor failing to collect receivable with due promptness liable for interest from due date. Receivables generally, supra § 6.11-1 ff.
[9] Collection of assets, supra Ch. VI.
[10] Infra § 7.7-2.
[11] Infra § 7.6-1a ff.

§ 7.2-1. *Tangibles; in general.* In accordance with the general rule stated above, all tangible personal property forming a part of the estate must be taken into possession by the executor, or brought under his control, in order that it may be inventoried, protected, and preserved until it is distributed to legatees,[12] sold,[13] or otherwise disposed of,[14] as may be appropriate in the particular case. Such steps to obtain possession of the tangible, and such steps to protect it from depreciation, damage, and loss, whether by putting it into storage, depositing it in a safe or vault,[15] or otherwise,[16] must be taken as are necessary under the circumstances to carry out the executor's duty of protection and preservation; and a failure to act promptly or to take any such steps will render him liable to beneficiaries, as for any other negligence. Obviously, if the tangible is at the testator's death held in storage or safekeeping by a suitable custodian, and it is reasonable or necessary that it be so held, the executor need not take it from such custodian's possession but may continue *pro tem* the existing arrangement.[17] As a corollary to the rules as to his duty to protect and preserve, the executor is authorized to pay the reasonable expenses thereof out of the general estate, even though the tangible be specifically bequeathed.[18]

§ 7.2-2. ———; *"exempt" articles.* While statutes in a number of states specify certain kinds of tangibles that are declared to be exempt from creditors' claims and not to constitute a part of the estate,[19] it would appear that, except where such articles are already in the possession of the person or persons entitled to the exempt property, the executor has the same duty initially to reduce such articles to his possession, and to see to their protection or preservation, as he has with respect to any other tangible, inasmuch as such statutes ordinarily direct the executor to set apart the exempt property and deliver it to the spouse or children. To the limited extent of such duty, therefore, the exempt property may be said to constitute a part of the estate for purposes of administration, even if it is not such in any other respect.[20]

§ 7.2-3. ———; *sale or other disposition of residuary tangibles.* Tangible personal property that is not effectively specifically bequeathed, and falls into the residuary estate, usually must be converted into cash by the executor,[21] unless all residuary legatees prefer or are willing to receive such property in kind and so advise the executor.[22] If tangibles are to be distributed to the residuary legatees in

---

[12] Satisfaction of specific legacies, infra § 14.4-1 ff; of residuary legacies, infra § 18.6-1.
[13] Sale of tangibles, infra § 7.2-3; liquidation generally, infra § 7.6-1 ff.
[14] Narcotic drugs, supra § 6.20-3; contraband generally, infra § 7.2-5.
[15] Rental of safe deposit box, infra § 7.3-3.
[16] Insurance, infra § 7.2-4.
[17] Delivery of tangibles, infra § 14.4-9.
[18] See also infra § 7.2-4.
[19] Exempt property, in general, infra § 17.1.
[20] Availability for funeral expenses, infra § 9.2-1.
[21] Liquidation for distribution, infra § 7.6-2.
[22] Infra § 18.6-4.

CUSTODY, PRESERVATION, AND MANAGEMENT OF ASSETS 67

kind, the executor should, of course, continue to take the necessary steps to protect and preserve them,[23] and should keep them appropriately insured,[24] all at the expense of the estate, until distribution may be made. Unless, however, they are to be distributed in kind, the executor should proceed, as promptly as may be consistent with orderly administration and with realization of an adequate price, to sell the tangibles, and presumably may be held liable to beneficiaries for any depreciation or loss resulting from undue delay in effecting sale, as well as for storage, safekeeping, or insurance expense incurred during the period of delay. Except where an established rule of law or a provision of the will permits private sale, the executor must consider whether it is his duty on general principles, or advisably for his own protection, that a sale of tangibles be at public auction; where, however, he is not restricted by any of the considerations mentioned to a public sale, he must consider whether better prices are likely to be realized at private sale. He should in either case advertise or otherwise give notice of the sale, in such manner and to such degree as is reasonable under the circumstances, again to the end that best prices may be obtained. And sale must be made for cash unless the will or a statute authorizes sales on terms of credit.

§ 7.2-4. ———; *insurance*.[25] The executor's duty to protect and preserve tangible personal property,[26] pending its distribution or sale, extends to and includes the duty of covering such property with insurance, against loss or damage, of whatever kind is appropriate to the situation. The duty applies in the case of specifically bequeathed property[27] as well as that of property not so bequeathed, but as to the former may terminate earlier if specific bequests are or are proper to be satisfied before distribution is made of the residuary.[28] The amount of the insurance coverage should, of course, be not less than the full value of the property, or the valuation thereof with which the executor is chargeable. As in the case of other protection expenses,[29] the premiums on appropriate insurance policies are a proper administration expense and payable out of the general estate.[30]

§ 7.2-5. ———; *contraband*. Where an executor finds among the decedent's effects an article or item of property the possession of which is prohibited by law, or requires a special license or permit, he must take prompt action to protect himself and the estate against applicable penalties, usually by surrender of the article or item to proper authorities. In the case of narcotic drugs, for example, as is men-

---

[23] Supra § 7.2-1.
[24] See next following section.
[25] P-H Est. Plng. Serv. ¶ 2174. Insurance on or in respect of real property, infra § 7.5-4.
[26] Supra § 7.2-1.
[27] Right of specific legatee to insurance proceeds where loss or damage occurs after death, infra § 14.4-4c. This duty to insure is not inconsistent with the so-called "as is, where is" rule recognized in some circumstances as to tangibles specifically bequeathed (infra § 14.4-9), for it applies until the tangible is delivered or is released under such rule.
[28] Time of satisfaction of benefits, infra § 14.31-1 ff.
[29] Supra § 7.2-1.
[30] Administration expenses, in general, infra Ch. XX.

tioned elsewhere,[31] a federal regulation prescribes the procedure to be followed. If the article is a firearm, the possession or transportation of which is forbidden, the executor should surrender it to the police, but runs some risk of holding it or transporting it for surrender, unless a statute covers the case.[32] Where gold coins are found,[33] the executor should surrender them through a bank, and in practice it appears that if that is done no penalty accrues. Other contraband articles should be disposed of in such manner as is practicable under the general principles reflected in the examples here given.

§ 7.3-1. *Securities; in general.* The rule stated in a preceding section as to obtaining control of assets[34] must receive the executor's immediate attention with respect to securities belonging to the decedent that at the time of his death were in the possession of a broker or other agent,[35] or indeed any other third person. The executor is particularly not justified in allowing a broker to maintain possession or custody of securities that had been deposited or left by the decedent with the broker under the usual arrangement entitling the broker to hold them in his own name or in such form that they will pass by delivery, to pledge them to secure the broker's borrowings, to lend them to cover "short" sales, or the like, or, for those and additional reasons, in allowing a margin account to continue; it is obvious that special risks of loss to the estate exist in all such circumstances.[36] Similar considerations apply in the case of securities left with any other agent of or custodian for the decedent, including an investment advisor, where the agent has it within his power to dispose of the securities, whether because they are in bearer form or otherwise can pass by delivery or because they are accompanied by instruments of transfer which would be accepted by a person ignorant of the decedent's death. Apart from the possibilities of misappropriation or unauthorized dealing with securities on the part of a broker or agent, there is also the factor that if the executor does not have securities in his own possession or control he may be unable to make prompt delivery to carry out a desirable or necessary sale and loss to the estate may accordingly result. For dereliction of duty in obtaining possession of securities, therefore, the executor is surchargeable under the principles governing negligence,[37] and, as noted in a preceding section, may have the liability of an insurer for any loss or depreciation in value because he violated his duty.[38]

§ 7.3-2. ———; *margin accounts.* Where at his death the decedent had a margin account with a broker,[39] that is, one in which were held securities that had been

---

[31] Supra § 6.20-3.
[32] See, e.g., N.Y. Penal L. sec. 265.20.
[33] Unless they qualify as collectors' items, the possession of which is not forbidden.
[34] Supra § 7.1.
[35] Closing decedent's brokerage accounts, supra § 6.12.
[36] See next following section.
[37] Supra §§ 3.5-1, 3.6.
[38] Supra § 3.7-1.
[39] Closing decedent's brokerage accounts, supra § 6.12.

pledged to the broker to secure an advancement of a part of their purchase price or of the purchase price of other securities in the account, the rules stated in the last preceding section are applicable, but other and even more important considerations also apply. So long as the executor allows such pledge arrangement to continue he is speculating on the maintenance or increase of the market values of the pledged securities,[40] and accordingly is liable to beneficiaries for any loss that occurs as a result of the decline of the fund. The executor must, therefore, promptly direct the broker to sell securities held in the account to the extent necessary to provide funds to pay off the debit balance, or, possibly, use funds of the general estate to make such payment; but, of course, if he uses such other funds he is making a new or additional investment, and he must therefore consider whether he is authorized to make investments[41] and, if he is, not only whether the securities that are in effect purchased by payment of the debit balance are of a nature or category permitted for the investment of estate funds, but also whether they are of suitable investment quality and are suited to the investment needs and situation of the estate. As soon as the debit balance is paid off, the executor should, under the rules previously referred to,[42] recover possession of the remaining securities from the broker.

§ 7.3-3. ———; *rental of safe deposit box.* Where the securities of an estate are not sufficient in number or value, or other circumstances are not such, as to justify the opening of a custodian or advisory account for their keeping and management,[43] the executor who does not have adequate facilities of his own may and ordinarily should rent a safe deposit box or the like for the storage and safekeeping of securities, and the rental of such a box is in such case a proper administration expense.[44] A box may also be rented, in the absence of such suitable facilities, for safekeeping of jewelry and other small tangibles needing protection.[45]

§ 7.3-4. ———; *establishment of custodian or advisory account.* The rules hereinabove stated as to the duty of an executor to obtain possession of securities belonging to the decedent, and not to leave them in the custody of an agent or other third person who may lose them or dispose of them without authority, and the rules as to delegation of his authorities,[46] of course, do not preclude the executor from opening a custodian account, or investment advisory account, in a proper case and with a responsible institution or organization. Indeed, the establishment of arrangements with a suitable bank or trust company for custody and safekeeping may be an appropriate and advisable means of sustaining the executor's responsibility to safeguard securities. At least if the securities are of considerable number or value,

---

[40] Speculation, supra § 3.5-3.
[41] Infra § 7.7-2.
[42] See last preceding section.
[43] See next following section.
[44] Administration expenses, in general, infra Ch. XX.
[45] Supra § 7.2-1.
[46] Supra § 3.4-1.

the cost of such a custody account is ordinarily a proper administration expense;[47] but the contrary would probably be held where the securities were few or of small value, or where for other reasons storage in a safe deposit box or the like would be adequate.[48] In some cases an investment advisory account, which may or may not couple physical custody of securities with the rendition of investment advice, may be appropriate, particularly if there are important problems of timing sales of securities or other problems of liquidation, and substantial values are involved; but unless large values or difficult problems are involved it would seem unlikely that the fees of an investment advisor would be allowed, as against objection by any affected beneficiary, as a charge against the estate or an expense of its administration, inasmuch as procedures for proper liquidation, and investment matters generally, are an inherent part of the responsibility of the executor and so deemed to be covered in his compensation. The maintenance of a custodian or advisory account is, of course, to be distinguished from a delegation of authority to do other than ministerial acts,[49] as a custodian or advisor under such an account does not have as such (and should not be given by the executor) any authority to act on his own initiative in selling or purchasing securities; but the executor who opens or maintains such an account takes certain inherent risks of loss, as in safekeeping of the securities or performance of duties by the custodian, and, particularly, risks of mismanagement or misappropriation where the securities are in bearer form, or where the executor furnishes the custodian in advance with instruments of transfer to be used when a sale is directed, and the executor should accordingly use great care on the selection of a custodian.

§ 7.3-4a. ———; ———; *corporate executor distinguished.* The principles stated in the preceding section as to payment out of the estate of the expenses of a custodian or advisory account ordinarily do not apply where the executor is a bank or trust company, if for no other reason than that it holds itself out as qualified to be a fiduciary and as having the facilities necessary to enable it to carry out its duties without the assistance of others in such matters as preservation of assets and proper resolution of investment problems.

§ 7.3-5. ———; *registration in nominee's name.* Where he is permitted so to do by law[50] or by the terms of the will, it is ordinarily advisable for an executor to transfer stocks and other registered securities from the name of the decedent into the name of a nominee of the executor, at least other than those securities that are specifically bequeathed[51] and those that the executor definitely plans to retain for distribution in kind.[52] Securities that are registered in the name of a decedent usually cannot be transferred of record until there are furnished to the transfer agent or

---

[47] Administration expenses, in general, infra Ch. XX.
[48] See last preceding section.
[49] Supra § 3.4.
[50] So in Unif. Prob. Code sec. 3-715 (14).
[51] Infra § 14.4-1.
[52] Infra §§ 14.27-1, 18.6-4.

officer evidence of the appointment and qualification of the executor,[53] and either evidence of payment of state estate or inheritance taxes or a consent by the relevant tax authority to the transfer.[54] While the problems and difficulties of furnishing additional documentation formerly associated with the transfer of securities by a fiduciary have been greatly reduced by the enactment in every state of the Uniform Act for Simplification of Security Transfers,[55] that Act is permissive only and is not followed in practice by all corporations or transfer agents, some of which are unwilling to effect a transfer without further documentation and evidence; and where that is the case considerable time and bother may be required to comply with their requirements, and the resulting delay may be such as to cause the loss of a desirable sale. Problems of this character are obviated where the securities sold are registered in the name of a nominee, and effecting such registration, where permissible, at an early stage of the administration, and free of pressures of time, will enable sales to be promptly effected when necessary or proper[56] and also will facilitate eventual distribution of securities remaining unsold. Of course, the nominee in such a case is an agent of the executor, and the latter is responsible under ordinary principles of agency for any fault or negligence on the part of the nominee; the executor should therefore cause the nominee to execute instruments of assignment in blank and to re-deliver the securities to the executor with such assignments, lest there be any violation of the principles stated above as to leaving securities in the possession or under the control of a third person.[57] The executor should not cause securities to be registered in his individual name, because of the possibility of confusion with his own assets upon his death, the enforcement of a personal creditor's claim, or otherwise, as well as because of the danger of laying himself open to a charge of conversion of the securities to his own use and consequent liability as an insurer for any depreciation in their value;[58] and in some jurisdictions such registration is specifically prohibited or penalized by statute.[59]

§ 7.4-1. *United States government bonds; in general.*[60] Certain classes of bonds of the United States, where held in an estate, require special attention on the part of the executor, as noted in the following sections.

§ 7.4-2. ———; *bonds applicable at par on Federal estate tax.* United States bonds of certain issues are, under the statute providing for them, eligible to be ap-

---

[53] Under Unif. Prob. Code sec. 8–402, issuer or transfer agent may require "appropriate evidence of appointment or incumbency". But cf. Unif. Act for Simplification of Security Transfers, secs. 2 and 3, obviating such duty.

[54] Infra § 12.11.

[55] Cf. note 53 supra. See comment by Scott, Recent Statutory Trends in the Law of Trusts, 45 The Trust Bulletin 33, 36, as to whether the Uniform Act is superseded as to such transfers by the Unif. Commercial Code.

[56] Liquidation, infra § 7.6-1 ff.

[57] Supra § 7.3-1.

[58] Liability as insurer, supra § 3.7-1.

[59] Commingling moneys, infra § 7.7-1.

[60] Co-owner registration of U. S. Savings Bonds, supra § 6.16-2c.

plied at par to payment of the Federal estate tax on the estate of the bondholder. If the decedent owned such bonds at his death, and his estate is subject to such tax, the bonds up to the maximum possible amount of the tax should be set apart by the executor and retained unsold, so that they may be used for payment of or application upon such tax, when the time arrives for the payment thereof, if the market price of such bonds is then less than par. The statutory provision for application of such bonds at par against the tax gives the executor the opportunity, even though their price on the general market is less, to obtain full face value for them, up to the amount of Federal estate tax payable; in this sense they have a special market value of par,[61] and if the executor fails to take advantage of his opportunity to realize that value he is liable to the beneficiaries, on the general principle of waste,[62] for the resulting loss. It is to be emphasized that such special applicability applies only to bonds of certain issues, and only to bonds owned by the decedent at the time of his death; a purchase of such bonds by the executor after the decedent's death (even if the purchase order had been given before death) would not qualify them. There is, however, no requirement that they shall have been owned by the decedent for any prescribed length of time, and bonds acquired by him even immediately before his death, provided only that ownership of them passed to him while he lived, are applicable as hereinabove mentioned.

§ 7.4-3. ———; *Savings Bonds redeemable at par.* Certain United States Savings Bonds, which during the lifetime of the owner are redeemable, in advance of maturity, only at a discount from their face amount, may by the terms of the governing statute be redeemed at par within a limited period of time after the death of the holder. Thus the executor is afforded a special opportunity to receive a higher amount for the bonds, by taking steps for their redemption within the limited period, than he could obtain at any later time or a beneficiary could obtain after distribution of the bonds to him (unless their maturity date were then at hand); and, on the same principles as those relating to bonds applicable at par on the Federal estate tax,[63] the executor is liable for such loss as results from his failure to take advantage of such opportunity.

§ 7.5-1. *Real property; in general.*[64] In practically every jurisdiction, title to real property that was owned by the decedent,[65] whether specifically devised[66] or

---

[61] Bonds so eligible and not exceeding the amount of the Federal estate tax payable, whether or not applied to such tax, are to be valued for the purposes of the tax at par (*Bankers Trust Co. v. U.S.*, 284 F.2d 537) and therefore are to be so valued for accounting purposes also; but any bonds, although eligible for application on the tax, that exceed the amount of tax payable are to be valued only at market.

[62] Supra § 3.5-2.

[63] See last preceding section.

[64] West Dig., Exrs. & Admrs. Key No. 129 ff.

[65] Ascertainment of fact and nature of decedent's ownership, supra § 6.15-1; property owned jointly or by entireties with survivor, supra § 6.16-1.

[66] Infra Ch. XV.

CUSTODY, PRESERVATION, AND MANAGEMENT OF ASSETS 73

passing under the residuary clause,[67] except in some instances a cemetery lot,[68] vests immediately upon the testator's death in the devise; and in either such case the executor does not have title,[69] although in some states he may be required to execute a confirmatory conveyance to the devisee. Also in every jurisdiction, however, the executor is given some powers over devised property;[70] in some states his powers or possession and control are broad, and in other states limited to special circumstances, as, for example, where there is no heir or devisee in possession, or the property passes to more than one devisee, or there is a will contest, or growing crops are involved, or where resort to the land or its rents is necessary for the payment of charges or expenses.[71] In any case, except to the extent that powers are conferred upon him by statute or by the will, the executor has no control over land or power to deal with it, and his duties and responsibilities are, as in every other connection, co-extensive with his powers and limited thereby. As to all these matters, like others involving real property,[72] the law of the situs of the land governs, regardless of the law of the testator's domicile or that of the place of administration.

§ 7.5-2. ———; *collection of rents.* As a part of the rights of control conferred upon him by statute, the executor may have the right, either generally or in particular circumstances, to collect the rents of real property.[73] Under the rule that rents belong to the devisee,[74] the executor who collects them must pay them over to the devisee, except if and to the extent that they are under applicable law available for and are used for payment of charges or expenses.[75]

§ 7.5-3. ———; *sale.*[76] By statute in every state an executor is given power to sell real property if, but in most states (unless the will otherwise provides) only if, under the rules relating to the availability of realty for the purpose[77] and to the abatement of devises in an insolvent estate,[78] such sale is necessary to raise money

---

[67] Infra § 18.3-5.

[68] Infra § 7.5-6.

[69] Although an executor is sometimes spoken of as having (only) a "qualified title", this would seem to mean little more than that he has power in appropriate circumstances to manage the real property, collect its rents, or sell it. Cf. Unif. Prob. Code sec. 3-711, providing that executor has "power over the title" to the property of the estate, and Comments to that section and sec. 3-709 to the effect that such provision obviates questions of the executor's title.

[70] See next following sections. Where the executor does have management duties as to real property in the estate, he may find useful a check list of the kind set forth in Appendix C, infra, which of course should be adapted to the law and practice of the particular jurisdiction.

[71] Infra §§ 15.7, 19.5-2, -2a.

[72] Infra § 25.4-3.

[73] Cf. *Hodgkinson v. Hodgkinson,* 281 Mass. 463, 183 N.E. 708 (executor has nothing to do with real property except to collect rents).

[74] Infra § 15.6.

[75] Generally, infra § 15.7. In insolvent or insufficient estate, infra § 19.7.

[76] West Dig., Exrs. & Admrs. Key Nos. 136–149, 319–407.

[77] Infra § 15.7.

[78] Infra § 19.5-7.

for the payment of charges or expenses.[79] The executor also has power to sell real property to enable the payment of legacies charged on the land,[80] inasmuch as the imposition by the will of such a charge implies a power to sell if necessary, and he may by statute or by will be given power to sell residuary real property for investment or other reasons.[81] In effect, therefore, in at least some situations the executor may "recapture" property from a devisee in whom title has vested.[82] In many jurisdictions, however, the sale may be made only with the permission or approval of the court,[83] obtained on appropriate application therefore; but in other jurisdictions statutes have removed such a requirement, and it may also be waived by the terms of the will, or by the designation of an "independent executor" in jurisdictions recognizing that or a like concept.[84] Powers of sale are, of course, like other matters affecting real property, governed by the law of the situs of the land and not by that of the place of administration, where the two are different.[85] It is to be emphasized that, as pointed out below, a sale of real property should not be made without a prior appraisal to ascertain its market value and so enable a judgment to be made of the adequacy of an offered price.[86]

§ 7.5-4. ———; *liability and casualty insurance.* Where and so long as, under applicable law, an executor has control of or responsibility for real property of a decedent,[87] the executor's duty to protect and preserve assets of the estate[88] requires him to put into force adequate insurance against losses and damage by casualty,[89] and for his own protection and that of the estate he should also obtain adequate public liability insurance.[90] Where, instead, real property does not become subject to administration by the executor, the executor would not seem to have any duty to provide any casualty insurance, or indeed to have any insurable interest in the premises, at least unless, under proper authorization so to do, he takes over the management of the property, in which case he should ascertain whether under local law he has an insurable interest therein or a duty to obtain insurance. The same

---

[79] At common law, real property could not be sold for such purpose. *First Trust & Sav. Bank v. Henderson,* 109 Fla. 175, 147 S. 248.

[80] Infra §§ 14.9-1, -2.

[81] In a few states, sale is permitted where that is in the best interest of the estate. Sale of unproductive real estate, supra § 7.7-2a.

[82] Title as vesting in devisee at death, supra § 7.5-1.

[83] Cf., e.g., *Cass v. Eliassen,* 94 Cal. App. 175, 270 P. 745; *Burnham v. Kelley,* 299 Mich. 452, 300 N.W. 127.

[84] Supra § 1.3-2.

[85] Infra § 25.4-3.

[86] Infra § 8.5-1.

[87] Generally, supra § 7.5-1.

[88] Supra § 7.1.

[89] Insurance on tangible personal property, supra § 7.2-4.

[90] Cf. *Reiff's Est.,* 49 D. & C. (Pa.) 119, pointing out that in considering the payment out of estate funds of premiums on liability insurance the question is whether the insurance is for the benefit of the estate or that of the fiduciary, but that the fact that the executor may initially be held liable for damage does not make the insurance for his benefit rather than that of the estate since (in absence of personal fault) the executor could recoup the amount from the estate.

principles would seem to apply as to liability insurance, but, even where real property is not treated as a part of the assets administered by the executor, some courts hold that the executor, although perhaps not under a duty to do so, may properly expend estate funds for liability insurance to protect the interests of persons interested in the estate, at least where the real property is not specifically devised.

§ 7.5-5. ———; *realty in another jurisdiction.* The law of a state ordinarily does not permit an executor appointed in another state to deal with real property situate in the former,[91] and the appointment of an ancillary executor, or ancillary administrator,[92] is therefore usually necessary before rents of real property therein may be collected, sale of it may be made, or other acts of administration may be had with respect to it. Accordingly, the only powers and responsibilities of the domiciliary executor with respect to real property in a state other than the state of his appointment, apart from those with respect to Federal estate taxation, are usually no greater than to see to it in a proper case that an ancillary representative is appointed in the state of the situs or, if ancillary proceedings are not required, that such state's inheritance or estate taxes are paid. It is to be noted that under statutes in some states, if nothing is required to be done with respect to real property situate therein that is disposed of by a will probated in another state except to settle state death taxes and clear title in the devisee, the filing in such state of duly exemplified copies of the will and of the decree admitting it to probate, or of the proceedings for its probate, is sufficient to evidence the devolution of title to the devisee, without an ancillary proceeding.

§ 7.5-6. ———; *cemetery lots.* As is pointed out elsewhere,[93] the disposability and devolution of cemetery lots are governed in some jurisdictions by special statutes; and so the law of the jurisdiction in which any cemetery lot that belonged to the decedent is situate must be consulted to determine what if any power of sale or other powers, and hence what responsibilities, the executor may have with respect thereto.

---

[91] Cf. § 1.7, supra.

[92] Ibid. Necessity of ancillary administration, in general, supra § 6.21-1.

[93] Devises of cemetery lots, supra § 15.8; includibility in residuary estate or residuary clause, infra § 18.3-5a.

VII

CUSTODY, PRESERVATION, AND MANAGEMENT OF ASSETS

Part B—Liquidation, Investment, Other Management Problems

§ 7.6-1. *Liquidation of assets;*[1] *for cash requirements.* At a very early stage of his administration of the estate the executor should estimate the amount of cash he will require and take steps to raise such cash to the extent it is not already on hand, either as such or in the form of assets equivalent to cash.[2] The cash requirements include estate and inheritance taxes,[3] funeral expenses and debts of the decedent,[4] expenses of administering the estate,[5] and cash legacies.[6] While most of these items cannot be computed with exactness until a later stage of the administration, a reasonably close estimate of most of them can usually be made at the outset; in making such an estimate doubtful items should be taken at their maximum amounts or on the most unfavorable basis, and a reasonable addition should be made to the computed amount for contingencies. From the total so arrived at there should be deducted not only the amount of cash on hand but also the amount of such assets on hand as are non-fluctuating in value and can be converted into cash almost immediately when desired, such as United States Treasury bills; and such parts of the cash requirements as will not be payable for a significant period of time, such as death taxes, some cash legacies[7] (including deferred legacies[8]), and the executor's

---

[1] West Dig., Exrs. & Admrs. Key Nos. 157–168, 321–331, 414; P-H Est. Plng. Serv. ¶ 2301 ff.
[2] 1964 Proc. A.B.A. Sec. Real Prop., Prob. & Tr. L. Part I, 55–56. See also Price, Postmortem Estate Planning Up to Date, 20 N.Y.U. Inst. on Fed. Taxation 301.
[3] Infra Ch. XII.
[4] Infra Ch. IX.
[5] Infra Ch. XX.
[6] Infra Ch. XIV.
[7] Infra § 15.31-1.
[8] Infra § 14.12-1.

CUSTODY, PRESERVATION, AND MANAGEMENT OF ASSETS

compensation,[9] attorney's fees,[10] and some other administration expenses, may be provided for without liquidation of assets if there are held obligations of high quality that have maturity dates not later than the time the cash will be needed. If the executor does not provide for his cash requirements within a reasonable time, he is in effect speculating upon the continued maintenance of existing values of assets of the estate;[11] and it is to be kept in mind that a reasonable time for liquidation may be a very short time, as, for example, in the case of securities having an active market. So an executor who does not carry out the necessary liquidation with all promptness practicable under the circumstances may be surcharged by beneficiaries if, by reason of a decline in market levels or otherwise, a lesser sum is eventually obtained for assets than could have been obtained, or a greater amount of assets has eventually to be sold to raise a given amount than would have had to be sold to raise that amount, if timely liquidation had been effected. In accordance with the general rules as to the order of availability of various kinds of property for payment of debts and expenses, in most states personal property must be exhausted before real property is sold, and residuary property before property specifically bequested or devised.[12] Within these rules, where they apply, the judgment of the executor as to what assets shall be sold where the sale of all is not required is ordinarily final, at least in the absence of bad faith; but the executor may well think it preferable to sell unproductive or under-productive property before productive property where the choice exists.[13]

§ 7.6-1a. ———; ———; *redemption of corporate stock.* Where an estate consists largely or substantially of stock of a closely-held corporation,[14] the often difficult problems of liquidation of such stock, or a part thereof, to raise cash requirements may be eased or obviated by causing a redemption of such stock by the corporation.[15] A special provision[16] of the Federal income tax law allows such a redemption to be made to such extent (only) as to provide for death taxes and funeral and administration expenses, without incurring the income tax consequences of stock redemptions generally,[17] if certain conditions are met; and the statute should be consulted in the light of the particular circumstances to determine whether its

---

[9] Infra § 20.4-3.

[10] Infra §§ 20.3-4, -4a.

[11] Speculation, supra § 3.5-3.

[12] Infra §§ 15.7, 19.5-1. Contribution to beneficiary whose property is sold from other beneficiaries of same class, infra § 19.2.

[13] Selection as option available to executor, infra § 13.6. Sale of unproductive property for investment of proceeds, infra § 7.7-2a.

[14] Duties with respect to closely-held corporations, in general infra § 7.8-1 ff.

[15] Redemption of its shares by corporation, see Price, Postmortem Estate Planning Up to Date, 20 N.Y.U. Inst. on Fed. Taxation 301, 303 ff.

[16] I.R.C. sec. 303. See Levenfeld, Postdeath Planning under Section 303, 51 A.B.A.J. 495. Redemption under that section as means of getting cash into estate even though liquidation not otherwise necessary, infra § 13.6 note 33.

[17] I.R.C. sec. 302.

provisions are applicable. Apart from or in addition to the tax aspects of a redemption, however, is the matter of the power or ability of the corporation to redeem its own stock, which under many corporation laws depends upon whether it has a surplus sufficient to cover the redemption price; and therefore the executor will also have to ascertain the facts in that regard. Where, however, such a redemption is available it may prevent the sale of the stock at a sacrifice, and also may obviate the necessity of seeking a postponement of payment[18] of an estate or inheritance tax because of inability to find a purchaser of the stock by the due date of the tax.

§ 7.6-1b. ———; ———; *borrowing.* Borrowing money for cash requirements may be thought of as a substitute for liquidation,[19] but usually is instead merely a deferment of liquidation until some future time when money for repayment of the loan is to be raised. Unless expressly authorized by statute or the will, an executor is without power to borrow,[20] and if he does so without authorization, or if he borrows for a purpose not authorized, he will be personally liable on the loan.[21] Borrowing, where permitted, is usually effected for payment of death taxes,[22] claims,[23] or administration expenses;[24] it is doubtful that any provision in a will, however broad, will be held to authorize borrowing for satisfaction of cash legacies,[25] at least in any but a most exigent situation, or borrowing for reinvestment.[26] Even where borrowing is within the executor's authority, and the purpose is a proper one, the executor should be very chary about exercising the power. In most cases where he is tempted to do so it is because assets are difficult to market, or their value is felt to be depressed at the time or to be likely to increase in the future; but it is obvious that any such situation involves elements of the speculation which is a violation of duty and may result in liability on the part of the executor if the hoped-for improvement does not occur. The executor must also consider the possibility that interest on the loan may exceed the income from the assets that are retained instead of being liquidated, or the rate of return on the estate as a whole. It is to be noted that postponement of payment of an estate or inheritance tax, under statutory provision therefor, is a form of borrowing and, as elsewhere discussed,[27] involves many of the considerations hereinabove mentioned.

§ 7.6-2. ———; *for distribution.* Historically it was the function of an executor to liquidate and distribute the assets of the estate not specifically disposed of

---

[18] Infra § 12.6.
[19] See last preceding section.
[20] But he probably can recoup from the estate, if it actually benefited; 1964 Proc. A.B.A. Sec. Real Prop. Prob. & Tr. L., Part I, 55.
[21] Ibid.
[22] Infra § 12.4-1 ff.
[23] Generally, infra §§ 9.5, 9.8-1.
[24] Infra § 20.2 ff.
[25] Cash legacies and payment thereof, infra §§ 14.6, 14.31-1 ff.
[26] Investment by executor, infra § 7.7-2.
[27] Infra § 12.6.

CUSTODY, PRESERVATION, AND MANAGEMENT OF ASSETS 79

by the will,[28] and, except where a statute permits him to do so,[29] it would seem doubtful that an executor may compel a general[30] or residuary[31] legatee to take distribution in kind unless the will contains an express provision permitting such distribution. In some states, however, the historical rule has been reversed by statute, in that an executor is without power to liquidate assets otherwise than as necessary to meet cash requirements.[32] Except for assets that, under the will or under such a statute, or by consent of the beneficiaries,[33] are to be distributed in kind,[34] the principles mentioned in the last preceding section require the executor to liquidate promptly, lest he be surcharged for a decline in values before liquidation is actually made.

§ 7.6-3. ————; *sale to executor or beneficiary*.[35] The matter of the sale of an estate asset to, or its purchase by, the executor himself, in its relation to his duty of faithfulness and impartiality, have been discussed elsewhere,[36] and it is there pointed out that such a purchase is usually voidable on the demand of any beneficiary even without a showing of unfairness or bad faith. The principles there involved, of the opportunity for unfairness, overreaching, or fraud, are also applicable in the case of a sale to a beneficiary, although to a somewhat less rigorous degree; a sale of the latter kind is not so readily voidable as that to an executor, but will be carefully scrutinized when questioned by any other beneficiary claiming to be affected by it, and if the consideration is found to have been inadequate, or in any other respect the transaction is found to have been unfair to others interested in the estate, it will be set aside; indeed, the degree of proof of unfairness sufficient to cause the sale to be set aside will probably be less than would be required if the sale had been to a disinterested person. Sometimes, of course, a beneficiary is the only available purchaser of a particular asset or interest, or a more favorable sale can be made to a beneficiary than to any third person; but in any such circumstance the executor should make sure that he will be able to establish such facts if the transaction should be questioned, and the general principle that an independent appraisal of the asset by a competent appraiser should first be obtained[37] applies here with special force.

---

[28] Liquidation of unproductive assets, infra § 7.7-2.
[29] Cf. Unif. Prob. Code sec. 3-906 (b), permitting cash legacy to be satisfied in property unless legatee demands money or a residuary legatee requests retention of property; and Comment thereto, saying that the section "establishes a preference" for distribution in kind, with conversion into cash to be made "only where there is a special reason for doing so".
[30] Satisfaction of cash legacy in property, in general, infra § 14.27-1.
[31] Satisfaction of residuary legacy in property, infra § 18.6-4 ff.
[32] Liquidation for cash requirements, supra § 7.6-1.
[33] Infra §§ 14.27-1, 18.6-4.
[34] Retention for distribution in kind, infra § 7.6-5.
[35] West Dig., Exrs. & Admrs. Key No. 163.
[36] Supra § 3.9-4b.
[37] Infra § 8.1.

§ 7.6-4. ———; *corporate executor's own securities; "divided loyalty rule".* In an increasing number of jurisdiction the rule is becoming established that, unless a contrary intention is evidenced in the will, securities of or issued by a bank or trust company which is the executor or one of the executors of the decedent's will may not be retained, but must be disposed of within a reasonable time.[38] This rule, known as the "divided loyalty rule," is based on the theory that the corporate executor cannot take an objective view of the value or investment merit of its own capital stock or other securities, or the desirability of the sale thereof, including the possible effect of a sale on the market price of the corporation's stock as a whole, and the rule accordingly requires the sale of such securities wholly without regard to the considerations which in general govern a fiduciary in determining whether to retain or to dispose of investments. It is to be pointed out that the "reasonable time" within which under the rule disposal of such securities is required may be a very short time, as where the securities are traded actively or fairly frequently, and that failure to dispose of a corporate executor's securities with considerable promptness may accordingly be held to constitute an infringement of the rule and therefore may cause not only the corporate executor but also its co-executors, if any, to be surchargeable for any amount by which the eventual sale price falls below the price at which the securities could have been sold at any earlier time. It is therefor very important, where securities of the corporate executor are among the estate assets, to determine at an early date whether the rule referred to is recognized in the jurisdiction or is likely to be applied, and, if so, whether any provision contained in the will, such as a grant of general power to retain the decedent's assets or some more explicit provision, is sufficient to waive or to prevent application of the rule.

§ 7.6-4a. ———; ———; *officer or director of corporation.* By an extension of the divided loyalty rule,[39] or on principles analogous to those on which that rule is founded, an executor who is an officer or director of a corporation securities of which are held in the estate is in a position where self-interest may, or may be deemed to, affect his decisions with respect to the retention, voting, or disposition of such securities; and, although it does not appear to have been held (as it has in the case discussed in the preceding section) that the securities must for that reason be sold, situations may readily be envisaged in which the relationship between the executor and such corporation is so close as to risk application of the same rule as if the corporation were itself the executor.[40] At the least, the executor in such case is open to a suspicion of lack of impartiality and so is especially vulnerable to surcharge if the stock declines in value or any action on the part of the corporation adversely affects the estate or its beneficiaries.

---

[38] *City Bank Farmers Tr. Co. v. Cannon*, 264 A.D. 429, 35 N.Y.S.2d 870, affd. 291 N.Y. 125, 51 N.E. 674.

[39] See last preceding section.

[40] Cf. *Cashman v. Petrie*, 14 N.Y.2d 426, 252 N.Y.S.2d 447, 201 N.E.2d 24.

CUSTODY, PRESERVATION, AND MANAGEMENT OF ASSETS

§ 7.6-5. ———; *retention for distribution in kind*. If under applicable law the rule of liquidation for distribution is recognized,[41] an authorization in the will to make distribution in kind to residuary legatees relieves the executor from the duty otherwise incumbent upon him to liquidate merely for distribution, but he may nevertheless liquidate if he sees fit; and even though the will does not authorize distribution in kind he may make such distribution if the beneficiaries so request, or if they consent to receive their shares wholly or partly in kind. Therefore, the executor will ordinarily consult the beneficiaries as to their preferences in this regard, if they are *sui juris*. If, on the other hand, the governing law directs that assets be not liquidated merely for purposes of distribution,[42] the executor may still liquidate if the beneficiaries so request or agree, although before proceeding in such a case the executor should consider, or call to the attention of the beneficiaries, the possibility that capital gains or losses realized on a sale made at the instance of beneficiaries may be treated for income tax purposes as realized by the beneficiaries, rather than by the estate, on the theory that in making the sale the executor acted as their agent.[43] The question of liquidation or retention for eventual distribution usually comes up at a fairly early stage of the administration, when the executor must consider promptness of sale to avoid possible declines in value;[44] and because a considerable length of time may elapse before distribution can properly or safely be made, the executor may be unwilling to assume the risks of declining values in the meantime, at least where he has the power or option to liquidate. Accordingly, where residuary beneficiaries prefer to receive property in kind, the executor in consideration of acceding to their wishes should obtain from them an express agreement relieving him from liability, or estopping themselves from asserting liability, for any diminution of value of the property.[45]

§ 7.6-6. ———; *liquidation of unauthorized or unsuitable investment*.[46] Apart from considerations of the kinds discussed in the preceding sections, an executor must consider his duty to dispose of investments, received from the testator, that are not within the class in which, by statute or court rule, or the terms of the will, he is himself authorized to invest estate funds,[47] or that, under the usual principles applicable to trust funds generally, are not deemed safe, prudent, or suitable.[48] Where a statute or rule of court permits the retention of "unauthorized" investments for only a reasonable time, the executor should recognize that under some circumstances such

---

[41] Cf. § 7.6-2, supra.

[42] Ibid.

[43] Partial distribution in kind as making estate's income for year taxable to beneficiary, infra § 18.6-3.

[44] Supra § 6.1.

[45] Distribution in kind, in general, infra § 18.6-4; where a beneficiary fails or is unable to agree thereto, infra § 18.6-4b.

[46] West Dig., Exrs. & Admrs. Key No. 105.

[47] *Taylor's Est.*, 277 Pa. 518, 121 A. 310. Investment by executor, in general, infra § 7.7-2.

[48] Sale of unproductive property, infra § 7.7-2a. Disposition or liquidation of business, infra § 7.9.

a time may be very short. A failure on the part of the executor to make timely disposition of assets which it is his duty to liquidate will render him liable to beneficiaries for any loss, as for any other negligence in the performance of his duties.

§ 7.7-1. Money; opening bank account; commingling.[49] The executor should open a bank account in his name as executor, or in the name of the estate, and deposit therein all moneys received during the course of administration of the estate, including cash held by the decedent at death,[50] moneys received upon the closing of accounts in the decedent's name,[51] proceeds of sales of assets,[52] and all other receipts and collections, whether of principal or of income.[53] Moneys of the estate must at all times be kept separate and distinct from the executor's own funds and from the funds of every other estate or trust, so that no commingling can occur; therefore, the title of the account in which estate funds are deposited should be such as clearly to indicate its fiduciary character, and, of course, the executor should not deposit in such account any moneys not belonging to or constituting assets of the estate.

§ 7.7-2. ———; duty to make productive; investments.[54] Having in mind the executor's basic duties of collecting, administering, and disposing of the estate, often epitomized in the statement that his duty is to liquidate and distribute,[55] it is apparent that his functions differ basically from those of a trustee so far as concerns the investment of estate funds, and in general he is without authority to invest, in the sense of any long-term or "permanent" deployment of funds, at least unless the will authorizes him so to do.[56] However, because it is his duty to effect prompt liquidation of at least sufficient assets to cover his cash requirements,[57] an executor may have in his hands a substantial amount of money considerably in advance of the time for its expenditure or distribution. His duty of diligence,[58] which may be translated as the duty of administering the estate to the best advantage of its beneficiaries, makes it improper for him to retain a fund of any considerable amount for any significant period of time without making it productive of income.[59] Accordingly, notwithstand-

---

[49] West Dig., Exrs. & Admrs. Key Nos. 104 (3), 105; P-H Est. Plng. Serv. ¶ 2180.
[50] Supra §§ 6.5, 6.6.
[51] Supra §§ 6.7-1, -2.
[52] Supra § 7.6-1 ff.
[53] Principal and income, in general, infra Ch. XVI.
[54] West Dig., Exrs. & Admrs. Key Nos. 101–104.
[55] Supra § 7.6-2.
[56] It is argued by some authorities that, because of the inherent nature of the executorial function, a will cannot effectively authorize the executor to make other than temporary investments of estate funds, except where some sort of trust is intended; whether this argument be valid or not, an executor may be held imprudent or acting beyond his proper function, even under a will provision authorizing investment in unrestricted terms, if he makes an investment other than a purely temporary one and a decline in value ensues.
[57] Supra § 7.61.
[58] Supra § 3.1.
[59] *Lare's Est.*, 436 Pa. 1, 267 A.2d 556, held an executor surchargeable for holding funds uninvested for an extended period, notwithstanding a statute providing that an executor has no duty to invest. For a detailed discussion of the duty to invest, see 1964 Proc. A.B.A. Sec. Real Prop. Prob. & Tr. L., Part I, 57–67.

CUSTODY, PRESERVATION, AND MANAGEMENT OF ASSETS 83

ing his general lack of power to invest funds in the sense that a trustee would have power or owe a duty to invest them, an executor should make appropriate investments of any substantial amounts of money,[60] or deposit them in a savings or other interest-bearing bank account where that is otherwise proper,[61] so as to make them productive of reasonable income,[62] after first applying for and obtaining judicial authorization so to do if such authorization is required under applicable law. In choosing investments the executor must, of course, observe any restrictions prescribed by statutory or judicial rules, or by the will, relating to the investment of estate funds. Within such limitations, and even where the will purports to relax or remove them, the duty of care and prudence would seem to make it appropriate, if not indeed requisite, for the executor to confine himself to short-term investments, of high quality and such as not to fluctuate significantly in value,[63] for his primary duty is to make sure that the funds will be available immediately or on short notice when needed and will not diminish or disappear by a shrinkage in value in the interim period. The rate or amount of income obtainable on such investments will, of course, ordinarily be less than that obtainable on longer-term investments or those involving more risk, but will be commensurate with the nature and purpose of the investment as above mentioned, in which the production of income is secondary to considerations of safety and liquidity. This somewhat secondary nature of an executor's duty to make funds productive of income while they await disbursement or distribution does not, however, mean that the duty does not exist or that it may be disregarded with impunity; and an executor who holds funds uninvested in significant amount for any extended period may be liable to beneficiaries as for any other want of diligence.

§ 7.7-2a. ———; ———; *sale of unproductive property*. The general principle that it is the duty of an executor to make funds productive of income[64] may by extension require that unproductive property be made productive by sale and investment of its proceeds.[65] While in most states an executor is not permitted to sell real property, unless the will otherwise provides, except for payment of debts or ex-

---

[60] Cf. Unif. Prob. Code sec. 3-715 (5).

[61] Such a deposit should not be made unless it is a "legal" or permitted investment of estate or trust funds under governing law. Also, if under local law a savings account of other interest-bearing account is subject to possible imposition of a requirement for advance notice of withdrawals, the executor must consider whether deposits of estate funds in such an account would be improper because he might not be able to obtain the funds when they were needed.

[62] On the same principle, as well as under basic doctrines of self-interest, by statute in some states a corporate fiduciary is required to pay interest on funds held uninvested on deposit with itself for longer than a specified period of time. It may be noted that a problem arises where such a statute conflicts with regulations of the Federal Reserve Board or a state banking board limiting or prohibiting payment of interest on demand deposits.

[63] United States Treasury bills, if obtainable in denominations not greater than the amount available for investment, are often regarded as a most suitable medium because they fill the requirements mentioned in the text and can be acquired and disposed of readily and expeditiously.

[64] See last preceding section.

[65] Liquidation of unsuitable investments, in general, supra § 7.6-6.

penses,[66] a few states permit its sale where that is for the best interests of the estate, and in the latter case it is within the power, although perhaps not ordinarily the duty, of the executor to sell unproductive realty that is not specifically devised, and invest the proceeds in accordance with the rules stated in the preceding section. As to unproductive personal property, not specifically bequeathed, it would seem, even absent from any other reason for its sale,[67] that its unproductivity may impose on the executor a duty to sell it,[68] so that its value may be turned into productive property by investment of the proceeds of sale, where a significant amount of time will elapse before distribution of the residue can be made.[69]

§ 7.8-1. *Closely-held corporations;*[70] *in general.* Where the decedent at his death was the owner of shares of stock of a closely-held corporation, the executor may have responsibilities greater than those he would have if the stock were instead that of a publicly-held corporation.[71] The nature and degree of such responsibilities depend principally upon the degree or extent of control of the corporation represented by or exercisable in virtue of the decedent's stock. Obviously, if the amount of stock coming into the hands of the executor is such a relatively small fraction of the corporation's outstanding stock as to give the executor no power to control corporate action, his responsibilities are minimal because they cannot exceed his power; but, by the same token, if the stock held by the executor gives him full working control of the corporation, his responsibilities are of the same scope as his power.[72]

§ 7.8-2. ———; *management, sale, merger, liquidation.* Within the limits of his power and responsibility,[73] or, more specifically, to the extent that by voting his stock or otherwise he can exert his efforts, it is the duty of the executor holding stock of a closely-held corporation to endeavor promptly to see to it that the corporation has adequate management and supervision, for at least a transition period, and then to consider whether it is in the best interest of the beneficiaries of the estate that the business of the corporation be continued or, instead, that the corporation's stock or its assets be sold, that it be merged with another corporation, or that it be liquidated. These considerations involve many factors, some of which are whether the business can be continued in view of the decedent's death, especially where he was a "key man", whether it should be continued, who can and will manage or operate it, whether

---

[66] Supra §§ 7.5-3, 7.6-1.

[67] Supra § 7.6-1 ff.

[68] Cumulative preferred stock on which dividends are not being currently paid would seem to come within the rule of the text, so that the executor should consider sale of the stock because of unproductivity, unless it affirmatively appears that dividend payments will be resumed or arrears discharged within a reasonable time.

[69] Distribution of residue, infra § 18.6-1 ff.

[70] P-H Est. Plng. Serv. ¶ 2193.1.

[71] Collection and protection of assets of closely-held corporation, supra § 6.9. Redemption of stock, supra § 7.6-1a. Valuation problems, infra § 8.6-2.

[72] The terms "closely-held" and "publicly-held" are, of course, relative, and the principles discussed in this and the following sections depend not so much upon the number of stockholders as upon the degree of control possessed by the decedent or represented by his stock.

[73] See last preceding section.

CUSTODY, PRESERVATION, AND MANAGEMENT OF ASSETS 85

adequate financing will be available, whether its profitability and stability will be such that beneficiaries should be left dependent (in whole or in part) upon it, whether it or its assets can be sold at a fair price, whether the corporation can be merged into another company and, if so, whether it should be, or whether it should be liquidated so that the risks of a going business are avoided and its value as represented by the proceeds may be put into safer or surer investments.[74] Unless the decedent during his lifetime has considered and has provided in his will or otherwise[75] for meeting the situation created by his death, the problems presented to the executor by ownership of stock of a closely-held corporation are likely to be difficult and of great importance, particularly where such stock is a chief asset of the estate; and the executor's duties and responsibilities are of corresponding urgency and importance.

§ 7.8-3. ———; *buy-and-sell agreements.* Where the decedent as a stockholder of a closely-held corporation has during his lifetime entered into a valid agreement with his fellow stockholders, or the corporation, or both, providing for the sale of the decedent's stock to and its purchase by the other stockholders or the corporation at his death,[76] the executor should carry out such agreement if it be mandatory, or, even if sale pursuant to it be optional on the part of the executor, if disposal of the stock pursuant to its terms is judged to be in the best interest of the estate under the circumstances.[77] If such an agreement is mandatory so far as the estate is concerned and fixes the sale price, either explicitly or by a formula, the executor is, of course, bound thereby, subject only to the principles upon which any contract may be rescinded or avoided, as in case it was induced by fraud, duress, mistake, misrepresentation, or the like. If, however, compliance with the agreement is not mandatory upon the estate, but is optional, or if the price or terms are not fixed but are subject to negotiation, the executor has the same kind of responsibilities for determining whether to sell pursuant to the agreement, or for determining the adequacy of the price or terms, as he has in connection with any other sale of estate assets.[78] Where the executor has an option to sell the stock, or to require the other contracting parties to purchase it, only upon a specified notice or demand, an executor who fails to give such notice or make such demand in a case where the sale is in the best interest of the estate is liable to beneficiaries for the whatever loss results.[79]

§ 7.8-4. ———; *fee or salary to executor as director or officer.* Under the general rule that a fiduciary is prohibited from making a personal profit from his trust,[80] an executor is not warranted in receiving a fee or salary for services as a director or

---

[74] Liquidation of assets, in general, supra § 7.6-1 ff. Powers of executor in connection with business, cf. Unif Prob. Code sec. 3-715 (24) and (25).
[75] See next following section.
[76] Agreement as establishing or affecting valuation for death tax purposes, infra § 8.6-3.
[77] Contracts of decedent, in general, infra § 7.13-1.
[78] Sale generally, supra § 7.6-1 ff.
[79] Negligence, in general, supra § 3.5-1.
[80] Supra § 3.9-4b.

officer of a closely-held corporation of which stock is held in the estate, and if he does receive any such compensation he must turn it over to the estate. The rule stated is, of course, subject to exception where the will clearly otherwise provides, but any provision of doubtful import will probably be construed against the executor, having in mind also that the regular compensation allowable by law to an executor is intended to be for all his services as such.[81] Presumably the rigorous rule herein stated does not apply to the executor who is a director or officer of a publicly-held company, especially if he was such, to the knowledge of the testator, when the will was executed, but the executor in such case is nevertheless subject to the general rules governing self-interest,[82] and must be aware of his special vulnerability.

§ 7.9. *Proprietorships and partnership interests.*[83] Where the decedent at the time of his death owned or operated a business or enterprise (as distinguished from a profession[84]) as a sole proprietor,[85] the duties and responsibilities of the executor with respect to the business or enterprise are largely of the same kind as those with respect to a corporation of which the decedent was sole stockholder,[86] and many problems facing the executor are of the same nature. Specifically, however, the excutor who proposes to continue the business for more than a comparatively brief transition period[87] must ascertain whether, under applicable law, he has power to do so; in some states statutes grant such power, or permit the court to authorize continuation in a proper case,[88] but in the absence of statute, or of effective provision in the will, the executor must dispose of the business or liquidate it with reasonable promptness.[89] Where, instead of being a sole proprietor, the decedent at his death was a member of a partnership, the executor must examine the partnership agreement, with particular reference to the extent of the decedent's interest in the partnership[90] and also with reference to the terms of the agreement as to liquidation of the decedent's interest, the continuance of his capital at risk in the business for some designated length of time, or the substitution of the estate as a partner, special or general, in the firm. Apart from the effect of provisions of the agreement and the fact that one or more partners survive to continue the firm's business or to effect its liquidation, so that the executor's problems may differ in degree from those present where the business was conducted as a corporation or a proprietorship, they do not differ in character. It is to be noted that even if the partnership agreement or the will authorizes or requires the executor to leave the decedent's interest in the firm at risk therein for a period of time, or provides that the estate shall succeed the decedent as

---

[81] Compensation, in general, infra § 20.4-1 ff.
[82] Supra § 3.9-4 ff.
[83] West Dig., Exrs. & Admrs. Key Nos. 93, 94; P-H Est. Plng. Serv. ¶¶ 2193, 2194.
[84] Estates of professional men, supra § 6.20-1 ff.
[85] Collection and protection of assets of proprietorship, supra § 6.9.
[86] Supra § 7.8-1 ff.
[87] Supra § 6.9.
[88] So in Unif. Prob. Code sec. 3-715 (24).
[89] Duty to dispose of unsuitable investment, in general, supra § 7.6.6.
[90] Valuation, infra § 8.8.

CUSTODY, PRESERVATION, AND MANAGEMENT OF ASSETS 87

a partner, the executor is ordinarily without power to invest in the business any additional funds out of the general estate,[91] unless clearly authorized by the will so to do.

§ 7.10. *Domestic and personal employees.* Persons in the employ of the decedent at the time of his death as domestic or personal servants or aids should be discharged by the executor with reasonable promptness, in order to end the burden to the estate of their wages or salaries. What is reasonable promptness depends upon the circumstances of each case. For example, it may be reasonable to continue for a considerable period of time the employment of a house servant for the purpose of protecting the premises or their contents, or of facilitating a sale of household furnishings or the like, even if, or for a period for which, it would be unreasonable to continue such employment in the absence of such considerations.[92] Similarly, a personal secretary, bookkeeper, or the like, may be of substantial usefulness to the executor because of special knowledge of the decedent's affairs, and the continuation of his employment for a period of time may therefore be warranted. In general, however, unless the employee performs functions useful or beneficial to the estate, or when he ceases so to do, his employment should be terminated at an early date. These rules do not require, however, that employees be discharged without notice or a payment in lieu of notice, and it seems to be accepted that the executor may properly pay from estate funds salary or wages for a period of time, or an amount of severance pay, comparable with that customary upon an individual employer's discharge of a corresponding employee without fault on the part of the latter.[93]

§ 7.11-1. *Apartment or rented home; in general.* Generally speaking, it is the duty of the executor, under the doctrine of waste,[94] to terminate the continuing liability of the estate for rent of an apartment or home of the decedent as promptly as feasible under the circumstance.[95] If the tenancy, whether under a lease or otherwise, is terminable upon proper notice to the landlord, the executor should promptly give such notice of termination, unless another person occupied the premises with the decedent and either such other person is willing to assume the rental payments or it is reasonable, or in conformity with a will provision, to allow such occupancy to continue and to charge the rental against benefits provided for such person in the will. If the tenancy is under an unexpired lease which is not by its terms cancellable

---

[91] *Matter of Muller*, 24 N.Y.2d 336, 300 N.Y.S.2d 341, 248 N.E.2d 164.

[92] In *Matter of Watson*, 86 Misc. 588, 148 N.Y.S. 902, affd. 165 App.D. 252, 150 N.Y.S. 776, rev. on other gds. 215 N.Y. 209, 109 N.E. 86, it was held that retention and support of all the decedent's servants for four months after death, and some of them for a longer period to preserve expensive home furnishings and exhibit the house in attractive form to prospective purchasers, was not too long in the circumstances.

[93] Ibid.; see also *Matter of Kaufman*, N.Y.L.J. Jan. 21, 1966, p. 16, holding payment of wages to cook, butler, secretaries, and handyman for 14 months improper but allowing payment for one month after death as reasonable severance pay.

[94] Supra § 3.5-2.

[95] Familiarization with nature and terms of tenancy, supra § 6.10. Decedent as landlord or lessor, supra § 6.15-2.

or terminable, the executor should, subject to the other considerations mentioned, endeavor to obtain to consent of the landlord to a surrender of the lease if such consent can be obtained on reasonable terms,[96] and, in the absence of such consent, endeavor to sublet the premises if not prohibited by the lease from so doing. An exception to the rules just stated exists where in the sound judgment of the executor it is more economical or otherwise more advantageous to the estate to leave furnishings or other tangibles in the premises for a time than to transfer them to other storage facilities, pending their sale or other disposition.[97] Also, the executor may reasonably decided to continue the tenancy, at the expense of the estate, for such reasonable time as is necessary or advisable to continue to provide a servant or companion with a home during the period proper for continuance of employment,[98] or where contents of the premises are to be sold and it appears that their sale will be facilitated, or better prices will be obtained, if they are left in the premises.

§ 7.11-2. ———; *cooperative apartment, or condominium.* The principles stated in the last preceding section as to termination or continuance of a decedent's tenancy of a rented apartment or home apply equally to a tenancy under a so-called proprietary lease held in virtue of ownership of shares of stock in a cooperative title-holding corporation, and to ownership of an apartment under a condominium arrangement, subject to the requirements and restrictions of the proprietary lease or the agreement among co-owners and to the additional fact in the case of condominium that the holder has a legal title rather than a leasehold. In the case of either a proprietary lease or a condominium the executor may not, because of conditions and restrictions in the basic agreements, be able to terminate the decedent's obligations, and hence the expense to the estate, in respect of the premises as easily or promptly, or to sublet, or dispose of the decedent's rights or interests in the premises, as freely, as in the case of a tenancy under a conventional rental or lease arrangement; nevertheless, the executor has the same kind and degree of responsibility, within the limits of the action available to him, to endeavor to terminate the continuing burden upon the estate in the one case as in the other, and it is his duty to take whatever steps to that end are within his power and advantageous to the estate.[99]

§ 7.12. *Suspension of utilities.* In line with the duty of an executor to avoid the incurrence of unnecessary expense,[100] he should proceed with promptness to suspend or discontinue utility services that were being supplied to the decedent before his death and are no longer needed for the benefit of the estate, unless a member of the family or other person who lived in the testator's home or occupied business premises with him continues so to do, in which case the executor should arrange for the expense of such services to be assumed by such person. Suspension of telephone serv-

---

[96] Compromise of claims, in general, infra § 9.9.
[97] Delivery of tangibles to legatee, infra § 14.4-9.
[98] See last preceding section.
[99] Incurrence of avoidable expense as waste, supra § 3.5-2.
[100] Ibid.

ice, where feasible in the light of the foregoing, may usually be accompanied by arrangements to have calls intercepted and referred to the executor's telephone, and this, as in the case of forwarded mail,[1] may assist the executor in obtaining knowledge of the decedent's affairs. Utilities or some of them may, of course, properly be continued where, for example, they conduce to the protection or preservation of the premises or its contents, or facilitate the inspection thereof by prospective purchasers or renters, or where an employee or servant is left in possession pending discharge or as a caretaker or otherwise to promote the affairs of the estate.[2]

§ 7.13-1. *Executory contracts of decedent;*[3] *in general.* As a general rule, to which, however, there may possibly be some exceptions,[4] the executor must carry out and perform all valid contracts that had been entered into by the decedent during his lifetime and remained unperformed at his death[5] (except contracts for the rendition by the decedent of personal services, which class of contracts under general rules of law become ineffective on his death), subject to any valid defenses that would have been available to the decedent or are available to the executor.[6] By the same token, he must enforce the obligations of the other contracting party under all agreements that are advantageous or beneficial to the estate,[7] or demand damages for non-performance of such contracts, as may be appropriate in the particular case. These duties make necessary, as is obvious, adequate investigation of the circumstances under which the decedent's undertaking was made, and of all other factors having a bearing on the validity or enforceability of his contract, and of the effect upon the estate of performance or non-performance by the other party. For a failure or default in making such investigations or in his duties under or with respect to the contract, including expenses of any unnecessary litigation,[8] the executor is liable to beneficiaries as for any other default or negligence.

§ 7.13-2. ————; *purchase or sale of land; equitable conversion.* The general rules as to executory contracts made by a decedent apply, of course, to contracts for the purchase or the sale of land.[9] In addition, where such a contract is in existence, the executor must consider, where the point is significant, whether under applicable law an equitable conversion is effected by it, as bearing on the rights *inter se* of lega-

---

[1] Supra § 3.51.
[2] Supra § 7.11-1.
[3] West Dig., Exrs. & Admrs. Key Nos. 95-100; P-H Est. Plng. Serv. ¶ 2196.
[4] Cf. Simes, Rights of Personal Representatives to Breach Executory Contracts of Decedent, 1958 Proc. A.B.A. Sec. Real Prop. Prob. & Tr. L., Part I, 4.
[5] Buy-and-sell agreements as to corporate stock, supra § 7.8-3. Charitable pledges of decedent, infra § 9.11.
[6] Cf. Unif. Prob. Code sec. 3-715 (3): Executor may complete, compromise, or refuse performance of contracts that continue as obligations of the estate, as he may determine in the circumstances.
[7] Non-beneficial contracts, cf. Simes, op. cit. supra note 4.
[8] Supra § 3.5-2.
[9] Duty of executor to discover and consider, supra § 6.15-4.

tees,[29] on the one hand, and devisees,[11] on the other, and perhaps also the availability of the property or funds involved for payment of debts and charges of the estate.[12]

§ 7.14. Contracts and undertakings of executor.[13] It is a general rule, in the absence of statute otherwise providing,[14] that any contract, promise, or undertaking made by an executor, even though he describes himself therein as such or executes it "as" executor, is deemed made by him personally and is not in and of itself binding upon the estate for which he acts;[15] but that the executor may claim over against the estate assets for any liability established against him thereon if the matter to which the contract, promise, or undertaking relates was within his authority and for the benefit of the estate. Thus when it is said, somewhat loosely, that the executor is personally liable on an unauthorized or otherwise improper contract, what is really meant is that the executor is without right to indemnification thereon out of the assets of the estate. Ordinarily, however, the parties to the arrangement may validly agree that the executor shall not be personally liable and that the other party will look solely to the estate for any breach or default, and while in such case the executor cannot be made to answer personally therefor, he may still be surcharged if the contract was beyond his authority or otherwise affected by fault on his part.

§ 7.15. Torts of executor.[16] Generally speaking, an executor is personally liable for torts committed by him, even if he purported to be acting in his representative capacity, but, as in the case of contracts made by him,[17] he may be entitled to indemnification from the estate, and, in the absence of personal fault on his part, as, for example, in the case of a defect in premises under his control, the liability may be that of the estate and not that of the executor.[18] As the legal problems are primarily those of the law of torts rather than of the law of estate administration, they are not further treated here.

§ 7.16. Exculpation from liability. Provisions in a will for the exculpation of the executor from liability are likely to apply particularly to matters of the kind to which this chapter relates, and the questions discussed above as to the efficacy and reliability of such provisions[19] should accordingly have particular consideration in those connections.

---

[10] Legacies, infra Ch. XIV.
[11] Devises, infra Ch. XV.
[12] Infra §§ 15.7, 19.5-2, -2a.
[13] West Dig., Exrs. & Admrs., Key Nos. 92, 95-100.
[14] Cf. Unif. Prob. Code sec. 3-808 (a): Executor not personally liable if he reveals in the contract his fiduciary capacity and the identity of the estate.
[15] This grows out of the fact that the estate is not an entity; supra § 1.11-2.
[16] West Dig., Exrs. & Admrs. Key No. 119.
[17] See last preceding section.
[18] So in Unif. Prob. Code sec. 3-808 (b).
[19] Supra § 3.10. Release by beneficiaries, infra Ch. XXI.

VIII

VALUATION OF ASSETS

§ 8.1. Necessity and purposes of valuation.[1] Whether or not an appraisal or valuation of assets of the estate is required for estate or inheritance tax purposes,[2] it is necessary that the assets be valued by the executor in order to determine or establish the amount of property for which he is responsible.[3] Such valuation is therefore that to be used for accounting purposes,[4] and fixes the base for measuring the executor's performance in his administration, as to whether he has allowed the value of the estate to be diminished by losses or declines in value, and as to the property or amount eventually distributable to beneficiaries, and accordingly as to each asset is called its "inventory value".[5] The determination of inventory value is, as will be apparent, necessary only as to the assets coming into the executor's hands or for which he is accountable, as a part of the assets administerable by him (the "probate estate"[6]). As to assets not administerable by him ("non-probate assets"[7]) his duty of valuation (if any) is solely for the purposes of an estate or inheritance tax on the estate, except where, as under some statutes, certain non-probate assets are to be taken into account in computing a spouse's statutory or elective share and determining whether it has been satisfied;[8] in either such case such non-probate assets must be valued by the executor but, as they do not come into his hands or under his control for purposes of administration, they do not enter into inventory value. It is to be noted that the determination of inventory value does not necessarily suffice for all purposes, and that a second valuation of some assets may be required to be made at a later time, as where a cash legacy is satisfied in property,[9] or where a residuary or

---

[1] West Dig., Exrs. & Admrs. Key Nos. 62–73 and Taxation Key No. 895; P-H Est. Plng. Serv. ¶ 2177.

[2] Tax valuation distinguished, see next following section.

[3] Responsibility for assets, in general, supra § 6.1.

[4] Accountability and accounting, infra Ch. XXIV.

[5] Basis and determination, infra § 8.3 ff.

[6] Supra § 1.11-1.

[7] Ibid.

[8] Infra § 17.4-1.

[9] Infra §§ 14.27-1, -2.

other legacy of a share or fraction of a group or aggregate of assets to each of two or more persons is satisfied other than by ratable distribution,[10] and also, as pointed out elsewhere, for his own protection and that of the beneficiaries, the executor must obtain an appraisal of an asset proposed to be sold in order to determine whether an offered price is adequate.[11]

§ 8.2. *Accounting and tax values distinguished.* It is apparent from the last preceding section that the inventory value of an asset, being the value of such asset at the time when or as of which the executor becomes responsible for it, may be its value as of a date considerably different from that governing values for purposes of an estate or inheritance tax. While the inventory value is usually the value as of the date of death of the decedent,[12] on the theory that the executor's appointment relates back to that date, it may be as of a later date, as in some instances where there is unusual delay in the appointment and qualification[13] of the executor and there are no special circumstances which would make the executor liable for assets as of any date earlier than that of his appointment;[14] and obviously the inventory value with which a successor executor is chargeable will not be the value at the date of the testator's death but instead the value when the successor executor comes into office.[15] Also, the value for purposes of a particular tax may be that of a date after the date of death; a familiar instance is the case of alternate or "optional" values for Federal estate tax purposes where the valuation date may be as much as six months after death.[16] It is, therefore, necessary in theory, and often (although not always[17]) in practice, to distinguish between the inventory value of an asset, which is the value with which the executor is charged and accordingly the value to be used by him for accounting purposes,[18] and the value for the purposes of a death tax, which may be different both from inventory value and from the value to be used for the purposes of another death tax.

§ 8.3-1. *Inventory value; basis and determination.* The inventory value, or value for accounting purposes,[19] of any asset of the estate is its fair market value on the date as of which the executor becomes chargeable with or responsible for it.[20] If as of that date there existed merely a right to receive the property at a future time or upon some contingency, the right, and not the property, is to be valued, although of course the value of the property will affect the value of the right. Market value may be readily or definitively ascertainable, as in the case of listed securities, but in other

---

[10] Infra § 18.6-4a.
[11] Cf. §§ 7.5-3, 7.6-3 supra.
[12] Infra § 8.3.
[13] Supra § 5.8-1 ff.
[14] Pre-probate responsibility to preserve assets, supra § 4.6.
[15] Successor executor as liable for values at time of appointment, infra § 23.4-2.
[16] I.R.C. sec. 2032.
[17] Infra § 8.3-2.
[18] See last preceding section.
[91] Supra § 8.1.
[20] Supra § 8.2.

VALUATION OF ASSETS

cases an appraisal will be necessary;[21] and for his own protection and that of the beneficiaries, as well as for tax purposes, the executor should be sure that the appraiser employed to determine values is both competent and reputable. For any negligence in determining inventory value the executor is, of course, responsible,[22] but in general an error in such determination is merely subject to correction.

§ 8.3-2. ———; *statutory inventory and appraisal.* In many states statutes require the executor to make, and file in the probate court, an inventory of the decedent's assets, and to appraise them, at fair market values, or cause them to be so appraised; and some statutes provide for the appointment by the court of appraisers who, as agents of the court, are charged with making such inventory and appraisal.[23] Such statutes may be in terms of ascertaining the assets with which the executor is chargeable or for which he is responsible, or instead in terms of fixing the state estate or inheritance tax on the estate. In either case the appraised values usually are determinative for both purposes, subject of course to correction, except in the case of a successor executor[24] and perhaps in the case of an executor qualifying only after substantial delay.[25] The converse approach is taken in still other statutes which allow the state estate or inheritance tax return to serve also the purpose of an inventory and appraisal, and in effect provide that the values finally fixed for the purposes of such tax shall be, or at least are presumptively, the values with which the executor is chargeable, again with exceptions of the kinds above mentioned.

8.4-1. Tangible personal property; in general. Except where statutes provide for an inventory and appraisal of estate assets by official appraisers or agents of the court,[26] the duty of the executor to ascertain the value of property coming into his possession or under his control ordinarily means, in the case of tangible personal property, that he must cause it to be evaluated by a competent appraiser;[27] and the executor should proceed with promptness to obtain such an evaluation in order to establish the amount with which he is chargeable or for which he is responsible in respect of the tangibles, and, as a corollary, in order that he may make sure that he provides adequate protection and safekeeping of the tangibles and adequate insurance upon them.[28] Since such appraisal will usually also determine the value at which the tangibles are reported by the executor for purposes of estate or inheritance taxation (except where "optional valuation" as of a later date is permitted and is used), and in arranging for the making of it the executor should accordingly be sure that any special requirements of the tax statute are complied with, in order to avoid an

---

[21] Tangibles, infra § 8.4-1; real property, infra §§ 8.5-1, -2.
[22] Generally, supra § 3.5-1 ff.
[23] The statutes as at the time in force are tabulated and analysed in 1963 Proc. A.B.A. Sec. Real Prop. Prob. & Tr. L., Part I, 24 ff.
[24] Infra § 23.4-2.
[25] Supra § 8.2.
[26] See last preceding section.
[27] Valuing a stamp collection, see Fox, Stamps in an Estate, 105 Trusts & Estates 1057.
[28] Supra §§ 7.2-1, 7.2-4.

unnecessary second appraisal and also to avoid the possibility of a discrepancy in the appraised valuations.

§ 8.4-2. ———; *exempt property*. Where a statute providing for the setting aside of property as "exempt" for the benefit of the decedent's spouse or children[29] specifies what is to be so set aside in terms of value, or a maximum value, rather than in terms of specified items or kinds of property, the executor must include exempt tangibles in the property to be appraised, even though under the statute they do not form any part of the estate for the purposes of administration. The executor will, of course, keep in mind that under the Federal estate tax law and some state or inheritance tax laws such exempt property is nevertheless includible in the gross taxable estate and that, as in the case of tangibles,[30] in such case the appraisal made for the purpose of determining what is to be set aside should comply with the requirements of the tax statute.

§ 8.5-1. *Real property; as such*. Inasmuch as in practically every jurisdiction real property[31] is held to vest directly and by operation of law in the devisee as of the date of death of the testator, and the executor does not have title to it (although he may be given a greater or lesser measure of control over it),[32] it may not be necessary for accounting or other administrative purposes that such real property be valued or appraised; but, of course, if real property should later be offered for sale by the executor[33] he will necessarily obtain a current appraisal of it both so that he may determine a proper offering price and for his protection in deciding whether to accept or reject a bid or offer of purchase. Where the estate is subject to an estate or inheritance tax an appraisal of land for the purpose of such tax is required, and, as in the case of appraisals of personal property,[34] the executor should make sure that any appraisal made complies with the requirements of the relevant tax laws.

§ 8.5-2. ———; *mortgages*. Where a mortgage or other encumbrance on real property is an asset of the estate, its value is usually not capable of being ascertained except by evaluating the real property covered by it, and if such is the case the executor should cause an appraisal of the property to be made.

§ 8.6-1. *Securities; in general*. Inasmuch as the effort in valuing any asset of the estate must be to arrive at fair market value,[35] the problem of valuation of securities revolves around the existence or non-existence of an ascertainable market for them.[36] In the case of securities listed on an exchange, trading is ordinarily reasonably active, and the value as of a particular date may usually be readily ascertained from

---

[29] Exempt property, in general, supra § 7.2-2.
[30] See last preceding section.
[31] Oil, gas, and mineral interests as real property, infra § 15.2-2a; valuation, infra § 8.9.
[32] Supra § 7.5-1 ff.
[33] Sale of real property, in general, supra § 7.5-3.
[34] Supra § 8.4-1.
[35] Supra § 8.3-1.
[36] Absence of ascertainable market, see next following section.

VALUATION OF ASSETS 95

reported quotations of sales made on the exchange or from so-called bid-and-asked quotations, the prices at which a buyer offers to buy and a holder offers to sell. Where the security in question, although not listed on an exchange, is traded reasonably actively "over the counter", so that a market for it is existent and available, its value may sometimes be readily ascertained from reported quotations, although they may be less readily available, and the spread between bid and asked prices may be greater, than in the case of listed securities; and in some instances quotations may be so scanty or difficult to obtain, or reflect such a wide "spread" between bid and offer, or indeed be purely nominal and not reflective of actual bids or offerings, that the executor will find it necessary to employ the assistance of one or more securities dealers, or an investment service, to ascertain values. Where the securities are to be valued for the purposes of an estate or inheritance tax as well as for the purpose of fixing inventory values, any special requirements of the tax law as to method of valuation, such as taking the mean between the high and low price for the valuation day, or interpolating between the last day preceding the valuation date upon which a sale occurred and the day next following such date, should be followed; and even if valuation for tax purposes is not required, or is not to be made as of the date as of which inventory value is to be ascertained, the method of valuation prescribed by the state estate or inheritance tax law or, in the absence thereof, by the Federal estate tax law will doubtless be accepted for all purposes and should be adopted.[37]

§ 8.6-2. ———; *stock of closely-held corporation.* The valuation of stock of a closely-held corporation, for which no ascertainable market exists and hence no quotation of market price is obtainable, may be very difficult and expensive. If an arm's length sale of such stock has occurred within a reasonable time before or after the death of the decedent, or whatever other valuation day is involved, the price at such sale is ordinarily highly persuasive as to value at the valuation day, in the absence of any developments in the interim that would tend to increase or decrease value; and, usually, if the value of stock of the corporation has been determined in another estate in the not too distant past, such determination is also persuasive. Estate and inheritance tax statutes or regulations ordinarily prescribe the method to be employed or the factors to be considered in arriving at the value of closely-held stock, at least where no such sale can be found, and as in the case of other securities,[38] it is ordinarily advisable to apply the tax rules[39] for purposes of determining inventory values even if a valuation for the purposes of such tax is not required or is not being made as of the same date. Whether or not the tax procedure is to be followed in arriving at value, the executor ordinarily must examine balance sheets and profit-and-loss statements of the corporation for the several years preceding the decedent's death, and the

---

[37] *Quaere*, however, whether there should be adopted for accounting purposes the valuation required for Federal estate tax purposes of U. S. Treasury bonds applicable at par against the tax (par rather than market; cf. supra § 7.4-2) and of mutual fund [regulated investment company] shares (issue price rather than redemption price or mean of the two (Reg. § 20.2031-8 (b)).

[38] See last preceding section.

[39] Rev. Rul. 59–60; 1959-1 Cum. Bul. 237.

record of the corporation as to dividend payments during those years, and must consider the upward or downward trend in values (or earnings as fixing or influencing values) disclosed by such records; he must also consider the relationship of book value of the corporation's assets as reflected in balance sheets to actual or market value of such assets, and in addition such factors as the effect of the decedent's death on the status or prospects of the corporation, especially where the decedent was a "key man" in its business.[40]

§ 8.6-3. ———; *buy-and-sell agreements.* Whether an agreement made by the decedent during his lifetime with other stockholders of a corporation, or with the corporation, for the sale and purchase of the decedent's stock in the corporation at his death,[41] has the effect of fixing the value of such stock for the purposes of an estate or inheritance tax depends upon the provisions of the taxing law as applied by the courts; and ordinarily similar principles are applicable in determining whether such an agreement fixes the value for accounting purposes. It is, however, to be kept in mind that a decedent may have entered into an agreement, such as to be binding upon his estate, to sell his stock at a clearly inadequate price, and that, while the executor may be required to carry out such agreement, the price fixed in the agreement will not necessarily be determinative of value of the stock either for tax purposes or for accounting purposes, but the excess of value over the stipulated price presumably constitutes, in effect, a gift or, if the will expressly directs performance of the agreement, a legacy to the other contracting party.[42]

§ 8.7. *Stock options, etc.* The valuation of an option held by the decedent at his death to purchase stock or other securities at a specified price ordinarily involves a determination of the market value of such stock or securities, which in turn is governed by the considerations discussed in preceding sections.[43] Such valuation is also affected, of course, by whatever restrictions are imposed by the option agreement upon time or manner or exercise of the option, and upon the disposition of the stock acquired upon such exercise, as such restrictions necessarily affect what a purchaser of the option would be willing to pay for it and hence its fair market value.[44]

§ 8.8. *Proprietorships and partnership interests.* The problems of valuation of a business or enterprise conducted as a proprietorship, or of a partnership interest,[45] are essentially similar to those of valuing stock of a closely-held corporation.[46] In arriving at the value of a partnership interest it is, of course, necessary to take into consideration the terms and provisions of the partnership agreement, which may pre-

---

[40] As affecting continuance or disposal of business, supra § 7.8-2.
[41] Duties and obligations of executor where such agreement exists, supra § 7.8-3.
[42] Direction in will for sale at inadequate price as general legacy, infra § 14.6-1.
[43] Supra §§ 8.6-1, -2.
[44] Fair market value as criterion, supra § 8.3-1.
[45] Proprietorship and partnership interest, in general, supra § 7.9.
[46] Supra § 8.6-2.

scribe, by formula or otherwise, the amount or value that is payable upon the decedent's death and the manner or terms of liquidation of his interest; and it may be said, therefore, that the analogy between valuation of a partnership interest and valuation of closely-held stock includes an analogy between a partnership agreement and a buy-and-sell agreement affecting stock.[47]

§ *8.9. Oil, gas, and mineral interests.* Interests of every kind in oil, gas, or minerals, including royalties, working interests, and others by whatever name known, are governed as to valuation by similar principles, and all present special problems of valuation. These stem not only from the difficulty in arriving at value in view of the imponderables involved, but also from the fact that an appraisal study of the kind that is made of other assets, particularly real properties,[48] usually would entail expense for engineers' reports and geologists' studies that would be entirely disproportionate in most cases to the value of the decedent's interest. It may be that sales of comparable interests in the same property, field, or deposit can be found, and if so the sales prices, as in the case of valuation of securities,[49] may have substantially definitive effect. Where if such a sale cannot be found, a broker or dealer in interests of the kind in question may be able to express an informed opinion as to the value of the decedent's interest, and to support it with available data from other sources; and such an opinion by a reputable and knowledgeable person or organization will ordinarily be sufficient to establish value for both accounting and tax purposes. Even without such evidence as that above mentioned, however, in some cases interests of the kind here referred to are sometimes valued as a multiple of annual royalties or other receipts.[50]

§ *8.10. Patents and copyrights.* A patent's value is ordinarily to be ascertained by a consideration of such factors as whether it has been availed of or put into practice, if so what royalties or other profits it has produced for the decedent and the trend, as toward an increase or a decline, during the period preceding his death, the length of the unexpired term of the patent, and the outlook for future profitability.[51] The value of a copyright[52] is governed to some extent by similar considerations, but it is in truth a bundle of rights[53] and accordingly its value depends largely upon the values of the individual rights.[54] Often, however, the value is to be found in the com-

---

[47] Supra § 8.6-3.

[48] Oil, gas, and mineral interests as real property, infra §15.2a; valuation of real property, supra § 8.5-1.

[49] Supra §§ 8.6-1, -2.

[50] In some instances multiples of as little as three to six have been treated as acceptable for tax purposes.

[51] Hoskold's formula for valuing patents, copyright, and the like, see P-H Fed. Tax Serv. ¶ 120, 318.1 note 12.

[52] Copyright as not subject to bequest, infra § 14.4-2d note 58.

[53] See Earl & Middleditch, Copyrights and the Author's Estate, 53 A.B.A.J. 366.

[54] For example, the right of renewal, which under 17 U.S.C.A. sec. 24 is exercisable after the author's death only by spouse or children, if any, otherwise by executor or intestate distributees.

mon-law "literary property" rather than in the statutory copyright is such.[55] Practically all authority as to valuation of patents and copyrights is in the connotation of taxes, and the rules applied in tax cases, to which the reader is referred, will almost surely govern valuation for accounting and other non-tax purposes.

---

[55] In practice, the value of literary property is often arrived at as a multiple of annual royalties being received; for this purpose, an average novel is sometimes regarded as having a productive "life" of 3 years, and an average textbook one of 6 years, but this varies with the circumstances.

IX

FUNERAL EXPENSES, DEBTS, AND CLAIMS

§ *9.1. Taxes and administration expenses.* This chapter excludes from its scope taxes (of every kind),[1] even though those are in a proper sense debts;[2] and it also excludes administration expenses.[3] Those categories are respectively dealt with at other places.

§ *9.2-1. Funeral expenses; in general.*[4] Expenses connected with the funeral of the decedent[5] are properly payable out of his estate, within reasonable limits of cost,[6] and, indeed, as is elsewhere pointed out, are payable in preference to most or all other charges and expenses;[7] and even "exempt" property[8] may, under some statutes, be used for such expenses if there is no other estate, or other assets are insufficient.[9] If the expenses have been paid by a member of the family or a third person, they are reimbursable to him to the same extent and subject to the same considerations as if they had been incurred directly by the executor.[10] An exception to the rule of payment of funeral expenses out of the estate is generally stated to exist in the case of a woman whose husband survives her, on the theory that the husband has a duty (at his own expense) to bury her body, unless he is insolvent; but this exception seems in

---

[1] Income taxes, infra Ch. X; gift taxes, infra Ch. XI; estate and inheritance taxes, infra Ch. XII.

[2] Taxes as "debts" owing to state or Federal government, within statutes establishing priorities of payment, infra § 19.4-4.

[3] Generally, infra Ch. XXI. Cf. *Catena's Est.*, 19 Fiduc. Rep. (Pa.) 82, holding that the Federal income tax is a debt but the Federal estate tax is an "administration expense" within the meaning of a statute making administration expenses payable in priority to debts.

[4] West Dig., Exrs. & Admrs. Key Nos. 109 (2), 214-215; P-H Est. Plng. Serv. ¶ 2221.

[5] Power and duty of executor with respect thereto, supra § 4.7.

[6] Infra § 9.2-3.

[7] Infra § 19.4-3.

[8] "Exempt" property generally, infra § 17.1.

[9] Infra § 19.8.

[10] Deduction of governmental allowance, infra § 9.2-4. Power and duty of executor to make funeral arrangements, supra § 4.7.

recent times to be largely ignored, at least in practice, where the wife had an estate or her own.[11]

§ 9.2-2. ———; *items included*. In considering payment of funeral expenses of his decedent the executor must take into account two aspects of the matter, namely, the kinds of costs or expenditures that are includible as part of the funeral expenses, and the overall amount involved.[12] Obviously, such items as embalming, coffin, religious services, cremation, and interment are a customary or inherent part of funeral procedures, and reasonable charges therefore are properly payable from the estate. A grave marker or stone is ordinarily also regarded as properly chargeable against the estate, again within reasonable limits as to cost.[13] The will may direct the construction of a tomb or mausoleum,[14] but in the absence of such a direction it would seem that the cost of such construction usually would not be a warranted expense and so would not be properly payable out of the estate. If the decedent was not the owner of a cemetery plot, and his body or its ashes are to be interred, the reasonable cost of acquisition of such a plot is a proper funeral expense; but if he owned a plot at his death, the cost of acquisition of another is not a proper charge against the estate, so that if a spouse or other family member entitled to select the place of burial[15] wishes to have interment made at another place, the cost of a new plot must be borne by such person. Whether a payment for perpetual care of grave or plot is a proper charge would seem, in the absence of express authorization therefore in the will, to depend largely on custom in the community and perhaps on whether payment for such care is a necessary condition of acquiring a cemetery plot, where such acquisition is necessary, or of making an interment therein; in general, it seems doubtful that, at least in the absence of such a requirement or of a well-established local practice of doing so, an executor is justified in expending estate assets for such care unless the will explicitly authorizes or directs such a payment.

§ 9.2-3. ———; *amount*. An executor who expends, or reimburses another who has expended, excessive amounts in connection with the funeral of his decedent is liable to surcharge on the same basis as for any other waste of estate assets;[16] and presumably, also, the priority of payment attaching to funeral expenses does not extend to unreasonably large amounts.[17] What is a reasonable amount and what is an excessive one depends, of course, on numerous factors, but the basic consideration is probably the size of the estate; what would be a reasonable expenditure in the case of a decedent with a large fortune would be grossly excessive in a modest estate, and the converse is also true. Apart from those considerations, funeral expenses may, of

---

[11] *Est. of Rubin*, N.Y.L.J. Apr. 20, 1962, p. 10; generally, see P-H Est. Plng. Serv. ¶ 2221.1.
[12] See next following section.
[13] Non-duty of executor to erect marker or stone in absence of direction in will, supra § 4.7.
[14] Directions as to funeral, etc., and effectiveness thereof, in general, supra § 4.7; in insolvent or insufficient estate, infra § 19.4-3 note 26.
[15] Supra § 4.7.
[16] Waste, in general, supra § 3.5-2.
[17] Generally, infra § 19.4-3.

FUNERAL EXPENSES, DEBTS, AND CLAIMS 101

course, vary considerably with other circumstances. The executor should, however, bear in mind that he must be prepared to justify the propriety and reasonableness of funeral expenses incurred or reimbursed by him in the same manner and on the same basis as any other expenditure made in administering the estate, and he should not pay out assets of the estate to reimburse a family member, for example, for funeral expenses that the executor regards as unreasonably high under the circumstances without first obtaining the consent of the residuary legatees,[18] or, in the absence thereof, submitting the matter to and obtaining the instructions of the appropriate court.

§ 9.2-4. ———; *governmental funeral allowance*. Where a payment or allowance on account of funeral expenses is made from a public or governmental source to a person who has incurred expenses in connection with the funeral of the decedent,[19] as in the case of a decedent who was in or a veteran of military service, or the case of such an allowance under the Social Security law, the executor must take such payment or allowance into account and in making reimbursement to such person[20] must deduct the amount received by the latter from the public source.

§ 9.3-1. *Debts and claims; in general*[21] Debts and other monetary liabilities of the decedent, and claims thereof against his estate, are payable, or must be provided for, whether or not the will contains any authorization or direction for their payment, and, of course, as in the case of taxes and administration expenses,[22] before any legacies are satisfied.[23] It is, nevertheless, to be noted that a provision in a will relating to payment of debts may have the effect of rendering items payable that otherwise would not be payable by or could not be collected from the estate,[24] or of making payable out of the general estate items which otherwise would be payable from a particular asset or by the recipient of particular property,[25] and vice versa.[26] Directions in wills for the payment of debts should, therefore, not be passed over by the executor as merely a statement of existing law or as surplusage, but must be considered in the light of their effect upon particular claims or obligations.

§ 9.3-2. ———; *unmatured or unliquidated liabilities*.[27] The rule that debts must be paid or provided for before any distribution may be made to beneficiaries[28] applies

---

[18] Consents or agreements by beneficiaries, in general, infra Ch. XXI.
[19] Facilitating collection of funeral allowance, supra § 6.14.
[20] Reimbursement, supra §9.2-1.
[21] West Dig., Exrs. & Admrs. Key Nos. 202–221, 258–287; P-H Est. Plng. Serv. ¶ 2213 ff.
[22] Infra § 19.4-1. Priorities of debts and claims *inter se*, infra § 19.4-5 ff.
[23] Satisfaction of legacies only after payment of or provision for prior charges, infra §§ 14.31-1, 19.4-1.
[24] Infra § 9.4-4.
[25] Secured debts, infra § 9.3-3a; life insurance policy loans, infra § 9.3-3b.
[26] Direction that claim or charge be paid out of particular fund or item of property, infra § 9.8-2; by particular legatee, infra § 14.10. Direction as to payment of death taxes, infra § 12.10-3. Specific bequests and devises of property encumbered by indebtedness as passing to beneficiaries *cum onere*, infra §§ 14.4-5, 15.3.
[27] West Dig., Exrs. & Admrs. Key No. 202.2; P-H Est. Plng. Serv. ¶¶ 2222, 2223.
[28] See last preceding section.

to unmatured as well as matured obligations, and to obligations that are unliquidated, contingent, or otherwise not of determinable amount at the time as well as those then fixed in amount. In the case of unmatured obligations the executor may have to postpone distribution of at least sufficient assets to cover the debt,[29] until it does mature, even though this may possibly result in payment of interest on legacies;[30] and the same may be true of unliquidated or uncertain debts and claims, although some statutes permit the court, upon proper application and notice to the creditor, to prescribe the amount to be retained to cover the claim and thus free the executor from risk in distributing the balance of the estate.[31] As a practical matter, where the residuary estate is to remain in trust,[32] for a period that will probably extend beyond the maturity of the debt or the liquidation of the claim, and the executor is also the trustee of such trust, the executor may deem it safe, and preferable for administrative convenience, not to set apart a reserve against the claim but instead to plan to pay the claim, when it becomes due or fixed, out of the trust principal; if the trust should, contrary to expectation, terminate before the claim matures or becomes fixed, the executor may then reclaim funds from himself as trustee and set them apart as a reserve, or if a statute of the character above mentioned exists may then apply pursuant to it; but before deciding to follow such a course the executor should consider the probable length of the waiting period, the risk of decline in value of trust assets during such period, and any possibility of invasions of principal thereof.

§ **9.3-3.** ———; *secured debts;*[33] *debts of business.* The effect of a specific bequest or devise of property mortgaged, pledged, or otherwise encumbered to secure an obligation or indebtedness, with respect to the burden of payment of the obligation or indebtedness in such case[34] and to the relative priority of the debt in question,[35] are discussed elsewhere herein. Also elsewhere, it has been suggested that debts of a specifically bequeathed proprietorship should be treated in the same manner as debts secured by personal property that is the subject of a bequest.[36] The otherwise applicable rules may, of course, be varied by the terms of the will.[37] It will be apparent that a question of the burden of payment of such a debt arises, in a solvent estate, only in connection with a specific bequest or devise, for if the encumbered property forms part of the residuary estate it is of no economic concern to a residuary legatee whether the indebtedness is paid out of the securing property or out of other assets

---

[29] Cf. administrative problems as to deferred and instalment legacies, infra § 14.12-2.
[30] Generally, infra § 14.31-3.
[31] Cf. Unif. Prob. Code sec. 3-810, providing that claim not due, contingent, or unliquidated, may be directed by court to be either paid *in praesenti*, if creditor consents, at present value, taking into account any uncertainty, or provided for by creating a trust, giving a mortgage or bond, "or otherwise."
[32] Testamentary trusts, infra Ch. XXVII.
[33] P-H Est. Plng. Serv. ¶ 2262.
[34] Infra §§ 14.4-5, 15.3.
[35] Order of priority of debts, infra § 19.4-5 ff.
[36] Infra § 14.4-5a.
[37] Infra § 9.3-3b.

FUNERAL EXPENSES, DEBTS, AND CLAIMS 103

of the estate, although the legatee may have a preference in this regard, which ordinarily the executor should heed. In the case, however, of an insolvent or insufficient estate, the problem may arise whether the securing property be specifically disposed of or be a part of the residuary estate, because of the priority of payment ordinarily afforded to secured creditors.[38]

§ **9.3-3a.** ———; ———; *effect of direction in will.* Frequently a will contains a general direction of some sort for the payment of the testator's debts.[39] Such a provision is too often inserted as a matter of routine, without adequate consideration of its possibly unintended or unfavorable effects; and an executor faced with a provision of the character mentioned may too often pass it over as surplusage. As elsewhere noted, it may be important in considering payment of debts barred by a statute of limitation.[40] The problem it may most often create, however, relates to the payment of secured debts. Thus, since the rule, where otherwise applicable, that a legatee or devisee of encumbered property takes it *cum onere*[41] may be changed by will, if the will contains a general or unqualified direction for payment of all debts out of the general estate, which in effect ordinarily means the residue, the executor must consider, and may have to seek the instruction of the court,[42] whether such direction is to be given the effect of relieving the specific legatee or devisee of the burden he otherwise would have to discharge the secured indebtedness out of his own pocket, and so of putting the burden of the debt upon the residuary takers.[43] The effect of such a direction on the payment of death taxes of a foreign country should also be considered, where such taxes are asserted.[44]

§ **9.3-3b.** ———; ———; *life insurance policy loans.* A special case of a secured loan is that of a loan secured by a life insurance policy payable on the testator's death to a designated beneficiary (other than the estate.) In many states the question depends on whether the loan was obtained from the insuring company or from a bank or other third person; it is held in such states that if the loan is one made by the insurer it is payable out of the proceeds of the policy and the designated beneficiary receives only an excess of such proceeds, but if the loan was one made by any other lender the debt is payable out of the insured's estate and the beneficiary receives the entire amount of the insurance proceeds. In some states, however, this somewhat dubious distinction has been abolished and the indebtedness is payable out of the insurance proceeds in both cases. As in the case of other secured debts,[45] however, provision in the will may make the debt payable out of the general estate.

---

[38] Infra § 19.4-5c.
[39] Direction for payment of expense or claim out of specified fund or property, infra § 9.8-2.
[40] Infra § 9.4-4.
[41] Infra §§ 14.4-5, 15.3.
[42] Instruction proceedings, in general, infra Ch. XXII.
[43] So held in *Est. of Moffat*, N.Y.L.J. May 3, 1965, p. 20. But see Unif. Prob. Code sec. 2-609 to contrary.
[44] Infra § 12.4-5a.
[45] See last preceding section.

§ 9.3-4. ———; *personal liability of executor for payment.* The executor is personally liable for the payment of debts and claims, in the sense that if he pays a claim before expiration of the time limited for presentation of claims[46] or before another claim of equal or greater priority,[47] and, *a fortiori*, if he distributes assets of the estate to beneficiaries without paying or providing for claims,[48] and in consequence a creditor is damaged, the executor is personally responsible to the injured creditor up to the amount of assets so paid or distributed.[49]

§ 9.4-1. *Presentation and consideration of claims; in general.*[50] Statutes ordinarily provide for the presentation or submission of claims by the claimants to the executor or their filing with a court clerk,[51] within a specified time,[52] or in a specified form or accompanied by proof of a specified kind.[53] Whether a claim not presented or filed in accordance with the statute may nevertheless be allowed or paid if the executor otherwise obtains knowledge of it would seem to depend upon the nature of the statutory provision,[54] with particular reference to whether it bars claims not properly submitted within the specified time.[55]

§ 9.4-2. ———; *time of presentation; limitation.*[56] Statutes prescribing the time within which claims are to be presented or filed[57] are of two distinct types. Under those of one type, claims not submitted within the prescribed period are barred;[58] and if such a statute applies the executor is, of course, precluded from allowing a claim first brought to his attention after the period has expired, and may be so precluded, if the language of the statute is broad, even though he had actual knowledge of the existence, nature, and amount of the decedent's liability to the creditor.[59] Under

---

[46] Infra § 9.4-2. So in Unif. Prob. Code sec. 3-807(b); cf. ibid. sec. 3-909, making payee liable to return improper payment or distribution.

[47] Priorities, in general, infra § 19.4-2 ff. Statutory liability as to debts owing to United States, 31 U.S.C.A. sec. 192.

[48] Infra §§ 14.31-1, 19.4-1.

[49] Ibid.; in insolvent estate, infra § 19.3. See also Unif. Prob. Code, loc. cit. supra note 46.

[50] West Dig., Exrs. & Admrs. Key Nos. 222 ff, 242 ff, 415–416.

[51] So in Unif. Prob. Code sec. 3-804.

[52] See next following section.

[53] Infra § 9.4-3a.

[54] Cf. Unif. Prob. Code sec. 3-807(b), authorizing payment of claims not formally presented, if not barred by time. Deductibility of unpresented claim for Federal estate tax purposes, see Rev. Rul, 60-247, 1960-2 Cum. Bul. 272.

[55] Effect of failure of timely filing, see next following section.

[56] West Dig., Exrs. & Admrs. Key No. 225; P-H Est. Plng. Serv. ¶ 2224.

[57] See last preceding section. It is to be noted that such statutes differ among themselves not only as to the length of the period for presentation of claims but also as to the commencement of such period or the time from which its length is measured. Time as measured from notice to creditors, see next following section. What law governs, in general, Goodrich & Scoles, Conflict of Laws, sec. 192; Beale, Conflict of Laws, sec. 495.1 ff.

[58] So in Unif. Prob. Code sec. 3-803.

[59] If not clearly answered by the wording of the statute, the problem would seem to turn on whether the primary purpose of the time limit is deemed to be to penalize dilatory creditors or to enable executors to expedite settlement of estates.

FUNERAL EXPENSES, DEBTS, AND CLAIMS 105

statutes of the other type, claims not timely presented are not barred, but so far as the executor is concerned,[60] are payable only out of such assets, if any, as remain in the hands of the executor when the claim is submitted. As will be apparent, the executor is not precluded or relieved by a statute of this second type from paying a claim not presented until after the statutory period has elapsed, if when it is presented he still has assets in his hands that are available therefor; but such a statute is protective to the executor, and to other creditors, in that when the statutory period expires the executor may safely assume that the claims of which he then has knowledge are the only claims against the estate, and may without further delay[61] pay or provide for them, and proceed to satisfy legacies or make distributions, without personal liability under the rules of relative priorities of claims[62] if the estate should later prove insufficient to satisfy late-presented claims in full and the principle that no legacies may be paid until all claims have been paid or provided for.[63] Under either of the two kinds of statutes herein referred to, there may or may not be a right on the part of an unpaid claimant to follow the assets or collect from beneficiaries, and the relevant statute should be consulted on the point.[64]

§ *9.4-2a.* ———; ———; *notice to creditors.*[65] In most states, but not all, an executor, upon his appointment, is required by statute to publish, in some prescribed manner, a notice to creditors, informing them of the death of the decedent and of the executor's appointment as such, and of the place where and the time within which claims are to be filed;[66] and under such a statute the period for presentation of claims[67] is measured from the time of such publication. A failure to publish such a notice, where required, in accordance with the terms of the statute will therefore not start such period running, and so there will not be a date when the executor can safely satisfy claims that have been brought to his attention and satisfy legacies, without the risk of personal liability to creditors later presenting claims.[68] The executor should therefore ascertain whether a notice to creditors is required in the jurisdiction of his appointment, and if so should be careful to comply strictly with its requirements as to the form and contents of the notice and as to its publication.

§ *9.4-3. Allowance or rejection.*[69] In many jurisdictions the allowance or rejection of claims against the estate is primarily and initially the responsibility of the executor; in other jurisdictions, it is instead a function of the probate court, or

---

[60] Under such a statute, the late-filing creditor may still be able to collect from beneficiaries if he can trace estate assets into their hands; see below, text at note 63.

[61] Time for payment of claims, infra § 9.5; of legacies, infra § 14.31-1 ff.

[62] Infra § 19.4-1 ff.

[63] Infra § 14.31-1, 19.4-1.

[64] Cf. Unif. Prob. Code sec. 3-1004 ff.

[65] West Dig., Exrs. & Admrs. Key No. 226.

[66] So in Unif. Prob. Code. sec. 3-801.

[67] See last preceding section.

[68] Supra § 9.3-4.

[69] West Dig., Exrs. & Admrs. Key Nos. 234–257; P-H Est. Plng. Serv. ¶¶ 2232–2235.

of a commissioner or other officer designated for the purpose, but even where that is the case the executor has a duty either to contest the claim before the court or commissioner, or admit it by failing to contest it. In both cases, as thus appears, the responsibilities of the executor are of the same nature. In either case, therefore, when a claim is presented to the executor or comes to his attention, it is his duty to consider it and decide whether it should be allowed, if it is valid in character and correct in amount, or rejected, if it is not valid or correct, or, if it is warranted in part or as to part of the amount claimed and unwarranted as to the balance, to approve it in part and reject it in part.[70] Allowance of a claim is to be distinguished from payment. When a claim is allowed it is recognized as a just and lawful obligation of the estate, in the amount claimed or the lesser amount allowed, as the case may be, but whether it will be paid in full, or only in part, or not at all, remains to be determined; if the estate is fully solvent the claim will, of course, be payable in full,[71] but if the estate is insolvent, (as that term is used in respect of estates[72]), and insufficient to pay all liabilities in full, the claim, however valid and although allowed as such, may be payable only in part, or may go unpaid, depending upon the degree of inadequacy of the estate and the relative priority of the claim as compared with the estate's other liabilities.[73] If, on the other hand, the claim is rejected, either in whole or in part, by the executor (as distinguished from rejection in a judicial proceeding), the claimant is not thereby entirely precluded from collecting, as the matter of presentment of claims to and their allowance or rejection by the executor is an administrative procedure only; the claimant continues to have a judicial remedy, which is usually either by bringing an action on his claim against the executor[74] or by later seeking a judicial determination of the claim on the executor's accounting.[75]

§ 9.4-3a. ———; ———; *basis of decision; proof of claim.* Statutes as to presentation or filing of claims ordinarily require that a claim be made, or supported, by a sworn statement of its validity,[76] or at least authorize the executor to demand such a statement; and the executor should for his own protection and that of the estate require compliance with such a statute in practically every instance, and certainly where he lacks knowledge as to the claim or has any doubt or question about it. Further, whether or not a statute expressly empowers him to do so, it would seem clear that the executor may properly ask a claimant to furnish appropriate additional proof of or evidence to sustain a claim as to which knowledge is lacking

---

[70] So in Unif. Prob. Code sec. 3-806.
[71] Payment, infra § 9.5.
[72] Infra § 19.1.
[73] Priorities and abatement in insolvent estate, infra § 19.2 ff.
[74] So in Unif. Prob. Code sec. 3-806.
[75] Infra § 24.5-4b. Under some statutes, unless an action is commenced within a specified period of time the claimant must await the accounting; or, as in Unif. Prob. Code sec. 3-806, claim is barred unless action is commenced within a specified period.
[76] Often called a "proof of claim"; but it is such only for administrative purposes, and not sufficient in a subsequent judicial proceeding referred to in the last preceding section.

FUNERAL EXPENSES, DEBTS, AND CLAIMS 107

or question exists, since a request for such proof evidences care and diligence on the part of the executor and the claimant, even if not required as a matter of law to furnish additional proof, may prefer to accede to a request therefore rather than to have his claim rejected. If the executor is not satisfied, by the claim and any additional evidence that may be supplied to him, that the claim is valid and the amount of it is justly payable, he should reject the claim,[77] or, as mentioned above,[78] in a proper case allow it in part and reject it as to the balance, and so put upon the claimant the burden of establishing the claim, or such balance, in such forum and by such type of proceeding as may be available under local law. By the same token, a just claim should be allowed by the executor,[79] and the claimant should not unnecessarily be required to resort to a judicial remedy. Inasmuch, however, as the executor can be held personally liable to beneficiaries, on principles of waste,[80] for any amount paid by him on an unwarranted or unsound claim, he should in general resolve doubts against the claimant and thus put the latter to his proof.

§ 9.4-4. ———; *claims barred by statute of limitation.*[81] It is the duty of an executor to reject any claim which at the testator's death was barred by a statute of limitation,[82] and to plead such statute in any action or proceeding by the claimant to enforce payment of the claim, unless all affected beneficiaries otherwise agree,[83] or unless the will contains a direction for the payment of claims notwithstanding such bar. There must not be overlooked, as has been referred to above,[84] the possibility that a general direction in a will to pay debts may preclude the executor from availing himself of a statute of limitation; although there is little authority on the point, such a direction may make debts payable that would otherwise be barred by such statute, inasmuch as a statute of limitation does not effect a discharge of the debt but merely prevents its collection if the statute be pleaded, so that the debt still subsists and may be within the direction for payment.

§ 9.4-5. ———; *claims of foreign creditors.* It is laid down as a general rule that a creditor may present his claim to and receive payment from a legal representative appointed in any jurisdiction, whether or not the creditor is a resident of that jurisdiction.[85] The rule stated is certainly true in the case of claims presented to the domiliary executor. It may, however, be subject to an exception in the case of an ancillary administrative;[86] since ancillary administration is often regarded as primarily

---

[77] See last preceding secton.
[78] Ibid.
[79] Duty to creditors, in general, supra § 3.9-2.
[80] Supra § 3.5-2.
[81] West Dig., Exrs. & Admrs. Key No. 213.
[82] So in Unif. Prob. Code sec. 3-802. Barring of claim not presented within statutory period, supra § 9.4-2.
[83] Agreements by beneficiaries, infra Ch. XXI.
[84] Supra § 9.3-3a.
[85] Restatement, Conflict of Laws 2d, sec. 342.
[86] Op. cit. sec. 343. Ancillary executor or administrator, supra § 1.7.

for the protection of local creditors, the court having control of the ancillary proceeding may, at least if no local creditors present claims, direct the remittance of the local assets to the domicile[87] and creditors may accordingly need to submit their claims there.

§ 9.5. *Time for payment of claims*.[88] The statutory provisions prescribing a time within which claims of creditors may be presented,[89] taken in combination with the rule of personal liability of an executor[90] and the principles of priorities of claims as among themselves and over legacies,[91] mean that the executor should not pay any claim before the expiration of the statutory period unless he is willing to assume personally whatever risk there may be that the estate will be sufficient to pay all claims that may be asserted within the period,[92] for until such period expires the executor cannot know with assurance that other valid claims may be presented within the period which would render the estate insolvent[93] or be entitled to priority over claims already presented.[94] Furthermore, under a statute which does not bar claims not presented within the statutory period but merely protects the executor in distributing after the period has elapsed,[95] the executor should not make a distribution even after the end of such period without first making sufficient provision for a claim of which he has knowledge or information but which has not yet been formally presented or asserted. Subject to the considerations hereinabove mentioned, the executor should proceed with reasonable diligence to pay claims,[96] and, in view of his duties to creditors,[97] can of course be held liable to one damaged by undue delay. In some states interest is payable on allowed claims after a specified period.[98] It is to be noted, however, that a creditor is usually prevented by statute from bringing action to enforce payment of his claim until after the expiration of a specified time, at least unless his claim has sooner been affirmatively rejected.[99]

---

[87] The terms "domicile" and "domiciliary executor" are used here to refer to the place of original probate and the principal executor, whether the will be probated at the testator's domicile or at some other place; cf. §§ 5.4-1, 5.5-1 supra.

[88] West Dig., Exrs. & Admrs. Key Nos. 277, 278.

[89] Supra § 9.4-2.

[90] Supra § 9.3-4.

[91] Infra § 19.2.

[92] It would not seem that a direction in a will for payment of debts "promptly", or "as soon as practicable", or the like, would protect the executor against liabilities of the kind referred to in the text, if he pays a claim before expiration of the statutory period, as the principles involved are for the protection of creditors and in general their rights cannot be diminished by the testator. On the other hand, it would not seem that such a direction would entitle a creditor to compel payment of his claim sooner than if such direction were not contained in the will (infra text at note 99). Directions in will as to payment of debts, in general, supra § 9.3-3a.

[93] Insolvency, infra § 19.1.

[94] Infra § 19.4-1 ff.

[95] Supra § 9.4-2.

[96] Statutory period for payment, Unif. Prob. Code sec. 3-807.

[97] Supra § 3.9-2.

[98] Infra § 9.7.

[99] Remedies after rejection, supra § 9.4-3.

FUNERAL EXPENSES, DEBTS, AND CLAIMS 109

§ 9.6. *Personal claim of executor.*[100] Where the executor in his individual capacity has a claim against his decedent, he is precluded by statute in some jurisdictions from paying such claim until after applying to and receiving permission from the probate court so to do. The purposes of such a statute is obvious when there is taken into account the divided interest[1] of one who is both an alleged creditor, eager to establish his claim, and an executor, duty bound to reject unwarranted or excessive claims.[2] Even in the absence of such a statute, it would seem on the same principle that an executor making claim against the estate should enter in his files and records, and eventually include in his account,[3] a full and complete disclosure of all the facts relating to the claim and to its payment, so that any person in interest may be made fully aware of the situation and have full opportunity to raise questions or objections. Ironically, a statute of the kind mentioned, intended to protect the estate against a conflict of interest, itself raises an additional conflict where the executor's claim is interest-bearing, as one for money lent, for interest continues to run on the claim until it is paid[4] and the statute delays its payment; the executor therefore would seem to have a duty to apply promptly for the required permission to pay the claim and so cut off the further running of interest.

§ 9.7. *Interest on debts and claims.*[5] It is necessary in considering the liability of an estate for interest on debts or claims to distinguish between two kinds of circumstances. Where an indebtedness or obligation of the decedent was by its terms (as in the case of a promissory note or other express obligation) or by law (as in the case of a judgment rendered against him) one that bore interest, the interest is a part of the debt, and continues to run until the debt is discharged by payment, although so much of the interest as accrues after death is ordinarily payable out of income,[6] rather than, as in the case of the claim itself and the interest accrued thereon at death, out of principal.[7] In the case, however, of ordinary open accounts and other liabilities of which interest is thus not a part, the claim does not bear interest, at least in the absence of undue delay in payment or, as often statutes provide, only if it remains unpaid after a specified length of time;[8] and, under the usual principles of diligence and negligence, if the creditor becomes entitled to interest by reason of a delay which is the fault of the executor the latter may be surchargeable with the interest.[9]

---

[100] West Dig., Exrs. & Admrs. Key Nos. 219, 221 (10), 263, 265.
[1] Conflict of interest as creditor, supra § 3.9-4a.
[2] Supra § 9.4-3.
[3] Disclosure in account, in general, infra § 24.3-3.
[4] Interest on claims, in general, see next following section.
[5] West Dig., Exrs. & Admrs. Key No. 267; P-H Est. Plng. Serv. ¶ 2236.
[6] Infra § 16.5-2.
[7] Source of payment of debts and claims, see next following section.
[8] Statutes providing for interest after specified period, supra § 9.5.
[9] Liability for negligence, in general, supra § 3.5-1.

§ 9.8-1. *Source of payment of claims;*[10] *in general.* Subject to the rules hereinabove mentioned as to secured debts,[11] claims against an estate are ordinarily payable out of the general estate,[12] which in effect means out of the residuary estate (if the estate is solvent[13]), inasmuch as the latter by definition comprises only such assets as remain after prior charges, including expenses and claims, are paid.[14] This is, however, subject to the rules as to setting off counterclaims of the estate against the claimant.[15] As pointed out above, "exempt" property which by statute is not a part of the estate is not available for payments of claims,[16] except under some statutes where all other assets are exhausted.[17]

§ 9.8-2. ———; *provision in will.* Where the will directs that particular expenses or claims, or particular classes or categories thereof, be paid from a specified fund or property,[18] such expenses and claims are payable from such specified fund or property to the extent that it is sufficient therefor, and as to any excess are payable out of the general estate.[19]

§ 9.8-3. ———; *property subject to power of appointment.* Property over which the testator at the time of his death possessed a power of appointment is, of course, not for that reason his own property and so is not, in general, available for payment of claims of his creditors or of any other charges or expenses of the estate.[20] As discussed elsewhere,[21] however, the appointive property may be made part of the testator's estate by appointment (where the power so permits) thereto or to his legal representatives, and where it so becomes a part of the estate it is available as any other property for such payments; and, in some jurisdictions, even where appointed to others the property may be subject to creditors' claims where the power was a general one and the testator's own estate is insufficient.[22]

§ 9.8-4. ———; *counterclaims.*[23] It is a general rule that an executor may, and should, set off against any claim made against the estate the amount of any claim or right the estate has against the creditor, whether growing out of the same or a different transaction.[24] The counterclaim is, thus, in effect a source of payment of the claim against the estate, and indeed the first source.[25]

---

[10] West Dig., Exrs. & Admrs. Key No. 270 ff.; P-H Est. Plng. Serv. ¶ 2219.
[11] Supra § 9.3-3 ff.
[12] Borrowing to pay claims, supra § 7.6-1b. Effect of will directions as to payment, supra § 9.3-3a.
[13] Insolvency, infra Ch. XIX.
[14] Order of applicability of assets to payment, infra § 19.5-1 ff.
[15] Infra § 9.8-4.
[16] Supra § 7.2-2.
[17] Availability for funeral expense, supra § 9.2-1, and infra § 19.8.
[18] Direction in will as to payment of debts, in general, supra § 9.3-1.
[19] As source of payment, in general, see last preceding section.
[20] *Low v. Bankers Trust Co.*, 270 N.Y. 134, 200 N.E. 674.
[21] Infra § 18.3-8.
[22] Infra § 19.6. Collection by executor of appointive property which is subject to creditors' claims, supra § 6.19.
[23] West Dig., Exrs. & Admrs. Key No. 434.
[24] So in Unif. Prob. Code sec. 3-811.
[25] Right of retention or set-off against legatee-debtor, infra § 14.16-2.

FUNERAL EXPENSES, DEBTS, AND CLAIMS   111

§ 9.9-1. *Compromise of claims;*[26] *in general.* The power of an executor to compromise claims against the estate[27] is expressly granted by statute in some jurisdictions,[28] but even in the absence of statute would seem to exist as an inherent part of the executor's function to settle and pay claims. In any case it is, of course, like every other function of the executor, reviewable by a court in an appropriate proceeding,[29] and the executor must therefore be prepared to establish the facts justifying the making of the compromise, as such, and the amount of the payment made pursuant to the compromise.[30]

§ 9.9-2. ————; *creditor's acceptance of bequest.* It is noted elsewhere that a creditor's acceptance of a bequest to him that is deemed to be intended as in satisfaction of his claim amounts to a discharge of the debt,[31] and such a bequest and its acceptance may therefore be regarded as a species of compromise.

§ 9.10-1. *Liability of decedent as a fiduciary; in general.* Where the decedent was an executor, trustee, guardian, or other fiduciary in his lifetime, his liability to persons in interest for any improper acts or omissions as such fiduciary may be regarded as equivalent to a claim, or potential claim, against his estate, and one against which ordinarily no statute of limitation runs,[32] probably including a statute limiting the time for presenting claims.[33] Accordingly, unless the decedent was during his lifetime discharged in a proper proceeding from any liability as such fiduciary,[34] the executor must consider whether he should not institute a proper proceeding for the settlement of the decedent's account and his discharge from liability,[35] and this would seem to be true even where no accounting by the decedent would have been mandatory under the applicable law if he had lived; for until a discharge from liability is obtained, the estate may remain liable, and after distribution of its assets the executor may be personally liable, to beneficiaries of the decedent's fiducium for anything for which the decedent could have been surcharged or otherwise held liable, and such liability may continue indefinitely if, as suggested above, no statute of limitation applies.

§ 9.10-2. ————; *legal life tenant.* Considerations similar to those applicable as to a decedent who was a fiduciary in the usual sense[36] apply also to one who was a legal life tenant or the like of property, whether personal or real, and, as such, is un-

---

[26] West Dig., Exrs. & Admrs. Key Nos. 87, 269; P-H Est. Plng. Serv. ¶ 2232.
[27] Compromise of claim held by estate, supra § 6.11-3.
[28] So in Unif. Prob. Code secs. 3-715(17), 3-813.
[29] Cf. op. cit. sec. 3-810, providing *inter alia* that the court may direct an unmatured or contingent claim to be paid at present value, taking into account any uncertainty, if the creditor so consents.
[30] Accountability, in general, infra § 24.1.
[31] Infra § 14.15.
[32] Infra §§ 24.1, 24.6.
[33] Generally, supra § 9.4-2.
[34] Infra § 24.5-5.
[35] Infra § 24.10.
[36] See last preceding section.

der applicable law to be regarded as a fiduciary (in the general sense) because of accountability to remaindermen for his management of the subject-matter during his lifetime.[37]

§ 9.11. *Decedent's charitable pledges.* Questions often arise as to the executor's duty, or even his power, to satisfy pledges made by the decedent during his lifetime to a charitable institution or cause. On the basic principle that a promise to make a gift is unenforceable, it would often seem improper for the executor to satisfy a pledge, at least without the consent of the beneficiaries affected by the payment, and in the latter case it may be that the charitable gift should be deemed to be one made by such beneficiaries rather than by the decedent or pursuant to his pledge. In some cases, however, courts have found a contractual basis for the pledge, the consideration being deemed to be the concurrent pledges of others.[38] In the absence of a statute governing the matter,[39] the executor usually should refrain from satisfying a charitable pledge by the decedent until expressly authorized so to do by beneficiaries or by the court. A provision in the will directing satisfaction of such a pledge is, of course, effective, but probably as a bequest to the charity rather than as giving the pledge the dignity of a debt, and would seem to be subject to any applicable rules as to the rights of family members as against charitable gifts,[40] whether or not the pledge itself is so subject.[41]

---

[37] Infra § 24.10.

[38] Contracts and undertakings of decedent, in general, supra § 7.13-1.

[39] Cf. Unif. Prob. Code sec. 3-715(4): Executor "may" satisfy decedent's written charitable pledges, irrespective of whether they constitute binding obligations or were properly presented as claims, "when, in the judgment of the [executor], the decedent would have wanted the pledges completed under the circumstances."

[40] Infra § 17.7.

[41] Ibid.

X

INCOME TAXES

§ 10.1. Priority of payment. The relative priority in order of payment accorded by statutes to taxes[1] applies, under every such statute, to income taxes of the decedent, including such taxes for the year of his death[2] and those of prior years not barred by a statute of limitations.[3]

§ 10.2-1. Final return of decedent; in general. It is the duty of the executor[4] to make timely filing of all required income tax returns in respect of the decedent for the tax year in which the decedent's death occurred,[5] and to pay all taxes thereby shown to be due. Accordingly, the executor is surchargeable, on general principles of negligence,[6] for any interest and penalties assessed in consequence of a failure to make such filing and payment.[7]

§ 10.2-2. ——; joint return with spouse. Where a spouse survived the decedent and a joint income tax return of the spouse is permitted by statute to be filed for the year of the decedent's death (or for the year preceding that of his death where the decedent's death occurred before the filing of a return for such year), the executor must consider whether to join with the spouse in a joint return.[8] Where the decedent had the larger income of the two spouses, it is ordinarily to the advantage of the estate that a joint return be filed; and the same may be true where the income of the two were comparable but the spouse is entitled to substantial deductions

---

[1] Infra § 19.4-4; lien for Federal taxes, ibid.
[2] See next following sections.
[3] Infra § 10.3.
[4] I.R.C. sec. 6012(b) (1).
[5] Time for filing returns and making payments of Federal income tax in case of absentee presumed dead, see Rev. Rul. 66-286, 1966-2 Cum. Bull. 485. Presumption of death of absentee, supra § 5.1.
[6] Negligence and remedies therefor, supra §§ 3.5-1 ff., 3.6.
[7] Failure of decedent to file returns, infra § 10.6.
[8] I.R.C. § 6013(a). Joint returns with surviving spouse, in general, Price, Postmortem Estate Planning Up to Date, 20 N.Y.U. Inst. on Fed. Taxation 301, 316, Right of spouse to have returns for certain later years treated for rate purposes as if joint return with decedent, I.R.C. § 2(a).

that reduce the combined taxable incomes. Where, however, the surviving spouse had the larger income, it is ordinarily not to the advantage of the estate to join in a return with the spouse, especially when it is in mind that under tax statutes each signer of a joint return is severally liable for the entire tax on the combined incomes of the spouses, including any deficiencies that may be assessed and any interest and penalties;[9] an executor is not justified in exposing the estate to the risk of liability for a greater tax than it would incur on a separate return,[10] and accordingly not justified in joining in a return with the spouse in such a case. The case is even stronger against a joint return if there is any reason to suspect that the spouse's full income is not reported in the return, or any of the spouse's claimed deductions are not allowable; apart from any other factors, such as possible charges of fraud or concealment, the principles just mentioned make it improper in such case for the executor to join in a return with the spouse, at least unless the executor can be affirmatively indemnified to his satisfaction against all possible liabilities.

§ *10.2-2a.* ———; ———; *division of tax on joint return.* Where a joint return is filed, the liability of the estate and the spouse is joint and several, so that, as mentioned in the preceding section, the estate is liable to the Treasury for the full amount of the tax on the year's income, plus any interest and penalties. As between the estate and the spouse, however, while it is apparent (if both had income) that the entire tax should not be borne by either alone, there is no affirmative rule in most jurisdictions as to the method of dividing the tax between them. In that state of the law, the amount deductible by the estate for Federal estate tax purposes[11] furnishes a guide and the executor would seem to be protected in making the division on that basis.

§ *10.3.* **Examination of prior returns.** The executor should examine copies of the decedent's income tax returns for at least the number of years preceding his death specified in any statute of limitation of the period for additional assessments, and for any earlier years that appear to be "open" for additional assessment by reason of waiver of limitations or otherwise, in order to estimate the probability, if any, of a deficiency assessment for any such prior year and so to be able to make provision for payment of such an assessment if made.[12]

§ *10.4.* **Fraud of decedent.** The executor should have in mind that an audit of a decedent's income tax return, whether made during his lifetime or after his death,

---

[9] I.R.C. § 6013 (d) (3); unless decedent innocent, ibid ¶ (e).

[10] Incurrence of unnecessary charge or expense as waste, supra § 3.5-2.

[11] The portion of the tax on the joint return computed by multiplying the tax on the return by the same percentage that a separate tax computed for the decedent is of the total of the taxes computed for each spouse separately. Reg. 20.2053-6(f); Rev. Rul. 56–290, 1956-1 Cum. Bull. 445; Rev. Rul. 57–98, 1957-1 Cum. Bull. 300.

[12] Examination of returns as aid in ascertainment of assets, supra § 6.3. Filing notice of fiduciary relationship with I.R.S. to assure receipt of communications regarding tax matters, supra § 6.2.

INCOME TAXES

and whether pursuant to a request for prompt audit[13] or in normal course, does not bar a subsequent assessment of a deficiency based upon fraud, or of a fraud penalty. If the executor discovers patent fraud on the part of the decedent,[14] his duty to disclose it to the relevant taxing authority would appear to be clear. A more difficult case is presented where there is indication of possible fraud but no certain evidence thereof; the executor faces the dilemma of the need to protect himself against personal liability for such deficiency or penalty, and his civic duty, on the one hand, and, on the other hand, his duty not to traduce his decedent's reputation or to expose his estate to needless difficulty and expense in an intensive and perhaps lengthy investigation. In such a case the executor should seek an opportunity, in connection with a normal audit, to bring the pertinent facts to the auditing agent's attention, in writing, but without accusing his decedent of affiirmative wrongdoing, and try to obtain an affirmative reference to such facts in the audit report.

§ 10.5. *Failure of decedent to file returns.* Where the executor finds that his decedent has failed to file required income tax returns for any year or years prior to his death, he should bring the facts promptly to the attention of the relevant taxing authorities, to the end that the tax liability may be established and paid. It may be possible in such a case to reconstruct the income and deductions of the decedent for the missing years, at least with reasonable approximation, on the basis of his records or of evidence of his assets at the beginning of the period involved and its end or the time of the decedent's death. If, as sometimes is the case, records for the years in question are nonexistent, that fact should be made clear to the taxing authorities and the best possible estimate or compromise of liability should be worked out with them.[15] Certainly the executor is not justified in remaining silent in such a case or in assuming that the decedent's default will never be discovered.

§ 10.6. *Income taxes of estate.*[16] It is, of course, the duty of the executor to prepare and file income tax returns in respect of the estate for the period from the date of the decedent's death[17] to that of final distribution,[18] and to pay any taxes shown by such returns.[19] While the law of taxation is beyond the scope of this work, it will be in mind that, briefly stated, under at least the Federal income tax law taxable in-

---

[13] Infra § 10.7-1.

[14] Failure of decedent to file returns, see next following section.

[15] In an instance that came to the author's attention, a wife received certain securities from her husband's estate; she died some twenty years later, holding an entirely different (and smaller) group of securities. She had filed no income tax returns during her survivorship, and no records of income, or of gains and losses, were found. As the executor and the I.R.S. were equally unable to establish any facts, an arbitrary compromise was effected and tax paid on the basis thereof.

[16] West Dig., Taxation Key No. 1024.

[17] Including "income in respect of [the] decedent" under I.R.C. sec. 691.

[18] Distribution, in general, infra § 18.6-1 ff; prolongation of administration, infra § 18.13. Income during period of administration, in general, infra § 16.4-2.

[19] Estate income tax returns and problems, see 1965 Proc. A.B.A. Sec. Real Prop. Prob. & Tr. L., Part I, 179–184.

come which is distributed or distributable during a tax year[20] is not taxable to the estate (but rather is taxable to the distributee), but that income not so distributed or distributable in the year, as often in the case particularly, although not exclusively, of capital gains, is taxable to the estate.[21]

§ *10.7-1.* *Request for early audit; of decedent's returns.* The executor should consider in each case whether it is advisable for him, usually at the time of or shortly after filing the decedent's final income tax return,[22] to make due request to the Internal Revenue Service for early audit of that return and of returns for all prior "open years",[23] and a like request to state income tax authorities if provided for by state law. Audit of such returns within the limited period specified in the statute providing for such a request[24] will both protect the executor in making distribution to beneficiaries without waiting for the expiration at some later date of the ordinary period of limitation on additional assessments, and benefit the estate by establishing earlier than might otherwise be done its liability, if any, for additional tax and thereby permitting the running of interest on the deficiency to be shortened; and failure to receive an additional assessment within the limited period referred to may enable distribution to beneficiaries at an earlier date than would otherwise be practicable.[25] As against any opposition by beneficiaries to the making of such a request for early audit based upon fear that the audit will disclose irregularities in the returns, the executor may justly observe that it is not his function to assist in evasion of lawful tax liabilities. If, however, there is no reason for the executor to believe that the returns involved are other than correct, and the ordinary period of limitation on additional assessments will in any event expire as to all the decedent's returns before distribution of the estate's assets can be made, the executor may determine that a request for early audit would serve no useful purpose and may be omitted.

§ *10.7-2.* ———; *of estate's returns.* As in the case of returns of the decedent,[26] the executor should consider, before making final distribution of the estate, whether it is advisable to request an early audit of the income tax returns of the estate for the period of its administration.[27] The theoretical considerations here are much the

---

[20] Selection of fiscal year for tax purposes, infra § 12.5.
[21] Capital gains taxes as payable out of principal, infra § 16.3-2.
[22] Supra § 10.2.
[23] In at least some collection districts, however, the volume of requests for early audit of Federal returns at times becomes so great that the requests cannot be complied with within the statutory period, with the result that the Internal Revenue Service demands a waiver or extension of time under implied threat of an immediate "jeopardy" assessment. The executor should accordingly consider whether a request for early audit will accomplish a useful purpose and so whether it is really advisable.
[24] In case of Federal income tax, I.R.C. sec. 6501(d), which is in terms of a request for prompt assessment of any deficiency.
[25] Time for satisfaction of legacies, infra § 14.31-1; for distribution of residuary estate, infra § 18.6-3.
[26] See last preceding section.
[27] Supra § 10.6.

INCOME TAXES 117

same as those in the former case, with particular emphasis on freedom to make payment of legacies and distribution of the residue without withholding a reserve to cover possible tax deficiencies. In the usual case, however, if the executor is fully satisfied as to the correctness of his returns and no special problems exist, he may decide that no substantial risk exists of a deficiency assessment against him or the estate and so may omit the making of such a request.

§ 10.8. *Closing agreements.* In a proper case the executor may deem it advisable to request a closing agreement,[28] to settle or terminate finally any liabilities in respect of income taxes of the decedent. In the case of the Federal income tax a closing agreement may be obtained only where good and sufficient reason is shown, and accordingly closing agreements are not usual in estates.[29]

---

[28] As to Federal taxes, see I.R.C. sec. 7121.

[29] The Internal Revenue Service will, however, usually consider an executor's request for a closing agreement where that is necessary in order that he may be discharged by the court. Discharge from liability on general, infra § 24.9.

XI

GIFT TAXES

§ 11.1. In general.[1] It is the duty of the executor, as a part of his responsibility to pay lawful debts and discharge legal obligations of the decedent, to file any gift tax return that the decedent should have filed during his lifetime, or would have been required by law to file if he had lived, and to pay any tax that is shown by such return to be payable.[2] The fact that individuals frequently neglect to file returns of taxable gifts increases the responsibility that falls upon the executor to make due investigation as to taxable gifts by the decedent, and an omission by the decedent at some past time to file a required return or pay a gift tax lawfully due does not relieve the executor of the duty of ascertaining the facts and of preparing and filing a return upon discovering that a taxable gift was made.[3] The executor will, of course, in this connection have in mind that the mere fact that property which formed the subject matter of a gift by the decedent in his lifetime is includible in his estate for the purposes of an estate or other death tax does not necessarily indicate that no gift tax return in respect of the gift was required to be filed or that no gift tax was required to be paid.

§ 11.2. Gifts in quarter of death and preceding quarter.[3a] As his first step toward satisfying any gift tax liabilities of the decedent, the executor should promptly investigate as to whether the decedent made any gifts, not covered by allowable annual exclusions,[4] in the calendar quarter in which his death occurred and, if he died before the due date of gift tax returns in respect of the preceding quarter, whether he made any such gifts in such preceding quarter, and to file a return in respect of any such gift, even if no tax is payable on the return by reason of the availability, as in the case of the Federal gift tax,[5] of the decedent's specific or "lifetime" exemption in an

---

[1] West Dig., Taxation Key Nos. 906.101–.113.

[2] Priority of taxes, and tax liens, infra § 19.4-4.

[3] Personal liability of executor, 2 Real Prop. Prob. & Tr. J. 250 ff.; as to Federal taxes generally, 31 U.S.C.A. sec. 192.

[3a] Returns, formerly annual, are now required quarterly.

[4] Under Federal law, I.R.C. sec. 2503(b).

[5] I.R.C. sec. 2521.

GIFT TAXES

amount sufficient to cover the taxable gift. Any tax shown by such a return to be payable should be paid by the executor promptly, in order to prevent or cut off the accrual of interest thereon, and in case of any undue delay the executor may be held liable to beneficiaries for the amount of interest that was incurred by reason of the delay.[6]

§ 11.3. Past gifts. Where a Federal estate tax return is required to be filed by the executor, he will necessarily investigate, in order that he may complete such return, what if any gifts taxable for estate tax purposes, or gifts (whether or not deemed so taxable) of substantial parts of the decedent's estate, were made by the decedent in his lifetime, and whether gift tax returns were required and were filed in respect of such gifts; and it would seem that, upon assembling sufficient information as to such matters to enable completion of the Federal estate tax return, the executor need not make further investigation as to past gifts unless he has reason to believe that gifts not required to be reported in such estate tax return were or may have been made.[7] Where the filing of a Federal estate tax return is not required, the executor should make at least the same kind of investigation as to past gifts and gift tax returns as would be necessary for the purposes of such an estate tax return. If it comes to the knowledge of the executor that a gift was made at any time by the decedent which was required to be reported in a gift tax return, and that such a return was not filed, the executor should prepare and file a return of such gift, at least if a taxable amount remains after applying any available exclusion or other exemption, and should pay the tax shown by such return. Ordinarily, it would not seem that the executor in making such a payment should include any interest thereon or any penalty in respect of late filing, but he should make sure that, until the expiration of the applicable statute of limitation, he retains sufficient funds to provide for any interest or penalty that may be assessed.

---

[6] Waste generally, supra § 3.5-2.
[7] Invalid or ineffective gifts and other transfers, supra § 6.18.

XII

ESTATE AND INHERITANCE TAXES

Part A—In General; Payment

§ 12.1. Priority. The priority of taxes generally, including estate and inheritance taxes, over other debts,[1] and the priority of Federal taxes over those imposed by states,[2] are elsewhere discussed. A question of relative priority between estate or inheritance taxes of two states, as, for example, that of the state of domicile and that of another state in which an asset has a situs for tax purposes, ordinarily will not arise. This is, basically, because an asset taxable by either state is not taxable by the other. The state of the decedent's domicile, and only that state, has power to impose an estate or inheritance tax on the decedent's estate, except that property having a situs in another state is taxable by such other state and not by the domiciliary state.[3] If ancillary administration[4] is had in the non-domiciliary state, the ancillary executor or administrator will be required to pay the tax of such state, out of the assets coming into his hands, before he can make any distribution to beneficiaries or remittance to the domiciliary representative; and even if no ancillary proceeding be had, the asset in the non-domiciliary jurisdiction ordinarily cannot, under its laws, be recovered by the domiciliary executor without first satisfying its tax. In either case, therefore, the tax based on situs of an asset in another jurisdiction than that of the domicile is in effect payable out of such asset, and not out of the domiciliary estate as such, and a question of relative priority of the taxes of the two estates does not exist because such taxes are not "competitive" as to payment but are payable from separate and distinct funds.

§ 12.2. Contest as to domicile and right to tax. Where the domicile of a decedent as between two states is doubtful or in dispute,[5] and each state asserts a right to tax

---
[1] Infra § 19.4-4; lien for Federal taxes, ibid.
[2] Infra § 19.4-5a.
[3] So as to tangible personal property, as well as real property: *Frick v. Pennsylvania*, 268 U.S. 473, 45 S.Ct. 603, 69 L.ed. 1058, 42 A.L.R. 316; *City Bank Farmers Trust Co. v. Schnader*, 293 U.S. 112, 55 S.Ct. 29, 79 L.ed. 228.
[4] Supra § 5.5-4.
[5] Domicile problems in general, supra § 5.4-2.

ESTATE AND INHERITANCE TAXES

the estate as one of its own domiciliary, the problem presented to the executor may be very serious.[6] Some states have enacted reciprocal statutes authorizing their fiscal or taxing officials, in cases of disputed domicile, to confer with corresponding officials of other states having like statutes and to enter into agreements with them compromising the tax or determining the amount of tax payable to each; and where such statutes exist in both or all jurisdictions involved in a dispute and are applied, the matter may be resolved without excessive difficulty or expense to the estate. Such statutes, however, being permissive only, cannot be invoked by the executor, and the mere fact that they exist does not necessarily mean that a compromise will be sought or had. In the absence of such a statute in either of the states involved in a dispute as to right to tax, the executor has little hope of being able to get the point settled by agreement between the states because of the absence of power on the part of their respective taxing authorities to compromise, so that one or another must recede wholly from its assertion of a right to tax, and such a recession is unlikely except in the clearest case. The executor is thus put into the position where he must argue his case separately with each state involved; in so doing, he runs the risk of an adverse decision in each, and indeed the risk that an argument used in one state against its claim to have been the domicile will, after such argument has failed, be turned against him as conclusory by the other state.[7]

§ *12.3. Preliminary investigations; notices and returns.* Statutes imposing estate or inheritance taxes universally require the executor to file, at or within a specified time, a return or other prescribed report of assets and deductions,[8] or to institute a proceeding to determine the facts with respect thereto, so that the amount of the taxable estate may be ascertained and the tax in respect thereof may be determined; and the executor also may be required to file, at an earlier date, a notice of the existence of a taxable or possibly taxable estate and an approximation of the amount or value of its taxable assets.[9] Not only for the purposes of such a notice but on more general principles,[10] an executor should, at an early stage, make a reasonably full investigation of the decedent's affairs and transactions to discover the existence, nature, and amount of assets includible in the taxable estate that do not come into the executor's hands ("non-probate" or "non-testamentary" property[11]), as well as the assets of the testamentary estate, for purposes of estimating the amounts of

---

[6] Cf. *In re Dorrance's Est.* 309 Pa. 151, 163 A. 303, cert.den. (sub nom. Dorrance v. Penna.) 287 U.S. 660, 53 S.Ct. 222, 77 L.ed. 570, and affd. 172 A. 900, cert. den. (sub nom. Dorrance v. Penna.) 288 U.S. 617, 53 S.Ct. 507, 77 L.ed. 990; *In re Dorrance's Est.*, 115 N.J.Eq. 268, 170 A, 601, supp. 116 N.J.Eq. 204, 172 A. 503, sustained (sub nom. Dorrance v. Martin) 13 N.J.Misc. 168, 176 A. 743, cert. den. 298 U.S. 678, 56 S.Ct. 949, 80 L.ed. 399, reh. den. 298 U.S. 692, 56 S.Ct. 957, 80 L.ed. 1410; *Camden Safe Dep. & Trust Co. v. Martin*, 298 U.S. 678, 56 S.Ct. 949, and 950, 80 L. ed. 1399.

[7] Cf. New Jersey decision in *Dorrance*, supra.

[8] Federal estate tax, form 706; see L.R.C. sec. 6018(a).

[9] The Federal preliminary notice, Form 704, is no longer required.

[10] Identification of assets and familiarization with decedent's affairs, in general, supra § 6.3.

[11] Supra § 1.11-1.

cash that will eventually be required for tax purposes and the liquidation that will be required to raise such cash.[12] Inasmuch as penalties are prescribed by tax laws for failure to file required returns or notices within prescribed periods, an executor who fails to make such a filing by the proper time may be held liable to beneficiaries for the amount of any penalty assessed or other damage suffered as a result of such failure,[13] unless adequate reason therefor be established.[14]

§ *12.4-1. Payment of tax; in general.*[15] Just as estate and inheritance tax statutes require the executor to file, by a prescribed time, a return or report of assets and deductions so that the tax payable may be ascertained, they require him to pay such tax,[16] within a prescribed period,[17] and impose interest charges or other penalties for failure to make timely payment.[18] On general principles, therefore, an executor who fails to pay such a tax within the prescribed period is personally liable to the beneficiaries for interest or penalties resulting from such failure, and surchargeable accordingly,[19] unless there is adequate excuse for the delay.[20] The matter of postponement of payment pursuant to a statute providing therefor is considered at a later point.[21]

§ *12.4-2. ———; source of initial payment.* Estate and inheritance taxes are, of course, payable out of principal,[22] and are initially payable wholly out of the decedent's "testamentary" or "probate" estate[23] (ie., the property administerable by the executor[24]), to the extent that such property is sufficient therefor,[25] where, as is the

---

[12] Liquidation for cash requirements supra § 7.6-1.

[13] Cf. *Lohm's Est.*, 440 Pa. 268, 269 A.2d 451, where executor was held liable for loss of availability of alternate Federal estate valuation as result of late filing of return. Negligence in general, supra § 3.5-1.

[14] In the case of the Federal estate tax, I.R.C. sec. 6018(b) provides in substance that if the executor cannot make a complete return as to a part of the gross taxable estate, he shall include a description of such part and the persons interested therein, and on notice from the I.R.S. such persons shall make a return as to such part of the estate. Accordingly, it would seem that any penalties and other liabilities in respect of the tax attributable to such part of the estate should fall upon the persons interested in the latter and not upon the executor.

[15] Estate and inheritance taxes, in general, West Dig., Taxation Key Nos. 856–906.

[16] I.R.C. sec. 2002: "The tax . . . shall be paid by the executor." Personal liability of executor for tax until paid, infra § 12.7.

[17] Time for filing returns and making payments in case of absentee presumed dead, see Rev. Rul. 66–286, 1966-2 Cum. Bul. 485. Presumption of death of absentee, supra § 5.1.

[18] Infra § 12.4-3a. Allowance of discount for early payment, or addition to tax if not paid early, infra § 12.5.

[19] Supra § 3.6.

[20] Insufficiency of testamentary assets, infra § 12.4-4.

[21] Infra § 12.5.

[22] (1962) Rev. Unif. Prin. & Inc. Act sec. 5(a).

[23] See I.R.C. sec. 2205, stating it to be "the purpose and intent" of the Federal estate tax law that, so far as practicable, and unless otherwise directed in the decedent's will, such tax shall be paid out of the estate before its distribution; and providing for reimbursement out of the testamentary estate of a taker of non-testamentary property that is used for payment of or application on the tax. State tax laws, even if less explicit, are to the same effect.

[24] Supra §1.11-1.

[25] Resort to non-testamentary property in case of insufficiency, infra § 12.4-4.

ESTATE AND INHERITANCE TAXES

usual case, the non-probate property is not within the executor's control. Thus, the payment is, in effect, made out of the residuary estate;[26] and this is true even where, in the case of an estate tax, the amount of tax is to be equitably apportioned among the takers of the property includible in the taxable estate,[27] or, in the case of an inheritance tax, there is to be collected from each recipient of an item of taxable property the amount of tax on such item.[28] Thus where, as is often the case at least as to an estate tax, the tax payment must be made before shares of the tax can be computed or can be collected from recipients of property, the executor may be required to liquidate assets of the testamentary estate in order to make the payment[29] even though at a later time he will be entitled to collect some or all of the amount paid from such recipients[30] and thus replenish the funds in his hands.

§ 12.4-2a. ———; ———; *time; premature payment.* Emphasis upon the duty of the executor to make payment of an estate or inheritance tax by its due date,[31] or before expiration of the time within which payment will entitle the estate to a discount or prevent an addition to the tax,[32] should not be allowed to obscure the impropriety of making payment at an unnecessarily early date, and thereby depriving the estate of the use of and income from the tax moneys sooner than need be.[33] The general principle of waste[34] applies as well to an avoidable loss of income as to an unnecessary expenditure of principal, and at least if the amount of the payment is significant the executor should carefully time the payment to avoid both prematurity and lateness.

§ 12.4-3. ———; *deficiency assessments.* The rule above stated that an executor is personally liable, and may be surcharged, for damage resulting from unexcused failure to make timely payment of an estate or inheritance tax[35] applies not only to the case of his failure to make any payment by the prescribed time but also to his unwarranted failure to make a sufficient payment, as where he negligently or fraudulently omits taxable assets from his return, or claims therein deductions that clearly are not allowable, with the result that at some time after the due date of the tax, on audit of the return or otherwise, an additional amount of tax is determined to be payable and interest or penalties are imposed on the estate.[36] This, however, is not to say

---

[26] More accurately, out of property that would fall into or constitute the residuary estate if it were not required for the tax payment.

[27] Apportionment, infra § 12.10-1 ff.

[28] Infra § 12.10-2.

[29] Liquidation for cash requirements, in general, supra § 7.6-1. Borrowing to pay taxes, supra § 7.6-1b. Postponement of payment, infra § 12.6.

[30] Collection of apportioned shares of tax, infra §§ 12.10-5, -5a; disposition of amounts collected, infra § 12.10-5b.

[31] Supra § 12.4-1. Postponement of payment, infra § 12.6.

[32] Infra § 12.5.

[33] Duty to make funds of estate productive, supra § 7.7-2.

[34] Supra § 3.5-2.

[35] Supra § 12.4-1.

[36] See next following section.

that an executor is surchargeable, in every case of a deficiency assessment of tax, for the interest on the deficiency; on the contrary, where there is room for reasonable doubt as to the includibility of an asset in the taxable estate, or the value at which it should be included, or as to the allowability of a deduction, it is ordinarily the duty of the executor to resolve such doubts in favor of the estate, and in such a case he is not liable to beneficiaries for the interest on a tax deficiency that is thereafter determined. Penalties assessed in respect of a tax[37] are subject to similar principles, although, as they are usually prescribed for gross or willful negligence or other misfeasance, the executor is more likely to be personally liable for a penalty than for interest.

§ 12.4-3a. ———; ———; *interest and penalties.* In many if not most jurisdictions, interest on an estate or inheritance tax deficiency, or a penalty payable in respect thereof, is not payable out of income of the estate,[38] but is to be regarded as a part of and an addition to the tax, and so payable from the same sources and subject to the same principles as to apportionment or allocation among beneficiaries as the tax itself,[39] unless, of course, the interest or penalty is incurred under which circumstances that the executor is personally liable, by way of surcharge, for its amount. An exception to the general rule may exist where the interest or penalty results from the omission or improper treatment in the return of a non-testamentary asset whose existence or value was unknown to or unascertainable by the executor because of non-cooperation on the part of its take or holder in supplying information to the executor;[40] in such case, as also in the case of interest or a penalty resulting by reason of delay or failure of a person taking or holding non-testamentary property in contributing to the tax where the testamentary estate is insufficient,[41] it would seem that the burden of the interest or penalty should fall upon the person at fault.

§ 12.4-4. ———; *insufficiency of testamentary assets.*[42] The rules hereinabove stated as to the duty of an executor to pay an estate or inheritance tax when it is due, and his liability for failure to make timely payment of such a tax,[43] apply only to the extent of the assets that come into his hands or under his control, or should have so come. The taxable estimate may, of course, include property not passing under the will or administerable by the executor, but instead passing by operation of law, or under lifetime transfers, or pursuant to beneficiary designations, and the value of such "non-testamentary" property[44] may be so large in relation to the probate estate, or may cause such a high tax rate to be applicable, that the taxes pay-

---

[37] Ibid.
[38] (1962) Rev. Unif. Prin. & Inc. Act sec. 5(a).
[39] Supra § 12.4-2.
[40] Investigation as to non-testamentary property, supra § 12.3.
[41] See next following section.
[42] Insolvent or insufficient estate, generally, infra Ch. XIX.
[43] Supra § 12.4-1.
[44] Supra § 1.11-1.

ESTATE AND INHERITANCE TAXES

able exceed the assets available to the executor for application thereon. Inasmuch as the executor has no control over such non-testamentary property, and so cannot require that it be applied to the tax payment,[45] he is not liable to taxing authorities for the consequences of failure to pay that portion of an estate or inheritance tax that remains after exhaustion of the assets within the executor's control nor liable to beneficiaries or others against whom interest or penalties may be imposed for delay in payment of the balance of tax. The executor should, however, in such a case, endeavor to arrange with the respective holders of the non-testamentary property for the contribution, not later than at the due date of the tax, of either such holders' apportionable shares of the tax (where apportionment is eventually to be made[46]) or at least of the balance of tax remaining unpaid after exhaustion of the testamentary assets; even if unsuccessful in this effort,[47] the executor may thus build a positive defense against any attempt later made to surcharge him for interest or penalties, in respect of the unpaid portion of the tax, if under an apportionment statute those are treated as part of the total apportionable amount and hence increase ratably the amount eventually apportioned against takers of the testamentary estate.

§ 12.4-5. ————; *death taxes of foreign state or country.*[48] In accordance with principles stated in a preceding section,[49] where assets of an estate are subject to an estate or inheritance tax imposed by a state of the United States other than that of the domicile of the decedent, in a case other than that of disputed domicile or right to tax,[50] such tax is ordinarily payable by the ancillary executor or administrator if one has been appointed in the taxing state (and in some states it may be necessary, as elsewhere noted,[51] to obtain an ancillary appointment in order that the tax may be settled and paid) or otherwise out of the property in the taxing state; in addition, a number of states have reciprocal statutes permitting the enforcement or collection of one another's taxes where no ancillary appointment has been made and the tax is not collected out of the property itself. In the case of a death tax or death duty imposed or asserted by a foreign country, however, the situation may be different. In each such case the executor must consider whether he has any responsibility for the payment of such tax or duty and, indeed, whether he has any right to pay it. In general, unless the will otherwise directs,[52] he must not pay a foreign tax or duty except

---

[45] Collection from holder after payment of tax, infra §§ 12.10-5, -5a.

[46] Apportionment, in general, infra § 12.10-1 ff.

[47] It is to be recognized that the trustee of an inter vivos trust includible in the taxable estate, or any other fiduciary holding "taxable" property, may feel unable to make a contribution at the time the tax becomes payable, on the theory that he is without right to expend trust funds, and hence diminish the income of his trust, until he is compelled to contribute either by demand of the taxing authority or under an order of apportionment, which usually is not made until after the total tax has been finally settled; cf. § 12.10-1, infra. See also infra § 12.10-5d note 43.

[48] P-H Est, Plng. Serv. ¶ 2276.

[49] Supra § 12.1.

[50] Supra § 12.2.

[51] Supra § 1.7.

[52] Effect of direction in will, see next following section.

out of such assets, if any, of the decedent as can be reached or seized by the foreign country to satisfy such tax. This follows from the principle that a foreign country cannot avail itself of judicial process in this country to reach property held here; and so the executor who pays any such tax or duty out of the general assets of the estate is making a voluntary payment and wasting the assets of the estate,[53] at least unless a treaty or convention between the United States and the foreign country contains provisions for the facilitation by each of the collection of the other's tax. Accordingly, if an asset of the estate is located or kept in such foreign country and can be collected by the executor if, but only if, such country's tax or duty is paid, and the value of the asset exceeds the amount of the tax or duty involved, the executor may and should make the necessary payment and collect the asset. If, however, the tax or duty asserted exceeds the value of such assets, if any, of the decedent as are located or kept within the foreign country, as where under the law of the latter the decedent is regarded as its resident or national and the entire estate is therefor treated as taxable by it, the executor is not required to pay the tax out of the general assets of the estate,[54] and, it would follow, is without power to make such a payment, except *pro tanto* by way of abandonment to the foreign country of such assets,[55] if any, as are located or kept therein, unless, as noted above, a treaty or convention otherwise requires.

§ *12.4-5a.* ———; ———; *effect of direction in will.* A foreign death tax not otherwise payable by an executor under the principles discussed in the preceding section may, of course, be directed to be paid by the decedent's will. In this connection it is not to be overlooked that a general direction to pay "all" estate or inheritance taxes may have the effect, however unintended, of making the estate liable for a tax of a foreign country that, but for such direction, would not be payable except out of property in the foreign country.[56]

§ *12.5. Discounts; additions to tax.*[57] Some statutes provide that a payment on account of an estate or inheritance tax, made by a prescribed time which is earlier than the due date of the tax, entitled the estate to a discount on the tax, or gives it a credit against the tax for a greater amount than that paid. Some other statutes provide a like incentive for early payment of the tax by imposing a percentage addi-

---

[53] Waste, supra § 3.5-2.
[54] *Est. of McNeel*, 170 N.Y.S.2d 892.
[55] Such abandonment may, of course, result in damage or inequity to one who is a devisee or legatee of the foreign assets and not also the residuary beneficiary, but a greater inequity would result to residuary beneficiaries if their benefits were reduced or wiped out by payment of the foreign death duty merely in order that such devisee or legatee could receive the foreign property. The executor may wish for his own projection to obtain judicial approval of the abandonment before it is effected; and he should also consider whether the harmed devisee or legatee may be entitled to equitable adjustment out of the general estate or from other beneficiaries, but in general the existence or non-existence of such a right should not be determinative of the question of abandonment rather than payment.
[56] See last preceding section.
[57] Deficiency assessments, supra § 12.4-3.

tion to the tax except as to amounts paid on account thereof by a prescribed time before the due date. It is the duty of the executor under any such statute to obtain for the estate the benefit of such discount or credit, or to avoid liability for such addition, as the case may be, by making an appropriate advance payment on account, or of the estimated tax, if it is feasible for him to do so and a net advantage to the estate will result; and it follows that, unless adequate reason for failure to make such an advance payment can be shown, an executor may be held liable to beneficiaries, under his duty of diligence[58] and the doctrine of waste,[59] for the amount of tax ultimately required to be paid that, but for such failure, would not have been payable. As in other instances of advance payment,[60] however, the executor should consider what earnings from the amount of money that might be used to make the payment could be realized down to the ordinary due date of the tax if the payment were not made, and to compare such earnings with the discount of tax saving; but if any trust or life interest is created under the will he should have in mind that the tax saving would enure to the benefit of the principal or remainder interest[61] while the earnings would benefit persons entitled to income,[62] so that if he makes the early payment the executor may have later to make an equitable adjustment between principal and income.[63]

§ *12.6. Postponement of payment.* A statute imposing an estate or inheritance tax may provide for postponement of payment of the tax, beyond its normal due date,[64] in certain circumstances and upon specified terms and conditions; the Federal estate tax law is an example.[65] In a proper case the executor is justified in availing himself of the statutory privilege, and may indeed, under his duty of care and prudence, have a duty to do so.[67] It should, however, be recognized that cases for the exercise of the privilege are rare, and that in most instances its exercise may subject

---

[58] Supra § 3.1.

[59] Supra § 3.5-2.

[60] Attorneys' fees, infra § 20.2-4a; executor's compensation, infra § 20.4-3a. Premature payment of tax distinguished, supra § 12.4-2a.

[61] Tax as payable from principal, supra § 12.4-2.

[62] Persons entitled to surplus income, infra § 18.4-1 ff.

[63] Cf. adjustment as to deductions taken for estate tax instead of income tax purposes, infra § 13.3.

[64] Payment by due date in general, supra § 12.4-1; in time to take discount or prevent addition to tax, see last preceding section. Premature payment, supra § 12.4-2a.

[65] I.R.C. sec. 6161(a) (2); tax attributable to future interest held by decedent, ibid. sec. 6163. Postponing payment of Federal estate tax, in general, see Price, Postmortem Estate Planning Up to Date, 20 N.Y.U. Inst. on Fed. Texation 301, 307 ff.

[66] Supra § 3.1.

[67] It might be argued, from the general principle of an executor's duty to manage the affairs of the estate to the greatest benefit of its beneficiaries (cf. § 3.2-2, supra), that in a period of high yields on even short-term investments the executor should elect installment payments of Federal estate tax, in every case "qualifying" under I.R.C. sec. 6166, even where funds are available for an outright payment, in view of the relatively low interest rate prescribed by that section. It would seem, however, that such an argument would distort the statutory purpose and should not be sustained.

the estate to loss or damage and the executor to liability for surcharge. The privilege of postponement is designed, generally speaking, to meet cases of special hardship,[68] and a postponement pursuant thereto is ordinarily for the purpose of avoiding forced liquidation of an asset to enable payment of the tax at its normal due date.[69] It is difficult in most instances to distinguish a postponement of liquidation and of tax payment from any other case of retention of an asset in the hope that its value will increase or that a readier market for it will exist at a later time, and hence from "speculation" as that term is used within the framework of fiduciary duty.[70] When it is kept in mind that the value of the asset in question may decrease, or its marketability may not improve, and that in the meantime interest on the postponed amount of tax runs at a statutory rate which may exceed the return on the retained asset, it is apparent that the privilege of postponement of payment is one to be exercised only after very careful consideration of all factors and with full appreciation of the risks involved.

§ *12.7. Personal liability of executor for tax.* The Federal statute,[71] and at least some state statutes, provide in effect that the executor shall be personally liable for a death tax, until it is paid, to the extent of the assets at any time coming into his hands that are available for payment thereof. Such a provision is, of course, closely connected with the rules as to priority of taxes over most other charges.[72] Having in mind that such taxes are ordinarily not payable until the expiration of a considerable period of time after the decedent's death, and may not be finally fixed in amount, upon audit or otherwise, until a much later date, the executor must make sure that he retains at all times, until final settlement of the taxes, sufficient assets to cover any possible deficiency or additional assessment, including interest and penalties; and if before such final settlement he had paid charges of a lower order of priority than taxes,[73] or has made distributions to beneficiaries, and as a result there do not remain in his hands sufficient funds to pay a balance of tax, including interest and any lawful penalties, he must himself pay such balance, and can only hope that he may be able to obtain a reimbursement from recipients of payments or distributions previously made. The personal liability of the executor under such a statutory provision ordinarily exists side by side with a further provision permitting the collection of the tax from any holder or recipient of property included in the taxable estate, under principles of "transferee liability", but is independent thereof,[74] and the executor

---

[68] It appears that the I.R.S. is reluctant to grant an extension of time under I.R.C. sec. 6161 and requires a strong demonstration of actual hardship.

[69] Such postponement is, of course, a species of borrowing and as such is subject to the considerations applicable thereto; cf. supra § 7.6-1b.

[70] Supra § 3.5-3.

[71] 31 U.S.C.A. sec. 192. See Liability of Fiduciaries and Transferees for Federal Estate and Gift Taxes, 2 Real Prop. Prob. & Tr. J. 250 ff.

[72] Supra § 12.1.

[73] Order of priority of charges and expenses, in general, infra § 18.4-1 ff.

[74] Cf. *Grieb v. Commr.*, 36 T.C. 156, 16, distinguishing fiduciary liability from transferee liability. Lien for tax on property in hands of legatee or distributee, infra § 19.4-4.

ESTATE AND INHERITANCE TAXES

cannot insist that the taxing authority exhaust its remedies against such holders or recipients before proceeding against him.

§ 12.8. Additional state tax to utilize Federal credit. Most state estate and inheritance tax laws provide that, if the aggregate of state death taxes on the estate is less than the maximum amount of state taxes for which a credit against the Federal estate tax is allowable,[75] there shall be an additional tax on the estate equal to the excess of such allowable credit over the state taxes otherwise payable. The effect of such a provision is, of course, to shift the benefit of such "excess" from the federal government to the state, without changing the aggregate tax liability of the estate.

§ 12.9. Establishment of credit against Federal tax for state tax paid. Where the estate is subject both to the Federal estate tax and to a state estate or inheritance tax, it is the duty of the executor, after having paid the state tax, to establish the credit therefore to which the estate is entitled under Federal law[76] against the Federal estate tax, and to obtain any refund or reduction of the latter tax to which such credit entitles the estate.

---

[75] Credit for state death taxes, I.R.C. sec. 2011. Establishment of such credit, see next following section. The credit is often referred to as "the 80% credit" because originally the maximum allowable credit was 80% of the tax imposed by the Revenue Act of 1926.

[76] See last preceding section.

XII

ESTATE AND INHERITANCE TAXES

Part B—Apportionment; Waivers

§ 12.10-1. *Apportionment of taxes;*[1] *in general.* Because, as elsewhere pointed out, the general testamentary estate is subject to the payment of estate taxes, and is the initial source of payment thereof,[2] in most, but not all,[3] jurisdictions such taxes are payable wholly out of the residuary estate (to the extent it is sufficient therefor) and the takers of the residuary accordingly bear the whole brunt of them, in the absence of statute otherwise providing.[4] In many states, however, statutes provide that the aggregate amount of the estate tax shall be apportioned equitably among all[5] or most[6] recipients of property includible in the taxable estate, unless the

---

[1] P-H Est. Plng. Serv. ¶¶ 2271-2274.

[2] Supra § 12.4-2.

[3] *Doetsch v. Doetsch*, 312 F.2d 323; *Trimble v. Helcher's Exr.*, 295 Ky. 178, 173 S.W.2d 985, both holding that the tax should be equitably apportioned among beneficiaries, even though no statute so provided. Cf. *Gesner v. Roberts*, 48 N.J. 379, 225 A.2d 697, holding a widow's share, qualifying for the marital deduction, not to be liable for a share of the estate tax, even though no statute provided for its exclusion from apportionment, on the ground that a testator normally intends to make the maximum bequest to his wife and such presumed intent overrides the otherwise general rule (under the state statute in force at the time) that the tax should be borne by everyone interested in the estate.

[4] The federal estate tax law (I.R.C. sec. 2202, providing that the tax shall be paid by the executor) does not require that the tax be borne by the residue. *Riggs v. Del Drago*, 317 U.S. 95, 63 S.Ct. 109, 87 L.ed. 106, 142 A.L.R. 2d 1131. The matter is one governed by state law, even as to the Federal estate tax, except only that the Federal statute provides that the executor may recover a ratable portion of the tax from life insurance beneficiaries (I.R.C. sec. 2206) and recipients of appointed property (ibid., sec. 2207), after due allowance for the marital deduction when applicable; as to whether the two sections cited merely confer a right of recovery or instead impose a duty to proceed for recovery, see Liability of Fiduciaries and Transferees for Federal Estate and Gift Taxes, 2 Real Prop. Prob. & Tr. J. 250, 269.

[5] So in Unif. Prob. Code sec. 3-916(b); that section copies the Uniform Estate Tax Apportionment Act.

[6] Some statutes exclude, for example, apportionment against a recipient of a cash legacy of specified amount, or of a specific legacy or devise, and provide that the share of tax attributable to such recipient shall be paid out of the residuary estate, in order not to diminish the amount or value presumably intended by the testator to pass to such recipient.

ESTATE AND INHERITANCE TAXES

will otherwise directs, or, under some statutes, if the will directs such apportionment;[7] usually subject, however, in both kinds of such statutes, to provisions excluding from sharing in such apportionment any recipients of such nature that their benefits do not generate any part of the tax (i.e., benefits that are deducted in computing the net taxable estate), as for example charitable bequests and marital deduction bequests.[8] Such statutes commonly contemplate that the tax will first be paid out of the general testamentary estate, in accordance with the rule hereinabove stated, but that after the amount of tax, including any interest and penalties payable by the estate,[9] has been finally determined and full paid, and after the amount or value of taxable property received or held by each person interested in the taxable estate, including the amount passing to residuary beneficiaries,[10] has been finally ascertained, an equitable share of the tax, for the judicial determination of which the statutes commonly make provision,[11] will be collected by the executor from each such person.[12] This has the sometimes unfortunate result, as noted in a preceding section,[13] of requiring the executor to liquidate some or all assets of the estate to enable payment of the tax even though he will eventually receive the return of perhaps a large fraction of the amount realized on the liquidation. It may also present problems to the executor of collection of apportioned amounts, as noted in a following section.[14] The theory of apportionment, where provided for, is that the ultimate burden of the tax should fall equitably on each recipient instead of being (in effect) borne wholly by residuary beneficiaries.[15]

§ *12.10-2.* ———; *inheritance taxes.* The doctrine of apportionment has no application to an inheritance tax, which, instead of being (as is an estate tax) a tax on

---

[7] Direction in will as to apportionment, infra § 12.10-3.

[8] Formulae for computation of both Federal and state taxes are set forth in *In re Casey's Est.*, 287 N.Y.S.2d 745; I.R.S. Supplemental Instructions for Form 706 for Computation of Interrelated Death Taxes and Marital or Charitable Deduction; and P-H Est. Plng. Serv. ¶ 120,576. Computation of marital bequest to be made before taxes, infra § 14.8-1. "Greeley formula" (where no marital deduction involved), CCH Fed. Tax Reptr. ¶ 2023.99.

[9] Where treated as addition to and parts of the tax, see supra § 12.4-3a.

[10] Where a charitable or other "exempt" bequest is of a share of the residuary estate, the amount of tax and the amount of the residue (and hence of the bequest) are interdependent; formulae for computation, cf. supra note 8.

[11] Cf. Unif. Prob. Code sec. 3-916(c).

[12] Retention or recovery of apportioned share, infra § 10.5 ff.

[13] Supra § 12.4-2.

[14] Supra § 12.10-5a.

[15] It will of course be apparent that, because the amount to be apportioned is the whole of the tax, and the tax is computed at progressive rates, the difference in sizes of two taxable estates may cause a legacy under one will to bear (through apportionment) a larger, or smaller, amount of tax than an identical legacy under another will; and that the inclusion in a taxable estate of non-testamentary property may, because of the progressive rates, cause the effective rate of tax on the estate as a whole, and hence the amount to be apportioned against each legatee under the will, to be unexpectedly high. Because in either case the result as to at least some beneficiaries may be quite different from what the testator expected or intended, the inclusion in or omission from a will of a general and inclusive direction for apportionment or non-apportionment should not be a matter of routine in drafting a will but the circumstances of each case should be carefully considered.

the passage of the entire taxable estate, is a separate charge on each recipient's receipt of taxable property. A will may, however, direct that inheritance taxes be paid out of the residuary estate,[16] and apparently, at least in most of the jurisdictions imposing such a tax, such a direction is not treated as increasing the amount of property receivable by the recipient and hence increasing the inheritance tax. In the absence of such a direction, an executor who has paid inheritance taxes in the first instance[17] has a right and duty, similar to that in the case of an apportioned estate tax,[18] to withhold, or collect, from each beneficiary the amount of the tax on his legacy or devise, and in both cases the means available to the executor are similar.

§ *12.10-3.* ———; *direction in will as to apportionment.* Where a statute provides for equitable apportionment of estate taxes among the recipients of the taxable property, a testator may direct in his will that such apportionment be not made,[19] either as against particular legatees or devisees, or generally as against takers of property passing under the will, or as against takers of any of the property includible in the gross taxable estate, including property not passing under the will; and where such a direction is given, the burden of the tax, or of so much of it as is so directed not to be apportioned, falls upon the residuary estate. Conversely, in the absence of a statute requiring apportionment, or under a statute prescribing non-apportionment, the testator may nevertheless direct that apportionment be made.[20] The matter for the executor to determine on this score is, therefore, whether the will contains any provision as to apportionment of taxes and, if it does, what is the effect of such provision. Obviously, a mere direction in a will that estate taxes be paid, without specification of the source of payment, seems merely a statement of what is required by law, and so should not prevent the application of a statute providing for apportionment. Such statutes ordinarily are by their terms to be applied in the absence of a clear direction in the will to the contrary, and so, in any case of doubt as to the intended scope or effect of a direction against apportionment where the statute would require apportionment, the direction will ordinarily be strictly construed, and may be deemed to relate only to legacies and devises under the will and not to any property passing outside the will if the latter is not mentioned. An executor should, therefor, ascertain with assurance the meaning and effect of any tax-payment provision before proceeding, but in case of doubt the more conservative course is, of course, to assume that an apportionment will be made, and to protect himself and the estate by retention or collection of tentatively apportioned shares, unless and until a court otherwise instructs him. Where there is a clear direction against apportionment even as to property not passing under the will, or a statute or rule of law to that effect is clearly left applicable by the will, of course no calculation of apportionable amounts or shares is necessary, subject in a proper case to the consideration discussed in the

---

[16] Direction in will as to apportionment of estate tax, see next following section.
[17] Source of initial payment of tax, supra § 12.4-2.
[18] Infra § 12.10-4.
[19] The statutes uniformly permit a testator to alter the otherwise prescribed treatment.
[20] Supra § 12.10-1 note 4.

ESTATE AND INHERITANCE TAXES 133

next following section; but if under an apportionment statute a will direction is only against apportionment as to property passing under the will, or only against apportionment as to property passing under particular bequests or devises, or if under a non-apportionment rule the will directs only such limited apportionment, a first apportionment must be made as between the part of the taxable estate which is not to bear a share of the tax, on the one hand, and the several parts (collectively) of the taxable estate against which apportionment is to be made, on the other hand, and a sub-apportionment must then be made among such latter parts. The tax in respect of any property as to which the will or the law effectively directs non-apportionment is, of course, borne by the residuary estate.[21]

§ 12.10-4. ————; *apportionment within residue.* Where any amount of an estate tax is payable out of the residuary estate, whether such amount be the whole of the tax, under a statute or will provision for non-apportionment, or be itself an apportioned share of the tax, under a statute or will directing apportionment, and there are two or more residuary legatees or devisees, there obviously is no need, in many cases, to make an apportionment of such amount of tax as between or among the residuary takers, in order to do equity, for distribution of the net residue after payment of the tax necessarily effects a ratable sharing of the tax burden among the residuary takers. Such a necessity does arise, however, where the parts or shares of the residue passing to the respective takers are subject to different treatment for the purposes of the tax; the apportionment then to be made is spoken of as an "apportionment within the residue", and is not affected by any direction in the will for non-apportionment[22] and, at least under most statutes, even by a statutory non-apportionment rule. Thus, if a part or share of the residuary estate passes to or in trust for charitable purposes, or to or for the benefit of the spouse, and another part or share is left to or in trust for another or others, so much of the charitable bequest as is deductible for the purposes of the tax, or so much of the property left to or in trust for the spouse as qualifies for a marital deduction in the case of the Federal estate tax law or a similar state statute, should not bear any part of the tax, since it did not "generate" tax, and an apportionment within the residue is necessary in order to relieve such property from in effect contributing to payment of a tax based upon property passing to others.[23] Such apportionment is thus to be made by excluding the deductible or "non-taxable" property from the total residue and apportioning the amount of tax in question to or among the remaining "taxable" parts, only, of the residue.

§ 12.10-4a. ————; ————; *payment "as expense" distinguished.* It is pointed out in the preceding section that an appointment of tax within the residue, where some parts or shares of the residuary estate are "non-taxable" and others are "tax-

---

[21] Residuary as source of payment, supra § 12.4-2.
[22] *Matter of Shubert*, 10 N.Y.2d 461, 225 N.Y.S.2d 13, 180 N.E.2d 410; *Erieg Est.*, 439 Pa. 550, 267, A.2d 841.
[23] Ibid.

able", is not precluded by a will provision, and perhaps not by a statutory provision, against apportionment of taxes. There is, however, to be distinguished from such a provision a direction in the will that estate taxes be paid out of the residuary estate as, or as if they were, an expense of administration. Under such a direction, the tax is deducted in arriving at the residue (just as would any expense of administration[24]), and the result is that all residuary beneficiaries bear ratably the burden of the tax, even if such beneficiaries include a charity or a spouse whose share of the residue, because of applicable deductions, does not itself generate any tax. It will be noted that such a direction for payment of the tax as an expense requires the making of a "circular" computation where a charitable deduction or a marital deduction in respect of a share or fraction of the residue (as distinguished from a dollar amount thereof) is involved, as in such case the amount of the tax and the amount of the deduction are reciprocal and interdependent.[25]

§ 12.10-5. ———; *retention or recovery of apportioned shares; in general.* It is true that in most cases the amount or value of the residuary estate (and in some instances even that of pre-residuary legacies) cannot be ascertained with exactness until the estate is ready for final distribution, and, of course, the amount of the estate tax, and hence the amount of each apportioned share thereof (under a statute or will providing for apportionment[26]), and also, in the case of a deductible residuary share, the amount of such deduction (which itself affects not only the amount of tax but also the calculation of the relative fractions or percentages to be used in making the tax apportionment[27]), cannot be known with assurance until the tax has been finally determined. Statutes contemplating postponement of the apportionment of an estate tax until all these things have been accomplishd, perhaps long after the payment of the tax, and then the collection by the executor of shares of the tax from the respective recipients of property, at least some of whom had or otherwise would have theretofore received distribution of all or parts of their benefits, accordingly cannot be charged with illogicality or with adopting a plainly non-realistic approach, although a plausible argument might be made that the necessity for payment of the taxes initially out of the general estate, with perhaps the necessity of liquidating (often at a sacrifice) a large portion of its assets in order to raise funds which will be in larger or smaller part recoverable later from beneficiaries,[28] is unjust to residuary beneficiaries. Nevertheless, an executor, by the time he is ready to satisfy (in whole or in part) any legacy[29] which will have to bear a share of the estate tax, usually can make a fairly close estimate of the tax and of the legatee's ratable share thereof, and, by allowing appropriately for contingencies and adjustments, can arrive at a tentative apportionment of the tax, and take steps to collect or

---

[24] Administration expenses in general, infra Ch. XX.
[25] For method of computation, see supra 12-10-1 note 8.
[26] Generally, supra § 12.10-1.
[27] See last preceding section, text at note 25.
[28] Supra § 12.4-2.
[29] Time for satisfaction of legacies, infra § 14-31-1.

ESTATE AND INHERITANCE TAXES 135

secure the respective estimated amounts. In the case of a legatee of cash, or of a residuary legatee to whom cash or liquid assets are to be turned over as a partial distribution, the executor should withhold[30] such legatee's tentatively apportioned amount of tax, including not only the share of tax apportionable in respect of the legacy being paid but also shares apportionable in respect of any other property, real or personal, of or passing to him, whether under other provisions of the will or outside the will. In the case of a legatee of tangibles only, the executor should withhold delivery of the tangibles, or of a sufficient part of them to secure the legatee's tentatively apportioned share of tax, unless and until the legatee contributes money to or posts other security with the executor[31] to cover, as in the case of a cash legatee, not merely the tax in respect of the tangibles but also that in respect of any other property of or passing to such legatee. Additional possible procedures in respect of a share of tax apportionable against a devisee of real property are mentioned elsewhere.[32] It is to be emphasized, generally, that the executor not only may have opportunities of providing for the apportioned shares of tax, but owes an affiirmative duty to avail himself of such of them as are feasible or open to him under the circumstances;[33] he may thereby avoid later problems of collection and perhaps litigation to compel contribution, and also may protect himself against any later assertion by a residuary beneficiary, where an apportioned amount of tax proves to be uncollectible, that the executor was negligent in failing to protect the residuary estate by withholding or collecting funds when it was possible for him to do so.[34] Any amount withheld from distribution to or deposited with the executor by a beneficiary or another that proves to be in excess of the share of tax apportionable to such person is, of course, payable over to him as soon as final apportionment is made.

§ 12.10-5a. ———; ———; *collection by litigation.* As is implied in the preceding section, an executor ordinarily has no means of protecting himself, and the estate, against the possibility that he will not be able, when definitive apportionment is made, to collect the share of an estate tax apportioned to one who is a recipient of property not passing under the will and who is not a beneficiary under the will to an extent sufficient to permit withholding of such share of tax out of testamentary benefits. The problem arises frequently with respect to a surviving joint owner, a beneficiary of life insurance, or the beneficiary of a lifetime transfer. A problem of the same kind arises in the case, for example, of a devisee of real property who is not a legatee or whose legacy is not large enough to cover his total share of the tax.[35] In any such case, unless the executor is able to persuade the recipient in question to

---

[30] Unif. Prob. Code sec. 3-916(d) (1).
[31] Op. cit., sec. 3-916(d) (2) and (g).
[32] Infra § 15.10.
[33] See Shriver, The Multi-State Estate, 3 Real Prop. Prob. & Tr. J. 189, 190.
[34] In *Matter of Lupoff*, N.Y.L.J. Oct. 30, 1964, p. 20, an executor was surcharged for failure to withhold a share of the tax in paying a legacy, where the legatee failed to remit his apportioned share after fixation thereof.
[35] Collection from devisee, infra § 15.10.

make a voluntary contribution or deposit, his remedy is only that of legal action against the recipient.[36] Since it is the duty of the executor to collect apportioned shares of tax if possible, he must pursue his legal remedies, unless it is demonstrable that they would be futile, and for a failure to do so he may be held liable to the residuary beneficiaries of the estate, on the same principles as for any other failure to collect assets of the estate. It is to be in mind in this connection that special problems may arise in respect of litigation against a recipient residing in another state, by reason of the general rule, elsewhere referred to,[37] that the standing and authority of an executor are usually not recognized outside the jurisdiction in which he was appointed,[38] so that he is incapable of suing in another state,[39] except where its statute permits him to do so. In some instances action may lie in a federal court, under the diversity rule or otherwise.[40]

§ 12.10-5b. ———; ———; *disposition of amounts recovered.* While statutes contemplating the collection by or return to the executor of apportioned amounts of estate tax after payment of the tax seldom if ever specify the disposition to be made of the amounts so recovered, it is apparent that such amounts should be treated as repayments of moneys advanced for account of the respective recipients of taxable property and so should be used to replace the moneys used for the payment of the tax. The result in the usual case is that the recovered amounts should be added to or treated as part of the residuary estate.[41]

§ 12.10-5c. ———; ———; *inability to recover.* If an executor after due diligence is unable to collect an apportioned share of an estate tax, such share is in effect paid out of the residuary estate, since the moneys initially used to pay the tax came from the general estate,[42] thus reducing the residue, and the inability to recoup them means that the residuary estate is not replenished.

§ 12.10-5d. ———; ———; *interest on apportioned share.* It has been held that, where non-testamentary property is included in the taxable estate, the holder of such property is liable to the residuary beneficiaries for interest on such holder's ultimately apportioned share of the tax, computed from the date of the tax pay-

---

[36] Unif. Prob. Code sec. 3-916(d) (1). See Shriver, op. cit. supra note 33, at 190–191.

[37] Supra § 1.7.

[38] Suits by foreign executor, in general, Currie, The Multiple Personality of the Dead: Executors, Administrators, and Conflict of Laws, 33 Univ. of Chicago L. R. 429. See also Restatement, Conflict of Laws 2d, secs. 354, 355; Ehrenzweig, Conflict of Laws, secs. 14, 15; Leflar, American Conflicts Law (1968 rev.) sec. 204. Generally, see West Dig., Exrs. & Admrs. Key No. 120 ff.

[39] In a growing number of jurisdictions, statutes have been enacted permitting "foreign" executors to sue, either generally or for particular purposes. So in Unif. Prob. Code sec. 3-916(h).

[40] It may be considered whether I.R.C. secs. 2206 and 2207 (supra § 12.10-1 note 4) confer jurisdiction on the federal courts to enforce contribution by life insurance beneficiaries and recipients of appointed property, so far as concerns the Federal estate tax.

[41] Infra § 18.3-4.

[42] Supra § 12.4-2.

ment;[43] this on the theory that, in effect, the residuary advanced the money for payment of such share of tax[44] and should be reimbursed for the loss of income resulting during the period the advance remained unpaid. While the decision is logical, such liability for interest is ordinarily not imposed.

§ 12.10-6. ———; *insufficiency of residue.* Where a statute provides for the apportionment of an estate tax unless the will otherwise directs, and the will directs its payment out of the residuary estate, without apportionment, but the residue is insufficient to enable payment of the whole amount of the tax, or there is no residue, the balance of tax not paid out of the residue is apportionable among the recipients of property includible in the taxable estate, including non-testamentary property, in the same manner as if such balance constituted the entire tax and there were no direction in the will as to apportionment; this is, of course, on the theory that an ineffective direction against apportionment is equivalent to no direction at all and leaves the statute in force. Where, instead, the statute provides for payment of an estate tax out of the residuary estate unless the will otherwise directs, and the will contains no contrary direction, any balance of tax remaining after exhaustion of the residue causes an abatement of other legacies and devises in accordance with the usual rules relating to insolvent or insufficient estates,[45] unless the statute provides for apportionment of such a balance, in which case, as in the one first mentioned, non-testamentary property may be required to contribute. In determining whether the residue is sufficient or insufficient in this connection, and, if insufficient, the method of apportionment or abatement, it seems clear that property not forming a part of the residuary estate, but disposed of by or pursuant to the terms of the residuary clause,[46] such as insurance payable to a testamentary trustee of the residue,[47] or property appointed to the residuary legatees or trustee,[48] is not to be treated as a part of the residue, so that its liability, if any, for payment of or contribution toward the payment of the tax is the same as if it were payable, or appointed, as the case may be, to any other third person.

§ 12.11. *Waivers and consents to transfer.* The transfer, whether by sale or otherwise, of personal property that belonged to a decedent, by the executor or any other person having possession of it, is often prohibited by state estate and inheritance tax laws until a notice of the proposed transfer has been given to the taxing

---

[43] *Est. of Forsheim*, 235 N.Y.S.2d 945. It will be noted that this holding implies (i) that it is the duty of the taker or holder of included property to contribute his share of the tax at the date of the payment thereof and (ii) accordingly that where (as in the cited case) such holder is a trustee, he has power to make such a contribution without waiting for an adjudication of his apportioned share and the equivalent of a judgment against him therefor. Neither of these two points appears to have been squarely decided in a reported case, however. Cf. supra § 12.4-4 note 47.

[44] General estate as initial source of payment, supra § 12.4-2.

[45] Abatement in insolvent or insufficient estate, infra § 19.5-1 ff.

[46] Generally, infra § 18.3-1.

[47] Infra § 18.3-7.

[48] Infra § 18.3-8.

authorities and they have thus been offered an opportunity to examine or evaluate it and to collect the tax out of it, or, alternatively, until a waiver of such notice or a consent to transfer has been issued by such authorities. Both waivers and such consents are often called "tax waivers". In some states the waiver or consent can in some or most cases be obtained only after the tax return has been filed and the tax, if any, paid; in other states, it may be obtained without prior return and payment, at least in the estate of a resident. The requirement of notice or consent, where it exists, applies to transfers or deliveries of taxable property to the executor by third persons, as well as to transfers or deliveries by the executor. Thus, without such a waiver or consent, a bank may not permit withdrawal by the executor of funds from an account in the name of the decedent (except, under some statutes, where the account does not exceed a specified amount) or permit opening of the decedent's safe deposit box[49] or removal of its contents, a person holding property belonging to the decedent may not deliver or release it to the executor, and transfer agent may not effect a transfer of securities out of the decedent's name; and, as has noted elsewhere, it is the duty of the executor to obtain and furnish required waivers or consents[50] in collecting any property of the decedent. It may thus be necessary, for example, for the executor first to furnish a bank with a waiver covering all items contained in a safe deposit box, in order to obtain a release to him of the contents, and, later, to furnish a transfer agent with a waiver covering a particular security included among such contents, in order to obtain a transfer of the security into the name of the executor or that of a legatee, distributee, or purchaser; where, as in such case, two waivers covering the same property are obtained, the executor in applying for the second should make it plain that it is a duplication, so that he will not later be called upon, when waiver applications are checked against a tax return, to account for (apparently) two items of the security or other property in question. The necessity in most cases of obtaining consents or waivers, and the possibility of delay in obtaining them, are among the reasons making it advisable for the executor to cause registered securities to be transferred into the name of a nominee, where that is permissible, at an early stage of the administration.[51]

---

[49] Opening box to ascertain contents, supra § 6.4.
[50] Generally, supra § 6.24.
[51] Supra § 7.3-5.

XIII

OPTIONS AND ELECTIONS

§ 13.1. In general.[1] There are usually various options and elections available to to an executor in his fiduciary capacity, which are often grouped under the designation "post mortem planning".[2] Some of such options or elections relate directly to taxes and others relate to administrative matters. Each of them, however, necessarily has substantive effects, in that its exercise or non-exercise affects the quantum of benefits to a person or persons interested in the estate; and, as in the case of any other power or discretion possessed by a fiduciary, the availability of an election connotes a duty to exercise it when so to do is in the best interest of the estate.[3] It is to be borne in mind in this regard that an omission to elect an optional course of action is as much an "election" as would be an affirmative election of such course of action, inasmuch as the omission itself constitutes the making of a choice between alternatives. The executor's duty of impartiality as among beneficiaries[4] applies especially where options or elections are concerned, and the executor must take care to avoid any appearance of favoring one beneficiary over another.

§ 13.2. Estate tax optional valuation date. Where, as in the case of the Federal estate tax, a statutory provision[5] permits the executor to elect to value assets of the taxable estate as of a date other than the date of the decedent's death,[6] the exercise or non-exercise of such election may have very substantial effects upon the amount

---

[1] Elections of surviving spouse or children, infra §§ 17.4-1 ff., 17.7.

[2] For a concise listing and discussion of such options and elections, see Dalton, Exercise of Elections by Personal Representatives, 43 The Trust Bulletin 53. A more extended treatment, with emphasis on income tax elections, may be found in Price, Postmortem Estate Planning Up to Date, 20 N.Y.U. Inst. on Fed. Taxation 301. See also Barnett, Tax-Saving Elections Available to Executor, 17 Jour. of Taxation 93; Peschel, Postdeath Marital Deduction Planning, 56 A.B.A.J. 398; and Lewis, Tax Elections by Executors and Trustees, N.Y.L.J. Feb. 11, 1965, p. 1 (which, while revolving around New York law, has matter of more general applicability).

[3] Generally, supra § 3.2.2.

[4] Supra § 3.9-3.

[5] I.R.C. sec. 2032.

[6] Generally, see Price, op. cit. supra note 2, at 322–323.

of estate tax payable by the estate, and incidental effects upon beneficiaries in other respects. Thus, the valuation of an asset established for Federal estate tax purposes becomes, for Federal income tax purposes, the cost basis of the asset for the computation of computing capital gains and losses realized by the estate or, in certain cases, by a legatee to whom the property is distributed;[7] and the difference between aggregate valuations as of the date of the decedent's death and the "optional" date causes a change equal to half such difference in the amount of the maximum allowable marital deduction. Such incidental effects, as well as the direct effect upon the amount of the estate tax, must be considered by the executor, in the light of the facts and circumstances of the particular case, in determining whether to elect the optional valuation; and as to such direct effects upon estate tax the executor must not overlook the fact that his election as to valuation date applies to the taxable estate as a whole, which is to say, to non-testamentary property includible in the gross taxable estate as well as to the testamentary assets, and that values of some of the non-testamentary assets may have changed, since the decedent's death, in a direction opposite to that in which the values of testamentary assets have changed. The executor must also consider whether it is his duty to elect the valuation method which will produce the *higher* valuation of the estate, where the will bequeaths an amount equal to the "maximum" allowable marital deduction,[8] since the allowable deduction will be smaller if the lower valuation is used.[9] The election as to the optional valuation is made by filing a return claiming or failing to claim it,[10] and, as in case of other options and elections,[11] a failure to elect is a choice of valuations no less than would be an election.

§ *13.3. Claiming deductions for estate tax or income tax purposes.*[12] Where certain deductions allowable for estate tax purposes are permitted by statute to be claimed instead for income tax purposes,[13] the result of an election to claim such deductions for income tax purposes has the effect of increasing the net taxable estate for estate tax purposes and hence the estate tax, with the result that less property will remain to pass as principal of the estate, and of decreasing the net taxable income and hence the income tax, with the result that more property will be available

---

[7] I.R.C. sec. 1014.

[8] Marital deduction "formula" legacies, supra § 14.8-2. Cf. next following section as to corresponding duty as to claiming deductions for income tax rather than estate tax purposes.

[9] While it may perhaps be unlikely that such a literal construction would be given to a bequest in that form, the possibility must be considered, and unless there is clear authority to the contrary in the applicable jurisdiction the executor may deem it advisable to seek a judicial determination of the point, or to consider whether under local law a consent by the spouse to the use of the lower valuation method will protect him in so doing, i.e., will be binding upon appointees (if any) or, in absence of appointment, upon takers in default.

[10] I.R.C. sec. 2032(c).

[11] See last preceding section.

[12] Cf. Lewis, Estate Administration Expenses—Shall They be Taken as Income or Estate Tax Deductions?, 40 Taxes 851; Price, op. cit. supra § 13.1 note 2, at 317 ff.

[13] Generally, I.R.C. sec. 642(g); election to take medical expenses as income tax instead of estate tax deductions, ibid. sec. 213(d)(2).

OPTIONS AND ELECTIONS   141

to pass as income.[14] Conversely, a failure to exercise the election (which failure is, as pointed out above,[15] itself a choice between alternatives) results in more property passing as principal and less as income. The question as to which treatment of the deductions in question should be used ordinarily arises with special force (although not exclusively[16]) where the executor needs to distinguish between principal and income,[17] but if such is the case the executor must be conscious of the risk that in making his decision he may violate his fiduciary duty of impartiality as between income beneficiary and remainderman.[18] In some states the risk is obviated by a rule requiring in substance that, where the election has been made to claim such deductions for income tax purposes, there must (unless the will otherwise provides) be transferred from income account to principal account an amount equal to the "additional" estate taxes resulting from such treatment;[19] and where such a rule exists the decision is ordinarily to be based upon relative tax brackets. If under the law governing the estate the executor is not permitted to make such equitable adjustment, he probably cannot justify an election to claim the deductions for income tax purposes, under the rule of impartiality just mentioned, unless the persons interested in principal consent[20] or the will expressly authorizes such treatment. An executor confronted with a bequest of an amount equal to the "maximum" allowable marital deduction[21] must consider whether he is thereby required to claim deductions (as to which he has an option) for income tax purposes rather than for estate tax purposes, as thereby the adjusted gross estate, and hence the allowable marital deduction, are increased.[22]

§ 13.4. *Increment on United States Savings Bonds.* Where the decedent was the owner at his death of United States Savings Bonds of a type on which increment in lieu of interest accrues, and during his lifetime had elected not to report such increment as current income, the executor has the option of continuing that treatment or of reporting, in the decedent's final return or in any return of the estate, the total of all accruals to date.[23] The latter, of course, makes such total taxable in a single year, and may be disadvantageous accordingly. If, however, the other taxable income reportable in the decedent's final return, or that reportable in a return of the estate for the year of death or a later year, is relatively small, or offsetting deductions are

---

[14] But cf. *Republic Natl. Bank of Dallas*, 39 T.C. 85, as to illusory tax saving (value of charitable remainder of residuary trust is reduced by administration expenses paid, notwithstanding that they are claimed as income tax rather than estate tax deductions). Principal and income in general, infra Ch. XVI.
[15] Supra § 13.1.
[16] See the last sentence of this section.
[17] Necessity of distinguishment, infra § 16.2.
[18] Generally, supra § 3.9-3.
[19] Cf. *Matter of Warms*, 140 N.Y.S.2d 169.
[20] Agreements and consent of beneficiaries, in general, infra Ch. XXI.
[21] Marital deduction "formula" bequests, infra § 14.8-2.
[22] So held in *Matter of Kennedy*, 39 Misc.2d 688, 241 N.Y.S.2d 894. See last preceding section as to possible duty under such bequest to use higher of date-of-death and optional valuations.
[23] I.R.C. sec. 454(a).

available, the aggregation of the accruals and payment of a tax thereon may result in tax economy to the estate or a beneficiary as compared with the taxability otherwise of the entire increment on top of other income at the time of the maturity of the bonds. In this connection, of course, as in the case of all other options and elections, the executor must be conscious of his duty of impartiality among beneficiaries[24] and may not make an election as to such increment that will benefit one beneficiary at the expense of another or others.

§ *13.5. Administrative elections affecting income taxation.* The executor should have in mind that his elections or decisions as to some administrative matters, particularly the selection of the fiscal year of the estate[25] and the timing of distributions, may have a substantial effect on the amounts of income taxable to the estate and the amounts taxable to the beneficiaries[26] and so upon the aggregate amount of taxes thereon. Inasmuch as a distribution of property, even of tangibles, to a beneficiary other than a specific legatee or an outright legatee of cash is treated for the purposes of at least the Federal income tax as constituting a distribution of the estate's income (up to the value of the property distributed) for the full tax year in which the distribution is made,[27] the executor may be able substantially to reduce the ultimate tax burden on estate and beneficiary by proper timing of the setting up of trusts[28] or of a partial or final distribution of residuary assets.[29] Similar income tax effects may ensue from the timing of an executor's payment of administration expenses.[30] Because of both kinds of considerations an executor who has a choice of closing the estate before the end of a given tax year or after the beginning of the next following

---

[24] Supra § 3.9-3.

[25] Since the estate is a new taxpayer, it can select its fiscal period; and its first and last periods may be less than a year. So the executor can control the number of months in the first and final returns of the estate, and, to a degree, the amount of income shown in those returns as distributed or retained, and so can control to like degree the amounts of income for such periods taxable to the estate. Also, in view of the fact that a beneficiary is taxable on income distributed to him in his tax year in which the estate's fiscal year ends, the executor by suitably "straddling" the calendar year can postpone the time of taxation of income to the beneficiary until the year after its realization, and the time of payment of the beneficiary's tax until the year after that.

Again, where a substantial amount of non-recurring income is received shortly after death, the executor by choosing a "short" initial fiscal period may cause such amount to be taxed in the bottom brackets, where if the short initial period were not chosen the non-recurring amount and the bulk of the year's investment income would be aggregated for tax purposes.

Obviously, it is usually necessary to make a series of alternative and laborious projections to determine what fiscal period should be selected for best advantage. Generally, see 1965 Proc. A.B.A. Sec. of Real Prop. Prob. & Tr. L., Part I. 183; Price, Postmortem Estate Planning Up to Date, 20 N.Y.U. Inst. on Fed. Taxation 301, 311 ff.

[26] Supra § 10.6.

[27] I.R.C. sec. 663(a).

[28] Infra § 14.31-4.

[29] Distribution of residuary, infra § 18.6-1 ff. Tax timing in distribution, see 1964 Proc. A.B.A. Sec. Real Prop. Prob. & Tr. L., Part I, 51–52, and 1965 Proc. ibid., Part I, 183; Price, op. cit. supra note 25, at 314. Excess ("unused") deductions in last year of estate's administration as available to beneficiaries, I.R.C. sec. 642(h).

[30] Attorney's fee as chief example, 1964 Proc., supra note 29, at 47–48; see also infra § 20.3-4.

OPTIONS AND ELECTIONS 143

year should compare the relative advantages to the beneficiaries and govern his actions accordingly.[31]

§ 13.6. Other fiduciary elections. As other places in this work there have been discussed the factors to be taken into account by an executor in determining whether to exercise certain fiduciary elections other than those referred to in the last preceding sections, including the selection of the items of property to be liquidated for cash requirements,[32] the redemption of corporate stock in lieu of a sale thereof,[33] the filing of a joint income tax return with the surviving spouse for the year of the decedent's death,[34] the making of a request for prompt audit of the decedent's income tax returns,[35] the advance payment of estate or inheritance taxes in order to obtain a discount or prevent an addition to the tax,[36] and the postponement of payment of such a tax.[37] A less frequent problem, but one of importance where it is presented, is that of the taxation of a small business corporation shares of which come into the hands of the executor and which has elected to be taxed as a partnership for Federal income tax purposes;[38] unless the executor promptly files a consent to such treatment,[39] the corporation ceases to be so taxed, and in deciding whether to consent or not the executor must consider not only the effect upon the estate but also the effect upon other stockholders, and further must consider, if the will creates a trust to which the shares are to be distributed, the time when the election, if still in force, will terminate by establishment of the trust, since a corporation of which a trust is a shareholder is not eligible to make or continue such election.[40]

§ 13.7. Non-fiduciary elections. Apart from the elections available to an executor in his fiduciary capacity,[41] he may have certain non-fiduciary elections, as, for example, an election to waive compensation for his service,[42] or to renounce a special compensation provision[43] or a bequest made in lieu of compensation[44] and claim the compensation allowable by law. While such elections, like those of a fiduciary nature,

---

[31] Undue prolongation of administration, infra § 18.13.
[32] Supra § 7.6-1.
[33] Supra § 7.6-1a. Generally, see Levenfeld, Postdeath Planning Under Section 303, 51 A.B.A.J. 495. The executor holding stock of a closely-held corporation may consider whether he should not redeem the shares pursuant to I.R.C. sec. 303 (where that is possible as a matter of corporate law) as a means of getting money out of the corporation without adverse tax consequences, even though cash may be available in the estate for payment of the taxes and expenses referred to in the section cited.
[34] Supra § 10.2-2.
[35] Supra § 10.7-1.
[36] Supra § 12.5.
[37] Supra § 12.6.
[38] I.R.C. sec. 1372. A corporation so electing is commonly referred to as a Subchapter S corporation.
[39] I.R.C. sec. 1371.
[40] Ibid.
[41] Supra this chapter, passim.
[42] Infra § 20.4-2d.
[43] Infra §§ 20.4-2a, -2b.
[44] Infra § 20.4-2c.

discussed above, may have substantive effects upon the amounts of property passing to beneficiaries, they are personal to the executor and are not governed by the rules applicable to fiduciary elections, so that in deciding whether to exercise them, the executor is not required to consider the best interests of the estate but may make his decision on the basis of personal considerations alone.

XIV

SATISFACTION OF LEGACIES

Part A—General Principles

§ 14.1-1. Classification of legacies;[1] in general. Legacies are commonly classified into four categories, and in the following order: (a) specific legacies,[2] (b) demonstrative legacies,[3] (c) general legacies,[4] and (d) residuary legacies.[5] Such classification has its chief importance where an estate is insufficient to satisfy in full all legacies bequeathed by the will.[6] The classification, with particular reference to the distinction between specific legacies and others, is also important in the computation of executors' commissions in those jurisdictions in which specifically-bequeathed property is to be excluded in fixing commissions.[7]

§ 14.1-2. ———; legacies in trust; conditional and deferred legacies. The classification of legacies as in the preceding section, and its consequences in the respects mentioned, as well as in most other respects discussed in this chapter, are unaffected by such considerations as whether the bequest is outright or in trust,[8] whether it is absolute or subject to a condition precedent or subsequent,[9] and whether it is payable at once or is deferred for future payment or payable over a period of time.[10]

§ 14.2. Abatement, ademption, lapse.[11] An otherwise valid and effective legacy may fail to take effect for any of three reasons: abatement, ademption, or lapse.

---

[1] Legacies generally, West Dig., Exrs. & Admrs. Key Nos. 298–318; P-H Est. Plng. Serv. ¶ 367. This chapter, as indicated by its title, deals solely with bequests of personal property; as to real property and devises thereof, sec. Ch. XV infra.

[2] Infra § 14.4-1 ff.

[3] Infra § 14.5-1 ff.

[4] Infra §§ 14.6-1, -2.

[5] Infra § 14.7; generally, infra Ch. XXII.

[6] Insolvent and insufficient estates generally, infra Ch. XIX.

[7] Infra § 20.4-5.

[8] Legacies in trust, and pour-over to existing trust, infra Ch. XXVII; cf. constructive trusts, infra Ch. XXVI.

[9] Infra §§ 14.10, 14.11.

[10] Infra § 14.12-1, -2.

[11] P-H Est. Plng. Serv. ¶¶ 428–431. As to devises, infra §§ 15.4, 15.5-1, 15.7.

Abatement refers to the case of insufficiency of assets to satisfy a particular legacy. Where, under principles elsewhere discussed,[12] there are no assets that can be used to satisfy the legacy,[13] or the assets available for application upon it are insufficient to satisfy it in full, the legacy "abates", either entirely or pro tanto, as the case may be. The principle applies not only in the case of an "insolvent" estate[14] but also in the case, for example, of a spouse entitled or electing to take a statutory share of the estate against the will,[15] or a child entitled to an intestate share,[16] or the somewhat similar case of a share by forced heirship;[17] it is apparent that such share can be made up only by reducing the shares of some or all legatees named in the will, and their shares accordingly abate to the extent necessary for that purpose.

Ademption is a term ordinarily applicable only to a specific legacy; in general,[18] such a legacy "adeems", and fails to be effective, if its subject matter is not in existence, or not owned by the testator, at the time of his death, either because it has been lost or destroyed, or because he has disposed of it, during his lifetime. The term is also used, however, in certain cases of lifetime gifts to a legatee, which are said to "adeem by satisfaction".[19]

Lapse[20] designates the failure of a legacy to be effective because the designated legatee is not in existence, either through non-survival[21] or otherwise,[22] or is unwilling to take the legacy,[23] or is as a matter of law unable to take it,[24] and no alternative taker (other than perhaps residuary legatees) is designated.[25] It may be said that a legacy lapses when it fails to be effective for any reason other than abatement or ademption,[26] and accordingly a legacy is also said to lapse when it cannot be given effect because it violates some rule of law or public policy.[27]

While each of the three concepts involves the failure of a legacy to be effective according to the will, either wholly or in part, the distinctions among them are of some importance in describing the event or situation that causes the failure and also because of a difference, in some instances, in the consequences of the failure.[28] It will be observed that "abatement" and "ademption" pertain to a failure having to do with

---

[12] Infra § 19.2 ff.
[13] Failure of "excessive" or otherwise voidable gift to charity as abatement, infra § 17.7.
[14] Defined, infra § 19.1.
[15] Infra § 17.4-5.
[16] Infra § 17.6-4.
[17] Infra § 17.8.
[18] Infra § 14.4-4 ff.
[19] Ademption by satisfaction, infra § 14.6-3; "advancement" distinguished, infra § 14.30.
[20] Lapse, in general, infra § 14.23-1.
[21] Survival, in general, infra § 14.22-1.
[22] *Cy pres* where charitable organization no longer exists, infra § 14.14-2.
[23] Renunciation, infra § 14.36-1.
[24] Infra § 14.18-1 ff.
[25] Anti-lapse statutes, infra § 14.23-2.
[26] Election by surviving spouse as causing lapse of will provision for her, infra § 17.4-5.
[27] Infra § 14.23-1.
[28] Infra this chapter, passim.

SATISFACTION OF LEGACIES

the asset bequeathed and "lapse" pertains to a failure having to do with the legatee or with the aim or terms of the legacy.

§ 14.3. *When title to legacy vests.* Although in most or all jurisdictions, as elsewhere mentioned, title to real property belonging to a decedent vests in the devisee or heir immediately upon the death of the owner,[29] it is the rule, except where changed by statute,[30] that ownership of or title to personal property, even that which is specifically bequeathed, does not vest in the legatee until the property is paid or distributed to him (or otherwise put into his possession or control) by the executor.[31] In the case of a specific bequest, however, upon the receipt of the property by the legatee his title relates back to the date of the testator's death, at least in the sense that he is entitled to the income (if any) from the property from and after that date[32] and is entitled to proceeds of insurance on the property if it is lost, damaged, or destroyed after the testator's death.[33]

§ 14.4-1. *Specific legacies;*[34] *definition.* A specific legacy is a legacy of specified personal property other than money, or of a specified class or category of such property.[35] The term is not limited to a legacy of tangibles; a legacy of a bank account is specific,[36] and securities and other intangibles[37] may be the subject of a specific legacy. In the case of securities, however, the executor should be cautious in assuming that a bequest is specific merely because it refers to those of a specified corporation or issuer; at least in the case of securities readily obtainable in the open market, the tendency appears to be to regard the bequest as general[38] unless the testator has

---

[29] Supra § 7.5-1.

[30] Under Unif. Prob. Code sec. 3-11, all property "devolves" at death of testator, subject to administration; cf. Code sec. 3-709, providing that executor has right to and shall take possession and control of all property. The Comments to the two sections state the intention to be to obviate any question of an executor's title by giving him a "power" which makes it unnecessary to consider his "title."

[31] Time of satisfaction of legacies, infra § 14.31-1 ff.

[32] Infra § 14.4-3.

[33] Infra § 14.4-4c.

[34] West Dig., Wills Key Nos. 752–754.

[35] The term "specific legacy" is sometimes misused to refer to a cash legacy of specified amount, in controdistinction to a legacy of a share of a fund or of the residuary estate. Correctly, such a cash legacy is termed a general legacy (infra § 14.6-1) inasmuch as it is payable out of the general assets of the estate. At least where the classification of legacies is important, as in applying rules of abatement, ademption, etc., the distinction of general legacies from both specific and demonstrative legacies should be observed.

[36] *Matter of Rubenstein*, 169 Misc. 273, N.Y.S.2d 311. So also of a legacy of a share of a particular bank account; *ibid*. And so of a legacy charged on an account where the intention appears to burden only that fund with its payment; *Matter of Strasenburgh*, 136 Misc. 91, 242 N.Y.S.2d 453. An example of a specific bequest of a bank account is where the testator was a sole proprietor and bequeathes the business or the assets of the business, including the business bank account. Demonstrative legacy distinguished, infra § 14.5-2.

[37] For example, where the decedent was in business as a sole proprietor, a bequest of "the business" would seem to be a specific bequest of its receivables, good will, etc., as well as of its inventory, equipment, and other tangibles.

[38] Bequest of securities as specific or general, infra § 14.6-2. Question as affecting ademption, infra § 14.4-4a.

evinced an explicit intention to make it specific, as for example by referring to "my" stock, bonds, or the like. Under some statutes, as is mentioned at a later place, specific bequests do not enter into the base for computing the executor's compensation,[39] and specific bequests have a higher priority in payment than general legacies in insolvent or insufficient estates,[40] so that the question whether a legacy is specific or general may have importance in those connections as well as in determining the the right to the income, if any, from the subject property.[41]

§ 14.4-2. ———; *identification of property bequeathed.* The difficulty that most frequently arises in connection with a specific legacy is the identification of the property that is the intended subject-matter of the bequest, because of an inadequate, ambiguous, or otherwise unclear description thereof in the will,[42] and hence the risk that the executor may be charged with having failed properly to satisfy the bequest or with having delivered property to one legatee that passed to another under a different provision of the will. Not to be overlooked is the risk that the intended item was no longer in existence or owned by the testator at his death, with the result that the legacy is adeemed, even though there was owned at death another item which would fit the description in the will.[43] Questions as to whether extrinsic evidence is admissible to resolve or obviate any questions as to the particular property covered by or passing under a bequest are beyond the scope of this work, but must be taken into consideration by the executor in deciding or obtaining a determination of the effect of the bequest.

§ 14.4-2a. ———; ———; *description by provenance or location.*[44] A bequest of an item of personal property, usually a tangible, identified only as that formerly belonging to a named ancestor or other person, or as having been acquired by the testator from a designated person or at some specified time or in some particular manner, or as being kept in a specified place, may present serious problems to the executor. The author of a bequest of, for example, "Aunt Mary's ring", or of "the (pearl) ring kept in my jewel box",[45] presumably had no question as to what was meant, but the executor may have considerable difficulty in ascertaining, with full assurance, which (if any) of two or more rings owned by the decedent passes under the bequest, and submission of the problem to a court may be necessary to resolve doubts. Unless, therefore, all persons who might claim to be legatees of the property in question are *sui juris* and can agree as to the matter,[46] the executor may find a

---

[39] Infra § 20.4-5.
[40] Infra § 19.5-6.
[41] Infra § 14.4-3.
[42] So seemingly simple a bequest as one of "books" raised a question in an author's estate as to its inclusion of his manuscripts, notebooks, and papers; these were held not to pass under the bequest, except a manuscript bound as a book and kept with books. *Est. of Wright*, 177 N.Y.S.2d 410, 421. Identification of subject matter of legacy in particular cases, see following sections.
[43] Infra § 14.4-4.
[44] West Dig., Wills Key No. 573; P-H Est. Plng. Serv. ¶ 381.
[45] Bequest of contents of box, etc., see next following section.
[46] Agreements with or among beneficiaries, infra Ch. XXI.

SATISFACTION OF LEGACIES 149

judicial proceeding to be the only solution, especially as ordinarily there is no reason why the executor, not otherwise interested in the actual or potential controversy, should assume risk of individual liability to a dissatisfied beneficiary.

§ 14.4-2aa. ———; ———; ———; *contents of box, room, etc.* Bequests of property described only as the contents of, or as that contained in, a safe deposit box, a cabinet or chest, a room, or other "container", are ordinarily given effect; and this notwithstanding the somewhat doubtful logical basis for so doing in view of the general principle that dispositions at death may be made only with prescribed formalities and of the fact that the testator by adding or removing articles from the designated place may change the property that passes under the bequest and indeed the persons who receive the articles so added or removed.[47] Where, however, the designated keeping place is adapted or used for property of a particular kind of character and there is found in it at death an item of entirely different nature, the question whether such article passes under the bequest of "contents" would seem to depend upon intention as deduced from the will and from any admissible evidence as to the circumstances under which or the reasons for which the article was placed where it is found.[48]

§ 14.4-2b. ———; ———; *description by nature: "jewelry", "personal effects", "household effects".* A bequest of "jewelry" may at the least raise a question as to whether the legatee thereof takes costume jewelry and similar articles of personal adornment as well as items of precious metals and gem stones; and in addition it may give rise to controversy between the legatee of jewelry and a legatee of "personal effects" (or between the former and a residuary legatee if personal effects are not specifically bequeathed) as to whether particular articles fall into the one category or the other.[49] Somewhat similarly, questions as to what is included in the term "personal effects" as such may arise,[50] and a bequest of "personal effects" to one legatee or class of legatees and of "household effects" to another may well cause difficulty in determining under which bequest a particular article passes.[51] As in the case of the problem referred to in the last preceding section, the executor may find it necessary

---

[47] Possibly the rule may be justified by application of the doctrine of "facts of independent significance," i.e., acts or circumstances which have significance apart from their effect upon dispositions made by the will; cf. § 18.5 infra.

[48] In an unreported case, where the bequest was of the contents of a china cabinet, which consisted entirely of china except for a bond also found in the cabinet, the bond was held not to pass with the china. Possible distinction between "small" and "large" containers, see *Lamb Est.*, 21 Fiduc. Rep. (Pa.) 412.

[49] *Est. of Bernstein*, N.Y.L.J. Apr. 5, 1966, holding that a bequest of personal effects did not include jewelry that had not been purchased by the testator for his own use and had not been used by him to adorn his person.

[50] "The test in each case must be whether the articles are used in or by the household or for the benefit and comfort of the family" or instead were for the personal use of the testator. *Est. of Wright*, 177 N.Y.S.2d 410, 421.

[51] In the case last cited, the court was required to decide whether a gold fountain pen passed to the taker of personal effects or the taker of jewelry, and whether a pair of binoculars passed to the taker of personal effects or the taker of household effects.

to submit the matter for judicial determination, unless all persons having possible rights in the property can and do agree among themselves.[52]

§ 14.4-2bb. ———; ———; ———; *coin or stamp collections, works of art, etc.* Where the testator was at his death the owner of a collection of coins, stamps,[53] or other items, or of paintings, prints, or other works of art, and his will does not contain a specific bequest of such property *eo nomine*, the executor must carefully consider where the property does or does not pass under a bequest of "personal effects" or "household effects". In at least some jurisdictions, such collections, art objects, and the like are held not to be embraced within either of the last quoted terms, and therefore not to pass under such a bequest. Apart from that consideration, it may often be difficult to determine whether a particular item or group of items constitutes a "collection" within the meaning of the rule or is to be treated merely as an aggregation of individual items. Similarly, it is often difficult to determine whether a particular item should be regarded as a part of personal or household effects, as the case may be, or instead should be regarded as a work of art; for example, a silver pot might be either a household effect or a work of art, depending partly on value and perhaps partly on how it was used, kept, or regarded by the testator, and an article of personal adornment might be a personal effect or a work of art, in the light of similar considerations. There may also be noted the difficulty that may exist in determining the identity of a particular painting or other work of art referred to in a bequest, where the description in the will is not clear and accurate,[54] if the testator owned more than one such work, and also the possible risk that the object referred to in the will was no longer owned or no longer existed at the testator's death and the bequest was therefor adeemed.[55]

§ 14.4-2c. ———; ———; *bequest of "all tangibles"*. A bequest of "all tangible personal property", or a like inclusive bequest of tangibles, may have unintended results. For example, under some decisions bonds, notes, and other obligations, being themselves property, and tangible in character (as distinguished from stock certificates or the like, which are merely evidences of property which itself is intangible), are to be deemed to be tangible property. Again, where a testator owning the stock of a business or manufacturing corporation, and executing a will bequeathing such stock to someone other than the legatee of tangibles, afterward dissolves the corporation and, having received its inventory, equipment, machinery, and the like in a liquidating distribution, conducts the business as a proprietorship at the time of his death, a bequest of tangibles, if literally applied, would cause such property to pass thereunder, even though the property may be the chief value of his estate and did not exist as owned tangibles when the will was made. In cases of such serious doubt as to true intention, the executor will not want to make any distribution of the assets in

---

[52] Agreements with or among beneficiaries, infra Ch. XXI.

[53] For an information discussion of problems relating to stamp collections in estates, see Fox, Stamps in an Estate, 105 Trusts and Estates 1057.

[54] Generally, supra § 14.4-2.

[55] Infra § 14.4-4.

question, either to the legatee of tangibles or to anyone else, without first resolving the question in a judicial proceeding[56] or by agreement among all persons interested in the result.[57]

§ 14.4-2d. ———; ———; *bequest of "all personal property".* The executor must be wary of possible entrapment under a will containing a bequest of "all personal property" belonging to the testator at the time of his death. It may be that by such provision the testator meant personal effects only, or tangible personal property only, but the quoted words (or words of like inclusiveness) of course extend to and cover intangibles as well as tangibles, and everything the testator owned that is subject to bequest[58] except real property. The executor thus is not justified in assuming, or in taking the burden of deciding, the meaning or scope of the bequest, and making distribution in accordance with his own decision, as a different construction may later be urged by a person who would benefit therefrom. In any case of such a provision, as of that referred to in the preceding section, the executor should obtain a judicial construction of the provision in question, considered, of course, in conjunction with other relevant provisions of the will, unless the problem can effectively be solved by agreement among all persons having any possible interest in the result. It may be noted at this point, as a separate phase of the matter herein discussed, that in most if not all jurisdictions the considerations elsewhere discussed in connection with a devise of real property[59] do not apply in the case of a bequest of "all" the testator's personal property, or of "all" his personalty of a particular kind or nature, and such a bequest of either kind passes personal property acquired after the date of the will as well as that owned at such date.

§ 14.4-2e. ———; ———; *corporate stock after capital changes.* Except where the question is settled by statute,[60] difficult questions may arise as to the effect of a bequest of a specified number of shares of stock of a particular corporation[61] where, after the execution of the will but before the death of the testator,[62] stock dividends were issued, the stock was split (or a "reverse split", changing two or more old shares

---

[56] Construction proceedings, infra Ch. XXII.

[57] Agreements with or among beneficiaries, infra Ch. XXI.

[58] "Exempt" property, supra § 7.2-2, infra §§ 17.1, 18.3-2. Narcotic drugs, supra § 6.20.3. A copyright, being renewable after the author's death only by specified persons (spouse or children, if any, otherwise executor or intestate distributees; 17 U.S.C.A. set. 24), is in that sense at least not the subject of a bequest. Cf. matter of cemetery lot under general devise of real estate, infra § 15.8.

[59] Infra § 15.2-2.

[60] As to specific bequests, cf. Unif. Prob. Code sec. 2-607.

[61] As specific or general bequest, supra § 14.4-1; so far as concerns ademption, infra § 14.4-4a.

[62] A stock dividend, split, or other change after death is to be distinguished. This, in *Est. of Reisinger*, N.Y.L.J. Aug. 26, 1966, p. 9, where a testator owning a large number of shares of A-B corporation made bequests of 300, 1,000, and 500 shares of A-B, then by codicil shortly before his death increased the bequests to 500, 2,000, and 1,000 respectively, and shortly after his death A-B split its stock 2-for-1, it was held that, "whether the legacies are to be considered general or specific," the legatees were entitled to double the numbers of (new) shares specified in the codicil, because of the split; and this notwithstanding that testator was a director of A-B and presumably knew of and had in mind the plans of A-B to effect the split when he made the codicil.

into one new share, was effected), the corporation merged with another, or some other change in its capital structure occured. As the author has elsewhere emphasized,[63] the problem is one that can and should be obviated by proper draftsmanship; but where that has not been done a court must endeavor to determine, not what the testator probably would have intended if the question had been submitted to him, but what intention can be gathered from the will itself. The answers to the question accordingly depend in the first instance on the provisions and scheme of the will, considered as a whole. It would seem, howevver, that, in the absence of statute or any indication of a contrary intention, (i) the number of shares passing under such a bequest should be unchanged by a stock dividend, notwithstanding that the dividend has "diluted" pre-existing shares; (ii) where a true stock split has been effected, however, (and it must be recognized that the line between a dividend and a split is often far from sharp) the shares resulting therefrom should stand in the place of those held immediately before the split and pass under the bequest; and (iii) the question whether shares of stock of a merged corporation pass under the bequest or the bequest adeems should depend largely on whether the character or purposes of the corporation whose stock was held at the time of execution of the will have been substantially changed by the merger. Under any of such circumstances, however, the executor proceeds at his peril in satisfying the bequest; usually (except in the case of a "reverse split") he may safely deliver the number of shares specified in the will, exclusive of any additional shares received as a dividend or in a split, but otherwise, or so far as concerns any greater number of shares in such a case or any shares at all in case of a merger or like change, he should ordinarily obtain a judicial determination of the meaning and effect of the bequest,[64] in connection with an accounting proceeding or otherwise, unless, of course, all persons affected in any way by the question are in existence and *sui juris* and agree as to the solution of the problem.[65]

§ *14.4-3.* ———; *income from date of death.*[66] Under the rule that title of a specific legatee to the subject matter of his legacy, when the property is delivered or released to him, relates back to the date of death of the testator,[67] a specific legatee of income-producing personalty is entitled to the net income from it after such date.[68] In applying this rule, however, particularly in the case of a bequest of corporate stock, the executor must first make sure that the bequest is specific.[69] Also, in the case of a cash dividend on corporate stock specifically bequeathed, a dividend pay-

---

[63] Tomlinson, Planning for Administration of Estates and Trusts, 13 Drake L.R. 113, 119.
[64] Construction proceedings, infra Ch. XXII.
[65] Agreements with or among beneficiaries, infra Ch. XXI.
[66] P-H Est. Plng. Serv. ¶ 434.
[67] Supra § 14.3.
[68] (1931) Unif. Prin. & Inc. Act sec. 3-A (3) (a); (1962) Rev. Unif. Prin. & Inc. Act sec. 5 (b). Rents from specifically devised realty as belonging to devisee, infra § 15.6. Abatement of legacy as abating income from it, infra § 19.7.
[69] Supra § 14.4-1; see also infra § 14.6-2.

SATISFACTION OF LEGACIES

153

able after death does not belong to the legatee where the record date, or date as of which the dividend is in contemplation of law set aside out of corporate funds and the right to receive it becomes fixed, was before the death of the testator.[70]

§ 14.4-4. ———; *ademption*.[71] As indicated above,[72] a specific legacy is ordinarily adeemed if the property constituting its intended subject-matter is not owned by the testator at the time of his death, either because such property was disposed of, or was lost or destroyed, during his lifetime; but the rule is subject to some qualifications, as noted in the following sections.[73] A possible trap for the executor exists under the rule of ademption where at the testator's death there is owned an object fulfilling the description contained in the will but not owned at the date of the execution of the will; in such a case, because the object owned at death is not the object covered by the bequest, ademption occurs.[74]

§ 14.4-4a. ———; ———; *open-market securities*. Where a testator bequeaths a specified number of shares of a particular stock, and at his death owns none of such shares, or only a lesser number thereof, the question arises of the effect to be given to the bequest.[75] The general rule of ademption,[76] under which the bequest would adeem, in whole or pro tanto as the case may be, is sometimes applied, and it would seem it should be applied if under applicable law and the terms of the will the bequest is deemed to be a specific one.[77] As above pointed out, however, where the subject stock is one readily obtainable in the open market, as where it is traded on a securities exchange, many cases treat the bequest as a general one, in the absence of any indication of contrary intention,[78] with the result that the executor must purchase the number of shares needed to satisfy the bequest and transfer them to the legatee, or pay the legatee an amount equal to their value. If at the time of executing his will the testator did not own the number of shares specified in the bequest, or did not own any shares of the stock, the case is probably even stronger for deciding that the legatee must be supplied with the shares or their equivalent in money.

---

[70] Cf. Comment to Unif. Prob. Code sec. 2-607 that that section, dealing with accession to specific legacies and omitting reference to dividends as of record date prior to death, is intended to codify existing law as stated in the text. Dividend in such case as principal of estate, not income, infra § 16.4-1; need for separate accounting, infra § 16.6-2.

[71] P-H Est. Plng. Serv. ¶ 429.

[72] Supra § 14.2.

[73] Cf. also Unif. Prob. Code sec. 2-608(b), providing that specific legatee is entitled to unpaid balance of purchase price where the property was sold in testator's lifetime, any unpaid condemnation award, and unpaid proceeds of fire or casualty insurance on the property, and, in the case of a specifically bequeathed secured obligation, any property obtained by the testator by or in lieu of foreclosure. As to specifically bequeathed corporate stock after capital change in testator's lifetime, supra § 14.4-2e.

[74] Similar rule in case of devise of "home," infra § 15.5-1.

[75] Effect of capital changes after execution of will, supra § 14.4-2e.

[76] Supra § 14.2.

[77] Bequest of securities as specific or general, infra § 14,6-2.

[78] Cf. § 14-4-1 supra.

§ **14.4-4b.** ———; ———; *property sold by guardian of incompetent.* As another exception to the rule that a specific legacy adeems if the subject matter is not owned by the testator at death,[79] it is the rule in a number of jurisdictions that where after the execution of the will the testator became incompetent, and the property referred to in the bequest was sold by his guardian or committee, the legacy does not adeem and the legatee is entitled to the proceeds of the sale or the property into which they can be traced.[80] The theory of the rule would seem to be that a competent testator who disposed in his lifetime of property he had specifically bequeathed must be deemed to know that he thereby prevented the bequest from being effective and so must have intended that result, whereas an incompetent did not make a voluntary disposition and could not have formed or given effect to such an intention. The rule presents problems to the executor, who, knowing that the decedent had been adjudged incompetent, must ascertain whether the "missing" property was sold before incompetency supervened, by the testator, or afterward, by the legal representative. It may also be noted that, during the period of incompetency, the executor or another having custody of the will may have a difficult ethical and legal problem to determine: whether he may communicate the fact of the existence of the specific bequest (or the contents of the will generally) to the guardian or committee so that the latter may take its terms into account in deciding to sell property for investment reasons or in selecting property to be sold to raise funds needed for the incompetent's maintenance.[81]

§ **14.4-4c.** ———; ———; *insurance proceeds.* Where property which is the subject of a specific bequest is lost or destroyed before the death of the testator, it is usually held that the intended legatee is not entitled to receive, in lieu of the property, proceeds of insurance on it, even where the loss or destruction occurred shortly before the death, and the insurance is collected by the executor.[82] In some jurisdictions, however, the rule is to the contrary,[83] and in those jurisdictions it may be said that the legacy accordingly does not adeem but merely changes in form, provided

---

[79] Supra § 14.4-4.

[80] So in Unif. Prob. Code sec. 608(a), which extends the rule also to condemnation awards and proceeds of casualty insurance paid to guardian, unless ward is declared competent at least one year before death. In case of devise of real property, infra § 15.5-2.

[81] Cf. *Matter of Riegel*, N.Y.L.J. Feb. 27, 1963, p. 14 (holding that incompetent's committee was not entitled to the will or a copy).

[82] The rule is presumably based on the theory that the bequest adeems if the specifically bequeathed item was completely destroyed and so does not exist at death, and that if the item was damaged but not destroyed the legatee takes it but as it existed at death, i.e., in its damaged condition. Cf. *In re Barry's Est.*, 208 Okl. 8, 252 P.2d 437, holding that where a specifically bequeathed car was damaged in an accident that caused the death of the testatrix, and executor assigned the damaged car to the insurance company and received an amount equal to its value before the accident, the legatee was thus prevented by the executor's action from receiving the car in its damaged condition and so was entitled to so much (only) of the insurance proceeds as equalled the car's value immediately after the accident. Insurance collected by guardian or committee of incompetent, cf. Unif. Proc. Code sec. 2-608(a).

[83] So in Unif. Prob. Code sec. 2-608(b).

SATISFACTION OF LEGACIES 155

the loss or destruction occurred after the making of the will.[84] The case of loss or destruction before death, is of course, to be distinguished from that of loss or destruction occurring after death;[85] under the rule that title to a specific legacy relates back to the testator's death,[86] the legatee in the latter case is entitled to receive the insurance proceeds. The same result has been held to follow where the loss or destruction and the death of the testator were simultaneous.[87]

§ 14.4-5. ———; *property subject to encumbrance.*[88] Where the subject-matter of a specific bequest is subject at the testator's death to a lien, mortgage, pledge, or other encumbrance, the executor must consider the question as to whether the legatee takes the property free of the encumbrance, or instead *cum onere*. The law seems to be less uniform in the various jurisdictions than in the case of encumbered real property.[89] In some of them it is held, with somewhat doubtful logic, that the question depends upon whether the encumbrance was created before the execution of the will, in which case the legatee takes free of it, or was created after the will was executed, in which case he takes *cum onere*. In other jurisdictions, however, the legatee in all cases takes *cum onere* unless the will evidences an intention to the contrary.[90] It is of course true, under general principles of law, that, whether or not the legatee takes the property burdened with the encumbrance and the debt it secures, the debt remains that of the testator and an obligation of the estate,[91] and the executor must protection himself under the principles applicable to unmatured or contingent obligations generally,[92] until such time, if any, as the estate's liability to the creditor is terminated, as where the creditor does not present a claim for his debt and his rights are barred by passage of time,[93] or distribution without making provision for payment to the creditor is directed in an accounting proceeding to which he is a party;[94] nevertheless, where under applicable law the legatee takes subject to the encumbrance, and the will does not contain any provision to the contrary, it would seem that the executor is not warranted in using funds of the estate to discharge the encum-

---

[84] Where, however, the loss or damage occurs before the making of the will, and the testator knows of it, the will passes the property as damaged, or whatever is left of the property, and there is nothing either to adeem or to be substituted for, so that the legatee is not entitled to the benefit of the insurance even though the insurance proceeds are collected after the testator's death. *Matter of Cramm*, 27 A.D.2d 8, 275 N.Y.S.2d 769.

[85] Duty of executor to insure, supra § 7.2-4.

[86] Supra § 14.3.

[87] *Matter of Buda*, 197 N.Y.S.2d 824.

[88] West Dig., Wills Key Nos. 827–834.

[89] Infra § 15.3.

[90] Unif. Prob. Code sec. 3-814 seems so to imply; see infra note 95. Effect of direction in will for payment of debts, supra § 9.3-3a.

[91] In the absence, of course, of a novation whereby the creditor accepts the legatee as the debtor and releases the estate. In a few states, if the creditor resorts to the securing property he must, or thereby does, release the estate.

[92] Supra § 9.3-2.

[93] Supra § 9.4-2.

[94] Infra § 24.5-5a.

brance,[95] except to the extent, if any, that a deficiency remains after the creditor's recourse to the securing property, and if he does so is liable to residuary legatees (or, if as a result of insufficiency of assets there is no residue, to legatees whose legacies have been caused to abate[96]) for the amount so used. If not only the subject-matter of the legacy but also other property is subject to a single encumbrance, the burden of the encumbrance, if the legatees do not take free of it, is to be allocated ratably between or among the several items of property or the legatees thereof, unless, of course, the will otherwise provides.

§ 14.4-5a. ———; ———; *obligations of business specifically bequeathed.* Where a decedent bequeaths a business enterprise of which he was the proprietor at the time of his death, and such business at that time had indebtedness or other obligations, the question may arise,[97] unless the will is explicit on the point,[98] whether the legatee of the business takes it *cum onere*, and must himself discharge its indebtedness, or the indebtedness is payable out of the general estate, as would be the case if the business had not been specifically bequeathed. It would seem that the case is analogous to that of a bequest of encumbered personal property,[99] and should be governed by the same considerations.

§ 14.4-6. ———; *availability for debts and expenses.* Subject to the considerations referred to in the two preceding sections in the case of property subject to a lien or other encumbrance, a specific legacy is not available for the payment of debts or administration expenses, unless and until all other personal property of the estate is exhausted. This results from the rule, elsewhere discussed,[100] that specific legacies are entitled to priority of payment over all other classes of legacies, and are the last class of legacies to abate if the estate is insufficient for the payment of all legacies and prior charges.

§ 14.4-7. ———; *letter or memorandum as to distribution.* A frequent source of difficulty is a direction in a will, or a bequest coupled with a direction or request, that all or certain property, usually tangibles, bequeathed to one (whether the executor or another) be distributed by him to others in accordance with the testator's wishes as expressed in a letter or memorandum. In some jurisdictions such a bequest is valid and effective, and the letter or memorandum governs the disposition, provided it meets certain conditions, as that it was in existence at the time of the execution of the will and is adequately identified therein,[1] or is in the testator's hand-

---

[95] Cf. Unif. Prob. Code sec. 3-814, permitting executor to pay the encumbrance, or transfer the securing property in partial or total satisfaction, if it appears for the best interest of the estate so to do, but providing that such a payment shall not increase the share of the legatee if the latter under general rules takes *cum onere*.
[96] Abatement in insolvent or insufficient estate, infra § 19.5-1 ff.
[97] Cf. § 9.3-3 supra.
[98] Supra § 9.3-3a.
[99] See last preceding section.
[100] Infra § 19.5-6.
[1] Cf. Unif. Prob. Code sec. 2-510.

writing or signed by him.[2] In other cases, however, and in those jurisdictions where the more general rule obtains that a writing not executed or attested in accordance with the formalities required of wills cannot be incorporated in, or in effect made a part of, the will by reference to it therein, the question whether the legatee takes the bequest free of restrictions except for such moral duty as he may feel, or instead the bequest fails entirely, is governed by principles very similar to those discussed at another place in connection with bequests to an executor *eo nomine*,[3] to which the case referred to in this section bears a close resemblance.

§ 14.4-7a. ———; ———; ***wishes orally expressed.*** The principles stated in the last preceding section apply, *a fortiori*, to the case of a bequest accompanied by a request or direction for disposition of the subject matter by the legatee in accordance with wishes or instructions communicated orally to him by the testator in the latter's lifetime, or, as wills sometimes say, "known" to the legatee from discussions with the testator.

§ 14.4-8. ———; ***division among legatees.*** Where securities, a group of identical items of tangible personal property, or other items capable of division, are specifically bequeathed to two or more legatees in shares (usually directed to be equal), the principles as to the division and distribution of funds and other aggregations of property apply and, as suggested in the discussion elsewhere thereof,[4] ordinarily a ratable number of each group or block of like assets should be delivered to each such legatee. In the usual case of a bequest of tangibles, however, it is impracticable if not impossible to follow such rules strictly, as obviously individual tangibles cannot be separated into parts, and even if there are, e.g., a pair or set of identical objects for distribution their purpose or usefulness may be frustrated or their desirability largely impaired if they are separated or are disposed of to different persons. Furthermore, an allocation to each legatee of an undivided interest in the whole group is ordinarily impracticable, if not indeed in contravention of the terms of the will. Accordingly, special problems may arise under such bequests. If the legatees are all *sui juris* they may agree among themselves on the division,[5] or perhaps on a round of choices in specified order, or even upon a sale of the tangibles and division of the proceeds;[6] and the executor should endeavor in the usual case to obtain such an agreement.[7] If for any reason agreement is not obtainable, and if the executor is given power by the will to determine the method of division, he may allocate items into groups as nearly as possible equal in value and desirability, and make distribution accordingly, and his action in good faith will ordinarily be conclusive; but where values of individual items are so disparate as to make that procedure impracticable,

---

[2] Ibid., sec. 2-513.
[3] Infra § 14.17.
[4] Infra §§ 14.28, 18.6-4a.
[5] Capital gain or loss to estate or legatee where non-ratable distribution made, infra § 18.6-4.
[6] In lieu of sale to third persons, an alternative may be a private "action" among legatees, with each thus given an opportunity to acquire the items or articles he most desires.
[7] Agreements with or among beneficiaries, infra Ch. XI.

or any friction exists among the legatees, the executor for his own protection may postpone satisfying the legacy until he can obtain the instructions of the court, in his accounting proceeding or otherwise.[8] Of course, if the executor himself is one of the legatees, he should be very chary of making any allocation or distribution in which his impartiality might be called into question by any other legatee.[9]

§ 14.4-9. ———; *delivery of tangibles.*[10] Where a tangible is specifically bequeathed, it is normally the duty of the executor to deliver it, at the proper time,[11] to the legatee, at the risk and expense of the estate. Where, however, the tangible does not come into the actual possession of the executor, as where at the testator's death it was in storage or safekeeping and is allowed to remain there,[12] a rule prevails in some states that is known as the "as is, where is" rule. Under that rule, the executor is not required to obtain possession of the tangible and make delivery of it to the legatee; when he is ready to satisfy the bequest he need do no more than notify the legatee of the whereabouts of the tangible and that it is at the legatee's disposal, and notify the custodian of the tangible that thenceforth it is to be held for the account of the legatee and subject to his instructions.[13] The estate incurs no expense of delivery, and within a reasonable time after such notification the estate's liability for storage or custody charges ceases. The executor must accordingly, in a case to which the rule relates, ascertain whether it is in force in the jurisdiction governing his actions for if it is he is without authority, under general principles forbidding the incurrence of unnecessary expense,[14] to expend estate funds in making a delivery.

§ 14.4-10. ———; *bequest or disposition of body or organs.* It is usually stated that there is no property in a dead body, and in general it is not subject to disposal by will.[15] In most states, however, statutes have been enacted[16] which permit one effectively to direct that upon his death his body, or parts or organs thereof, be turned over to a hospital, medical school, or other institution for use in research and teaching, or for purposes of enabling transplants into the bodies of living persons.[17] or to a physician for delivery to such an institution or use for such a purpose. Such statutes

---

[8] Instruction proceedings, infra § 22.2.
[9] Executor's own interest as beneficiary, in general, supra § 3.9-4a.
[10] West Dig., Exrs. & Admrs. Key No. 300.
[11] Time for satisfaction of legacies, infra § 14.31 ff.
[12] Property of such arrangement, supra § 7.2.
[13] *Matter of Columbia Tr. Co.*, 186 A.D. 377, 174 N.Y.S. 576.
[14] As waste, supra § 3.5-2.
[15] Rights with respect to dead bodies, in general, see Forzio, The Transplant Age, 84 ff. Directions in will as to funeral, burial, cremation, and the like, are of course to be distinguished from the matters referred to in the text; see § 4.7 supra. Cf. Unif. Prob. Code sec. 3-701 (executor may carry out written instructions of decedent relating to body; this may relate only to burial etc.)
[16] Usually, the Uniform Anatomical Gift Act, under which bequests or dispositions of a body or organs thereof made pursuant to the terms of the Act by the decedent (or in absence thereof directions given by spouse, adult child, parent, etc.) create rights paramount to those of any other person.
[17] Fact and time of death in transplantation cases, supra § 5.2-1.

usually provide for such a direction either by will, or by an instrument in writing executed with formalities closely resembling or identical with those required in the case of a will. Such a statute would seem to create a species of property in the body, although only for the limited purposes contemplated by the statute. Whether, however, an instrument of the second character above mentioned is to be treated as a will,[18] and also whether in either case the direction as to disposition of the body or its parts is to be regarded as a legacy, are open to question; if and to the extent that such a disposition is to be thought of as a legacy it clearly is a specific one, but equally clearly it is not within the rules of availability of legacies for debts and expenses[19] or the principles of abatement.[20] The direction would, however, seem to empower the executor, and impose upon him some duty, akin to that with respect to funeral and interment[21] and also akin in some degree to that relating to delivery of specific legacies,[22] to deliver the body, or make it available, in accordance with the direction, if the body is under the executor's control, or to see that the person having possession or control is informed of the direction and is at least encouraged to comply with it.[23] This assumes that the executor knows of the existence of the direction or is chargeable with notice of it; if he does not have such knowledge, or reason to believe that a direction may exist, it would seem unlikely that he would be held to any duty to search or inquire for one, or responsible for proceeding[24] without regard to it.

§ *14.5-1. Demonstrative legacies;*[25] *definition.* A demonstrative legacy is a legacy of money payable out of a specified fund. An example is a bequest of a specified amount to be paid out of insurance proceeds receivable by the estate, or out of a savings account.[26] The demonstrative legacy differs from a general legacy[27] only in that the former is coupled with a specification of the source of payment. It would seem that in modern times courts tend to construe a bequest as one either of a specific legacy or of a general legacy, rather than of a demonstrative legacy, and in some jurisdictions, at least for some purposes, the concept of the demonstrative legacy appears to be largely ignored.[28]

---

[18] It seems obvious, from references in some such statutes to an "instrument" or "writing" and avoidance of the term "will," that the instrument does not require, and indeed is not eligible for, probate. This fact, of course, is not of itself decisive as to whether the instrument is to be regarded as a will or the disposition as a legacy, under the general principle that the validity of a will does not depend on probate. As further bearing on the question of will *vel non*, it may be noted that under some statutes there appears to be doubt that the direction may be revoked.

[19] Supra § 14.4-6.

[20] Infra § 19.5-1 ff.

[21] Supra § 4.7.

[22] See last preceding section.

[23] *Quaere* as to the existence, extent, and enforceability of a duty on the part of such person.

[24] Supra § 4.7.

[25] West Dig., Exrs. & Admrs. Key No. 755.

[26] Bequest of bank account, as such, distinguished, see next following section.

[27] General legacies, supra § 14.6.

[28] Cf. § 19.5-5. infra.

§ *14.5-2.* ———; *bequest of bank account*[29] *distinguished.* As has been pointed out above,[30] a bequest of a bank account, as such, is a specific legacy, and is distinguished from a demonstrative legacy by the fact that it passes whatever balance is in the designated account at death, rather than some specified amount payable out of the account; and thus the rule as to satisfaction of a demonstrative legacy out of the general estate to the extent that the fund designated as the source of payment is not sufficient[31] has no application.

§ *14.5-3.* ———; *general legacy to extent fund insufficient.* If and to the extent that the fund out of which a demonstrative legacy is directed to be paid is insufficient for its payment, the legacy is a general legacy, unless the will limits the legacy to the amount of the specified fund. As has been indicated above,[32] the question whether or to what extent a legacy is demonstrative or general, in the absence of such an express limitation, is ordinarily of importance only where the net estate is insufficient to pay all legacies in full.[33]

§ *14.5-4.* ———; *ademption.* It follows from the rule stated in the last preceding section that a demonstrative legacy is not adeemed[34] merely because the specified fund out of which it is to be paid is non-existent or insufficient at the death of the testator, unless by the terms of the will the legacy is to be paid only out of such fund or only to the extent that such fund is sufficient.

§ *14.5-5.* ———; *availability of fund for charges and expenses.* In accordance with the rules as to priority and abatement of demonstrative legacies[35] in jurisdictions in which they are distinguished for those purposes from general legacies, so much of a fund as is bequeathed as a demonstrative legacy should not be availed of by the executor for the payment of charges and expenses until other moneys of the estate available for such payment have been exhausted.

§ *14.6-1. General legacies;*[36] *definition.* A general legacy is ordinarily a legacy of money,[37] payable out of the general estate, rather than (as in the case of a demonstrative legacy[38]) out of a specified fund. It may be effected not only by an explicit bequest in the will, but also, as elsewhere pointed out, by a forgiveness of an indebtedness[39] or by a direction to sell property at less than its value.[40] A general legacy may, of course, abate by reason of insufficiency of assets in the estate,[41] but, because of its

---

[29] P-H Est. Plng. Serv. ¶ 432.8.
[30] Supra § 14.4-1.
[31] See next following section.
[32] Supra § 14.1-1.
[33] Order of abatement of demonstrative legacy, infra § 19.5-5.
[34] Ademption generally, supra § 14.2.
[35] Infra §19.5-5
[36] West Dig., Wills Key No. 756; P-H Est Plng. Serv. ¶ 432.9.
[37] Legacy of securities as general, see next following section.
[38] Supra § 14.5-1.
[39] Infra § 14.16-1.
[40] Supra § 8.6-3.
[41] Abatement, supra § 14.2.

SATISFACTION OF LEGACIES

nature, there can be no application of the principle of ademption,[42] except what is called ademption by satisfaction.[43]

§ 14.6-2. ———; *legacy of securities*. There is noted above the tendency of modern decisions to treat a bequest of securities as general, rather than specific.[44] This treatment is accorded, however, principally but not solely,[45] where the securities that are the subject of the bequest were not owned by the decedent, or the bequeathed number of them were not owned by him, at his death, and is applied merely to preclude the operation of the principle of ademption[46] that would apply if the legacy were treated as specific.[47] Inasmuch, however, as the legacy in such case is to be satisfied first out of the described securities held, to the extent any are held, and only any lacking are to be supplied by purchase or by payment of monetary equivalent out of the general estate, the analogy to a demonstrative legacy would seem to be closer.[48]

§ 14.6-3. ———; *ademption by satisfaction*. Where a will contains a general legacy,[49] especially one of money, to one for some specified purpose, and after the execution of the will the testator makes a gift to the same person for the same purpose (whether or not the amounts of the gift and the legacy are the same), the legacy is said to be adeemed by satisfaction, and does not take effect, except as a statute may otherwise provide.[50] While this rule seems somewhat to extend the doctrine of ademption,[51] it can be brought within the latter by regarding the lifetime disposition as re-

---

[42] Ademption, ibid.

[43] Infra § 14.6-3.

[44] Supra § 14.4-1. Bequest of corporate stock where capital change occurs, supra § 14.4-2e.

[45] See *Est. of Reisinger*, N.Y.L.J. Aug. 26, 1966, p. 9, where bequests of specified numbers of shares of a particular corporation, out of a much larger number held by the testator, were held to be general, so that the legatees were not entitled to cash dividends received by the executor during the statutory pre-distribution period; right of general legatee to income earned during period of administration, in general, infra § 16.6-3. The trend toward treatment as a general legacy has not, however, been extended, so far as has been found, to an insolvent estate so as to make the bequest abate as a general legacy rather than a specific one; relative order of abatement of general and specific legacies, infra §§ 19.5-4, 19.5-6.

[46] Ademption, in general, supra § 14.2; of bequest of open-market securities, supra § 14.4-4a; inapplicability in case of general legacy, see last preceding section.

[47] Cf. Unif. Prob. Code sec. 2-607; specific bequest of securities passes so much of such securities as are owned at death, but (as to those so owned) also passes any additional or other securities of the same issuer distributed by it to the testator (excluding purchase options), securities of another entity held by the testator as a result of a merger, consolidation, reorganization, or other similar action of the issuer, and, in case of a regulated investment company, additional securities acquired by the testator under a reinvestment program.

[48] Non-ademption of demonstrative legacy, supra § 14.5-4.

[49] Defined, supra § 14.6-1. Residuary legacy, infra § 18.10.

[50] Such statutes uniformly require a written declaration or admission, and under at least many of them it must be contemporaneous with the gift; *Hirning v. Webb*, 91 Ida. 229, 419 P.2d 671; *Elliott v. Western Coal & Min. Co.*, 243 Ill. 614, 90 N.E. 1104; *Arthur v. Arthur*, 143 Wis. 126, 126 N.W. 550. So parole evidence is not admissible; *Stark v. Stark*, 128 Neb. 524, 259 N.W. 523. Under Unif. Prob. Code sec. 2-612, the same rules that apply in case of advancement (infra § 14.30) as to the necessity of a contemporaneous declaration by donor or acknowledgment by donee are made applicable to the case of ademption by satisfaction.

[51] Ademption in general, supra § 14.2.

sulting in non-ownership of the subject matter by the testator at his death; but it would seem that satisfaction, rather than ademption, is the better explanation of the rule. The doctrine of ademption by satisfaction is somewhat analogous to that of advancement,[52] and indeed has been affected by the latter to the extent that some authorities indicate it applies not merely in the case mentioned above but more generally where the testator is a parent of the legatee or stands *in loco parentis* to him, or where the legacy and the gift are *ejusdem generis*; and an ademption by satisfaction is sometimes referred to as an advancement, but, as appears hereinafter, advancement differs in important respects.[53] It may be observed that there is no controlling reason why the doctrine of ademption by satisfaction, ordinarily applied only in the case of a general legacy, should not also be applicable in the case of a specific legacy where the subject matter is given to the legatee in the testator's lifetime, but the ordinary rule of ademption[54] is sufficient to cover the latter case without resorting to the slightly more esoteric rule of satisfaction.[55]

§ 14.7. Residuary legacies; definition. A residuary legacy is a legacy of all or part of such personal property as may remain after the satisfaction in full of all charges and of all other legacies.[56]

---

[52] Infra § 14.30. Obviously, the doctrine can have no application where the will shows that the testator in making the bequest has taken into account his lifetime gifts to the legatee.

[53] Ibid. "Although Courts traditionally can this [lifetime satisfaction of a bequest] 'ademption by satisfaction' when a will is involved and 'advancement' when the estate is intestate, the difference in terminology is not significant" Comment to Unif. Prob. Code sec. 2-612, which, however, also points out that where an anti-lapse statute is involved (infra § 14.23-2) issue take the same benefit as their ancestor and so if the bequest is reduced under the doctrine of ademption by satisfaction it is automatically reduced as to the issue, producing in this respect a different result than in the case of an advancement, where the issue would take directly as heirs.

[54] Ademption as based in general on non-ownership or non-existence of subject matter at testator's death, supra § 14.2. Ademption of specific legacy, supr § 14.4-4 ff.

[55] *Beck v. McGillis*, 9 Barb. (N.Y.) 57, 58. "If the devise [legacy] is specific, a gift of the specific property during lifetime would adeem the gift by extinction rather than by satisfaction. . ."; Comment to Unif. Prob. Code sec. 2-612.

[56] Ascertainment of residuary estate, in general, infra § 18.1. What passes under residuary clause, infra § 18.2 ff.

XIV

SATISFACTION OF LEGACIES

Part B—Special Problems

§ 14.8-1. "Marital deduction" legacies; in general. A legacy intended to entitle the testator's estate to the benefit of a "marital deduction" under the Federal estate tax law or under some state laws may, depending upon the terms of the will, be a specific, demonstrative, or general legacy,[1] or, at least so far as concerns the application of rules of priority of payment and abatement,[2] may be a residuary legacy.[3]

§ 14.8-2. ———; formula clauses: "pecuniary" and "share" formulae. Formulae prescribed by wills for determining the amount or size of a "marital deduction" legacy, and usually intended to obtain the full allowable marital deduction, fall into two classes, (a) the "pecuniary" or "amount" formula and (b) the "share" or "fraction" formula. The first is a legacy of an amount in money (although it may be satisfiable in property[4]) determined by the calculation in an estate tax return of the amount of the deduction allowable;[5] it is a general legacy,[6] although if it is directed that its amount be paid or set aside from the residuary estate it may be junior in priority of payment to all legacies except that of the "balance" of the residuary.[7] The second kind of formula is of a fractional share of assets, not measured in dollars or amount of value;[8] it partakes of the nature of a residuary legacy because of this feature, but may also be regarded as having characteristics of a specific legacy in view of the general rules of law governing the satisfaction of legacies of shares of any group of assets.[9] Either type of formula is, of course, to be applied, and the computation under it to be made, before the deduction of estate or inheritance taxes.

---

[1] Classification of legacies, supra § 14.1-1.
[2] Generally, infra Ch. XIX.
[3] Residuary legacies, supra § 14.7.
[4] Infra § 14.27-2.
[5] Problems under bequest of amount equal to "maximum" allowable marital deduction, supra § 13.3.
[6] Defined, supra § 14.6-1.
[7] Infra § 19.5-3a.
[8] Legacies of shares or fractions, in general, infra § 14.28.
[9] Infra § 14.8-2b.

§ 14.8-2a. ———; ———; *importance of determining nature of formula.* It is clear from their differing natures[10] that a "pecuniary" formula for fixing the size of a marital deduction legacy produces a fixed and unchanging amount as soon as valuations for the purpose of the estate tax are finally fixed or determined, whereas a "share" formula results instead in a fraction that becomes fixed as soon as such valuations are so determined but is then applied to assets whose value may have changed since the valuation date for the purposes of the tax (and such application is unaffected by and without regard to any such changes). It is therefore important to the executor for both substantive and administrative purposes[11] to ascertain the nature and effect of a formula contained in a will, as to whether it is to be construed as a legacy of an amount in money or value or as a share or fraction of a group of assets. Unfortunately, the will often is ambiguous on this score. For example, a bequest of that "portion" of the residuary estate which is "equal to" the allowable marital deduction would seem properly construable as a pecuniary legacy, as the allowable marital deduction is an amount and a thing equal to an amount must itself be an amount; but courts have frequently found in such a provision an intention to bequeath a share or fraction of the estate or residue. It may be noted that these decisions have been rendered in a period of rising values, where it was apparently felt that the surviving spouse should have the benefit of post-mortem increases; whether the same result would be reached in a period of declining values is problematical.

§ 14.8-2b. ———; ———; *administrative problems under formulae.* The administrative problems under a formula measuring a marital deduction bequest differ considerably with the nature of the formula.[12] Under a pecuniary formula, no problems arise other than those involved in the satisfaction of any other general legacy,[13] except in some cases where the bequest is satisfied in property,[14] and except that the amount of the legacy cannot be determined with accuracy until after audit of the estate tax return or other final determination of the property taxable and the aggregate value thereof. The executor must, however, estimate the amount of the bequest, as best he can, at an early stage of his administration of the estate, in order to carry out his duty to provide promptly for his probable cash requirements,[15] or at the least must make sure, if he is authorized to satisfy the legacy in property, that he has on hand property that will be available and suitable for that purpose. Under a share formula,[16] no special problems arise where the share or fraction is expressed to be one of the residuary estate[17] (or of the residue before deduction of death taxes), and

---

[10] See last preceding section.
[11] See next following section.
[12] Generally, see Stevens, Administrative Problems of Fiduciaries in Working with Formula Clauses, 1965 Proc. A.B.A. Sec. Real Prop Prob. & Tr. L., Part I, 14.
[13] Infra passim. Pecuniary formula as general legacy, supra § 14.8-2.
[14] Infra § 14.27-2.
[15] Liquidation for cash requirements, in general, supra § 7.6-1.
[16] Legacy of share or fraction of fund, in general, infra § 14.28.
[17] Share or fraction of residue, infra § 18.6-4a.

SATISFACTION OF LEGACIES

the estate may be administered in the normal manner down to the point where the residuary estate can be ascertained and is ready for distribution.[18] Where, however, the will refers to a share or fraction of the testamentary estate as a whole, rather than merely one of the residuary estate, the bequest partakes, as has been pointed out,[19] of the nature of a specific bequest;[20] and accordingly the executor is in theory required (by the rule that a specific legacy is not available for payment of debts or administration expenses until all other personal property shall have been exhausted[21]) at the outset to compute the amount of the taxable estate and of the allowable marital deduction and (by the rules governing the method of satisfying a legacy of a share or fraction of a fund or group of assets[22]) to set aside for the marital deduction bequest the appropriate fraction (determined by such computation) of each testamentary assets, so that all taxes, administration expenses, and prior legacies may be paid out of the remaining assets and none of the allocated "specifically bequeathed" assets are used for that purpose (assuming that the remaining assets are sufficient). Obviously it is not possible, until estate taxes have been finally determined, to do this with accuracy, but the executor must make as close an estimate as possible and tentatively set aside, for use eventually in satisfying the marital deduction legacy, such portion of each asset as will at all events be sufficient for that purpose, to the end that no part of the assets required to pass to the marital deduction legatee will be used for other charges.[23] Where, as occasionally is the case, the will instead directs the setting aside of a fraction of the *taxable* estate, and non-testamentary assets[24] are includible in the taxable estate, the executor is faced with a situation in which it is impossible for him to comply strictly with the rules above referred to, inasmuch as the non-testamentary assets do not come into his hands or under his control as executor and he cannot allocate a ratable part of each thereof to the marital share; under such a provision the executor's only means of obtaining protection would ordinarily be to apply to the appropriate court for instructions,[25] in a proceeding to which all interested persons were made parties, unless an agreement by all such persons is obtained.[26]

§ 14.8-2bb. ———; ———; ———; *non-qualifying assets.* The Federal estate tax law disallows a marital deduction in respect of assets, or the proceeds of assets,

---

[18] Distribution of residue, in general, infra § 18.6-1 ff.
[19] Supra § 14.8-2.
[20] Casner, Fractional Share Marital Deduction Gifts, 39 The Trust Bulletin 42: "The [fractional share marital deduction gift], whether the fraction is produced by the application of a formula or not, is a gift of the described fractional share of each item in the fund against which the described fraction is to be applied."
[21] Infra § 19.5-6.
[22] Infra § 14.28.
[23] So long, of course, as there are other assets entitled to remain unused therefor under the rules of priority and abatement; cf. § 19.5-1 ff., infra.
[24] Defined, supra § 1.11-1.
[25] Instruction proceedings, infra § 22.2.
[26] Agreements with or among beneficiaries, infra Ch. XXI.

not "qualifying" for such deduction;[27] and under a share formula[28] assets or proceeds of that character might be included among the property passing under the share bequest. To avoid the consequent possibility of partial loss of the deduction, wills commonly provide that no non-qualifying assets be included in the share or that other assets be substituted therefor. Under such a provision, the executor must value the non-qualifying assets and the assets to be substituted for them, to obtain equality, and to that extent the supposed "share" formula is converted into a pecuniary one.

§ 14.9-1. *Legacies charged on land;*[29] *in general.* As elsewhere discussed, in most states real property is not ordinarily available for sale to raise cash for payment of pecuniary legacies,[30] and so such legacies may go unpaid if there is not sufficient personal property to enable their payment. A contrary intention may, however, appear from the will, and may be evidenced by explicit provision or implied from circumstances, as, for example, that at the time of executing his will the testator knew he had insufficient personalty to satisfy the bequests made by the will. Accordingly, where personal property is not sufficient to provide for the cash legacies bequeathed by the will, after, of course, payment of all prior items,[31] the executor must consider whether the will as a whole and the surrounding circumstances may be sufficient to indicate an intention that real property in the residuary estate be sold to pay the legacies. Such an intention, however, will not readily be implied, and if it is not expressed, but is merely to be deduced or inferred, the executor will seldom if ever feel justified in having resort to real property without first obtaining a judicial determination of the point involved.

§ 14.9-2. ———; *charge on specific devise.*[32] To be distinguished from the case, referred to in the preceding section, of an intention (express or implied) that residuary real property be sold to make possible the payment of cash legacies for which personal property is insufficient, is the specific devise[33] of land subject to or accompanied by a direction for payment of a cash amount to another out of the land or by the devisee. In one sense, there may be room for argument as to whether such a provision truly constitutes a bequest to the "legatee" or instead creates merely a personal liability toward him on the part of the devisee, who must pay the specified amount as a condition to having the devise; but even the latter would seem within the concept of a legacy as being a right created by will with respect to personal property, and in any case such a provision is ordinarily termed a legacy and treated as such for most if not all purposes. So treated, the question may arise, in an insol-

---

[27] I.R.C. sec. 2056(b) (2). The most frequent reason for such non-qualification is a "terminable interest" type of asset.
[28] Supra § 14.8-2.
[29] West Dig., Wills Key Nos. 891–826; P-H Est. Plng. Serv. ¶ 435.
[30] Infra § 15.7.
[31] Order of payment and abatement, generally, infra § 19.5-1 ff.
[32] Devise of encumbered real property, infra § 15.3.
[33] Specific devises, infra § 15.2-2b.

SATISFACTION OF LEGACIES 167

vent or insufficient estate,[34] whether it is a species of demonstrative legacy (with the land as the "fund" from which it is primarily payable)[35] or a specific legacy (because attached to and a part of a specific disposition).[36] In a solvent estate, however, if the devisee, for whatever reason, should renounce the devise,[37] or if the devise should lapse because of non-survival of the devisee,[38] there may be a problem as to whether the legatee's right ceases, or the charge remains on or "runs with" the land, so that liability for its discharge falls upon the alternate devisee, residuary devisee, or heir, as the case may be, who then takes the land. Similarly, if the legacy should exceed the amount realizable from the land, the question would be whether the excess is lost to the legatee, or is to be treated as a general legacy,[39] by analogy to the portion of a demonstrative legacy not covered by the source-fund.[40] These questions may be affected by the presumed intention of the testator, as deduced from the reason or inducement for the making of the charge on the land and perhaps the identities and relationship to the testator or devisee of the legatee. Thus, in all such cases the executor may have to obtain a judicial determination of the points involved,[41] unless all parties in interest agree.[42]

§ *14.10. Legacies subject to condition precedent.*[43] When a legacy is by its terms to be effective only in the event of the existence or non-existence of a particular fact or circumstance, the executor must, of course, satisfy himself, at his peril, as to the validity of the condition, and, if it be valid, as to its fulfillment, before either paying the legacy or distributing the assets of the estate without having paid the legacy. A bequest to one if he be in the testator's employment at the time of the latter's death, or if he shall have been so employed for a specified period of time, ordinarily presents no administrative difficulties other than those always present in ascertaining the facts of any matter. A bequest to one if unmarried, or if not remarried, requires a determination of the question whether the condition violates public policy against restraints on marriage and, if it does, whether the bequest fails or, as some courts hold, the condition is to be disregarded and the bequest given effect without regard to it. A bequest to one if living at the expiration of a specified period of time after the testator's death (for example, the six-months' period permitted in the marital deduction provisions of the Federal estate tax law[44]), or if living at the probate of

---

[34] Infra § 19.5-6a; insolvent or insufficient estate, infra § 19.1.
[35] Demonstrative legacies, in general, supra § 14.5-1 ff.
[36] Specific legacies, supra § 14.4-1.
[37] Infra § 15.9.
[38] Infra § 15.4.
[39] So in Unif. Prob. Code sec. 3-902.
[40] Supra § 14.5-3.
[41] Construction and instruction proceedings, infra Ch. XXII.
[42] Agreements with or among beneficiaries, infra Ch. XXI. In acting under such an agreement, the executor should consider its effectiveness under an inheritance tax statute imposing tax at rates differing with the relationships of takers to the decedent, if the agreement produces a result (as to persons who take or the amounts received by them) different from that which might be produced under rules of law.
[43] P-H Est. Plng. Serv. ¶¶ 375.4, 375.6 ff.
[44] I.R.C. sec. 2056(b) (3).

the will, the distribution of the estate, or some other indefinite time, requires first a determination whether the proviso infringes the applicable rule against perpetuities or a cognate rule or statute. A somewhat different kind of condition precedent is a requirement annexed to a bequest that the legatee satisfy a specified obligation of the decedent or make a specified payment or transfer to a third person;[45] this, as will be apparent, is closely analogous to a legacy charged on a specific devise of land, and similar considerations apply.[46]

§ 14.11. *Legacies upon condition subsequent;*[47] *life estates; responsibility of executor.* Ordinarily a provision that a legacy shall cease to be effective, or shall be cancelled, if a particular set or circumstance is done or arises, or is not done or does not arise, as the case may be,[48] is effective only where followed by a gift over of the subject-matter of the legacy to another. As in the case of a condition precedent,[49] the possibility of violation of the rule against perpetuities or a statutory substitute for it may have to be considered. Absent any invalidity on that score, if the provision for gift over comes into effect after the executor has made distribution, as of a tangible, the question arises as to whether he is under any duty to obtain the subject-matter of the legacy and deliver it to the alternate taker, or in some other way to see to it that the alternate taker receives the benefit of the legacy. Similarly, where personal property is bequeathed to one for life,[50] with remainder to another, the executor may or may not have a duty to inform himself of the death of the life tenant and to see to it that the subject property then passes into the hands or control of the remainderman. In each case the existence *vel non* of such a duty may be affected by the language of the will, and subject thereto is governed by local law. The problems are mentioned here merely in order that they may not be overlooked.

§ 14.12-1. *Deferred legacies;*[51] *in general.* Where payment of a legacy is to be deferred, either as to the whole or as to a part of the legacy, there is first to be determined the time when the legacy vests or becomes payable,[52] and then whether there is any violation of the applicable rule against perpetuities or of a statute or rule of similar purpose. The usual kinds of deferred legacies are those directed to be paid in instalments, and, closely related thereto, testamentary annuities.[53] Ordinarily

---

[45] Will provision making item payable from particular assets instead of general estate, or vice versa, supra § 9.3-1.
[46] See last preceding section.
[47] P-H Est. Plng. Serv. ¶ 375.5 ff.
[48] *In terrorem* provisions as to probate and contests, supra § 5.10-2.
[49] See last preceding section.
[50] A legal life estate, and not an estate in trust, is here referred to.
[51] P-H Est. Plng. Serv. ¶ 413.
[52] Attainment of specified age, see Cantrall, The Careful Draftsman and the Problem of Age, 47 A.B.A.J. 41; Leach, The Careful Draftsman: Watch Out!, op. cit. 259.
[53] The term "testamentary annuities" is used to refer to annuities payable by the executor as a form of bequest under the will, as distinguished from an annuity purchased by the executor, pursuant to a direction or authorization in the will, from an insurance company or another; the latter is, of course, an "immediate" and not a "deferred" legacy. Direction or authorization to purchase annuity, infra § 14.13.

SATISFACTION OF LEGACIES

in case of such a legacy there is no violation of a rule or statute relating to vesting or alienability,[54] unless the commencement of payment is unlawfully deferred, although if the annuity or legacy is payable to a succession of persons a violation might result under familiar rules relating to postponement of vesting. The deferred legacy, whether an annuity or not, is to be distinguished from a trust[55] to provide for periodic payments to a beneficiary; the former is payable from principal of the estate, like any other legacy, whereas payments under a trust may be directed by its terms to be made wholly or partly from income.

§ *14.12-2.* ———; *administrative problems.* Special administrative problems arise in connection with a deferred legacy, their nature depending upon the nature of the bequest. If a legacy is one payable in instalments but is of a specified total amount, or the instalments are to be of specified amounts and number (as over a fixed period of time), so that the total or maximum amount of funds required for its satisfaction is known or can be definitely computed, the executor is protected if he sets apart a fund equal to such total or maximum amount, and, of course, protects it against diminution;[56] and his only special problems grow out of the fact that final closing of the estate, or at least termination of the executorial function, may have to be postponed to a date later than would be necessary if instalment payments did not have to be made. If, however, the instalment legacy is one of a specified annual or other periodic sum for the life of the beneficiary, or some other period not ascertainable at the outset, the executor is faced with the problem (unless he is authorized to purchase a commercial annuity[57]) of determining what amount of assets should be set aside or reserved to provide for such payments. This involves, where payments are to be made for life, a consideration of the age of the beneficiary and hence of his life expectancy; but it is, of course, necessary that the executor provide a fund sufficient to cover the prescribed payments if the beneficiary should live far beyond his normal or statistical expectancy, since the beneficiary is entitled under the terms of the legacy to payments for life, however short or long that may be. Similar considerations apply where the payments are to be for an uncertain term other than life. Upon setting aside a fund to provide for payments under either annuity-type of legacy, the executor ordinarily is not justified in holding the fund in cash or uninvested, in view of a fiduciary's general duty to make funds productive,[58] but must confine himself to a relatively nonfluctuating type of investment, such for example as short-term or serially-maturing government obligations, if he is to make sure cash will be available as and when it becomes payable to the annuitant, and also to protect himself against possible loss of capital and consequent liability, on the one hand, to the annuitant if the fund should prove to be inadequate to cover the legacy payments, and, on the other hand, to whomever becomes entitled to

---

[54] Perpetuities and related problems, infra § 15.35-2.
[55] Testamentary trusts, in general, infra Ch. XXVII.
[56] Infra this section.
[57] See next following section.
[58] Supra § 7.7-2.

such portion of the fund as remains at the death of the annuitant—ordinarily residuary beneficiaries, unless the will otherwise provides. Similarly, the executor must determine to whom income earned on the fund is lawfully payable; such payee may be the residuary legatee if the will does not otherwise provide.[59] It is, of course, sometimes the case that a will directs the setting aside of a fund of such size as will provide, from both principal and income, the lifetime annuity payments; under such a provision the executor (who is carrying out the provision becomes a trustee in fact if not in name) in determining the amount to be set aside must consider, in addition to the factors mentioned above, the probable yield on the corpus, taking into account the diminishing or wasting character of the latter; inasmuch as most of the factors he must consider are speculative or uncertain, an executor ordinarily should if possible obtain an instruction from the court as to the amount to be set aside, and such an instruction obtained in a proper proceeding should protect him from liability even if the amount determined by the court should prove to be insufficient. If, instead of being a bequest of an amount or annuity or the like, the deferred bequest is of a tangible, the problem arises as to the source of payment of expenses of safekeeping, insurance, and the like, and, unless appropriate provision is contained in the will, it may be necessary for the executor to seek instructions from the court on the point; and if the bequest is one of securities or other income-producing property, the question arises, unless the will is explicit, as to the disposition of income during the period of the deferment; here, again, judicial instructions may have to be obtained. It will be noted from the foregoing discussion that many of the administrative problems with respect to deferred legacies are not dissimilar to those with respect to unmatured or unliquidated claims against the estate.[60]

§ 14.13. *Direction or authorization to purchase annuity.* A direction or authorization in a will to the executor to purchase, from a company engaged in the business of writing annuities, an annuity of a specified periodic amount, or to expend a specified sum in the purchase of an annuity, for the benefit of a designated person or persons is a legacy of the amount used for such purchase.[61] Administrative problems frequently arise in connection with such a provision because of failure of the will to specify exactly the kind of annuity to be purchased, with particular reference to such matters as guaranteed number of payments, survivorship or refund features, and the like; and, inasmuch as such factors may considerably influence the cost of an annuity of a specified amount, or the size of an annuity that may be purchased for a specified amount, the problem is important. In any case of an incomplete or ambiguous direction, or other doubt as to the effect of the direction, the executor must protect himself, and protect the respective rights of beneficiaries, by obtaining a judicial construction,[62] unless, of course, all persons in interest (usually the annuitant and

---

[59] Disposition of income from estate assets, in general, infra § 16.6-1 ff.
[60] Supra §9.3-2.
[61] "Testamentary" annuities and other instalment legacies distinguished, supra § 14.12.1.
[62] Infra Ch. XXII.

SATISFACTION OF LEGACIES 171

the residuary legatees under the will) can and do agree among themselves and with the executor.[63]

§ 14.14-1. *Charitable legacies; in general.* The problem most frequently arising in connection with bequests to charity is that of identifying the organization or institution intended to receive the legacy.[64] Such a problem can grow out of the use in the will of a popular name or description of the organization or institution rather than its true name, but is usually the result of the use of a name merely approximating, more or less closely, the correct name, where the difference may be so considerable as to give rise to doubt as to what was meant, or of a name which resembles to some degree the name of each of two or more organizations or institutions, so that there is doubt as to which one was intended. The executor in any such case makes payment of the legacy at his peril, unless he first obtains a judicial determination of the effect of the bequest; and accordingly in every case where the name used in the will is not the correct name of an existing organization or institution the executor should not assume that any particular organization or institution was intended without having satisfied himself, first, that there is no other whose name is such that it could have been intended, or could claim to have been intended, by the name used in the will, and, second, that the name in the will is not that of an organization or institution which has gone out of existence since the will was executed and the existing organization of resembling name is not a different, and, to the testator, unknown, entity. A somewhat different kind of problem may arise where there are both a national organization and a local or regional organization of similar names[65] and the will does not make it clear which the testator meant to be the recipient of his bequest. The executor should not overlook the fact that, in any proceeding involving the identification of a charitable legatee, the attorney general of the state in which the will was probated is ordinarily a necessary party.

§ 14.14-2. ———; *cy pres.* The doctrine of *cy pres* applies where a general charitable intent is found[66] but either the charitable organization or institution named in a will has gone out of existence or the particular charitable purpose expressed in the will cannot be accomplished. In a proper case, therefore, it is the duty of the executor to submit the matter of a charitable legacy to the appropriate court and seek a determination as to whether *cy pres* is to be applied, or a determination as to the disposition to be made of the legacy. The comment made in the preceding section

---

[63] Infra Ch. XXI.

[64] There may also arise, however, a question of ineffectiveness or voidability of an "excessive" provision for charity or one made shortly before death (infra § 17.7), or a question as to the capacity of the charity to receive the bequest (infra § 14.18-4).

[65] Names often raising such problems include, e.g., American Red Cross, Boy Scouts of America, etc., and those of a number of public health organizations.

[66] Where the intent was merely to benefit a particular institution or organization, rather than primarily to accomplish a charitable purpose, the doctrine of *cy pres* does not apply and, if the bequest cannot take effect according to its terms, it fails. See, e.g., *Bowden v. Brown*, 200 Mass. 269, 86 N.E. 351. Lapse where intended beneficiary non-existent, in general, supra § 14.2.

as to the necessity of making the relevant attorney general a party to a proceeding involving a charitable disposition is, of course, applicable to such a proceeding.

§ 14.14-3. ———; *"honorary trusts"*. Related to the charitable bequest, but distinguished by the fact that it is not charitable in the legal sense, is the so-called "honorary trust". It involves a bequest to one with the direction or condition that its principal or income, as the case may be, be applied directly for some such purpose as maintenance of pet animals, preservation of a non-public structure, promotion of a sport, or a comparable end. It is apparent that such a bequest, having no human beneficiary and not being charitable as a matter of law, has no one who can enforce its carrying out, and accordingly cannot be given effect as a trust.[67] If, however, the legatee is willing to accept the bequest on the terms of the will, most jurisdictions will permit the bequest to be paid.[68] The arrangement is known as an honorary trust because its performance rests upon the honor and moral responsibility of the legatee. While as a general rule an executor is of course not justified in paying a bequest for a purpose or for disposition outside the established principles of law, the honorary trust, although anomalous,[69] is so well established that, as indicated by the foregoing, it will usually be given effect if its purpose is not illegal or capricious.[70] The executor faced with such a bequest is well advised, however, not to satisfy it until authorized to do so by the appropriate court or by all persons in interest (usually the residuary legatees), and then only if the legatee of the bequest suitably manifests his willingness to accept it and carry out its purposes.

§ 14.15. *Bequest to creditor.* A bequest by a testator to his creditor raises a question whether it is to be deemed to be merely in discharge of the debt or is of the nature of a voluntary gift or bounty (like any other legacy) and leaves the creditor in a position to accept the legacy and still to enforce his claim against the estate.[71] The matter depends upon local law, but the general rule appears to be that such a bequest, without further expression of intention, does not prevent the creditor from claiming repayment of the debt.[72] Where, however, the bequest is indicated in the will to be in satisfaction of the debt, it appears that the creditor is put to an election to claim either as legatee or as creditor—i.e., to accept the legacy as a discharge of

---

[67] Testamentary trusts, infra Ch. XXVII.

[68] Restatement, Trusts 2d, sec. 124, comment c.

[69] "While as against the grantee [trustee] the cestui has no enforceable rights, still if the grantee chooses to carry out his 'moral' obligation, even his creditors cannot complain. . . If the grantee cannot be compelled to carry out the trust, his recognition of it is as voluntary as if there were no trust. The whole doctrine is anomalous . . . [but too well established to be questioned now]." *Bryant v. Klatt*, 2 F.2d 167, 168–169.

[70] Restatement, Trusts 2d, sec. 124.

[71] Debts and claims in general, supra § 9.3-1 ff.

[72] Obviously, where the creditor is also the sole residuary beneficiary the question (in a solvent estate) is of no importance, except only as to the deductibility of the claim for inheritance or estate tax purposes; as to the latter, in the case of the Federal estate tax, cf. Rev. Rul. 60–247, 1960-2 Cum. Bull. 272.

SATISFACTION OF LEGACIES

the debt,[73] or to renounce the legacy[74] and assert his claim; he cannot have both. If the estate is insufficient to pay legacies in full,[75] it is obviously to the creditor's advantage to renounce the legacy and maintain his standing as a creditor, but the converse election would be preferable in some cases: for example, if the estate were insolvent but the testator exercised in favor of the creditor a power of appointment over property or a fund not otherwise subject to creditors' claims.[76]

§ 14.16-1. Bequest to debtor; forgiveness of debt. A bequest by a testator to his debtor may or may not be such a forgiveness of the debt as to preclude the executor from collecting the indebtedness, either by offsetting it against the legacy[77] or otherwise. It would seem that normally such a bequest, without other indication of intention, is not to be regarded as a forgiveness of the debt. An express forgiveness of an indebtedness is, of course, a legacy to the debtor of the amount of the debt,[78] and should be treated as such for such purposes as allocation of inheritance taxes[79] and apportionment (where required) of estate taxes;[80] also, for purposes of determining the abatement of legacies in an insolvent estate[81] the debt should presumably be treated as forgiven only in part and to the same degree as if the will had contained an express legacy equal in amount to the amount of the debt.

§ 14.16-2. ———; right of set-off or retainer.[82] Where a bequest to a debtor of the testator is not such as to amount to a forgiveness of the debt,[83] the right of the executor to set off the amount of the legacy against the amount of the debt, and thus to recover the latter (in full or *pro tanto*, as the case may be), is universally recognized.[84] Because it involves retaining the amount of the legacy (up to the amount of the debt), it is often referred to as a "right of retainer".[85] It exists even though the debt is unmatured at the time[86] (in which case the executor may have to

---

[73] Acceptance as in effect a compromise, supra § 9.9-2.
[74] Renunciation, infra § 14.26-1.
[75] Insolvent and insufficient estates, in general, infra Ch. XIX.
[76] Liability of appointive property for payment of debts, infra § 19.6.
[77] See next following section.
[78] Supra § 14.6-1.
[79] Supra § 12.10-2.
[80] Supra § 12.10-1.
[81] Infra § 19.5-1 ff.
[82] West Dig., Exrs. & Admrs. Key Nos. 275, 294, 434.
[83] See last preceding section.
[84] So in Unif. Prob. Code sec. 3-903. In intestate estate, debt is set off against share of debtor only, not those of his issue if he fails to survive; op. cit. sec. 2-111.
[85] Set-off or counterclaim against claimant, supra § 9.8-4.
[86] *Matter of Flint*, 120 Misc. 230, 198 N.Y.S. 190, 191–192 (affd. w/o op. 206 A.D. 778, 200 N.Y.S. 922): "That the legatee or heir should fulfill his obligation to the estate before receiving the bounty is clear, just, and equitable, and the Court should enforce it. The principle that the distributee is not entitled to his distributable share, while he retains in his own hand a fund out of which that and other legacies and shares ought to be paid, governs the instant case [of an unmatured debt]." As to a contingent claim, however, the right may not exist; cf. Unif. Prob. Code sec. 3-903.

postpone payment of the legacy until the debt matures, even though such postponement results in the incurrence of interest on the legacy[87]), and in logic it should exist against a legatee even though the debt in question is one owing by him jointly with another. The right also may exist even though collection of the debt is barred by a statute of limitation,[87a] or by a mortgage foreclosure "moratorium" statute.[88] In other respects, however, the debtor has all the defenses that would be available to him in a direct action to recover the debt.[89] Clearly, an executor who pays a legacy to a debtor of the testator without availing himself of such right, and then is unable to collect the debt, is surchargeable for the amount of the legacy or the amount of the debt, whichever is less, under the general principles governing liability for negligence or dereliction of duty.[90]

§ *14.17. Bequest to executor eo nomine.* It is possible that a bequest made to the executor, designating him as such, will be held to be beneficial to him, so that its subject matter becomes his individual property to do with as he wishes. Before such a bequest can be held to pass the property to the executor as an individual, however, an intention to that effect must be plainly manifested, and ordinarily the bequest will be held to be to the executor in an official or fiduciary capacity, on some secret trust. *A fortiori*, this result will tend to be reached where the bequest is accompanied by some expression of wish, hope, or confidence that the subject matter will be disposed of by the executor in some indicated way or to some indicated person or persons. If the language attached to the bequest is plainly precatory only, imposing no more than a moral duty, and the bequest can be construed as one to the executor individually, it will not fail merely because he is referred to as the executor; but if there is no clear indication that a personal benefit was intended the bequest will fail, on the theory that it attempts to create a trust (in the general sense) of which there is no ascertainable beneficiary or which there is no person entitled to enforce, and which therefore, under the general rules of trusts, cannot be given effect. In applying these principles it would seem quite unlikely, where the executor is a bank or trust company, that a legacy to it was intended to be beneficial and also unlikely that the testator intended to impose on it merely a moral obligation when he must have been aware of the general principle that a corporation cannot give away its property, and so a bequest to an executor which is a bank or trust company is even more likely to fail than one to an individual executor. In summary, however, it should be noted that in few other kinds of problems facing an executor are the decisions less consistent[91] and the results less predictable than in the case of a bequest to an executor *eo*

---

[87] Interest on legacies, infra § 14.31-3.
[87a] *Fleming v. Yeazel*, 379 Ill. 343, 40 N.E.2d 507.
[88] *Matter of Geiger*, 184 Misc. 518, 53 N.Y.S.2d 219. The right of retainer is equitable in nature, and distinct from the technical right of set-off in actions at law.
[89] So in Unif. Prob. Code sec. 3-903.
[90] Supra § 3.5-1.
[91] For that reason, citation of cases here has been deemed unhelpful, for want of space to analyze and discuss them individually.

SATISFACTION OF LEGACIES

nomine, and in almost every case of such a bequest it will be found very advisable, if not indeed essential, to obtain a judicial determination of its meaning and effectiveness, either in a construction or instruction proceeding or in connection with the approval of a proposed distribution of the estate on the executor's accounting or otherwise.

§ 14.18-1. *Legatees not capable of taking; subscribing witness.* In some jurisdictions a subscribing witness to a will, at least if his testimony was necessary to prove it, is barred by statute from taking any benefit under the will, and accordingly a legacy to him is ineffective.[92] Such a statute is, of course, to be distinguished from one taking what may be thought of as the converse approach that a beneficiary under a will is disqualified from being a subscribing witness.[93]

§ 14.18-2. ———; *unincorporated associations.* Ordinarily an unincorporated association is not a legal entity capable of taking and holding property, and accordingly a bequest to such an association is ineffective. The problem often arises in connection with bequests to social clubs, fraternity chapters, and various other voluntary groups and associations, that are not corporations. A statute in some states validates such a bequest if the association becomes incorporated within a specified time, as one year after probate of the will. Apart from such a statute, or in its absence, it is held in some jurisdictions that if the association has a "parent" organization which can take and hold property, as in the case of a national church or a bishopric whose unincorporated local congregation or parish is the intended legatee, the legacy may be paid to such parent under a promise that it will be held for the use and benefit of the local organization, and the legacy thereby given effect; but an executor should ordinarily not make payment pursuant to this rule without the approval of the appropriate court, obtained in an accounting proceeding or otherwise.

§ 14.18-3. ———; *person responsible for death of decedent.* Under the rule of public policy that a person will not be permitted to profit by his own wrong, a legatee who is responsible for the testator's death ordinarily cannot receive his legacy, and the bequest fails.[94] Similarly, in an intestate estate, an heir or distributee responsible for his decedent's death cannot inherit.[95] A criminal conviction of homicide will usually be conclusive as to the fact of the killing;[96] but, as the "wrong" against which the rule is directed presumably is a wrong against the decedent, or tort, rather than a wrong against the state, or crime, it should follow that neither is a criminal

---

[92] Devisee under will who was a witness to a codicil cutting down his benefit held not precluded from taking the reduced benefit; *Matter of Moore*, N.Y.L.J. Dec. 28, 1961, p. 16.

[93] Under statute requiring attestation of will by witnesses "not beneficially interested" under it, probate was denied to a will containing a bequest of $ 5 to each witness "as a token of appreciation"; *Re Will of Moody*, 155 Me. 325, 154 A.2d 165, 73 A.L.R.2d 1225.

[94] So in Unif. Prob. Code sec. 2-803(a).

[95] Ibid.

[96] So in Unif. Prob. Code sec. 2-803(e). Cf. *Larendon Est.*, 439 Pa. 535, 266 A.2d 763, where a conviction in another state was accepted by both the trial court and the appellate court as conclusive of status as a slayer.

conviction necessary to cause failure of the bequest or inheritance[97] nor is an acquittal on a criminal charge decisive against such failure. Whether, when the wrongdoer is the spouse, so-called "exempt" property, or other share or amount of the estate that by statute passes to a spouse outside the administerable estate,[98] can take effect is a question on which authority is apparently lacking. It would seem to depend in part, at least, on whether the spouse's right is or is not to be regarded as of the nature of an inheritance.[98a]

§ 14.18-4. ———; *charitable or religious corporation*. An occasional statute prohibits a charitable or religious corporation from receiving, or from holding, property exceeding a specified amount or value.[99] Where such a statute applies, the bequest fails to the extent that it exceeds the permitted maximum, and the executor may therefore be required, before satisfying the legacy, to ascertain what property the corporation already holds; obviously this is a matter that the executor ordinarily will not be able or willing to decide himself, and a judicial proceeding for instructions,[100] or an appropriate raising of the issue in an action by the corporation to compel satisfaction of the legacy, will be required.

§ 14.19-1. *Legatees not permitted to receive*;[1] *in general*. In the immediately preceding sections there have been considered cases of a legatee disqualified from being such, so that the legacy fails. Such cases are to be distinguished from those now about to be discussed, where the legatee is not disqualified but payment to him is not permitted, and must be made to another for his benefit.[2]

§ 14.19-2. ———; *infant legatees*.[3] An infant legatee is not precluded by law from taking or holding property; a legacy to him is valid and effective, but an executor is not protected in paying the legacy to the infant because an infant is not legally competent to receive and manage property and so cannot effectively receipt for the legacy or discharge the executor from liability as to it. Payment may be made, if the executor is to protect himself against possible future question, only to a guardian duly authorized to receive it, either by virtue of a judicial appointment or (under a statute providing therefor) an appointment by will, or, in some jurisdictions, by virtue of a statute making a parent the "natural guardian" of the property of his infant child.[4] A statute of the latter character, however, usually permits the parent as such natural guardian to receive property only up to a specified amount or value, and an executor proposing to pay an infant's legacy to the parent pursuant to

---

[97] So in Unif. Prob. Code sec. 2-803(e).
[98] Exempt property in general, infra §§ 17.1, 18.3-2.
[98a] Apparently so regarded in Unif. Prob. Code sec. 2-803(a).
[99] See Restrictions on Charitable Testamentary Gifts, 5 Real Prop. Prob. & Tr. J. 290, 295–297. Devise to corporation, infra § 15.4.
[100] Infra Ch. XXII.
[1] West Dig., Exrs. & Admrs. Key No. 304.
[2] Problems as to incompetent and possibly incompetent legatees, infra § 14.20.
[3] P-H Est. Plng. Serv. ¶ 2508.
[4] Cf. Unif. Prob. Code sec. 3-915.

such a statute must ascertain whether he would be protected in making the payment, even though the legacy does not exceed the statutory maximum, if the parent already holds other property for the infant of such amount that the addition to it of the legacy would cause the statutory limit to be exceeded. Somewhat similarly, an executor before paying to a guardian appointed by court or will must assure himself not only that the guardian has been duly appointed (and, if the guardian was appointed in another jurisdiction, that the executor is protected by the law of his state in paying to a foreign fiduciary[5]) but also that the guardian either is not required to give bond or has furnished bond in an amount sufficient to cover the legacy as well as any other property held; and an executor making payment to a guardian appointed by a will other than that of the executor's decedent must satisfy himself that under applicable law a guardian so appointed may receive the legacy and is not restricted to property passing to his ward under the will in which his appointment was made.

§ 14.19-2a. ———; ———; *will provision for payment to parent or another*. A will sometimes provides that a legacy bequeathed to an infant may be paid or delivered to the infant's parent, or another third person, for the infant's benefit. The effectiveness of such a provision is open to serious question, unless a statute clearly permits such dealing with an infant's property, and may constitute a trap to the executor. The provision is plainly not intended to pass the property to the parent or third person in beneficial ownership, and yet it does not create an active trust, nor can it constitute the recipient a guardian;[6] the infant is thus deprived of the protection that would be given him by the judicial control over trustees and guardians, and the public policy that is reflected in guardianship statutes is violated. The result may well be that an executor who satisfies a bequest to an infant by payment or delivery to the parent or another in reliance upon such a provision may find himself personally liable to the infant when the latter, upon attaining majority (or a legal guardian later appointed for him during his minority), asserts that the subject matter of the bequest was misapplied, lost, or dissipated by the recipient and did not enure to the benefit of the infant.

§ 14.19-2b. ———; ———; *powers of management during minority*. In at least some jurisdictions a testator may effectively provide in his will, in substance, that any property passing thereunder to a person who is a minor shall vest in the minor but may in the executor's discretion be retained by him during the minor's minority and be administered in much the same manner as a trust fund; the executor while retaining property under such a provision may be authorized to accumulate its income (subject to any statutory limitations on accumulation) or to apply income or principal, or both, to the benefit of the minor as deemed necessary or advisable. Since legal title is vested in the minor, the executor is not a trustee, but is the holder of a power, which is sometimes referred to as a "power in trust" because it is held in a fiduciary

---

[5] If not, the executor may and ordinarily should insist upon the appointment of a guardian in his own state before making the payment.

[6] Such a statute would not seem to be equivalent to one making the parent a "natural" guardian of the infant; see last preceding section.

capacity, i.e., for the benefit of the minor and not that of the executor. An executor of a will containing such a grant of power must satisfy himself that a power of that character is recognized by the applicable law, and, if it is, must further satisfy himself what administrative powers are conferred upon him as donee of the power and, in particular, what powers of investment and management of the fund he is given by the will or by law, bearing in mind that he is not acting as executor or as testamentary trustee in respect of the property held under the power, and so does not have the inherent or statutory powers of those fiduciaries, but rather is acting only as donee of a power. Also, if the terms of the will do not grant a merely discretionary power to retain the minor's property, but instead are mandatory in form, so as to purport to require such retention, the executor must consider whether the provision amounts to a power or instead creates a trust, and, if the latter, whether the executor must "qualify" as a trustee (where qualification of some nature by a testamentary trustee is required[7]) before acting under the provision.

§ 14.19-3. ———; *persons in "iron curtain" countries.* In some jurisdictions statutes provide in substance that, if it appears that a legatee resides in a foreign country and would not have the personal benefit of the legacy, the legacy shall not be paid to the legatee; some statutes provide that the bequest shall lapse, others that it shall be paid into court or to a specified public officer, to be held until the legatee appears in person or otherwise demonstrates that he can have its benefit. Such statutes are intended for the protection of legatees in countries "behind the iron curtain" or elsewhere whose governments would presumably confiscate the legacy, either directly or by compelling its conversion into local funds at an unfavorable rate of exchange. Efforts of consular officers of such foreign countries to obtain payment to them of legacies to their nationals, under the usual rules permitting foreign consuls to represent their nationals interested in American estates, have generally been frustrated by the courts. There is a question as to the constitutionality of at least some statutes of this character;[8] but unless or until invalidity is established, it would seem that the executor should not make payment to a legatee or anyone representing him in a case to which such a statute applies, and in every case of a legacy to a person residing abroad the executor should make sure whether such a statute exists in the state whose law governs the administration and distribution of the estate.[9] It will, of course, be apparent that a statute providing for payment into court or a public officer does not disqualify the legatee or render him incapable of taking the legacy, for he may obtain it if and when he can fulfill the statutory conditions.

---

[7] Infra § 27.3.

[8] *Zschernig v. Miller,* 389 U.S. 429, 88 S.Ct. 664, 19 L.ed. 683, holding an Oregon statute unconstitutional, apparently on the ground that it constituted an unwarranted interference by a state in foreign affairs; *Demczuk Est.,* (Pa.) 282 A.2d 700, holding a Pennsylvania statute invalid. But cf. *Pet. of Mazurowski,* 331 Mass. 33, 116 N.E.2d. 854, upholding a Massachusetts statute, and *Matter of Leikind,* 22 N.Y.2d 346, 292 N.Y.S.2d 681, 239 N.E.2d 550, upholding a New York statute.

[9] What law governs, in general, infra § 25.4-4b.

§ *14.20. Incompetent and possibly incompetent legatees.*[10] As in the case of an infant,[11] an incompetent is not disqualified from or incapable of being a legatee. However, an executor is, of course, not protected in making payment of a legacy to a legatee who has been adjudged incompetent, and may pay only to a duly appointed guardian, committee, or other legal representative (by whatever name known) authorized to receive and deal with the property of the incompetent;[12] and, if such legal representative was appointed in another jurisdiction, the executor must (again as in the case of a guardian of an infant) satisfy himself that the representative was lawfully appointed and that the executor is protected in paying to the foreign representative. If the incompetent does not have a guardian or other representative who is authorized to receive the incompetent's property and to whom the executor may safely pay or deliver the legacy, the executor must ordinarily insist upon the appointment of a qualified representative before the legacy may be satisfied. Similarly, in the case of a legatee who is in a mental institution, by whatever name known, even though he has not been adjudged incompetent, the executor ordinarily will refrain from making payment of the legacy to the legatee unless or until he can be satisfied that the legatee is in fact capable of managing his own affairs. Very difficult practical problems often arise, however, in the case of a legatee who has not been adjudged incompetent and is not in an institution but whose competency the executor has reason to doubt. The executor is probably not protected in making payment to a *de facto* incompetent where the executor is on notice or inquiry as to the fact, but the executor ordinarily is not in a position, and has no legal standing, to institute an investigation into the legatee's competency or to have a guardian or representative appointed for him, and the legatee's family seldom wishes to have such a proceeding brought or will cooperate in bringing it. In few if any jurisdictions does the law make any provision for such a case, so that the executor has no clear remedy or means of obtaining protection. Where a judicial proceeding for settlement of the executor's account[13] is to be had, it may be possible, through suggestion in that proceeding of possible inability of the legatee to manage his own affairs, to have a guardian ad litem or special guardian appointed therein for the legatee, so that the judgment or decree will instruct the executor as to payment of the legacy and furnish protection to him as against any further questions.[14]

§ *14.21-1. Location and identification of legatees; in general.* The executor, as part of his duties in carrying out the will, has the responsibility of locating and iden-

---

[10] P-H Est. Plng. Serv. ¶¶359–366.
[11] Supra § 14.19-2.
[12] So in Unif. Prob. Code sec. 3-915.
[13] Infra §24.5-2.
[14] The executor will, of course, be cautious in so proceeding, lest he harm the legatee in standing or reputation, or lay himself open to criticism. If, however, the facts are such as to cause the executor reasonably to doubt the legatee's competence, the executor is entitled to protection in satisfying the legacy and it seems unlikely that he could justifiably be criticized for seeking it, unless there is a family member who can and will adequately indemnify him.

tifying the persons designated therein to receive legacies or other benefits thereunder, at the risk of failing to pay a legacy to a person entitled to receive it or of paying it to the wrong person.[15] He must take all reasonable steps to determine the whereabouts, identities, and continued existence of intended legatees, and is warranted in expending estate funds for that purpose.[16] While ascertaining the whereabouts of a legatee may usually present no problem, in some cases the executor may have serious difficulty in that regard, especially where the will was executed long before the testator's death and the legatee's location has changed, or where the legatee's name has changed as a result of marriage, divorce, or otherwise; and it may even be impossible in some cases to locate a legatee.[17] Associated with the problem of locating legatees is that of identification of the persons intended; here again serious difficulty may occur, with the problem perhaps particularly troublesome where the legacy is to persons by description (as relatives of a stated degree, or issue,[18] of the testator or another) rather than to individuals *nominatim*. A somewhat different problem of identification arises out of a bequest to the "wife" (without naming her) of a designated person; the executor must ascertain whether a wife of such person survived the testator, whether she is the same person who was the wife at the execution of the will (and if not how the bequest is to be construed), and perhaps even, if the term "wife" be regarded as indicating a status rather than as merely descriptive of an individual, whether the marriage was valid. Similar to the problem, elsewhere mentioned, of the identification of an intended charitable institution[19] is that arising where the name of an individual is incorrectly or incompletely given, or where there is room for doubt as to which of two persons of the same name or similar names was intended. A related problem that may arise is whether a particular person is truly the person mentioned in the bequest.[20] Apart from questions as to identity, there may arise a question as to the shares in which two or more legatees are intended to take the legacy, particularly where they are issue of the same person and it is not made clear in the will whether they are to take *per stirpes* or *per capita*; in some states there is a statutory or judicial rule of construction that may solve such a problem. Plainly, where there is doubt as to any of such matters as are discussed in this section, the executor proceeds at his peril in making a distribution, and if he errs he is liable to persons damaged by it and has no recourse except to endeavor to recover the overdistributions or improper distributions from the recipients thereof; and so, unless agreement by all persons in interest is obtained, he may need to obtain a judicial determination for the protection of all concerned. Such matters as the distinction in these matters between latent and patent ambiguities in a will, and the admissibility

---

[15] Identifying charitable legatees, supra § 14.14-1.
[16] As administration expense, infra § 20.1.
[17] See next following section.
[18] Adopted or illegitimate children as "issue" etc., infra § 14.21-3; class gifts, infra § 14.24-1 ff.
[19] Supra § 14.14-1.
[20] Cf. *Matter of Dimond*, N.Y.L.J. Aug. 12, 1966, p. 7 (where legatee was clearly not a relative of testator, was identified in the will only by name, and the name was not uncommon).

SATISFACTION OF LEGACIES 181

vel non of extrinsic evidence to resolve them, should be in mind in connection with the problems discussed.[21]

§ 14.21-2. ———; *inability to locate legatee.*[22] Where, after due diligence, an executor is unable to discover the whereabouts or existence of a legatee, he may have available a statutory procedure[23] for deposit of the subject matter of the bequest in court or with a specified public officer, pending appearance of the legatee or, alternatively, proof that he did not survive the testator. At least if such procedure is unavailable, the executor should apply to the appropriate court for instructions[24] in any such case, and he proceeds at his own risk if he disposes of the property to which the legacy relates on the assumption that the legatee predeceased the testator and the legacy accordingly has lapsed.[25] Where, however, the legacy is not a specific one,[26] and its subject matter would fall into the residue if the legatee failed to survive,[27] and the residue is left in trust,[28] the executor may decide to postpone the problem by treating the subject matter as a part of the residue, subject to an appropriate refunding agreement on the part of the trustee, with the thought that by the time the trust terminates the legatee may have been located or his non-survival established.[29]

§ 14.21-3. ———; *illegitimate or adopted children as "issue", etc.* It is an established rule that the terms "issue", "children",[30] "descendants", and the like,[31] do not extend to illegitimate children, in the absence of indication of a contrary intention.[32] Whether adopted children are included within such terms is frequently a question of considerable difficulty and the authorities are far from uniform. At common law they were not so included. In some states the question is affected by a statute, usually designed to permit such inclusion only if it does not preclude taking by blood relatives or does not dilute their benefits; but such a statute, like the common law rule of exclusion, gives a way to a contrary intention. It would seem more likely that persons adopted by the testator himself, even if after the execution of the will, will be so included than persons adopted by others; and, in the case of adoption by another, it would seem that persons adopted before the execution of the will are more likely to be so included than those adopted afterward. The question thus usually turns upon intention, as deduced from such things as whether the testator knew of

---

[21] Latent and patent ambiguities in general, 57 Am. Jur., Wills, secs. 1042–1044.
[22] West Dig., Exrs. & Admrs. Key No. 303(3).
[23] Cf. Unif. Prob. Code sec. 3-914.
[24] Proceeding for instructions, infra § 22.2.
[25] Lapse of legacy on non-survival of legatee, infra §§ 14.23-1, -2, Doubt as to survivorship, in general, infra §14.22-1.
[26] Defined, supra § 14.4-1.
[27] Lapsed legacies as falling into residue, infra § 18.3-3.
[28] Testamentary trusts, infra Ch. XXVII.
[29] The analogy to the case of an unmatured or unliquidated claim will be apparent; supra § 9.3-2.
[30] "Children" and "issue", in general, supra § 1.14.
[31] Class gifts, infra § 14.24-1 ff.
[32] *Byers v. Womack*, 37 F.2d 816.

the adoption, if so when he learned of it (as bearing on the making of the will or failure to change it), his attitude toward the adopted child and perhaps the adoptive parent, and the like, and as a practical matter each case must be resolved on its own particular factual situation.[33] The modern tendency appears to be toward the inclusion of adopted persons in the class of beneficiaries under such language; but in almost every case where the question arises the executor, unless all interested persons are in agreement,[34] must submit the matter for a judicial determination.[35] In all matters having to do with the rights of illegitimate or adopted children, the executor should have in mind that many such persons are unaware that they are not lawful and natural children, and that unnecessary or untactful disclosure to them of the facts may result in serious psychological trauma.

§ *14.22-1. Doubt as to survivorship;*[36] *in general.* In view of the rule that a legacy lapses[37] if no beneficiary qualified to receive it survives the testator,[38] it is necessary for the executor to make sure whether a designated legatee did or did not survive. At common law, in cases of uncertainty various presumptions were indulged. In nearly all states, however, such presumptions have been superseded by adoption of the Uniform Simultaneous Death Act, under which, if there is no sufficient evidence that two persons died otherwise than simultaneously, the property of each is to be disposed of as if he had survived the other, unless the will otherwise provides.[39] It is to be emphasized, however, that neither such a statute, nor a will provision to like effect,[40] relieves the executor of the duty to ascertain the facts if possible; instead, it applies only where after due diligence it has not been found possible to determine the facts. It is also to be recognized that it may not be possible to determine whether there is "no sufficient evidence" until a hearing on the point is had, and the executor accordingly should not proceed in any case of doubt without taking appropriate steps to have the question judicially determined.

§ *14.22-2.* ———; *"common disaster" provisions of wills.*[41] The rules otherwise governing the disposition of a legacy when the order of deaths of the testator and the legatee is in doubt or not determinable[42] may be altered by the terms of the will, as by a provision that the testator, or the legatee, shall be deemed to have sur-

---

[33] Cf. *In re Day's Trust*, 10 A.D.2d 220, 198 N.Y.S.2d 760 (where a child adopted by a son of testator seven years before the latter's death was held to be included within the term "issue" as used of trust remaindermen; and to prevent obvious inequality a child who had been adopted by another son ten years after testator's death was also held so included).

[34] Agreements with or among beneficiaries, infra Ch. XXI.

[35] Construction and instruction proceedings, infra Ch. XXII.

[36] P-H Est. Plng. Serv. ¶¶ 370, 371.

[37] Supra § 14.2.

[38] Fact and time of testator's death, supra § 5-1 ff.

[39] Cf. Unif. Prob. Code secs. 2-104, 2-601 under which one not surviving for 120 hours is to be deemed not to have survived.

[40] "Common disaster" provisions, see next following section.

[41] P-H Est. Plng. Serv. ¶2697.4.

[42] See last preceding section.

vived;[43] and in numerous wills the provision calls for one result in the case of, for example, the spouse and the contrary result in the case of other legatees.[44] Such a provision is properly to be regarded as a rule of construction, directing that the provisions of the will that are to be operative are those that speak in terms of the survivorship, or nonsurvivorship, as the case may be, of the spouse or other legatee.[45] A provision as to survivorship may, however, present problems to the executor and in some instances may entrap him. A provision, for example, relating to death "in" a common accident or disaster may not apply where testator or legatee, or both of them, survive the accident or disaster but die from injuries received therein; and a provision relating to death "as a result of" the common accident or disaster gives rise to questions where one or both survive but die a considerable time, perhaps even months or years, after the accident or disaster but as a result of injuries therein sustained. Further, the conventional common disaster provision often fails to contemplate the possibility that testator and legatee will die from causes other than a common accident or disaster, and perhaps at widely separated places, but within such a short space of time of one another that doubt exists as to which survived; if the clause does not cover such an occurrence the executor is, of course, relegated to the statutory or judicial rules otherwise applicable. A clause in the will following the language of the statute that would apply if the will were silent on the point does not aid in the solution of a problem as to survivorship. Probably the problem is most eased by a clause which refers to or speaks in terms of reasonable, or substantial, doubt as to the order of deaths (without limitation to cases of common accident or disaster); but even under such a clause the executor must determine at his peril what is reasonable, or substantial, doubt and so, in a case where the facts are open to argument, he may wish before satisfying the legacy or refusing to satisfy it to obtain a judicial determination of the question or judicial approval of his proposed action.

§ 14.23-1. *Lapse;*[46] *in general.* As mentioned in a preceding section,[47] a bequest lapses[48] where it fails to be effective for a reason pertaining to the legatee, or to rules of law or policy, rather than (as in the case of abatement or ademption) for a reason pertaining to the subject matter of the bequest. The most usual case of lapse is that of the failure of the designated legatee to survive the testator; in such case the bequest fails for want of a legatee to take it, except of course where an alternate legatee is designated in the will or is supplied by a non-lapse statute.[49] A somewhat

---

[43] Effectiveness of provision for purposes of Federal estate tax marital deduction, see Regs. 20.2056(e)-2(e).

[44] Particularly where a marital deduction is desired, the will often provides that in any case of doubt the spouse is to be deemed to have survived, but any other legatee is presumed to have predeceased the testator. As to problems and considerations involved, see Brown, Planning Against Simultaneous Death, N.Y. State Bar J., Feb. 1970, 119.

[45] *Est. of Currier*, N.Y.L.J. Mar. 20, 1967, p. 17.

[46] West Dig., Wills Key Nos. 889–866.

[47] Supra § 14.2.

[48] Lapse of devises, infra § 15.4.

[49] See next following section, Cf. also somewhat analogous "residue of the residue" rule, infra § 18.7-2.

similar case is that of the renunciation of the bequest by the legatee,[50] or that of a legatee incapable of taking the bequest.[51] Lapse may, however, occur in other situations; for example, where the bequest is for an illegal purpose, or (except in certain cases of charitable bequests[52]) a purpose impossible of being carried out, or is for a purpose or upon terms contrary to rules of public policy.[53] This latter category includes a bequest which is such as to be void *ab initio* because of violation of the rule against perpetuities or a statute of like nature;[54] and by the same token a bequest which violates such rule or statute as to one or more interests created but is not such as to be wholly void lapses in part and as to the violative provisions. In cases of the kinds referred to in the two preceding sentences the lapse occurs, in a sense, not because there is no beneficiary to take but because the law does not permit the bequest to be effective; but in another sense it may be said that even in such cases the failure pertains to the beneficiary, in that a beneficiary who cannot be allowed to take must be regarded as non-existent, and in that sense lapse always results from absence of a legatee. In all cases discussed, therefore, the subject matter of the bequest does not pass to the designated legatee, but, with the exceptions noted, the property is to be disposed of as if the bequest were not contained in the will.[55] It has been suggested that questions of occurrence and consequences of lapse should be governed by the law of the testator's domicile at the time of the death of the legatee or other operative event.[56]

§ *14.23-2.* ———; *non-lapse statutes.* References are made in the preceding section to statutes, in some jurisdictions, intended to prevent the lapse of legacies[57] in certain cases of failure of the designated legatee to survive. Such a statute, where one exists, ordinarily applies only in such one cause of lapse, and not to lapse caused by any other circumstance.[58] Some statutes apply to every legacy, but most statutes apply only where the legatee is of some specified kind or degree of relationship to the testator, as a child or kindred.[59] In all cases the statute is to the effect that if issue of the deceased legatee survive the testator, the legacy shall not lapse but shall pass to such issue, unless, of course, a contrary intent appears in the will.[60] All such statutes that have been enacted apply the non-lapse rule to the legatee's failure to survive the testator, and some make it also apply to legatees who, even if they survive the testator, fail to survive the termination of a precedent estate, as in the case of remaindermen dying before a life tenant. A non-lapse statute may be regarded as somewhat

---

[50] Infra § 14.26-1.
[51] Supra § 14.18-1 ff.
[52] Cy. pres, supra § 14.14-2.
[53] As to "honorary trusts," supra § 14.14-3.
[54] Perpetuities violations, infra § 14.35-2.
[55] Lapsed legacies as falling into residuary estate, infra § 18.3-3.
[56] Ehrenzweig, Conflict of Laws, p. 675. Questions of governing law, in general, infra Ch. XXV.
[57] And usually devises also; infra § 15.4.
[58] Other causes of lapse, see last preceding section.
[59] Under Unif. Prob. Code sec. 2-605, grandparent or descendants of grandparent.
[60] Where legacy is a "class gift," infra § 14.24-4.

SATISFACTION OF LEGACIES 185

analogous to a statute of descent and distribution in that it disposes of property that, in the event that has occurred, the testator has not disposed of (except perhaps by a residuary clause), and carries out what may be thought to have been the probable intent of the testator or, more accurately, supplies an intent to him.[61] Therefore, as indicated above, such a statute does not apply where a contrary intent appears, as where the legacy is expressly conditioned upon survivorship. In the absence of such a condition, it is incumbent upon the executor, in every case of a predeceased legatee, to determine whether issue of the legatee survived, if so whether a non-lapse statute exists in the relevant jurisdiction, and if so whether the legatee was within the class of legatees to whom the statute relates.

§ 14.24-1. *Class gifts;*[62] *in general.* Where a legacy is bequeathed to two or more persons in common, or to be divided between or among them, and any such person fails to survive the testator, or the termination of a precedent life estate or the like, the executor may have to determine whether the bequest constitutes a "class gift".[63] This is because a class gift is an exception to, or does not fall within, the rule that a legacy lapses if the legatee does not survive to take it.[64] So, while a bequest of a share of property to each of two or more individuals, either *nominatim* or by description, lapses in part if one of them fails to survive, and the share he would have taken if living therefore does not pass under the bequest, the non-survival of a member of a class to which a legacy is bequeathed does not cause a lapse of any share or part of the legacy and instead (in the absence of an applicable anti-lapse statute[65]) those members of the class who do survive take the entire legacy, the number of shares into which it is divided being thus reduced and the size of each share correspondingly increased. Further, if a bequest is to be regarded as a class gift, and additional persons come into being, after the testator's death or the termination of the precedent estate as the case may be, who are within the description of the class, or newly come within the description for any other reason, the executor may have to determine whether the class opens to admit such additional persons.[66] As implied above, any problem of class gift created by the failure of a member of the class to survive may be obviated if there is an applicable anti-lapse statute; but any problem created by afterborn or after-qualifying persons will still remain.

§ 14.24-2. ———; *what is a class gift.* Generally speaking, the factor that distinguishes a class gift from individual gifts is the intention, as manifested in the will, to pass the subject matter of the bequest to those who shall constitute a designated or described class, group, or aggregation of persons at the time for ascertainment of the

---

[61] For two theories as to purpose of anti-lapse statutes, ibid.
[62] West Dig., Wills Key No. 634(14); P-H Est. Plng. Serv. ¶¶ 363, 369.
[63] Nature and features, see next following section.
[64] Supra § 14.23-1.
[65] Non-lapse statutes in general, see last preceding section; applicability to class gifts, infra § 14.24-4.
[66] When class is to be ascertained, infra § 14.24-3.

legatees, with the number of shares dependent upon the number of such persons, rather than to give a fixed share of fraction of the property to each of certain persons.[67] Obviously, if the bequest is in terms to named persons, in specified shares, there is no intent to make a class gift; and if the bequest is to such of the named persons as survive, or there is designated an alternate taker of the bequest to any such person who fails to survive, an intention not to make a class gift is apparent. In other cases, however, many problems can arise, and in a number of respects the authorities are not in full agreement. Some of the questions that may face the executor are whether there is a class gift only where the class is a "natural" one, as the issue of a designated person or a set of persons already in some way related to associated, or whether a class gift results from a bequest to any group treated by the testator as a class, regardless of any common characteristic in its membership; whether a bequest to a named person and a described group constitutes a class gift in the sense that the named person is a member of the class so that his failure to survive does not cause a partial lapse;[68] and whether a bequest to persons identified by name with some descriptive term added, as "my children", is to be treated as a class gift. Because, as mentioned above, the answers to such questions as these depend in the first instance on the testator's intention as ascertained or inferred from the will, any guidelines deducible from other cases are at most persuasive in any particular case and not decisive or controlling.

§ 14.24-3. ———; *when class to be ascertained.* In the case of an outright bequest to a class, the members of the class are, by the weight of authority, to be ascertained as of the time of the testator's death, unless a contrary intention appears; "the roll is called" at that time and the class membership is fixed. This has been called a rule of convenience,[69] to facilitate the administration of estates and the distribution of property; but as the convenience is to the executor and the then members of the class, and not to persons afterward qualifying for membership or even to the testator, courts have tended to find evidence of a contrary intention when they feel that the testator would have intended otherwise if he had considered the problem. In the case of a future interest, as a remainder to a class after a life estate, it is usually held that the class is to be ascertained when the prior estate terminates, although some authorities apply the same rule as in the case of immediate gifts. Where, however, payments are directed to be made periodically or from time to time among a class (as distinguished from a lump sum payment in satisfaction of a legacy), the reason for the rule of convenience mentioned above disappears and the persons constituting the class are accordingly to be determined anew at each distribution date.[70]

---

[67] The principles may be epitomized by saying that if under the provisions of the will the persons to take are ascertained before the death of the testator there is not a class gift, whereas if they are ascertainable only at or after his death the bequest does or may constitute a class gift. Cf. *Lacy v. Murdock*, 147 Neb. 242, 22 N.W.2d 713.

[68] Non-survival of legatee as resulting in lapse, in general, supra § 14.2.

[69] *Cole v. Cole*, 229 N.C. 757, 51 S.E.2d 491.

[70] *In re Wenmoth's Est.*, 37 Ch. Div. 266.

SATISFACTION OF LEGACIES

§ 14.24-4. ———; *applicability of non-lapse statute.* There is some difference of opinion among the authorities as to whether a non-lapse statute,[71] where one exists, applies in the case of a class gift, so that on the death of a member of the class before the time for its ascertainment,[72] leaving issue then living, the share that the deceased member would have taken if living does not go to increase the shares of the surviving members[73] but instead passes to the issue of the deceased member. Those courts taking the view that the purpose of a non-lapse statute is to prevent intestacy in case of lapse hold that the non-lapse statute is not applicable to a class gift because failure of a class member to survive does not cause a lapse.[74] The courts viewing the non-lapse statute as intended to protect the issue of a deceased legatee hold, instead, that the statute applies as well to a class gift as to an individual gift. The weight of authority appears to be that such a statute does so apply.[75] It is apparent, however, that an executor confronted with the question must ascertain the law in the relevant jurisdiction.[76] Of course, any question of applying a non-lapse statute to a class gift can arise only where the statute would be applicable if the gift were to the deceased legatee as an individual; that is, the deceased legatee must be within the degree of relationship, if any, to which the statute is confined, the statute must be such as to apply not merely at the testator's death but at the time of ascertainment of the class, where that is after the testator's death, and issue of the deceased legatee must survive the time for such ascertainment.

§ 14.25. *Pour-over legacies.* Where "pour-over" or "spill-over" bequests to an existing *inter vivos* trust are recognized, such a bequest may be a general or demonstrative one. Because, however, such bequests most often involve dispositions of the residuary estate or part of it, they are for convenience discussed in that connection.[77]

§ 14.26-1. *Renunciation or disclaimer;[78] of legacy.* On the basis that no one may be required to accept a gift or other benefit from another, and that a bequest is of the nature of an offer of the subject matter to the legatee, a legatee may renounce or disclaim,[79] presumably in part as well as in whole, a legacy bequeathed to him, and refuse to accept it;[80] and an effective renunciation or disclaimer causes a lapse, with the same consequences as any other lapse,[81] except that the renounced legacy may not be

---

[71] Generally, supra § 14.23-2.
[72] Time for ascertainment of class, see last preceding section.
[73] As general rule of class gifts, supra § 14.24-1.
[74] Ibid.
[75] So in Unif. Prob. Code sec. 2-605.
[76] What law governs, in general, infra Ch. XXV.
[77] Infra § 18.5. Distinguished from "testamentary trust," infra § 27.5.
[78] P-H Est. Plng. Serv. ¶ 451.
[79] Except, under Unif. Prob. Code sec. 2-801, where an assignment, conveyance, pledge, or transfer of the subject matter, or a contract therefor, has been made, or right to renounce has been waived in writing. Disclaimer problems in general, and proposed legislation, see Disclaimer of Testamentary and Nontestamentary Dispositions, 3 Real Prop. Prob. and Tr. J. 131, and 4 ibid. 658.
[80] Refusal by executor to accept legacy in lieu of compensation, infra § 20.4-2c.
[81] Lapsed or renounced legacy as falling into residue, infra § 18.3-3. Tax consequences as in case of lapse, see Price, Postmortem Estate Planning Up to Date, 20 N.Y.U. Inst. on Fed. Taxation 301, 326.

"saved" by a non-lapse statute if, as is usual, such statute is in terms only of the non-survival of the legatee,[82] and, similarly, a designation in the will of an alternate taker in case of the non-survival of the renouncing legatee may not pass the legacy to such alternate,[83] unless, as to each such case, it is clear by statute or decision that a renounced legacy is to be treated for all purposes as if the renouncing legatee had failed to survive.[84] The rule is usually stated that a legacy may be renounced only if the legatee has not accepted or received any of its benefits; but it is doubtful that, except in some instances of benefits under a trust,[85] the rule means more than that if the legatee attempts to refuse the legacy after he has accepted any of its benefits he will be deemed to have accepted the subject matter and then made a gift of it to the person who succeeds to the property as a result of the "renunciation". Because, however, of the rights of others resulting from a renunciation by the named legatee, the executor must assure himself as to the effectiveness and, subject to the comment above, the timeliness of a purported or attempted renunciation or disclaimer of a legacy, and also, of course, must determine the disposition to be made of the subject matter of the bequest in the light thereof.

§ *14.26-2.* ————; *of intestate share.* While a legacy or other benefit under a will may be renounced by the legatee, it is usually held that one to whom property descends as an heir or intestate distributee, whether because of absence of a will or because the will fails to dispose of such property, is without power to renounce or disclaim, since in such case the property passes to him by operation of law which he cannot prevent or frustrate. In several jurisdictions, however, the rule has been changed by statute.[86]

§ *14.27-1.* *Satisfaction of cash legacy in property; in general.* An executor has no right to require a legatee of a pecuniary bequest[87] to accept property, in lieu of cash, in satisfaction of the bequest, unless the will otherwise provides. Wills often do otherwise provide, particularly in the case of a "marital deduction" bequest,[88] either outright or in trust, and either of a specified amount of money or under a pecuniary

---

[82] Supra § 14.23-2.

[83] It would seem clear that a legatee cannot renounce the legacy "in favor of" the alternate taker, but that he either (a) effectively renounces the legacy and it therefore passes to whomever is then entitled to it under the will or law, or (b) he accepts the legacy and assigns it to the alternate. Assignments by legatees in general, infra § 14.29.

[84] So in Unif. Prob. Code sec. 2-801(e); cf. Comment to that section that non-lapse statute accordingly applies.

[85] Where, as in the case of a "spendthrift trust," or by express statute, an income interest under a trust is non-assignable, the designated income beneficiary may renounce or refuse to accept the interest if he acts before receiving any income, but ordinarily if he accepts any distribution of income he is deemed to have accepted the benefit conferred upon him by the will and this is unable thereafter to renounce, as that would be in effect an assignment to the person who succeeded to the interest in question.

[86] So in Unif. Prob. Code sec. 2-801.

[87] Share legacies, infra § 14.28; residuary legacies, infra § 18.6-4.

[88] See next following section.

SATISFACTION OF LEGACIES

formula;[89] it is usual in making such bequests, especially because they are usually of relatively large size, to include explicit authorization to satisfy them in cash or in property. A legatee may, of course, even in the absence of such a provision, agree or consent to receive securities or other property in lieu of cash.[90] In any case where a cash legacy is to be satisfied in property, the property delivered must be of a fair market value, as of the date of transfer, equal to the amount of the legacy, and in this connection, as discussed in the next following section, special requirements may apply in the case of a marital deduction legacy under a pecuniary formula. A gain or loss for income tax purposes is, of course, realized by the executor in satisfying a pecuniary legacy is property, and is measured by the difference between the tax basis of the property used and the valuation at which it is turned over to the legatee, just as if the property had then been sold and its proceeds paid to the legatee.[91]

§ 14.27-2. ———; *marital deduction legacy*. As noted in the preceding section, wills containing a pecuniary bequest intended to qualify for the marital deduction under the Federal estate tax law or a state statute frequently authorize the legacy to be satisfied in property. Sometimes, however, such wills proceed to direct or permit the property used for the purpose to be applied by the executor to the legacy at the values determined for the purposes of the tax. An executor faced with such a provision must have in mind the possible disallowance of the deduction by reason thereof, and also must ascertain whether a statute of the governing estate overrides such provision. It is apparent that, where values of some estate assets are less at the time of satisfying the pecuniary bequest than their values as fixed for tax purposes, the provision would enable the executor to select for application upon the legacy those assets which had depreciated most, so that the spouse or her trust would receive less in value of property than the amount of the marital deduction allowed to the estate.[92] Accordingly, the deduction for at least Federal estate tax purposes is denied unless under the will or state law any assets used for satisfaction of a pecuniary marital deduction bequest must be applied at their current values, or be fairly representative of appreciation and depreciation in the values of all distributable assets.[93] In order to avoid the loss of such deduction, a number of states have enacted statutes intended

---

[89] Formulae bequests, supra § 14.8-2.

[90] Cf. Unif. Prob. Code sec. 3-906(a)(2), permitting a cash legacy to be satisfied in property unless the legatee demands money or a residuary legatee requests retention of the property.

[91] Tax considerations in distributions in kind, see Price, Postmortem Estate Planning Up to Date, 20 N.Y.U. Inst. on Fed. Taxation 301, 316–317.

[92] It will be obvious that no problem of this character arises under a "share" bequest, inasmuch as in the latter dollar values do not enter into the satisfaction of the legacy (supra §§ 14.8-2, 14.8-2b). Satisfaction of legacies of shares or fractions, see next following section and infra § 18.6-4a.

[93] Rev. Proc. 64-19, 1964-1 Cum.Bull. 682, so providing, but making an exception as to wills executed before Nov. 1, 1964, if the executor and spouse enter into agreement for such treatment. As to problems generally thereunder, see 1964 Proc. A.B.A. Sec. Real Prop. Prob. & Tr. L., Part I, 51 ff; problems of such agreements and authority of executor to execute them, see Lauritzen, The Marital Deduction, 103 Trusts and Estates 318, and Straus, When Should Agreements be Made?, op. cit. 911, and cf. comment in 1965 Proc. of Sec. cited supra, Part I, 53–64.

so to provide; unfortunately, some of such statutes appear to raise additional problems. An executor faced with a statute on the point must comply with its terms, notwithstanding the will provision, and will be liable for negligence[94] if his failure to do so causes denial of the deduction to the estate.

§ 14.28. Legacy of share or fraction. A bequest of a share or fraction of a group or class of assets, as of securities as a class, is to be clearly distinguished from a legacy of an amount, as in any but exceptional circumstances dollar amounts or values do not enter into the computation or satisfaction of such a bequest. As has been pointed out elsewhere, the distinction is particularly important, for both tax and administrative reasons, in the case of a "marital deduction" formula legacy,[95] but is not limited to that case.[96] Where the class of property to be divided under such a bequest consists of more than one kind of asset, as of securities of two or more kinds or two or more issuers, the principles relating to the division of the residuary estate are applicable.[97]

§ 14.29. Assignments by legatees. As assignment by a legatee of his legacy or interest under the will usually occurs only in the case of a residuary legatee, and is accordingly discussed herein in the chapter relating to distribution of the residue.[98] There is, however, no reason why any other legatee may not assign his legacy,[99] either absolutely or by way of security for an obligation, and the same considerations apply as in case of assignments of a residuary legacy.

§ 14.30. Satisfaction in lifetime; advancements.[100] Except within the boundaries of the doctrine of ademption by satisfaction,[1] a lifetime gift made by a testator, whether before or after the execution of his will, to a person named in the will as a general legatee has no bearing upon the legacy and the latter takes effect like any other legacy. As is mentioned elsewhere,[2] such a lifetime gift is sometimes referred to as an advancement. Advancement is, however, to be strictly distinguished from such a case, and the application of that term thereto is inaccurate. The primary distinction is that the doctrine of advancement applies only in an intestate estate, and thus not to a legacy; and, secondly, it applies only in the case of a gift by an intestate to his heir, whereas ademption by satisfaction can occur as to a cash legacy to any person. At common law, the doctrine of advancement was that a lifetime gift made by a parent to his child was presumed to be intended as an advance payment

---

[94] Negligence in general, supra § 3.5-1 ff.
[95] Supra § 14.8-2a.
[96] Division of tangibles, supra § 14.4-8.
[97] Infra § 18.6-4a. Legacy of amount out of residue, infra § 19.5-3a.
[98] Infra § 18.10.
[99] Attempted renunciation of legacy after its acceptance as equivalent to assignment, supra § 14.26-1.
[100] P-H Est. Plng. Serv. ¶¶ 427–428, 2700.1.
[1] Ademption of general legacy by satisfaction, supra § 14.6-3.
[2] Ibid.

SATISFACTION OF LEGACIES 191

of or on account of the child's eventual intestate share of the parent's estate,[3] unless a contrary intention was shown. In some jurisdictions the doctrine is extended to gifts to collateral heirs;[4] and statutes in some states in effect reverse the presumption mentioned by treating a lifetime gift as an advancement only if contemporaneously declared or acknowledged to be such.[5] One to whom an advancement has been made does not participate in the distribution of the donor's estate,[6] except only if and to the extent that the donee's intestate portion (including the advancement in hotchpot[7]) exceeds the lifetime gift,[8] and with that exception the estate passes wholly to the other heirs.

§ 14.31-1. *Time of payment or satisfaction;*[9] *in general.* Numerous factors are appropriate for consideration by an executor in determining when to satisfy legacies,[10] and whether to satisfy them wholly or in part only[11] at a given time. The first prerequisite is payment of or provision for all prior charges.[12] Statutes ordinarily prescribe a period for the presentation of claims against the estate,[13] and an executor who makes any payment or distribution to a legatee before the expiration of such period does so at his own risk, for if thereafter an unexpected claim or a claim in an unexpected amount should be timely presented the executor may find himself without sufficient funds to satisfy all claims.[14] For similar reasons, an executor must at all times retain enough assets in his possession to cover unmatured or contingent claims.[15] Obviously, he must also retain enough assets to cover all possible death taxes and deficiency assessments, including interest and penalties, until such taxes have been finally determined and paid;[16] and where such taxes are to be apportioned

---

[3] On the supposition that the parent would not intend a child to receive a "double portion."

[4] So in Unif. Prob. Code sec. 2-110; but see next following text and note.

[5] Ibid. Under such a statute a declaration or notation made after the making of the gift is ineffective. *In re Rawnsley's Est.*, 94 Cal. App. 2d 384, 210 P.2d 888; *Hirning v. Webb*, 91 Ida. 229, 419 P.2d 671; *Elliott v. Western Coal & Min. Co.*, 213 Ill. 614, 90 N.E. 1104; *Stark v. Stark*, 128 Neb. 524, 259 N.W. 523; *Arthur v. Arthur*, 146 Wis. 126, 126 N.W. 550.

[6] But if an heir whom an advancement was made predeceases the donor, such heir's issue, who take in their own right as heirs and not through their parent, are not chargeable with the advancement. *Person's App.*, 74 Pa. 121; so under Unif. Prob. Code sec. 2-110. Difference in result under doctrine of ademption by satisfaction when a non-lapse statute applies, supra § 14.6-3 note 53.

[7] Hotchpot to adjust advances, in general, P-H Est. Plng. Serv. ¶ 2700.1. But the heir who received an advancement exceeding his intestate share is not required to return the excess or to adjust it with other heirs.

[8] There may be a question whether the advancement is to be valued for this purpose as of the date of its receipt by the heir or as of the date of the decedent's death. Under Unif. Prob. Code sec. 2-110 it is the earlier of the two; cf. sec. 2-611 prescribing the same rule in case of ademption by satisfaction.

[9] West Dig., Exrs. & Admrs. Key Nos. 295, 309.

[10] Cf. 1965 Proc. A.B.A. Sec. Real Prop. Prob. & Tr. L., Part I, 43–44 See also supra § 13.5.

[11] Partial satisfaction, see next following section.

[12] Priority of claims over legacies, supra § 9.3-1; in insolvent estate, infra § 19.4-1.

[13] Supra § 9.4-2 ff.

[14] Personal liability of executor, supra § 9.3-4.

[15] Generally, supra § 9.3-2.

[16] Priority over legacies, supra § 12.1.

among takers of taxable property, he may be compelled further to delay satisfaction of a legacy to provide for or secure the legatee's apportioned share of taxes.[17] If a right of election by a spouse to take a share of the estate exists, delay may be necessary until the time for the exercise of such right expires.[18] Further the executor must have in mind the tax effects of a distribution of particular property as at a particular time.[19] Subject to considerations of the kinds mentioned, however, and to his duty of set-off or retainer as against a legatee-debtor[20] and subject also, of course, to any provision of the will for deferment of a legacy,[21] it is the duty of the executor to proceed with reasonable promptness to satisfy legacies (including residuary legacies[22]), and he may be held liable for waste[23] if he allows storage or safekeeping charges or insurance premiums to be incurred for an unnecessary length of time while he delays satisfaction of a specific legacy, or liable to any legatee who is damaged by an unreasonable delay;[24] and in an appropriate case of excessive delay he may be denied compensation,[25] removed from office,[26] or otherwise penalized.

§ 14.31-2. ———; *partial satisfaction.* On the same principles as those applying to residuary distribution,[27] where an executor for any reason is not in a position to make full payment or satisfaction of a legacy he should endeavor, where it is feasible so to do, and subject to the considerations discussed in the last preceding section, to make a partial payment or distribution on account of the legacy. This is consistent with the duty of promptness,[28] and in addition has the virtues of putting at least part of the legacy into the hands of the legatee, so that he may deal with or enjoy it, and of freeing the executor from further concern with the amount or property distributed; and in addition a partial distribution, where delays must occur in satisfying the bequest in full, tends to dissipate much of any anxiety or irritation that may be felt by a legatee, particularly one who does not understand estate problems and procedures.

§ 14.31-3. ———; *interest on cash legacies.*[29] Statutes frequently provide for the payment of interest on cash legacies that are not paid within a specified time after death or after qualification of the executor.[30] Unlike the penalties referred to

---

[17] Retention or collection of apportioned share, supra § 12.10-5.
[18] Rights of election in general, supra § 17.4-1 ff.
[19] Supra § 13.5.
[20] Supra §14.16-2.
[21] Deferred legacies, supra § 14.12-1.
[22] Distribution of residue, in general, infra § 18.6-1 ff.
[23] Generally, supra § 3.5-2.
[24] Liability for interest, infra § 14.31-3.
[25] Denial of compensation, in general, infra § 20.4-8.
[26] Removal, in general, infra § 23.3.
[27] Infra § 18.6-3.
[28] See last preceding section.
[29] West Dig., Exrs. & Admrs. Key Nos. 313, 315(8); P-H Est. Plng. Serv. ¶¶ 433–433.19.
[30] So in Unif. Prob. Code sec. 3-904. Sharing in income earned by estate distinguished, infra § 16.6-3.

SATISFACTION OF LEGACIES 193

in a preceding section,[31] the liability for interest under such statutes does not depend on fault of the executor, and the interest is ordinarily payable out of income of the estate[32] and not by the executor personally. Nevertheless, for gross negligence or nonfeasance resulting in excessive delays, an executor presumably may be compelled to pay such interest, or at least some part of it, out of his own pocket, at the instance of a residuary beneficiary (upon whose share of the estate the interest burden would otherwise fall), under general principles of liability for surcharge for negligence.[33] Where interest is payable, it may be at a rate prescribed by statute, or at or measured by the average rate earned by the estate during its administration,[34] and the applicable statute should be consulted. Liability for interest on legacies is not, however, a matter of public policy and so the estate may be exonerated therefrom by the testator by appropriate provision in his will.[35]

§ 14.31-4. ———; *establishment of trusts.* Where the will creates a trust,[36] particularly by a pre-residuary bequest, the executor should, of course, take into account the general considerations applicable to the satisfaction of other legacies,[37] and also give special consideration to the time of the establishment of such trust as affecting income taxation of the estate and of the trust or its beneficiaries.[38]

§ 14.32. *Duty of simultaneous payments or distributions.* Under his duty of impartiality as among beneficiaries,[39] an executor must not pay or satisfy, in whole or in part, a particular legacy without simultaneously paying or satisfying (ratably, if a partial payment is involved) all other legacies of the same class or order of priority.[40] The principle stated applies also, of course, to distributions of, or on account of, shares or fractions of the estate or a fund,[41] including the residuary estate;[42] in such case all persons entitled to share therein must receive ratable portions or amounts when any distribution is made.[43] Where, as sometimes is the case, there is no reason to delay satisfaction of one legacy but a legacy of the same class to another legatee must be temporarily delayed for a reason personal to the legatee, as,

---

[31] Supra § 14.31-1.

[32] Infra § 16.5-2.

[33] Supra § 3.6. Liability for interest in case of non-simultaneous payment of legacies, infra § 14.32.

[34] In some instances the interest rate exceeds the average income of the estate, so that residuary beneficiaries bear a loss. In such a case, their right to recover from the executor should be considered, if the delay was caused by his negligence or fault.

[35] Exculpatory provisions, in general, supra § 3.10.

[36] Testamentary trusts, in general, infra Ch. XXVII.

[37] See preceding sections.

[38] Administrative elections affecting income taxation, in general, supra § 13.5. Cf. 1964 Proc. A.B.A. Sec. Real Prop. Prob. & Tr. L., Part I, 51–52.

[39] Generally, supra § 3.9-3.

[40] Classification as to order of priority or abatement, infra § 19.5-1 ff.

[41] Legacies of shares or fractions, in general, supra § 14.28.

[42] Distribution of residue, infra § 18.6-1 ff.

[43] Distribution of ratable share of each asset or class of assets in fund, infra § 18.6-4a. Distribution to one legatee in kind and another in money, infra § 18.6-4b.

for example, where he is a minor and appointment of a guardian is being awaited[44] or where a supporting document, an estate tax waiver, or the like is not yet in hand, the executor ordinarily should not penalize or inconvenience the one legatee merely because the other cannot simultaneously receive corresponding satisfaction, and may carry out his duty of impartiality by making the one payment or delivery and setting aside the other amount or property in a separate account, segregated from the balance of the estate and appropriately labeled with the name of such other legatee, to be actually released to him when the existing impediment is removed. An executor who makes a payment (in whole or in part) of a cash legacy to one legatee without making (or segregating) a corresponding payment to another legatee of the same class may be required to pay interest to the latter for the period of delay.[45]

§ *14.33. Payment to legal representative of afterdying legatee.* Where a legatee survived the testator[46] but dies before the legacy is paid, the executor may not, in the absence of statute otherwise providing, pay the legacy to anyone other than a duly qualified legal representative of the deceased legatee. Accordingly, he must obtain appropriate evidence that the representative has been appointed and has qualified, and that his bond, if one was furnished,[47] is sufficient to cover the amount or value of the legacy in addition to whatever other property belonged to the legatee; and, if the representative was appointed in another jurisdiction, the executor must determine whether under the law of the state in which he is acting he is protected in paying to a foreign representative or must withhold payment until an ancillary representative is appointed to receive it.[48]

§ *14.34. Revocation of legacy by later instrument or by law.* A legacy contained in a will may be revoked by a codicil, either by explicit provision therein or, at least in the case of a specific legacy or devise, by a disposition therein of the same asset to another person or in a different manner; or of course, by revocation of the will in which it is contained.[49] A legacy may also be revoked by operation of law, as in the case, for example, in some states, of a legacy to a spouse where the marriage is dissolved after the execution of the will.[50] Legacies to persons who are precluded by law from taking,[51] and a legacy to a charity in excess of that permitted as against the objection of a spouse or child,[52] may also be thought of as revoked by law. A legacy revoked in any of these ways ordinarily falls into (or, more accurately, remains in) the residuary estate and is to be disposed of as a part thereof.[53] In the case, however,

---

[44] Legacies to infants, in general, supra § 14.19-2 ff.
[45] *Matter of Foster*, N.Y.L.J. Aug. 1, 1966, p. 8, Interest on legacies, in general, supra § 14.31-3.
[46] Non-survival as causing lapse of legacy, supra §§ 14.23-1, -2.
[47] Requirement of bond, supra § 5.8-2.
[48] Ancillary administration generally, supra § 1.7.
[49] Determination of "last" will, supra § 5.3-1 ff.
[50] Infra § 17.5.
[51] Supra § 14.18-1 ff.
[52] Infra § 17.7.
[53] Cf. § 18.3-3 infra.

SATISFACTION OF LEGACIES

of a revoked specific legacy or devise, the property may be otherwise specifically disposed of by a later instrument, or by another provision of the will itself, as where the revoked bequest is of one article of a kind or class and another provision of the will contains a bequest in general terms of articles of such kind or class; in the latter case a question of construction arises, as to whether such second provision is to be deemed to "pick up" the subject matter of the lapsed bequest or is effective only as to the other or remaining articles of the designated kind or class.

§ *14.35-1.* *Construction questions; in general.* There frequently arise questions of construction of bequests, as to such matters as identification of legatees or what persons are included in a class of intended legatees,[54] what property is the intended subject-matter of a bequest or the identification of the particular asset or item attempted to be disposed of,[55] the amount or share of money or property passing to a legatee or to each of a group or class of legatees,[56] and the like,[57] and the executor should at an early stage of his administration of an estate[58] consider whether any such questions, either patent or latent, exist and require answers. If such a question does exist, the executor should refrain from making any distribution, or taking any other steps, which would or might require change or reversal under any possible construction, until the problems are resolved. Statutes usually afford a reasonably expeditious means of submitting such questions to the appropriate court and obtaining a judicial determination of them.[59] In some instances it may be possible to resolve a question of this kind by agreement, where all persons having any possible interest in the problem are *sui juris* and join in the agreement.[60] In the absence of such agreement, the executor should seek a judicial determination at the proper time and in the proper manner, considering in that connection the general principles as to time and expense that are elsewhere discussed.[61]

§ *14.35-2.* ———; *perpetuities problems.* Where a will provides for a conditional or deferred legacy, or creates a trust or successive legal interests, and because thereof or for any other reason there is any possibility, whether turning on a factual situation or a construction question, that there may be a violation of the applicable rule against perpetuities or a statute of similar purpose, the executor should seek a judicial determination of the validity and effect of the provisions before distributing any property or taking other steps in relation to the doubtful provision, having in mind that dispositions which violate such a rule or statute may be void *ab initio*.

---

[54] Supra § 14.31-1 ff.
[55] Supra § 14.4-2 ff.
[56] Supra § 14.24-1.
[57] Constructive trusts, infra Ch. XXVI.
[58] Preliminary review of will, in general, supra § 5.9.
[59] Construction by or accompanying settlement of account, infra § 24.5-5a. Construction proceedings generally, infra Ch. XXII.
[60] Agreements with or among beneficiaries, in general, infra Ch. XXI.
[61] Infra §§ 22.4-1, -2. Incurrence of unnecessary expense, in general, supra § 3.5-2.

§ 14.36-1. *Estate and inheritance taxes; waivers and consents.* The executor in satisfying any legacy, other than in money, should have in mind the requirements under most state estate and inheritance tax statutes of obtaining waivers or consents to transfer from the relevant tax authorities.[62]

§ 14.36-2. ———; *apportionment.* The possibility that a share of estate taxes may be apportionable against a legatee, the necessity of the executor's protecting himself as to any such apportionment in satisfying legacies, and methods of obtaining such protection, all of which are discussed elsewhere,[63] should have timely consideration by an executor in preparing to satisfy any legacy.

---

[62] Supra § 12.11.
[63] Supra § 12.10-1 ff.

XV

DEVISES

§ 15.1. *Importance of law of situs.* The executor should always keep in mind that, under the general principles as to what law governs testamentary dispositions of, or the descent of, real property,[1] devises[2] are governed in all respects, as to their validity, construction, and effect, by the law of the jurisdiction in which the real property is situate.

§ 15.2-1. *Description and identification; in general.* It is not necessary, in order that a devise of real property be effective, that the property be described by metes and bounds, or lot and block numbers, or the like, as it would be described in a deed; it is sufficient if the will identifies the property in such manner that there can be no doubt as to what is devised. Problems similar in some respects to those having to do with the identification of tangible personal property referred to in a specific bequest[3] may accordingly arise in connection with specific devises; for example, a devise of real property described merely by reference to the time, manner, or source of its acquisition may to some degree at least be open to the same kind of questions as a similar bequest of personal property. Apart from such matters, a question that perhaps arises more often than is generally recognized is of the kind created by a devise of "my home" or the like;[4] such a devise is universally regarded as passing the plot of land upon which the dwelling house stands, but if, in addition to the particular plot upon which the dwelling house stands, the testator owned an adjoining plot, or a plot separated from the dwelling house by a street or alley, there may be room for real doubt as to what or how much of the property passes under the devise; the question may be affected by the factual situation as to the character of the "other" plots, and the use made of them by the testator during his lifetime, including such factors as the presence or absence of buildings thereon and the nature or use of any

---

[1] Generally, infra Ch. XXV.
[2] "Devise" as designating disposition of real property, supra § 1.13.
[3] Supra § 14.4-2 ff.
[4] Ademption of such a devise, infra § 15.5-1.

such buildings, and probably by the identity of the devisee, as a devise to a spouse or close relative who lived with the testator might well be given a broader construction than a devise to a stranger. In any event, the executor should consider the possible existence of any questions of identification of the subject-matter of the devise and, at least where undevised real property is to be sold,[5] or where a conveyance by the executor is necessary or customary to pass title to the devisee, the executor should have such questions resolved before taking any affirmative steps.

§ 15.2-2. ———; *devise of "all" real property*. A devise of "all" the testator's real property, as distinguished from one of designated tracts or parcels, may give rise to questions, both as to certain kinds of real property[6] and also, as is likely to be overlooked, as to property acquired after the date of the will. While historically such a devise was held to pass only such real property as the testator owned at the time of executing his will (and still owned at his death), in most, if not all, states that doctrine has long since been abandoned as to a devise of "all" real property, without qualification, and such a devise is held to cover real property acquired after the making of the will as well as that owned at its date. A devise, however, of "all" the testator's real property situate in, for example, a particular city, county, or other geographical area may not be construed, in the absence of any other indication of intention, to pass property in the specified area that was not owned by the testator at the time the will was executed, on the theory that in referring to the specified area the testator in effect referred to and intended to dispose of the particular parcels, only, therein that he then owned, just as if he had designated or described such parcels by any other language specifically identifying them. Under any devise in general terms, therefore, it may not be assumed in every case that the words of the devise are to be applied to the factual situation existing at the testator's death, where that is not the same as the one that existed at the date of the will. Questions of this character, like others relating to real property,[7] must be decided under the law of the situs of the property.

§ 15.2-2a. ———; ———; *oil, gas, and mineral interests*. The executor should not overlook the fact that an inclusive devise will presumably include (whether or not the testator actually intended it to do so) many kinds of royalty and working interests in oil, gas, and mineral production from lands situate in those states under whose laws such interests, and the receipts therefrom, are real rather than personal property.[8] The executor having any such interest must, therefore, first determine whether under the law of the situs[9] such interests are real property. Moreover, in the case of any such interest in lands situate in Louisiana, the executor in another

---

[5] Sale of real property, in general, supra § 7.5-3.
[6] See next following section, and infra § 15.8.
[7] Generally, infra Ch. XXV.
[8] Such states appear to be in the majority.
[9] As governing, supra § 15.1.

DEVISES 199

jurisdiction must have in mind the applicability of the "forced heirship" rules of that state.[10]

§ 15.2-2b. ———; ———; *as specific devise.*[11] It appears that an inclusive devise of real property, as well as a devise of specifically identified property, will be regarded for purposes of determining rights of devisees to rents,[12] order of abatement in insolvent estates,[13] and probably all other matters, as a specific rather than a general devise,[14] and indeed that there are only two kinds of devises, specific and residuary.[15] It thus may be that an inclusive devise, or devise in general terms, appearing before the residuary clause may have different consequences than one made by the same language in a residuary clause.

§ 15.3. *Encumbrances.*[16] Where real property is subject at the testator's death to a mortgage or other encumbrance, applicable state law[17] must be consulted to determine whether, as is the case in most jurisdictions, the property passes to the devisee *cum onere*,[18] so that the devisee takes subject to the encumbrance and must eventually discharge it out of his own funds if he wishes to accept the devise, or, instead, the devisee is entitled to require that the encumbrance be satisfied out of the general estate, so that he will hold the property free of it. The will may, of course, contain explicit provision on the point, and, as pointed out elsewhere, the question may also be affected by a general direction in the will to pay debts.[19] The encumbrances as to which the problem here involved arises are usually mortgages, taxes on the land, mechanics' liens, or the like, and even may include an executory contract of sale;[20] the rule may be different as to such more general liens as those of judgments entered on personal obligations of the testator, statutory liens for taxes other than those on the land, and other non-specific encumbrances. In the case of liens which attach also to other property of the estate, it may be necessary for the executor to seek a judicial determination of the amount, if any, thereof payable out of the general estate or by

---

[10] Infra § 17.8. Thus an executor who uses or distributes royalty payments or other receipts from such interests without realization of the rights of the testator's descendants or parents may find himself surchargeable in their favor.

[11] West Dig., Wills Key No. 751.

[12] Infra § 15.6.

[13] Infra § 19.5-7.

[14] The terms "specific" and "general" hereunder connote the same kind of distinction as in the case of bequests; cf. supra §§ 14.4-1, 14.6-1.

[15] Residuary devises in general, infra § 18.3-5.

[16] West Dig., Wills Key Nos. 827–848; P-H Est. Plng. Serv. ¶¶ 432.25, 436.

[17] Law of situs as governing, infra § 25.4-3.

[18] So in Unif. Prob. Code sec. 2-609; the common law was otherwise. Cf. op. cit. sec. 3-814, permitting the executor to discharge the encumbrance, or transfer the securing property in partial or total satisfaction thereof, if it appears for the best interests of the estate so to do; but providing that such payment shall not increase the share of the devisee.

[19] Supra § 9.3-3a.

[20] *Matter of Fogarty*, 165 Misc. 78, 82, 300 N.Y.S. 231, 237. Executory contracts for sale and purchase, in general, supra § 6.15-4.

the takers of the other property. If the devised property passes *cum onere* the estate is not absolved from ultimate liability for the indebtedness but subject to the considerations mentioned in the last preceding sentence, the executor is liable, on general principles,[21] to surcharge if he applies assets of the general estate to the discharge of the encumbrance, except if and to the extent that a deficiency remains unpaid after the lien has been enforced against the devised land.[21a]

§ 15.4. *Lapse; incapacity to take.* The rules of lapse[22] apply to devises as well as to bequests. Where, for example, the devisee is an individual and fails to survive the testator, lapse occurs in the absence of any applicable non-lapse statute;[23] and, as in the case of a legatee,[24] a devisee responsible for the testator's death cannot take under the will. In addition, however, in the case of a devise to a corporation, particularly one of charitable or religious nature,[25] or to a governmental body, or to an alien, it is necessary to ascertain whether under the law of the situs of the property[26] the devisee is capable of taking or holding title to the real property, and if not the devise lapses.

§ 15.5-1. *Ademption; in general.* The doctrine of ademption[27] applies to devises as well as to bequests, and so, just as a specific legacy is adeemed if the subject matter has been disposed of by the testator before his death, so a specific devise of real property adeems if the realty has been so disposed of.[28] A special case is that of a home; if the home owned at the time of execution of the will is sold, the devise is adeemed, even though another home is owned at death,[29] unless, of course, the devise is in terms of, or plainly made applicable to, whatever home is owned by the testator at his death, or a statute provides that it shall be so construed.

§ 15.5-2. ———; *sale by incompetent's guardian or committee.* An exception to the general rule that specific devise is adeemed if the property covered by it is not owned at the testator's death exists in a majority of jurisdictions, where, by statute or decisional law, the rule is that where the owner of real property had been adjudged

---

[21] Waste, supra § 3.5-2.
[21a] Unless estate released; supra § 14.4-5 Note 93.
[22] Generally, supra §§ 14.2, 14.23-1.
[23] Non-lapse statutes, supra § 14.23-2.
[24] Supra § 14.18-3.
[25] Right of such corporation to receive or hold property, see Restrictions on Charitable Testamentary Gifts, 5 Real Prop. Prob. & Tr. J. 290, 295–297. Legacy to charitable or religious corporation, supra § 14.18-4.
[26] As governing, supra § 15.1.
[27] Supra §§ 14.2, 14.4-4.
[28] Cf. Unif. Prob. Code sec. 2-608 (b), under which any balance unpaid at death on a contract for sale of the property, any proceeds then unpaid of fire or casualty insurance on damaged or destroyed property, and any unpaid amount of a condemnation award for the property, pass to the devisee.
[29] It will be in mind that the problem discussed in this section is in some respects the converse of that dealt with in § 15.2-2. That section deals with property acquired after the making of the will, and this section with property disposed of after the making of the will.

DEVISES

incompetent and a guardian or committee had been appointed for him, and real property that is the subject of a specific devise in his previously executed will was sold by such guardian or committee, the proceeds of sale or the property into which they are traceable stand in the place of the realty and pass to the devisee.[30] If the proceeds have been used for the testator's support and maintenance, it has been held that other beneficiaries under the will whose bequests or devises were equally or preferentially available for such purpose, under the general rules as to priorities,[31] must contribute to the devisee whose devise has thus failed.[32] Where such rule of non-ademption, or *a fortiori* such rule of contribution, obtains, the executor in the case of any specific devise of property not held at death should make sure, before distributing the estate, that the testator did not at any time after making the will have a guardian or committee who sold the property in question.

§ 15.5-3. ———; *damage or destruction.* As in the case of specifically bequeathed personal property,[33] it would seem that a devisee of real property is not entitled to receive the proceeds of insurance covering a loss or damage occurring to buildings or improvements on the land before the testator's death, even if such proceeds are collected after death, unless a statute otherwise provides.[34]

§ 15.6. **Rents as belonging to devisee.** From the rule that title to devised real property vests in the devisee by operation of law on the death of the testator,[35] it logically follows that rents accruing from the property after the testator's death should belong to the devisee.[36] This is the case in all jurisdictions where the devise is a specific one, and in at least most jurisdictions where the devise is a residuary one;[37] and in some jurisdictions it has been extended even to the case of real property used to satisfy a pecuniary legacy in trust,[38] so that the rents follow the land.[39] As elsewhere noted, however, the executor may by statute have the right to collect rents;[40] and rents, like the property from which they are derived,[41] may be available,

---

[30] *Lewis v. Hill*, 387 Ill. 542, 56 N.E.2d 619; *In re Bierstedt's Est.*, 254 Iowa 772, 119 N.W.2d 234, 51 A.L.R.2d 770; *Walsh v. Gillespie*, 338 Mass. 278, 154 N.E.2d 906. So in Unif. Prob. Code sec. 2-608 (a). Similar rule in the case of a specific bequest, supra § 14.4-4b.

[31] Infra § 19.5-1 ff.

[32] *In re Mason's Est.*, 62 Cal.2d 213, 42 Cal. Reptr. 13, 397 P.2d 1005.

[33] Supra § 14.4-4c.

[34] *Matter of Cramm*, 27 A.D.2d 8, 275 N.Y.S.2d 769, holding inapplicable a statute abrogating the rule of ademption where property is destroyed before death and insurance proceeds collected after death, in a case where building was destroyed by fire before execution of will and testatrix knew of the fact, on the ground that there was nothing to adeem and therefore purpose of the statute was absent. Cf. note 28 supra.

[35] Supra § 7.5-1.

[36] (1931) Unif. Prin. & Inc. Act sec. 3-A (3) (a); (1962) Rev. Unif. Prin. & Inc. Act sec. 5 (b). Income from specifically bequeathed personalty as belonging to legatee, supra § 14.4-3.

[37] Income from specific legacies and devises, in general. infra § 16.6-2.

[38] Supra § 14.27-2, infra § 16.6-3a.

[39] See, e.g., N.Y. E.P.T.L. sec. 11-2.1 (d) (3). The purpose of such an enactment is presumably to avoid the possibility of loss of the Federal estate tax marital deduction in such a case.

[40] Supra § 7.5-2.

[41] See next following section.

and under some statutes are explicitly made available,[42] to the executor for payment of charges and expenses.[43] If rents belonging to the devisee under the rules hereinabove stated are collected by the executor, they are by him payable over to the devisee, at or before settlement of the estate, except to the extent that they are properly used for payment of charges or expenses. If any rents do not, under such rules, belong to the devisee, they fall into the residuary estate and are to be disposed of in accordance with the principles applicable thereto.[44]

§ 15.7. ———; *availability for charges, expenses, and legacies.*[45] There are dealt with at another place[46] the rules as to the order of abatement of legacies and devises where necessary to enable payment of debts and other charges, administration expenses and pecuniary legacies; as appears therefrom, real property, except where a statute or the will otherwise provides, is not available for any of these purposes so long as personal property exists, and may not be available at all for the satisfaction of cash legacies, except where they are charged on the land.[47] Accordingly, it follows that real property is not subject to sale by the executor[48] for such purposes, except within the rules referred to, unless a statute or the will so provides; and the rents from land are affected by the same considerations.[49]

§ 15.8. *Cemetery lots.*[50] There are discussed elsewhere[51] the questions whether a cemetery lot is to be treated as a part of the estate or as separate therefrom, and, if a part of the estate, whether it is disposable by will. In any case, as there pointed out, it is the general rule that a cemetery lot may be disposed of only by a specific devise and not by a merely general or inclusive devise of real property, which accordingly is ineffective for the purpose.

§ 15.9. *Renunciation.*[52] It is generally held that a devise of land, like a bequest of personal property,[53] may be renounced by the devisee,[54] and that under a timely renunciation title does not vest in the devisee. On the other hand, it would seem that an

---

[42] Such statutes, specifying the conditions under which income may be collected and used by the executor and the procedure to be followed in that connection, are presumably designed to make it unnecessary to sell the land to raise needed cash where the rents are sufficient for the purpose.

[43] Under (1962) Rev. Unif. Prin. & Inc. Act sec. 5 (b), there are to be deducted taxes, ordinary repairs, and other expenses of management and operation of the devised property and an "appropriate portion" of interest accrued after the testator's death and of income taxes (excluding capital gains taxes) during the period of administration. Expenses payable out of income, in general, infra § 16.5-1 ff.

[44] Infra § 18.4-1 ff.
[45] West Dig., Exrs. & Admrs. Key Nos. 321–326; P-H Est. Plng. Serv. ¶¶ 432.21–.23.
[46] Infra §§ 19.5-2, -2a.
[47] Legacies charged on land, supra §§ 14.9-1, -2.
[48] Generally, supra § 7.5-3.
[49] See last preceding section.
[50] West Dig., Cemeteries Key No. 15.
[51] Infra § 18.3-5a.
[52] P-H Est. Plng. Serv. ¶ 451.
[53] Supra § 14.26-1.
[54] So in Unif. Prob. Code sec. 2-801.

DEVISES

heir to whom land descends, like a distributee of personal property,[55] in an intestate estate or where the will fails to make an effective disposition, cannot renounce the inheritance unless a statute otherwise provides.[56]

§ 15.10. *Estate tax apportionment.* Where estate taxes are to be apportioned among beneficiaries,[57] the problems of recovering a devisee's apportioned share thereof are essentially of the same nature as in the case of a legatee,[58] but may be somewhat more difficult because real property, unlike personal property, does not usually pass through the hands of the executor and the latter cannot withhold the share of tax from the land, or withhold the passage of title to the devisee[59] until the latter contributes his share of tax moneys. As in the case of a legatee, the executor must use whatever means are appropriate and available to him under the circumstances to obtain or hold sufficient assets to cover the maximum amounts of the taxes (including interest and penalties) that may eventually be apportioned against the devisee. If the devisee is also a legatee under the will, his tax liability in respect of the real property as well as in respect of the personal property bequeathed to him may be covered, at least up to the amount of the personalty, by withholding payment or delivery of all or part of the bequest; and, of course, it may be possible to obtain a deposit or indemnification from the devisee. If under applicable law[60] the executor has the right of possession and control of the real property until he releases or conveys it to the devisee,[61] he may perhaps refrain from making such release or conveyance until the devisee contributes or deposits an amount sufficient to cover his apportionable share of the tax. If none of these, nor any similar, means is available, the executor may find himself compelled eventually to bring action against the devisee for the latter's apportioned share of the tax after the apportionment has been made;[62] and the filing of a lis pendens at an early stage may afford protection to the executor against the devisee's disposition of the land and its proceeds before the apportionment can be made.

§ 15.11. *Establishing title to real property in another state.* Where real property that belonged to the decedent is situate in a state other than the one in which the will is probated, the executor should ascertain whether, for the purposes of establishing title or the passage thereof to the devisee, as well as for purposes of state death taxes, the appointment of an ancillary executor or ancillary administrator in such state is necessary,[63] or, instead, as under some statutes, it is sufficient to file an exemplified copy of the decree or other documents in the original probate proceeding.

---

[55] Supra § 14.26-2.
[56] Unif. Prob. Code, loc.cit. supra note 54, so provides.
[57] Apportionment of estate taxes, in general, supra § 12.10-1 ff.
[58] Supra § 12.10-5.
[59] Title as vesting by operation of law, supra § 7.5-1.
[60] As law of situs, supra § 15.1.
[61] Supra § 7.5-1.
[62] Collection of apportioned share by litigation, in general supra § 12.10-5a.
[63] Ancillary administration in general, supra § 1.7.

XVI

PRINCIPAL AND INCOME

§ *16.1.* *Tax and accounting computations distinguished.* Problems in an estate as to principal and income, and as to the ascertainment or computation of each, arise, first, for income tax purposes, and secondly, for what may be called accounting purposes,[1] that is, for determining the disposition to be made by the executor of income coming into his hands and the ascertainment of what is income for that purpose. This distinction must be kept in mind at all times, for questions as to what is income and the treatment of income in computing income taxes, and the determinations of what is income and what is to be done with it for accounting purposes, are not necessarily the same and, indeed, are often quite different. Income tax questions are outside the scope of this work; the matter herein dealt with is the congeries of problems that hereinabove have been referred to for convenience as accounting questions: more exactly, the substantive rights of beneficiaries under the will as to income and to principal, respectively.

§ *16.2.* *Need for separate ascertainment.* While the executor will always need to separate income accrued at the testator's death from that accruing afterward,[2] in all other respects the matter of what is income and what is principal may or may not, except for income tax purposes,[3] be of consequence.[4] If, for example, no specific legacy or devise of income-producing property[5] is contained in the will, and the residuary estate passes outright, all net income earned during the period of administration will pass to the residuary beneficiaries along with the principal of the residue,[6] and so it makes no economic difference to them, except so far as taxation is concerned, how much of what they receive is income and how much is principal, their

---

[1] Accountability and accounting, in general, infra Ch. XXIV.
[2] Accruals at death as principal, infra § 16.4-1.
[3] Importance of distinguishing between ascertainment of income for tax purposes and for accounting purposes, see last preceding section.
[4] Similarly as to expenses payable out of income, infra § 16.5-1.
[5] Income from property specifically bequeathed or devised as belonging to legatee or devisee, supra §§ 14.4-3, 15.6; determination of net income in such case, infra § 16.5-1.
[6] Infra § 18.4-2.

PRINCIPAL AND INCOME

only concern being that their total amount is correct. If, however, the will contains any specific bequest or specific devise, the income, if any, therefrom must be kept separate, under the rules as to the persons entitled to receive it;[7] and if any trust or any legal life estate is created by the will, it is ordinarily requisite that the executor keep appropriate account of income and principal separately inasmuch as the persons interested in income and those interested in principal are or may be different.[8] Moreover, where the will creates a trust and a trustee would be required under applicable law to make adjustments as between principal and income, as in cases of non-productive assets, so-called salvage operations, and depreciation or depletion reserves, the executor must consider whether he should make corresponding adjustments in such a case.

§ 16.3-1.   *What is income; in general.* Questions as to what is income and what is principal in estates have been largely resolved in nearly every state by the enactment of either the Uniform Principal and Income Act[9] or the Revised Uniform Principal and Income Act,[10] or by other statutory enactment, and the executor should in each instance consult the statutes and decisions of the governing jurisdiction. The rules thereby prescribed will, of course, determine what is income accrued at the date of death[11] as well as what is income thereafter accruing.[12] In general, as is explicit in the Revised Act,[13] the rules applicable in estates are the same as those governing trusts, and judicial decisions relating to principal and income problems in trusts are therefore usually applicable to estates also.

§ 16.3-2.   ———; *capital gains and losses.* One important difference (but by no means the only one) between the ascertainment of income for an executor's accounting purposes and for income tax purposes[14] is the treatment of capital gains and losses. Gains on the sale of assets of the estate constitute capital of the estate and do not in any way enter into the computation, for accounting purposes, of income earned during the period of administration; and capital losses do not in any way reduce the amount of income distributable to beneficiaries.[15] It follows that any income taxes payable by the estate[16] in respect of capital gains realized during the administration are chargeable against principal of the estate, and not against income;[17] but any sav-

---

[7] Supra §§ 14.4-3, 15.6.

[8] Generally, infra § 18.4-3 ff. Adjustment between principal and income where deductions claimed for income tax purposes instead of estate tax purposes, supra § 13.3.

[9] "The 1931 Act," with the addition of Sec. 3-A relating specifically to estates.

[10] "The 1962 Act."

[11] For accounting purposes, not for income tax purposes. Such accruals are principal of the estate; infra § 16.4-1.

[12] "Income during period of administration," infra § 16.4-2.

[13] Sec. 5(b). Cf. Sec. 3-A of the 1931 Act, to the same effect.

[14] Cf. § 16.1, supra.

[15] (1931) Unif. Prin. & Inc. Act sec. 3(2); (1962) Rev. Unif. Prin. & Inc. Act sec. 3(b)(8).

[16] Income taxes of estate, supra § 10.6.

[17] 1931 Act, sec. 3-A (2)(d); 1962 Act, sec. 13(c)(4). Expenses payable out of income, infra § 16.5-1.

ing of income taxes resulting from deduction of a capital loss in computing taxable income inures to the benefit of income beneficiaries and does not result in, or make proper, any converse adjustment as between income and principal.

§ 16.4-1. *Income received by executor; accruals before death.* An amount that would have constituted income[18] to the decedent if he had survived, and that has been earned or has become payable before his death, or is accrued at the time of his death, even though such amount is payable or is received after his death, is principal of his estate and forms part of the corpus thereof,[19] just as do moneys at any time received as income by the testator during his lifetime and remaining on hand at his death. It is, therefore, necessary for the executor to include in principal not only all uncollected sums that had become payable by the time the testator died but also that portion, determined by the usual methods of computation, of any income of a character that accrues from day to day (as, for example, interest on receivables, rents from real property, and wages of the decedent), and dividends on corporate stock, where the testator's right to receive it became fixed on or before the date of his death.[20] Such accrued amount should be treated, until received, as a receivable constituting an asset of the estate,[21] and when payment thereof is received the amount of the before-death accrual should be credited to principal and the balance, which accrued after death, to income.[22]

§ 16.4-2. ———; *accruals after death; "income during period of administration".*[23] That part, and only that part, of day-to-day income that accrues after the decedent's death,[24] plus all other income earned after his death, whether from investments or otherwise, is "income earned during the period of administration" and is the only property constituting "income" for accounting purposes. Such income includes the yield on funds later used to pay taxes, claims, expenses, and legacies, as well as that on funds retained for eventual distribution.[25] Each reference in this work to

---

[18] In the accounting sense, not necessarily in the income tax sense; cf. § 16.1 supra.

[19] (1962) Rev. Unif. Prin. Inc. Act sec. 4 (b). Income tax treatment of such accruals, supra § 10.6.

[20] Dividends on stock to be treated as "due" on record date or, if none, date of declaration, (1962) Rev. Unif. Prin. & Inc. Act sec. 4 (e). Dividend as not part of specific bequest of stock where record date preceded death, supra §4.4-3.

[21] Collection of receivables, supra § 6.11-1.

[22] It should of course, be borne in mind that before-death accruals are under Federal law subject to both income taxation, as income in respect of the decedent (I.R.C. sec. 691) and estate taxation, as part of the corpus of the estate (ibid. sec. 2031), but that a deduction in respect of the estate tax may be allowable for income tax purposes (ibid. sec. 691 (c) (4)); there may be similar results under state tax laws.

[23] P-H Est. Plng. Serv. ¶¶ 434.7–434.10. Called "probate income" in (1931) Unif. Prin. & Inc. Act sec. 3-A.

[24] (1962) Rev. Unif. Prin. & Inc. Act sec. 4 (b) (2). Cash dividends on stock received after death where record date was before death, ibid. sec. 4 (e). As to whether stock dividends, stock splits, and subscription rights are principal or income, or partly each, local statutes and decisions differ and should be consulted; cf. ibid. sec. 6.

[25] (1931) Unif. Prin. & Inc. Act sec. 3-A (2) (b); (1962) Rev. Unif. Prin. & Inc. Act sec. 5 (b).

PRINCIPAL AND INCOME 207

income means only income as hereinabove described, unless the context otherwise requires.

§ 16.5-1. *Expenses payable out of income; in general.* Income earned during the period of administration[26] that is allocable to a legatee of personal property specifically bequeathed[27] or a devisee of real property,[28] and income attributable to a marital deduction trust fund,[29] are (except in the case of residuary real property the rents of which may be made available for charges and expenses generally in lieu of a sale of the land[30]) subject to deduction of such expenses only as are deductible from gross income in arriving at net income under ordinary concepts, namely, expenses that relate to the property from which the income is derived or to the income therefrom[31] and are not payable out of principal.[32] The matter of expenses payable out of the balance of the income earned during the period of administration depends, in the real sense, upon the disposition made by the will of the residuary estate. If the residue passes outright, it makes no economic difference whether a particular item of expense is paid out of funds received as income or out of funds received as principal, inasmuch as in such case income and principal are to be disposed of together and as a whole or aggregate fund.[33] If, however, the residuary estate or a part of it is to be held in trust, or as subject-matter of a legal life estate,[34] then it follows from the necessity previously discussed to maintain income separate from principal[35] that it is also necessary to pay out of income those expenses, and only those, that under usual principles applicable to trusts are payable out of gross income in arriving at net income,[36] unless principal had been exhausted.[37] These rules are now embodied in the Uniform Principal and Income Acts,[38] one or the other of which is in force in a number of states, and in statutes of similar import in some other states.

---

[26] Defined, see last preceding section.
[27] Supra § 14.4-3.
[28] Supra § 15.6.
[29] Infra § 16.6-4.
[30] Supra § 15.6.
[31] See 1964 Proc. A.B.A. Sec. Real Prop. Prob. & Tr. L., Part I, 54. Cf. (1931) Unif. Prin. & Inc. Act sec. 3-A (2) (d) (income taxes other than capital gains taxes, and that share of administration expenses which is properly paid out of probate income); (1962) Rev. Unif. Prin. & Inc. Act sec. 5 (b) (2) (taxes, ordinary repairs, and other expenses of management and operation of property, interest accrued after testator's death, and income taxes other than capital gains taxes). Capital gains and taxes thereon, supra § 16.3-2.
[32] Items payable out of principal: Administration expenses, infra § 20.2; capital gains taxes, supra § 16.3-2; interest and penalties on estate taxes, supra § 12.4-3a. Abatement of income with principal to pay prior charges, infra § 19.7.
[33] Generally, infra § 18.4-2. Similarly as to need for separate ascertainment of income, supra § 16.2.
[34] Disposition of surplus income in such case, infra § 18.4-3 ff.
[35] Supra § 16.2.
[36] Interest on death taxes as payable from principal rather than income, supra § 12.4-3a.
[37] Infra § 19.6.
[38] Supra note 31.

§ 16.5-2. ———; *interest on debts and legacies.* While there appears to be little authority on the point, it would seem proper that the interest payable, in respect of a period after the testator's death,[39] on a claim against or obligation of his estate, whether such obligation be itself interest-bearing or not, should be paid out of income, rather than (as a part of the debt) out of principal;[40] but, as elsewhere, noted, the contrary is often true as to interest on an estate tax deficiency.[41] It is plain that where interest is payable on a cash legacy, for undue delay in its satisfaction,[42] such interest is payable out of income, on the theory that the estate had the use, during the period of the delay, of the funds eventually used to satisfy the legacy.

§ 16.5-3. ———; *alteration of rules by will; attempts to define net income.* The general rules as to expenses payable out of income, as stated in the preceding section, may, of course, be altered or varied by provisions of the will. Any such variance usually is found in a will creating a trust and attempting to specify or define net income, and is probably inadvertent more often than intentional. While the concepts of income, and of net income, are well understood and subject in most cases to little doubt or argument, they are very difficult to define accurately and comprehensively. Accordingly, where a will refers to the amount of income remaining after deduction therefrom of specified kinds or items of expense, difficult problems are often created because it is very likely that the specification is either too narrow, and omits items that under general rules are payable from income, thus raising a question as to the source of payment of those items, or too broad, and includes items that under general rules are payable out of principal (for example, "all income taxes", which language is broad enough to include taxes on capital gains, or "the expenses of administering my estate", which would include many kinds of expenses ordinarily constituting principal charges). Any will containing a definition or description of net income, or otherwise appearing to change the rules otherwise applicable in determining it, must therefore be studied carefully in connection with each kind of receipt and disbursement.

§ 16.6-1. *Disposition of net income; in general.* The term "net income" in estate administration means the amount of income remaining for disposition to beneficiaries after payment of all expenses properly payable out of income. It therefore includes, and is ascertained before deduction of, the amounts of income distributable under the principles discussed in the sections next following, and is to be distinguished from "surplus income" as discussed in a later section.[43]

§ 16.6-2. ———; *income from specific legacies and devises.* The "net income" from personal property specifically bequeathed, and that from real property devised

---

[39] Interest accrued at death as part of debt and payable out of principal, supra § 9.7.

[40] (1962) Rev. Unif. Prin. & Inc. Act sec. 5 (b). The (1931) Unif. Prin. & Inc. Act does not contain a provision on the point explicitly applicable to estates, but cf. sec. 12 (1).

[41] Supra § 12.4-3a.

[42] Supra § 14.31-3.

[43] Infra § 16.6-4.

either specifically or as part of the residuary estate, which under principles discussed above belongs to the legatee or devisee,[44] is the amount of gross income therefrom remaining after deduction of those expenses, only, that pertain to the property itself or its income.[45] It is thus apparent that in the case of such bequests and devises the income and expenses must be segregated in the executor's records so that the amount of net income distributable to the legatee or devisee may be correctly computed. Such net income, so computed, as passes through the executor's hands is distributable to the legatee or devisee, as a separate quantum or category of income.

§ 16.6-3. ————; *general legacies; outright.* It is the uniform rule that no part of the net income earned during the period of administration of an estate is payable to the legatee of an outright pre-residuary cash bequest;[46] the legatee is entitled to receive only the amount specified in the bequest, regardless of any income earned by the estate on that amount (or on any other asset of the estate) pending the satisfaction of the legacy. The same rules apply to other general legacies, as of securities.[47] Any right of a legatee to interest on his legacy where it is not satisfied within a prescribed period, or without undue delay,[48] is to be distinguished from a right to share in the income from the estate; such interest is of the nature of a penalty to the estate for late payment of the legacy, or compensation to the legatee for the withholding of amounts to which he is entitled, and is not of the nature of a sharing in the income earned during the period of administration, even though under some statutes the rate of interest payable may be measured by or fixed with respect to the average earnings of the estate. There is, however, to be noted an argument, on grounds of presumed intention, that at least a bequest intended to qualify for the marital deduction should share in income.[49]

§ 16.6-3a. ————; ————; *in trust.*[50] For most purposes, as has been elsewhere noted, the principles governing the satisfaction of bequests and the rights of legatees are not affected by whether the bequest is outright or in trust.[51] In most states, however, the rule that a cash legatee is not entitled to participate in income or earn-

---

[44] Supra §§ 14.4-3, 15.6. Where legacy or devise abates, income as abating also, infra § 19.7.

[45] (1931) Unif. Prin. & Inc. Act sec. 3-A (3) (a); (1962) Rev. Unif. Prin. & Inc. Act sec. 5 (b) (1). As to problems raised by those sections for deduction of a portion of the estate's income taxes, see Covey, Allocation of Income Earned During Estate Administration, 2 Real Prop. Prob. & Tr. J. 1, 5–7. Expenses payable in arriving at net income, in general, supra § 16.5-1.

[46] (1931) Unif. Act cit., sec. 3-A (3) (b); (1962) Rev. Unif. Act cit., sec. 5 (b). Note that this rule applies in the case of an outright "pecuniary formula" marital deduction bequest, inasmuch as it is a bequest of a dollar amount (supra § 14.8-2); but see infra text at note 48.

[47] See *Est. of Reisinger*, N.Y.L.J. Aug. 26, 1966, p. 9, where bequests of specified numbers of shares were held to be general legacies and the legatees accordingly not entitled to cash dividends received by the executor during the statutory pre-distribution period. Legacy of securities as specific or general, supra § 14.6-2.

[48] Interest on cash legacies, supra § 14.31-3.

[49] Cf. 1963 Proc. A.B.A. Sec. Real Prop. Prob. & Tr. L., Part I, 33–34. Where the bequest is in trust, see next following section.

[50] P-H Est. Plng. Serv. ¶ 434.3.

[51] Supra § 14.1-2.

ings of the estate during its administration[52] does not apply where the bequest is in trust rather than outright.[53] In those states a cash bequest in trust carries with it a ratable share of the estate's income,[54] or income at a prescribed rate[55] or at the average rate earned by the estate,[56] from the date of the testator's death to the date of satisfaction of the bequest. Where that view has been adopted, it applies, of course, not only to a bequest in trust of a specific amount of money but also to "pecuniary formula" marital deduction bequests in trust.[57]

§ *16.6-3aa.* ———; ———; ———; *payment to trustee or beneficiary.* Under some statutes the amount of income allocable to a trust under the will, or to its beneficiary, is payable by the executor to the trustee of the trust,[58] and under other statutes is payable directly to the income beneficiary;[59] but even where the latter is the case the executor may be required to make the payment to the trustee, as where under the terms of the trust the trustee is given discretion as to such a matter as the time of payment of income, the selection of the beneficiary (as in the case of a "sprinkling" trust), or the like, or as to whether to pay out or accumulate trust income, for the executor cannot exercise a discretion committee to the trustee.

§ *16.6-4.* ———; *surplus income.* So much of the net income of an estate as remains after any payments or allocations required by the principles discussed in the three preceding sections hereof is referred to as "surplus income".[60] The concept of surplus income is somewhat analogous to that of a residuary estate;[61] it is the balance of income not payable to others than residuary legatees. Its disposition there-

---

[52] See last preceding section.

[53] So in (1931) Unif. Prin. & Inc. Act sec 3-A (3) (b) (iv), and (1962) Rev. Unif. Prin. & Inc. Act sec. 5 (a). The adoption of this view, or change in the general rule, is said to reflect what a testator would normally intend, and was undoubtedly spurred by a fear that without such treatment a trust intended to qualify for the marital deduction would not do so and a wish to preserve such deduction for testators. Cf., however, Covey, Allocation of Income Earned During Estate Administration, 2 Real Prop. Prob. & Tr. J. 1, 4, as to whether the deduction would not be allowable even in absence of the change in question.

[54] (1931) Unif. Act cit., sec. 3-A (3) (b); (1962) Rev. Act. cit., sec. 5 (b). Problems as to determination of share, see 1963 Proc. A.B.A. Sec. Real Prop. Prob. & Tr. L., Part I, 36–38.

[55] Some statutes refer to this as "interest" but it is imposed differently from interest for delay in payment of an outright legacy; see, e.g., Pa. Fiduciaries Act of 1949 sec. 320.753.

[56] Problems of determining average rate of earnings or return during administration, see Covey, op. cit. supra note 53, at 7–8; Dodge & Sullivan, Estate Administration and Accounting, 417 ff.; see also infra § 18.4-3a.

[57] Cf. note 53, supra. Formula bequests, supra § 14.8-2. Residuary trust as sharing in "surplus income," infra § 18.4-3b.

[58] So in (1931) Unif. Prin. & Inc. Act sec. 3-A (3) (b) (i) and (iv), and (1962) Rev. Unif. Prin. & Inc. Act sec. 5 (b), each further providing that income received by a trustee shall be treated as income of the trust.

[59] The purpose of such a provision is presumably to avoid circuity and, perhaps more particularly, to prevent the inclusion of the income in computation of the trustee's commission, with consequent "double" commissions on the same income.

[60] The (1931) Unif. Prin. & Inc. Act sec. 3-A (3) (b) refers to "net probate income," and the (1962) Rev. Unif. Prin. & Inc. Act sec. 5 (b) to "the balance of the income" earned by the estate.

[61] Residuary estate as property not otherwise disposed of, infra § 18.1.

fore depends chiefly upon the disposition to be made of the residuary estate itself, and it is convenient to refer to it as falling into the residue; but, as will be seen in a following chapter, that is not entirely descriptive of the disposition to be made of it.[62] The distinction between "net income"[63] and "surplus income" must be observed if confusion is to be avoided.

§ 16.7.   *Expenses payable out of principal.* In general, all expenses and charges not payable out of income under the rules hereinabove stated[64] are payable wholly out of principal of the estate.[65] Occasional exceptions as to certain administration expenses are noted at a later place.[66]

---

[62] Infra § 18.4-1.
[63] Supra § 16.6-1.
[64] Supra § 16.5-1 ff.
[65] Cf. (1962) Rev. Unif. Prin. & Inc. Act sec. 5 (a).
[66] Infra § 20.2.

XVII

RIGHTS OF SURVIVING SPOUSE OR CHILDREN

§ *17.1.* *"Exempt" property and allowances.*[1] Statutes usually provide in substance that certain property, usually specified kinds of tangible property, referred to as "exempt" property, or (perhaps in addition) a specified amount of money,[2] usually called a family allowance or homestead allowance, shall be set aside and turned over to the decedent's spouse or children.[3] Under such a statute, property covered thereby is not disposable by will[4] and does not constitute a part of the estate for purposes of administration[5] (once it has been identified and set aside[6]), and so is exempt from claims of creditors[7] (although not, under some statutes, from funeral expenses[8]) and from availability for payment of administration expenses;[9] it is not, however, excluded from the gross taxable estate for purposes of the Federal estate tax, and may not be so excluded for the purposes of a state estate or inheritance tax. In some other respects, the nature of the benefit provided for by such a statute may not be entirely clear. It would seem that a testator may provide in his will a benefit expressly in lieu of the right to the statutory benefit or the exempt property, and that in such case the spouse or child, as the case may be, must elect between the two or at least waives the statutory benefit if he or she accepts the testamentary benefit. Under other statutes the statutory benefit is not effective unless claimed by the spouse or child. Except in a case of the kind last mentioned, it should be considered whether

---

[1] West Dig., Exrs. & Admrs. Key Nos. 53, 173 ff.; P-H Est. Plng. Serv. ¶¶ 2505, 2506, 2700.

[2] As to selection of exempt items, and amount and source of payment of a pecuniary allowance or exemption, the relevant statutory provisions should be consulted. See Unif. Prob. Code sec. 2-404, further providing that property specifically devised or bequeathed shall not be availed of if other assets are available. What law governs exemptions and allowances, see Goodrich & Scoles, Conflict of Laws sec. 193.

[3] Under Unif. Prob. Code sec. 2-403 the death of a person entitled to such an allowance terminates his right as to any payments not yet made.

[4] As not passing under residuary clause, infra § 18.3-2.

[5] Consequent "priority" in insolvent estate, infra § 19.8.

[6] Duty of executor as to exempt property, supra § 7.2-2.

[7] Source of payment of claims, in general, supra § 9.8-1 ff.

[8] Generally, supra § 9.2-1; cf. § 19.8 infra.

[9] Generally, infra § 20.2.

RIGHTS OF SURVIVING SPOUSE OR CHILDREN 213

the benefit can be waived by the person entitled to it,[10] for if not, and at the instance of such person the property in question is not set aside but is retained for treatment as part of the testamentary estate,[11] there may in effect be a gift, for tax purposes, to the persons who receive additional property as a result. A further question that can arise with respect to "exempt" property is whether the benefits of the statute are forfeited by a spouse or child who was responsible for the death of the decedent,[12] as would be a legacy or devise to or an intestate share of such person.[13] Both of these and perhaps other questions may depend, if not settled by statute, upon whether the provision for exemption or allowance is to be regarded as creating a statutory legacy, or a special kind of intestate share or "forced heirship",[14] or possibly neither and is *sui generis*.

§ 17.2. *Widow's quarantine*.[15] The widow's quarantine, provided by statute in some states, is not an interest in property of the estate in the usual sense, but instead is a possessory right, a right to occupy the home, for a limited period of time. The home accordingly is not excluded from the estate as is exempt property,[16] but remains a part of the estate for all purposes, and passes under the decedent's will, subject only to such right of occupancy.

§ 17.3. *Dower and curtesy*. In some states a surviving spouse possesses by law dower or curtesy in the decedent's property or parts thereof, or by statute is given interests comparable to or in lieu of dower or curtesy. An executor in any of the states referred to, and an executor in any other jurisdiction having property which has a situs in any such state,[17] must accordingly ascertain the nature and extent of the statutory rights or interests of such character before dealing with such property.

§ 17.4-1. *Spouse's election to take statutory share;*[18] *in general*. In some states,[19] in lieu of dower and curtesy or statutory modifications thereof, a spouse is given the right to elect to take, as against the terms of the decedent's will, a prescribed share of his estate,[20] similar to (but sometimes not exactly the same as) that to which the

---

[10] Unif. Prob. Code sec. 2-204 permits waiver of rights by spouse. Renunciation of legacy, supra § 14.26-1; of intestate share, supra § 14.26-2.

[11] Defined, supra § 1.11-1.

[12] So in Unif. Prob. Code sec. 2-803.

[13] Supra §§ 14.18-3, 15.4.

[14] Infra § 17.8.

[15] West Dig., Exrs. & Admrs. Key No. 175; P-H Est. Plng. Serv. ¶ 2700.

[16] See last preceding section.

[17] Law of situs as governing, infra § 25.4-3.

[18] West Dig., Wills, Key Nos. 778–803; P-H Est. Plng. Serv. ¶ 2700.

[19] Statutes of the various states on the point are collected and discussed in Powell, Real Property, sec. 970.

[20] The Unif. Prob. Code distinguishes between the general case of a spouse's right of election (sec. 2-201) and the particular case of a spouse married to the testator after the execution of the will and not provided for by him (sec. 2-301); in the latter case the spouse is to take an intestate share, and the provisions as to satisfying the elective share and the intestate share are different (secs. 2-207, 2-301 (b)). For a detailed study of the right of election see Election by Surviving Spouse, 2 Real Prop. Prob. & Tr. J. 310. Measure of elective share, see next following section; waiver of right, infra § 17.4-3.

spouse would have been entitled if the decedent had died intestate, or, under some statutes, the excess of such prescribed share over the provision made for the spouse in the will.[21] The existence and extent of such a right are governed as to personal property by the law of the testator's domicile,[22] and, under most authorities, as to real property by the law of its situs.[23] Such an election must be made strictly in the manner and within the time prescribed by the statute conferring it;[24] and it is held to be personal to the spouse, so that in case of the death of a spouse without having exercised such right the election cannot be made by the spouse's legal representative, although during the lifetime of an incompetent spouse it may in some circumstances be made by the spouse's guardian or committee.[25] Where a statute provides such a right, the executor acts at his peril if he makes any distribution to others, that could be affected by an election by the spouse, before the time for election has expired; but he acts equally at his peril if he distributes to the spouse pursuant to or on the basis of a notice of election if under the particular will and the facts of the instant case the spouse does not have a right of election or her[26] right is of more limited quantum or scope than that asserted in her notice of election. So the executor may find it necessary to obtain a judicial determination before he acts. It is, of course, necessary for the executor to ascertain whether the electing survivor was indeed the spouse of the decedent within the meaning of the statute granting the right of election. Further, under some statutes a right of election otherwise available to the spouse may be lost or barred by her abandonment of the testator, a judicial separation from him, or her procurement of a decree of divorce, annulment, or dissolution even though it be not recognized as valid in the state of the testator's residence;[27] and under such statutes the executor must ascertain the facts in such regard, or obtain a judicial determination as to them, before making any distribution pursuant to an attempted exercise of the right of election.[28]

---

[21] Limited right of election, infra § 17.4-2a.

[22] See *Matter of Clark*, 21 N.Y.2d 478, 288 N.Y.S.2d 993, 216 N.E.2d 152 (husband domiciled in Virginia, where statute gave wife broad right to elect, provided in his will that the disposition of his estate be governed by New York law, where securities were kept and where statute gave wife only a limited election; held, Virginia law governed). Cf. Shriver, The Multi-State Estate, 3 Real Prop. Prob. & Tr. J. 189, 195–196. What law governs as to personal property in general, infra § 25.4-4.

[23] Law of situs as governing, in general, infra § 25.4-3. But under Unif. Prob. Code sec. 2-201 (b) the law of the domicile would govern as to real as well as personal property.

[24] Requirements and procedure, see Unif. Prob. Code sec. 2-205.

[25] Op. cit. sec. 2-203. Cf. *Est of Pearson*, (Fla.) 192 So. 89, holding that where incompetent spouse died after her guardian had filed her election but before required court action had been taken thereon, the right of election terminated.

[26] The use in this and following sections of the feminine pronoun in referring to the surviving spouse is for convenience only and not intended to imply that a surviving husband does not have like rights.

[27] One who obtains or consents to invalid divorce, etc., as not entitled to rights as spouse, Unif. Prob. Code sec. 2-802.

[28] Effect of election on marital deduction, and other tax considerations, see Price, Postmortem Estate Planning Up to Date, 20 N.Y.U. Inst. on Fed. Taxation 301, 327.

§ 17.4-2. ———; *measure of elective share; in general.* It would seem clear that a right of election by a surviving spouse is not affected, either as to its existence or as to its extent, by the right of the spouse to receive "exempt" property under a statute providing that such property shall not be deemed to be a part of the estate.[29] The extent of the right is also, under many statutes, not affected by the fact that the decedent in his lifetime transferred portions of his assets to or in trust for the spouse or another, unless, in the case of a transfer to or for the benefit of one other than the spouse, the decedent retained such degree of control or of beneficial enjoyment of the transferred assets as to render the transfer "illusory" as against the spouse.[30] Under a number of statutes, however, some kinds of property disposed of by the testator during lifetime, and property, such as life insurance proceeds, passing at his death, are to be aggregated with property owned by him at his death in determining whether a right of election exists and, if so, the amount of the elective share;[31] the aggregate thus obtained is referred to as the "augmented estate", and its aggregation for this purpose with property owned at death not only protects the spouse against lifetime transfers to others for purpose of defeating her right but also prevents from the taking, as against other beneficiaries, the benefits of both a non-testamentary transfer or payment to her or for her benefit and an elective share of the testamentary estate.[32] On the other hand, it would appear that, subject to the principles of the augmented estate, the right to elect can apply only to property which the testator could have bequeathed or devised to the spouse or for her benefit, and not to property which, although owned by the testator, he was precluded from so bequeathing or devising.[33] The elective share should be computed before estate taxes, in a jurisdiction in which taxes are to be apportioned,[34] if it qualifies for the marital deduction and so bears no share of the tax; but if apportionment is not recognized the share is presumably intended to be of the net estate, unless the statute otherwise provides, and therefore is to be computed after death taxes.[35]

§ 17.4-2a. ———; ———; *"limited" right of election.* If the statute conferring a right of election on a surviving spouse does not otherwise provide, the election by the spouse to take her statutory share works a forfeiture of all her benefits under the will and the provisions for her benefit lapse.[36] Where, however, the right of election is a limited one, to take only the excess of the statutory share over the provision

---

[29] Supra § 17.1.
[30] *Newman v. Dore*, 275 N.Y. 371, 9 N.E.2d 966, 112 A.L.R. 643.
[31] Cf. Unif. Prob. Code sec. 2-202.
[32] Cf. op. cit. sec. 207, providing that property included in the augmented estate and passing to the spouse shall be first applied to satisfy the elective share.
[33] *Rubenstein v. Mueller*, 19 N.Y.2d 228, 285 N.Y.S.2d 845, 225 N.E.2d 540, holding that where the testator had executed with his (deceased) first wife a joint will that was binding upon him at his death, his second wife (surviving him) could not take by election any of the property disposed of by the will. Joint wills, in general, supra § 5.3-6.
[34] Apportionment, in general, supra § 12.10-1 ff.
[35] 1964 Proc. A.B.A. Sec. Real Prop. Prob. & Tr. L., Part I, 52.
[36] Lapse, in general, supra § 14.2.

made in the will,[37] the will remains in effect so far as the spouse is concerned[38] and, while of course she may renounce its provisions for her benefit,[39] she cannot thereby obtain any benefit, under the statute, greater than would that to which she would have been entitled thereunder if she had not so renounced.[40]

§ 17.4-3. ———; *waiver of right during testator's lifetime.* Under some statutes a spouse may, during the testator's lifetime, waive any right of election against a particular will, or against any will that the testator may leave.[41] In the absence of such a statute, it would seem doubtful that any such waiver, at least if made without consideration, would be effective.[42] It will be noted, however, that a joint and mutual will, if of such nature as to amount to a contractual arrangement between the parties, may in effect deprive the survivor of them of a right to elect against it.[43]

§ 17.4-4. ———; *withdrawal of election.* In some states an election, once made, is held to be irrevocable,[44] except as the court may relieve the spouse of it on a showing that it was made without due consideration or knowledge of the facts. In some other jurisdictions, however, such authority as exists indicates that the electing spouse may at her option withdraw or cancel her election, even in the absence of statutory provision for such withdrawal or cancellation,[45] and that the election is thereupon to be treated as a nullity.[46] Apparently such a withdrawal or cancellation, where permitted, is not required to be made before the expiration of the time permitted by statute for making the election, but may be made at any time before (but presumably not after) any distribution of the estate has been effected in reliance upon the notice or assertion of election or rights of others have intervened. It is to be noted that, where under applicable law the effect of the election is to entitle the spouse to share ratably in the surplus income earned during the administration of the estate,[47] and interim distributions of income have been made in reliance upon the election and

---

[37] Statutes adopting the doctrine of "augmented estate" (see last preceding section) normally provide that all property, testamentary or non-testamentary, included therein and passing to the spouse shall first be applied to satisfy the elective share; so in Unif. Prob. Code sec. 2-207. Problems under "limited election" statutes, see Biskind & Scanlon, Boardman's Estate Management and Accounting, secs. 195–197.04.

[38] Effect on other beneficiaries, infra § 17.4-4.

[39] Renunciation of legacy or benefit, in general, supra § 14.26-1.

[40] Where, for example, under such a statute a trust for the spouse's benefit "qualifies" for the elective share but is less in amount than such share, the spouse may elect to take the amount of the deficiency but cannot disavow the trust and thereby receive her whole statutory share outright.

[41] So in Unif. Prob. Code sec. 2-204. Ante-nuptial agreements in general, West Dig., Exrs. & Admrs. Key No. 185.

[42] Obviously, a right of election, like any other personal right, may be waived after the testator's death, either expressly or by failure to assert it.

[43] The principle was carried a step further, to prevent a second wife from electing on the death of her husband in *Rubenstein v. Mueller*, 19 N.Y.2d 228, 285 N.Y.S.2d 845, 225 N.E.2d 540; cf. supra § 17.4-2 note 33. Joint wills, in general, supra § 5.3-6.

[44] *In re McCutcheon's Est.*, 283 Pa. 175, 128 A. 843.

[45] Statutory provision for withdrawal, cf. Unif. Prob. Code sec. 2-205 (c).

[46] *Matter of Allan*, 5 A.D.2d 453, 172 N.Y.S.2d 447.

[47] Disposition of surplus income, in general, infra § 18.4-1 ff.

RIGHTS OF SURVIVING SPOUSE OR CHILDREN 217

in the relative shares required by virtue of the prospective distribution of principal assets resulting from it, a withdrawal or cancellation of the election and the retroactive nullification of the latter may result in the discovery that an overpayment of income has been made to the spouse, and the executor may not be able to recover the overpayment.[48]

§ 17.4-5. ———; *source of satisfaction of elective share.* Where a surviving spouse exercises a right of election, her elective share (or, in the case of a limited election, the amount thereof) is to be made up, not merely or wholly out of the residuary estate, but ratably out of the legacies to other beneficiaries,[49] or, in the case of a statute providing for an "augmented estate" for purposes of the election, also out of the non-testamentary property.[50] The result of an exercise of the election, except in case of a limited one,[51] is of course that by reason of lapse of whatever provision is made in the will for the spouse[52] the residuary estate is increased,[53] and its size as so increased would seem to be the proper basis for computation of the ratable portions of the elective share as between residuary and other legacies. As is obvious, the effect of the requirement of contribution by other legacies to make up the elective share is the abatement[54] *pro tanto* of such other legacies.

§ 17.4-6. ———; *informing spouse of right to elect.* Whether it is incumbent upon, or proper for, an executor or his attorney to inform a surviving spouse of the possible or probable existence of a right of election against the decedent's will is a question of some difficulty. On the one hand, there is the fact that the spouse is often unaware of her rights and may feel reliance upon the executor or his attorney, who has usually told her of the provision made for her in the will, for full information as to or protection of her rights under it. On the other hand is the executor's duty of impartiality as among beneficiaries[55] and the fact that shares of other beneficiaries in

---

[48] In such a case there might be a question whether the executor was personally liable, for the "error," to others interested in income, or their remedy would be solely against the spouse.

[49] *Matter of Byrnes,* 149 Misc. 449, 267 N.Y.S. 627 (without distinction between outright legacies and legacies in trust); *Kilcoyne v. Reilly,* 249 F. 472 (specific as well as general legacies abate ratably). In the case, however, of a spouse entitled to an intestate share (as distinguished from one exercising a right of election; supra § 17.4-1 note 20), Unif. Prob. Code sec. 2-301 provides that such share shall be satisfied in accordance with the ordinary rules as to order of abatement (infra § 19.5-1).

[50] Cf. Unif. Prob. Code sec. 2-207, providing that property included in augmented estate that passes or has passed to spouse is applied first to satisfy the elective share and reduce the amount due from other recipients of portions of the augmented estate; the analogy to a "limited" right of election will be apparent. Augmented estate, in general, supra § 17.4-2.

[51] Limited right of election, supra § 14.4-2a.

[52] Where a provision so lapsing is a trust for the benefit of the spouse, with vested remainders, the remainders are accelerated, so that the remaindermen take without waiting for the spouse's death; *Matter of Roschelle,* N.Y.L.J. Feb. 17, 1967, p. 19. Election as causing lapse, supra § 17.4-2a.

[53] Infra § 18.3-3.

[54] Abatement, in general supra § 14.2. Rights of other beneficiacies, West Dig., Wills Key No. 802; of creditors, ibid. Key No. 803.

[55] Supra § 3.9-3.

the estate will be reduced if an election is made.[56] The tendency of opinion, in recent times appears to be toward at least a moral duty, and possibly a legal duty, to bring to the spouse's attention the possible existence of the right to elect and the limitation of the time within which election may be made, and to advise her to consult counsel with respect thereto.[57]

§ 17.5. *Dissolution of marriage.* Where the testator has been divorced, or his marriage has been annulled or otherwise dissolved, since the execution of his will, the executor must consider whether under applicable law the will is to be deemed revoked, either in whole or, as under statutes in a number of states, so far (only) as concerns its provisions for the former spouse,[58] and, if the latter, what disposition is to be made of the property devised or bequeathed to such spouse.[59] If the spouse is appointed in the will as an executor, or in another fiduciary capacity, it should also be considered whether, under the governing law, (if the will is not deemed revoked as a whole) such appointment is revoked by the dissolution of the marriage.[60]

§ 17.6-1. *Rights of children unprovided for; in general.* In nearly all states children omitted from a decedent's will may under some circumstances be entitled to share in the estate. The relevant statutes differ substantially among themselves, and different considerations may apply in the case of children born after the execution of the will than in the case of children living at the time of execution.[61] While in no state is a testator required to make provision in his will for his children,[62] the law may in effect presume that he forgot them, or the omission was unintentional, unless the will at least recognizes their existence. Accordingly, in every case of a child not provided for in the will, the executor should ascertain the rights, if any, of such child before any distribution of the estate is made.

§ 17.6-2. ———; *children living at execution of will.* In some states a child who was living at the testator's death and is not provided for in the will has no right to share in the estate. In other states, however, he is entitled to the share he would have received if the parent had died intestate unless, under some statutes, it appears that

---

[56] See last preceding section.

[57] This is especially so where there is any relationship, personal or professional, between the spouse and the attorney (Assn. of Bar of City of New York, Ops. on Prof. Ethics, No. 373), and even in the absence thereof (*Matter of Mescall*, 51 Misc.2d 751, 753, 273 N.Y.S.2d 778, 780, where the court referred to the fact that an officer of the corporate executor had explained to the widow the benefits she would receive under the will without also advising her to seek counsel). If reliance, however unwarranted, and the usual assumption by one when being informed of the provision for him or her under the will that he is being fully informed as to all his rights, create a duty, then it is only in the exceptional case that the executor or his attorney does not have a duty to inform or advise a widow accordingly.

[58] Supra § 5.3-5.

[59] Under Unif. Prob. Code sec. 2-508, such property is to be disposed of as if the spouse had not survived the testator. Disposition of lapsed legacies, in general, infra § 18.3-3.

[60] So under Unif. Prob. Code, loc, cit.

[61] See two following sections.

[62] But see next following sections. "Forced heirship" distinguished, infra § 17.8.

the omission was intentional, or only, under other statutes, if it appears that it was unintentional.[63] Apart from the matter of a right to share, the absence in a will of provision for a living child may, of course, lend plausibility to a contest of the will on the ground of lack of testamentary capacity or undue influence.

§ 17.6-3.   ———; *after-born or after-adopted children.* [64] Where the testator is survived by a child born after the execution of the will, whether before or after the testator's death, or adopted by him[65] after the execution of the will, the child may be entitled by statute to a share of or interest in the estate, although not provided for therein. The statutes vary considerably among themselves. Thus it is often provided that the after-born child is entitled to the same share of the estate to which he would have been entitled if the decedent had died intestate, unless he is provided for in the will, or unless he is mentioned therein even though not provided for, or unless his mother is a principal beneficiary under the will, or unless it appears that the omission to provide for him was intentional.[66] Under other statutes the omitted child may be entitled to share in the estate only if at the time of the will's execution there were children living who were provided for in it; or, if there were such other children, the omitted child, instead of being entitled to an intestate share of the estate, may take only on the same basis or to the same extent as such living children, or take a ratable share of so much of the estate as is bequeathed to them collectively.[67] It is thus apparent that an executor must ascertain whether any child was born after the will was executed and, if so, must refrain from making any distribution affecting children until the rights, if any, of the after-born child have been determined or provided for.

§ 17.6-4.   ———; *sources of satisfaction of child's share.* Where under the principles discussed in the two preceding sections an omitted child is entitled to take an intestate share of the testator's estate, the statute conferring such right ordinarily provides from what source the child's share shall be satisfied, as that it shall be made up, ratably, out of the property passing to the other children, or, at least if there is no other child, out of the property passing to other beneficiaries, rather than wholly out of the residuary estate;[68] and the result is that the provisions for the other children, or other beneficiaries, as the case may be, abate accordingly.[69] It has been held that even where appointive property is subject to claims of creditors of the donee,[70] it is not for that reason available to satisfy the share of a pretermitted child.[71]

---

[63] Cf. Unif. Prob. Code sec. 2-302 (b), entitling to an intestate share a child erroneously believed by the testator to be dead and omitted because of that belief.

[64] P-H Est. Plng. Serv. ¶ 432.27.

[65] Adopted child of another as "issue," supra § 14.21-3.

[66] Cf. Unif. Prob. Code sec. 2-302 (a), applying somewhat different exceptions.

[67] See also next following section.

[68] But under Unif. Prob. Code sec. 2-302 (c) ordinary rules as to abatement (infra § 19.5-1 ff.) are to apply, so that the residuary estate will be used, to the extent it is sufficient.

[69] Abatement, in general, supra § 14.2.

[70] Infra § 19.6.

[71] *Fiske v. Warner*, 99 N.H. 236, 109 A.2d 37.

§ 17.7. "Excessive" or "late" gifts to charity.[72] In some states the amount or fraction of his estate that may be left to charity or for charitable purposes by a testator who is survived by a close family member, as a spouse,[73] child, or parent, is limited by statute, and is voidable as to any excess at the election of the family member; and under some statutes the right to attack such a bequest is extended to any person adversely affected by it. In other states a lifetime gift,[74] a pledge,[75] or a testamentary provision[76] to a charity or for a charitable purpose[77] made within, or contained in a will[78] executed within, a specified period before death is similarly voidable, or is completely void. To the extent that such a bequest is avoided or void, it is said to abate,[79] and so far as ineffective it lapses;[80] but in the case of partial avoidance under a statute of the first type mentioned, if there are bequests of different classes[81] to each of two or more charities, or a devise to one and a bequest to another, it should be considered whether under local law the usual rules as to order to abatement[82] are to be applied or instead, as would seem more proper, all the charitable provisions abate ratably. An executor faced with a provision for charity which is or may be voidable under any statute should, of course, refrain from satisfying the bequest until the time allowed by the statute for interested persons' election has elapsed, unless the right to elect is expressly waived by all persons possessing it.

§ 17.8. Forced heirship. In Louisiana, where the disposition of property of decedents is based upon the civil law concept of legitime, the decedent's descendants, or, if he has none, his parents, are entitled to specified portions of his estate, the amount varying with circumstances, so that only the balance of the estate is subject to testamentary disposition. A somewhat similar and in some respects even more rigorous system obtains in Puerto Rico.[83] Because these jurisdictions are unique in the United

---

[72] Validity of legacies and devises to charitable and religious corporations, in general, supra §§ 14.18-4, 15.4.

[73] Under some statutes the "protected" persons do not include the spouse, whose right of election (supra § 17.4-1 ff.) is deemed adequate protection to her as against charitable bequests. Where the doctrine of "augmented estate" for purpose of the election obtains (supra § 17.4-2) the elective right may also protect, at least to some degree, as to lifetime charitable gifts.

[74] Collection by executor of invalid or ineffective lifetime transfers, supra § 6.18.

[75] Satisfaction of decedent's charitable pledges, supra § 9.11.

[76] Generally, see Restrictions on Charitable Bequests, 5 Real Prop. Prob. & Tr. J. 290, 295. Charitable legacies, in general, supra § 14.14-1 ff.

[77] Some states extend the principle even to a bequest to an individual with the request that he make a charitable gift.

[78] The possibility should be considered that the execution of a codicil to a will that contains such a bequest will cause the statutory period to be measured from the codicil's date.

[79] Abatement generally, supra § 14.2. The term is correctly applied in a case of the kind referred to in the text in the sense that under such a statute there are insufficient assets, or no assets, that are lawfully applicable for satisfaction of the bequest.

[80] Lapsed legacies and devises as part of residuary estate, infra § 18.3-3; lapse of part of residue, infra § 18.7-1, -2.

[81] Classification of legacies, supra § 14.1-1 ff.

[82] Infra § 19.5-1 ff.

[83] Cf. Segall et al., Estate Planning Comes to Puerto Rico, 55 A.B.A.J. 464, 466. It is also to be noted that Puerto Rico has a special system of community property, which may complicate the problems discussed in this section; op. cit., at 465.

States, such "forced heirship" may be a trap for the executor of a non-resident of Louisiana or Puerto Rico who owned real property in either jurisdiction,[84] particularly in the case of oil, gas, or mineral interests and the proceeds therefrom.[85] There is, of course, no abatement[86] required, in the correct sense, to satisfy the forced heirs' shares, because only assets other than or in excess of such share can be disposed of by the will and the will has no or limited operation over the forced share; but the provisions of a will that, as too often may happen in the case of a non-resident, does not take this into account and purports to dispose of the entire interest are ineffective *pro tanto* and so in a sense may be said to abate. Statutes in other jurisdictions providing for "exempt" property or a family allowance,[87] or for the passage of an intestate share to an omitted or after-born child,[88] may be thought of as creating a species of forced heirship, but are not usually so regarded.

§ *17.9. Community property.*[89] While problems relating to community property[90] on the death of one member of the community may in a sense be within the scope of a discussion of the rights of a surviving spouse, they are not treated at this point, nor elsewhere herein, for the reason that the spouse's rights in community property are those of continuing ownership,[91] whereas the matter with which this work deals is not the ownership of property, as such, or the owner's rights therein during his lifetime, but the administration after an owner's death of the property that belonged to him at his death or passes by reason of his death.

---

[84] Law of situs as governing, supra § 15.1.

[85] Such interests as real property, supra § 15.2–2a.

[86] Abatement, in general, supra § 14.2.

[87] Supra § 17.1.

[88] Supra § 17.6-1 ff.

[89] West Dig., Hsb. & Wife Key Nos. 246–276; P-H Est. Plng. Serv. ¶ 2698.2.

[90] States having a community property system (but differing in various respects among themselves) are Arizona, California, Idaho, Louisiana, Nevada, New Mexico, Texas, and Washington. A special form exists in Puerto Rico; see last preceding section, note 83. ,

[91] Continuing character of property as separate or community on change of domicile, supra § 25.2.

XVIII

ASCERTAINMENT AND DISTRIBUTION OF RESIDUARY ESTATE

Part A—Residuary Clause; Property Passing

§ 18.1. *Ascertainment of residuary estate*.[1] As the term indicates, the residuary estate, or residue,[2] consists of the property disposable by will[3] that is not used for the payment of debts, charges, and expenses[4] and does not pass under any pre-residuary legacy[5] or devise[6] or pursuant to a requirement of law.[7] It is obvious that there will be no residuary estate if all assets coming into the hands of the executor or included in the testamentary estate have been required to satisfy prior items. It will also be apparent that, because administration expenses, at least, cannot be fully known or finally determined until the end of the period of administration and, often, the settlement of the executor's account,[8] it is not possible to determine the amount of the residue with precision until that time; but in most cases it may be closely estimated prior thereto, and at least an approximation at as early a date as practicable will be useful, if not indeed necessary, to the executor's planning of his administration as to such matters as the choice of assets for liquidation,[9] the tentative apportionment of taxes,[10] and the solvency of the estate.[11]

---

[1] West Dig., Wills Key Nos. 586–588, 857–860; P-H Est. Plng. Serv. ¶ 414.

[2] "True residue," infra § 18.4-3a.

[3] It will be in mind that some kinds of property are not or may not be disposable by will; e.g., copyrights (supra § 14.4-2d, note 58), cemetery lots (supra § 15.8; cf. also infra § 18.3-5a), and exempt property (supra § 17.1.).

[4] Including funeral expenses, debts, and claims (Ch. IX), taxes (Chs. X, XI, and XII), and administration expenses (Ch. XX).

[5] Supra Ch. XIV.

[6] Supra Ch. XV.

[7] Supra Ch. XVII.

[8] Accounting and settlement, infra Ch. XXIV.

[9] Generally, supra § 7.6-1 ff.

[10] Supra § 12.10-1 ff.

[11] Insolvent or insufficient estates, infra Ch. XIX.

§ *18.2. Nature and effect of residuary clause.* Strictly speaking, what property constitutes the residue of an estate,[12] and what property passes under or is disposed of by the residuary clause of a will, are different and distinct concepts. Often the property is the same in both cases, and ordinarily the two concepts are treated as interchangeable; but in some circumstances both conceptual and practical problems may arise from a failure to recognize the distinction. The problem is partly semantic: it is easy to assume from its common designation that a "residuary clause" disposes of all property not disposed of by a preceding provision of the will, and to overlook the fact that this may not be so. On the other hand, a residuary clause may dispose of, or govern the disposition of, property that was not held by the testator at the time of his death, or that did not belong to him.[13] An executor sometimes faces possibilities of entrapment by an apparently clear or simple residuary clause, and should assure himself as to the scope and effect of the clause before proceeding with distribution under it. Some of the kinds of considerations to be kept in mind and problems that may arise are discussed in following sections.

§ *18.3-1. Particular kinds of property; preliminary statement.* Whether or not property coming into the hands of the executor and not disposed of by any provision of the will preceding or taking precedence over the residuary clause constitutes a part of the residuary estate, and whether or not such property is disposed of by the residuary clause, which as noted in the last preceding section may be different matters, the executor has responsibilities with respect to such property and its disposition. He must also consider whether, in the case of property that did not come into his hands, and did not form part of the residuary estate, but that nevertheless is disposed of by or pursuant to the residuary clause, he does or does not have responsibilities. Because the nature and degree of responsibility, if any, may differ in different cases, and may depend upon the particular terms of the will and upon the nature of the particular property, categorization is not possible and all relevant facts and circumstances have to be considered in each case.[14]

§ *18.3-2. ———; "exempt" property and allowances.* So-called exempt property, family allowances, and the like, which by statute in some states are directed to be set apart for the decedent's wife or children and declared not to be a part of the estate,[15] are *a fortiori* not a part of the residuary estate, and not affected by the residuary clause.

§ *18.3-3. ———; lapsed, renounced, and revoked legacies and other dispositions.* A legacy devise that has lapsed,[16] or has been renounced[17] or revoked,[18] falls into

---

[12] See last preceding section.
[13] Cf. infra §§ 18.3-6, -7, -8; and, as to property becoming part of estate after testator's death, infra § 18.11.
[14] Generally, see following sections.
[15] Supra § 17.7-1.
[16] Supra §§ 14.23-1, 15.4.
[17] Supra § 14.26-1.
[18] Supra § 14.34.

the residuary estate and becomes a part thereof,[19] at least unless the disposition is itself one of a part of the residue.[20] Under the general principle in the construction of wills that the law favors completeness of testamentary disposition and will not readily adopt a construction which would result in partial intestacy, the subject matter of such a disposition will ordinarily be within, and be disposed of by, the residuary clause. The language of a residuary clause may, however, in some instances be so narrow, or so specific, or hedged with such exceptions or references to prior provisions of the will,[21] that it raises doubts on the point, or even conduces to a contrary conclusion.[22] In any case of possible doubt or question, the executor, because of the risk of partial intestacy and the assertion of rights by intestate distributees, should before making and distribution obtain an agreement by all persons interested in or affected by the question,[23] or, if that is not obtainable or not feasible, a judicial determination.[24]

§ 18.3-3a. ———; *revocation or ineffectiveness by operation of law.* The rules as to lapse of revoked legacies or devises, and disposition of their subject matter,[25] apply to those revoked by operation of law,[26] or prevented by law from being given effect.[27]

§ 18.3-3b. ———; ———; *revocation of "bank account trust".* Where a so-called "bank account trust" is revoked by the will,[28] but without a demonstrative[29] or otherwise explicit bequest of the funds thereof, such funds fall into the residuary estate and pass under the residuary clause, subject to the same considerations as those applying in the case of a lapsed or revoked bequest.

§ 18.3-4. ———; *estate and inheritance taxes recouped.* There has been discussed elsewhere the duty of the executor who has advanced or paid estate or inheritance taxes to recover apportioned shares of the estate tax (where apportionment is had), or the amounts of the inheritance tax, from recipients of taxable property.[30] Where, as in the usual case, such tax payments were initially made out of the general

---

[19] Unif. Prob. Code sec. 2-606 (a).

[20] Lapse of residuary disposition, infra §§ 18.6-1, -2.

[21] For example, where it speaks in terms of "all other property," "the balance of my estate," or the like, so that there is doubt whether it means only property not mentioned above in the will, or extends to property mentioned above but not effectively disposed of there; or where it mentions various classes of property and they do not include that referred to in a bequest that lapses or is revoked by codicil or operation of law or is renounced or disclaimed by the legatee. As to similar problem as to lapse of residuary share, infra § 18.7-1 text at note 47.

[22] Technically, of course, in such case the clause is not truly a "residuary" cause, in that it does not dispose of the residue of the estate.

[23] Agreements with or among beneficiaries, infra Ch. XXI.

[24] Construction proceedings, infra Ch. XXII.

[25] See last preceding section.

[26] Supra § 14.34.

[27] "Excessive" or "late" gift to charity, supra § 17.7; legatees not capable of taking, supra § 14.18-1 ff.

[28] Supra § 6.16-2b.

[29] Demonstrative legacies, supra § 14.5-1.

[30] Supra § 12.10-5.

ASCERTAINMENT AND DISTRIBUTION OF RESIDUARY ESTATE 225

estate, thus in effect temporarily depleting the residue, amounts so recovered or recouped are added to the residuary estate as a replenishment, *pro tanto*, thereof[31] and constitute a part of the funds available for distribution to residuary beneficiaries.

§ 18.3-5. ———; *real property; in general.* With the exception under some laws of a cemetery lot,[32] real property that was owned by the decedent and is not devised by any preceding provision of the ordinary will forms a part of the residuary estate, and so passes under the residuary clause, if not in any way excluded therefrom by the language of the latter;[33] and, as discussed above,[34] a lapsed, renounced, or revoked devise also passes under the residuary clause, or fails so to pass, under the same considerations as those applicable to legacies. Real property in the residue or passing under the residuary clause is subject to the principles, elsewhere stated, applying to other devises.[35]

§ 18.3-5a. ———; ———; *cemetery lots.*[36] In some states cemetery lots appear to be regarded as not part of the estate, but as somewhat resembling exempt property,[37] and in such case they obviously are not disposable by will, either by specific devise or by the residuary clause. Generally, however, a cemetery lot is deemed to be a part of the estate, but in some jurisdictions it is not disposable by will if there has been an interment in it, and in most jurisdictions, even if it can be devised, that can be done only by specific devise, from which it follows that a cemetery lot does not pass under a residuary clause unless expressly mentioned therein.[38] A cemetery lot not effectively disposed of by will may descend as intestate property in accord with ordinary rules of descent and distribution,[39] but under some statutes it devolves differently, usually to close members of the family, under what may be thought of as a special and distinct rule of descent. While as to a cemetery lot the executor normally has few if any duties or responsibilities, and perhaps fewer than in the case of other real property,[40] general considerations require that he ascertain what rules govern its disposition under the law of its situs,[41] so that his own position may be clear.

§ 18.3-6. ———; *life insurance payable to estate.* Insurance on the life of the testator that under the terms of the policy is payable to his legal representatives, or

---

[31] Where the residue was insufficient for payment of the tax and funds bequeathed to other beneficiaries were used (supra § 12.10-6), recouped amounts are of course to be equitably allocated among such other beneficiaries.

[32] See next following section.

[33] A residuary clause worded in terms of personal property will, of course, not pass real property, unless the court finds an intention, from a consideration of the will as a whole, and from the general disfavoring of intestacy, to dispose of the entire residuary estate.

[34] Supra § 18.3-3.

[35] Devises generally, supra Ch. XV.

[36] West Dig., Cemeteries Key No. 15.

[37] Supra § 17.1.

[38] Generally as to the disposition of cemetery lots see 1965 Proc. A.B.A. Sec. Real Prop. Prob. & Tr. L., Part I, 55–56, where it is pointed out that the problems in connection therewith stem mainly from the fact that the nature of the title or right to a cemetery lot is not entirely clear.

[39] Intestacy as to property not disposed of by residuary clause, infra § 18.8.

[40] Generally, supra § 7.5-1 ff.

[41] Law of situs of real property as governing its disposition, supra § 15.1.

his estate, either as the primary or designated beneficiary, or as alternate beneficiary because of failure of the primary beneficiary to survive, becomes a part of the residuary estate and in most jurisdictions passes as a part thereof under the residuary clause. In at least one jurisdiction, however, it is held not to pass under a residuary clause unless specifically mentioned;[42] and where that rule obtains an executor not familiar with it is particularly subject to entrapment by a conventional residuary clause.

§ 18.3-7. ———; *life insurance payable to testamentary trustee.* Where a statute permits the trustee of a trust created by will[43] to be named as the beneficiary of insurance on the testator's life,[44] the proceeds of insurance so made payable to a residuary trust[45] do not pass through the hands of the executor for any purpose and are not a part of the residuary estate.[46] Because, however, they become a part of the funds of the residuary trust, or at least are to be administered as if they were a part thereof, they may be said to be disposed of by or pursuant to the residuary clause of the will.

§ 18.3-8. ———; *appointive property.* Where a testator at the time of his death possesses a power of appointment that by its terms is exercisable by will (whether or not also exercisable by deed), it may be exercised by the residuary clause as well as by a pre-residuary provision. Indeed, in some jurisdictions a general power (but not a special or limited power) not explicitly exercised by another provision of the will is deemed to be exercised by the residuary clause[47] unless an intention to the contrary appears from the will; but in other jurisdictions the converse rule is applied and a residuary clause is held not to exercise a power unless an intent to do so affirmatively appears.[48] Assuming that such an appointment is within the terms or scope of the power, the testator may appoint to his legal representatives, or his estate, in which case the property subject to the power (the "appointive property") becomes a part of the general estate for all purposes and any of it not otherwise disposed of or ex-

---

[42] *Hathaway v. Sherman,* 61 Me. 466.

[43] Testamentary trusts, in general, infra Ch.XXVII.

[44] In the absence of such a statute, it would seem at least doubtful that such a beneficiary designation would be effective, inasmuch as a testamentary trustee is not in existence as such at the time of the insured's death.

[45] Note that under such a statute the designation of the trustee as beneficiary is ordinarily not limited to the case of the trustee of a residuary trust, and principles similar to those discussed in in this section apply where the trust is one created by a pre-residuary provision of the will.

[46] As to taking such proceeds into account in determining sufficiency of residue for payment of estate taxes, supra § 12.10-6, text at note 23; in ascertaining or satisfying spouse's elective share, supra § 17.4-2, text at note 31.

[47] More exactly, at least in some jurisdictions, a power not explicitly exercised nor negated is deemed to be exercised by the will as a whole; thus if the residue is non-existent or the other estate is insufficient for the payment of general legacies in full the appointive property is available to pay them, on the theory that any operative clause of the will exercises the power, and not merely the residuary clause. Appointive property in insolvent or insufficient estate, in general, infra § 19.6.

[48] So in Unif. Prob. Code sec. 2-610.

pended becomes integrated with the passes as a part of the residuary estate. Accordingly, as mentioned above,[49] where such an appointment is made, the executor must recover or collect the appointive property just as if it were property owned by the testator. Where, however, the appointment is to any one other than the legal representative or the estate, the appointive property forms no part or the testamentary estate and, *a fortiori*, no part of the residuary estate, although in some jurisdictions, as noted below,[50] it may under some circumstances be available for application upon the testator's debts. It is to be emphasized that an appointment (assuming that it is permitted under the terms of the power) to the testator's residuary legatees, or to the trustee of his residuary estate,[51] comes within the rule of the last preceding sentence, and such an appointment does not make the appointive property a part of the residuary estate,[52] or subject it to administration by the executor, even though its disposition is governed by the residuary clause. In the case of a retained power,[53] of course, if the power is not effectively exercised and no different provision is made for the case of such failure, the appointive property reverts to (or, more correctly, remains as a part of) the residuary estate and is to be disposed of accordingly.

§ 18.4-1. *Surplus income; in general*.[54] Surplus income[55] is, by its nature, in a real sense a part of the residuary estate, in that it is property not otherwise disposed of. In the next following sections is discussed the disposition to be made of it therein.

§ 18.4-2. ———; *where entire residue passes outright*. It follows from the principle stated in the last preceding section that if the entire residuary estate passes outright, the taker or takers of the residue receive the surplus income. If there is more than one residuary beneficiary, whether they take the residue in equal shares or otherwise, the surplus income is distributable among them ratably, that is, in the same proportions as their respective shares of the residue itself. In many such cases, therefore, the concept of surplus income loses much of its significance, as all income not payable to others merely adds to or augments the total available for distribution to the residuary taker or takers. Where, however, there is more than one residuary beneficiary and the property passing to one of them is and that passing to another is not subject to payment of death taxes,[56] further problems arise, as discussed in a following section.[57]

---

[49] Supra § 6.19.
[50] Supra § 9.8-3.
[51] Testamentary trusts, infra Ch. XXVII.
[52] As not taken into account in determining sufficiency of residue for payment of estate taxes, supra § 12.10-6, text at note 24.
[53] I.e., a power retained by the testator in making a lifetime transfer to another, as distinguished from a power granted to the testator by another or by the testator to another.
[54] P-H Est. Plng. Serv. ¶¶ 434.7–.10.
[55] Defined, supra § 16.6-4.
[56] Supra § 12.10-4.
[57] Infra §18.4-4.

§ 18.4-3. ———; *where residuary trust or life estate is created.*

Where the whole or any part of the residuary estate is to be held in trust,[58] or is subjected to a legal life estate or the like, the disposition or surplus income depends primarily, as appears from the next following sections, upon whether the so-called "true residue" rule obtains under applicable law.[59]

§ 18.4-3a. ———; ———; *true residue rule.*

The "true residue" rule, governing the disposition of surplus income earned during the period of administration, was formerly everywhere applied where the residuary estate or any part of it passed in trust or subject to a life estate or the like; and even in those states in which it has been abolished[60] it may still have some lingering significance, and its principles apply in the computation of the amount of the estate's income that is to be allocated to beneficiaries of a pre-residuary trust.[61] The rule contemplates that a period of time will necessarily elapse after the testator's death before payment is made of such items payable before ascertainment of the residue as debts, taxes, administration expenses, and general legacies; that during such period income will accrue or be earned on assets later used to make such payments; and that if all surplus income passed to the income beneficiary or life tenant, as the case may be, of part or all of the residuary estate, he would receive not only a larger (perhaps much larger) amount of income in, or in respect of, the initial period after the testator's death than later, but also a larger income than the testator intended. Accordingly, the true residue rule is, in effect, that, unless the will discloses a contrary intention, income earned during the period of administration on assets eventually used for the payment of pre-residuary items of the kind above mentioned shall be added to the corpus of the residuary estate, and only the balance of the surplus income (income on the "clear residue") shall be allocated to the income beneficiary or life tenant.[62] In order to arrive at the amount so to be added to corpus, calculations, often lengthy and laborious, must be made.[63] Briefly, the usual steps are as follows: The assets on hand from day to day are computed, starting with the original inventory,[64] adding any further assets re-

---

[58] Testamentary trusts, infra Ch. XXVII.

[59] See 1963 Proc. A.B.A. Sec. Real Prop. Prob. & Tr. L, Part I, 30–32.

[60] See next following section.

[61] See Harris, Estates Practice Guide, sec. 682 (at p. 1200 ff.). Pre-residuary trust as carrying with it ratable share of estate income at average rate of return, supra § 16.6-3a.

[62] Originally the income beneficiary was held not to be entitled to any of the income earned during the period of administration of the estate, and all such income was to be added to the principal of the residuary estate. The rule as stated in the text has, however, been uniformly accepted since 1837, when a decision pointed out that the English case on which the former holdings were based had been misinterpreted; *Williamson v. Williamson*, 6 Paige (N.Y.) 298.

[63] For a detailed example of the computation to be made, see Dodge & Sullivan, Estate Administration and Accounting 426–431; a simplified example may be found in Harris, loc. cit. supra note 61. While both works cited refer to the former law of New York, which has been abolished by statute (E.P.T.L. sec. 11-2.1 (d) (2)), the examples would seem to be of value in jurisdictions where the true residue rule still obtains, and also, as pointed out supra this section, in computing the income distributable in respect of a pre-residuary trust.

[64] Inventory value, supra § 8.3-1.

ceived and any gains realized, and subtracting amounts paid out for purposes mentioned above; then is counted the number of days each intermediate value thus shown remained unchanged, and the average value for the whole period is computed. To such average value is applied the amount of surplus income for distribution, thus arriving at the average yield for the period. Such average yield, applied to the average amount or value (computed in similar fashion, and discounted for futurity as of the date of the testator's death by the average time for which payment was deferred) of pre-residuary payments as above mentioned, gives the amount of the surplus income that is to be added to the corpus of the residuary estate, to make the "true residue". The balance of the surplus income then remaining is distributable ratably[65] among the residuary beneficiaries, and, as to the portions of the residue in trust or subject to a life estate, constitutes income to the trust beneficiary or the life tenant, as the case may be.

§ *18.4-3b*. ———; ———; *majority rule.* The trust residue rule is not recognized, or has been abolished by statute, in a majority of the states, and in those states the surplus income of the estate in its entirety continues to be treated as income and is distributable accordingly.[66] Thus a ratable portion of surplus income enures to the benefit of the income beneficiary[67] of each residuary trust, and the life tenant of each portion of the residue subject to such a tenancy; as to parts of the residue passing outright, a ratable portion goes to each outright taker.

§ *18.4-4*. ———; *allocation among residuary beneficiaries.* Once it is determined whether any part, and, if any, what amount, of the surplus income of an estate is allocable to principal,[68] the rule that the remaining or distributable income shall be allocated ratably among residuary beneficiaries[69] gives rise to no difficulty where all residuary shares or takers also bear ratably the death taxes or so much thereof as is payable out of the residuary estate.[70] Where, however, a residuary portion or share does bear a part of such taxes and another portion or share, because of a marital or charitable deduction or a different relationship of the taker to the testator, does not bear any of such taxes[71] or bears a tax computed at a higher or lower rate, further questions may remain. There are three chief possibilities; that the income in question shall be allocated on the basis of the shares specified in the will, without regard to the incidence of death taxes; that the average-yield method be applied to each share,

---

[65] Infra § 18.4-4.

[66] Restatement of Trusts 2d, sec. 234 comment g. So in (1931) Unif. Prin. & Inc. Act sec. 3-A (3) (b), and (1962) Rev. Unif. Prin. & Inc. Act. sec. 5 (b). Even in such case, however, a computation of average value and average yield, made in the same manner as where the rule applies, is necessary in order to determine the amount of income allocable to the beneficiary of a pre-residuary trust; see the last preceding section hereof, and cf. supra § 16.6-3a.

[67] Payment to trustee or to beneficiary, supra § 16.6-3a.

[68] See two last preceding sections.

[69] Ibid.

[70] Payment of death taxes wholly or partly out of residue, supra § 12.10-1; apportionment within residue, supra § 12.10-4.

[71] Supra § 12.10-4.

involving a computation of the kind required in the case of the true-residue rule;[72] and that the allocation be made on the basis of the net distributable amounts of residue, after deduction from each of its portion, if any, of the taxes. The first of these approaches is administratively simplest, and is the one reflected in the Uniform Principal and Income Acts.[73] Where neither of those Acts, nor any statute of like import, applies, there is little authority on the problem, with good arguments for and against each of the three possible treatments and a diversity of practice among the states and even, it appears, within some states.[74]

§ 18.5. "Pour-over". A direction in a will that property of the estate, usually (but not necessarily[75]) all or a share of the residue, shall be added to a trust created by another instrument, or a bequest to the trustee of such a trust to be held as part of his trust fund, is commonly referred to as a "pour-over" bequest.[76] Most or all states now permit pour-over, either by statute[77] or by decision, but there still may be difficult questions as to its validity and effectiveness in some circumstances.[78] Where the recipient trust is one created by the will of another person who had died prior to the execution of the will containing the bequest, there would not seem to be any reason why the bequest is not effective;[79] and such a bequest may also be effective, although the matter is open to more doubt, where the testator whose will creates the trust is living at the execution of the will containing the bequest, if he dies before the latter takes effect by death of its maker.[80] Where, instead, the recipient trust is one created by agreement *inter vivos*, the problems arise chiefly out of the classical rule in many jurisdictions[81] that an instrument not executed with the formalities required of wills cannot be incorporated by reference into a will; where that rule is applied the bequest cannot be effective, in the absence of statute, except on the theory, applied in some of the states that have considered the problem, that an existing *inter vivos* trust is a "fact of independent significance",[82] as to which no incorporation into

---

[72] Supra § 18.4-3a.

[73] (1931) Unif. Prin. & Inc. Act sec. 3-A (3) (b); (1962) Rev. Unif. Prin. & Inc. Act sec. 5 (b) (2).

[74] Cf. 1963 Proc. A.B.A. Sec. Real Prop. Prob. & Tr. L., Part I, 38–46, 109.

[75] Supra § 14.25.

[76] Distinguished from "testamentary trust," infra § 27.5.

[77] So in Unif. Prob. Code sec. 2-511, which is the same as Uniform Testamentary Additions to Trusts Act sec. 1. The latter is discussed in Osgood, The Pour-Over Will, 104 Trusts and Estates 768, and a brief comment upon it appears in Scott, Recent Statutory Trends in the Law of Trusts, 45 The Trust Bulletin 33, 37–38.

[78] Cf. Marcus, Pour-Over Provisions and Estate Planning, 70 Dick. L. R. 158.

[79] So in Unif. Prob. Code sec. 2-511.

[80] Op. cit. sec. 2-512 provides that execution or revocation of will of another person is an event of independent significance by reference to which the testator may govern the disposition of his property.

[81] But. cf. Unif. Prob. Code sec. 2-510, permitting incorporation by reference of any writing in existence when the will is executed.

[82] "[A]cts and events which have significance apart from their effect upon the dispositions made in the will"; Unif. Prob. Code sec. 2-512. Doctrine as possible basis of "container" rule, supra § 14.4-2aa note 47.

the will is necessary or occurs. Such theory is based, as appears from its statement, upon the existence of the *inter vivos* trust when the will is executed, and so it must have been created (both by execution of the governing instrument and by creation or transfer of a corpus or res) before the execution of the will. On the same principle, a problem arises where, after the execution of the will, the trust instrument is altered or amended; in some jurisdictions pour-over is not permitted in such case,[83] and in others it has been held that the terms of the trust instrument as it existed when the will was executed governs the pour-over property, without regard to subsequent changes. Under some statutes, amendments of the trust instrument subsequent to the execution of the will, whether before or (at least if the will so provides) after the death of the testator, are applicable to the pour-over property and do not impair the effectiveness of the bequest,[84] and, in some cases, it is even immaterial that the recipient trust was not in existence at the time of the will's execution, if it is thereafter executed.[85] The law governing the validity and effectiveness of the pour-over provision is in the case of personal property that of the testator's domicile, and in the case of real property that of the situs of the land.[86] If an attempted pour-over is invalid for any reason, the usual rules of lapse[87] apply, in the absence of any valid alternative disposition in the will, and the subject-matter is to be disposed of accordingly.[88]

---

[83] *Pres. and Directors of Manhattan Co. v. Janowitz,* 260 A.D. 174, 21 N.Y.S.2d 232 (rule of which has been since changed by statute in New York).

[84] So in Unif. Prob. Code sec. 2-511.

[85] Ibid.

[86] What law governs, in general, infra Ch. XXV.

[87] Lapse of legacy, supra § 14.23-1; of devise, supra § 15.4.

[88] Disposition of property on lapse of pre-residuary bequest, supra § 18.3-3; of residuary bequest, infra § 18.7-1.

XVIII

ASCERTAINMENT AND DISTRIBUTION OF RESIDUARY ESTATE

Part B—Distribution Problems

§ 18.6-1. *Distribution of residuary estate;[1] in general.* The rules applicable to the satisfaction of legacies in general,[2] and to problems connected therewith, are applicable in the case of residuary legacies and the distribution of the residuary estate,[3] subject to such special considerations in respect of the latter as grow out of the nature of a residuary bequest and as are created by statutes having particular application to the distribution of the residuary estate. The following sections are accordingly confined chiefly to a discussion of such special considerations.[4] It should, however, be emphasized at this point that the rules of promptness in the satisfaction of other legacies[5] apply equally to the distribution of the residuary, and so the executor should proceed therewith, or with obtaining an order permitting distribution where that is required,[6] without unnecessary or unwarranted delays;[7] it will be apparent that if he delays after the executorial function is completed, that is, when there is no remaining reason not to make distribution and thus wind up the estate, the executor may thereby convert himself into a trustee *de son tort* as to the assets remaining in

---

[1] West Dig., Exrs. & Admrs. Key Nos. 288 ff., 418; P-H Est. Plng. Serv. ¶ 2400 ff.

[2] Supra Ch. XIV.

[3] Distribution to testamentary trustee, infra § 27.2; pour-over, infra § 27.5.

[4] It will be apparent that the rules discussed in the following sections apply not only to the distribution of the residuary estate where the decedent died testate, but also to the distribution of the net distributable estate of an intestate, which in effect is his "residuary" estate in that it is what remains for disposition after payment of debts, charges, and expenses.

[5] Supra § 14.31-1.

[6] See next following section.

[7] For a detailed discussion of time of payment, remedies for delays, and related matters, see 1964 Proc. A.B.A. Sec. Real Prop. Prob. & Tr. L., Part I, 50 ff. (where, however, it is noted, as against undue hastiness, that "From an analysis of the laws throughout the country, it would appear that a personal representative has much less to fear from delaying the distribution of an estate's assets than from promptly distributing them but erroneously"; p. 52). See also 1965 Proc., ibid., Part I, at 43 ff. Distribution but impounding share of unborn child pending birth alive, *Cattell Trust*, 21 Fiduc. Rep. (Pa.) 653. Prolongation of administration by delaying distribution, infra § 18.13.

his hands and so be liable as an insurer for subsequent losses or declines in value of such assets.[8]

§ 18.6-2. ———; *necessity of order of distribution*.[9] In many states the executor is precluded from making distribution, or at least complete distribution, of the residuary estate until he has first applied to the court for and obtained an order permitting or directing distribution,[10] which order is ordinarily made on the settlement of his account.[11] In other states, however, there is no provision for, or at least no requirement of, an order of distribution,[12] and the executor may proceed on his own initiative with distribution of the residue, leaving settlement of his account to be effected thereafter.

§ 18.6-3. ———; *partial distributions*. Partial distributions of residuary assets can often be made considerably before the time for final distribution and closing the estate, and are desirable when feasible, not only for getting assets into the hands of the beneficiaries but also for the purpose of getting them out of the hands of the executor and thereby shifting the burdens of management and investment risks to the beneficial owners of the assets,[13] and, in some cases, for income tax advantage.[14] Accordingly, subject to any statutory requirement of obtaining an order of distribution,[15] or after obtaining such an order where it is required, the executor should make a partial distribution at as early a time as he can safely do so, and in such amount or to the extent of such portion of the residue as he can safely relinquish at the time. In this connection the executor must, of course, make sure that he retains in his possession assets sufficient in amount or value to provide for all unpaid or undetermined taxes[16] and other charges[17] and for the expenses of administration,[18] including those of his final accounting.[19] The assets to be retained for these purposes should ordinarily be those most liquid in nature and most stable in value. It may be, of course, that unsatisfied obligations, or uncertainties as to liabilities, will prevent any distribution, or at least any more than a nominal distribution, until their resolution and that final distribution can be made as soon as such matters are resolved. Moreover, in deciding to make a partial distribution, the executor should keep in mind the rule that for

---

[8] Liability as insurer, in general, supra § 3.7-1.

[9] West Dig., Exrs. & Admrs. Key Nos. 314, 315.

[10] A discussion in detail of orders of distribution and the requirements thereof is contained in 1964 Proc. A.B.A. Sec. Real Prop. Prob. & Tr. L., Part I, 44 ff.

[11] Accounting and settlement, in general infra Ch. XXIV.

[12] Cf. Unif. Prob. Code secs. 3-1001, -.1002, -.1003.

[13] For a discussion of some of the situations where a need for partial distributions to residuary legatee may arise, and accounting and other problems in connection therewith, see Dole, A Technique for Making Distributions from Principal and Income to Residuary Beneficiaries During Administration of Estates, 79 Harv. L.R. 765.

[14] Cf. 1965 Proc. A.B.A. Sec. Real Prop. Prob. & Tr. L., Part I, 51–53, 56. Timing distributions, in general, supra § 13.5.

[15] See last perceding section.

[16] Supra §§ 10.4 ff., 11.3, 14.3.

[17] Supra Ch. IX.

[18] Infra Ch. XX.

[19] Infra § 24.8-1.

Federal income tax purposes a distribution to residuary legatees, whether in kind or in money, is deemed to be a distribution (up to the amount or value of property distributed) to them of the estate's net distributable income for the entire tax year in which the distribution is made,[20] with the result that such income becomes taxable to the beneficiaries instead of to the estate, and in pursuance of his duty with respect to his options and elections[21] the executor should consider the tax effects upon the estate and upon the beneficiaries.[22] Subject, however, to considerations of the kinds mentioned in this section, the executor is not warranted in delaying the making of a partial distribution for other than sound reasons, and as a matter of proper stewardship as well as of legal duty he should proceed accordingly. Where a partial distribution is made, all residuary legatees must share in it ratably.[23]

§ 18.6-4. ———; *distribution in cash or in kind.* There has been discussed at another place the matter of the authority of an executor to retain residuary assets for distribution in kind instead of selling them and distributing the proceeds.[24] It is no doubt unnecessary to point out here that distribution in kind of a share or fraction of the residue does not result in any gain or loss for income tax purposes, except perhaps in the case of a non-ratable distribution among two or more legatees,[25] whereas a sale for purposes of distribution may result in realization of a gain or loss either by the estate or by legatees, depending on the circumstances.[26] It is also to be kept in mind that the rule, mentioned in the preceding section, that a distribution to residuary legatees is treated as a distribution to them of the estate's income for the current tax year applies as well to distributions in kind as to those in money. All these considerations should be taken into account by the executor, under his general duty as to the exercise of his administrative elections,[27] in deciding whether to make a distribution of residuary assets in cash or in kind; and the additional considerations relating to the satisfaction in property of pre-residuary legacies[28] apply also in the case of distributions of the residue.[29]

§ 18.6-4a. ———; ———; *shares or fractions of residue.* Where under the terms of the residuary clause (or, as has been noted above, any other bequest of a fund or group of assets[30]) the property thereby disposed of is to be distributed in

---

[20] Supra § 13.5.
[21] Generally, supra Ch. XIII.
[22] Too early distribution, 1964 Proc. A.B.A. Sec. Real Prop. Prob. & Tr. L., Part I, 51.
[23] *Matter of Foster,* N.Y.L.J. Aug. 1, 1966, p. 8, directing executor who paid $5,000 to one of two residuary legatees without paying the other to pay interest to the latter. Simultaneity of satisfying legacies, in general, supra § 14.32.
[24] Supra § 7.6-5.
[25] See next following section.
[26] Supra § 7.6-5.
[27] Supra § 13.5.
[28] Supra § 14.27-1.
[29] Cf. Unif. Prob. Code sec. 3-906, which, as is said in the Comment thereto, "establishes a preference" for distribution in kind, with conversion into cash to be made "only where there is a special reason for doing so." Liquidation for distribution, supra § 7.6-5.
[30] Supra § 14.28.

fractions or shares,[31] equal or unequal, between or among two or more persons, and the executor makes distribution wholly or partly in kind, he must consider whether, at least in the absence of a statute or will provision[32] expressly authorizing a different treatment, he is not required to transfer to each legatee a proportionate share of each asset or class of assets included in the distribution.[33] Although the practice in some jurisdictions is otherwise,[34] it is difficult to justify any method of distribution under which (except perhaps, as elsewhere noted, in the case of tangibles[35]) certain assets are allocated wholly or disproportionately to one legatee and other assets wholly or disproportionately to another. The problem may arise most frequently in the case of securities: Where bonds and stocks are among the distributable assets, it would seem necessary on both logical and equitable grounds that a ratable share or fraction of the bonds and a like share or fraction of the stocks be allocated to each legatee; further, where securities of different issues or different issuers are being distributed, it seems necessary on the same principle that a ratable share or fraction of each block or issue of securities be allocated to each legatee. In any case where the block or issue is not capable of division into the required shares or fractions, this rule requires the sale of the "odd" pieces, except where the beneficiaries agree among themselves[36] or where the values (present and potential) of the latter are so small that the executor, after consideration of the personalities of beneficiaries, is willing to take whatever risk may be involved in distributing them in kind. A failure to make such a ratable allocation seems plainly to be a violation of the executor's duty of impartiality as among beneficiaries,[37] and to render him vulnerable accordingly; for if one legatee receives securities of one issue or issuer and another receives those of another issue or issuer, even though relative values are the same at the time of the allocation, it is not to be expected that the values will remain equal, and the legatee whose distribution declines in value as compared with (or increases in value less than) the distribution to another may legitimately charge the executor with discrim-

---

[31] Legacy of amount out of residue, infra § 19.5-3a.

[32] Any will provision of this character should be carefully considered, as to its clarity and effect, inasmuch as a distribution other than a ratable one, as discussed in the next following text, may have adverse effects upon one or more of the takers; and a draftsman of such a provision should consider, in addition, the possible tax effects thereof and particularly, if a marital deduction bequest is involved, the complicated area of Rev. Proc. 64–19. Direction in marital deduction bequest for replacement of non-qualifying assets with others, supra § 14.8-2bb.

[33] "The [fractional share gift] . . . is a gift of the described fractional share of each item of the fund against which the described fraction is to be applied."; Casner, Fractional Share Marital Deduction Gifts, 39 The Trust Bulletin 42. "It is implicit in . . . this section [preferring distribution in kind] that each residuary beneficiary's basic right is to his proportionate share of each assets constituting the residue."; Comment to Unif. Prob. Code sec. 3-906. While the problem here discussed has received increased attention as a result of the frequent use of "share" formulae in marital deduction bequests (supra § 14.8-2), it is by no means limited to such bequests.

[34] A comment seemingly approving such contrary practice appears in 1965 Proc. A.B.A. Sec. Real Prop. Prob. & Tr. L., Part I, 50–51.

[35] Supra § 14.4-8.

[36] But see infra this section, text at note 39.

[37] Supra § 3.9-3.

ination. It is also to be kept in mind that any departure from this rule of ratable distribution requires a determination of comparative values, and to that extent converts the "share" distribution directed in the will into a "pecuniary" one;[38] and it must therefore be considered whether a capital gain or loss for income tax purposes may not be realized by the estate, or, if the departure is requested or consented to by legatees, realized by them, in each case on the theory that assets have been "sold" (for a consideration in other assets).[39] Even where, as in some jurisdictions, a statute permits distribution to be made other than ratably among the legatees, it is possible for similar tax problems to arise; but apart from those, the executor who proceeds under the statute must at his peril ascertain the relative values of the assets involved, and incurs a risk of liability in that respect of the same nature and degree as in any other case of evaluation.[40]

§ 18.6-4b. ———; ———; *cash distribution to one beneficiary.* The principles as to ratable distribution of assets discussed in the preceding section do not preclude distribution of any beneficiary's share of the residue in cash instead of in kind where that is necessary or he so prefers. The principles of equitable allocation[41] and simultaneity of distribution[42] are maintained in such a case by setting apart for each beneficiary a ratable share of each asset in accordance with the principles referred to, and delivering one such share in kind to a beneficiary who is to take in kind, and selling the share of a beneficiary who is to take cash and distributing the proceeds to him.

§ 18.7-1. *Lapse of residuary legacy;*[43] *in general.* Where the sole residuary legatee fails to survive the testator, and no non-lapse statute[44] is applicable, the entire residuary bequest lapses.[45] Partial lapses of residuary provisions are more usual, however, occurring where the residue is to be distributed between or among two or more legatees, of whom fewer than all survive, and in such case whether a lapse occurs under a particular residuary clause depends largely on its language. If the provision is for division among and distribution to such ones of designated persons, or such members of a designated class,[46] as survive the testator, the failure of any such person or member to survive does not create any lapse so long as at least one other

---

[38] So in marital deduction share bequest where non-qualifying assets are replaced by others, supra § 14.8-2bb.

[39] I.R.C. sec. 1001 (a), (b). If that theory be applied, inequality among legatees may result from the fact that the relative values at which the respective assets are taken into account in making the distribution may not as to all the assets bear the same relation to their tax bases, so that the measure of taxable gain or loss will not be the same to all legatees when they sell the assets received, and the executor may on that score be chargeable with lack of impartiality.

[40] Valuation in general, supra Ch. VIII.

[41] See last preceding section.

[42] Supra § 14.32.

[43] West Dig., Wills Key Nos. 861-863.

[44] Supra § 14.23-2.

[45] Failure of legatee to survive testator as causing lapse, supra § 14.23-1. Intestacy as to lapsed residuary bequest, infra § 18.8.

[46] Class gifts, in general, supra § 14.24-1 ff.

ASCERTAINMENT AND DISTRIBUTION OF RESIDUARY ESTATE

does survive, the only effect of a non-survival being to reduce the number of shares into which division is to be made. If, however, the direction is for distribution of the residue among designated persons in specified portions or fractions, which together make up the whole, and any one of such persons fails to survive, a lapse occurs as to the non-survivor's share, unless a non-lapse statute applies or the "residue of the residue" rule[47] obtains in the governing jurisdiction. A kind of provision that may partake of the character of either of the two just mentioned is that bequeathing specified portions or shares of the residue to designated persons and what then remains to another; if the latter survives, the failure of one of the designated persons to survive will not result in a lapse if it is clear that all property of the residue not effectively bequeathed to one of the designated persons is to pass to such other, but if such other is given merely the "balance" of the residue a question may exist as to whether the quoted term, or one of similar nature, is to be construed to refer to all residuary property not effectively bequeathed to the others, or instead to refer only to so much of the residue as would have remained if all bequests to others had been effective;[48] if the latter is the case a lapse occurs, subject to the same considerations as those mentioned in the last preceding sentence. It is therefore very important to give careful consideration to the wording of a residuary clause which contemplates distribution to more than one person, as small differences in language may produce substantially different results.

§ 18.7-2. ———; *disposition of lapsed share; "residue of residue"*. Although a lapsed pre-residuary legacy falls into the residuary estate and is ordinarily disposed of by the residuary clause with other residuary property,[49] it must not be assumed that a similar result occurs where the lapsed legacy is itself a part of the residue. In some states, where the residue is bequeathed in two or more shares, and one such share lapses under the principles stated in the last preceding section, but other shares take effect, it is the rule, by statute or decision, that the lapsed share does not become intestate property but is distributable among the surviving residuary beneficiaries, in proportion to their respective shares, under the terms of the residuary clause, of the residuary estate;[50] this rule is known as the "residue of the residue" rule, and presumably is based upon the assumption that the testator would have preferred his surviving residuary beneficiaries to receive larger shares of his estate than to have a part thereof pass to his intestate heirs or distributees.[51] In a majority of jurisdictions, however, that rule does not obtain, and a lapse of a legacy of a share of the residue results in intestacy as to such share.[52] Under either rule, of course, intestacy as to the entire residuary estate results if no share thereof is effectively disposed of.

---

[47] See next following section.
[48] Similar problem as to residuary clause as a whole, supra § 18.3-3 note 21.
[49] Supra § 18.3-3.
[50] So in Unif. Prob. Code sec. 2-606 (b).
[51] The analogy between the rule and the conventional "non-lapse" statute (supra § 14.23-2) will be apparent.
[52] See next following section.

§ **18.8.** *Partial intestacy.*[53] Where, because of lapse or otherwise, a portion of the testamentary estate fails to be disposed of by the will as a whole, including its residuary clause,[54] the decedent is intestate as to such portion, but such portion only; and it descends or is distributable to the persons and in the manner prescribed by the applicable law of descent and distribution, usually as if such undisposed of property constituted the entire estate of an intestate decedent.[55] The partial intestacy may result from failure or inadequacy of the residuary clause to dispose of all property falling into or forming a part of the residuary estate, as its omission to cover property the bequest or devise of which by a previous provision has lapsed or been renounced; but it occurs most often where a bequest or devise of part or all of the residuary estate itself fails, by reason of the non-survival of a beneficiary to take it.[56]

§ **18.9-1.** *Assignment by legatee; in general.* A residuary legacy, like any other legacy,[57] is assignable by the legatee[58] prior to payment of the legacy to him. The assignment may be of the whole of the assignor's share of the residue, or of a specified amount or fraction thereof, and may be absolute or by way of security. Ordinarily an assignment is not effective, as against the executor, until he receives actual or constructive notice of it, as by delivery to him of the assignment or a duplicate original thereof or, if a statute provides therefor, by filling or recording the assignment in the probate court or other public office. Under a valid assignment the assignee is substituted for the legatee as beneficiary of the amount or share assigned and the executor must pay such amount or share to the assignee instead of to the legatee. An assignment presents certain risks to the executor, however, and he must use considerable caution in satisfying any legacy which is or may be affected by an assignment of which the executor has notice. He must first determine whether the instrument of assignment is valid and effective on its face and appears to be properly executed by the legatee, including compliance with any statutory requirement, such as notarial acknowledgment. He must further determine from the face of the instrument whether it is absolute in terms or is given by way of security only, and where the latter is the case the executor must obtain confirmation from the legatee as to the amount, if any, payable under it and agreement by the assignee as to such amount. Wherever possible even in the case of an assignment outright in terms, the executor should obtain the assent of the legatee to payment of the assigned amount or share to the assignee; and if the legatee refuses such assent, or if in the case of an assignment by way of secu-

---

[53] West Dig., Wills Key Nos. 864–866.

[54] Special rules as to cemetery lots, supra § 18.3-5a.

[55] Thus, in absence of statute otherwise providing, the shares of heirs and distributees in such property are computed under the rules of descent and distribution without reduction because of any provisions for them in the will that remain effective.

[56] Supra § 18.7-1. The "residue of the residue" rule, where recognized (see last preceding section), of course may or may not result in there being a surviving beneficiary to take.

[57] Supra § 14.29.

[58] The matter of assignment by a legatee is to be distinguished from that of assignments by trust beneficiaries of their rights in the trust fund or its income; the latter is in some jurisdictions restricted by statute or rule of law, or may be restricted by an effective "spendthrift" provision in the will.

rity the legatee and assignee do not agree as to the amount payable to the latter, the executor should withhold payment until the matter is resolved. In those jurisdictions in which an order of distribution is, or is required to be, obtained,[59] or a proceeding for construction or instructions[60] or for settlement of the executor's account[61] is had, before final distribution is made, and persons interested are entitled to notice of the proceeding, the executor should make parties thereto, and give notice to, both the legatee and the assignee so that a judgment or decree in the proceeding will protect the executor as to the satisfaction of the legacy.

§ 18.9-2. ———; *revocability; direction for payment distinguished.* An assignment by a legatee is ordinarily irrevocable, unless otherwise provided by its terms. It is in this respect to be distinguished from a mere order or direction by the legatee to the executor to make payment or distribution of some part or the whole of the legatee's share of the estate to a third person; such an order or direction is revocable,[62] so far as it concerns the executor, at any time when or to the extent that the executor has not yet acted under it. However, where there is room for doubt as to whether in the particular case the legatee has effected an assignment or has only given a direction for payment to another, the executor acts at his peril if he honors either the original instrument or the revocation, and unless both parties agree as to his course the executor should withhold payment until the question is judicially resolved.

§ 18.9-3. ———; *assignment before death of testator.* It is a general rule that a mere expectancy of receiving part of the estate of a living person at his death, either under his will or by inheritance, is not assignable, and so an attempted or purported assignment by a legatee made before the death of the testator is without effect. An executor faced with such a situation may nevertheless, in some circumstances, feel it advisable to delay payment or distribution until he obtains a judicial determination or approval[63] in a proceeding to which the purported assignee is made a party.

§ 18.10. *Satisfaction in lifetime; advancements.* As is elsewhere pointed out,[64] the doctrine of advancements is limited to cases of intestacy, and in such case of course applies to the net distributable estate, or "residuary" estate, as a whole. In cases of testate estates, the somewhat analogous doctrine of ademption by satisfaction,[65] which is sometimes inaccurately referred to as advancement, can apply to a residuary legacy, but since the doctrine usually is recognized only in case of a legacy for a specified purpose and a lifetime gift for the same purpose, instances of such application are rare if not indeed non-existent.

---

[59] Supra § 18.6-2.
[60] Generally, infra Ch. XXII.
[61] Infra § 24.5-5a.
[62] That is, so far as the executor is concerned. There may be some contractual arrangement between assignor and assignee that gives the latter rights as against the former, but the executor is not bound thereby, at least in the absence of actual notice thereof.
[63] Supra § 18.9-1, text at notes 59, 60. Construction and instruction proceedings, generally, infra Ch. XXII.
[64] Supra § 14.30.
[65] Supra § 14.6-3.

§ *18.11. After-acquired or after-discovered property.*[66] There are to be distinguished two different cases of "after-acquired" property, meaning property that comes into the hands of the legal representative at some stage after his original collection of estate assets.[67] The first is that of property that was not owned by the testator at the time of his death and the acquisition of which he did not contemplate, but which falls into his estate after his death; it is usually held that property so acquired is within general residuary language and so is disposed of by the residuary clause, even though the testator in executing his will could not have consciously intended to bequeath it; but there is authority to the contrary.[68] The second case is that of property which did belong to the testator at the time of his death but the existence or ownership of it was then unknown, and only late in or after completion of the administration of the estate is it discovered, or is then unexpectedly received, as, for example, by realization upon a supposedly worthless or uncollectible asset that the executor had previously abandoned.[69] In this second case there is no question that such property (unless the subject of a specific bequest[70]) forms a part of the residuary estate,[71] and the only questions that can arise relate to its administration. In either of the two cases, if the executor is still in office when such additional property is acquired or received, it is his responsibility to administer it as any other estate asset and dispose of it to whomever is entitled to receive it; if, instead, the executor has been discharged from office,[72] it may be necessary to obtain the appointment of an administrator d.b.n.[73] to receive and distribute the property.

§ *18.12. Worthless property; abandonment.* Where property falling within the residuary clause is worthless, or so nearly so as not to be worth the expenses of collecting or distributing it, the executor may obtain the approval of the court supervising the estate, on his accounting[74] or otherwise,[75] that such property be abandoned. Without such approval, however, or in its place the agreement of all persons having any interest in the residue that the property may be abandoned,[76] the executor should not treat it as without value but should distribute it, or the evidence of its owner-

---

[66] West Dig., Wills Key No. 578.

[67] Generally, supra Ch. VI.

[68] *Braman Will*, 435 Pa. 573, 258 A.2d 492, holding that residuary clause did not pass property left to testatrix or her "estate" (treated by the Court as a substitutional gift) under will of her sister dying after death of testatrix, and such property descended as intestate property of testatrix; but cf. dissenting op.

[69] See next following section.

[70] Generally, supra § 14.4-1 ff.

[71] If the estate was insolvent, and the residuary estate non-existent, the after-discovered property is distributable to the beneficiary whose devise or bequest was the last to abate; infra § 19.5-1, text and note 51. Cf. rule as to contribution among beneficiaries under doctrine of ratable abatement, infra § 19.2.

[72] Distinguished from discharge from liability, infra § 24.9.

[73] Generally, supra § 1.4-2.

[74] Accounting and settlement, in general, infra § 24.5-1 ff.

[75] Instruction proceedings, infra § 22.2.

[76] Agreements with or among beneficiaries, in general, infra Ch. XXI.

ship, in accordance with the terms of the will, if that can be done without expense, for it at some later time it becomes of value the executor who has abandoned it without proper authorization will be liable to the legatees.[77] As an alternative to abandonment, and as protection to legatees, the executor may be able to obtain an agreement by the residuary legatees, or even an authorization or direction by the court, for its delivery or transfer to one of their number, so that if value exists at some later time the recipient may realize upon it for the benefit of all;[78] such an agreement, while not fully satisfactory in all circumstances, is much preferable to a complete discarding or destruction of the item of property or its evidence. If a worthless item is not so delivered, the executor (and perhaps in particular a corporate executor, because of its continuing existence) should seldom if ever fail to retain the item indefinitely, as against the possibility of its subsequently acquiring value, even where authorization or approval to "abandon" it has been given. It is to be noted here that the doctrine of abandonment applies only to personal property, and that real property cannot be abandoned, in the strict sense of discarding it or relinquishing title or ownership, but the same result may usually be reached by allowing the property to be sold for taxes, and so the term "abandoned" is often used in the present connotation with reference to real property as well as to personal property.

§ *18.13. Prolongation of administration.* Apart from his general duty of promptness,[79] an executor must not refrain from distributing the residuary estate, and so keep the estate open for any unnecessary or unduly lengthy period of time, merely or principally for the purpose of obtaining income tax advantages;[80] and in any case an attempt to do so will usually prove futile in that after a reasonable time the income tax authorities will "look through" the estate and tax its income to the beneficiaries as if received directly by them.[81] At the same time, on principles hereinabove discussed,[82] the executor should consider the income tax effects of distribution at a particular time, and to the extent that reasonable cause exists for postponing final distribution he should take advantage thereof if it is for the best interest of the beneficiaries to do so.[83]

---

[77] Cf. last preceding section.

[78] Cf. *Matter of Meyers*, N.Y.L.J. Aug. 4, 1966, p. 8, where on objection by one of residuary legatees to abandonment of a claim it was held that it would be an abuse of discretion to compel the executor to litigate what the latter believed was a worthless claim, but equally an abuse to preclude recovery on what the objectant regarded as a valuable claim, and accordingly that the claim be assigned to the objectant to be prosecuted by him for the benefit of all persons entitled to share in any recovery.

[79] Supra § 18.6-1.

[80] Note that income accumulated in an estate during the period of administration is not subject to the throwback rule applied to income accumulated in trusts by I.R.C. sec. 668 as amended by the Tax Reform Act of 1969, sec. 331. Carry-over to beneficiaries of estate's unused deductions in year of termination, I.R.C. sec. 642 (h).

[81] Disregard of unduly prolonged estate and taxation of income directly to beneficiaries, Reg. 1.641 (b) (3).

[82] Supra § 13.5.

[83] Cf. 1964 Proc. A.B.A. Sec. Real Prop. Prob. & Tr. L., Part I, 50–52.

XIX

INSOLVENT OR INSUFFICIENT ESTATES

§ 19.1. When estate "insolvent".[1] As do the terms "negligence"[2] and "waste",[3] the term "insolvent" as applied to estates has a meaning or connotation somewhat different from that in other connections. An estate is said to be insolvent not only when its assets are not sufficient to pay debts, charges, and expenses, but also when, although those can be fully paid, any legacy or devise, other than a residuary disposition, cannot be satisfied in full because of insufficiency of assets. So the term "insufficiency" may in some instances better indicate the problem involved. It is obvious that there may be degrees of insolvency ranging from an amount of assets almost sufficient to permit satisfaction of all pre-residuary provisions[4] down to an almost complete absence of assets. It will also be apparent that insolvency may exist at the time of the testator's death, or may occur later by reason of losses or declines in value of assets; by the same token, insolvency at death may be obviated by increases later realized. Generally speaking, therefore, the question of solvency or insolvency, and the degree of insolvency if any, are to be determined when payments or distributions are to be made.[5] In any case in which, at such time, there are some assets in the estate but not enough to cover all needs, questions arise as to what items or dispositions are to be satisfied first or so far as possible and what ones must wholly or partly fail to be satisfied or to be given effect; and it is primarily with those questions that this chapter deals. It is to be noted, however, that the principles of priority and abatement that are herein discussed in terms of an insolvent or insufficient estate are, as has been indicated at other places in this work, applicable in determining the relative

---

[1] West Dig., Exrs. & Admrs. Key Nos. 408–419.
[2] Supra § 3.5-1.
[3] Supra § 3.5-2.
[4] Concept of "abatement" as inapplicable to residuary bequest, infra § 19.5-3.
[5] This principle reenforces the necessity, adverted to at various places supra, that the executor not satisfy any debt, charge, or expense before assuring himself that there is no other of equal or greater priority not paid or provided for, and not satisfy any disposition if any of equal or higher rank remains unsatisfied or unprovided for, lest insolvency supervene before the items of superior standing become payable.

availability as among themselves of different kinds of assets or dispositions for the satisfaction of debts, charges, and expenses even in a solvent estate; but it is equally to be kept in mind that, as also indicated elsewhere, there are some matters as to which such general principles do not apply.[6]

§ 19.2. Priority and abatement.[7] Where the estate is insolvent (as defined above), it must be determined what priorities of payment exist, that is, what items or classes of items are entitled to have available assets applied to their satisfaction in preference to other items or classes of items.[8] This is another way of expressing the problem as to what dispositions made by the will must fail to be given effect where the assets are insufficient to permit all dispositions to be satisfied[9] and also, if the degree of insolvency is great enough, what items of charge or claim must remain unpaid. The general principles are (a) that no charge or disposition may be satisfied, either in whole or in part, until all charge and dispositions of higher priority have been fully satisfied, and (b) that, if there are insufficient assets to satisfy in full all charges or dispositions having a particular degree of priority, the available assets must be applied to such items ratably.[10] Where any disposition made by the will cannot, under the principles just stated, be fully satisfied, it is said to abate,[11] either partially (if there are assets which can be applied to its partial satisfaction) or wholly (if there are no assets available for application upon it); and where there are two or more dispositions of the same class they abate ratably, from which it follows that if property of one beneficiary of such class is used for the satisfaction of a superior charge or disposition he is entitled to contribution from other beneficiaries of the class.[12] It will be apparent from the foregoing that priority and abatement are reciprocal concepts, which may be thought of as approaches to the problem from opposite directions.

§ 19.3. Liabilities of executor. In view of the principles stated in the last preceding section as to priority of payment or satisfaction, an executor who satisfies a particular charge or disposition, or applies assets toward its satisfaction, is liable (to the extent of the assets so used or applied) to anyone damaged by a resulting inability to satisfy a charge or disposition of an equal or higher degree of priority.[13] It is thus very important that the executor use great care in determining relative priorities whenever the estate is or may be insolvent (as that term is used in respect of estates[14]), and indeed the executor should refrain from paying any charge or expense, or satisfying any legacy or other disposition under the will, even where the

---

[6] Infra § 19.5-1.
[7] West Dig., Wills Key Nos. 804–818.
[8] Order of priorities, infra § 19.4-1 ff.
[9] Order of abatement, infra § 19.5-1 ff.
[10] Restatement, Conflict of Laws 2d, secs. 344, 348–350.
[11] Abatement generally, supra § 14.2.
[12] So under Unif. Prob. Code sec. 3-922 (b).
[13] So by statute as to debts due the United States; 31 U.S.C.A. sec. 192. In case of taxes, personal or "fiduciary" and transferee liabilities distinguished, *Grieb v. Comm.*, 36 T.C. 156, 160.
[14] Supra § 19.1.

estate is believed to be fully solvent, not only, as has been elsewhere observed, until the time permitted or prescribed by law for presentation of creditors' claims has expired,[15] but also until he has then assured himself (recognizing that it is at his own risk) that there are at least sufficient assets available for all charges and dispositions of the same or a higher order of priority. Except as to debts owing to the United States,[16] matters of priority of payment, and the order of abatement of legacies and devises, are governed by law in each jurisdiction, and, where a will is probated in a jurisdiction other than that of the testator's domicile,[17] or where the question involves real property in such another jurisdiction, it must be considered whether there is any conflict of laws and, if so, what law governs.[18]

§ *19.4-1. Charges and expenses;*[19] *in general.* Under the principles outlined above,[20] all debts, expenses, taxes, and other charges against an estate must be paid in full before any assets may be applied toward the satisfaction of any legacy or devise;[21] and this is so whether or not the will of the decedent contains any provision to that effect.[22] In other words, all such charges and expenses have priority of payment over all beneficial provisions. Where there are sufficient assets to enable payment in full of all charges and expenses, no question of priority as among the items thereof arises, regardless of the existence or non-existence of assets for application toward the satisfaction of legacies and devises; but where the assets are not, or may not be, sufficient in amount to cover all charges and expenses, the relative priorities of various items or classes of items thereof must be considered by the executor, lest he incur personal liability by satisfying an item of a particular ranking or priority without having paid or provided for an item of equal or higher ranking or priority. Such relative priorities are prescribed by statute in each jurisdiction, and, while there are differences in detail among the various states, a general pattern exists,[23] as discussed in the following sections.

§ *19.4-2.* ———; *administration expenses.* Apparently on the theory that it is socially desirable that estates of deceased persons be administered in an orderly manner, and that administration is necessary if taxes and creditors are to be paid, expenses of the administration of the estate[24] are usually entitled, under statutes, to either the highest priority ranking or to a priority just below that of funeral expenses.

---

[15] Supra § 14.31-1.
[16] Infra § 19.4-5a.
[17] Supra § 5.5-1.
[18] Governing law, in general, infra Ch. XXV.
[19] West Dig., Exrs. & Admrs. Key Nos. 258–287, 415–417.
[20] Supra § 19.2.
[21] Generally, see West Dig., Exrs. & Admrs. Key No. 289.
[22] Effects of directions in will, supra § 9.3-3a.
[23] See 1964 Proc. A.B.A. Sec. Real Prop. Prob. & Tr. L., Part I, 53, where the order is said to be generally as follows: (a) administration expenses, (b) funeral expenses, (c) expenses of last illness, (d) family allowance, (e) wage claims, (f) debts having preference under Federal or state law, and (g) other claims. Under Unif. Prob. Code sec. 3-805, claims are to be paid in the following order: (i) administration expenses, (ii) funeral expenses and expenses of last illness, (iii) debts and taxes having preference under Federal or state law, and, (iv) all other claims.
[24] Defined, infra § 20.1. See also infra § 19.4-4 note 28.

§ 19.4-3. ———; *funeral expenses.* Under the law of most states, expenses of the funeral of the decedent,[25] in view of social and sanitary considerations as well as considerations of general public policy, are of a high order of priority, second only, if at all, to administration expenses. Of course, as in the case of every expense in a decedent's estate, funeral expenses are subject to the requirement of reasonableness, and may come under special scrutiny in this regard where the estate is insolvent.[26]

§ 19.4-4. ———; *taxes.* Ranking usually only below administration expenses and funeral expenses in order of priority of payment are taxes. Such priority may be based upon a statute explicitly referring to taxes, or may be based upon one referring to debts owing to the Federal or state government,[27] as the case may be, since unpaid taxes of the decedent are in a proper sense debts of his and taxes upon or in respect of the estate are "debts" of its.[28] A statute of either kind ordinarily includes within its scope all manner of taxes, and makes such taxes payable prior to the payment of any other debt; in the case of Federal taxes, the priority of payment is buttressed by statutory liens,[29] which may give rise to difficult problems as to relative rankings of liens.[30] The priority relates, of course, to taxes as finally determined, including any deficiency assessed and including any interest and penalties. As between Federal and state taxes, those owing to the Federal government are, by its laws, prior in payment to those owing to a state.[31]

§ 19.4-5. ———; *debts of decedent.*[32] All debts of a decedent are payable in full ahead of any legacies and devises, and so must be paid or provided for before any distribution may be made to beneficiaries under the will. As among themselves, however, in addition to the preferred treatment accorded to taxes.[33] an order of priority may exist, as discussed in the next following sections.

---

[25] Generally, supra § 9.2-1 ff.

[26] Thus, if the testator's will should direct unusual or especially expensive funeral arrangements, as for example the construction of a mausoleum, or disposal of body or ashes at a remote place, it is doubtful that the cost thereof over what would normally be recognized as reasonable funeral expense would be entitled to priority, and if not the direction probably could not be carried out unless upon contribution by beneficiaries either directly or by consenting that their benefits abate to make up the additional or super-normal expense.

[27] Infra § 19.4-5a.

[28] But the latter are sometimes treated instead as administration expenses. See *Matter of Begent*, —A.D.2d—, 325 N.Y.S. 2d 317 (unpaid withholding, social security, and unemployment taxes of business continued during period of administration were regarded as administration expenses, and so preferred over other debts, even though continuance of business exceeded executor's authority); *Catena Est.*, 19 Fiduc. Rep. (Pa.) 82 (where there were unpaid both Federal income taxes of the decedent and Federal estate tax on his estate, which was insufficient to pay both, the United States had no right of election to apply available assets on the income tax rather than the estate tax, for the latter is an "administration expense" and the former a debt; and the executor had no right to elect because a state statute gave priority to administration expenses).

[29] I.R.C. sec. 6321, taxes generally; sec. 6324 (a), estate taxes; sec. 6324 (b), gift taxes. Lien for income taxes, West Dig., Taxation Key No. 1090.

[30] Cf. 2 Real Prop. Prob. & Tr. J. 256–267.

[31] It has been pointed out elsewhere that questions of priority as between states do not arise; supra § 12.1.

[32] P-H Est. Plng. Serv. ¶ 2261.

[33] See last preceding section.

§ 19.4-5a. ———; ———; *debts to Federal or state government.* By Federal statute,[34] debts owing to the United States are entitled to priority over all other debts and must be paid in preference to the latter; and corresponding statutes exist in some states as to debts owing thereto. As noted above, such statutes presumably apply to taxes of all kinds,[35] since a tax obligation is in the general sense a debt, but they ordinarily are broad enough to apply also to any other kind of obligation. The applicable state statute, as well as the Federal statute, should, of course, be consulted by the executor.

§ 19.4-5b. ———; ———; *expenses of last illness.* Under some statutes expenses of the last illness of the decedent,[36] or medical expenses incurred within a specified period before death, are preferred in payment over some other obligations of the estate. It is therefore necessary for the executor to ascertain whether there is any statutory preference as to such expenses and, if so, its nature. If the statute is in terms merely of last illness rather than relating to a time period, it may be further necessary for the executor to determine whether particular expenses were indeed those of the last illness or were merely coincidentally related in time to the testator's death.

§ 19.4-5c. ———; ———; *secured debts.*[37] Where an estate is insufficient to pay all debts of the decedent in full, a debt secured by mortgage, pledge, or other lien,[38] can be enforced by the creditor, through foreclosure or other recourse to the securing property, even if, as a result, unsecured creditors go unpaid. In that sense, therefore, a secured debt is entitled to priority over unsecured debts, to the extent of the amount realizable out of the securing property.[39] Any deficiency remaining after recourse to the security ranks as an unsecured debt.[40]

§ 19.4-5d. ———; ———; *other debts.* While debts of the decedent that are not entitled to priority under the principles discussed in the two preceding sections are the class of the lowest order of priority of payment among all charges against the estate, they are, of course, payable in full before any beneficiary under the will is entitled to receive any property or to have it held or used for his benefit. As among themselves, such debts are satisfied ratably,[41] where the property available for application upon them is insufficient for their full payment, except if and to the extent, if any, that applicable state law may grant some preference, within the class, to sealed obligations, judgments, or other categories. The debts to which these principles apply

---

[34] 31 U.S.C.A. sec. 191.
[35] Supra § 19.4-4.
[36] Supra § 19.4-1 note 23.
[37] West Dig., Exrs. & Admrs. Key No. 264.
[38] Liens for taxes, supra § 19.4-4.
[39] The rationale of this result may be that the testator is to be treated for the purpose of determining priorities as not owning the pledged or mortgaged asset except to the extent its value exceeds the debt it secures, so that (subject to that exception) such asset does not form part of the assets out of which other creditors are entitled to be paid.
[40] To this effect, Unif. Prob. Code sec. 3-809.
[41] Supra § 19.2.

include, of course, unmatured obligations and unliquidated accounts[42] as well as debts due and of fixed amounts.

§ 19.5-1. Legacies and devises;[43] in general. The doctrine of abatement[44] of legacies and devises in an insolvent or insufficient estate is, as has been heretofore pointed out,[45] the reciprocal of the doctrine of priority of payment, and, on the same principle as the latter, means that no assets may be applied to or toward the satisfaction of any beneficial provision until all items having priority over it have been satisfied in full. Inasmuch as charges and expenses are collectively entitled to full payment before any beneficial provision may be satisfied,[46] it follows that legacies and devises abate *in toto* where assets are not sufficient to pay charges and expenses or where, after payment of those, no balance of assets remains. Where, instead, assets do remain after full payment of all charges and expenses but are not sufficient in amount to cover all dispositions made by the will, partial abatement, or abatement of some (but perhaps not all) dispositions occurs; so the relative priorities of such disposition, or of various classes of dispositions,[47] as among themselves, must be considered by the executor, and those of the lowest priority are the first to abate.[48] The process of abatement continues until the descending scale of priorities and the upward erasure of benefits meet—in other words, until, as the executor applies assets to each lower rank of disposition in turn, the assets are exhausted. It is thus apparent that, in any insolvent or possibly insolvent estate, it is essential for the executor to determine the order of abatement, i.e., to determine what dispositions fail to take effect and what ones may be satisfied; for, as has been pointed out at an earlier place,[49] if an executor distributes assets under a disposition which must abate, wholly or partially, under the rules herein discussed, he is liable to surcharge in order to make the estate able to cover dispositions of higher priority, that is, of lower ranking in order of abatement. By an extension of the same principles, if after-discovered assets[50] of an estate are of a character such that, if they had been on hand at the time, they would have been applicable to satisfy a charge of obligation ahead of assets that were actually used for that purpose, the persons who would have been entitled to the assets so used are equitably entitled to restitution out of the after-discovered property.[51] It is, however, to be emphasized here that, as appears at other places in this

[42] So under Unif. Prob. Code sec. 3-805. Such claims generally, supra § 9.3-2.
[43] West Dig., Exrs. & Admrs. Key Nos. 270 ff., 418; P-H Est. Plng. Serv. ¶¶ 432.20–.23, 432.29.
[44] Generally, supra § 14.2.
[45] Supra § 19.2.
[46] Supra § 19.4-1.
[47] Classification of dispositions, supra §§ 14.1, 15.2-2b.
[48] As to order of abatement, in general, cf. Unif. Prob. Code sec. 3-902.
[49] Supra § 19.3.
[50] Supra § 18.11.
[51] Thus, if real property is not available under applicable law to satisfy a charge or claim until personal property is exhausted, and the after-discovered property is personalty, the devisee of real property used is entitled to such restitution; or if a specific legacy was sold to satisfy a claim or charge, and the after-discovered property is not the subject of a specific bequest, the specific legatee is entitled to restitution. For a statute embodying the principle stated, cf. N. Y. S.C.P.A. sec. 1919. Cf. rule of contribution among beneficiaries under doctrine of ratable abatement, supra § 19.2.

work, the general rules as to order of abatement do not always apply in making up exempt property,[52] family or homestead allowances,[53] elective shares of spouses,[54] shares of pretermitted children,[55] and estate taxes payable out of the residuary estate but for the payment of which the latter is insufficient.[56]

19.5-2. ———; *devises; common law rules.* Historically, it is apparent that when the common law was taking shape the bulk of the wealth in England was in land, and real property had a regard in the law that in numerous respects was superior to that held for personal property; so, much of the structure of the law and of our legal institutions evinces a purpose to protect and perpetuate ownership of land. One manifestation of this purpose is the rule of the common law that all personal property of a decedent must be exhausted, before resort may be had to any real property,[57] for the payment of debts, charges, and expenses; accordingly, at common law devises are the last to abate in an insolvent estate, and, by analogy to specific legacies,[58] specific devises abate only after general or residuary devises. *A fortiori*, under the classical rules, unless a contrary intention appears in the will,[59] a devise of any kind does not abate to enable the payment of a legacy, with the result that, even if all personal property is exhausted by charges and expenses, devisees still take the real property, or so much thereof as remains after any balance of the debts, charges, and expenses have been paid. Although in most parts of this country wealth is now represented much more often and to much greater degree by securities and other personal property than by land, the common law rule still prevails except where it has been altered by statute.

§ *19.5-2a.* ———; ———; *statutory changes.* In an increasing number of jurisdictions, recognition that the historical reasons for the preferential treatment of devises over bequests, referred to in the preceding section, no longer exist, or have lost most of their force,[60] has resulted in the enactment of statutory provisions having the effect of putting real property on a parity with personal property as far as concerns availability for cash needs of estates. Under such a statute, a devise, of any

---

[52] Supra § 17.1.
[53] Ibid.
[54] Supra § 17.4-5.
[55] Supra § 17.6-4.
[56] It will be apparent that, except to a degree in the case of taxes, the items mentioned in the text at this point do not involve insolvency, but merely an adjustment for dispositions which the testator had no effective power to make as against statutory rights of the persons affected.
[57] Generally, supra § 15.7. Restitution to devisee out of after-acquired personalty, see last preceding section, note 51. Sale of land, available for payment of charges in one state, where personal property remains in another state, Restatement, Conflict of Laws 2d, sec. 335; where assets in other state are insufficient, ibid. sec. 336.
[58] Supra § 19.5-6.
[59] Legacy charged on land, supra §§ 14.9-1, -2.
[60] In modern times, it would seem likely that a testator is normally little interested in perpetuating ownership of land, and that, on the contrary, most testators would prefer to have land (other than any thereof specifically devised) disposed of as necessary to meet cash requirements, and securities and other personalty retained for his beneficiaries, than the converse.

class,[61] abates to enable the payment of debts, charges, and expenses,[62] and, under some of the statutes, payment of legacies also, whenever and at the same time or in the same order as does a bequest of the same class. Under such a statute, of course, if only a part, and not the whole, of the real and personal property covered by dispositions of a particular class is needed in order to enable the making of the payments in question, there is a partial abatement, only, of the class as a whole, and the executor will normally have discretion as to what particular items of such property, real or personal without preference, are to be converted into money[63] or used for the purpose of such payments.[64]

§ 19.5-3. ———; *residuary legacies.* The term "abatement" is not strictly applicable to a residuary legacy where the legacy is of the entire residuary estate or a share or fraction thereof,[65] inasmuch as a residuary legacy by its nature embraces only so much personal property as remains after all items entitled to priority have been paid in full. Thus the amount of a legacy of the residue, or one of a share or fraction of the residue, is affected only by the amount of property so remaining and the doctrine of abatement has no proper application; the doctrine is also not correctly applicable to the case of entire failure of a residuary estate (that is, the exhaustion of all assets by charges and prior dispositions, so that nothing remains to pass under the residuary provision of the will), for here there cannot be a residuary legacy. It is, however, convenient in speaking of relative priorities of payment of legacies, or relative orders of abatement, to say that a residuary legacy abates before any other disposition made by the will,[66] and that the residuary personalty (or, where the distinction between real and personal property has been abolished for purposes of abatement,[67] the residuary dispositions as a whole) must be exhausted before there is any abatement of any other legacy.

§ 19.5-3a. ———; ———; *legacy of amount out of residue.*[68] While, as noted in the last preceding section, the doctrine of abatement is not strictly applicable to the case of a legacy of the residuary estate or of a share or fraction thereof, the doctrine is applicable in the case of a residuary provision which directs payment out of the residue of specified amounts (rather than shares or fractions) to specified persons, and disposes of the "balance" of the residuary estate[69] to others. Under such a provision such "balance" is to be treated as actually the residuary estate for purposes of determining priorities of payment and order of abatement, and the specified sums, while payable only out of such assets as remain after payment of all charges against the

---

[61] Classification of dispositions as specific, general, etc., supra §§ 14.1-1, 15.2-2b.

[62] So in Unif. Prob. Code sec. 3-902, unless will otherwise provides, or the testamentary plan, or the purpose of the legacy or devise, would be defeated.

[63] Liquidation for cash requirements, in general, supra § 7.6-1.

[64] Contribution by other beneficiaries of same class, supra § 19.2.

[65] Legacy of specified amount out of residue, see next following section.

[66] Intestate property, infra § 19.9.

[67] See last preceding section.

[68] West Dig., Wills Key No. 587 (6).

[69] Bequest of balance of residue, West Dig., Wills Key No. 588.

estate and all preceding bequests, nevertheless are payable in full before any legatee of such "balance" is entitled to receive any payment or distribution. Thus it may be said that such "balance" of the residue abates before the specified sums, and the legatees of such sums do not suffer any diminution of the amounts directed to be paid to them merely because there are no or few assets remaining for distribution to the legatees of the "balance" of the residue; but such specified sums abate (ratably, as among themselves) before there is any abatement of any preceding legacy.

§ 19.5-4. ———; *general legacies.* General legacies[70] abate where, and to the extent that, available assets remaining after payment of charges and expenses, and satisfaction of legacies entitled to priority of payment,[71] are insufficient to pay all legacies in full; thus a general legacy is the first (after exhaustion of the residuary[72]) to abate. As among themselves, where all cannot be satisfied in full, the several general legacies abate ratably, subject to the consideration mentioned in the next following section.

§ 19.5-4a. ———; ———; *legacy for specified purpose.* Where a general legacy is specified to be for a particular purpose, as for education, support, or maintenance of the legatee, it may in some jurisdictions be entitled to priority of payment over other general legacies not expressed to be for specified purposes; and, if so, it will not abate except to the extent, if any, that a deficiency of assets remains after abatement *in toto* of such other general legacies.

§ 19.5-4b. ———; ———; *legacy to wife or child; marital deduction legacy.*[73] By extension of the principles referred to in the last preceding section, it is often held, even in the absence of statute, that a general legacy to or for the benefit of the testator's wife, particularly one qualifying for the marital deduction,[74] or to a child or other person toward whom the testator stood in *loco parentis*, is to be preferred in payment over other general legacies, where the estate is insufficient to pay all of them in full, and so is the last general legacy to abate. This is upon the theory that such would accord with the probable intention of the testator.[75]

§ 19.5-5. ———; *demonstrative legacies.* In all jurisdictions demonstrative legacies[76] have a special ranking so far as concerns order of abatement, but the principles applied are not uniform as among the various jurisdictions. In some of the latter, a demonstrative legacy ranks as a specific legacy to the extent that the fund designated as its source of payment is sufficient, and, as a general legacy to the extent, if any, that it exceeds such fund;[77] where that rule obtains, demonstrative legacies, to

---

[70] Defined, supra § 14.6-1.
[71] Infra §§ 19.5-5, -6.
[72] See last preceding section.
[73] P-H Est. Plng. Serv. ¶¶ 432.10, 432.13.
[74] Marital deduction legacies, in general, supra § 14.8-1 ff.
[75] So as to Unif. Prob. Code sec. 3-902, permitting departure from the otherwise applicable rules as to order of abatement if the "express or implied purpose" of the legacy would be defeated, according to the Comment to that section.
[76] In general, supra § 14.5-1 ff.
[77] So in Unif. Prob. Code sec. 3-902. Payment of excess over designated fund as general legacy, supra § 14.5-3; general legacy as first to abate, supra § 19.5-4.

the extent of such fund, and specific legacies abate together, as a single class.[78] In other jurisdictions, demonstrative legacies form a class intermediate between general legacies and specific legacies, and the order of abatement is before specific legacies but after general legacies, to the extent of sufficiency of the designated fund; but here also, as under the rule previously stated, the legacy is to be treated as general if and to the extent that it exceeds the fund. Thus, under either of the two rules, where the estate is insufficient to pay general legacies in full, a demonstrative legacy may have full effect, or partial effect, depending on the size of the source fund, and abate partially or wholly to the extent of its excess (if any) over such fund.

§ 19.5-6. ———; *specific legacies*. Specific legacies[79] are of the highest degree of priority in payment of all bequests of personal property,[80] and abate only if a balance of charges or expenses remains unpaid after exhaustion of all personal property not specifically bequeathed—in other words, after abatement of all residuary bequests of personalty, all general legacies, and all demonstrative legacies. The rule, elsewhere stated,[81] that specifically bequeathed personalty is not subject to sale to raise funds for charges or expenses until all other personal property of the estate, including cash, has first been exhausted, is of course applicable in an insolvent estate, and accordingly (if or to the extent that the specific personalty has not had to be sold for those purposes) the specific legatee is entitled to receive his bequest even if no assets are available to pay cash legacies. If it is necessary, for the payment of charges or expenses, to sell some, but not all, of the personal property specifically bequeathed by the will, and there are two or more specific legatees, the principle hereinabove stated of parity as within a class of dispositions having equal priority[82] would presumably be applied to require the legatee of an unsold item to contribute equitably to the legatee of an item that was sold, so that the burden would be borne ratably among the specific legatees as a class.[83]

§ 19.5-6a. ———; ———; *legacy charged on specific devise*. It is not entirely clear whether, as mentioned above,[84] a legacy charged upon a specific devise of land, or upon the devisee thereof, is properly to be treated for purposes of abatement as a demonstrative legacy, with the land as the source of payment, or as a specific legacy, because liked to a specific disposition of land.[85] It would seem, for the latter reason, more logical that it be treated as specific in determining the order of abatement

---

[78] *Kilcoyne v. Reilly*, 249 F.2d 472; *Matter of Byrnes*, 149 Misc. 449, 267 N.Y.S. 627. Priority of specific legacies over others, see next following section.

[79] Generally, supra § 14.4-1 ff.

[80] Devises of real property, supra §§ 19.5-2, -2a.

[82] Supra § 19.2.

[83] So in Unif. Prob. Code sec. 3-902 (c).

[84] Supra § 14.9-2.

[85] Cf. Unif. Prob. Code sec. 3-902 (a), providing that for purposes of abatement rules a legacy charged on "any specific property or fund" is a specific legacy to the extent of the value of such property and a general legacy to the extent of any insufficiency thereof; it will be noted that this provision appears to eliminate, at least for the purposes mentioned, the concept of demonstrative legacies as a separate class but maintains the concept as to any insufficiency of the designated source-fund.

in the case of an insolvent or insufficient estate, but in either case it is apparent that such a legacy has priority over general legacies and does not abate until the latter have been exhausted.

§ 19.6. *Appointive property*.[86] While it is not accurate to speak of the abatement of an appointment of property made by the testator under a power possessed by him at his death, or of the order of abatement thereof, it has been mentioned above[87] that such appointive property may in some circumstances be subject to or available for application on the testator's debts, and it is appropriate at this point to consider whether and when it is so available. Of course, if the property is validly appointed to the testator's own estate or executor, it becomes and is to be treated as an addition to and an integral part of the estate for all purposes,[88] including payment of charges and expenses and of legacies. In some jurisdictions, however, it is held that where the power was a general one and is exercised by the testator, although otherwise than by appointing to his own estate, the appointive property by virtue of the exercise of the power becomes subject to claims of the testator's creditors,[89] but only after exhaustion of his own assets. Thus, even where that rule obtains, it may be said that appointive property is of a "priority" exceeding that of all testamentary assets, in that it is not available to creditors until all such assets have been applied to claims and an unpaid balance of the latter remains. In all jurisdictions, however, property subject to a general power that is not exercised, and property subject to a special or limited power, whether or not exercised, is not available for payment of creditors' claims, and cannot be reached by creditors or by the executor, even though the estate be insolvent and the claims go unpaid.[90] In no jurisdiction, it is emphasized, is appointive property available for payment of legacies unless, as above mentioned, the appointment is to the estate.

§ 19.7. *Income*. It has been mentioned above that under some statutes an executor may collect and use the rents from real property for payment of or application

---

[86] P-H Est. Plng. Serv. ¶ 443.

[87] Supra § 9.8-3.

[88] Supra § 18.3-8; executor's duty to collect, supra § 6.19.

[89] The rationale of the rule is either that the donee could and should have appointed to his creditors in preference to a volunteer ("one must be just before being generous"), or that when the power is exercised the property momentarily passes into the ownership of the donee and then is disposed of by him and that creditor's rights attach during such passage. *U.S. v. Field*, 255 U.S. 257, 41 S.Ct. 256, 65 L.ed. 617, 18 ALR 1461; *Gilman v. Bell*, 90 Ill. 144; *Prescott v. Wordell*, 319 Mass. 118, 65 N.E.2d 19; cf. *Vinton v. Pratt*, 228 Mass. 468, 117 N.E. 919, LRA 1918D 343 (appointment to one creditor made the appointive property available to all creditors). The executor accordingly has a duty to collect and administer appointive property to the extent it is required to pay debts payable from it; *U.S. v. Field*, supra (saying that this is a matter of convenience, wherein the executor represents the rights of creditors, and not a part of the executor's administration of the decedent's assets); see also supra §6.19.

[90] This follows from and is explained by the reasoning cited in the preceding footnote. So in feudal England, where land was the chief wealth and most of it was held by a feoffee to uses for the benefit of the real owner, who retained a general power of appointment, the failure of such owner to execute a will exercising his power prevented the collection of their claims by his creditors, by whom he was accordingly referred to as a "stinking intestate."

INSOLVENT OR INSUFFICIENT ESTATES

upon debts and charges.[91] Apart from such cases, where a specific bequest or devise abates, the income therefrom that otherwise would be payable to the specific legatee or devisee[92] abates also, and is available for the payment of charges and expenses in the same manner and to the same degree as the corpus of the bequest or devise, for if the disposition made by the will cannot be given effect for want of available assets there can be no attribution of income thereto. On similar principles, if the residuary dispositions abate entirely, or, more accurately, if there is no residue after payment of debts, charges and prior dispositions any income that otherwise would fall into the residue or pass to residuary beneficiaries[93] must be applied toward prior items on the same basis as the corpus of the residuary and as a part hereof, and accordingly dispositions of higher priority do not abate until after such income is so applied.

§ 19.8. *"Exempt" property and allowances.* As has been discussed above,[94] so-called "exempt" property directed by a statute to be set apart and turned over to the spouse or children of the testator is under such a statute not a part of the administerable estate, and so is not available for payment of charges, expenses, or creditor's claims;[95] and therefore no problem of abatement or the order thereof arises with respect to such property. Similarly, where statutes provide for a pecuniary payment to spouse or children, commonly called a homestead allowance, family allowance, or the like, the amount of which also is to be excluded from the administerable estate, no problem of abatement arises, except where, as under some statutes, such moneys may be reached for the payment of funeral expenses if there are no other assets;[96] if the latter kind of provision exists, a priority of highest degree may be said to attach to the allowance in question. Where the assets of the decedent are insufficient to make up both or all forms of exemption and allowance provided by applicable statute, the latter usually prescribes their order of priority *inter se*.[97]

§ 19.9. *Totten trusts.* It has been held that a so-called Totten trust, or savings bank trust,[98] is subject to a lien or charge, where the estate is insufficient to pay creditors in full, for the deficiency.[99]

§ 19.10. *Intestate property.* The foregoing discussion has dealt with the abatement of devises and legacies, and so assumes that the decedent died fully testate as to his entire estate. If, instead, he died intestate as to any property,[100] as where the residuary clause does not in terms or in effect cover it,[1] or where a residuary bequest

---

[91] Supra § 15.6.
[92] Supra §§ 14.4-3, 15.6.
[93] Supra § 18.4-1 ff.
[94] Supra § 17.1.
[95] So in Unif. Prob. Code secs. 2-401, -402, -403.
[96] *Matter of O'Rourke*, 223 N.Y.S.2d 725.
[97] Unif. Prob. Code, secs. cited supra note 95, provides for (i) homestead allowance, (ii) exempt property, and (iii) family allowance, in that order of priority.
[98] Supra § 6.12-2b.
[99] *Matter of Baker*, 48 Misc.2d 732, 265 N.Y.S.2d 816. Some analogy between such a trust and a general power of appointment (supra § 19.6) will be apparent.
[100] Partial intestacy, in general, supra § 18.8.
[1] Supra §§ 18.3-3, -5. Special rules as to cemetery lots, supra § 18.3-5a.

itself fails to be effective in whole or in part,[2] such intestate property is the first available for payment of debts and charges,[3] and no disposition made by the will abates until after exhaustion of the intestate property.[4] This rule is presumably founded upon the theory that the will should be given effect so far as possible.

---

[2] Supra §§ 18.7-1, -2.

[3] "Intestate property should first be applied."; Atkinson, Wills (2d ed. 1953), sec. 136. *Re Hall's Est.*, 183 Cal. 61, 190 P. 364. Cf. *Hays p. Jackson,* 6 Mass. 149 (under rule making real property liable for debts and charges only after exhaustion of personalty, intestate real property should be resorted to, after such exhaustion, before devised realty).

[4] So in Unif. Prob. Code sec. 3-902.

XX

ADMINISTRATION EXPENSES; FEES AND COMPENSATION

§ 20.1. *Administration expenses*[1] *defined*. The term "administration expenses" refers in general to all expenses necessarily or properly incurred by the executor or in his behalf in administering the estate. It includes not only the fees of the executor's counsel and his own compensation, which are discussed in this chapter, but also expenditures for many other purposes,[2] as referred to or implicit in other portions of this work. While some expenditures of income are within the term, those involved merely in arriving at net income[3] are ordinarily not treated as within the term. Both for purposes of priority of payment[4] and those of accounting,[5] administration expenses are to be distinguished from funeral expenses, death taxes, and, of course, debts of the decedent.

§ 20.2. *Source of payment*.[6] The reasonable and proper expenses of administering the estate are in almost all instances payable out of the estate as a whole, which in effect usually means they are borne by the residuary beneficiaries.[7] This is true in most circumstances even as to expenses that relate to, or are generated by or connected with, assets passing to or problems affecting only a particular beneficiary or class of beneficiaries, as in storing or protecting a particular asset,[8] locating or identifying a particular legatee,[9] or obtaining a construction of the will as to a particular devise or bequest.[10] On the same principle, expenses incurred in determining estate or

---

[1] West Dig., Exrs. & Admrs. Key Nos. 108–111.

[2] For example, collecting, protecting, and valuing assets, finding or identifying legatees, settling tax controversies or questions, making distributions, proceedings for construction or instructions, and settling the executor's account.

[3] Expenses payable out of income, supra § 16.5-1 ff.

[4] Supra § 19.4-2.

[5] Generally, infra Ch. XXIV.

[6] West Dig., Exrs. & Admrs. Key No. 218.

[7] Borrowing for payment of expenses, supra § 7.6-1b.

[8] Supra §§ 7.2-1, 7.2-4, 7.3-3.

[9] Supra § 14.21-1.

[10] Infra § 22.7.

inheritance taxes or questions relating thereto are payable out of the general estate, even if the matter involved relates only to a particular item of property or affects only a particular beneficiary, and even though the property involved or affected is property that, while includible or asserted to be includible in the taxable estate, does not come into the hands of the executor and does not pass under the will. The general rule is subject to occasional exception where a point for construction or determination relates solely to or affects only the rights or interests of a particular group of beneficiaries *inter se*, and no other beneficiary is affected by the result; in such a case the expense involved is sometimes directed to be borne by such beneficiaries or paid out of the assets in which they are interested. As an extension of this latter principle, in a few instances where a distinction between principal and income of the estate is necessary[11] and a problem relates solely to income, the expense generated by the problem may be payable out of income; but such cases are rare. With that possible exception, and excluding expenses payable out of income under general principles in arriving at net income,[12] administration expenses are payable solely out of principal of the estate.[13]

§ 20.3-1. *Counsel fees;*[14] *in general*. It is universally recognized that an executor is entitled to retain counsel to advise him, and that the fees of such counsel are payable out of the estate as an expense of the administration thereof. The amount of such a fee is, like every other expenditure by the executor,[15] governed by the rule that it must be reasonable, and is, like all other items charged as administration expenses, subject to judicial review and control.[16] The services for which counsel fees are payable out of the estate may include those rendered before the probate of the will,[17] as well as those connected with probate proceedings, whether or not a contest is involved,[18] the administration of the estate,[19] and the settlement of the executor's account,[20] and even, in most cases, those rendered in defending the executor against an objection to the account[21] or a claim for surcharge,[22] at least where the defense is successful.

---

[11] Supra § 16.2.
[12] Supra § 16.5-1 ff.
[13] (1962) Rev. Unif. Prin. & Inc. Act sec. 5 (a). This is implicit in (1931) Unif. Prin. & Inc. Act sec. 3-A (2) (d).
[14] West Dig., Exrs. & Admrs. Key Nos. 111, 216 (2); P-H Est. Plng. Serv. ¶ 2451.1.
[15] Infra § 20.6.
[16] Court may *sua sponte*, although no objection is made by a party in interest, pass on reasonableness of fee. *Lohm Est.*, 440 Pa. 268, 269 A.2d 451.
[17] Infra § 20.3-5.
[18] Contested probate, in general, supra § 5.10-1.
[19] Fees of attorney in settling estate tax are payable out of estate even though the tax return was required because of non-probate assets. *Andrews Est.*, 20 Fiduc. Rep. (Pa.) 163.
[20] Expenses of accounting and settlement, infra § 24.8-1.
[21] Objections, in general, infra § 24.5-4 ff.
[22] *Browarsky Est.*, 437 Pa. 282, 263 A.2d 365, 366: "The executors were placed in the position to be sued because of duties they had performed for the estate. . . . This it is clear that the estate is obligated to pay the reasonable costs of defending against the attempted surcharge of the executors by the residuary beneficiaries." Surcharge in general, supra § 3.6.

§ 20.3-2. ———; *amount and fixation.* In some states, the fees of the executor's counsel are fixed by statute or rule of court, usually as a percentage of the estate. In some other states or localities, customary rates of fee, also usually computed on a percentage basis, may be so recognized or acceded to by the courts as to attain almost to dignity of an established scale. Basically, however, the fee of counsel must be in some rational way commensurate with the services rendered;[23] a statutory or judicial scale, or acceptance of a customary scale, implies reasonableness, but even where such a scale exists provision is usually made for departure from it where it is either excessive or inadequate.[24] Because such a prescribed or recognized rate or scale exists in most places, the attorney may have less difficulty in fixing his fee in estate matters than in many other matters. Whether the percentage basis is a proper approach to the question of amount of the fee in estates has been and continues to be a subject of consideration by bar associations and others, but thus far it appears to be generally accepted as such, and, whether it be viewed as reflecting the relative amount or degree of the lawyer's responsibility or as a measure of relative ability to pay, it seems proper in fixing a fee to give weight to the size of the estate; but where, as in some localities, property comprising part of the taxable estate but not part of the testamentary estate is regarded as appropriate to be included in arriving at the size for fee purposes, such property should perhaps be given less weight, particularly where it forms a substantial, and possibly a major, part of the taxable estate. Subject to considerations of the kinds hereinbefore mentioned, it would appear that, under general principles,[25] the lawyer may also justifiably take into account the amount of time and efforts usefully expended, his experience and competence in the area of decedent's estates, his customary rates of charges and those of other lawyers in the community, and the results achieved in any out-of-the-ordinary, especially difficult, or contested matter affecting the estate or its beneficiaries.

§ 20.3-2a. ———; ———; *agreement by executor.* Because the fees of the attorney for the estate are subject in the last analysis to judicial review and control, the executor is without power to bind the estate by an agreement with his counsel as to the amount of the latter's fee. The executor may properly agree with counsel that he will submit or recommend a particular figure to the court or the beneficiaries, or will not object to an application by the attorney for a fee of a particular amount, if (but only if) in his judgment such amount is reasonable under the circumstances, but he should not contract or agree to pay any specified amount; if he does so, and the court later finds the agreed amount to be excessive, the estate will not be bound to pay any amount exceeding that allowed or approved by the court and the executor may be personally liable as on his own undertaking for the excess.[26]

---

[23] Cf. A.B.A. Code of Prof. Responsibility, EC2-18 and DR2-106.

[24] It is obvious that a percentage rate that is customary and reasonable in an estate of medium size may be grossly excessive in a very large estate, and may be quite inadequate in a very small estate even after the limited ability of the latter to pay is properly taken into account.

[25] Loc. cit. supra note 23.

[26] Contracts of executor, in general, supra § 7.14.

§ 20.3-3. ———; *co-executors' separate counsel.* While each of two or more co-executors is entitled to counsel of his own choosing, and hence each may retain separate counsel if he wishes to do so, it is a general rule that the aggregate of the fees allowable out of the estate to such counsel may not exceed the amount that would have been reasonable if both or all executors had been represented by the same counsel, and that such aggregate must be shared among the several counsel as they may agree or in proportion to the services rendered by them respectively. Ordinarily the retention of separate counsel serves no useful purpose, and instead may tend to impede the orderly administration of the estate, and therefore executors should endeavor to agree upon counsel to represent both or all of them. Where that is not feasible, the executors should encourage the attorneys to arrive promptly at a clear understanding as to the portions of the work to be handled by each of them, so as to fix responsibilities and to minimize confusion or differences of opinion.

§ 20.3-4. ———; *time of payment.* Because the fee of the executor's counsel is to cover all services to the executor through the final winding up of the estate and distribution of its assets, such fee ordinarily does not become payable until the end of the period of administration; and, within appropriate limits of circumstance and discretion, the executor should give due regard to tax consequences in choosing the time to make the payment.[27] Moreover, because, as has been mentioned in a preceding section, the amount of the fee is subject to judical control,[28] the executor who pays a fee before it has been allowed or approved, on the executor's accounting or otherwise, where the local practice provides therefor, risks the possibility that the amount paid will be found to be excessive and he will be surcharged for the excess;[29] and he may find it difficult or impossible to recoup the amount of the surcharge, especially if the attorney has meanwhile died or retired from practice. If it is necessary in an executor's accounting to show all expenses paid or the entire estate distributed, or, even if not necessary, it is desirable so to do or, by having the account settled, to obtain an approval of the payment,[30] the executor may protect himself by arranging to have the amount of the fee, or at least an appropriate portion of it, held in escrow, by the executor or another, so that recovery of any amount determined to be excessive may be readily obtained.

§ 20.3-4a. ———; ———; *partial payments.* The considerations discussed in the last preceding section do not preclude the making by the executor of a partial payment, or payment on account, of his counsel's fee, subject to obtaining advance judicial approval if required by statute or court rule. In making any partial payment the executor should take care that the amount thereof (when added to that of any previ-

---

[27] Cf. 1964 Proc. A.B.A. Sec. Real Prop. Prob. & Tr. L., Part I, 47–48. Tax considerations affecting time of payment of administration expenses, in general, supra § 13.5.
[28] Supra § 20.3-1.
[29] Surcharge, in general, supra § 3.6.
[30] Settlement as approval, in general, infra § 24.5-5.

ous payment) is not so large as to create any risk of exceeding the amount that eventually will be allowed or approved by the court or the beneficiaries.[31] Moreover, the amount of any partial payment should not be so large that if, for any reason, the attorney should fail or be unable to render the remaining services required of counsel in completing the administration of the estate, the aggregate of the amount or amounts paid to him and the additional amount that would be payable to a successor or substituted attorney would exceed the compensation that would have been payable to a single attorney for all services. In general, even apart from the foregoing considerations, a payment on account should not be made unless the period of administration has run and will continue for a sufficiently long period, and the probable amount of the fee already earned is large enough, to make a payment on account fair or reasonable. Originally, as in other cases of advance payment,[32] such as a payment is to be avoided where it is feasible to do so, having in mind that the moneys used to make the payment would or could, if not paid out, be made productive of income for the remaining period of administration; and in view of this latter consideration the executor before making any payment of a substantial amount not directed or approved by the court should consider obtaining the approval of the beneficiaries entitled to surplus income[33] to the making thereof.[34]

§ 20.3-5. ———; *pre-probate services.* An attorney may be entitled to compensation for services rendered prior to the appointment of the legal representative,[35] where such services are necessary and inure to the benefit of the estate.[36]

§ 20.3-6. ———; *contested probates.* On the theory that it is the general duty of the executor named in a will to defend it, counsel fees incurred by the executor in a contested probate proceeding are, in most jurisdictions, payable out of the estate, unless the executor acted in bad faith or did not have just cause to believe in the validity of the will.[37] In a minority of states, however, the contrary view prevails, on the theory that the executor does not have a duty to defend the will;[38] and in some cases, where the executor is himself a beneficiary under the will, that fact is regarded as

---

[31] Supra § 20.3-1.
[32] Estate or inheritance tax, supra §§ 12.4-2a, 12.5; executor's compensation, infra § 20.4-3a.
[33] Supra § 16.6-4.
[34] Agreements with or among beneficiaries, in general, infra Ch. XXI.
[35] Pre-probate powers and duties of executor, supra Ch. IV.
[36] *Est. of Baumgartner*, 274 Minn. 337, 144 N.W.2d 574, 579: ". . . attorneys are often required [before the appointment of a legal representative] to locate and preserve the assets of the estate; to investigate joint tenancy holdings; to determine the status of insurance policies; to ascertain various estate and inheritance tax situations that may arise; to look after rental of properties; to order emergency repairs to real estate; to insure preservation of crops; to provide for the care of stock and to perform numerous other tasks of like nature", and it would be unjust not to compensate them for their services where the work inures to the benefit of the estate and tre legal representative (in his capacity as such).
[37] See 1965 Proc. A.B.A. Sec. Real Prop Prob. & Tr. L. Part I, 165–167, where authorities are collected.
[38] Ibid, 166, criticizing this view.

reason for holding that he must personally bear all or at least a part of the costs of resisting a contest.[39] The fees of the attorney for the contestant may be payable out of the estate, where the contest is successful and others than the contestant himself are benefited by denial of probate; but they usually are not so payable where the contest is unsuccessful, and in general are allowed out of the estate more infrequently than are the fees of the executor's counsel in defending the contest.

§ 20.3-7. ———; *executor as attorney.* Although it was otherwise at common law, the rule in most states now is that, where the executor is a lawyer, he may act as attorney for himself and receive fees as attorney apart from his compensation as executor, or at least may receive more than normal compensation where he acts as his own attorney;[40] he may, however, be precluded from paying or receiving fees for legal services until they have been allowed by the court. Conversely, the mere fact that an executor is a lawyer does not, in most states, render it improper for him to retain independent counsel and compensate him out of the estate. In several states, however, the common law rule is still adhered to; and the doctrine is carried so far in a few jurisdictions as to require an executor who is a lawyer to render all necessary legal services to the estate without additional compensation. It is obvious that when an executor acts as his own attorney and is entitled to fees or additional compensation for legal services, and also where he retains his law partner as his attorney, the principles of conflicts of interest between executor and beneficiaries,[41] on which it seems the common law rule is based, apply with special force. So an executor must not as attorney render (or permit his partner to render) unnecessary legal services and thereby increase his compensation at the expense of the estate and its beneficiaries, or purport to perform as attorney (and as such receive compensation for) services which are part of the duty or function of an executor and so are covered by his compensation in the latter capacity.[42]

§ 20.4-1. *Compensation of executor;*[43] *in general.* In every jurisdiction an executor is entitled to compensation for his services, usually even though the will otherwise provides,[44] and such compensation is payable as an expense of administration. Since the lawful compensation, in whatever manner computed or fixed, is intended to cover all executorial services,[45] an executor is ordinarily precluded from receiving any additional or separate fee for any such services, either out of the estate or from oth-

---

[39] *Succession of Bradford*, (La. App.) 130 S.2d 702.

[40] The statutes and decisional rules are surveyed and their application discussed in 1964 Proc. A.B.A. Sec. Real Prop. Prob. & Tr. L., Part I, 44–49.

[41] Supra § 3.9-4. Interests of executor's attorney as governed by like principles, supra § 3.9-5.

[42] Executor's compensation as covering all executorial services, see next following section.

[43] West Dig., Exrs. & Admrs. Key Nos. 488–501.

[44] Infra § 20.4-2b.

[45] The statute or court rule may provide for or permit additional compensation, over and above that routinely allowed, for special or extraordinary services, but any such additional compensation is part of the "lawful compensation" in the sense of the text.

ers,[46] and from paying others for services comprised within his own duty or function as executor; but in most instances his compensation is not treated as covering services for which experts or specialists must be or customarily are retained, as legal counsel,[47] brokers in the sale of real or personal property,[48] and, in appropriate cases, but not as a general rule, investment advisers[49] and accountants.[50] The rule that all services are covered by his compensation does not, of course, preclude reimbursement of the executor for necessary and proper out-of-pocket expenses.[51]

§ 20.4-2. ———; *basis, rate, and amount*.[52] In some jurisdictions the compensation of an executor is a commission, in the true sense, in that it is a percentage of the amount or value of assets administered by him.[53] In other jurisdictions, the compensation is to be determined by the court in which the estate is administered, on the basis of the nature and degree of the services rendered.[54] The basis of compensation, as well as the rate at which a commission is to be computed or the factors to be weighed in determining an amount, are governed by the law of the place of administration of the estate (rather than by the law of the decedent's domicile, where that is different),[55] unless the will otherwise provides.[56]

§ 20.4-2a. ———; ———; *specification in will*.[57] Where the will provides that for his services the executor shall receive compensation which is at a rate or in an amount exceeding that to which he would be entitled by applicable law, such amount is payable to the executor, but if it plainly exceeds the normal amount the excess may, in case the estate is insolvent,[58] or for estate or inheritance tax purposes, be treated not as an administration expense but rather as a legacy to the executor. Where, instead, the compensation provided for in the will is less than that allowable by law,[59] it is ordinarily the rule that, in the absence of contract made by the executor with the testator or possibly with the beneficiaries,[60] the executor is not bound by the terms of the will, but may renounce its provisions, at least if he does so before

---

[46] So in Unif. Prob. Code sec. 3-719. Fee or salary as director or officer of corporation held in estate, supra § 7.8-4.

[47] Supra § 20.3-1 ff.

[48] Infra § 20.5.

[49] Supra § 7.3-4.

[50] Infra § 24.8-2.

[51] Infra § 20.5.

[52] West Dig., Exrs. & Admrs. Key Nos. 495–497.

[53] Assets included in commissions base, infra § 20.4-5; income as so included, infra § 20.4-4.

[54] So in Unif. Prob. Code sec. 3-719.

[55] Generally, infra § 25.4-4b.

[56] Will provision that compensation be governed by law of executor's residence or location, see next following section.

[57] West Dig., Exrs. & Admrs. Key No. 490.

[58] Priority of administration expenses over legacies, supra § 19.4-2.

[59] Will provision for service without compensation, see next following section.

[60] Any such contract may be regarded as a partial waiver of compensation; cf. § 20.4-2d infra. Agreements as to compensation, generally, West Dig., Exrs. & Admrs. Key No. 491.

qualifying, and claim the compensation to which he would be entitled by law in the absence of the will provision;[61] and this rule is usually applied even though the will purports to make the appointment of the executor conditional upon his acceptance of the compensation therein prescribed. The theory of the rule is that, since the administration of a decedent's estate is necessary for the protection of creditors and of beneficiaries, the legal representative cannot be denied proper compensation for performing the services that law and policy require to be performed; and since by definition the proper measure of compensation is that provided for by law, the rule applies no less in case of a will provision for sub-normal compensation than in the case of one for service without compensation. Where, however, the executor resides or is located in a jurisdiction other than that of the testator's domicile, it would seem that the will may effectively provide that the executor's compensation shall be that prescribed by the law of such residence or location rather than the law of the domicile or place of administration,[62] whether as a result the compensation be greater or less than otherwise.

§ 20.4-2b. ———; ———; *will providing for service without compensation.* While an executor may waive compensation for his services,[63] a provision in a will that he shall serve without compensation, like one that he shall serve for less than the compensation allowable by law,[64] is usually not binding upon him and so he may claim his lawful compensation notwithstanding the provision of the will.

§ 20.4-2c. ———; ———; *legacy in lieu of compensation.* On the same principle as that applicable in the case of a bequest to a creditor that is expressed to be in lieu of or in satisfaction of his claim,[65] it is usually the rule that an executor has an election to accept a bequest stated to be in lieu of compensation, and thereby waive compensation, or to renounce the legacy[66] and claim the compensation to which he is entitled by law. Ordinarily, however, any such renunciation should be made promptly, lest the executor be deemed by silence to have accepted the legacy and so to have lost the right to compensation under the law.

§ 20.4-2d. ———; ———; *waiver of compensation.* Although a testator may not be able by provision in his will to deprive his executor of compensation for services,[67] the executor by his voluntary act may waive all or part of the compensation to which he would otherwise be entitled.[68] The executor not desiring to receive com-

---

[61] So in Unif. Prob. Code sec. 3-719.

[62] Compensation of executor as governed by law of place of administration, in general, infra § 25.4-4b.

[63] Infra § 20.4-2d. Waiver as a non-fiduciary election, permissible on basis of personal considerations, supra § 13.7.

[64] See last preceding section.

[65] Supra § 14.15.

[66] Renunciation generally, supra § 14.26-1.

[67] See three preceding sections.

[68] So in Unif. Prob. Code sec. 3-719. Waiver as a non-fiduciary election, supra § 13.7.

pensation,[69] or not desiring to receive the whole of it,[70] should be sure that his waiver is affirmatively evidenced[71] and timely made if he is to avoid having the full amount, notwithstanding the waiver, included in his taxable income under the doctrine of constructive receipt and perhaps in addition being held to have made a taxable gift to the residuary beneficiaries of the estate.[72]

§ 20.4-2e. ———; ———; *executor dying, resigning, or removed during administration.*[73] Even in a jurisdiction in which the compensation of executors is prescribed by statute or court rule at a fixed rate or scale, where an executor dies without having completed the administration of the estate his legal representative is not necessarily entitled to payment for the deceased executor's services[74] on the basis of such prescribed rate or scale, but may be allowed only such amount as represents reasonable compensation for the services rendered by the deceased executor. Where an executor resigns during the period of administration, he will ordinarily be allowed the amount of compensation earned to the date of resignation, on whatever basis such compensation be computed in the particular jurisdiction. An executor removed from office may often be denied compensation, for the same reasons upon which his removal is based;[75] but if he is removed for a reason other than culpability, as in case of incapacitating illness or accident, it would seem that he should be allowed compensation on the same basis or to the same extent as if he had then resigned.

§ 20.4-3. ———; *time of payment; allowance or approval.*[76] Where an executor's compensation is payable on a statutory scale of percentages or the like, no less than where his compensation is to be fixed by the court on the basis of services rendered, it is not payable until allowed by the court, or at least approved or authorized by all persons having an interest in the residuary estate.[77] Ordinarily such judicial allowance is not made until the closing of the estate and the final accounting by the executor.[78] A partial payment on account of commissions may in a proper case be au-

---

[69] It will be observed that if the executor, or his spouse or dependent child, is sole residuary beneficiary under the will, it may be to his advantage (where the estate is solvent) to waive compensation, as in such case the amount waived will pass to the family free of income tax; but, as such amount correspondingly will not be a deduction for purposes of an estate or inheritance tax, and will therefore result in an increase in such tax, the effective rates of the two taxes must be compared to determine whether an advantage exists.

[70] Consent by executor to accept subnormal compensation as partial waiver, supra § 20.4-2a. Waiver of compensation by one of two executors distinguished from agreement that one shall receive all or greater share, infra § 20.4-6a.

[71] Under some statutes mere failure to collect or retain compensation is not a waiver.

[72] Rev. Rul. 66–167, 1966-1 Cum, Bull. 20.

[73] West Dig., Exrs. & Admrs. Key No. 499. Death, designation, and removal in general, infra Ch. XXIII.

[74] Collection by executor of commission of his decedent as a fiduciary, supra § 6.11-2.

[75] Grounds for removal, infra § 23.3. Denial of compensation, in general, infra § 20.4-8.

[76] West Dig., Exrs. & Admrs. Key No. 501.

[77] Premature payment, see next following section.

[78] Accounting and settlement, in general, infra § 24.5-1 ff.

thorized in an earlier proceeding, either for the settlement of an intermediate account[79] or, under a statute providing therefor, for an allowance of commissions; but no more may be allowed in any such proceeding than the commissions earned prior to its date. In proposing an advance payment the executor should take into account not only its effects upon income taxes of the estate or its beneficiaries[80] but also, as in the case of partial payments on attorneys' fees,[81] the loss to the beneficiaries of income on the amount so paid for the balance of the period of administration, as his duty of faithfulness to the estate must be weighed against, and may indeed outweigh, his personal advantage.[82]

§ 20.4-3a. ———; ———; *premature payment.* It follows from the rule that an executor's compensation is not payable until allowed by the court or authorized by all interested persons[83] that an executor who takes compensation prior to or without such allowance or authorization may be compelled to restore to the estate the amount so taken, with interest thereon,[84] usually at the legal rate, or to credit interest against the balance of compensation ultimately allowed to him; and in a flagrant case such unauthorized taking of commissions may be ground for denial of compensation to the executor.[85]

§ 20.4-4. ———; *commissions on principal and income.* The compensation of an executor, like other administration expenses, is payable out of principal;[86] and this is the case even where, as is explicit under some statutes, the base for computing a commission includes income received as well as principal of the estate. Where, however, income is included in the commissions case, and it is necessary in the estate to differentiate between principal and income,[87] there should be charged against income, or transferred as a charge from principal to income, an appropriate share of the total commission, measured by or attributable to income, so that income will bear its proper share or portion thereof. Where the compensation is a commission, and to be computed at a graduated scale of rates, it seems appropriate to apply such scale first to principal, in order to arrive at the amount of commissions chargeable to principal account, and then, commencing with the rate bracket thus reached, continue to apply the scale to income earned during the period of administration, in order to arrive at the amount of commissions chargeable to income account.

§ 20.4-5. ———; *assets includible in commissions base.*[88] Where the commission or other compensation of the executor is based upon the value of assets admin-

---

[79] Generally, infra § 24.4-1.
[80] Supra § 13.5.
[81] Supra § 20.3-4a.
[82] Conflicts of interest between executor and beneficiaries, supra § 3.9-4 ff.
[83] See last preceding section.
[84] *Matter of Frothingham,* 36 Misc.2d 778, 232 N.Y.S.2d 561; *Matter of Wright,* 177 N.Y.S.2d 410.
[85] Generally, infra § 20.4-8.
[86] (1962) Rev. Unif. Prin. & Inc. Act sec. 5 (a).
[87] Supra § 16.2.
[88] West Dig., Exrs. & Admrs. Key No. 495.

istered,[89] the executor must determine what assets enter into the base for determining such compensation and what assets are to be excluded therefrom. Thus in some jurisdictions personal property specifically bequeathed,[90] and real property not sold by the executor,[91] are excluded from such base, and in such jurisdictions the executor does not receive any compensation in respect of such property, except that, under some statutes, if he is required to manage and collect the rents of real property[92] he is entitled to a commission on rents collected.

§ 20.4-5a. ———; ———; *uncollected assets; assets subject to pledge.* Under statutes providing compensation to the executor by way of a commission on assets, an executor is ordinarily not entitled to a commission on assets which, although forming a part of the estate for which he is responsible, are not actually collected by him. For example, where a receivable is not collected but is set off against a legacy to the debtor,[93] the amount of the receivable may not enter into the commissions base; and, on a similar principle, a commission is usually not allowable on an asset that at the decedent's death was pledged to secure a debt, as in the case of life insurance payable to the estate that is subject to a policy loan, or securities held in a margin account, except to the extent that the value of such assets exceeds the amount of the debt so secured.

§ 20.4-6. ———; *compensation of co-executors.*[94] Where two or more executors act together, they may be required by law to share the commission that would be payable to a sole executor, or the aggregate compensation allowable to them may not exceed the amount that would be proper if only one were in office, unless the will otherwise provides. Under some statutes, however, each of two or more executors may be entitled to a full commission in at least certain circumstances, as where the estate exceeds a specified size. Where sharing of compensation is required, statutes or rules usually provide that it be on the basis of services rendered by the respective co-executors, but in the absence of a showing to the contrary an equal division is ordinarily proper.

§ 20.4-6a. ———; ———; *agreement; waiver by one.* Where, as mentioned above,[95] an aggregate of compensation allowed to two or more co-executors is to be shared between or among them on the basis of their respective services to the estate, the executors may agree for the sharing or allocation on a different basis, or that the whole shall be paid to one of them, and such an agreement will ordinarily be given effect. Such an agreement is to be distinguished from a waiver by one of two or more executors of all or part of his share of such an aggregate;[96] such waiver is held to

---

[89] Income as included, see last preceding section.
[90] Specific bequests, in general, supra § 14.4-1 ff.
[91] As ordinarily not administerable by executor, supra § 7.5-1.
[92] Supra § 7.5-2.
[93] Supra § 14.16-2.
[94] West Dig., Exrs. & Admrs. Key No. 498.
[95] See last preceding section.
[96] Waiver of compensation, in general, supra § 20.4-2d.

enure to the benefit of the estate and not to that of the other executor or executors, so that the amount of compensation receivable by the latter is not thereby increased.

§ 20.4-7. ———; *assignment of compensation.* It is regarded as against public policy for an executor to assign to a third person his compensation for service, or his right to receive compensation, in advance of the time it has been earned or he becomes entitled to payment. This rule, which is to be distinguished from the right of an executor to waive compensation[97] and also from an agreement between co-executor as to the division of an aggregate amount of compensation,[98] is based upon the theory that an executor who assigns compensation to be earned in the future will lose part or all of his incentive and hence may neglect his duties, and possibly also upon the theory that his actions may to some extent be controlled or influenced by his assignee, whose avails under the assignment could be affected by a decision or action by the executor that would have the effect of increasing or decreasing his compensation.

§ 20.4-8. ———; *denial of compensation.*[99] As in the case of any other fiduciary, an executor may be denied all or part of the compensation to which he would otherwise be entitled if in the judgment of the court having jurisdiction of the administration of the estate he has been guilty of such neglect of duty or improper conduct as to disentitle him to compensation, or cause forfeiture of his right thereto, in whole or in part.[100]

§ 20.5. *Out-of-pocket disbursements.*[1] Administration expenses include amounts disbursed by the executor or his counsel for required or incidental expenses, including, for example, such items as filing fees, publication of notices, premiums on his surety bond (if any),[2] necessary travel, appraisal expenses, postage or other charges for shipping assets of the estate, storage or safekeeping charges,[3] and insurance,[4] the cost of obtaining advice and assistance where warranted, including custody and management services,[5] and the costs of accounting[6] and construction[7] proceedings and other judicial proceedings. The concept of administration expense is broad enough to include, also, brokerage commissions paid on sales or purchases of securities or other property, but as such commissions are usually deducted from the proceeds of a sale, or added to the cost on a purchase, they ordinarily result merely in an adjustment of the price and are not separately regarded; it will be obvious that, because administra-

---

[97] Ibid.
[98] See last preceding section.
[99] West Dig., Exrs. & Admrs. Key No. 500.
[100] *Lohm Est.*, 440 Pa. 268, 269 A.2d 451 (executors guilty of "supine negligence" in failing to file estate tax return on time). Removal for like cause, infra § 23.3.
[1] West Dig., Exrs. & Admrs. Key Nos. 108–109, 217–218.
[2] Requirement of furnishing bond, supra § 5.8-2.
[3] Cf. § 7.3-3 supra.
[4] Supra § 7.2-4.
[5] Supra §§ 7.3-4, -4a.
[6] Infra § 24.5-1 ff.
[7] Infra Ch. XXII.

tion expenses are payable out of the general estate,[8] the effect on beneficiaries of either treatment is the same.

§ 20.6. *Judicial review.* The general principle that an executor is subject in all his proceedings to the control of the court having supervision of the administration of the estate, in that he is accountable to beneficiaries for all receipts and expenditures,[9] apply to administration expenses;[10] the executor is liable for unauthorized or excessive expenditures in connection with the administrative of the estate no less than for any other waste of its assets.[11] Such review ordinarily occurs on the settlement of the executor's account showing the payment or proposed payment of the expenses.[12]

---

[8] Supra § 20.2.
[9] Infra § 24.1.
[10] Review by court *sua sponte, supra* § 20.3-1 note 16.
[11] Waste, in general, supra § 3.5-2.
[12] Infra § 24.5-1 ff.

XXI

AGREEMENTS WITH OR AMONG BENEFICIARIES

§ 21.1. *Utility and advisability.* Many times, when questions of construction of a will, or of the powers or duties of an executor, arise for decision, a judicial proceeding for construction or for instructions[1] may be avoided by the making of an agreement with the executor by the beneficiaries affected by the question, or by the making of an agreement between or among two or more beneficiaries that has the effect of solving the problem so far as the executor is concerned. Where such an agreement is obtainable and the issue or problem at hand can be settled by it, it is usually preferable to proceed on that basis than to institute a judicial proceeding, and thus to avoid or minimize delay and expense. As is pointed out in following sections, an agreement may not be effective, either because of the nature of the matter involved,[2] or because joinder of all persons who have or might have an interest in the result cannot be had;[3] but an executor faced in the administration of the estate with a problem that might require solution by a court should first consider whether it is feasible to obtain an agreement that will settle or obviate it. If the executor is a party to such an agreement, he should be certain that there is no person unfavorably affected by it or by the result of it who does not join in it; and if the agreement is one purely between or among beneficiaries the executor should make sure that, either by explicit provision therein or otherwise, it will enure to his benefit and may be relied upon by him.

§ 21.2-1. *Scope and effectiveness; in general.* While a testator may be unable, by provision in his will, effectively to relieve his executor from responsibilities or liabilities inherent in the fiduciary relationship,[4] beneficiaries of the estate have somewhat more scope in the extent to which they may, by consent or waiver, protect the executor against liability for or relieve him of the consequences of an act or omission that otherwise would or might render him liable to surcharge. It would seem clear, by anal-

---

[1] Generally, infra Ch. XXII.
[2] Infra §§ 21.2-1, -2.
[3] Infra §§ 21.3-1, -2.
[4] Exculpatory provisions, in general, supra § 3.10.

ogy to the limitations on a testator's power, that a beneficiary may not relieve the executor from his lawful responsibilities generally, or for the future; nor, unless and to the extent permitted by an express statute authorizing compromises in contested probates, may beneficiaries by agreement modify a will in any general sense, although this may in reality mean no more than that they cannot change an income or estate tax treatment otherwise applicable, or perhaps avoid the incurrence of a gift tax.[5] It is equally clear, however, that, at least so long as he does not attempt to modify or disregard important terms of a will or the testator's intent, or violate any rule of public policy,[6] a beneficiary may relieve the executor from liability in respect of a past act or omission, or a specific act or omission contemplated to be taken currently,[7] or at least may estop himself to complain of the consequences of the act or omission.[8] Moreover, in a number of jurisdictions, in some of them by express statute,[9] beneficiaries may agree among themselves to alter the dispositions made in the will, as to their respective interests, shares, or amounts, subject to the rights of creditors and taxing authorities and to rules of public policy;[10] and the executor may proceed in accordance with such an agreement, so long as it does not adversely affect any other beneficiary or interest.[11] In each case, however, the executor should assure himself that all relevant facts are fully known or disclosed to the beneficiary and that by that or other means the beneficiary is fully apprised of or advised as to his rights, as otherwise the agreement or consent may be ineffective or at least subject to being set aside or treated as wholly ineffective.

§ *21.2-2.* ———; *public policy.* The ability of beneficiaries in many cases to free an executor of liability for acts or omissions that would otherwise render him culpable,[12] or to alter their benefits under the will,[13] does not permit them to validate any will provision that is against public policy or to induce or condone any act or omis-

---

[5] For example, where the rate or amount of an inheritance tax depends upon the relationship of the taker to the testator or the amount of property passing to the taker, an agreement under which property passes to a taker taxable at a lower rate or in a lower bracket than another may not be effective for tax purposes. The question will doubtless be affected by the degree of uncertainty, ambiguity, etc., under the will provision involved in the agreement and of course if an agreement changes the disposition of property under a will provision that is clear and free of doubt it would seem that not only should the inheritance tax be assessed as under the will, without consideration of the agreement, but also that a taxable gift may be involved by the taker under the will to the person receiving the property under the agreement.

[6] Cf. next following section.

[7] Agreement that executor retain assets for distribution in kind without liability for loss of value, supra § 7.6-5; agreement for non-ratable allocation of assets in distributing share or fraction, supra § 18.6-4a. Consents or agreements by beneficiaries are often sought and obtained as to past or proposed action under doubtful or ambiguous administrative or dispositive provisions of a will, or under an uncertain power or discretion of the executor.

[8] An agreement settling the account of the executor is within this rule; cf. § 24.5-2 infra.

[9] So in Unif. Prob. Code sec. 3-912.

[10] See next following section.

[11] Who must join in agreement, in general, infra §§ 21.3-1, -2.

[12] See last preceding section.

[13] Ibid.

sion that violates public policy. They cannot, for example, by any consent or agreement allow a violation of the rule against perpetuities or other judicial or statutory rule of similar purpose, or protect an executor in doing an unlawful or criminal act, or condone or excuse an otherwise wrongful or unauthorized act or omission in which the public, in the sense of the body politic, has an interest. Where, as in many jurisdictions, it is regarded as against public policy, or is a prohibited act, to terminate a testamentary trust (in whole or in part) by agreement,[14] the consent of remaindermen that the executor under a will creating a trust pay principal to the income beneficiary[15] is presumably as lacking in efficacy and in protection to the executor as it would be in the case of the trustee. Before acting under any consent or agreement by beneficiaries of his estate, therefore, the executor should assure himself that the action or non-action thereby contemplated is not against public policy.

§ 21.3-1. *Who must join; in general.* The effectiveness of an agreement or assent by beneficiaries to the doing or omission by the executor of any act which would or might otherwise render him liable to surcharge, or of any release by beneficiaries of the executor from such a liability, ordinarily rests, as has been indicated above,[16] upon the principle of estoppel, and it is therefore elementary that it cannot bind any person other than its makers. Accordingly, such an agreement, assent, or release, or an agreement altering benefits under the will,[17] if it is to protect the executor, must be made or joined in by all persons adversely affected by it or having an interest in its subject matter that may be unfavorably affected in any way, or possibly, according to indications in some jurisdictions, by all whose interests are affected in any way, even favorably.[18] This includes persons whose interests are in any way conditional or contingent, as well as persons having present or vested interests. Where, for example, a legacy is subject to a condition precedent[19] or subsequent,[20] all persons affected by the condition, or by its performance or non-performance, must join in any agreement relating to or affecting the property that is subject to the legacy, if the executor is to be protected; and if a trust is created by the will[21] and the executor is also the trustee thereof, any agreement that might or could affect the trust must in most jurisdictions be joined in by all possible income beneficiaries and remaindermen, contingent or

---

[14] Cf. *Matter of Becker,* N.Y.L.J. May 18, 1966, p. 18, where the court refused to approve an agreement of compromise as to the widow's right of election, despite absence of any objection, on the ground that no legal basis existed for the elimination (as would be done under the agreement) of a trust under the will for the widow's benefit.

[15] Such a payment would, of course, be a termination *pro tanto.*

[16] Supra § 21.2-1.

[17] Ibid., text at note 10.

[18] The theory appears to be that weight should be given to the testator's directions and provisions, and that a beneficiary has the right (unless he waives it by joining in the agreement) to have those directions and provisions carried out even though at the time or in seemingly every respect the proposed change appears favorable to him.

[19] Supra § 14.10.

[20] Supra § 14.11.

[21] Generally, infra Ch. XXVII.

otherwise, since the trustee cannot effectively pass upon his own acts as executor.[22] If there is any question as to whether a power of appointment was effectively exercised by the testator, or as to the persons to whom or for whose benefit an appointment was made, it is usually necessary that the agreement be joined in not only by all persons having any interest under the appointment, but also by all persons who would take in default of the exercise of the power. Where the question relates to a pre-residuary legacy whose subject-matter, if the bequest is not effective, would or might fall into the residue,[23] all persons interested in the residuary estate would normally have to join in any agreement under which the legacy is to be paid, wholly or partly. On the same principle, where the question relates to or affects the residuary estate or any part thereof, the joinder of intestate distributees is usually necessary.[24] These rules may in many cases prevent questions that arise in the administration of an estate from being resolved by the agreement, for if any person whose interest is or might be unfavorably affected by the result is a minor or an incompetent, or may be a person at present unknown or unborn, no agreement or assent can bind such person, even if (as may be the case in some jurisdictions) a determination in a judicial proceeding would bind him without the appointment of a guardian to represent his interests.[25]

§ 21.3-2. ———; *joinder of fewer than all beneficiaries.* While, as stated in the preceding section, an executor is not protected by a consent or agreement with or among beneficiaries unless at least all adversely affected beneficiaries join therein, a consent or agreement made by some but not all such beneficiaries is not nugatory, and may affect the rights of the makers or signers thereof to hold the executor liable, unless, of course, it is expressly contingent upon the joinder of all other beneficiaries. On the same principle as that applying where some but not all beneficiaries successfully object to an account of the executor,[26] the beneficiaries who consent or agree on a particular matter or question are ordinarily precluded from sharing in the benefits of an objection later made by other beneficiaries and sustained in their favor,[27] and if so a surcharge otherwise imposable on the executor will be adjusted accordingly.[28] Thus the executor is protected *pro tanto* by the "partial" consent or agreement.

---

[22] Infra § 24.5-3a.
[23] Supra § 18.3-3.
[24] Cf. § 18.7-2, supra, and § 22.5-2 infra.
[25] Under the doctrine of "virtual representation" or a variant of it (infra § 22.5-1 note 18). Cf. Unif. Prob. Code sec. 3-1101, under which any agreement compromising a controversy as to validity, effect, or construction of a will or rights under it may be made binding upon persons unable to contract by being approved by the court.
[26] Infra § 24.5-4a.
[27] *Matter of Hall,* 164 N.Y. 196, 58 N.E. 11.
[28] Where all interests are vested, no problem as to such adjustment arises. Where any interest is contingent, the usual method is to require the whole amount for which the executor would have been surchargeable if all beneficiaries had objected to be paid by the executor into a segregated fund, and held until the persons entitled to share in it become known, whereupon any share in respect of a non-objecting beneficiary is returnable to the executor.

§ *21.4. Indemnification agreements.* Executors are sometimes too ready, it would seem, to take or refrain from taking some action in reliance upon an agreement by a beneficiary to indemnify them against liability in respect thereof. The question of the ability of the indemnitor to fulfill his obligation, perhaps after a considerable period of time, or the ability of his estate to do so after his death, is not to be ignored, nor are the expense, delay, and perhaps undesirable publicity[29] that might be involved in enforcing such an obligation. In addition to these considerations, the executor should take into account, first, that the very fact that an indemnification is taken suggests that there is question or doubt as to the propriety or legality of the action or nonaction in question and invites attention thereto, and, second, that the indemnification agreement may be void or unenforceable for reasons of public policy. An indemnification agreement relating to a proposed act or omission is to a degree governed in that regard by the same kind of considerations as those bearing upon the validity and efficacy of any agreement, assent, or release by a beneficiary,[30] but going even beyond those is the indication in the law, at least in some jurisdictions, that an indemnification agreement made to induce a breach of trust, that is, an act or omission contrary to the law governing the executor's duty or to the terms of the will, is void or unenforceable as a matter of public policy; and since the executor's relationship is one of trust, in the broad sense, and almost every departure from his lawful duties and obligations may therefore be said to be a breach of his trust, the executor may find the indemnification agreement much less protective to him than he had assumed. A more fundamental view is that the executor should not take any action of such doubtful propriety or legality that an indemnification is necessary, but should seek a judicial construction of the will, or the instructions of the court as to his powers and duties,[31] if it is necessary to make a decision; and, while that as a general principle is doubtless somewhat too broad, considerations of that character deserve careful consideration. In summation, it would seem that the taking of indemnity should be a "last resort" of the executor, and should be done only where both real doubt or uncertainty exists and no other avenue of protection is feasible or available.

---

[29] An executor who must resort to litigation to enforce an indemnification agreement thereby publicly admits that he was in error in the act or omission to which the indemnity relates.
[30] Supra § 21.2-2.
[31] Generally, infra Ch. XXII.

XXII

CONSTRUCTION AND INSTRUCTION PROCEEDINGS

§ 22.1. In general.[1] At a number of places in this work reference is made to the necessity or advisability in various circumstances of obtaining a judicial construction of a will, or judicial instructions as to the powers or duties of the executor, unless agreement by all persons in interest can be obtained. In some states statutes expressly provide a procedure, usually relatively simple and expeditious (at least as compared with a conventional equity proceeding), for obtaining a construction, or instructions,[2] during the course of administration of the estate, and even in the absence of explicit statute such a procedure is usually available under more general statutes as to the supervisory powers of courts over decedents' estates. In the following sections, some of the problems connected with such proceedings are considered. As is discussed in a later chapter, in some instances a necessary or desired construction or instruction may in effect be obtained in a proceeding for settlement of the executor's account;[3] and in some circumstances an accounting is necessary to raise the question involved or to enable its determination.[4] It is to be emphasized that in seeking a construction or instructions the executor must take an objective approach; while it may be proper in some instances for him to indicate to the court what he believes to be correct as a matter of law, he must be conscious that the determination made in the proceeding will often affect the rights of one beneficiary or class of beneficiaries as against those of another and the executor must accordingly be careful to maintain impartiality as between them.[5]

---

[1] West Dig., Wills Key Nos. 695–707.

[2] Differentiated, see next following section.

[3] Infra § 25.5-5a.

[4] Also, without an accounting and steps for its settlement, the application may be regarded (in absence of a specific statute) as a declaratory judgment proceding, not within the jurisdiction of the probate court or not entertained except in unusual circumstances.

[5] In order to adhere to this principle the executor sometimes must resist a conscious or unconscious effort on the part of his attorney, because of the latter's personal or professional relations with a family member or a particular beneficiary, to seek a particular result. Duty of impartiality in general, supra § 3.9-3.

§ 22.2. *Proceeding for instructions.* A proceeding by an executor to obtain the instructions of the court as to what the executor has power to do, or lawfully should do, in a particular situation or as to a particular matter is available or recognized in at least some jurisdictions. It is in a number of respects similar in purpose and effect to a construction proceeding but is properly distinguishable therefrom. A proceeding for a construction is appropriate where the terms of the will are ambiguous or otherwise unclear, or the meaning or effects of its terms as applied to a particular factual situation is uncertain. A proceeding for instructions is the method of determining questions that arise, not because terms of a will are of doubtful meaning or effect, but, instead, because the will does not provide for or cover the matter involved, or because uncertainty exists either as to what principles of law are to be applied or as to what is the law on the point at issue, whether that be a substantive point or a problem of administrative authority. It will be obvious that there is no clear line of demarcation between the two kinds of proceedings, and the difference between them is often of little significance; they are governed by substantially the same principles, and both are often referred to without distinction as construction proceedings. It is, of course, to be kept in mind that an executor cannot use a proceeding for instructions as a device to obtain the court's directions or advice upon matters committed by the will or by law to the judgment or discretion of the executor; the most that a court will or should do in such a case is to determine whether the matter is or is not so committed to the executor, and the executor cannot expect the court to substitute its judgment for his or to make his decisions for him.

§ 22.3-1. *Matters for construction; in general.* References have been made at various places in preceding chapters to provisions to be construed and problems of construction, and specific comment has been made as to some of such problems. This chapter deals chiefly with the time for and method of obtaining a construction, rather than with construction problems as such or rules of construction; as to these latter reference should be made to texts on wills.

§ 22.3-2. ———; *precatory provisions.* It is seldom, if ever, necessary or appropriate to seek a construction of purely precatory provisions—those which merely express a hope or wish without imposing any duty on the executor. Very frequently, however, it is necessary to determine whether a particular provision is purely precatory or instead is mandatory or directive, for the form of language used does not necessarily settle the question; and such a determination may not be possible except by a judicial proceeding for construction or a proceeding in which, in effect, a construction is obtained.[6] It is to be emphasized that an executor should not assume that a provision precatory in form does not have binding effect, and entrapment may result from such an assumption, especially in view of the fact that where the effect of a particular provision is open to doubt the courts tend to favor a mandatory rather than a merely precatory construction. The problem as to whether a provision is pre-

---

[6] Cf. § 24.5-5a infra.

CONSTRUCTION AND INSTRUCTION PROCEEDINGS 275

catory or mandatory is not limited to provisions directed to the executor, but may affect him even when directed to a legatee because of questions that then arise as to the validity or effect of the bequest and the consequent responsibility of the executor.[7]

§ 22.4-1. *Time; interim or special proceeding.* It is pointed out above that in some jurisdictions an application for construction of a will, or for instructions as to the executor's power or duty, in a particular connection may be made either in an action or proceeding brought for the specific purpose or in connection with a proceeding for settlement of the executor's account.[8] Where an option exists, which course should be pursued in a particular case depends chiefly upon the immediacy of the problem. If the problem affects an action that must be taken, if at all, at once, or involves a question that must be resolved before the executor can proceed with steps necessary to be taken without delay, a proceeding to obtain the necessary construction or instruction should be instituted promptly; an example is a doubt as to the power of the executor, under the will or the law, to sell a particular asset where its continued retention may result in loss or diminution of value or where cash is required for payment of taxes or other charges.[9] In such a case the executor should promptly institute an appropriate proceeding, and may be liable to beneficiaries for loss or damage ensuing from failure to get the problem resolved. Unless, however, the problem is one to which a solution is essential at the time, the executor is ordinarily not justified in subjecting the estate to the expense of a proceeding for the purpose,[10] and should postpone seeking a judicial decision with respect to it until his final accounting; for example, where the question is as to the amount or subject matter of a bequest, or the identity of a legatee, or the shares or manner in which distribution of the residuary estate should be made, there is usually no necessity of resolving such question until the time arrives when distribution is required, and accordingly its resolution may and should be deferred until the time of the final accounting. A possible exception to this general rule exists where, for some other valid reason, an intermediate accounting proceeding[11] is instituted; in such case it may be appropriate

---

[7] A familiar example is a request appended to a legacy that the subject matter be distributed by the legatee to another or others. If the provision be treated as purely precatory, the legatee is entitled to receive the legacy and the executor has no concern about the request. If, instead, the provision be treated as mandatory, it may not be proper for the executor to satisfy the legacy, for in effect such a mandatory provision creates a trust (as the legatee is not the beneficial taker) and, unless it effectively designates the beneficiaries of such trust, the bequest may fail entirely under the rule that a trust without an ascertainable beneficiary is nugatory; and may also be invalid as substituting the will of the legatee for that of the testator (cf. Bowe & Parker, Page on Wills, secs. 40.5–.7). Similar considerations may arise under a bequest of tangibles with a provision that they be disposed of in accordance with a letter or other unattested writing or an oral direction (supra § 14.17). The executor must, therefore, determine whether to satisfy the legacy or not, i.e., whether it is valid and effective, and his determination depends on the effect to be given to the "precatory" provision or request.

[8] Supra § 22.1.

[9] Liquidation, in general, supra § 7.6-1 ff.

[10] Incurrence of unnecessary or avoidable expense as waste, supra § 3.5-2.

[11] Generally, infra § 24.4-1.

to raise questions of the kind last referred to in such proceeding, especially if their solution therein may simplify or make unnecessary an eventual final accounting proceeding.

§ 22.4-2.   ———; *on final accounting.* As appears from the preceding section, many if not most questions of construction of a will may and should be deferred for submission and decision at the time of, and in connection with, the final accounting of the executor.[12] This is especially the case where any conditional or contingent interests have existed during the period of administration of the estate; by the time of the final accounting proceeding the conditions and contingencies, which might have existed and been required to be taken into account in any interim special proceeding,[13] have usually been either eliminated or reduced in scope, so that the number of persons required to have notice of the proceeding[14] may be less than it would earlier have been, and there is no risk that the proceeding will be held to be premature as raising moot questions.[15] Moreover, on his final accounting an executor should submit, expressly or by implication, and obtain a decision upon, all construction problems that remain pertinent and unresolved, as otherwise he will not be discharged from liability to any person adversely affected by his action or choice of alternatives.[16]

§ 22.5-1. *Necessary parties; in general.* In accordance with general principles of due process of law, a judgment or decree on the construction of a will, or for the instruction of the executor, like an order or decree settling an executor's account,[17] is binding only upon persons who are parties to the proceeding or are represented therein.[18] It is therefore essential to the full effectiveness of the judgment or decree in such a proceeding, so far as concerns its protective value to the executor, that proper notice be given to or served upon all persons who (or those represented by whom) could have any interest in the subject matter under any possible construction of the will, or in the result under any possible application of the relevant rules of law.

§ 22.5-2.   ———; *heirs or next of kin.* In connection with any problem as to the construction of a will provision relating to or affecting the disposition of any share or asset of the estate, the executor must not overlook any possibility that the construction could be such that such share or asset would be undisposed of by or as a result of the provision. For example, where under a devise or bequest there is a question whether the property passes to one or the other of two persons or classes,

---

[12] Settlement of account as construction, infra § 24.5-5a.
[13] See last preceding section.
[14] See next following section.
[15] Infra § 22.6.
[16] Scope of account, and disclosure, infra § 24.3-3.
[17] Infra § 24.5-3.
[18] As under the doctrine of "virtual representation," where, by statute or decisional law, a parent is treated as representing his issue or existing members of a class are treated as representing persons later becoming members thereof.

or under a subjoined condition or overriding provision there is a question whether the rights or benefits of a legatee or devisee are restricted or cancelled in the circumstances that have occurred, or there is a question whether a bequest or devise has lapsed,[19] there may be also room for a construction under which neither of such persons or classes would take the devise or bequest, or no one is designated to take the cancelled or lapsed benefit. In considering whether any such possibility exists the executor must, of course, for his own protection, resolve all doubts in favor of its existence, and so must cause appropriate notice to be given to, or otherwise join as parties to the construction proceeding, the residuary beneficiaries if the property involved is not itself part of the residuary estate; and if the property is a part of the residuary estate, and, even though it is not, if there is room for any possible doubt as to whether it, if not otherwise effectively disposed of, would pass under the residuary clause,[20] such notice should also be give to, or there should also be joined as parties, the decedent's statutory heirs or next of kin, so that the court may have all parties in interest before it, and all will be bound by the determination.

§ 22.6. *Prematurity; moot questions.* Ordinarily, a court will refuse to decide questions submitted to it that do not actually arise at the time, even though they may perhaps arise at some later time. Where the factual situation is such that a particular question does not exist at the time, an application for construction or instructions is ordinarily premature, and the question is moot, because the question may never in fact arise or have to be decided, and, if it does arise, the problem or the persons interested or affected by it may be different. In some instances, however, the courts will decide questions that do not directly or immediately affect the administration of the estate, and in that sense are moot, as where problems of estate or inheritance taxation depend upon the construction or effect to be given to a disposition or administrative provision in the will, or even where a beneficiary under the will needs a determination as to his rights or interests in the estate in order that he may satisfactorily plan the disposition of his own estate.[21]

§ 22.7. *Expenses.*[22] The reasonable and proper expenses of a proceeding for a construction or for instructions are included in the category of administration expenses and payable in accordance with the rules relating thereto.[23]

---

[19] Lapse generally, supra §§ 14.2, 15.4.
[20] Disposition of lapsed legacy, supra § 18.3-3, 18.7-1; partial intestacy, supra § 18.8.
[21] *Matter of Faber*, N.Y.L.J. Oct. 18, 1966, p. 17, where an application for construction was entertained to enable testator's widow to dispose of her estate in an equitable manner premised upon the proper construction of her husband's will.
[22] West Dig., Wills Key No. 707.
[23] Generally, supra Ch. XX.

XXIII

DEATH, RESIGNATION, OR REMOVAL OF EXECUTOR; SUCCESSORS

§ 23.1. Death.[1] Where an executor dies before completion of the administration of the estate,[2] a vacancy occurs[3] unless, under applicable law, the deceased executor's legal representative succeeds to his office or has power to complete the administration of the estate. In only a few states is that the case, except that, under some statutes, if nothing remains to be done at the executor's death except to make distribution, his legal representative may do that without being appointed as a successor.[4]

§ 23.2. Resignation.[5] Unless a power to resign is expressly conferred upon the executor by the will, it is usually held that he may not resign his office without first obtaining the permission of the court having jurisdiction over the administration of the estate. Where that rule obtains, any attempted resignation without such permission is nugatory and the executor continues to have all the responsibilities of his office, so that neither can he be free of them, nor can any successor executor[6] possess them, until an appropriate order or decree of court has been obtained. It is to be noted that a mere provision in a will for the coming into office of a successor executor in case of the resignation of his predecessor, or other reference to the possibility or consequences of resignation, will not necessarily, or even usually, be given effect as a grant of power to resign. Where application is made to the court for permission to resign, an adequate reason for the request is ordinarily required, inasmuch as the interests of persons interested in the estate are involved and are entitled to first

---

[1] West Dig., Exrs. & Admrs. Key No. 36.

[2] Compensation of deceased executor, supra § 20.4-2e. Accounting on executor's death, supra § 21.4-2.

[3] Necessity for appointment of successor, infra § 23.4-1.

[4] Powers and responsibilities of legal representative of deceased executor, in general, West Dig., Exrs. & Admrs. Key No. 128.

[5] West Dig., Exrs. & Admrs. Key No. 33; P-H Est. Plng. Serv. ¶ 2542.

[6] Successors, in general, infra § 23.4.

consideration,[7] and therefore an executor is usually not permitted to resign merely for reasons of personal convenience or preference. Upon an executor's resignation, his letters testamentary cease to be in force and are deemed revoked.[8]

§ 23.3. Removal.[9] An executor may be removed from his office, and his letters testamentary revoked,[10] by the court having jurisdiction over the administration of the estate, where he has become no longer able to serve, or has become disqualified to be executor,[11] or where he has forfeited his right to continue in office. The grounds for removal are usually prescribed by statute, and, apart from legal disqualification, range from physical or mental incapacity to act, to malfeasance or nonfeasance. Thus removal may be of the nature of a penalty for wrongful action or for neglect or inefficient performance of duties,[12] or may be without obloquy and merely for the purpose of enabling the administration of the estate to be taken over and completed by another[13] where the removed representative cannot continue. Removal is ordinarily effected by an order or decree made in a proceeding brought for the purpose by a beneficiary or, in some instances, by a co-executor, and because of its nature removal will ordinarily be directed only upon an affirmative showing of good cause. The discharge of an executor, upon rendition and settlement of his account,[14] is to be distinguished from removal.[15]

§ 23.4-1. Successors; appointment. Where a vacancy occurs in the office of an executor by reason of his death, resignation, or removal during the administration of the estate, it must be considered whether the appointment of a successor to fill such vacancy is necessary.[16] Obviously, if the executor acted alone, and the administration has not been completed (at least if more remains to be done than merely distributing the remaining assets[17]), a successor must be appointed. If another executor remains in office, however, it may or may not be necessary that the vacancy be filled;[18] ordinarily a successor will not be appointed in such a case, unless the will indicates an intention to the contrary, or an intention that there always be more than one executor in office, or a statute otherwise provides,[19] or, perhaps the remain-

---

[7] Resignation should be permitted where refusal to permit it would be prejudicial to the estate (application to resign so that non-resident of state could be appointed, thereby giving federal court jurisdiction of wrongful death action); *Barch v. Avco Corp.*, 30 A.D.2d 241, 291 N.Y.S.2d 422.

[8] Revocation of letters, supra § 5.8-3. Compensation of resigning executor, supra § 20.4-2e. Accounting, infra § 24.4-2.

[9] West Dig., Exrs. & Admrs. Key Nos. 31–33, 35; P-H Est. Plng. Serv. ¶¶ 2543, 2544.

[10] Revocation of letters, in general, supra § 5.8-3.

[11] Supra § 4.5-3 (ineligibility to act; distinguished from formal qualification, supra § 5.8-4).

[12] Denial of compensation for like cause, supra § 20.4-8.

[13] See next following section.

[14] Accounting and settlement, in general, infra § 24.5-1 ff.

[15] Infra § 24.9. Accountability on removal, infra § 24.4-2.

[16] Appointment of substituted or successor representative after discharge of executor from office upon final accounting, infra § 24.9.

[17] Supra § 23.1.

[18] Co-executors and the survivor of them, in general, West Dig., Exrs. & Admrs. Key Nos. 123–127.

[19] So in Unif. Prob. Code sec. 3-718.

ing executor's interests in some way so conflict with those of other persons interested in the estate that it is felt that he could not impartially exercise certain discretionary powers or make certain elections.[20] Where a new or successor representative is to be appointed, one nominated in the will to fill a vacancy is entitled to be appointed, unless disqualified under general rules. If no successor is so nominated, or all persons so nominated fail or refuse to accept or qualify,[21] a successor will be appointed by the court. As has been elsewhere mentioned, a successor who was nominated in the will is usually referred to as a substituted or successor executor,[22] and one appointed by the court is designated an administrator c.t.a.[23]

§ 23.4-2. ———; *powers and responsibilities.*[24] A successor executor appointed on the death, resignation, or removal of a predecessor is responsible for the assets that he receives upon his appointment and qualification, at their then values,[25] and is not directly responsible for acts or missions of his predecessors, including diminutions in value previously occurring or losses previously realized. He does, however, like an executor originally appointed,[26] have a duty to collect all assets that are includible in the estate at the time he takes office, which means among other things that he has a duty to collect all assets that his predecessor would have on hand if the predecessor's administration of the estate had been proper in all respects. Thus the successor has the duty to enforce all lawful surcharge liability[27] that may exist against the predecessor or the latter's estate, and in that sense he is responsible for the predecessor's negligence, waste, wrongful expenditures or distributions, and culpable losses;[28] he therefore should require that an accounting of the predecessor's proceedings be prepared and submitted for settlement,[29] and should assert appropriate objection[30] as to any act or omission as to which surcharge liability may exist, under penalty of himself being eventually surcharged for failure to collect all assets that he should have collected. Apart from the foregoing, a successor executor has the same powers and responsibilities as the primary executor,[31] except that discretions given by the terms of the will may be regarded as personal to the primary executor, and so not exercisable by a successor, unless the will evinces a contrary intention or a statute otherwise provides.[32]

---

[20] Conflicts of interest, supra § 3.9-4 ff. Options and elections, in general, supra Ch. XIII.
[21] Renunciation of appointment, supra § 4.5-2; qualification, supra § 5.8-1 ff.
[22] Supra § 1.3-4.
[23] Supra § 1.4-2.
[24] West Dig., Exrs. & Admrs. Key Nos. 120, 464.
[25] Inventory value, in general, supra § 8.3-1.
[26] Supra § 6.1.
[27] Surcharge and basis thereof, supra § 3.6.
[28] Generally, supra § 3.5-1 ff. Cf. West Dig., Exrs. & Admrs., Key No. 128.
[29] Accounting on death, resignation, or removal of executor, infra § 24.4-2; compulsory accounting, infra § 24.7.
[30] Objections to account, in general, infra § 24.5-4.
[31] "Primary executor," supra § 1.3-4.
[32] Unif. Prob. Code sec. 3-716 provides that successor has the same powers as the original representative unless the will "expressly" makes a power personal to the latter.

XXIV

RECORDS AND ACCOUNTS; SETTLEMENT

§ 24.1. Accountability.[1] The principle that a fiduciary is accountable to beneficiaries for his stewardship[2] is so much the essence of the fiduciary relationship that, without it, such a relationship probably could not exist in a legal, as distinguished from a moral, sense. The fact that an executor will or may in due course be required to render to the persons interested in the estate an accounting of his stewardship affects all that he does or omits to do in his official capacity, and is at the same time the source of protection to beneficiaries and the threat of liability to the executor who in any way fails in or violates his duties and responsibilities. Accordingly, it seems that an executor can no more be effectively exonerated by a will from a duty to account[3] than from duties of care, diligence, and prudence.[4] Even in those states providing by statute for an "independent" executor[5] and relieving such an executor from a requirement to render an accounting as a normal or routine procedure, the principles hereinabove stated are recognized by provisions permitting beneficiaries to compel an accounting,[6] and for that and other reasons careful lawyers may often advise independent executors to account notwithstanding their statutory exemption from a duty so to do. The duty of an executor to account is a continuing one, not barred by lapse of time,[7] and a statute of limitations does not run in the executor's favor,[8] unless it is one explicity relating to the administration of estates.[9]

---

[1] West Dig., Exrs. & Admrs. Key No. 458 ff.; P-H Est. Plng. Serv. ¶¶ 2440, 2441.

[2] Restatement, Conflict of Laws 2d, secs. 362, 363.

[3] *Matter of Curley*, 151 Misc. 664, 272 N.Y.S. 489, mod. on other gds. 245 A.D. 255, 280 N.Y.S. 80, affd. 269 N.Y. 548, 199 N.E. 665. Cf. *Est. of Brush et al.*, N.Y.L.J. Mar. 26, 1965, p. 16, applying the rule to attempt of testatrix who was beneficiary under another will to relieve fiduciaries under the latter from duty to account to estate of testatrix.

[4] Supra § 3.10.

[5] Cf. § 1.3-2 supra.

[6] Compulsory accounting, in general, infra § 24.7.

[7] *In re Clark's Est.*, 203 Cal. 335, 264 P. 242.

[8] Ibid.; *Hays v. Nat. Surety Co.*, 169 Miss. 676, 152 S. 515; *McGovern's Est.*, N.Y.L.J. May 14, 1946, p. 1916.

[9] Cf. Unif. Prob. Code sec. 3-1005.

§ *24.2. Records.* It follows from the executor's accountability for his proceedings that he must keep full and accurate records of his acts and doings, as only from records can his acts and omissions be ascertained or an account be prepared. Because he alone has access to the facts concerning his executorship, he cannot take advantage of his own failure to keep adequate records, and he may be held personally liable for any loss or expense resulting from such failure. The records necessarily kept for income tax purposes will supply part of the information the executor must be prepared to furnish to beneficiaries, but not all of it, and the executor's records must therefore go beyond the minimum necessary for tax purposes, and in some respects must be prepared on a different basis,[10] inasmuch as the purpose is different.

§ *24.3-1. Accounts; in general.*[11] An account of an executor consists in essence of a report to beneficiaries of the executor's acts and proceedings, such as to give them all information necessary to enable them to know what has been done or omitted, so that they may form a judgment as to whether there was any improper or unauthorized act or omission on the part of the executor. While the formal requirements as to accounts vary considerably from jurisdiction to jurisdiction, as do the practice and procedure for the settlement of accounts,[12] certain basic requirements, as discussed in following sections, are inherent.

§ *24.3-2. ————; definitive and informational accountings distinguished.* A distinction must be kept in mind between, on the one hand, the rendition by an executor of an account of his proceedings, and approval or settlement thereof by decree of a court, or agreement of beneficiaries,[13] that is binding upon beneficiaries and therefor protective to the executor,[14] and, on the other hand, a mere periodic or other reporting to the court by the executor of the latter's acts and transactions, as is required in some jurisdictions, for the purpose of enabling the court to maintain supervision of the estate, or supervision over estates generally, but without such an approval or settlement as is *res judicata.* The latter procedure, where it exists or is required by statute or court rule, is ordinarily not protective to the executor as against a beneficiary who has ground for complaint or question as to any act or omission, and references in this work to an executor's account and its judicial settlement contemplate an account of adequate scope[15] and an order, judgment, or decree made upon appropriate notice to beneficiaries[16] and having conclusory effect.[17]

§ *24.3-3. ————; scope of account, and disclosure.* In order for an executor's account to be sufficient in the sense that its settlement will preclude beneficiaries from

---

[10] Cf., e.g., §§ 8.2, 16.1, supra. Cost of keeping records, infra § 24.8-2.
[11] Form and requirements of account, in general, West Dig., Exrs. & Admrs. Key No. 502; charges and credits, ibid. Key Nos. 475–487.
[12] Settlement of accounts, infra § 24.5-1 ff.
[13] Judicial or voluntary settlement, infra § 24.5-2.
[14] Infra § 24.5-5.
[15] See next following section.
[16] Infra §§ 24.5-3, -3a.
[17] Infra § 24.5-5.

RECORDS AND ACCOUNTS; SETTLEMENT

raising objections or asserting liability against the executor at a later time, it must be sufficiently full, and be stated in sufficient detail, as to give the beneficiaries full information as to what the executor has done and to enable them to form a judgment as to whether he has fully and satisfactorily carried out his duties and responsibilities. As the rule is often stated, an account is effective against beneficiaries only as to matters therein disclosed. The account therefore must contain a statement or showing of all assets that came into the hands of the executor and their values,[18] all property of the decedent not collected, all property sold or otherwise disposed of, usually all claims made against the estate and the allowance or rejection thereof, all disbursements made, all gains and losses realized (or information from which those may be ascertained), all investments made[19] and all changes of investment, and all property distributed or available for distribution, including in some jurisdictions a showing of the persons to whom and the manner in which or terms on which the distribution of any undistributed balance is proposed to be made.[20] Closely coupled with the necessity for such statements is that of fair and adequate disclosure of all other material matters affecting the estate or its administration, which may include reference to or explanation of omissions by the executor. Just what is adequate disclosure under particular circumstances may be a question of considerable difficulty, but, having in mind that the purpose of an account is to inform the beneficiaries as to all material matters in connection with the estate and that the account protects the executor only as to matters disclosed therein, it is apparent that the more complete the disclosure the better protection the account will afford to the executor against any subsequent attack.[21]

§ 24.4-1. *Time for accounting;*[22] *intermediate and final accounts.* The normal and appropriate time for an executor to account is at the conclusion of his administration of the estate, and the accounting at that time may be the necessary basis of an order for distribution of estate assets, where that is required,[23] as well as for the discharge of the executor[24] and the release of his bond if one has been given.[25] Ordinarily, an intermediate accounting[26] is unnecessary, and an executor who insti-

---

[18] Inventory value, supra § 8.3-1.

[19] Investment by executor, in general, supra § 7.7-2.

[20] Settlement or approval of account as "construction" of will, infra § 24.5-5a. Necessity for order of distribution, supra § 18.6-2.

[21] Infra § 24.5-5.

[22] West Dig., Exrs. & Admrs. Key No. 459.

[23] Supra § 18.6-2.

[24] Infra § 24.9.

[25] Bond of executor, supra § 5.8-2.

[26] The term "intermediate account" is used to describe an account rendered during the course of administration of the estate, and before completion thereof, and hence covering only acts and transactions down to a date "intermediate" between the opening and closing of the estate. The term thus merely distinguishes such an account from a "final" account, which covers acts and transactions (from the beginning of the executor's administration, if, as is usual, there has been no intermediate account, or, if there has been the latter, from the end of the period covered by it) down to the closing of the estate. In all respects except as to period covered the two accounts are governed by identical principles and the terminology has no significance except a descriptive one.

tutes an unneeded accounting proceeding may be held liable to the estate as for the incurrence of any other unnecessary expense[27] or may be required to pay some part of or all the cost and expense, including attorney's fees, out of his own pocket. An intermediate accounting may, of course, be appropriate in some circumstances, as where the administration of the estate is complex or protracted, and it clearly is appropriate where a necessity exists to have a construction question decided, or to obtain instructions, during the administration of the estate[28] and that cannot be done except on the basis of an account.

§ 24.4-2. ———; *death, resignation, or removal of executor.*[29] Where an executor dies, resigns, or is removed from office during the period of administration of the estate,[30] an accounting of his proceedings[31] is ordinarily desirable, if not indeed necessary, both for the purpose of discharging such executor or his estate from the possibility of future liability to beneficiaries[32] and for the purpose of protecting his successor from liability for acts or omissions of the predecessor.[33] In some jurisdictions permission to an executor to resign[34] is accompanied by a requirement that he account promptly.

§ 24.5-1. *Settlement of account; in general.* The term "settlement" as used with respect to an executor's account refers to a judicial determination, or voluntary agreement by beneficiaries, to the effect that the executor has in or by his account adequately informed the beneficiaries of his acts, proceedings, and omissions, and has satisfactorily performed his duties and carried out his responsibilities as to the matters disclosed by the account.[35]

§ 24.5-2. ———; *judicial or voluntary settlement.*[36] In some jurisdictions an executor is required by statute to render an account to the court by which he was appointed, at the conclusion of his administration of the estate, and to have the account settled by decree of the court. Even if there be no such statutory requirement, an executor is entitled to obtain a judicial settlement of his account if he wishes to do

---

[27] As waste, supra § 3.5-2.

[28] Supra § 22.4-1.

[29] West Dig., Exrs. & Admrs. Key No. 469 (2).

[30] Generally, supra Ch. XXIII.

[31] If another executor or other executors remain in office, it is usual for him or them to join with the deceased executor's legal representative, or the resigned or removed executor, as the case may be, in rendering an accounting, which is then a "final" accounting as to the deceased, resigned, or removed executor and an "intermediate" account as to the executor or executors remaining in office, making it unnecessary for them again to account for the period of such account; cf. supra § 24.4-1, text at note 26.

[32] Infra § 24.5-5.

[33] Supra § 23.4-2.

[34] Permission as requisite, supra § 23.2.

[35] As limited to matters disclosed, supra § 24.3-3 and infra § 24.5-5. For a detailed discussion of accounts of trustees and their settlement, much of which is applicable also in the case of executors, see Settling the Trustee's Accounts: Why, When, How, and Where, 1963 Proc. A.B.A. Sec. Real Prop. Prob. & Tr. L., Part I, 175.

[36] West Dig., Exrs. & Admrs. Key No. 515; P-H Est. Plng. Serv. ¶¶ 2444, 2445.

RECORDS AND ACCOUNTS; SETTLEMENT 285

so. Where there is no mandatory requirement of a judicial settlement,[37] the executor may have his account settled by agreement of the beneficiaries, if they are all *sui juris;*[38] such a settlement appears to be effective upon principles of estoppel or release,[39] and may in many cases be more convenient and less expensive than a judicial settlement if all beneficiaries accept and approve the account as submitted to them.[40]

§ 24.5-2a. ———; ———; *"general release" without account.* It follows from the rule that an account is protective,[41] and a settlement of it effective,[42] only as to matters therein disclosed that the rendition of an account is a prerequisite to any discharge of the executor from liability, and so a "general release" without an accounting is usually of little or no effectiveness, at least unless it can be demonstrated that the beneficiary signing the release was as fully informed about all matters of the estate and its administration as he would have been by a proper account.[43]

§ 24.5-3. ———; *parties.*[44] A settlement of an account is effective only as against persons who are duly made parties to or represented in a judicial proceeding or have joined in a voluntary agreement of settlement. It is accordingly essential for the protection of the executor that all persons having any interest in the estate join in the settlement, except, usually, specific legatees,[45] and legatees of specified amounts of money, whose legacies have been satisfied as demonstrated by receipts or vouchers submitted with the account or in the hands of the executor. Where the estate passes outright, there is little problem as to the persons to be made parties to the accounting; and even where a trust is created by the will, the trustee is ordinarily the only necessary party in respect of such trust if he is completely independent of the executor.[46]

§ 24.5-3a. ———; ———; *same person executor and trustee.* While the trustee of a trust under the will represents the interests of the trust beneficiaries, in a proceeding for settlement of the executor's account, if the trustee is fully independent of the executor, different considerations may apply where the executor, or one of two or more executors, is also the trustee, or one of the trustees, under the will. Obviously, one cannot account to himself, or discharge himself from liability, and it is therefore clear that a sole executor who is also sole trustee can have his account effectively settled only by making parties to the settlement all beneficiaries of the

---

[37] As in case of "independent" executor; supra § 24.1.

[38] Ineffectiveness of agreement where a beneficiary not *sui juris*, even though he would be concluded in a judicial proceeding under doctrine of virtual representation, supra § 21.3-1 note 25.

[39] As in case of other agreements by beneficiaries; supra § 21.2.

[40] Objection by any beneficiary as precluding voluntary settlement, infra § 24.5-4.

[41] Supra § 24.3-3; cf. infra § 24.5-5.

[42] Supra § 24.5-1.

[43] Such ordinarily would of course, be the case where the releasing beneficiary is also one of two or more executors, or possibly where he is attorney for the executor, but usually not in any other case.

[44] West Dig., Exrs. & Admrs. Key No. 473 (2).

[45] Specific legacy defined, supra § 14.4-1.

[46] Same person as executor and trustee, see next following section.

trust. The situation is less clear where there is at least one co-trustee who is not an executor. The view has been taken by some courts that in such case it is unnecessary to bring in the trust beneficiaries as parties to the settlement; but other courts take the contrary view, on the ground that there is no independence or objectivity of action on the part of the trustee who is not an executor, and hence no protection to trust beneficiaries, because one is unlikely to object to acts or omissions in one capacity of a person who is his co-fiduciary in another capacity and with whom he will have to continue to act in the future. In the converse situation, where there is at least one co-executor who is not also a trustee, it has been held, on the basis of somewhat similar principles, that even the non-trustee executor cannot have his account effectively settled unless the trust beneficiaries are parties to the proceeding.[47]

§ 24.5-4. ———; *objections to account*.[48] In a judicial proceeding for the settlement of the account of an executor, a beneficiary or creditor[49] contending that any act or omission was improper, unauthorized, or wrongful, to his detriment, or that in any respect the account is erroneous or incomplete, asserts his contention by filing or submitting what is usually known as an objection to the account; and that is ordinarily the appropriate way for the beneficiary to establish his rights in respect of the estate and assert any liability on the part of the executor.[50] In such objection the objectant specifies the matter as to which his contention relates and the nature or ground of his contention. Statutes or court rules ordinarily prescribe the time within which any objection must be made, and an objection not made within such time, or any authorized extension thereof, is barred. By the same token, any matter as to which no objection is made is not open to further question.[51] Where an objection is made,[52] it may be denied by the court, in which case the account stands as submitted; or instead it may be sustained, in whole or in part, in which case the account may be modified by the court, or directed to be restated by the executor, to give effect to the objection as sustained, or, as more usually occurs, the executor is surcharged in respect of the action or omission to which the sustained objection relates.[53] The rules or practice relating to objections do not of course, apply where an account is settled by agreement, as in such case a complaining or dissident beneficiary will merely refuse to join in the agreement, unless his contentions are accepted; and so where any beneficiary is dissatisfied in any way with the executor's administration of the estate a settlement of the account by agreement is ordinarily not possible.

---

[47] *Matter of Miles*, 221 N.Y.S.2d 43.
[48] West Dig., Exrs. & Admrs. Key No. 504 ff.; P-H Est. Plng. Serv. ¶¶ 2449, 2450.
[49] Creditor's right to determination on rejected or unpaid claim, infra § 24.5-4b.
[50] While a beneficiary may be able, under general principles, to enjoin a threatened or proposed act or omission on the part of the executor, he usually is not required to take any steps before the submission of the executor's account for settlement, and not precluded from objecting at that time by the mere fact that he knew in advance of the act or omission in question, unless, of course, he expressly or impliedly agreed to it or waived objection to it (cf. Ch. XXI, supra).
[51] Effect of settlement, in general, infra § 24.5-5.
[52] Burden of proof, supra § 3.6.
[53] Surcharge as remedy for negligence or wrongdoing, in general, supra § 3.6.

RECORDS AND ACCOUNTS; SETTLEMENT

§ 24.5-4a. ———; ———; *objection by fewer than all beneficiaries affected.* On the principle above stated that if no objection is made to an account further attack is precluded, it is usually held that where one or more beneficiaries object and their objection is sustained, only the objectants may share in the resulting recovery and other beneficiaries, likewise interested, who did not object do not share therein.[54] The rule that non-objecting beneficiaries do not benefit is, however, subject to exception in some cases, as where the dereliction infringes the basic duties of the executor,[55] or in the case of infants, to whom the courts tend to grant the benefit of the objection even though no objection was made in their behalf.[56]

§ 24.5-4b. ———; ———; *determination on rejected or unpaid claim.* As has been noted at an earlier place,[57] a claimant against the estate whose claim is rejected, in whole or in part, and who has not brought action on the claim against the executor,[58] may, unless a statute otherwise provides,[59] object to the executor's account showing the claim unpaid, or not showing it payable, and have the claim tried and decided in the accounting proceeding. A creditor may also object, and so obtain relief, where by reason of the improper payment by the executor of another claim of equal or lower priority[60] or the making of an improper distribution[61] the estate has been rendered insufficient to satisfy his claim in full.

§ 24.5-5. ———; *effect of settlement.*[62] The settlement, or approval, of an account, whether in a judicial proceeding or by voluntary agreement, precludes the persons who were duly made parties to such proceeding, or who are *sui juris* and have joined in such agreement, as the case may be, from thereafter raising any objections as to any act or omission of the executor, or thereafter asserting any liability against the executor, as to any matter disclosed in the account,[63] except in case of fraud or manifest error. As to any matter not so disclosed, the situation is as if no account had been rendered.[64]

---

[54] Adjustment of surcharge as to beneficiaries precluded from participating therein, supra § 21.3-2.

[55] Supra § 3.1. The courts take the attitude that a fiduciary is always held to the duty of exercising care and judgment, regardless of the wishes or views of beneficiaries, so that failure of some beneficiaries to object does not reduce the liability of the fiduciary for failure to perform his basic duties.

[56] This is on the theory that the courts have a general duty to protect the interests of infant beneficiaries, although adults ordinarily have the responsibility of protecting their own interests. See *Matter of Badenhausen*, 237 N.Y.S.2d 928, where a surcharge was imposed to protect rights of infant remaindermen even though no objections were filed in their behalf, while non-objecting adult beneficiaries were denied participation in the surcharge.

[57] Supra § 9.4-3.

[58] Election as to action on claim or determination on accounting, ibid.

[59] Cf. Unif. Prob. Code sec. 3-806 (a), barring claim unless action commenced against executor within 60 days after rejection.

[60] Priorities of payment in insolvent or insufficient estate, supra § 19.2 ff.

[61] Claims as payable before distribution, supra § 19.4-1.

[62] West Dig., Exrs. & Admrs. Key Nos. 512–514.

[63] Order for distribution, on settlement of account, supra § 18.6-2; for payment of executor's compensation, supra § 20.4-3.

[64] Failure to have account settled, infra § 24.6-1. General release without account, infra § 24.5-2a.

§ 24.5-5a. ———; ———; *as construction of will or determination of rights.* Where an executor's account as submitted for either judicial or voluntary settlement shows a particular act or omission effected or proposed, or a particular treatment of a bequest, whether as to identity of the legatee,[65] the amount or subject matter,[66] the manner or terms of its satisfaction,[67] or the effect and effectiveness of an assignment of it,[68] or in any other way reflects the result of a conclusion drawn as to the rights of a beneficiary, creditor,[69] or other person in interest[70] or an interpretation of the will or of law, and the account is duly settled by the court, either without objection by any person in interest or after denial of objections made, or is approved and accepted by agreement of all persons in interest, it is apparent that such settlement or approval amounts in effect to a construction of the will or a determination of rights as to the matter involved, or at the least to a demonstration that no person in interest wishes to question the construction or the result.[71] Thus, a construction of rights as to the matter involved, or instructions,[72] may often be avoided and the matter or question settled more economically and perhaps more expeditiously on the accounting. On general principles,[73] of course, the executor must be sure that the point in question is adequately brought out or reflected in the account. In some instances nothing more will be needed for this purpose than a mere showing in the account, in the usual manner, of a payment made or of property delivered to a designated person, or other routine entry of what the executor in fact did; but in other instances it may be necessary, or at least advisable, if the executor is to be fully protected, to include in or append to the account an explanatory statement calling attention to the provision or problem involved or the action taken with respect to it, or to include in a petition for settlement of the account, in the case of a judicial settlement, an express prayer for a construction or determination with respect to the problem.[74] The essential criterion to be applied in deciding how to handle the matter is, of course, that no beneficiary be misled by concealment of some material factor affecting his rights. Obviously, the relegation thus of construction and other questions to the accounting proceeding will not be possible where irrevocable action has to be taken, or an irrevocable decision made, at an earlier time, and a special proceeding for construction or instructions may in such a case have to be instituted; but even as to actions or decisions earlier taken or made it may often be found practicable to hold property in escrow, or otherwise suspend the irrevocability of the action, pending an eventual determination at the time of accounting, so that the executor is

---

[65] Supra § 14.21-1 ff.
[66] Supra § 14.4-2.
[67] Supra §§ 14.4-7 ff., 14.10–14.13.
[68] Supra § 14.29.
[69] Determination on rejected or unpaid claim, supra § 24.5-4b.
[70] Propriety of counsel fees and other administration expenses, supra § 20.3-2 ff., 20-6.
[71] Conclusiveness, see last preceding section.
[72] Generally, supra Ch. XXII.
[73] Supra § 24.3-3.
[74] Accounting proceeding as an appropriate time for obtaining construction, supra § 22.4-2.

protected against the possibility of a determination that his action was erroneous. Subject to the foregoing considerations, a "construction by accounting" offers in many instances a satisfactory mean of resolving problems of construction and of rights of parties and should be kept in mind accordingly.

§ 24.6. *Failure to have account settled.* [75] An executor remains open to attack for any failure of due performance of his duties until he has duly accounted and his account is settled. This follows as a necessary corollary to the basic rule of accountability.[76] Accordingly, even where an accounting is not mandatory under the statute,[77] a cautious executor will usually deem it nevertheless advisable to render his account and have it duly settled. On the same principle, and because of his own resulting liability, a successor executor or administrator will ordinarily insist upon the rendition and settlement of his predecessor's account.[78]

§ 24.7. *Compulsory accountings.* [79] An executor, like any other fiduciary, may be compelled by the court having jurisdiction of the estate, either upon its own motion[80] or, as more usually is the case, on application by a beneficiary, to render an account of his proceedings and submit it for judicial settlement.[81] Ordinarily, an intermediate accounting[82] will not be compelled, unless special reason is shown, as there is usually no necessity for any accounting until final closing of the estate. A resigning or removed executor, however, or the legal representative of a deceased executor, may be compelled to account[83] if he does not do so voluntarily; an account in such a case, while it covers only a part of the period of administration of the estate, is "final" so far as it pertains to the executor whose acts are being accounted for.

§ 24.8-1. *Expenses of setting account;*[84] *in general.* Subject to the rule relating to an unnecessary accounting,[85] the proper expenses of settling the account of an executor, whether by judicial proceeding or by voluntary agreement of beneficiaries, including fees of the executor's counsel in connection with the settlement,[86] are payable out of the general estate, as a necessary expense of administration.[87]

§ 24.8-2. ———; *cost of keeping records and preparing account.* [88] The rule stated in the preceding section relates to the expenses of settlement of an account

---

[75] West Dig., Exrs. & Admrs. Key No. 467.
[76] Supra § 24.1.
[77] As in case of "independent" executor, or "unsupervised" administration, supra § 1.3-2.
[78] Supra § 23.4-2. Compelling accounting, see next following section.
[79] West Dig., Exrs. & Admrs. Key Nos. 460, 472–473.
[80] Except ordinarily in case of "independent" executor, supra § 1.3-2. In case of resignation or removal, supra § 23.4-2.
[81] Compelling account by fiduciary of estate or trust of which decedent was a beneficiary, supra § 6.11-2.
[82] Defined, supra § 24.4-1 note 26.
[83] Supra § 23.4-2.
[84] West Dig., Exrs. & Admrs. Key Nos. 473 (b), 511.
[85] Supra § 24.4-1.
[86] Counsel fees, in general, supra § 20.3-1 ff.
[87] Administration expenses as payable out of general estate, supra § 20.2.
[88] West Dig., Exrs. & Admrs. Key No. 487.

rather than to the keeping of financial records[89] and the preparation of the account. Since an executor's compensation is ordinarily regarded as covering all executorial services,[90] a payment to him, or by him to another, for accounting services is usually not allowed as a charge against the estate. This rule follows from the doctrine of accountability.[91] Where, however, the size or complexity of the estate seems to the court to necessitate or justify the employment by the executor of professional assistance, an exception is made to the rule; and in general there seems in recent times a tendency even in other instances to allow accounting fees as an administration expense, and even to allow an executor who is also an accountant to be compensated in the latter capacity for accounting services.[92] Thus far, however, in most jurisdictions, accounting services rendered to the executor are not chargeable against the estate as a general rule,[93] and may perhaps be less often so chargeable in the case of a corporate executor than in that of an individual.

§ 24.9. Discharge of executor from liability or from office.[94] As appears from the preceding discussion, the ultimate purpose of an accounting by an executor and its settlement is to obtain the executor's discharge or release from liability in respect of matters disclosed by the account,[95] and enable the release of his bond, if any.[96] In some jurisdictions, the settlement of the executor's final account goes no further than that, and the executor remains in office, so that he remains authorized to receive any asset that at a later time may be discovered or become deliverable to the estate, or to enforce any after-discovered right of the estate.[97] In other jurisdictions, however, the settlement of the account is accompanied by or effects the executor's discharge from office;[98] and where that is the case the executor ceases to be such upon the settlement of his account, and a new legal representative[99] must be appointed if occasion later arises for dealing with any matter of the estate.[100] The

---

[89] Supra § 24.2.
[90] Supra § 20.4-1.
[91] Supra § 24.1.
[92] *Matter of Tuttle*, 4 A.D.2d 310, 164 N.Y.S.2d 573, affd. 4 N.Y.2d 159, 173 N.Y.S.2d 279, 149 N.E.2d 715, analogizing the case to that of an attorney-executor (cf. § 20.3-1 supra) in an estate having serious income tax difficulties with respect to the testator. But see next following note.
[93] Cf. *Est. of Binswanger*, N.Y.L.J. Apr. 21, 1967, p. 17, where the court, even in absence of any objection, questioned such a payment and directed that its amount, except so far as it related to preparation of estate tax returns (because those required a knowledge of tax regulations and accounting practices), be offset against the executor's commissions.
[94] P-H Est. Plng. Serv. ¶¶ 2545–2548.
[95] As effect of settlement, supra § 24.5-5.
[96] Cf. Unif. Prob. Code sec. 3-1007. Bond of executor, supra § 5.8-2.
[97] After-discovered or after-acquired property, in general, supra § 18.11.
[98] Removal from office distinguished from discharge, supra § 23.3.
[99] Ordinarily an administrator d.b.n. or c.t.a.; supra § 1.4.-2.
[100] So in Unif. Prob. Code sec. 3-1008; but cf. ibid. sec. 3-1001 providing for order on final accounting discharging the executor "from further claim or demand of any interested person," and sec. 3-1002 containing similar language, in each case without any reference to discharge from office.

executor should, of course, ascertain which rule prevails in the jurisdiction in which he is appointed, so that he may be governed accordingly.

§ *24.10. Accounting in respect of decedent as fiduciary or life tenant.* It is pointed out at another place that as part of the executor's duties to settle claims against or liabilities of the estate he may render an account of the acts or proceedings of his decedent as a fiduciary, and have such account settled,[1] and that the same is true where the decedent was a legal life tenant and under applicable law is treated as a fiduciary for the remainderman.[2] Such an accounting, while distinguishable from an accounting by the executor of his own acts and proceedings, is governed by the same principles and affected by the same considerations as the latter.

§ *24.11. "Small" estates.* The statutes enacted in an increasing number of states providing a simplified procedure for the administration and settlement of small estates,[3] as defined therein, dispense with the usual requirements as to proceedings for accountings,[4] and should be consulted in that connection as to any estate coming within their purview.

---

[1] Supra § 9.10-1.
[2] Supra § 9.10-2.
[3] Supra § 5.11.
[4] So in Unif. Prob. Code sec. 3-1204.

XXV

WHAT LAW GOVERNS

§ *25.1. In general.*[1] With the increasing mobility of the population and changes of domicile often accompanying movement from one state to another, and with reforming and other changes, sometimes radical, in statutes relating to wills and estates, problems as to what law governs various aspects and phases of the administration of decedents' estates arise much more frequently than in past times and the executor's problems in that regard are correspondingly greater in number. Questions as to governing law may arise in two kind of cases: One, where the problem is with respect to what time is that as of which the law is to be determined, as where the law has changed after the execution of the will;[2] and, the other, where the problem is with respect to the jurisdiction whose law is to be applied, as where the will is probated in,[3] or property is located or situate in,[4] or was acquired in,[5] a jurisdiction other than that of the testator's domicile at death, or the dispositions are contained in a will executed when the testator was domiciled in a jurisdiction other than that in which was his domicle at death. The body of authorities dealing in general with the ascertainment of governing law, and conflict of laws, is large, complex, and often not entirely clear; and the difficulties may be especially acute in problems arising in connection with the administration of decedents' estates, as to which case authority is largely lacking and problems have received less attention from courts and writers alike than in many other areas.[6] In the following sections the chief principles, so far as they can be ascertained, in relation to estates are adverted to and effort is made to sug-

---

[1] West Dig., Exrs. & Admrs. Key No. 2.

[2] Infra §§ 25.3-1. -2.

[3] Supra § 5.5-1.

[4] Infra § 25.4-1 ff.

[5] Continuing character as separate or community property, see next following section.

[6] Cf. Restatement, Trusts 2d, Introductory Note to Ch. 14, Topic 1: "Problems here have been less worked on by legal writers than many, perhaps most, other areas of the subject. There are many gaps in the adjudicated cases; in some instances even where a specific problem must have arisen and been dealt with in the handling of estates." The Restatement itself deals with few of such problems.

gest their proper application;[7] and at various places in preceding chapters the law governing particular matters is mentioned. It must be emphasized, however, that the present work, with its limitations of space, can offer no more than a brief and sometimes categorical discussion, that statutes in a number of states have altered common law rules,[8] and that when a question arises in an estate administration a thorough examination of the law must be made. In particular, the executor should not assume that the law at the time he is acting is the same as that at the time when the will was executed or necessarily is determinative where a change has occurred,[9] nor should be assume that the law of the state in which he is acting is the same as to any given matter as that of another state where the testator's domicile was or any of his property is located, or governs with respect to such matter.[10]

§ 25.2. Problems as to character or ownership distinguished. The classes of questions with which this chapter deals, as mentioned in the preceding section, are to be distinguished from those questions that relate to the kind or nature of the decedent's ownership of or interest in property. For example, where property was acquired by the decedent and his spouse while their domicile was in a community property property state and under such circumstances that it was community property, and the decedent died domiciled in a common law state, or where the decedent and his spouse acquired property while domiciled in a common law state and the decedent died domiciled in a community property state, the executor must satisfy himself, before dealing with such property, or with the proceeds of its disposition or property into which such proceeds can be traced, whether the original character of its ownership continues or such character has changed. It is very likely that, in many cases such as these, property has inadvertently been treated as community property when it was not, or, even more often, as not community property when it was. Once the nature or extent of the decedent's ownership or interest in the property is determined, however, the rules apply thereto that are applicable to any other like asset of the decedent, including those of governing law in the sense in which that concept is treated in this chapter.

§ 25.3-1. As between laws in force at different times;[11] execution requirements. A change of law occurring between the date of execution of a will and the date of the testator's death may give rise to a question as to what law governs. The question ordinarily involved is as to the formalities of execution, such as the number of witnesses required. It is held in most jurisdictions that the law in force at the date of death governs in determining the validity of the will's execution. In other

---

[7] "Wherein if I happen to be unaccurate or miftaken, the Obfcurity of the Subject will, I fuppofe, procure me Excufe amongft candid readers." I Madox, History and Antiquities of the Exchequer of the Kings of England, 84.

[8] The Unif. Conflict of Laws Act contains provisions relevant to estate administration that have been adopted in some states, but in other states statutory provisions differ therefrom or are absent.

[9] Infra § 25.3-1 ff.

[10] Infra § 25.4-1 ff.

[11] P-H Est. Plng. Serv. ¶ 282.

states, however, there is taken the contrary view, that the law as it existed at the time of execution of the will is to be applied, at least to the end that a will validly executed under the law in force at its date is entitled to probate even if at the date of death the requirements are different. In some cases courts appear to have been influenced by whether the change was in the direction of decreasing the requirements or of increasing them, and in the former case to have applied the law that existed at the date of death and in the latter case that which existed at the date of execution.

§ 25.3-2. ———; *administrative powers.* While there is not a great deal of authority on the point, it seems that an executor will be held to possess administrative powers granted by a statute that is in force at the time of the proposed exercise of the powers, notwithstanding that the statute was enacted after the death of the testator. Such is the rule generally applied in the case of an enlargement of the categories of property in which a fiduciary is permitted to invest funds[12] where the instrument does not otherwise provide, and the principle would seem applicable generally.

§ 25.4-1. *As between laws of different jurisdictions;*[13] *in general.* The fundamental principle to be regarded in considering what law governs a will or estate is that each state has sovereign power to control the disposition, at the death of its owner, of property, real or personal, that is within[14] or deemed to be within[15] its borders. In some states, fairly detailed statutes exist, some of them embodying or modeled upon the portion of the Uniform Conflict of Laws Act relevant to estates. Subject to such statutes, if existing, the kinds of problems that arise are, therefore, of two kinds: First, whether property is within, or is to be treated as within, a particular state; and, second, what problems are substantive and relate to disposition of property, as distinguished from those of a merely administrative character.[16]

§ 25.4-2. ———; *formalities of execution.*[17] In the absence of statute otherwise providing, the law of the place where a will is offered for probate ordinarily governs as to the formalities of execution, as, for example, the number of subscribing witnesses, if any, required, except as to its dispositions of real property situate in another jurisdiction.[18] Under this rule, where a will offered for probate in the state of the testator's domicile is not validly executed under its laws, it must be denied probate, regardless of where it was made or where the testator resided at the time of its execution;[19] and where a will is offered for probate in a state other than that of the domicile,[20] or effects property situate in such other state, and is not validly

---

[12] Investments by executor, supra § 7.7-2.
[13] P-H Est. Plng. Serv. ¶ 283.
[14] Real property, infra § 25.4-3.
[15] Personal property, infra § 25.4-4.
[16] Infra § 25.4-4b.
[17] In general, see Ehrenzweig, Conflict of Laws, p. 666 ff.
[18] See next following section.
[19] Change of testator's domicile as effecting nullification of will, supra § 5.3-5.
[20] Probate of non-resident's will, supra § 5.5-1 ff.

executed under the law of the forum, it is immaterial that it was validly executed under the laws of the domicile. In a majority of states, however, statutes have been enacted under which a will executed in accordance with either the law of the testator's domicile, or the law of the place where it was made, is to be treated as validly executed even though it does not comply in that regard with the law of the place of probate.[21]

§ 25.4-3. ———; *real property.* It follows, from the general principle that each state has power to control the disposition of property situate within its borders,[22] that all matters relating to the testamentary disposition of real property, and the descent of such property,[23] are governed by the law of the situs of the property.[24] Therefore the law of the situs governs as to all such matters as the formalities of execution of the will,[25] whether it has been revoked,[26] the essential validity of its provisions so far as they relate to the real property, the construction and effect of its terms so far as they so relate, including the identification of members of classes described by such terms as "next of kin" or "heirs",[27] the right of a spouse to elect against the will[28] so far as such real property is concerned, the capacity or eligibility of a named executor to serve as such in the state of situs,[29] the necessity for the appointment of an ancillary legal representative[30] where the will has been probated in another state, and the powers and duties of the legal representative with respect to the real property.[31]

---

[21] So in Unif. Prob. Code sec. 2-506. It will, of course, be recognized that the statement in the text is not an exception to the rule that formalities of execution are to be determined under the law of the state of probate, for a statute of the kind referred to is a part of the law of such state and it is by such statute that the sufficiency of the execution is to be judged.

[22] Supra § 25.4-1.

[23] Infra § 25.5

[24] Generally, see Ehrenzweig, Conflict of Laws, p. 658 ff.; Goodrich & Scoles, Conflict of Laws, sec. 166; Leflar, American Conflicts Law (1968 rev.) sec. 196. Cf. *Est. of Schneider*, 96 N.Y.S.2d 652, where the court discussed the meaning in this context of the "law of the situs"—"whether it means only the internal or municipal law of the country in which the property is situated or whether it also includes the conflict of laws rules to which the courts of that jurisdiction would resort in making the same determination." See also *In re Gallagher's Est.*, 169 N.Y.S. 2d 271 (affd. 7 A.D.2d 1029, 184 N.Y.S.2d 782 [if testator owned land in more than one state, law of each governs effect of will as to land in that state]).

[25] Cf. *French v. Short*, 207 Va. 548, 151 S.E.2d 354, where the holographic will of a Florida decedent, not valid under Florida law, was admitted to probate in Virginia (where holographic will was valid) for purpose of passing title to real property in Virginia, but not to personal property therein, on the ground that Florida law governed as to personalty, which accordingly passed as in intestacy.

[26] See Bozeman, The Conflict of Laws Relating to Wills, Probate Decrees and Estates, 49 A.B.A.J. 670, 671. Revocation, supra § 5.3-3 ff.

[27] Supra § 1.14. Generally, see Leflar, op. cit. supra note 24, sec. 198. But see infra § 25.4-6 note 66.

[28] *Matter of Clark*, 21 N.Y.2d 478, 288 N.Y.S.2d 993, 236 N.E.2d 152; *Pfau v. Moseley*, 9 Ohio St. 2d 13, 222 N.E.2d 639. Cf. Leflar, op. cit. sec. 199. Election, in general, supra § 17.4-1 ff.

[29] Supra § 5.8-1.

[30] Supra §§ 5.4-4, 15.11.

[31] Supra § 6.15-1.

§ 25.4-4. ———; *personal property; in general.* Under the maxim *mobilia personam sequuntur*, personal property is ordinarily deemed to exist at the domicile of its owner, regardless of where the property or evidence of ownership thereof may be located or kept; and accordingly the general principle is that all matters relating to the testamentary disposition of personal property, whether tangible or intangible, and the meaning and effect of the will as to personalty, are governed by the law of the testator's domicile.[32] Tangibles may have a situs in another jurisdiction for at least some purposes, including those of estate or inheritance taxation, as where they are employed in or used in connection with a business conducted there,[33] and so far as concerns the right of the domiciliary executor to collect them,[34] but it is at least doubtful that they are to be deemed to have a situs in such jurisdiction in a sense that makes its law govern their disposition at their owner's death. Accordingly, unless a situs for that purpose is to be deemed to exist, all the matters that, as to real property, are governed by the law of its situs,[35] except in some cases administrative powers and authorities,[36] are, as to personal property, governed by the law of the testator's domicile,[37] at least unless a contrary intention appears;[38] and it would seem that a contrary intention is not evidenced merely by the appointment of an executor located or resident in another jurisdiction.[39]

§ 25.4-4a. ———; ———; *direction that law of nondomiciliary state governs.* A direction in a will that it be offered for probate elsewhere than at the testator's domicile,[40] and that its dispositions be governed by the law of the jurisdiction in which it is so to be probated, will ordinarily be given effect, in that the law of such other jurisdiction will be applied, as to personal property,[41] at least in the absence of a requirement at the domicile of probate there,[42] if, but in general only if, a statute in such other jurisdiction so provides,[43] or, absent such a statute, such other juris-

---

[32] Generally, see Land, Trusts in the Conflict of Laws, sec. 18; Leflar, op. cit. supra note 24, Sec. 196 ff.

[33] Ibid., sec. 5.1.

[34] Supra § 6.21-1.

[35] See last preceding section.

[36] Infra § 25.4-4b.

[37] See *French v. Short*, supra note 25. Cf. *Est. of Strupp*, N.Y.L.J. Jan. 12, 1968, p. 18, where, in an ancillary proceeding involving securities kept in New York of a testator whose will created trust and who was domiciled in Argentina, in which country trusts were said to be invalid (under the civil law system there prevailing), the court refused to adjudge the validity of the trusts and directed that the assets be remitted to Argentina for determination as to their disposition.

[38] See next following section.

[39] But as to administrative matters, see infra § 25.4-4b.

[40] Probate of will of non-resident, in general, supra § 5.5-1 ff.

[41] But not as to rights given by law, rather than dispositions made by the will; see *Matter of Clark*, 21 N.Y.2d 478, 288 N.Y.S.2d 993, 236 N.E.2d 152, holding that a direction in the will of a Virginia testator, owning securities kept in New York, that law of New York should govern his dispositions (as permitted by a New York statute), did not prevent his widow from electing to take against the will where she had such right under Virginia law but not under New York law, on the ground that such right is governed by the law of the domicile; see supra § 17.4-1.

[42] Supra § 5.5-3.

[43] E.g., N.Y. E.P.T.L. sec. 3-5.1 (h): When a testator not domiciled in the state elects in his will to have the disposition of his property in the state governed by its laws, the intrinsic validity, interpretation, revocation, or alteration of such dispositions is determined by such law.

diction has some significant contact with the estate or its disposition, as to such matters as situs or physical location of substantial assets or evidences thereof, residence or location of the executor or the chief beneficiaries, or the like. Thus, while a testator is not free to choose among jurisdictions, without limitation, the one to govern his will and the disposition of his estate, he may be able to make a selection as between or among his domicile and another or other states where each of them has some degree of contact or concern with the matter.[44] Where such a direction or choice of a jurisdiction other than the domicile is made in a will the executor must, of course, satisfy himself as to its effectiveness whenever he is faced with a question as to which the law of the domicile and that of the chosen jurisdiction differ, and if there is reason for doubt the executor may need to obtain a judicial determination of the question before acting.[45]

§ 25.4-4b. ———; ———; *admininistrative powers and duties.*[46] Unlike the case of real property,[47] so far as personal property is concerned questions as to what law governs the administration of an estate and the powers and duties of the executor, as distinguished from the essential validity and effect of the will, arise where the will is admitted to probate in a jurisdiction other than the testator's domicile.[48] On the basis of the principles stated in a preceding section,[49] it may be argued that administrative matters, like substantive ones, relating to personal property should be governed by the law of the domicile; and there is some indication that such was the rule at common law. In modern times, however, the law of the place of probate and administration is generally applied to such matters;[50] and it would seem that a direction in a will for its probate in, and governance of its dispositions by the laws of, a jurisdiction other than that of the domicile[51] should *a fortiori* be treated as evidencing an intention that the administration also be governed by such laws.

§ 25.4-4bb. ———; ———; ———; *what is administrative or substantive.* Where, under the rules stated in the preceding section, administrative powers and duties are to be governed by the law of the place of administration of the estate rather than by that of the testator's domicile, there may often be difficulty in determining whether a particular matter is merely administrative, or is instead, or also, of a substantive nature and therefore, under general principles, governed by the law of the domicile.[52] This is because, as is apparent upon analysis, nearly every administrative power has some substantive content, in that it will or may affect to a

---

[44] Cf. Hendrickson, Planning Wills for Nonresidents, 105 Trusts and Estates 315.
[45] Instruction proceedings, supra § 22.2.
[46] West Dig., Exrs. & Admrs. Key No. 2.
[47] Supra § 25.4-3.
[48] Supra § 5.5-1.
[49] Supra § 25.4-1.
[50] Restatement, Conflict of Laws 2d, sec. 316; Ehrenzweig, Conflict of Laws, p. 678. So as to compensation of executor, supra § 20.4-2.
[51] See last preceding section.
[52] Supra § 25.4-4.

greater or lesser degree at least the quantum, if not the nature, of the rights of one or more beneficiaries. While in theory it may thus be impossible to make a definitive separation of administrative from substantive matters, some are so predominantly administrative in character, as, for example, powers as to retention or sale of personal property not specifically bequeathed,[53] or the giving of notice to creditors,[54] that there can be little doubt of the applicability, where the rules referred to obtain, of the law of the place of administration. Numerous other powers, however, are much less clearly of the one character or the other, and in case of significant differences between the relevant laws of the place of administration and the domicile it may be necessary, for the executor's protection, to institute a proceeding for instructions.[55]

§ 25.4-5. ——; *effectiveness of exercise of power of appointment.*[56] The question whether a will effectively exercises a power of appointment possessed by the testator over real property is, in accordance with general principles,[57] governed by the law of the situs of the property. The like question as to personal property, as, for example, whether the power is exercised by a bequest of the donee's residuary estate without express reference to the power,[58] is, except as a statute may otherwise provide,[59] governed by the law that governs the instrument by which the power was created, rather than the law of the donee's domicile where that is different.[60] Within the general principles just stated, however, several kinds of questions can arise,[61] and if the executor has any duties or responsibilities as to the appointive property,[62] or it is appointed to the estate,[63] he should carefully consider the applicable authorities.

§ 25.4-6. ——; *construction and interpretation.*[64] It has been stated as a general rule that in determining the meaning of such terms as "heirs" and "issue" the

---

[53] Supra §§ 7.6-1 ff., 18.6-4.
[54] Supra § 9.4-2a.
[55] Generally, supra § 22.2.
[56] West Dig., Powers Key No. 36 (2). Generally, see Durand, Conflict of Laws in Exercise of Powers of Appointment, 1956 Proc. A.B.A. Sec. Real Prop. Prob. & Tr. L., Part I, 151.
[57] Supra § 25.4-3.
[58] Supra § 18.3-8.
[59] E.g., N.Y. E.P.T.L. sec. 3-5.1 (g).
[60] *Sewall v. Wilmer*, 132 Mass. 131; *In re New York Life Ins. Co.*, 209 N.Y. 585, 103 N.E. 315. Cf. *Matter of Morgan Guaranty Trust Co.*, 28 N.Y.2d 155, 320 N.Y.S.2d 905, 269 N.E.2d 571, distinguishing between (a) validity of exercise of power created by New York trust, which was governed by New York law, and (b) construction of California will exercising the power, which was within the jurisdiction of California court to determine and determination of which by it was entitled to full faith and credit. See also Goodrich & Scoles, Conflict of Laws, secs. 175–177; Land, Trusts in the Conflict of Laws, secs. 20, 29.2; Leflar, American Conflicts Law (1968 rev.) sec. 200.
[61] A number of these are discussed in Durand and Herterich, Conflict of Laws and the Exercise of Powers of Appointment, XLII Cornell L. Q. No. 2, 185.
[62] Cf. § 6.19, supra.
[63] Supra § 18.3-8.
[64] West Dig., Exrs. & Admrs. Key No. 436; P-H Est, Plng. Serv. ¶¶ 326, 327.

law of the domicile governs.[65] Possibly, however, it would be more accurate, or at least more rational, to say that construction and interpretation questions should be governed by the law of the place where the testator was domiciled at the time of the execution of the will.[66]

§ 25.5. *Intestate property.* Under the principles hereinabove referred to, the question as to whether any property is for and reason not effectively disposed of by will, either because the decedent died without a will, or because his will fails to dispose of the property by reason of failure to provide for a contingency that occurs or by reason of lapse of a bequest or devise of the property and, in either such case, the absence of any other effective provision for disposition of such property,[67] and, where intestacy does exist, questions as to the identities of the persons entitled to take such property as heirs or next of kin of the decedent, and their respective shares or interests therein, depend, in the case of personal property, upon the law of the testator's domicile,[68] and, in the case of real property, upon the law of the situs thereof.[69]

---

[65] Land, op. cit. supra note 60, secs. 28.1, 32.1 (noting that as to laws in force at different times the decision are not uniform). As to interpretation generally, see Leflar, op. cit. supra note 60, sec. 198.

[66] Ehrenzweig, Conflict of Laws, pp. 671, 672. Cf. *In re Gallagher's Est.*, 169 N.Y.S.2d 271, 274 (affd. 7 A.D.2d 1029, 184 N.Y.S.2d 782): "The meaning of the language of the instrument must be ascertained by a reference to the law which the testator had in mind and with which he was familiar at the time of the execution thereof . . . no distinction need be made with respect to whether the property is personalty or realty."

[67] Lapse of residuary disposition, supra § 18.7-1 ff.; partial intestacy, in general, supra § 18.8.

[68] Ehrenzweig, Conflict of Laws, p. 675.

[69] As governing disposition of real property, in general, supra § 25.4-3.

XXVI

CONSTRUCTIVE TRUSTS

§ *26.1. Nature.*[1] A constructive trust is, essentially, one implied and enforced in a court of equitable jurisdiction in respect of property that has been acquired by one person by such conduct or under such circumstances that he will be treated as holding it for the benefit of another, and so may be required to deliver it to such other. In the area of wills, a constructive trust may arise when one induces the decedent to devise or bequeath property to him by a promise or representation, express or implied, that he will turn it over to or use it for the benefit of another, or where, by such a promise or representation, a beneficiary under a will induces the decedent to refrain from changing or revoking the will or an heir induces the decedent to refrain from making a will.[2] It is apparent from the foregoing that a constructive trust is a trust only in the broad sense of that term; and while it may arise with respect to property disposed of by will, it is not created by the will and hence is not a "testamentary trust".[3] It is at most a passive trust, in which the "trustee" is merely a conduit for passage of the property to the "cestui" as the true beneficial owner.

§ *26.2. Responsibility of executor.* By its nature a constructive trust involves only the legatee, devisee, or heir on the one hand, and the cestui, on the other, and so in general the executor has no direct concern with the matter. Clearly, an executor who has no knowledge of circumstances that may give rise to a constructive trust in respect of a legacy is protected in satisfying the legacy according to its terms,[4] and any rights of the cestui must then be asserted by him against the legatee. If, however before the satisfaction of the legacy, the executor does have knowledge or notice of the circumstances or conduct in question, or one claiming to be cestui of such a trust notifies the executor of his claim or asserts a right to the property, the

---

[1] West Dig., Trusts Key Nos. 97, 106–110.

[2] Iverson, Constructive Trusts in Probate Proceedings, 1957 Proc. A.B.A. Sec. Real Prop. Prob. & Tr. I., Part I, 20.

[3] Testamentary trusts, infra Ch. XXVII.

[4] Satisfaction of legacies, in general, supra Ch. XIV.

executor should not ignore the possible rights of the cestui and, while he is not required to, and should not, make his own decision as to the respective rights of the parties, he should not distribute the subject matter of the legacy until he has obtained a judicial determination. It may, of course, not be necessary for the executor to institute a proceeding for such determination, if the issue is decided in an action or proceeding brought by the legatee or the cestui; but, if the executor is not himself a party thereto, he should make sure that the judgment or decree entered in such action or proceeding is conclusory as to him, and enures to his benefit or protection, before he acts upon it.

XXVII

TESTAMENTARY TRUSTS

§ 27.1. In general.[1] The term "testamentary trust" merely distinguishes a trust created by a will from one created by declaration or agreement *inter vivos*; the "testamentary trustee" as the trustee appointed by or pursuant to the will receives assets from the executor or by virtue of the provisions of the will, and administers them in accordance with the relevant terms and provisions of the will. The trust may be created by a specific, demonstrative, or general legacy, or by a devise, or by a bequest of the residuary estate or part thereof;[2] or, as hereinbefore mentioned, the funds of the trust may be or include those passing to the testamentary trustee as beneficiary of life insurance[3] or by appointment of property to the trustee.[4] Apart from making sure, before distributing assets to the trustee,[5] that the trust is valid in its essence,[6] and that the trustee has duly qualified if and as required by law,[7] the executor's only substantial concern with the fact that a disposition of estate assets is in trust rather than outright is that, as discussed in a previous place, he ordinarily must maintain during the period of administration a distinction in his accounts between principal and income, where that otherwise might not be necessary.[8]

§ 27.2. Validity of trust; importance to executor. The executor should not satisfy a bequest in trust without first satisfying himself that the trust is essentially valid. If, for example, under principles applying to trust generally, the trust provided for in the will is a passive one, or is for a purpose that is unauthorized or forbidden by law or is contrary to public policy, or is void *ab initio* because violative of the rule

---

[1] West Dig., Wills Key Nos. 669–688; P-H Est. Plng. Serv. ¶ 2509.

[2] Cf. § 14.1-2, supra.

[3] Supra § 18.3-7.

[4] Supra § 18.3-8.

[5] Time of establishment of trusts, in general, supra § 14.31-4; income tax considerations, supra § 13.5.

[6] See next following section.

[7] Infra § 27.3.

[8] Except, of course, for income tax purposes, and for those often on a different basis; supra §§ 16.1, 16.2.

TESTAMENTARY TRUSTS 303

against perpetuities or a corresponding statute, or is ineffective for failure to designate a beneficiary,[9] the executor should not make payment or distribution to the trustee, but should dispose of its subject matter in whatever alternate way is proper under governing law and the general rules of lapse.[10] In any such case, however, the executor should do no more than refrain from distributing to the trustee, and should retain possession of the legacy, until he has obtained, in whatever manner is appropriate,[11] a judicial determination of the points involved or approval of a different disposition, for if he disposes of the property in question to another or in any different way he does so at his own risk. It will be apparent that a problem of the character hereinabove referred to arises for the executor only where the trust is or may be wholly invalid; if it has essential validity, even in part, any further problems as the management and disposition of the trust fund are for the trustee and not for the executor.

§ 27.3. *Qualification of trustee.* In some jurisdictions a testamentary trustee, like an executor,[12] is required to "qualify" as such in some prescribed manner, as by filing his acceptance of appointment or of the trusteeship, giving a bond for the faithful performance of his duties, obtaining the issuance to him by the relevant court of letters of trusteeship,[13] registering the trust with a court,[14] or the like. In such a jurisdiction the executor, before distributing any assets to the trustee, should require the furnishing to him of appropriate evidence that the trustee has so qualified.[15] In other states no formal qualification is required of testamentary trustees, and, instead, the trustee is treated by the probate court as if he were a legatee in his own right, to whom distribution may be made with no greater formalities than in the case of any other legatee. Even where this later rule obtains, however, some courts will not authorize or direct distribution by the executor to a trustee residing or located in another jurisdiction, the laws of which do provide for formal qualification by testamentary trustees, until the trustee so qualifies in his own jurisdiction.

§ 27.4. *Functions of executor and trustee distinguished.* Even where the same person or institution is both executor of a will and trustee of a trust created by it, the functions in the two capacities are entirely separate and distinct, and must not be confused with one another. Generally speaking, the functions of the executor are, as has been seen hereinabove, to collect the decedent's assets, settle death taxes, pay debts and other charges, and distribute the remaining assets; when that has been accomplished, the executor becomes *functus officio*. The trustee, however, is a legatee or

---

[9] "Honorary trusts," supra § 14.14-3.

[10] Supra §§ 14.23-1, 18.7-2. Payment of income to trustee or to beneficiary, supra § 16.6-3aa.

[11] Construction and instruction proceedings, supra Ch. XXII; construction on accounting, supra § 24.5-5a.

[12] Supra § 5.8-1.

[13] Such letters, issued in some jurisdictions, correspond as to the trustee to the letters testamentary issued to an executor; supra § 1.12.

[14] So in Unif. Prob. Code sec. 7-101 ff. It may be noted that Art. VII of that Code has as its primary purpose the bringing of all trusts, both testamentary and inter vivos, within controls of the same kind, similar to those now applied in most jurisdictions only to the former.

[15] Op. cit. sec. 3-913.

devisee;[16] again speaking generally, his duties and powers commence when he receives (or becomes entitled to receive) assets from the executor or otherwise, and his functions are to invest and manage the fund held by him so as to make it productive of income, to distribute or otherwise dispose of the net income during the term of the trust, and to distribute the principal of the fund at termination of the trust. As has been pointed out *supra,* an executor is ordinarily without power to make other than temporary investments,[17] and he should not infringe upon or assume the trustee's functions in that regard. Conversely, the testamentary trustee has no authority to settle estate or inheritance taxes, allow or reject claims, or perform any other executorial functions, although, of course, he may call the executor to account, as can any other legatee,[18] for any improper act or omission that results in the trustee's receiving less property than would have been turned over to him if the executor had properly performed his duties. The functions of the executor and the trustee may, of course, and often do, overlap in point of time, as where the trust is established, in whole or in part, before the administration of the estate is completed; but the executor bears alone the responsibility for carrying out his proper functions, and cannot rely upon the trustee for the performance of any of them, nor may he permit the trustee to interfere in any way with the executor's performance thereof. This is not to say, of course, that the executor should not consult with the trustee about any matters or that the two should not cooperate appropriately; on the contrary, executor and trustee should usually exchange views and where practicable arrive at a policy agreeable to both as to such matters as what assets are to be liquidated and what ones retained,[19] how surplus funds should be invested by the executor,[20] the timing of distributions for best tax advantage,[21] and other matters affecting the trustee and trust beneficiaries as well as the executor; nevertheless the executor should bear in mind that as to matters within his proper function he bears final responsibility and the decisions to be made are his own. By the same token, the executor has no duty or power to see to the performance of carrying out of the trust by the trustee.[22]

§ 27.5. *Pour-over to other trust distinguished.* A pour-over bequest or devise,[23] under which property of the estate passes to the trustee of a trust created by an instrument other than the testator's will, is to be distinguished from a trust under such will and hence from the term "testamentary trust" as used in this chapter. The trustee of a trust created by the testator's will holds the subject matter of his bequest or devise in trust under the will, and on the terms of and with the powers and dis-

---

[16] Cf. discussion in Comment to Unif. Prob. Code sec. 3-913.
[17] Supra § 7.7-2.
[18] By objection to executor's account; supra § 24.5-4.
[19] Supra §§ 7.6-1, -2.
[20] Supra § 7.7-2.
[21] Supra § 13.5.
[22] So in Unif. Prob. Code sec. 3-912.
[23] Supra § 18.5.

TESTAMENTARY TRUSTS

cretions contained in the will;[24] and it is such a trust that, in the connotation of any particular will or testator, is referred to as a testamentary trust. The recipient of a pour-over bequest, however, holds it as trustee under the instrument by which the trust was created,[25] as an addition to and an integral part of the corpus of such trust, and subject to the terms of and with such powers and discretions as are contained in that instrument;[26] the provisions of the testator's will have no further application to the property covered by the bequest or to its management or disposition. Just as in the case of a bequest to the trustee under the testator's will, nevertheless, the executor before satisfying the pour-over bequest will want to assure himself of the essential validity of the recipient trust,[27] and the due qualification, if required, of the trustee thereof;[28] further, the executor must ascertain, as in the case of any other legacy, the ability[29] and the willingness[30] of such trustee to accept and hold the subject matter of the legacy or devise.

---

[24] Supra § 27.1.

[25] But cf. Shriver, The Multi-State Estate, 3 Real Prop. Prob. & Tr. J. 189, 192, citing an instance of supposed invalidity of a pour-over bequest where the pour-over was to an inter vivos trust created in a jurisdiction other than the testator's domicile and its trustee was ineligible, because of non-residence, to be a trustee at the domicile; this seems to imply that the recipient trustee was to be treated as a trustee under the will or at least would have to be eligible to be such a trustee.

[26] So in Unif. Prob. Code sec. 3-511, which is same as Unif. Testamentary Additions to Trusts Act. sec. 1. That instrument may be either an inter vivos agreement or declaration of trust, or the will of a person other than the executor's testator; if the latter, the recipient trust is, of course, a "testamentary" trust under the will of its creator but is not such so far as concerns the will of the executor's testator.

[27] Supra § 27.2.

[28] Supra § 27.3.

[29] Incapacity to take, supra § 14.18-1 ff., 15.4.

[30] Renunciation, in general, supra § 14.26-1. It is, of course, only in a very rare case that a trustee-legatee would be justified in renouncing a pour-over bequest to him; conceivably renunciation might be justified if acceptance of the property or its addition to his trust would be in some manner prejudicial or disadvantageous to his beneficiaries or hamper the accomplishment of his trust purposes, but a renunciation for any reason personal to the trustee would seem impermissible.

APPENDICES

APPENDIX A

CALENDAR AND TICKLER

To be kept at top of file

[This form is illustrative only and should be modified as necessary in the light of each estate's own facts and of local law and practice.]

ESTATE OF _____

Date of death:

Testate [ ]   Intestate [ ]
 Date of Will:

Court and County:

Letters testamentary or of administration dated:

Is temporary administration necessary
 [ ] Yes   [ ] No

Inventory and appraisal due (date):

Federal estate tax:

 Return due:

Domicile:

Date of decree of probate or administration:

Attorney:

Co-fiduciary [ ] Yes   [ ] None
 Name and address:

Is ancillary administration necessary
 [ ] Yes   [ ] No
 Jurisdiction:

Decedent's final income tax return due:

State estate or inheritance tax:
 Initial/advance payment due:
 Return due:

. . . . . .

Is nominee registration of securities permitted:

 Consent of co-fiduciary obtained:

Will co-fiduciary claim commissions:

. . . . . .

Annual/periodic accountings due:
[Other fixed dates; specify]

Final accounting due:

APPENDIX B
CHECK LIST OF EXECUTOR'S DUTIES

[This check list covers the principal duties of an executor that are basic to his office or that arise in most jurisdictions and most estates. It details, however, the list may have to be modified in the light of local law and practice, and in special cases it may be necessary to add to it. Accordingly, the list that follows should not be used without due consideration of the factors mentioned.]

Pre-Probate Responsibilities

Establishment of fact and time of death

Locating Will and witnesses

Ascertainment of "last" Will

Examination of Will
    Special instructions
    Special provisions
    Determination of whether to qualify
        If not, renounce

Making or assisting in funeral arrangements

Steps necessary to protect estate pending probate

Determining necessity of temporary administration

Determining fact of intestacy if Will not found

Provide interim assistance to family as required

Probate and qualification; initial steps

Determine domicile of decedent

Determine place of probate or administration

Offer Will for probate or apply for administration

Arrange for bond (if required) and otherwise qualify

Obtain facsimile copy of Will

Obtain letters testamentary or of administration

Obtain copies of letters or certificates of issuance to enable collection of assets

Identification and protection of assets

Examine decedent's records (income tax returns, checkbooks, bank and brokers' statements, etc.) to locate assets

Open safe deposit boxes and take custody of contents

Get cash in decedent's possession at death

APPENDICES

Cancel open orders for purchase or sale of securities

Collect bank accounts
Consider interest dates on savings accounts

File claims for insurance, veterans' and social security benefits, etc., payable to estate

Search home and office for and take custody of valuables and records

Suspend unneeded utilities

Terminate margin accounts with brokers

Obtain securities in hands of brokers, custodians, etc.

Seal home or office (if necessary for protection)

Protect going business and its records and inventory

Open bank account of estate

Rent safe deposit box (if necessary); open custodian account (in proper case)

Examine employment contract, employee benefit plans, etc., as to amounts payable to estate

Obtain appraisals of real property, and of personalty as necessary

File inventory (if required)

Review of financial records and business affairs

Executory contracts for purchase or sale of property

Policies of casualty insurance on real and personal property
Adequacy of coverage
Endorsement of policies to estate

Title to real property (sole, joint, entireties)

Partnership agreements, buy-sell agreements, other business arrangements

Interest of decedent as fiduciary or beneficiary of other estates or trusts

Current bills and other obligations

Lease of home, apartment, office
Consider termination or sublease, if feasible

Continuance or discharge of business and personal employees
Withholding and social security taxes

Study of income tax returns for five years preceding death

Collection of data for preparation of decedent's final income tax returns

Ascertainment of any gifts made by decedent in lifetime:
For which return due
Which are reportable for estate tax purposes (date, motive, state of health, etc.)

Administration in general

Collection of all income, accounts, fees, other receivables

Estimate of cash requirements (expenses, taxes, debts, cash legacies)

Ascertainment and segregation of U.S. Treasury bonds eligible for application on Federal estate

Redemption of U.S. Savings Bonds redeemable at par within limited period after death

Liquidation if and as necessary:

    To provide for cash requirements
    For preservation of values
    For eventual distribution

Tax-free redemption of corporate stock

Making funds productive of income pending expenditure or distribution

Registration of securities in name of nominee (if permitted)

Examination and allowance or rejection of claims

Continuing, defending, or terminating pending litigation by or against decedent

Appropriate management or supervision of real property

Discovery proceedings to find or recover decedent's property in possession of others

Attention to non-probate assets

Obtaining information as to nature and amounts subject to death taxation

Information as to non-probate assets passing pursuant to residuary clause

Facilitating collection of insurance, social security benefits, joint bank accounts, etc., by taker or beneficiary

Tax returns and payments

(a) *Income taxes*

Notice of fiduciary relationship (I.R.C. § 6036)

File final return of decedent and return for preceding tax year (if not already filed)

    Consider joint return with spouse

Review open years as to possible deficiency assessments, fraud penalties

Prepare for audit of returns

    Consider request for prompt audit

Determine fiscal year of estate for income tax purposes

    Consideration of interests of and effects on beneficiaries

Determine whether to include accrued increment on U.S. Savings Bonds

Determination whether to take certain expenses as income tax or estate tax deductions

File returns of estate.

(b) *Gift taxes*

Determine whether taxable gifts were made in quarter of death (or preceding quarter)

File necessary returns

    Obtain consent of spouse to treat as joint gifts (in appropriate case)

APPENDICES

Determine whether taxable gifts were made in prior years for which returns were not filed

File necessary returns

(c) *Death taxes*

Obtain Form 712 in respect of each life insurance policy

Obtain release or consents as required to enable collection or transfer of securities or other assets

File Federal estate tax return

File state inheritance or estate tax return, or institute proceeding for fixation of tax

Make advance payment permitting discount on tax or precluding addition to tax

Establish credit against Federal tax for state death taxes paid

If taxes are to be apportioned, estimate apportionable shares and
    Withhold from legatees
    Collect from other takers

Compute and pay additional or "pick-up" state tax to take up unused balance of Federal credit

Determine definitive apportionment and adjust with beneficiaries as necessary

Debts and claims

Determine order of priority of expenses, debts, claims
    Determine solvency or insolvency of estate

Determine property applicable to payment of debts and claims

Timely payment of allowed claims
    Avoidance of interest

Rights of spouse and children

Ascertainment and segregation of "exempt" property and allowances

Determine rights of pretermitted children

Statutory election by surviving spouse

Distribution of assets

Satisfaction of legacies
    Attention to order of priority
    Time for satisfaction as affected by other factors
    Satisfaction of cash legacy in property

Partial distributions

Consideration of timing of distributions as affecting income taxation

Consideration of income tax effects of distributions to residuary beneficiaries

Reserves for expenses, contingencies, tax deficiencies, etc.

Distribution of residue in cash or in kind

Establishment of trust under Will

Pour-over to other trust

Partial intestacy

Accounts and accounting

Duty to keep full and accurate records

Duty to account to beneficiaries

    Periodic information accounts or reports to court or judge

    Intermediate accountings (only where necessary or proper)

    Final accountings

Necessity of disclosure of acts and omissions; adequacy of account

Settlement of account:

    By judicial proceeding

    By voluntary agreement of beneficiaries (receipt and release)

Payment of administration expenses, fees, and compensation

Compliance with final decree

Obtaining discharge of executor:

    From further accountability
    From office

Successor and substituted executors and administrators

Qualification of successor or substitute as in case of original executor

Requiring settlement of account of predecessor

Powers and duties generally as in case of original executor

    Duty to take all necessary steps not taken or completed by predecessor

    Discretionary powers exercisable unless personal to predecessor

APPENDIX C

SUPPLEMENTARY CHECK LIST
AS TO REAL PROPERTY HELD IN ESTATE

[The following illustrates the kind of check list, in addition to that as to an executor's duties generally, that may be advisable where real property is included in the estate. As in the case of any other check list, this is illustrative only and should not be used without adequate consideration of the law and practice of the jurisdiction in which the real property is situate. Important factors in this regard are those bearing upon the nature and extent of the powers and responsibilities of the executor or administrator with respect to real property, during the administration of the estate. It is to be kept in mind that such powers and duties may, in practice, be greater where the fiduciary may or does resort to real property for funds needed to meet cash requirements of the estate, or for any other reason sells the real property, than in cases where neither of those situations exists.]

ESTATE OF _____

Property: Location of identification:

Description (acreage, lot size, residential, business, store, apartment, unimproved, etc.):

Appraisal: Made (date):   Appraised value: $

Appraiser:

Management: Outside agent to be used   [ ] Yes   [ ] No

Name and address:

Will agent pay taxes, mortgage interest, insurance
[ ] Yes   [ ] No

Mortgage: Amount (as at death of decedent): $

Date: Due:

Name and address of mortgagee or holder:

Interest: %   Amortization payments due:
                                          $ each

To what date interest paid by decedent:

To what date amortization paid by decedent:

                  Arrears $

Taxes: Kinds: City [ ]   Town [ ]   County [ ]   School [ ]   Water [ ]

Other (specify):

When payable (each):

Open assessments:

Assessed valuation: Land $ Buildings $ Year:

Insurance: On building $ Furniture and fixtures $
          Public liability $ Elevator liability $
          Plate glass $ Workmen's compensation $
          Boiler $ Rents $
          Other (specify:)

Tenancy: Lease   [ ] Yes   [ ] No   Arrears $ Expires:
         Monthly [ ] Yes   [ ] No   Arrears $

             Names and addresses on reverse

         Is property to be occupied by life tenant
            or beneficiary   [ ] Yes   [ ] No
            Conditions:

Title: In whose name stands: Dower interest [ ] Yes   [ ] No
      Restrictions: (continue on reverse)

Managing agent at death: Name:
      Existing contract   [ ] Yes   [ ] No
      Bills payable   [ ] Yes*   [ ] No   * List on reverse

Employes: Names and capacities:

         Wages $ Dates payable: To what date paid:

Power of sale: Can property be sold   [ ] Yes   [ ] No
               Is sale desired   [ ] Yes   [ ] No
      Power to retain   [ ] Yes   [ ] No

Power to lease: [ ] Yes   [ ] No
           Can net lease be made [ ] Yes   [ ] No
           Special provisions (if any; list on reverse)

Inspection: Has property been inspected   [ ] Yes   [ ] No
         Date: By whom:
         Special comments:
         Violations:

Remarks:

Index

A

A Technique for Making Distributions from Principal and Income to Residuary Beneficiaries During Administration of Estates, 233*n*
A. B. A. Committee on Professional Ethics, 21*n*
Abandonment of worthless property included in residuary estate, 240–241
Abatement of dispositions in insolvent estates, 243
Abatement of legacy, 145–147
Acceptance by creditor of bequest, 111
Accountability of executor, 281
Accountant, particular problems of executor of estate of, 61
Accounting fees, admissability of as administration expense, 289–290
Accounting and tax computations distinguished, 204
   and tax values distinguished, 92
Accounts, executor's, 282–283
   compulsory, 289
   definitive and informational distinguished, 282
   disclosure, 283
   expenses of settling, 289–290
      of keeping records and preparing account, 289–290
   in general, 282
   intermediate and final, 283–284
   scope of, and disclosure, 282–283
   settlement of, 284–289
      effect of, 287–289 (see also "Settlement of account of executor")
      failure to make, 289
      in general, 284
      judicial or voluntary, 284–285 (see also "Settlement of account of executor")
      objections to account, 286 (see also "Objections to executor's account")
      parties, 285–286
   time for, 283–284
      death, resignation or removal of executor, 284
Accruals of income after decedent's death, 206–207
Additions to tax, duty of executor to avoid, 126–127
Ademption of demonstrative legacy, 160
   of devise, 200–201
      damage or destruction, 201
      sale by incompetent's guardian or committee, 200–201
   of legacy, 145–147
   by satisfaction of general legacy, 161–162
   of specific legacies, 146, 153–155
      guardian of incompetent, property sold by, 154
      insurance proceeds, 154–155
      open-market securities, 153
Administration, nature and phases of, 10–12
   draftsmanship, problems created or avoidable by, 12
   in general, 7, 10
   limitations, 10–11
   phases of, 11
   responsibilities therein, 10
   tickler and checklist, 11, 309, 310–314
Administration, meaning of, 7
   ancillary, 5–6
   independent, 2
   "supervised," 2
   "unsupervised," 2
Administration expenses, 255–267
   compensation of executor, 260–266
      assets includible in commissions base, 264–265
      assignment of, 266
      basis, rate and amount, 261–263 (see also "Executor, compensation of")
      of co-executors, 265–266
      commissions on principal and income, 264
      denial of compensation to, 266
      in general, 260–261
      time of payment, allowance or approval for, 263–264 (see also "Executor, compensation of")
   counsel fees, 256–260
      amount and fixation of, 257 (see also "Counsel fees and administration expense")
      co-executor's separate counsel, 258
      contested probates, 259–260
      executor as attorney, 260
      in general, 256
      pre-probate services, 259
      time of payment, 258–259
   defined, 255
   highest priority ranking of, 244
   judicial review, 267
   out-of-pocket disbursements, 266–267
   source of payment, 255–256
Administrative powers of executor under statute enacted after testator's death, 294
Administrative Problems of Fiduciaries in Working with Formula Clauses, 164*n*
Administrator, exact meaning of, 3–4
   ad colligendum, 4
   ancillary, 5–6
   cum testamento annexo, 4, 280

319

Administrator (*cont.*)
   d.b.n. or c.t.a., 4, 280
   de bonis non, 4
   de son tort, 4, 6
   domiciliary, 6
   and executor, comparison of, 6–7
   pendente lite, 4
   special, 5
   temporary, 4–5
Adopted children as "issue," consideration of for legacy, 181–182
Advancement, meaning of doctrine of, 190–191
Advancements, doctrine of re residuary legacy, 239
Advice and assistance for executor, 14–15
Advice of counsel, executor's reliance on, 22–23
Advices of death, executor's responsibility to issue, 45–46
After-acquired or after-discovered property, residuary estate and, 240
After-born or after-adopted children, rights of to estate, 219
Agreements with or among beneficiaries, 268–272
   (see also "Beneficiaries, agreements with or among")
"All personal property," bequest of by specific legacy, 151
"All" real property, devise of, 198–199
   oil, gas and mineral interests, 198–199
      "forced heirship" rules of Louisiana, 199
   as specific devise, 199
"All tangibles," bequest of by specific legacy, 150–151
Allocation of Income Earned During Estate Administration, 209n, 210n
Allocation of surplus income among residuary beneficiaries, 229–230
Allowance of claim and payment, difference between, 106
Allowance or rejection of claim on estate, 105–106
Allowances, insolvent estate and, 253
Allowances for decedent's wife and children, 212
American Conflicts Law, 136n, 295n, 298n
Amount and fixation of counsel fees, 257
   agreement by executor, 257
"Amount" formula for "marital deduction" legacy, 163
Ancillary executor, 5–6
   administration, meaning of, 38
   need for appointment of to handle out-of-state real property, 75, 295
   to pay taxes in foreign state or country, 125
   time of death and, 32
Ancillary probate, 38
Ancillary proceeding to obtain property in another jurisdiction, 62
Andrews Est., 256n
Annuity, direction or authorization to purchase, 170–171
Annulment of marriage of testator, effect of upon will, 34
   after execution of will, 218
Apartment of decedent, determining status of, 49–50
Apartment or rented home of decedent, responsibility of executor regarding, 87–88
   cooperative or condominium, 88

Appendices, 309–316
Appln. of Spitzmuller, 33n
Appointive property, executor's collection of, 58
   insolvent estate and, 252
   and residuary estate, 226–227
Appointment, effectiveness of power of, governed by law of situs, 298
Appointment, executor's decision to accept, 26–27
   in general, 26
   ineligibility, 27
   renunciation, 27
Apportionment of taxes, 130–137
   in general, 130–131
   inheritance taxes, 131–132
   residue, insufficiency, of, 137
   within residue, 133
      payment "as expense" distinguished, 133–134
   retention or recovery of shares, 134–137
      amounts recovered, disposition of, 136
      in general, 134–135
      inability to recover, 136
      interest on apportioned share, 136–137
      litigation, collection by, 135–136
   will, direction in regarding, 132–133
Art, works of, bequeathed by specific legacy, 150
Arthur v Arthur, 161n, 191n
"As is, where is" rule, 158
Assets, custody, preservation and management of, 65–90
   liquidation, investment and other management problems, 76–90
      apartment or rented home, 87–88
      cash requirements, list of, 76
      closely-held corporations, 84 (see also "Closely-held corporations...")
      contracts and undertakings of executor, 90
      employees, domestic and personal, 87
      executory contracts of decedent, 89–90
      liability, exculpation from, 22, 90
      liquidation of assets, 76–82 (see also "Liquidation of assets...")
      money, 82–84 (see also "Money, handling of by executor")
      proprietorships and partnership interests, 86–87
      torts of executor, 90
      utilities, suspension of, 88–89
   possession and control, 65–75
      duty, nature of, 65
      power and duty of executor to protect, 27–28
      real property, 72–75 (see also "Real property, executor's obtaining possession and control of")
      securities, 68–71 (see also "Securities, executor's possession and control of")
      tangibles, 66–68 (see also "Tangibles, custody, preservation and management of")
      United States government bonds, 71–72 (see also "Government bonds...")
Assets includible in commissions base, executor's compensation and, 264–265
   uncollected, 265
Assets and papers, collection of, 45–64
   in general, 45–52
      bank accounts, 47–48
      benefits payable to others, collection of, 52

INDEX

Assets and papers (*cont.*)
  brokerage accounts, 51
  business activities, 49
  cash and valuable, in box, home, office, etc., 47
  decedent's person, cash and valuables on, 47
  duty, existence and nature of, 45
  home or office, contents of, 48–49
  identification of assets and familiarization of affairs, 46
  insurance payable to state, collection of, 51–52
  preliminary steps, 45–46
  of proprietorship or close corporation, 49
  receivables, 50 (see also "Receivables of decedent, determining")
  rented home or apartment, 49–50
  safe deposit box, 46–47
  savings accounts, 48
  particular problems, 53–64
    appointive property, 58
    death tax waivers or consents, 64
    discovery proceedings, 63
    gifts, alleged, 56–57–58
    joint ownership and survivorship interests, 55
    jurisdiction, other, property in, 61–63
    legal life tenant, decedent as, 57
    personal property, joint tenancy in, 55–56 (see also "Personal property, determining joint tenancy of")
    professional men, estates of, 58–61 (see also "Professional men, collecting assets and papers of")
    real property, 53–55 (see also "Real property of decedent")
    reverse discovery, 63–64
    transfers, invalid or ineffective, 57–58
Assignment by executor of compensation, 266
Assignment by legatee of residuary legacy, 238–239
  before death of testator, 239
  direction for payment distinguished, 239
  in general, 238–239
  revocability, 239
Assignments by legatees, 190
Attorney of executor, conflicts of interest concerning, 21
"Augmented estate," meaning of, 215, 216*n*

B

"Bank account trust," revocation of by will, residuary estate and, 224
  collection of, 56
  in insolvent estate, 253
Bank accounts of decedent, 47–48
Bankers Trust Co. v. U.S., 72*n*
Barch v. Avco Corp., 279*n*
Barnett, 139*n*
Beale, 104*n*
Beck v. McGillis, 162*n*
Beneficiaries, agreements with or among, 268–272
  indemnification agreements, 272
  scope and effectiveness, 268–270
    in general, 268–269

public policy, 269–270
utility and advisability of, 268
who must join, 270–271
  of fewer than all, 271
Beneficiaries, conflicting interests of, 19–20
Beneficiary, executor's interest as, 20
Benefits payable to others, executor's task of facilitating collection of, 52
Bequest, meaning of, 8
Biskind & Scanlon, 216*n*
Bliss, 34*n*
Boardman's Estate Management and Accounting, 216*n*
Body or organs, bequest or disposition of, 158–159
Bond for qualification of executor, 41
Bonds, executor's obtaining possession and control of, 71–72 (see also "Government bonds . . .")
Bonds and stocks as distributable assets of residuary estate, 235–236
Borrowing money for cash needs rather than liquidation of assets, 78
Bowden v. Brown, 171*n*
Bowe & Parker, 275*n*
Bozeman, 35*n*, 38*n*, 295*n*
Braman Will, 240*n*
Brokerage accounts of decedent, 51
Browarsky Est., 256*n*
Brown, 183*n*
Bryant v. Klatt, 172*n*
Burnham v. Kelly, 74*n*
Business activities of decedent, protecting assets of, 49
Business obligations with encumbrances, specific legacy of, 156
Buy-and-sell agreements, effect of upon securities valuation, 96
Byers v. Womack, 181*n*

C

Calendar of dates and stages of administration, 11, 309
Camden Safe Dep. & Trust Co. v. Martin, 121*n*
Cantrall, 168*n*
Capital gains and losses, treatment of, 205–206
Care, diligence and prudence required of executor, 13
Cash distribution to one beneficiary of assets in residuary estate, 236
Cash legacy, satisfaction of in property, 188–190
  marital deduction legacy, 189–190
Cash requirements, list of, 76
Cash and/or valuables, executor's duty to locate and collect, 47
Cashman v. Petrie, 80*n*
Casner, 11*n*, 24*n*, 165*n*, 235*n*
Cass v. Eliassen, 74*n*
Casualty insurance on decedent's real property, 73–74
Catena's Est., 99*n*, 245*n*
Cattell Trust, 232*n*
Cavanaugh v. Dore, 28*n*
Cemetery lots, devise of, 202
  executor's responsibilities regarding, 75
  as part of residuary estate, 225

Cemetery lots (*cont.*)
   selection of other not justifiable expense for estate, 100
Charges and expenses of insolvent estate, 244–247
   administration expenses, 244
   debts of decedent, 245–247
     to Federal or state government, 246
     last illness, expenses of, 246
     other, 246–247
     secured, 246
   funeral expenses, 245
   in general, 244
   taxes, 245
     Federal, priority of over State, 245
Charitable legacies, 171–172
   cy pres, doctrine of, 171–172
   "honorary trust," 172
Charitable organization, inability of to receive legacy, 176
Charitable pledges of decedent, 112
Charity, "excessive" or "late" gifts to, 220
Check-list for administration, 11, 310–314
   supplementary for real property, 315–316
"Children," meaning of, 8–9
Children, surviving, rights of, 212–221 (see also "Surviving spouse or children, rights of")
Children unprovided for in will, rights of, 218–219
   after-born or after-adopted children, 219
   in general, 218
   living at execution of will, 218–219
   satisfaction of share, source of, 219
Choosing Foreign Forum for Probate and Administration, 35*n*
Christy v. Christy, 16*n*
Chrystie, 35*n*
City Bank Farmers Tr. Co. v. Cannon, 80*n*
City Bank Farmers Trust Co. v. Schnader, 120*n*
Claims, compromise of, 111
   acceptance of bequest by creditor, 111
Claims, interest on, 109
Claims on estate, presentation and consideration of, 104–108 (see also "Debts and claims" and "Funeral expenses, debts and claims")
   allowance or rejection of, 105–106
   creditors, notice to, 105
   executor, personal claim of, 109
   of foreign creditors, 107–108
   proof of, 106–107
   statute of limitations, barred by, 107
   time for payment of, 108
   time of presentation, limitation on, 104–105
Class gifts, consideration of bequest as, 185–187
   ascertainment of, 186
   convenience, rule of, 186
   non-lapse statute, applicability of, 187
   what is class gift, 185–186
Close corporation, protecting assets of, 49
Closely-held corporations, liquidation, investment and management problems of, 84–86
   buy-and-sell agreements, 85
   fee or salary to executor as director or officer, 85–86
   management, sale, merger, liquidation, 84–85
   valuation of stock of, 95–96
Co-executor, delegation of executorial functions to, 15

Co-executor's separate counsel, 258
Co-executors, compensation of, 265–266
   agreement; waiver by one, 265–266
Coin or stamp collections as bequeathed by specific legacy, 150
Cole v. Cole, 186*n*
Commingling of estate's money with executor's money forbidden, 82
Commissions on principal and income, executor's compensation and, 264
Committee on Ethics and Professional Responsibility, 21*n*
"Common disaster" provisions of will, 182–183
Community property, rights of surviving spouse and, 221
Compensation of executor, 260–266 (see also "Executor, compensation of")
Compromising claims, power of executor for, 51
Compulsory accountings by executor, 289
Concealment of will, 26
Condition precedent, legacy subject to, 167–168
Conditional legacies, 145
Condominium apartment of decedent, executor's responsibility concerning, 88
Confidentiality of executor, 18
Conflict of Laws, 38*n*, 104*n*, 136*n*, 184*n*, 212*n*, 294*n*, 295*n*, 297*n*, 298*n*, 299*n*
Conflict of Laws and the Exercise of Powers of Appointment, 298*n*
Conflict of Laws Relating to Wills, Probate Decrees and Estates, 38*n*
Conflicts of interest, 18–21
Consents to transfer of personal property, responsibility of executor to provide, 64
Construction and instruction proceedings, 273–277
   construction, matters for, 274–275
     in general, 274
     precatory provisions, 274–275
   expenses, 277
   in general, 273
   instructions, proceeding for, 274
   interim or special proceeding, 275–276
     on final accounting, 276
   necessary parties, 276–277
     heirs or next of kin, 276–277
   prematurity; moot questions, 277
   time for, 275–276
     on final accounting, 276
Construction problems of bequests, 195
   perpetuities problems, 195
Constructive trusts, 300–301
   executor, responsibility of, 300–301
   nature, 300
Constructive Trusts in Probate Proceedings, 300*n*
Contested probates, counsel's fees for, 259–260
Contests of wills, 43–44
   in terrorem provisions, 43–44
Contraband tangible personal property in decedent's estate, handling of by executor, 67–68
Contracts made by decedent, responsibility of executor concerning, 89–90
Contracts of purchase or sale made by decedent, 54–55
Contracts and undertakings of executor, 90
Convenience, rule of for ascertainment for "class gift" legacy, 186

INDEX

Cooperative apartment of decedent, executor's responsibility concerning, 88
Copyrights, valuation of, 97–98
Copyrights and the Author's Estate, 97*n*
Corday, 31*n*
Corporate executor's own securities, need for sale of, 80
Corporate stock, redemption of, 77–78
Corporate stock after capital changes, bequest of through specific legacy, 151–152
Correspondence of decedent, checking for greater familiarization, 46
Counsel, executor's reliance on advice of, 22–23
Counsel fees as administration expense, 256–260
    amount and fixation of, 257
        agreement by executor, 257
    co-executor's separate counsel, 258
    contested probates, 259–260
    executor as attorney, 260
    in general, 256
    pre-probate services, 259
    time of payment, 258–259
        partial payments, 258–259
Counterclaims, consideration of as source of payment of claim against estate, 110
Covey, 209*n*, 210*n*
Credit against Federal tax for state tax paid, establishment of, 129
Creditor, bequest to, 172–173
Creditor or beneficiary, executor's interest as, 20
Creditors, impartiality of executor regarding, 19
Creditors, publication of notice to by executor, 105
Currie, 136*n*
Custodian or advisory account, establishment of, 69–70
    corporate executor, exemption of, 70
    registration in nominee's name, 70–71
Cy pres, doctrine of, 171–172

D

Dalton, 139*n*
Date of death, ascertaining, 31–32
    at domicile, 32
    standard or daylight time, 32
Dead bodies, special bequests or dispositions of, 158–159
Death, fact of, establishment of, 30–31
Death of decedent, person responsible for incapable of receiving legacy, 175–176
Death of executor, 278–280 (see also "Executor, death, resignation or removal of")
Death tax value and accounting values, difference between, 92
Death tax waivers, executor's responsibility to provide, 64
    state, required for opening decedent's safe deposit box, 47, 47*n*
Debtor, bequest to, 173
    set-off or retainer, right of, 173–174
Debtor, executor as, 21
Debts and claims, 101–112 (see also "Claims on estate . . ." and "Funeral expenses, debts and claims")
    of business, 102–103
    direction in will, effect of, 103

executor, personal liability of for payment, 104
    interest on, 109
    life insurance policy loans, 103
    secured debts, 102–103
    unmatured or unliquidated liabilities, 101–102
Debts of decedent, priority of, 245–247
    to Federal and state government, 246
    last illness, expenses of, 246
    other, 246–247
    secured, 246
Debts and expenses, availability of specific legacy for, 156
Decision to accept appointment, executor's, 26–27
    in general, 26
    ineligibility, 27
    renunciation, 27
Deductions for estate or income tax purposes, claiming, 140–141
Deferred legacies, 145, 168–170
    administrative problems, 169–170
    and trust distinguished, 169
Deficiency assessments, 123–124
Definitive and informational accounting distinguished, 282
Delay by executor to be avoided in distribution of residuary estate, 232–233
    in liquidating assets, 77
Delegation by executor, 15
    to co-executor, 15
Delivery of tangibles, 158
    "as is, where is" rule, 158
Delivery of will to another than appropriate court, 25
Demczuk Est., 178*n*
Demonstrative legacies, 145, 159–160
    ademption, 160
    availability of fund for charges and expenses, 160
    bank account, bequest of, distinguished, 160
    definition, 159
    general legacy to extent fund insufficient, 160
    insolvent estate and, 250–251
Denial of compensation to executor, 266
Descent and distribution, statute of, and non-lapse statute, similarity of, 185
    rules of followed for distribution of intestate property, 238
Devises, 197–203
    ademption, 200–201
        damage or destruction, 201
        sale by incompetent's guardian or committee, 200–201
    cemetery lots, 202
    description and identification, 197–199
        of "all" real property, 198 (see also " 'All' real property, devise of")
        in general, 197–198
    encumbrances, 199–200
    estate tax apportionment, 203
    incapacity to take, 200
    lapse, 200
    law of situs, importance of, 197
    meaning of, 8
    rents as belonging to devisee, 201–202
        availability for charges, expenses and legacies, 202
    renunciation, 202–203

Devises (*cont.*)
  title to real property in another state, establishing, 203
Devises, abatement, common law, 248
  statutory changes, 248–249
Direction in will for payment of taxes to foreign state or country, effect of, 126
Discharge of executor from liability or from office, 290–291
  distinguished from removal, 279
Disclaimer of legacy, 187–188
  of intestate share, 188
Disclosure of pertinent estate matters in executor's accounts, 283
Discounts for payment of taxes, duty of executor to note, 126–127
Discovery proceedings, 63
Discretionary powers of executor, 14
Disqualification of executor, 42
Distribution, liquidation for, 78–79
  specific legacy and letter or memo concerning, 156–157
    wishes orally expressed, 157
Distribution problems of residuary estate, 232–241
  advancements, 239
  after-acquired or after-discovered property, 240
  assignment by legatee, 238–239
    before death of testator, 239
    direction for payment distinguished, 239
    in general, 238–239
    revocability, 239
  in cash or in kind, 234–236
    cash distribution to one beneficiary, 236
    shares or fractions of residue, 234–236
  in general, 232–233
  lapse of residuary legacy, 236–237
    in general, 236–237
    "residue of residue," disposition of, 237
  necessity of order of, 233
  partial, 233–234
  partial intestacy, 238
  prolongation of administration, 241
  satisfaction in lifetime, 239
  worthless property, 240–241
Distributions of legacy, executor's duty for simultaneous, 193–194
"Divided loyalty rule," meaning of, 80
Divorce of testator, effect of upon will, 34
  after execution of will, 218
Dodge & Sullivan, 210*n*, 228*n*
Doetsch v. Doetsch, 130*n*
Dole, 233*n*
Domicile, determination of, 35–36
  importance of determining, 36
  law of governing personal property, 297
    problems, 35–36
Domicile and right to tax, contest about, 120–121
Domiciliary administrator, 6
"Domiciliary" executor, meaning of, 2, 2*n*
Dower and curtesy, 213
Draftsmanship, problems created or avoidable by, 12
Drugs and medicines in office of medical decedent, particular problem of for executor, 60
Durand, 298*n*
Duty of executor to discover all decedent's assets, 45

Dying during administration, recompense to representative of executor, 263

E

Earl & Middleditch, 97*n*
Early audit of decedent's income tax returns, request for, 116
  of estate's returns, 116–117
Ehrenzweig, 38*n*, 136*n*, 184*n*, 294*n*, 295*n*, 297*n*, 299*n*
"80% credit" for state death taxes, allowance of, 129
Election by spouse to take statutory share, 213–218 (see also "Statutory share, election by spouse to take")
Elections, 139–144 (see also "Options and elections")
Elliott v. Western Coal & Min. Co., 161*n*, 191*n*
Employees of decedent, domestic and personal executor's responsibility concerning, 87
Encumbrance, property subject to, ademption of specific legacy regarding, 155–156
  business obligations specifically bequeathed, 156
Encumbrances upon decedent's property, 54
  on devise, 199–200
Equitable allocation, principle of in distribution of assets from residuary estate, 236
Erieg Est., 133*n*
Errors in judgment and negligence, difference between, 16–17
Est. of Baumgartner, 28*n*, 259*n*
Est. of Bernstein, 149*n*
Est. of Binswanger, 20*n*, 290*n*
Est. of Brush et al., 281*n*
Est. of Currier, 31*n*, 183*n*
Est. of Forsheim, 137*n*
Est. of McNeel, 126*n*
Est. of Moffat, 103*n*
Est. of Pearson, 214*n*
Est. of Reisinger, 151*n*, 161*n*, 209*n*
Est. of Rubin, 100*n*
Est. of Schneider, 295*n*
Est. of Strupp, 296*n*
Est. of Wright, 148*n*, 149*n*
Estate, meaning of, 7–8
  income taxes of, 115–116
  non-probate, 7
  not entity, 7–8
  probate, 7
  and "taxable estate," difference between, 7
  testamentary, 7
Estate Administration and Accounting, 210*n*, 228*n*
Estate Administration Expenses—Shall They Be Taken as Income or Estate Tax Deductions? 140*n*
Estate and inheritance taxes, 120–138
  apportionment and waivers, 130–138
    in general, 130–131
    inheritance taxes, 131–132
    residue, insufficiency of, 137
    within residue, 133
    retention or recovery of shares, 134–137
      (see also "Apportionment of taxes")
    waivers and consents to transfer, 137–138
    will, direction in regarding, 132–133

INDEX 325

Estate and inheritance taxes (*cont.*)
  in general; payment, 120–129
    credit against Federal tax for state tax paid, establishment of, 129
    discounts and additions to tax, 126–127
    domicile and right to tax, contest about, 120–121
    executor, personal liability of for tax, 128–129
    notices and returns, 121–122
    payment, 122–126 (see also "Payment of estate and inheritance taxes")
    postponement of payment, 127–128
    preliminary investigations, 121–122
    priority, 120
    state tax, additional, to utilize state Federal credit, 129
Estate Planning, 11*n*, 24*n*
Estate Planning Comes to Puerto Rico, 220*n*
Estate tax apportionment of devise, 203
Estate taxes recouped as part of residuary estate, 224–225
Estates Practice Guide, 228*n*
Evelyn Hickok, 47*n*
Examination of will, 26
"Excessive" or "late" gifts to charity, rights of surviving spouse or children to attack, 220
Exculpatory provisions in will, 22, 90
Execution, formalities of in different jurisdictions, 294–295
Execution requirements, law and, 293–294
Executor, agreement by for counsel's fee, 257
Executor, basic duties and responsibilities of, 13–23
  advice and assistance, 14–15
  advice of counsel, reliance on, 22–23
  care, diligence and prudence, 13
  confidentiality, 18
  delegation, 15
    to co-executor, 15
  discretionary powers, 14
  exculpatory provisions, 22
  impartiality and conflicts of interest, 18–21
    of beneficiaries, 19–20
    of creditors, 19
    of executor's attorney, 21
    executor's own, 20 (see also "Interest, executor's conflicts of")
  insurer, liability as, 17–18
    of third person participating, 18
  negligence, 16–17
    and errors of judgment, difference between, 16–17
    in general, 16
    speculation, 16
    surcharge, 17
    waste, 16
Executor, bequest to *eo nomine*, 174–175
Executor, checklist of duties of, 310–314
  supplementary for real property, 315–316
Executor, compensation of, 260–266
  assets includible in commissions base, 264–265
    uncollected, 265
  assignment of, 266
  basis, rate and amount, 261–263
    executor dying, resigning or removed during administration, 263
    legacy in lieu of compensation, 262
    service without compensation, will providing for, 262
    specification in will, 261–262
    waiver of compensation, 262–263
  of co-executors, 265–266
    agreement; waiver by one, 265–266
  commissions on principal and income, 264
  denial of compensation to, 266
  in general, 260–261
  time of payment, allowance or approval for, 263–264
    premature payment, 264
Executor, death, resignation or removal of, 278–280
  accounts of and, 284
  death, 278
  removal, 279
  resignation, 278–279
  successors, appointment of, 279–280
    powers and responsibilities, 280
Executor, exact meaning of, 2
  and administrator, comparison of, 6–7
  "domiciliary," 2, 2*n*
  "independent," 2
  literary, 3
  "preliminary," 2–3
  primary, 3
  substituted or successor, 3
Executor, liabilities of in insolvent estates, 243–244
Executor, personal claim of, 109
Executor, personal liability of for payment of debts, 104
  for tax, 128–129
Executor, qualification of, 40–42 (see also "Probate of will and qualification of executor")
  bond, 41
  disqualification, 42
  letters testamentary, 41–42
  "short-form certificate," meaning of, 42
Executor, responsibility of in constructive trusts, 300–301
Executor as attorney, 260
Executor and trustee, same person as, 285–286
  functions of distinguished, 303–304
Executor's decision to accept appointment, 26–27
  in general, 26
  ineligibility, 27
  renunciation, 27
Executory contracts of decedent, handling of, 89
  equitable conversion, 89–90
"Exempt" property, executor's responsibility to obtain possession and control of, 66
  and allowances not part of residuary estate, 223
  insolvent estate and, 253
Exercise of Elections by Personal Representatives, 139*n*
Expenses, availability of specific legacy for, 156
  construction of will and, 277
Expenses payable out of income, 207–208
  alteration of rules by will, 208
  in general, 207
  interest on debts and legacies, 208
  net income, attempts to define, 208
Expenses of settling accounts, 289–290
  of keeping records and preparing account, 289–290

F

Fact of death, establishment of, 30–31
"Facts of independent significance," doctrine of, 149n
Failure of executor to render account, 289
Familiarization with affairs, executor's duty of, 46
Family allowance, meaning of, 212
Federal government, debt of decedent to, 246
Federal taxes, priority of over State taxes, 245
Fees and compensation as administration expenses, 255–267 (see also "Administration expenses")
Fees due to professional, particular problem of collection of for executor, 61
Fetrow's Est., 8n
Fiduciary, decedent's commissions as, determining, 50
Fiduciary elections, 143
Fiduciary relationship of executor to beneficiaries impossible without proper care, diligence and prudence, 13
Final accounting, time of for questions of construction of will, 276
Final accounts of executor, 283–284
 definition of, 283n
Firearms as part of decedent's estate, disposition of by executor, 68
First Trust & Sav. Bank v. Henderson, 74n
Fiske v. Warner, 219n
Fleming v. Yeazel, 174n
Flomenhoft, 61n
"Forced heirship" rules of Louisiana, 199, 213, 220–221
Foreign creditors, acknowledging claims of, 107–108
Foreign state or country, payment of death taxes in, 125–126
 direction in will, effect of, 126
"Foreign will," execution of, 62–63
Forgiveness of debt and bequest to debtor, relationship between, 173
Formula clauses for "marital deduction" legacies, 163
 administrative problems under, 164–165
 non-qualifying assets, 165–166
 nature of, importance of determining, 164
Forwarding of decedent's mail, 45–46
Forzio, 158n
Fox, 150n
Fraction of assets, legacy of, 196
"Fraction" formula for "marital deduction" legacy, 163
Fractional Share Marital Deduction Gifts, 165n, 235n
Fraud of decedent in income tax returns, 114–115
French v. Short, 295n, 296n
Frick v. Pennsylvania, 120n
Fulrath, 59n, 61n
Funeral arrangements, provisions for in will, 28–29
Funeral expenses, debts and claims, 99–112
 charitable pledges of decedent, 112
 claims, presentation and consideration of, 104–108
 allowance or rejection, 105–106
 creditors, notice to, 105
 executor, personal claim of, 109
 of foreign creditors, 107–108
 limitations, statute of, claims barred by, 107
 proof of, 106–107
 time for payment of, 108
 time of presentation, limitation on, 104–105
 compromise of claims, 111
 acceptance by creditor, 111
 debts and claims, 101–104 (see also "Claims on estate . . .")
 of business 102–103
 direction in will, effect of, 103
 executor, personal liability of for payment, 104
 life insurance policy loans, 103
 secured debts, 102–103
 unmatured or unliquidated liabilities, 101–102
 funeral expenses in general, 99–101
 amount, 100–101
 governmental funeral allowance, 101
 items included, 100
 interest on debts and claims, 109
 liability of decedent as fiduciary, 111
 legal life tenant, 111–112
 payment of claims, source of, 110
 counterclaims, 110
 property subject to power of appointment, 110
 will, provision in, 110
 priority of, 245
 taxes and administration expenses, 99

G

General legacies, 145, 160–162
 ademption by satisfaction, 161–162
 definition, 160–161
 misunderstandings about, 147n
 securities, legacy of, 161
General legacies, income from, 209
 in trust, 209–210
 payment to trustee or beneficiary, 210
General legacies, insolvent estate and, 250
 for specific purpose, 250
 marital deduction legacy, 250
"General release" without account, 285
Gesner v. Roberts, 130n
Gift taxes, 118–119
 in general, 118
 past, 119
 in quarter of death and preceding quarter, 118–119
Gifts allegedly made by decedent, determining validity of questionable, 57–58
Gilman v. Bell, 252n
Gold coins as part of decedent's estate, disposition of by executor, 68
"Good faith" and lack of negligence, difference in meaning of, 16–17, 16n
Goodrich & Scoles, 38n, 104n, 212n, 295n, 298n
Government bonds, United States, executor's obtaining possession and control of, 71–72
 applicable at par on Federal estate tax, 71–72
 redeemable at par, 72
Governmental funeral allowance, 101

INDEX

"Greeley formula" for computation of taxes, 131*n*
Grieb v. Commr., 128*n*, 243*n*
Guardian of incompetent, sale of property by, ademption of specific legacy regarding, 154

H

Hardship cases, reason for provision for postponement of tax payment, 128
Harris, 228*n*
Hathaway v. Sherman, 226*n*
Hays v. Jackson, 254*n*
Hays v. Nat. Surety Co., 281*n*
Heirs as necessary party to construction of will, 276–277
Hendrickson, 37*n*, 297*n*
Herterich, 298*n*
Hirning v. Webb, 161*n*, 191*n*
History and Antiquities of the Exchequer of the Kings of England, 293*n*
Hodgkinson v. Hodgkinson, 73*n*
Hogan v. Curtin, 43*n*
Home or office, assessing contents of, 48–49
Homestead allowance, 212
"Honorary trusts," 172
Hoskold's formula for valuing patents and copyrights, 97*n*

I

Identification of assets by executor, 46
Identification of legatees, 179–182
  illegitimate or adopted children as "issue," 181–182
Identification of property bequeathed by specific legacy, 148
  "all personal property," bequest of, 151
  "all tangibles," bequest of, 150–151
  coin or stamp collections, works of art, etc., 150
  contents of box, room, etc., 149
  corporate stock after capital changes, 151–152
  nature of, description by, 149–150
  provenance or location, description by, 148–149
Illegitimate children as "issue," consideration of for legacy, 181–182
Immediate Pre-Mortem Check-list, 11*n*
Impartiality of executor, 18–21 (see also "Interest, executor's conflicts of")
Implied by Law Revocation of Wills, 34*n*
In re Barry's Est., 154*n*
In re Bierstedt's Est., 201*n*
In re Casey's Est., 131*n*
In re Clark's Est., 281*n*
In re Day's Trust, 182*n*
In re Dorrance's Est., 121*n*
In re Durston's Will, 21*n*
In re Gallagher's Est., 295*n*, 299*n*
In re Koster's Will, 56*n*
In re Mason's Est., 201*n*
In re McCutcheon's Est., 216*n*
In re New York Life Ins. Co., 298*n*
In re Rawnsley's Est., 191*n*
In re Robbins' Est., 21*n*

In re Wenmoth's Est., 186*n*
In terrorem clauses, 43–44
Income, 204–211 (see also "Principal and income")
Income, insolvent estate and, 252–253
Income from date of death, on specific legacy, 152–153
Income during period of administration, 206–207
Income received by executor, 206–207
  accruals after death, 206–207
Income taxation, administrative elections concerning, 142–143
Income taxes, 113–117
  closing agreement, 117
  early audit of decedent's returns, request for, 116–117
    of estate's returns, 116–117
  estate, taxes of, 115–116
  failure of decedent to file returns, 115
  final return of decedent, 113–114
  fraud of decedent, 114–115
  joint return with spouse, 113–114
    division of tax on, 114
  prior returns, examination of, 46, 114
  priority of payment, 113
Incompetent and possibly incompetent legatees, 179
Indemnification agreements, 272
"Independent" executor, meaning of, 2
Ineligibility of appointed executor to act, 27
Infant legatees not permitted to receive legacy, 176–178
  management, powers of during minority, 177–178
  parent or another, will provision for payment to, 177
Inferred death, probating will in cases of, 30–31
Informational and definitive accounting distinguished, 282
Informing spouse of right to elect against decedent's will, 217–218
Inheritance taxes, apportionment of, 131–132
  recouped as part of residuary estate, 224–225
Insolvent or insufficient estates, 242–254
  appointive property, 252
  charges and expenses, 244–247
    administration expenses, 244
    debts of decedent, 245–247 (see also "Debts of decedent, priority of")
    funeral expenses, 245
    in general, 244
    taxes, 245
  executor, liabilities of, 243–244
  "exempt" property and allowances, 253
  income, 252–253
  intestate property, 253–254
  legacies and devises, 247–252
    demonstrative, 250–251
    devises, common law and, 248 (see also "Legacies and devises of insolvent estates")
    general, 250 (see also "Legacies and devises of insolvent estate")
    in general, 247–248
    residuary legacies, 249–250 (see also "Legacies and devices of insolvent estate")
    specific, 251–252 (see also "Legacies and

Insolvent or insufficient estates (*cont.*)
    devises of insolvent estate")
      priority and abatement, 243
      Totten trust, 253
      when, 242–243
Insurance, liability and casualty, on real property, 74–75
Insurance payable to estate, collection of, 51–52
Insurance proceeds, ademption of specific legacy concerning, 154–155
Insurance on tangible personal property of decedent, 67
Insurer, executor's liability as, 17–18
    of third person participating, 18
Interest, executor's conflicts of, 18–21
    of beneficiaries, 19–20
    of creditors, 19
    of executor's attorney, 21
    of his own, 20
      as creditor or beneficiary, 20
      as debtor, 21
      self-dealing, 21
Interest on apportioned share of taxes, 136–137
Interest on debts and claims, 109
Interest on debts and legacies, question of payment from income or principal, 208
Interest on estate or inheritance tax deficiency, 124
Interest payable on cash legacies, 192–193
Intermediate and final accounts of executor, 283–284
    definition of, 283*n*
Intestacy, partial, 238
Intestate property, insolvent estate and, 253–254
    law and, 299
Inventory value of assets, determining, 91–98
    (see also "Valuation of assets")
    basis and determination, 92–93
    statutory inventory and appraisal, 93
Investment advisory account, opening of by executor, 69
    corporate executor, exception of, 70
    registration in nominee's name, 70–71
Investment of estate's moneys, executor's responsibility for, 82–83
"Iron curtain" countries, persons in not permitted to receive legacies, 178
Is an Unrealized Contingent Fee an Asset of a Deceased Illinois Attorney's Estate? 61*n*
"Issue," meaning of, 8–9
Iverson, 300*n*

J

"Jeopardy" assessment by Internal Revenue Service, 116*n*
Joint bank accounts, 56
Joint income tax return of decedent with spouse, 113–114
    division of tax on, 114
Joint ownership and survivorship interests, handling of, 55
Joint will, 35
Judgment, errors in, and negligence, difference between, 16–17
Judicial review of administration expenses, 267
Judicial or voluntary settlement of accounts, 284–285 (see also "Settlement of accounts...")
    "general release" without account, 285
Jurisdictions, different, laws of, 294–299
    (see also "What law governs")
    construction and interpretation, 298–299
    formalities of execution, 294–295
    in general, 294
    personal property, 296–298
      administrative powers and duties, 297–298
      direction that law of nondomiciliary state governs, 296–297
      in general, 296
    power of appointment, effectiveness of exercise of, 298
    real property, 295
Jurisdiction, other, property of decedent in, 61–63
    separate will, disposition of property by, 62–63

K

Kilcoyne v. Reilly, 217*n*, 251*n*
Kin, next of, as necessary party to construction of will, 276–277
Kinds of property, relationship of residuary clause to, 223–227
    appointive property, 226–227
    estate and inheritance taxes recouped, 224–225
    "exempt" property and allowances, 223
    lapsed, renounced and revoked legacies and other dispositions, 223–224
      "bank account trust," 224
      revocation or ineffectiveness by operation of law, 224
    life insurance payable to estate, 225–226
      testamentary trustee, payable to, 226
    preliminary statement, 223
    real property, 225
      cemetery lots, 225

L

Lacy v. Murdock, 186*n*
Lamb Est., 149*n*
Land, 296*n*, 298*n*, 299*n*
Land, legacies charged on, 166–167
    specific devise, charge on, 166–167
Lapse of legacy, 145, 146–147, 183–185
    non-lapse statutes, 184–185
Lapsed legacy devise as part of residuary estate, 223–224
    revocation or ineffectiveness by operation of law, 224
Lare's Est., 82*n*
Larendon Est., 175*n*
Last illness, payment of expenses of, 246
"Last" will, determination of, 32–35
    dependent relative revocation, 34
    joint will, 35
    other will or codicil, failure to discover, 33
    revocation of later will and "revival," 33–34
    revocation other than by later will or destruction, 34
Later discovery of will, danger of, 24
Lauritzen, 189*n*

INDEX

Law, what governs, 292–299
  execution requirements, 293–294
  in general, 292–293
  intestate property, 299
  as between laws of different jurisdictions, 294–299
    construction and interpretation, 298–299
    formalities of execution, 294–295
    in general, 294
    personal property, 296–298 (see also "Personal property in different jurisdictions, law governing")
    power of appointment, effectiveness of exercise of, 298
    real property, 295
  as between laws in force at different times, 293–294
    administrative powers, 294
  problems as to character of ownership distinguished, 293
Law of the domicile, matters relating to personal property governed by, 297
Lawyers, particular responsibilities of executors regarding estates of, 58–60
Leach, 168*n*
Leases and possessory claims upon decedent's property, 53–54
Leflar, 38*n*, 136*n*, 295*n*, 296*n*, 298*n*, 299*n*
Legacies, classification of, 145
  in trust, conditional and deferred, 145
Legacies, satisfaction of, 145–196
  abatement, ademption, lapse, 145–147
  annuity, direction or authorization to purchase, 170–171
  assignments by legatees, 190
  cash legacy, satisfaction of in property, 188–190
    marital deduction legacy, 189–190
  charitable, 171–172
    cy pres, doctrine of, 171–172
    "honorary trusts," 172
  class gifts, 185–187
    ascertainment of, 186
    convenience, rule of, 186
    non-lapse statute, applicability of, 187
    what are, 185–186
  condition precedent, legacy subject to, 167–168
  conditions subsequent, 168
  construction questions, 195
    perpetuities problems, 195
  creditor, bequest to, 172–173
  debtor, bequest to, 173
    set-off or retainer, right of, 173–174
  deferred, 168–170
    administrative problems, 169–170
    and trust distinguished, 169
  demonstrative, 159–160
    ademption, 160
    availability of fund for charges and expenses, 160
    bank account, bequest of distinguished, 160
    definition, 159
    general legacy to extent fund insufficient, 160
  to executor *eo nomine*, 174–175
  general, 160–162
    ademption by satisfaction, 161–162
    definition, 160–161
    securities, legacy of, 161
  incompetent and possibly incompetent legatees, 179
  land, as available for payment of, 166–167, 203
    specific devise, charge on, 166–167
  lapse, 183–185
    non-lapse statutes, 184–185
  legal representative of afterdying legatee, payment to, 194
  legatees not capable of taking, 175–176
    charitable or religious corporation, 176
    person responsible for death of decedent, 175–176
    subscribing witness, 175
    unincorporated associations, 175
  legatees not permitted to receive, 176–178
    in general, 176
    infant, 176–178 (see also "Infant legatees not permitted to receive legacy")
    "iron curtain" countries, persons in, 178
  life estates, 168
  location and identification of legatees, 179–182
    illegitimate or adopted children as "issue," 181–182
    inability to locate, 181
  "marital deduction" legacies, 163–166
    formula clauses, 163 (see also "Formula clauses . . .")
    in general, 163
  pour-over, 187
  principles, general, 145–162
    classification in general, 145 (see also "Legacies, classification of")
  problems, special, 163–196 (see also under particular problem)
  renunciation or disclaimer of legacy, 187–188
    of intestate share, 188
  residuary legacies, 162
  revocation by later instrument or by law, 194–195
  satisfaction in lifetime, 190–191
  of share or fraction, 190
  simultaneous payments or distributions, duty of, 193–194
  specific legacies, 145, 146, 147–159
    ademption, 146, 153–155 (see also "Specific legacies")
    availability for debts and expenses, 156
    body or organs, bequest or disposition of, 158–159
    definition, 147–148
    distribution, letter or memo concerning, 156–157 (see also "Distribution . . .")
    division among legatees, 157–158
    encumbrance, property subject to, 155–156
    identification of property bequeathed, 148–152 (see also "Identification of property bequeathed by specific legacy")
    income from date of death, 152–153
    misunderstandings about term, 147*n*
    tangibles, delivery of, 158
    "as is, where is"rule, 158
  survivorship, doubt as to, 182–183
    "common disaster" provisions of will, 182–183
  taxes, estate and inheritance, 196
    apportionment, 196
  time of payment or satisfaction, 191–193

Legacies, satisfaction of (*cont.*)
    interest on cash legacies, 192–193
    partial, 192
    trusts, establishment of, 193
    vesting of title to legacy, 147
Legacies and devises of insolvent estate, 247–252
    demonstrative, 250–251
    devises, common law rules and, 248
        statutory changes, 248–249
    general, 250
        marital deduction legacy, 250
        for specified purpose, 250
    in general, 247–248
    residuary legacies, 249–250
        of amount out of residue, 249–250
    specific, 251–252
        charged on specific devise, 251–252
Legacy, meaning of, 8
    in lieu of compensation for executor, 262
Legal life tenant, decedent as, 57, 111–112
Legal representative, meaning of, 1
Legatee, after-dying, payment of legacy to, 194
Legatees incapable of taking legacy, 175–176
    charitable or religious corporation, 176
    person responsible for death of decedent, 175–176
    subscribing witness, 175
    unincorporated associations, 175
Legatees not permitted to receive legacy, 176–178
    in general, 176
    infant, 176–177
        management, powers of during minority, 177–178
        parent or another, will provision for payment to, 177
    "iron curtain" countries, 178
Legitime, civil law concept of as basis for "forced heirship" in Louisiana, 199, 213, 220–221
Letters of administration, 8
"Letters patent," as historical origin of letters testamentary and of administration, 8
Letters testamentary, 8, 41–42
Levenfeld, 77n, 143n
Lewis, 139n
Lewis v. Hill, 201n
Liability of decedent as fiduciary, 111
    legal life tenant, 111–112
Liabilities, unmatured or unliquidated, satisfaction of, 101–102
Liability, exculpation from, 90
Liability of executor as insurer, 17–18
    of third person participating, 18
Liability insurance on decedent's real property, 73–74
Life-Death in Human Transplantation, 31
Life insurance payable to estate as part of residuary estate, 225–226
    testamentary trustee, payable to, 226
Limbaugh, 59n, 61n
Limitations, statute of, claims barred by, 107
Limitations inherent in administration, 10–11
Liquidation of assets, 76–82
    borrowing, 78
    cash requirements, list of, 76
    corporate stock, redemption of, 77–78
    for distribution, 78–79

"divided loyalty rule," 80
officer or director of corporation, 80
retention or distribution in kind, 81
sale to executor or beneficiary, 79
of unauthorized or unsuitable investment, 81–82
Literary executor, definition of, 3
"Literary property," value of copyright in, 97–98
Litigation, collection of apportioned taxes by, 135–136
Location of legatees, 179–182
    illegitimate or adopted children as "issue," 181–182
    inability to locate, 181
Lohm's Est., 13n, 23n, 122n, 256n, 266n
Low v. Bankers Trust Co., 110n

M

Management, powers of during infant's minority, 177–178
Marcus, 230n
Margin accounts of decedent, executor's responsibiliy to terminate, 68–69
"Marital deduction" legacies, 163–166
    formula clauses, 163
        administrative problems under, 164–165
        nature of, importance of determining, 164
    in general, 163
Marriage, dissolution of since execution of will, 218
Marriage of testator, revoking effect of on will, 34
Matter of Allan, 216n
Matter of Arrowsmith, 43n
Matter of Badenhausen, 287n
Matter of Baker, 253n
Matter of Becker, 270n
Matter of Begent, 245n
Matter of Buda, 155n
Matter of Byrnes, 217n, 251n
Matter of Clark, 214n, 295n, 296n
Matter of Columbia Tr. Co., 158n
Matter of Cramm, 155n, 201n
Matter of Curley, 22n, 281n
Matter of Deneff, 56n
Matter of Dimond, 180n
Matter of Faber, 277n
Matter of Flint, 173n
Matter of Fogarty, 199n
Matter of Foster, 65n, 194n, 234n
Matter of Frothingham, 264n
Matter of Geiger, 174n
Matter of Hall, 271n
Matter of Heller-Baghero, 37n
Matter of Kaufman, 87n
Matter of Kennedy, 141n
Matter of Krycun, 56n
Matter of Leikind, 178n
Matter of Lipsit, 21n
Matter of Lupoff, 135n
Matter of Mescall, 218n
Matter of Meyers, 241n
Matter of Miles, 286n
Matter of Moore, 175n
Matter of Morgan Guaranty Trust Co., 298n
Matter of Muller, 87n

INDEX

Matter of O'Rourke, 253n
Matter of Riegel, 154n
Matter of Roschelle, 217n
Matter of Rubenstein, 147n
Matter of Shubert, 133n
Matter of Strasenburgh, 147n
Matter of Totten, 56n
Matter of Tuttle, 290n
Matter of Warms, 141n
Matter of Watson, 87n
Matter of Wright, 264n
McGovern's Est., 281n
Medicines in office of medical decedent, particular problem of for executor, 60
Meinhard v. Salmon, 20n
Mineral interests, valuation of, 97
Mintz Trust, 22n
Mobilia personam sequuntur, doctrine of re personal property, 296
Model Small Estates Act, 44n
Monetary claim, inapplicability of discovery proceedings, 63
Money, handling of by executor, 82–84
    investments, making productive, 82–83
    unproductive property, sale of, 83–84
Moot questions, application for construction of will and, 277
Mortgages on real property as asset of estate, valuation of, 94
Multi-State Estate, 62n, 214n, 305n

N

Narcotics in decedent's estate, disposition of by executor, 60, 68
Nature of property bequeathed, identification by description of, 149–150
Necessary parties for construction of will, 276–277
    heirs or next of kin, 276–277
Negligence, lack of, and "good faith," difference in meaning of, 16–17, 16n
Negligence of executor, 16–17
    and errors of judgment, difference between, 16–17
    in general, 16
    speculation, 16
    surcharge, 17
    waste, 16
Net income, attempts of will to define, 208
Net income, disposition of, 208–211
    general legacies, 209
        in trust, 209–210
    from specific legacies and devises, 208–209
    surplus income, 210–211
Newman v. Dore, 215n
"1931 Act," Uniform Principal and Income Act, 205n
"1962 Act," 205n
Nominee of executor, transfer of stock and registered securities to, 70–71
Non-fiduciary elections, 143–144
"Non-intervention" will, meaning of, 2
Non-lapse statute, "class gift" legacy and, 187
Non-probate assets, valuation of by executor, 91

Non-probate estate, 7
Non-qualifying assets under formulae for "marital deduction" legacy, 165–166
Non-resident, determining place of probate for, 36–38
    ancillary probate, 38
    jurisdiction to tax not affected, 37
    statutes requiring original probate at domicile, 37–38
Non-testamentary assets, 7
Notice to creditors, publication of by executor, 105

O

Objections to executor's account, 286
    by fewer than all beneficiaries affected, 287
    rejected or unpaid claim, determination on, 287
Obligations of estate, unmatured or unliquidated, satisfaction of, 101–102
Office, ascertaining and preserving assets of, 48–49
Oil, gas and mineral interests, devise of, 198–199
    "forced heirship" rules of Louisiana, 199, 213, 220–221
    valuation of, 97
Open-market securities, ademption of specific legacy of, 153–154
Options and elections, 139–144
    deductions for estate or income tax, claiming, 140–141
    elections, administrative, affecting income taxation, 142–143
    in general, 139
    non-fiduciary elections, 143–144
    optional valuation date, estate tax, 139–140
    other fiduciary, 143
    Subchapter S corporations, 143
    United States savings bonds, increment on, 141–142
Order of distribution, necessity for, 233
Organs of body, bequest or disposition of, 158–159
Osgood, 230n
Out-of-pocket disbursements as administration expense, 266–267

P

Papers, collection of, 45–64 (see also "Assets and papers, collection of")
Parent of legatee, will provision for payment to, 177
Partial distribution of residuary assets, 233–234
Partial payments to counsel, 258–259
Partial satisfaction of legacy, 192
Partnership interests of decedent, executor's responsibility concerning, 86–87
Passive trust, constructive trust as, 300
Patents, valuation of, 97–98
Payment, source of for administration expenses, 255–256
Payment of claim and allowance of claim, distinguishing between, 106
Payment of claims, source of, 110
    counterclaims, 110
    property subject to power of appointment, 110

Payment of claims, source of (cont.)
   will, provision in, 110
Payment of claims, time for, 108
Payment of estate and inheritance taxes, 122–126
   deficiency assessments, 123–124
      foreign state or country, death taxes of, 125–126
         direction in will, effect of, 126
      in general, 122
      initial payment, source of, 122–123
         apportionable shares, 134–135
      interest and penalties, 124
      postponement of, 127–128
      premature payment, 123
      testamentary assets, insufficiency of, 124–125
      time, 122
Payments of legacy, executor's duty for, 193–194
"Pecuniary" formula for "marital deduction" legacy, 163
Penalty for estate or inheritance tax deficiency, 124
Perpetuities problems in construction of bequest, 195
Person's App., 191n
Personal profit from estate not allowed to executor, 21
Personal property, determining joint tenancy of, 55–56
   bank account trusts and revocation, 56–57
   joint bank accounts, 56
   United States Savings Bonds, 57
Personal property, tangible, valuation of, 93–94
   "exempt" property, 94
Personal property in different jurisdictions, law governing 296–298
   administrative powers and duties, 297–298
   direction that law of nondomiciliary state governs, 296–297
   in general, 296
Personal representative, meaning of, 1
Persons to receive notice of probate, 39
Peschel, 139n
Pet. of Mazurowski, 178n
Pfau v. Moseley, 295n
Physicians, particular responsibilities of executors regarding estates of, 60
Place of probate, determining, 36
Planning for Administration of Estates and Trusts, 152n
Planning Against Simultaneous Death, 183n
Planning Wills for Nonresidents, 35n, 37n, 297n
Plural wills, problem of in case of "foreign will," 62–63
Policy loan on life insurance as debt claim on estate, 103
Porzio, 30n, 31n
Postdeath Marital Deduction Planning, 139n
Postdeath Planning, 77n, 143n
"Post mortem planning," meaning of, 139
Postmortem Estate Planning Up to Date, 76n, 77n, 113n, 139n, 142n, 187n, 189n, 214n
Postponement of payment of taxes, 126–127
"Pour-over" bequest, residuary estate and, 230–231
   and testamentary trust distinguished, 304–305
Pour-over legacies, 187
Pour-Over Provisions and Estate Planning, 230n
Powell, 213n

"Power in trust" of executor for infant, 177–178
Precatory provisions of will, seeking construction of, 274–275
"Preliminary" executor, meaning of, 2–3
Premature payment of estate and inheritance taxes, 123
Premature payment of executor's compensation, 264
Prematurity of application for construction of will, 277
Pre-probate responsibilities, 24–29
   assets, power and duty to protect, 27–28
      examination of, 26
   executor's decision to accept appointment, 26–27
      in general, 26
      ineligibility, 27
      renunciation, 27
   funeral arrangements, 28–29
   in general, 24
   production of will, 25–26
      concealment of, 26
      delivery to another, 25
      in general, 25
      offer for probate, 25
   search for will, 24
      later discovery, peril of, 24
Pre-probate services of counsel, payment for, 259
Pres. and Directors of Manhattan Co. v. Janowitz, 231n
Prescott v. Wordell, 252n
Presumed death, probating will in cases of, 30–31
Price, 76n, 77n, 113n, 139n, 142n, 187n, 189n, 214n
"Primary" executor, definition of, 3
Principal and income, 204–211
   expenses payable out of income, 207–208
      alteration of rules by will, 208
      in general, 207
      interest on debts and legacies, 208
      net income, attempts to define, 208
   expenses payable out of principal, 211
   income, definition of, 205
      capital gains and losses, 205–206
   income received by executor, 206–207
      accruals after death, 206–207
   net income, disposition of, 208–211
      general legacies, 209 (see also "General legacies, income from")
      from specific legacies and devises, 208–209
      and surplus income, distinction between, 210–211
   separate ascertainment, need for, 204–205
   tax and accounting computations distinguished, 204
Prior income tax returns of decedent, examination of, 114
Priority of payments in insolvent estates, 243
Probate Decrees and Estates, 35n
Probate estate, 7
   assets within as responsibility of executor to value, 91
"Probate of heirship," meaning of, 39
Probate of will and qualification of executor, 30–44
   contests, 43–44
      in terrorem provisions, 43–44

INDEX 333

Probate of will (*cont.*)
   domicile and place of probate, determination of, 35–36
      importance of determining, 36
      problems, 35–36
   executor, qualification of, 40–44
      bond, 41
      disqualification, 42
      letters testamentary, 41–42
      "short-form certificate," 42
   fact of death, establishment of, 30–31
   in general, 38–39
   "last" will, determination of, 32–35
      dependent relative revocation, 34
      joint will, 35
      other will or codicil, failure to discover, 33
      revocation of later will and "revival," 33–34
      revocation other than by later will or destruction, 34
   of non-resident, 36–38
      ancillary probate, 38
      jurisdiction to tax not affected, 37
      statutes requiring original probate at domicile, 37–38
   persons to receive notice, 39
   place of, determining, 36
   "probate of heirship" distinguished, 39
   provisions, review of, 42–43
   "small estates" statutes, 44
   temporary administration, 39–40
      powers of, 40
   time of death, ascertaining, 31–32
      at domicile, 32
      standard or daylight time, 32
Proceeding for instructions, 274
Professional men, collecting assets and papers of, 58–61
   accountants, 61
   fees, collection of, 61
   lawyers, 58–60
   physicians and surgeons, 60
Promptness required of executor in distribution of residuary estate, 232–233
Proof of claim upon estate, 106–107
Property passing under residuary clause, 222–231 (see also "Residuary estate, ascertainment and distribution of")
Proprietorship, protecting assets of, 49
   of decedent, responsibility of executor concerning, 86–87
   valuation of, 96–97
Provisions of will, review of, 42–43
Public policy, inability of beneficiaries to condone acts against, 269–270

Q

Qualification of executor, 40–42 (see also "Probate of will and qualification of executor")
Qualification of testamentary trustee, determining, 303
Questions regarding governing law, 292–299 (see also "Law, what governs")

R

Ratable distribution of bonds, stocks and securities from residuary estate, 235–236
Re Hall's Est., 254n
Re Will of Moody, 175n
Real Property, 213n
Real property, executor's obtaining possession and control of, 72–75
   cemetery lots, 75
   checklist, supplementary, for, 315–316
   insurance, liability and casualty, 74–75
   jurisdiction, in other, 75
   rents, collection of, 73
   sale of, 73–74
Real property, valuation of, 94
   mortgages, 94
Real property of decedent, 53–55
   encumbrances, 54
   executory contracts of purchase or sale, 54–55
   leases and possessory claims, 53–54
Real property in another state, establishing title to, 203
Real property as part of residuary estate, 225
   cemetery lots, 225
Real property in different jurisdiction, law concerning, 295
Receivables of decedent, determining, 50
   accruals from fiduciaries, 50
   compromise, 51
Recent Statutory Trends in the Law of Trusts, 71n, 230n
Reciprocal statutes, requirement of for out-of-state executors, 27
Records and accounts, settlement of, 281–291
   accountability, 281
   accounts, 282–283
      definitive and informational distinguished, 282
      disclosure, 283
      in general, 282
      intermediate and final, 283–284
      scope of, and disclosure, 282–283
      time for, 283–284
   compulsory accountings, 289
   decedent as fiduciary or life tenant, accounting in respect of, 291
   discharge of executor from liability or from office, 290–291
   expenses of settling account, 289–290
      of preparing account and keeping records, 289–290
   records, 282
   settlement of accounts, 284–289
      effect of, 287–289 (see also "Settlement of accounts by executor")
      failure to make, 289
      in general, 284
      judicial or voluntary, 284–285 (see also "Settlement of accounts by executor")
      objections to account, 286 (see also "Objections to executor's account")
      parties, 285–286 (see also "Settlement of accounts by executor")
   "small" estates, 291
Recover apportioned shares of taxes, inability to, 136

Reiff's Est., 74n
Religious corporation, inability of to receive legacy, 176
Removal of executor, 278–280 (see also "Executor, death, resignation or removal of")
Removed during administration, executor, compensation to, 263
Renounced legacy devise as part of residuary estate, 223–224
Rented home or apartment, of decedent, determining, 49–50
   responsibility of executor regarding, 87–88
      cooperative or condominium, 88
Rents, collection of by executor, 73
   as belonging to devisee, 201–202
      availability for charges, expenses and legacies, 202
Renunciation of appointment as executor, 27
Renunciation of devisee, 202–203
Renunciation of legacy, 187–188
   of intestate share, 188
Republic Natl. Bank of Dallas, 141n
Residuary estate, apportionment of taxes within, 133
   payment "as expense" distinguished, 133–134
Residuary estate, ascertainment and distribution of, 222–241
   distribution problems, 232–241
      advancements, 239
      after-acquired or after-discovered property, 240
      assignment by legatee, 238–239 (see also "Distribution problems of residuary estate")
      in cash or in kind, 234–236 (see also "Distribution problems of residuary estate")
      in general, 232–233
      lapse of residuary legacy, 236–237 (see also "Distribution problems of residuary estate")
      necessity of order of, 233
      partial, 233–234
      partial intestacy, 238
      prolongation of administration, 241
      satisfaction in lifetime, 239
      worthless property, 240–241
   residuary clause and property passing, 222–231
      clause, nature and effect of, 223
      estate, ascertainment of, 222
      kinds of property, particular, 223–227 (see also "Kinds of property, relationship of residuary clause to")
      "pour-over," 230–231
      surplus income, 227–230 (see also "Surplus income as part of residuary estate")
Residuary estate, insufficiency of for payment of taxes, 137
Residuary legacies, 145, 162
   insolvent estate and, 249–250
   of amount out of residue, 249–250
Residuary tangibles, sale or other disposition of by executor, 66–67
"Residue of the residue" rule, 183n, 237
Resignation of executor, 278–280 (see also "Executor, death, resignation or removal of")

Resigning executor, compensation to, 263
Restatement of Property, 8
Retention of apportioned shares of taxes, 134–137
   amounts recovered, disposition of, 136
   in general, 134–135
   inability to recover, 136
   interest on apportioned share, 136–137
   litigation, collection by, 135–136
Reverse discovery, meaning of, 63–64
Revised Uniform Principal and Income Act, 205, 207, 230
Revocabliity of assignment by legatee, 239
Revocation of legacy by later instrument or by law, 194–195
Revoked legacy devise as part of residuary estate, 223–224
   "bank account trust," 224
   revocation or ineffectiveness by operation of law, 224
Riggs v. Del Drago, 130n
"Right of retainer," 173–174
Rights of Personal Representatives to Breach Executory Contracts of Decedent, 89n
Rodgers Est., 56
Rubenstein v. Mueller, 35n, 215n, 216n

S

Safe deposit box, rental of for protection of securities, 69
   executor's duty to locate and open, 46–47
Sale of assets to executor or beneficiary, 79
Sale of residuary tangibles, duty of executor to provide for, 66–67
Satisfaction of legacy in lifetime, 190–191
Satisfaction of residuary legacy, 239
Satisfaction of spouse's elective share, source of, 217
Savings accounts of decedents, handling, 48
Savings bank trust, insolvent estate and, 253
   collection of, 56
Savings bonds, handling increment on, 141–142
   United States, collection of, 57
Schlesinger, 11n
Scott, 230n
Search for will, 24
   later discovery, peril of, 24
Secured debts of decedent, 246
Secured debts, satisfaction of, 102–103
Securities, executor's possession and control of, 68–71
   custodian or advisory account, establishment of, 69–70
   corporate executor, exemption of, 70
   registration in nominee's name, 70–71
   margin accounts, 68–69
   safe deposit box, rental of, 69
Securities, legacy of, 161
   valuation of, 94–96
      buy-and-sell agreements, 96
      closely-held corporation, stock of, 95–96
Securities as distributable assets of residuary estate, 235–236
Segall et al., 220n
Self-dealing executor, 21

INDEX

Self-interest of executor, special rules against, 86
Separate ascertainment of tax and accounting computations, need for, 204–205
Service without compensation, will specification for executor's, 262
Settlement of account of executor, 284–289
    effect of, 287–289
        as construction of will or determination of rights, 288–289
        failure to make, 289
    in general, 284
    judicial or voluntary, 284–285
        "general release" without account, 285
        objections to account, 286
            by fewer than all beneficiaries affected, 287
            rejected or unpaid claim, determination on, 287
    parties, 285–286
        same person executor and trustee, 285–286
Sewall v. Wilmer, 298n
"Share" formula for "marital deduction" legacy, 163
Share or fraction, legacy of, 190
Sharing of compensation by co-executors, 265–266
    agreement; waiver by one, 265–266
"Short-form certificate," meaning of, 42
Shriver, 62n, 135n, 136n, 214n, 305n
Simes, 89n
Simultaneity of distribution, principle of in distribution of assets from residuary estate, 236
Simultaneous payments, executor's duty of, 193–194
Situs of land, real property governed by law of, 73, 74, 295
    important to devises, 197
"Small estates" statutes, 44
    accountings for, 291
Source of initial estate and inheritance tax, 122–123
Special administrator, 5
Specific legacies, 145, 146, 147–159
    ademptiton, 146, 153–155
        guardian of incompetent, property sold by, 154
        insurance proceeds, 154–155
        open-market securities, 153
    availability for debts and expenses, 156
    body or organs, bequest or disposition of, 158–159
    definition, 147–148
    distribution, letter or memo concerning, 156–157
        wishes orally expressed, 157
    division among legatees, 157–158
    encumbrance, property subject to, 155–156
        business obligations specifically bequeathed, 156
    identification of property bequeathed, 148–152
        "all personal property," bequest of, 151
        "all tangibles," bequest of, 150–151
        coin or stamp collections, works of art, etc., 150
        contents of box, room, etc., 149
        corporate stock after capital changes, 151–152
        nature of, description by, 149–150
        provenance or location, description by, 148–149
    income from date of death, 152–153
    misunderstandings about, 147n
    tangibles, delivery of, 158
        "as is, where is" rule, 158
Specific legacies, insolvent estate and, 251–252
    legacy charged on specific devise, 251–252
Specific legacies and devises, income from, 208–209
Specification in will regarding executor's compensation, 261–262
Speculation as negligence by executor, 16
"Spill-over" legacies, 187
Spouse, surviving, rights of, 212–221 (see also "Surviving spouse or children, rights of")
Stallings, 35n
Stamp collections bequeathed by specific legacy, 150
Stamps in an Estate, 150n
Stark v. Stark, 161n, 191n
State tax, additional, to utilize Federal credit, 129
Statutory share, election by spouse to take, 213–218
    informing spouse of right to elect, 217–218
    measure of elective share, 215–216
        "limited" right of election, 215–216
    satisfaction of elective share, source of, 217
    waiver of right during testator's lifetime, 216
    withdrawal of election, 216–217
Stevens, 59n, 164n
Stock, corporate, after capital changes, bequest of by specific legacy, 151–152
Stock options, valuation of, 96
Subchapter S corporation, definition of, 143, 143n
Subscribing witness not capable of taking legacy, 175
Substituted executor, meaning of, 3, 280
Succession of Bradford, 260n
Successor executor, meaning of, 3, 280
Successors to executor, 278–279, 280 (see also "Executor, death, resignation or removal of")
"Supervised" administration of estate, meaning of, 2, 7
Surcharge for negligence, 17
Surgeons, particular responsibilities of executors regarding estates of, 60
Surplus income and net income, distinction between, 210–211
Surplus income as part of residuary estate, 227–230
    allocation among residuary beneficiaries, 229–230
    where entire residue passes outright, 227
    in general, 227
    where residuary trust or life estate created, 228–229
        majority rule, 229
        "true residue" rule, 228–229
Surviving spouse or children, rights of, 212–221
    children unprovided for, rights of, 218–219
        after-born or after-adopted, 219
        in general, 218
        living at execution of will, 218–219
        satisfaction of share, source of, 219
    community property, 221

Surviving spouse or children, rights of (*cont.*)
   dower and curtesy, 213
   "excessive" or "late" gifts to charity, 220
   "exempt" property and allowances, 212–213
   "forced heirship," 220–221
   marriage, dissolution of, 218
   spouse's election to take statutory share, 213–218
     informing spouse of right to elect, 217–218
     measure of elective share, 215–216 (see also "Statutory share, election by spouse to take")
     satisfaction of elective share, source of, 217
     waiver of right during testator's lifetime, 216
     withdrawal of election, 216–217
   widow's quarantine, 213
Survivorship, doubts about, 182–183
   "common disaster" provisions of will, 182–183
Stocks as distributable assets of residuary estate, 235–236

T

Tangible personal property, valuation of, 93–94
   "exempt" property, 94
Tangibles, custody, preservation and management of, 66–68
   contraband, 67–68
   "exempt" articles, 66
   insurance, 67
   residuary, sale or other disposition of, 66–67
Tangibles of decedent held by another, recovery of through discovery proceedings, 63
Tax and accounting computations distinguished, 204
Tax Elections by Executors and Trustees, 139, 139*n*
Tax Reform Act of 1969, 241*n*
Tax return, failure of decedent to file, 115
Tax returns of decedent, request for early audit of, 116–117
   of estate's returns, 116–117
Tax-Saving Elections Available to Executor, 139*n*
Tax values and accounting distinguished, 92
Tax waivers, 137–138
"Taxable estate" and "estate," difference in a meaning between, 7
Taxes (see under particular tax)
Taxes, priority of, 245
   Federal, priority of over State, 245
Taylor's Est., 81*n*
Temporary administration, 39–40
   powers of, 40
Temporary administrator and preliminary executor, difference between, 2–3
Terminology, 1–9
"Testamentary annuities," meaning of, 168*n*
Testamentary assets, insufficiency of, 124–125
Testamentary estate, meaning of, 7
Testamentary trustee, life insurance payable to, and residuary estate, 226
Testamentary trusts, 302–305
   executor and trustee, functions of distinguished, 303–304
   in general, 302
   pour-over to other trusts distinguished, 304–305
   qualification of trustee, 303
   validity of trust, importance of to executor, 302–303
The Careful Draftsman: Watch Out! 168*n*
The Careful Draftsman and the Problem of Age, 168*n*
The Conflict of Laws Relating to Wills, Probate Decrees and Estates, 295*n*
The Lawyer's Estate, 59*n*
The Lawyer's Estate: Key Tax Problems in Disposition of Practice, 59*n*
The Lawyer's Estate: Responsibilities and Rights of Clients, 59*n*
The Marital Deduction, 189*n*
The Multi-State Estate, 62*n*, 135*n*, 214*n*, 305*n*
The Multiple Personality of the Dead: Executors, Administrators, and Conflict of Laws, 136*n*
The Pour-Over Will, 230*n*
The Practical Lawyer, 35*n*
The Transplant Age, 30*n*, 158*n*
Third person, condition of legacy as obligation or transfer to, 168
Tickler of dates and stages of administration, 11, 309
Time of death, ascertaining, 31–32
   at domicile, 32
   standard or daylight time, 32
Time of payment of counsel's fees, 258
   partial payments, 258–259
Time of payment of executor's compensation, allowance or approval for, 263–264
   premature payment, 264
Time of payment or satisfaction of legacy, 191–193
   interest on cash legacies, 192–193
   partial, 192
   trusts, establishment of, 193
Time of presentation of claims upon estate, limitation upon, 104–105
Torts of executor, 90
Totten trusts, 56, 224
   insolvent estate and, 253
Transfer, consents to, 137–138
Transfers during decedent's lifetime, invalid, handling, 57–58
Treasury bills excellent method of short-term investments for excess moneys in estate, 83
Trimble v. Helcher's Exr., 130*n*
True residue rule, meaning of, 228–229
Trust and deferred legacy distinguished, 169
Trustee and executor, functions of distinguished, 303–304
Trustee de son tort, 6, 6*n*
Trusts, establishment of, 193
Trusts in the Conflict of Laws, 296*n*, 298*n*

U

Unauthorized or unsuitable investment by decedent, liquidating, 81–82
Uniform Act for Simplification of Security Transfers, 71, 71*n*
Uniform Anatomical Gift Act, 158*n*

INDEX

Uniform Conflict of Laws Act, 293n, 294
Uniform Estate Tax Apportionment Act, 130n
Uniform Principal and Income Act, 205, 207, 230
Uniform Probate Code, 8
Uniform Simultaneous Death Act, 182
Uniform Testamentary Additions to Trusts Act, 230n, 305n
Uniform Time Act of 1966, 32
Unincorporated associations incapable of taking legacy, 175
United States government bonds, executor's obtaining possession and control of, 70–71 (see also "Government bonds...")
United States Savings Bonds, collection of, 57
United States Savings Bonds, handling increment from, 141–142
Unproductive property, sale of, 83–84
"Unsupervised" administration of estate, meaning of, 2, 7
U.S. v. Field, 252n
Utilities services to decedent, executor's responsibility to suspend, 88–89

V

Validity of testamentary trust, importance of to executor, 302–303
Valuation of assets, 91–98
  accounting and tax values distinguished, 92
  inventory value, 92–93
    basis and determination, 92–93
  necessity and purposes of, 91–92
    non-probate assets 91
    probate estate, 91
  oil, gas and mineral interests, 97
  patents and copyrights, 97–98
  personal property, tangible, 93–94
    "exempt" property, 94
  proprietorships and partnership interests, 96–97
  real property, 94–95
    mortgages, 94
  securities, 94–96
    buy-and-sell agreements, 96
    closely-held corporation, stock of, 95–96
  stock options, 96
Vesting of title to legacy, 147
Vinton v. Pratt, 252n
"Virtual representation," doctrine of, 271n, 276n

W

Waiver of compensation by executor, 262–263
Waivers and consents to transfer, 137–138
Walsh v. Gillespie, 201n
Waste, definition of, 16
What law governs, 292–299 (see also "Law, what governs")
Whitney v. Whitney, 20n
Widow's quarantine, 213
Will, direction in regarding apportionment of taxes, 132–133
Will, production of, 25–26
  concealment of, 26
  delivery to another, 25
  in general, 25
  offer for probate, 25
Will, provision in for payment of claims, 110
Will, search for, 24
  in general, 24
  later discovery, peril of, 24
Will, specification in of executor's compensation, 261–262
Will as property of client at all times, 60
Williamson v. Williamson, 228n
Withdrawal of election by spouse, 216–217
Worthless property and residuary estate, 240–241

Z

Zschernig v. Miller, 178n